MY EXPERIENCES
IN THE
FIRST WORLD WAR

MY EXPERIENCES
IN THE
FIRST WORLD WAR

JOHN J. PERSHING

WITH A NEW FOREWORD BY

Frank E. Vandiver

DA CAPO PRESS • NEW YORK

Library of Congress Cataloging in Publication Data

Pershing, John J. (John Joseph), 1860–1948.
  [My experiences in the World War]
  My experiences in the First World War / John J. Pershing; with a
new foreword by Frank E. Vandiver.—1st Da Capo Press ed.
    p.   cm.
  Originally published: My experiences in the World War. New York:
F. A. Stokes, 1931. 2. v. With new foreword.
  ISBN 0-306-80616-9
  1. Pershing, John J. (John Joseph) 1860–1948. 2. World War,
1914–1918—Personal narratives, American. 3. World War, 1914–
1918—United States. 4. Generals—United States—Biography. 5. United
States. Army—Biography. I. Title.
D640.P454 1995
940.54′214—dc20
                                                   94-48774
                                                     CIP

First Da Capo Press edition 1995

This Da Capo Press paperback edition of *My Experiences in the
First World War* is an unabridged republication of the edition
originally titled *My Experiences in the World War* and first
published in two volumes in New York in 1931. It is here
supplemented with photo inserts and a new foreword by
Frank E. Vandiver. It is published by arrangement with
HarperCollins Publishers.

Published by Da Capo Press, Inc.
A Subsidiary of Plenum Publishing Corporation
233 Spring Street, New York, N.Y. 10013

Manufactured in the United States of America

To

THE UNKNOWN SOLDIER

CONTENTS

CHAPTER V

CHAPTER VI

CHAPTER VII

CHAPTER VIII

CHAPTER IX

CONTENTS

CHAPTER X

CHAPTER XI

CHAPTER XII

CHAPTER XIII

CHAPTER XIV

CHAPTER XV

CHAPTER XVI

CHAPTER XVII

CHAPTER XVIII

CHAPTER XIX

CHAPTER XX

CHAPTER XXI

CHAPTER XXII

CHAPTER XXIII

CHAPTER XXIV

CHAPTER XXV

CHAPTER XXVI

CONTENTS

VOLUME II

CHAPTER XXVII

CHAPTER XXVIII

CHAPTER XXIX

CHAPTER XXX

CHAPTER XXXI

CHAPTER XXXII

CHAPTER XXXIII

CHAPTER XXXIV

CHAPTER XXXV

CHAPTER XXXVI

CHAPTER XXXVII

CHAPTER XXXVIII

CHAPTER XXXIX

CHAPTER XL

CHAPTER XLV

CHAPTER XLVI

CHAPTER XLVII

CHAPTER XLVIII

CHAPTER XLIX

CONTENTS

CHAPTER L

CHAPTER LI

FOREWORD

An odd alignment of circumstances has somehow made the First World War nearly a forgotten one for Americans. It was a war between wars, fitting between the Civil War and the Second World War. And although it reshaped the modern world in drastic and lasting ways—it killed over ten million people; drained the resources of France, the British Empire, Italy, Germany, the tottering Austro-Hungarian Monarchy, Imperial Russia; shattered ambitions and illusions—it looms dully from history. Perhaps it changed too much too violently for remembrance; perhaps, too, more recent violence has simply overshadowed it.

Most soldiers who survived the daily "wastage" of the "Western Front"—a 400-mile labyrinth of trenches scarring France from the Channel to Switzerland—or Russia, the Dardanelles, Gallipoli, Africa, Palestine, were strangely mute men. What they saw, endured, they kept peculiarly to themselves; rare, indeed, were stories from veterans for children to enlarge.

Unlike the Civil War or the Second World War, the battles of the "Great War" are not household names. The Marne, Verdun, the Somme, Passchendaele, Tannenberg, Caporetto, St. Mihiel, the Meuse-Argonne, all were vast and bloody battles stamped with honor, sacrifice, heroism, misery, waste, cowardice—all the marks of combat. But they are sunk now to the level of scholastic concern, topics for theses and treatises on how not to make war. Apparently mindless attacks of thousands into the red muzzles of machine guns winnowed several generations in a numbing harvest of death. Surely no humane lessons could be gleaned from such slaughter.

Do those battles deserve neglect? Are there things to be learned from those cauldrons of carnage? From the war years came a desperate need to believe that the "war to end all wars" had paved the way for an era of lasting peace. From those years, too, came a wide loathing of war, a surging triumph of appeasement that cast conflict into the dustbins of memory. For the few who still admitted interest in war-making, the First World War taught a good deal—about blind, obedient courage; about the changing nature of conflict in the halcyon days of industrialism; about the impact of technology on strategy, tactics, and especially logistics; about air and naval power, and the uncertainties of command.

Those battles, too, rewrote the world map, ushered in new ethnic hopes, reshaped such disciplines as engineering, finance, management, manufacturing, medicine, agriculture—and so primed us for the modern era. No other war matches the 1914-1918 conflict as an agent for change.

People made the war, of course; most of the soldiers were forgotten sacrifices to leaders floundering to grasp a war that ran past experience. Old strategies and tactics were outmoded by machines, gases, zeppelins, planes, long-range guns, even tanks—and new ideas lagged far behind. In the early days field commanders on both sides were taxed to deploy and use the swarms of men suddenly raised by the standing mobilization plans of nations long scheming for conflict.

Again, an oddity about the 1914-1918 war: Most of its generals are lost, too. Lee, Jackson, Grant, and Sherman loom brightly from the Civil War, as do Patton, Eisenhower, Rommel, von Rundstedt, Montgomery, Zhukov, and Yamamoto from World War II. Dim shadows linger from the earlier global conflict, dimmed not just by time but by the hecatombs piled around them.

Leaders of the First World War are neglected, too, because their tragedy was to command in a war that wrecked illusion, dented faith, and spread misery across fairways of progress. Most of them do not deserve obloquy, for they had to cope with changes beyond their knowing, to seek new ways of warring in the rubble of their precedents.

France's Joseph Joffre, Henri Philippe Pétain, Ferdinand Foch; Britain's John French, Horatio Herbert Kitchener, Douglas Haig, Edmund Allenby, T. E. Lawrence; Italy's Luigi Cadorna, Armando Diaz; Germany's Helmuth von Moltke, Paul von Hindenburg, Erich von Falkenhayn, Erich Ludendorff, Max Hoffman; Russia's Aleksei Brusilov, Yury N. Danilov—all these held high command at various times, all suffered surprises and discomforts, but many rose above circumstances to find new martial methods. Those of the Western Front—French, Haig, Joffre, Pétain, Foch, Falkenhayn, Hindenburg, Ludendorff—still wear a butcher's mantle. Some charity should go their way: They were leaders in a butcher's war. Trench systems, mass firepower, aerial reconnaissance, and terrible bombardments paralyzed them; by the time they did break the stalemates of mind and method, most had yielded place to others still to learn.

One came from America to lead the first massive United States commitment to a foreign war. John Joseph Pershing's career seemed unlikely to prepare him for Europe's endless meat grinder: Missouri-born in 1860, West Pointer, cavalryman, fighter of Indians, lawyer, founder of the Bureau of Insular Affairs during the Spanish-American War, long-time warrior against the Moros of the Philippines, brigade commander, and leader of the Punitive Expedition into Mexico against Pancho Villa. By 1917 Pershing boasted probably the best rounded fighting and command experience in the U.S. Army. Promoted from captain to brigadier general by President Theodore Roosevelt, Pershing discharged each task with energetic ability.

Marriage to Frances Warren, daughter of Francis Emory Warren, Wyoming governor, later U.S. senator and member of the Military Affairs Committee, gave the young officer unusual "connections" throughout the U.S. government. "Jack" Pershing's apparently charmed life shattered with the death of "Frankie" and three daughters in a fire at the San Francisco Presidio in August 1915—son Warren alone survived. Throwing himself into work, especially into the frustrating quest for Villa's banditos, Pershing restored his balance and by the time his expedition quit Mexico in early 1917, the new major general cast an anxious eye toward France and a burgeoning war.

A brief stint in San Antonio as commander of the Southern Department yielded to a summons to Washington in May 1917. As things worked out, Secretary of War Newton D. Baker and President Woodrow Wilson selected Pershing to command the American Expeditionary Forces—a command which would grow into the most immense force ever fielded by the United States of America up to that time.

By June 1917 Pershing and a small staff reached France—to be engulfed in a welcome that resonated through the scarred soul of a desperate nation. He brought hope—but no men! Keeping up the Poilu ranks taxed every sinew of France; big, strong American soldiers were wanted for strengthening French divisions. England, too, greeted Pershing with unrestrained cheer—Americans were needed there, also, to fill the divisions siphoning daily along those terrible ditches of the damned in France.

Neither French nor British authorities realized that the stern-faced American general (pooh-poohed behind his back as nothing but an antique fighter of Indians) came armed with specific orders from the President and the Secretary of War not to fritter American strength throughout Allied legions—work, they ordered him, towards the presence of a strictly American Army. "Amalgamation" became the main contention between the Allies; both French and British thought the idea of America building its own army hopelessly time-consuming and wasteful. Training staff and troops to reach modern trench efficiency would take at least two years, and in that time Germany might win the war, especially as Russia tottered toward defeat in the east. Pershing wavered only once; as his million-man army gathered, he hoarded it, except in the harsh crisis of Germany's spring 1918 offensive. He lent some troops to the British, helped counterattack Ludendorff's Marne drive at Belleau Wood and Chateau-Thierry, and at last launched his own attack against the St. Mihiel Salient in September 1918. Victory there spurred a regrouping of U.S. forces and a hard drive into a series of deeply dug trench lines in the hilly Meuse-Argonne sector.

Pershing understood and resisted Allied hopes of dimming America's impact at the peace table; America's aid to Allied shipping, its unstinting supplies of munitions, money, machinery, much less men, were ignored in the rush to exact tribute for France and Britain. With the Armistice Pershing made his presence felt, and he supported President Wilson's efforts at Versailles. Most of all, Pershing resented the slight recognition the AEF received for its massive effort in the war. As the joy of triumph faded, American contributions to victory were minimized, almost made to seem more irksome than essential.

Pershing himself had gone on to greatness, to the rank of General of the Armies—held before only by George Washington—but he kept the greatness of his men fresh in heart, and in the years after the war considered some kind of monument to his "doughboys" who did so well.

Several publishers wanted him to write his memoirs or something about the war. Busy with various duties—he served as Chief of Staff of the Army from 1921 to 1924—and irritated with the quarrelsome "battle of the books" raging among Allied and Central Powers generals, he resisted. He did begin gathering some notes, bits of his headquarters diary, and in 1924 scribbled a rough first draft. Long lapses occurred between fits of writing and as *My Experiences in the World War* developed it became a cumbersome burden to him and to a small cadre of young officers helping him. His early drafts were sparkling with his own brand of ironic wit, but the more he rewrote the book the more the objective changed, along with the tone.

Finally deciding to tell the whole of the AEF's story, Pershing set a rigid research standard, organizing the writing chronologically, so that topics were choppy and scattered. Always himself restrained, fair, and reasonable, he adopted that stance in the book. Although he disliked the wars of words flooding from the battlefields, he indulged himself in some criticisms of Allied leaders and of American colleagues on the home front. But, on balance, *My Experiences in the World War* is Pershing's personal statement, his memorial to the AEF. It is widely inclusive of people and units, preserves in detail American operations, and gives a fairly sound idea of what went on at AEF headquarters during the major campaigns. Reviewers who knew the general wondered what had happened to his passion, to the arguments so much his style? He subdued them in the interest of history. Despite controversies about the nature of his book, despite counter-books generated in response, *My Experiences in the World War* won the Pulitzer Prize for history in 1932.

Readers will find in the following pages a sometimes irritatingly sterile action account, an almost sanitized look at difficult issues. They will not find answers to some fascinating questions about behind-the-scenes AEF problems, such as supply, personnel shiftings, and the development of aerial reconnaissance. They will look in vain for personality sketches, for the kind of interplay between commanders that distinguishes coalition warfare.

They will find, though, Pershing's mind at its coldly logical best and, consequently, will see much of the war as he saw it, in the perspective of what he knew and guessed. And they will recognize, looking through his cool eyes, that sere facts have a truth which color might distort. They will note, as well, an iron honesty in recollection which makes this book a lasting historical source, one that stands as a foundation for any further studies of the American Expeditionary Forces.

General Pershing did what he so wanted—he created the solid memory of a great crusade and the army that gave it glory.

—FRANK E. VANDIVER
Texas A&M University
October 1994

INTRODUCTION

My primary purpose in writing this story of the American Expeditionary Forces in France is to render what I conceive to be an important service to my country. In that adventure there were many lessons useful to the American people, should they ever again be called to arms, and I felt it a duty to record them as I saw them.

The World War found us absorbed in the pursuits of peace and quite unconscious of probable threat to our security. We would listen to no warnings of danger. We had made small preparation for defense and none for aggression. So when war actually came upon us we had to change the very habits of our lives and minds to meet its realities. The slow processes by which we achieved these changes and applied our latent power to the problems of combat in Europe, despite our will, our numbers and our wealth, I endeavor to describe. Therein lie the lessons of which I write.

Once realizing their obligations, the American people willingly sent their sons to battle; with unstinted generosity, they gave of their substance; and with fortitude bore the sacrifices that fell to their lot. They, too, served, and in their service inspired the armies to victory.

I am grateful to President Wilson and Secretary Baker for having selected me to command our armies and for the whole-hearted and unfailing support they accorded me.

To my comrades of the Allied armies I would say that I am not attempting to write a history of the World War, or of the epic part they took in it. I write of our own army and for our own people, without consciously magnifying or minimizing the effort of any army or any people. There is credit for all of us in the final triumph of our united arms. The struggle of the Allies was much longer, their sacrifices much greater than ours.

The men of all ranks who served with me in France added a brilliant page to the record of the American soldier's devotion to country. This modest work can only outline the stirring narrative of their achievements. No commander was ever privileged to lead a finer force; no commander ever derived greater inspiration from the performance of his troops.

J. J. P.

Volume I

ON May 3, 1917, four weeks after the United States had declared war on Germany, I received the following telegram from my father-in-law, the late Senator F. E. Warren, in Washington:

"Wire me to-day whether and how much you speak, read and write French."

At this time I was in command of the Southern Department, and was stationed at Fort Sam Houston, which adjoins the city of San Antonio, Texas. Naturally, Senator Warren's telegram suggested that I was to be assigned to some duty in France, but as no intimation had been given out regarding the extent of our active participation in the war, the message was somewhat puzzling. However, I telegraphed the following reply:

"Spent several months in France nineteen eight studying language. Spoke quite fluently; could read and write very well at that time. Can easily reacquire satisfactory working knowledge."

My reply, to be sure, was rather optimistic, yet it was comparatively accurate and perhaps justified by the possibilities to be implied from Senator Warren's telegram. A few days later I received from him the following letter:

"DEAR JACK:

"This is what happened: Last night, about ten o'clock, the Secretary of War rang me up and wanted to know if I would call in and see him this morning, and I responded that I would if I could reach him at nine o'clock. This is the first time he has ever asked me to call for a consultation.

"When I reached him, he said, in the most distant and careless way: 'Oh, by the way, before I discuss the matter about which I asked you to call—do you happen to know whether Pershing speaks French?' (This is the first time your name was ever mentioned between the Secretary of War and me, direct.) I said I was not certain about that; that I knew he was a linguist along the lines of Spanish and, to some extent, Japanese, and all of the Philippine dialects (a pardonable exaggeration by one's father-in-law)—that perhaps my wife might know, as she speaks French a little and reads it readily. He said, 'Well, it is *of no special consequence,* only I happened to think of it at this moment.' I replied, 'Well, I'll ask my wife about it to-day and see whether she knows, and will let you know.' He then said, 'If you don't mind, do so.' And then he proceeded to discuss quite fully some appropriation matters on which I intended to go to work upon my arrival at the Capitol.

"Of course you will know what this means, the same as I do. It may mean nothing at all. But perhaps you have already written to the Department upon the subject or, rather, the one to which it pertains.

"I hope you will wire me promptly upon receipt of my telegram, so that I may tell the Secretary 'what my wife said about it(?).'

"Affectionately,

"F. E. WARREN."

Shortly after the receipt of the private wire and before the above letter reached me, a telegram, dated May 2d, came from Major General Hugh L. Scott, the Chief of Staff, containing the opening words, "For your eye alone," followed by a message in code:

"Under plans under consideration is one which will require among other troops, four infantry regiments and one artillery regiment from your department for service in France. If plans are carried out, you will be in command of the entire force. Wire me at once the designation of the regiments selected by you and their present stations. * * * "

I construed this message to mean that these troops were to form a division, which, together with such others as might be sent over at once, would be under my command.

Within a day or so after the receipt of Scott's telegram, I intimated to Colonel M. H. Barnum, my Chief of Staff, that we might be called upon for a recommendation, and after consultation with him I selected the 16th, 18th, 26th and 28th Regiments of Infantry and the 6th Field Artillery. These, together with two other artillery regiments and the necessary auxiliary units, were later organized as our 1st Division.

I had scarcely given a thought to the possibility of my being chosen as commander-in-chief of our forces abroad, as afterwards developed, although my old friend, Major General J. Franklin Bell, had written me that he thought my selection almost certain. After I left the Philippines, in 1913, where he was in command, he and I had kept up an intermittent correspondence in which we freely exchanged confidences on army matters. In one of his letters written early in April, 1917, he spoke of the possibility of our sending an army to France and gave a list of the general officers who might be considered for the supreme command. Discussing the chances for and against each one, he predicted, much to my surprise, that all the others, including himself, would be passed over and that I would be selected. I was the junior on the list of major generals, hence could not fully accept General Bell's view, but he was so strongly convinced that he was right that he requested an assignment under my command. The major generals senior to me at the time were, in order of rank, Leonard Wood, J. Franklin Bell, Thomas H. Barry, Hugh L. Scott and Tasker H. Bliss.

From the day of my entrance into West Point up to middle age I had hoped the time would come when I could return to civil life while still young enough to take up law or go into business. But successive assignments that offered chances for active field duty and adventure had held me in the Army. Now that there had come an opportunity for service to the country such as had fallen to the lot of but few men, I considered myself especially fortunate to have remained. Throughout my career I have never ceased to wonder whether, after all, we are not largely the creatures of destiny.

When the incident occurred at Sarajevo that caused the smoldering embers of hatred and jealousy in Europe to burst into flame, my command, the 8th Infantry Brigade, was stationed along the Mexican Border and I was on leave, spending a few weeks with my family in Cheyenne, Wyoming. My wife and I had been in France in 1908 and witnessed the excitement of the French people during the crisis that followed the seizure by Austria of the provinces of Bosnia and Herzegovina. It was suspected even then that Austria had similar designs against Serbia, and the animosity that had grown up between them, added to the fears and ambitions of the nations likely to be aligned on either side, furnished plenty of inflammable material to start a war. But the thought of a world war, impending, perhaps imminent, actually stunned one's senses.

And yet, in reviewing the previous ten years it could be seen that events had distinctly and unmistakably pointed that way. Without entering into a discussion of the more remote causes of the war, perhaps all European nations that were involved must share a certain responsibility. But it is an outstanding fact that during the history of the preceding fifty years, with its background of age-old racial and religious prejudices, its maze of shifting alignments, diplomatic entanglements and conflicting national ambitions, the attitude of United Germany had become more and more aggressive and dominating.

After the Franco-Prussian War Germany had emerged as the strongest military power of Europe and was the leader in the development of military science and tactics. During the decade prior to the World War the improvement and increase of her heavier artillery and the organization of machine gun units had gone forward rapidly. The very extensive expansion and use of these arms by the Japanese in Manchuria had not escaped the notice of German observers, and her experts were quick to take advantage of the lessons of that war. While these facts were commonly known in military circles, neither the extent of the growth of her land forces that had recently taken place nor the forecast that she would complete her military program about the year 1914 [1] had made sufficient impression on her possible adversaries to cause serious alarm.

Then came the action of the German Government following the Sarajevo incident that suddenly forced the conclusion upon other peoples that the leaders of Germany intended to avail themselves of the opportunity to establish their country, if possible, as the dominant power of Europe. If there had been any doubt of this purpose, it was removed by the outcome of the many conferences with Austria, covering a period of nearly a month, which culminated in German support of the very arbitrary and humiliating demands on Serbia, even in the face of the latter's conciliatory reply.

Although observing statesmen and military men, some vividly, others only vaguely, had sensed the situation as a menace of war, yet few seemed to appreciate that a resort to arms under the circumstances would involve practically the whole civilized world. Apparently none of the powers visualized what it would mean in its appalling destruction of human life, its devastation of countries, and in the suffering of populations. Even the men in the armies who lived through those terrible years got only a limited conception of it all. Looking backward, however, it now seems strange that the results of such a conflict could not have been generally foreseen.

As we now know, the German militarists held up to their people the fear of the Slav as one reason for going to war, and frightened the financial interests by pointing out the danger of losing national prestige and commercial advantage unless Slav ambitions were checked. The German people were led to believe

---

[1] The French Yellow Book 1914, quoting from a secret German report of March 19, 1913, on the Agadir crisis, says: "At that time the progress made by the French Army, the moral recovery of the Nation, the technical advance in the realm of aviation and of machine guns rendered an attack on France less easy than in the previous period. Further, an attack on the English fleet had to be considered. This difficulty opened our (Germany's) eyes to the necessity for an increase in the army."

that the army was invincible, and were no doubt flattered by the thought of the glory and the grandeur that success would bring to their country.

The German military machine itself was without doubt more nearly perfect and powerful than any that had ever before existed. Their Great General Staff had fully considered every condition necessary to military success, and even solemn treaty obligations were not to stand in the way. The hour for Germany to seize her opportunity had arrived. The details of what happened in the beginning are well known and the world has long since fixed the blame where it properly belongs—on the shoulders of the German Government of 1914.

The violation of Belgian neutrality afforded Germany the advantage of invading France from the most favorable quarter, yet it was no justification for her to claim that strategical considerations impelled her to take this action. In disregarding the Treaty of London of 1839 Germany presented the strongest kind of evidence of her war guilt. Moreover, this overt act served to give notice to all nations that Germany intended to brook no opposition in her purpose to conquer her ancient enemy once and for all. I cannot escape the conviction that in view of this defiance of neutral rights the United States made a grievous error in not immediately entering a vigorous protest.

The argument might be made that as our Government was not a signatory to the treaty its violation was none of our business. But one of the stronger members of the family of civilized nations, to which, broadly speaking, we all belong, had committed an outrage against a peaceful neutral neighbor simply because she stood in the way. The plea was advanced by the Germans that Belgium could have avoided trouble if she had not opposed the passage of their forces through her territory, but if she had failed to resist she would have forfeited the respect of the world, whereas by opposing she gained universal admiration.

The invasion of Belgium was in fact an open declaration of Germany's attitude toward all neutral rights. If our people had grasped its meaning they would have at least insisted upon preparation to meet more effectively the later cumulative offenses of Germany against the law of nations, one of the most inhumane of which was the sinking of the *Lusitania.* Here was provocation enough for very positive action by any government alive to its obligations to protect its citizens. The fact is that the world knew only too well that we had for years neglected to make adequate preparations for defense, and Germany therefore dared to go considerably further than she would have gone if we had been even partially ready to support our demands by force.

It will be recalled that after some diplomatic correspondence the question of the use of submarines as it affected us rested until the sinking, without warning, of the *Sussex,* a Channel steamer carrying American passengers, on March 24, 1916. Germany was then notified that unless she should immediately declare and effect an abandonment of such methods of submarine warfare against passenger and freight-carrying vessels there would be no choice for us but to sever diplomatic relations with her. In reply, Germany made a definite promise to sink no more vessels without warning, although she made reservations as to the future.

Germany was informed that her reply was unsatisfactory, and there the question was again dropped, apparently without our seriously considering the action that we necessarily would be forced to take in the event of her resumption of ruthless methods. Little more than a gesture was made to get ready for eventualities; in fact, practically nothing was done in the way of increasing our military strength or of providing equipment.

As to our navy, however, Congress did appropriate more than $300,000,000 in August, 1916, for expansion, and some progress was made in beginning the construction of small craft and the establishment of a better administrative organization. This same Congress also passed an act [1] providing for the reorganization of our military forces, but scarcely a move was made to carry it out prior to our actual entrance into the war. Thus we presented the spectacle of the most powerful nation in the world sitting on the sidelines, almost idly watching the enactment of the greatest

[1] See Act of Congress June 3, 1916.

tragedy of all time, in which it might be compelled at any minute to take an important part.

It is almost inconceivable that there could have been such an apparent lack of foresight in administration circles regarding the probable necessity for an increase of our military forces and so little appreciation of the time and effort which would be required to prepare them for effective service. The inaction played into the hands of Germany, for she knew how long it would take us to put an army in the field, and governed her action accordingly. In other words, the date of resuming indiscriminate submarine warfare, February 1, 1917, was timed with the idea that the greater part of neutral and British shipping could be destroyed before we could be ready, should we by any chance enter the war.

Let us suppose that, instead of adhering to the erroneous theory that neutrality forbade any move toward preparation, we had taken the precaution in the spring of 1916 to organize and equip an army of half a million combatant troops, together with the requisite number of supply troops for such a force. This could have been done merely by increasing the Regular Army and National Guard to war strength. Such action would have given us the equivalent of forty average Allied divisions, ready to sail at once for France upon the declaration of war. Preparation to this extent could have been carried out by taking advantage of the concentration of the Regular Army and National Guard on the Mexican Border in 1916.

The actual situation on the Western Front when we entered the war was more favorable for the Allies than at any previous time. The strength of the German forces there had been greatly reduced because of the necessity for supporting the Russian front. Although reports were filtering in regarding the beginning of the revolution, there was little to indicate that Russia was not still a factor to be reckoned with. Actually the Allies had an advantage of something over 20 per cent in numbers, French morale was high, owing to their successful defense of Verdun, and the British armies had reached their maximum power.

Under these conditions, it is not extravagant to assert that the addition of 500,000 American combat troops in early spring would have given the Allies such a preponderance of force that the war could have been brought to a victorious conclusion before the end of that year. Even without such aid, the confidence of the Allies led them to undertake a general offensive in April. Although it ended in defeat, especially for the French, the failure can be attributed to a large extent to lack of secrecy of the plans. A well-planned campaign with the assistance of half a million Americans would have told quite another story.

Thus, through a false notion of neutrality, which had prevented practically all previous preparation, a favorable opportunity to assist the Allies was lost, the war was prolonged another year and the cost in human life tremendously increased. But, from another viewpoint, it is not improbable that if we had been thus prepared, our rights would have been respected and we would not have been forced into the war. We shall see as we proceed how great were the difficulties to be overcome because of our inexcusable failure to do what common reason long before our entry into the war plainly indicated should have been done.

My service on the southwestern frontier had extended from early in April, 1914, to March 15, 1916, when the Punitive Expedition under my command entered Mexico in pursuit of the Mexican bandit, Pancho Villa, and his followers, who had made a night raid on Columbus, New Mexico, and the camp of Regular Army troops stationed there. The expedition, which eventually numbered over 15,000 men, was under the shadow of the World War and the danger of our becoming involved in a war with Mexico was necessarily a handicap to the operations.

The temper of the people on both sides of the line and the tense feeling between Mexican regular troops and our own were such that had we continued our activities there is little doubt that serious complications would have arisen which might have brought on a war between the two countries. After we had penetrated about 400 miles into Mexican territory and overtaken Villa's band and others, and scattered them, wounding Villa himself, the increasing disapproval of the Mexican Government doubtless caused the administration to conclude that it would be better to rest content that the outlaw bands had been severely punished and generally dispersed, and that the people of northern Mexico had been taught a salutary lesson.

Activities in Mexico were discontinued in June, the more advanced elements were withdrawn and the expedition thereafter held a line of communications reaching only about 150 miles south of the border. As there was then little work to do except to protect this line, a systematic scheme of training was inaugurated throughout the command. Thorough courses in musketry and battle tactics for all units, beginning with platoons and leading up to the brigade, were prepared, and the principles of attack and defense were applied through practical exercises. In following out this progressive program, the liveliest interest was aroused in both officers and men, with the result that when the command left Mexico it was probably more highly trained than any similar force of our army had ever been before.

The contingents of the Regular Army and about 156,000 National Guard troops that served on the border during this period learned much that was beneficial to them in the World War. Most commands were given some tactical training and the officers had the chance to learn something of camp life and to develop practical leadership in handling units up to the regiment. The training and experience the National Guard received during this service raised their relative efficiency considerably above that attained under ordinary circumstances. Thus the only training, except ordinary routine, any of our forces received during the year prior to 1917, was given to the troops then in Mexico and to those stationed along the border.

It was said that a greater number of men were not sent to the border for want of equipment and supplies. This fact should have prompted immediate corrective action, which, if taken, might have prevented the delay that occurred later for the same reason when the large numbers of men were called out to prepare for service in the World War.

The officers and men along the border and in my command followed closely the press reports from abroad and kept themselves informed as far as possible on the progress of the war. I recall that the German attempt to take Verdun excited deep interest, and the determination of the French to defend that fortress at all hazards was highly praised. The battle of the Somme, fought during the summer by the British and French mainly to relieve the pressure on Verdun, furnished fresh examples of the so-called warfare of position.

Many Allied writers had proclaimed that trench warfare was a development of the World War which had made open combat a thing of the past. But trenches were not new to Americans, as both the Union and Confederate armies in the Civil War had used them extensively. While my command in Mexico was taught the technique of trench fighting, it was more particularly trained in the war of movement. Without the application of open warfare methods, there could have been only a stalemate on the Western Front.

In each succeeding war there is a tendency to proclaim as something new the principles under which it is conducted. Not only those who have never studied or experienced the realities of war, but also professional soldiers frequently fall into the error. But the principles of warfare as I learned them at West Point remain unchanged. They were verified by my experience in our Indian Wars, and also during the campaign against the Spaniards in Cuba. I applied them in the Philippines and observed their application in Manchuria during the Russo-Japanese War.

It is true that the tactics of the battlefield change with improvement in weapons. Machine guns, quick-firing small-bore guns and rapid-fire artillery make the use of cover more necessary. They must be considered as aids to the infantryman, expert in the use of the rifle and familiar with the employment of hasty entrenchments. It is he who constitutes our main reliance in battle.

When the opposing armies in the World War took to the trenches and established themselves in parallel lines hundreds of miles long, neither was strong enough to dislodge the other. Their elements of attack and defense, the first line, the supports and the troops in immediate reserve simply dug in. It then became siege warfare and the continuance of this situation, with indecisive attacks from time to time, diverted the attention of some observers from the fact that the real objective was the enemy's army.

To bring about a decision, that army must be driven from the trenches and the fighting carried into the open. It is here that the infantryman with his rifle, supported by the machine guns, the tanks, the artillery, the airplanes and all auxiliary arms, determines the issue. Through adherence to this principle, the American soldier, taught how to shoot, how to take advantage of the terrain, and how to rely upon hasty entrenchment, shall retain the ability to drive the enemy from his trenches and, by the same tactics, defeat him in the open.

The Punitive Expedition was withdrawn early in February, 1917, and I returned to El Paso to resume command of that portion of the border. A few days after the death of Major General Frederick Funston on February 19th, I was assigned to the command of the Southern Department as his successor, with headquarters at Fort Sam Houston, Texas.

In the passing of General Funston the Army suffered a severe loss. With little military knowledge previous to the Spanish War, but with rare native ability, he had taken advantage of his opportunities and, through experience in Cuba and in the Philippine Islands had become a most efficient commander. He was daring and resourceful in the field and all his campaigns were successful. Funston was a first-class fighting man who served his country loyally and ably.

With the declaration of war against Germany there was much excitement in the Southwest and many were the demands for protection against sabotage. Our first concern was to guard Government property and railways. Military detachments were sent to the most critical points. Orders had already been given to military commanders directing them to take measures to protect military forts, important railroad bridges, tunnels, docks, munition plants, Government buildings and property, and to assert vigorously the Federal power should any acts of violence occur. With very few exceptions the sentiment of the people in the states of Louisiana, Texas, Oklahoma, New Mexico and Arizona, then included in the Southern Department, was strongly behind the Government. Men and women of all classes in that area were eager to aid and sought advice as to how they might do so to advantage. Their fine attitude gave every promise of the energy and patriotism with which our people throughout the country supported the war.

President Wilson recommended the draft as the best method of raising an army. In the discussions in Congress on the subject, many members spoke in favor of the volunteer system. Even the Speaker of the House, the Honorable Champ Clark, of Missouri, in a speech on the floor opposing the Draft Act, compared the conscript to the convict. With such strong opposition it looked as though the conscription law would fail to pass. Its opponents forgot that during the Civil War the volunteer system had given Mr. Lincoln and his commanders no end of trouble and that in order to provide manpower the North was finally forced to adopt conscription. Large numbers of shirkers were thus compelled to serve; hence the opprobrium that clung to the word "conscript." It was very important that a repetition of the experience in the Civil War should be avoided. The advocates of a volunteer army also ignored the experience of the British in the World War, who, after a year and a half of effort to recruit their armies under that system, had been obliged to resort to the draft. In my opinion, it was so vital to our success that while in San Antonio, contrary to my lifelong rule against meddling with legislation, I persuaded the Governor of Texas that conscription was sound in principle and got him to exert his influence with the Texas delegation in Congress in favor of it. In writing at the time to a friend of mine with reference to this subject, I said:

"We must avoid creating the impression that we are sending a political army to Europe—the day of political armies is past. It would be a whole lot wiser for us to stay at home until we are thoroughly prepared. Universal service is the only principle to follow that will lead to success in this war, and that should be well understood. We are in this thing for keeps and it is going to demand the utmost exertion and the best of preparation to win. We shall have to select the flower of the young manhood of this country and give them thorough training before we start. The only way we can hope to succeed is by dogged determination and perseverance. * * * No half-way measures are going to solve this problem. I am with the President in this matter, heart and soul. I am sincerely and deeply impressed with the necessity of clinging to rational lines in carrying out his policies. The President feels the importance of this situation and every honest American should stand right behind him and help to the utmost."

On the afternoon of April 29th, while busy at my desk at Fort Sam Houston, word came through the Associated Press that both houses of Congress had passed the Draft Act, although, as it turned out, amendments adopted by the two houses necessitated a conference, which delayed the passage of the Act in its final form until nearly three weeks later.

A number of local newspaper reporters called at once and wanted to know what I thought about it. I said that of course everybody had realized for some time that our actual participation with armed forces could hardly be avoided; that the responsibility that now rested upon the country was tremendous, and added: "The echo of that vote for conscription will be heard around the globe. It is a triumph of democratic government; a willing step taken by a free people under wise leadership. * * * It means that every man will have his rôle to play. To have a hand in affairs and know that he is a part of the system will make a better citizen of every man. * * * To witness the thing that has just happened is truly inspiring. I would rather live now and have my share to perform in the events of to-day than to have lived in any past period in the world's history. * * * This is the beginning of a wonderful era."

I ARRIVED in Washington on the morning of May 10th,
pursuant to orders, and called at once at the office of the
Chief of Staff, Major General Hugh L. Scott. He informed
me that, upon his recommendation, I had been selected to command a division to be sent to France. This confirmed the impression received from his message of May 2d. He spoke of the
other general officers who were then senior to me, whose names
were mentioned in the preceding chapter, and gave reasons why
each one had been passed over. I greatly appreciated the opinion
and action of the Chief of Staff, whom I have always held in
high esteem.

We discussed the military situation and he outlined the general plans in so far as anything definite had been determined.
The War College Division of the General Staff during the previous three months had presented a number of recommendations
for action in the event of war. One of these provided for the
enactment of a draft law, the study of which General Scott himself had initiated. Others were concerned with the size of the
army to be organized and the necessity for the procurement of
equipment and supplies. Some of the heads of supply departments had previously asked Congress for funds for the purchase
of supplies, and others had made estimates, but nothing definite
had been accomplished. On March 15th, acting under instructions of the Chief of Staff, the War College Division had submitted a rather general scheme which contemplated an army of
500,000 men. These were all eleventh-hour recommendations

and definite action was not taken until May 18th, when Congress passed the law authorizing the increase of the military establishment through the application of the draft.

I was really more chagrined than astonished to realize that so little had been done in the way of preparation when there were so many things that might have been done long before. It had been apparent to everybody for months that we were likely to be forced into the war, and a state of war had actually existed for several weeks, yet scarcely a start had been made to prepare for our participation. The War Department seemed to be suffering from a kind of inertia, for which perhaps it was not altogether responsible.

The war plans functions of the War Department were in the hands of the General Staff, which had been established just after the Spanish-American War, on the recommendation of Mr. Elihu Root, then Secretary of War. Specifically the General Staff was charged with the study of possible theaters of operations, and with the preparation of plans for the mobilization, organization, supply, transportation and strategic employment of the necessary forces to meet all possible contingencies. But until a few weeks before the declaration of war neither the General Staff nor the War College had received any hint or direction to be ready with recommendations, except as indicated above. The General Staff had apparently done little more, even after war was declared, than to consider the immediate question of organizing and sending abroad one combat division and 50,000 special troops, as requested by the Allies.

In view of the serious possibility of war that had confronted the nation since the sinking of the *Lusitania,* there was no apparent reason why the General Staff should not have developed definite basic plans for the organization and employment of our armies in anticipation of the rapidly approaching emergency and without waiting for instructions from the Administration. To find such a lack of foresight on the part of the General Staff was not calculated to inspire confidence in its ability to do its part efficiently in the crisis that confronted us.

The truth is that the General Staff had not yet been properly organized. It was too much the inarticulate instrument of the Chief of Staff, who often erroneously assumed the rôle of Commanding General of the Army. There were many senior officers on the General Staff who understood little or nothing of its duties. The prominent bureau chiefs who possessed the advantage of disbursing Government funds continuously opposed the development of this planning and coördinating agency superior to them. Furthermore, Congress had recently reduced the number of officers allowed on the War Department General Staff. In these facts we no doubt find the basis of many of the difficulties that arose later in connection with the preparation of our army at home and its shipment and supply abroad.

My next call was upon the Secretary of War, Mr. Newton D. Baker. I was surprised to find him much younger and considerably smaller than I had expected. He looked actually diminutive as he sat behind his desk, doubled up in a rather large office chair, but when he spoke my impression changed immediately. We talked of my recent experience in Mexico and of conditions on the border, which, fortunately, were quieter than they had been for several years. He referred to my appointment and said that he had given the subject very careful thought and had made the choice solely upon my record. I expressed my appreciation of the honor, mentioned the responsibility of the position, and said that I hoped he would have no reason to regret his action.

At this time it was my understanding that I was to go over in command of a division, and as no such unit then existed in our Army it was urgent that it be organized as soon as practicable. As directed, I had already designated the infantry and artillery regiments to form the division, but details of interior organization, including the size of smaller units, their armament, the kind of auxiliary troops, and many such matters had not been determined.

I left Mr. Baker's office with a distinctly favorable impression of the man upon whom, as head of the War Department, would rest the burden of preparing for a great war to which the wholly unready nation was now committed. He was courteous and pleasant and impressed me as being frank, fair, and business-like. His conception of the problems seemed broad and comprehensive. From the start he did not hesitate to make definite decisions on the momentous questions involved. Yet, naturally, he did not then fully appreciate the enormous difficulties that confronted his department.

Still proceeding under the assumption that I was to command only a division in France, my feelings may well be imagined when, a day or so later, the Secretary of War called me in to say that it had been decided by the President to send me abroad as Commander-in-Chief, and that I should select my staff accordingly and prepare to sail as soon as possible.

In our conversation the Secretary indicated that several divisions and other troops would be sent overseas as soon as they could be prepared. The numbers could not then be fixed, of course, as the plans of the War Department were not fully developed until later. Moreover, there was always the determining factor in any calculation that might be made, and that was the amount of tonnage available for the transportation and supply of an army.

The thought of the responsibilities that this high position carried depressed me for the moment. Here in the face of a great war I had been placed in command of a theoretical army which had yet to be constituted, equipped, trained, and sent abroad. Still, there was no doubt in my mind then, or at any other time, of my ability to do my part, provided the Government would furnish men, equipment and supplies.

The new decision materially broadened the scope of my duties, and it became necessary at once to discuss with the War Department the outlines of the organization of our forces. Naturally the consideration of personnel and the assembly of a field general staff was of first importance, and the foundation of the supply system as an integral part of the organization was to be next in order. The efficiency of the staff and supply departments would depend largely upon the ability and experience of their chiefs, so that the selection of capable officers for these positions was of the greatest moment. This was a difficult task because there was only a limited number of available officers who had received even theoretical training in the duties of the staff in war.

Obviously it was advisable to choose my chief of staff as soon as practicable. After studying the records of several officers of my acquaintance, and of others who were recommended for the position, I chose Major James G. Harbord. His efficiency in every grade from the day of his enlistment as a private in the Army, in January, 1889, was not only of record but was well known to those with whom he had served. The first time I had ever heard of him was shortly before he was promoted to the grade of first lieutenant in the 10th Cavalry. An officer who had known him as a sergeant said that he was a most promising youngster and that the regiment would be fortunate to get him. I had met him later during his service in the cavalry and in the Philippine Constabulary.

Apart from sheer ability, a chief of staff, to be highly efficient, should have tact, and he must have the confidence of his commander. He would be of small value without the courage to give his own views on any question that might arise, and he must have the loyalty to abide by the decisions of his chief.

Throughout the war Harbord never hesitated a moment to express his opinion with the utmost frankness, no matter how radically it might differ from my own, nor did he ever fail to carry out instructions faithfully even when they were not in accord with his views. Entirely unselfish, he labored incessantly for what he believed to be the best interests of our armies. His ability, his resourcefulness, his faculty for organization, and, above all, his loyalty, were outstanding qualities, and these together with a compelling personality made him invaluable to the nation in this important position.

After consultation with the permanent heads of staff and supply departments, and with no little insistence on my part in more than one instance, the corresponding representatives to accompany me were designated, and they in turn chose their assistants. Although the list did not include all whom I would have selected, as some were not available, yet all rose to important places in the final organization, except one or two who failed in health. Fifty-nine officers and 128 clerks, civilian employees and enlisted men accompanied me abroad.[1]

The Selective Service Act (Draft Act) as submitted to Congress was prepared by the Judge Advocate General's Office under instructions from the Secretary of War. The draft was strongly

[1] The Personal Staff (Aides-de-Camp) consisted of: *Capt. Nelson E. Margetts,* F.A., later Colonel, Field Artillery; *Capt. James L. Collins,* Cav., later Colonel, Field Artillery; *1st Lt. Martin C. Shallenberger,* Inf., later Colonel, General Staff.

The original members of the General Staff were: *Maj. James G. Harbord,* Cav., Chief of Staff, later Major General; *Maj. John McA. Palmer,* G.S.C., later Colonel, Infantry; *Maj. Dennis E. Nolan,* G.S.C., later Brigadier General and Chief of Intelligence, A.E.F.; *Maj. Fox Conner,* Asst. Inspector General (attached), later Brigadier General and Chief of Operations, A.E.F.; *Capt. Arthur L. Conger,* Inf. (attached), later Colonel, General Staff, and regimental commander; *Capt. Hugh A. Drum,* Inf. (attached), later Brigadier General and Chief of Staff, First Army.

The Administrative and Supply Staff was: *Col. Benjamin Alvord,* Adjutant General, later Brigadier General and Adjutant General, A.E.F. (invalided home); *Col. André W. Brewster,* Inspector General, later Major General and Inspector General, A.E.F.; *Lt. Col. Walter A. Bethel,* Judge Advocate, later Brigadier General and Judge Advocate General, A.E.F.; *Col. Daniel E. McCarthy,* Q.M.C. (invalided home); *Col. Alfred E. Bradley,* M.C., later Brigadier General and Chief Surgeon, A.E.F. (joined in London; invalided home); *Lt. Col. Merritte W. Ireland,* M. C., later Brigadier General and Chief Surgeon, A.E.F., relieving General Bradley; *Col. Harry Taylor,* C. of E., later Brigadier General and Chief of Engineers, A.E.F.; *Lt. Col. Clarence C. Williams,* Ord., later Brigadier General and Chief of Ordnance, A.E.F.; *Col. Edgar Russel,* S.C., later Brigadier General and Chief Signal Officer, A.E.F.; *Maj. Townsend F. Dodd,* Aviation Sec., later Colonel and Chief of Air Service, A.E.F., until Sept. 3, 1917.

The total number in my party that sailed on the S.S. *Baltic* was as follows:

Regular Army Officers.....................	40
Marine Corps Officers......................	2
O.R.C. Officers in active service.............	17
Enlisted Men	67
Field Clerks	36
Civilian Clerks	20
Civilian Interpreters	5
Civilians (Correspondents)	3
Total on *Baltic*	190

urged by the Chief of Staff, the Secretary of War, and the President, who had recommended it to Congress on April 2d. But it did not become a law until May 18th, thus deferring its application for forty-two days after the declaration of war. The question had been discussed in the press of the country for some time, with the result in the end that the principle of conscription was advocated by the majority of the leading newspapers. In doing so they rendered distinguished service to the nation by creating favorable public opinion to sustain the President and Congress in the enactment of this important law.

The administration of the draft was placed under the direction of Brigadier General E. H. Crowder, who was appointed to the position of Provost Marshal General for that purpose. The system of using polling places throughout the country and of having the registration under the supervision of local boards proved to be both simple and effective. The people of every community became directly interested in the creation of our armies, and were generally enthusiastic in their support of the war. The system of selecting men for service as worked out by the Judge Advocate General's Office was admirable and should stand as a model for the future.

The Act contained a provision authorizing the President to raise not to exceed four infantry divisions by voluntary enlistment. When Mr. Baker asked my view as to whether action should be taken under this provision I expressed myself against the principle except as to special or technical troops. While volunteer fighting units would naturally be composed of fine men, who would give a good account of themselves, there was no reason to suppose that they would be any better than those selected under the draft, similarly officered by their quota from the Regular Army. Moreover, the volunteers, as they had done in the past, would regard themselves as belonging to a special class and would expect priority both as to supplies and assignments. Any difference in the status of the various units such as would thus exist between volunteers and those who should come in through the draft would arouse jealousies almost certain to be subversive of discipline.

When one recalled the evils of the volunteer system in the Civil War, with the appointment of politicians to high command and the conferring of Medals of Honor upon whole regiments for a few days of extra service; and later, in the Spanish-American War, the insistent demands of the volunteers, politically and otherwise, that they should have preferential consideration, it was not difficult to foresee what would have happened in the World War.

The appeal of Colonel Roosevelt for permission to raise a volunteer division aroused popular sentiment in his favor throughout the country, but approval would have opened the door for many similar requests, and the policy would have interfered materially with the orderly and businesslike enforcement of the Draft Law. Moreover, the regular establishment would have suffered from the loss of an undue proportion of the best officers, who inevitably would have been selected for important positions in these special units at a time when their services were urgently needed in building more largely.

Another important reason for disapproving Colonel Roosevelt's application was that in such a war it was necessary that officers, especially those in high command, should be thoroughly trained and disciplined. Furthermore, he was not in the best of health and could not have withstood the hard work and exposure of the training camps and trenches. The Secretary of War, much to the disappointment of Colonel Roosevelt, wisely made an adverse decision in his case, which was confirmed by the President. It was evident that both Mr. Wilson and Secretary Baker were looking for trained leaders and were determined to avoid the embarrassment Mr. Lincoln experienced in the Civil War, when he was more or less driven to fill many high positions with political appointees who, in the end, had to be replaced by men trained in the military profession.

The following letter from Colonel Roosevelt will show his own fine attitude:

"May 20th, 1917.

"My dear General Pershing:

"I very heartily congratulate you, and especially the people of the United States, upon your selection to lead the expeditionary force to the front. When I was endeavoring to persuade the Secretary of War to permit me to raise a division or two of volunteers I stated that if you or some man like you were to command the expeditionary force I could raise the divisions without trouble.

"I write you now to request that my two sons, Theodore Roosevelt, Jr., aged 27, and Archibald B. Roosevelt, aged 23, both of Harvard, be allowed to enlist as privates under you, to go over with the first troops. The former is a Major and the latter a Captain in the Officers' Reserve Corps. They are at Plattsburg for their third summer. My own belief is that competent men of their standing and rank can gain very little from a third summer at Plattsburg, and that they should be utilized as officers, even if only as second lieutenants. But they are keenly desirous to see service; and if they serve under you at the front, and are not killed, they will be far better able to instruct the draft army next fall, or next winter, or whenever they are sent home, than they will be after spending the summer at Plattsburg. The President has announced that only regular officers are to go with you; and if this is to be the invariable rule then I apply on behalf of my two sons that they may serve under you as enlisted men, to go to the front with the first troops sent over.

"Trusting to hear that this request has been granted, I am, with great respect,

"Very sincerely yours,

"Theodore Roosevelt.

"P. S. If I were physically fit, instead of old and heavy and stiff, I should myself ask to go under you in any capacity down to and including a sergeant; but at my age, and condition, I suppose that I could not do work you would consider worth while in the fighting line (my only line) in a lower grade than brigade commander."

Although it was not generally known that I was to go abroad, there was a flood of applications to accompany me. One of them was a personal appeal for service in any capacity by my old friend, Robert Bacon, who had been Ambassador to France. He had already given valuable aid to the Allied cause and because of his intimate knowledge of the French people and his tact and discretion I was glad to have him. Major Bacon became garrison commander at Chaumont and later, as colonel and aide-de-camp on my staff, rendered exceptional service at British G.H.Q., where he was chief of our mission.   There is no doubt that his very strenuous activity in these various positions of trust and responsibility during the war shortened his life.

Another friend who was most anxious to join my headquarters was Willard D. Straight, whom I had known in Manchuria during the Russo-Japanese War.   Although his request could not be granted, he came to France within a few months and served efficiently in the Army and with the Peace Commission, being on duty with the latter at the time of his death.   Lloyd C. Griscom, with whom I had been pleasantly associated when he was our Minister and I was Military Attaché at Tokyo, asked to go with me, but it was impossible to arrange it.   When he came over later as adjutant of the 77th Division, I at once detailed him as my representative at the War Office in London.

A few days before my departure, while at lunch at the Metropolitan Club with Charles E. Magoon, ex-Governor of Cuba, Charles G. Dawes joined us.   The three of us had been friends in the days when we were together at Lincoln, Nebraska, Magoon and Dawes as young lawyers, the latter with a decided talent for business, and I as military instructor at the State University. Dawes was an applicant for a commission in one of the engineer regiments then being organized, under the direction of Mr. Samuel M. Felton, from volunteers with experience in railroading, and wanted me to help him get the appointment.   I asked him whether he knew anything about engineering, and he said that when a youth he had carried a chain a month or so for a surveyor out in Ohio.   I was not much impressed with his pretensions as an engineer or as a prospective military possibility, but I did have knowledge of his business ability and experience and knew that he would be valuable in some position requiring his qualifications, so I spoke to the Secretary of War in his behalf.

Requests from National Guard officers and from Governors for the early acceptance of their State units poured into the War

Department. The clamor became so general and so insistent that the Secretary of War happily conceived the idea of forming a composite division to include troops from every State in the Union. I thought the suggestion a good one and gave it my hearty endorsement. This was the origin of the 42d (Rainbow) Division, which was later to distinguish itself in many important engagements.

CHAPTER III

Conference on Munitions—Shortage of Guns, Ammunition and Airplanes
—Training Camps for Officers—Cantonments—French and British
Missions Want American Replacements—Attend Red Cross Confer-
ence—Call on President Wilson—Letters of Instruction

OUR deplorable situation as to munitions was fully discussed at a conference called by the Secretary of War
in his office on the afternoon of May 10th.[1] A general
survey of our requirements for the immediate future was made
as to rifles, machine guns, light and heavy artillery, ammunition
and airplanes. It was brought out that we had for issue, not
in the hands of troops, only about 285,000 Springfield rifles, 400
light field guns, and 150 heavy field guns.[2]

As it was impossible, because of manufacturing difficulties, for
our factories to turn out enough Springfield rifles within a reasonable time, the Secretary, after hearing the facts, decided to
adopt the Enfield rifle for our infantry. It was then being
manufactured for the British in large quantities at private factories in our country and a slight modification of the chamber
only was necessary to make it fit our ammunition. More than
2,000,000 of these rifles were manufactured during the war.

Although Congress had appropriated $12,000,000 for the pro-
curement of machine guns in 1916, it was reported to the conference that we had less than 1,500 guns and that these were
of four different types. This condition existed because the War
Department had not decided definitely which type to adopt for

[1] Those present were the Secretary of War; Major General Hugh L. Scott, Chief
of Staff; Major General Tasker H. Bliss, Assistant Chief of Staff; Major General
William Crozier, Chief of Ordnance; Major General Erasmus M. Weaver, Chief of
Artillery; Brigadier General Joseph E. Kuhn, President of the War College; and myself.
[2] We eventually had with the armies in France: 1,761,000 rifles; 2,106 75-mm.
field guns, and 1,485 heavy guns; besides about half as many of each at home.

our Army, although an order had been placed late in 1916 for a quantity of the heavy Vickers-Maxims. Tests of machine guns were held in May, 1917, and an entirely new type was pronounced acceptable and adopted by the Ordnance Department. Until these could be manufactured we had to purchase machine guns of the Hotchkiss type from the French.

Our capacity to manufacture small arms ammunition in large quantities was assured through the operations of private factories. As in the case of Enfield rifles, this was due to increased production for sale to the Allies prior to our entry into the war and not to any preparatory action by the War Department. Except for our 3-inch artillery ammunition, we did not have enough to provide for more than nine hours' supply, even for the limited number of guns on hand, firing at the rate ordinarily used in laying down a barrage for an infantry attack.

The situation at that time as to aviation was such that every American ought to feel mortified to hear it mentioned. Out of 65 officers and about 1,000 men in the Air Service Section of the Signal Corps, there were 35 officers who could fly. With the exception of five or six officers, none of them could have met the requirements of modern battle conditions and none had any technical experience with aircraft guns, bombs or bombing devices.

We could boast some 55 training planes in various conditions of usefulness, all entirely without war equipment and valueless for service at the front. Of these 55 planes, it is amusing now to recall that the National Advisory Committee for Aeronautics, which was then conducting a scientific study of the problem of flight, advised that 51 were obsolete and the other 4 obsolescent. We could not have put a single squadron in the field, although it was estimated later that we should eventually need at least 300 squadrons, each to be composed on the average of some 24 officers, 180 men and 18 airplanes, besides a large reserve of planes for replacements.

The expectations of the Allies concerning our assistance in the air are shown by the following cable from the French Prime

Minister, received about May 24, 1917, which formed the basis of War Department effort:

> "It is desired that in order to coöperate with the French Aeronautics, the American Government should adopt the following program: The formation of a flying corps of 4,500 airplanes—personnel and matériel included—to be sent to the French front during the campaign of 1918. The total number of pilots, including reserve, should be 5,000 and 50,000 mechanics.
>
> "2,000 airplanes should be constructed each month as well as 4,000 engines, by the American factories. That is to say, that during the first six months of 1918, 16,500 planes (of the latest type) and 30,000 engines will have to be built.
>
> "The French Government is anxious to know if the American Government accepts this proposition, which would allow the Allies to win the supremacy of the air.
>
> "RIBOT."

This message, in its appeal for such a large number of aviation personnel and airplanes, was really a most convincing confession of the plight of the Allied armies. But more than that, it strikingly brought home to us a full realization of our pitiful deficiencies, not only in aviation but in all equipment. The appropriation in July, 1917, of $640,000,000 for aviation indicated that Congress understood the predicament that confronted us, but what a commentary it was on the lack of that wisdom which should have prompted both the people and their representatives to earlier action.

Thus the deeper we went into the situation the more overwhelming the work ahead of us seemed to be. As the degree of its accomplishment within a reasonable time would be the measure of our aid to the Allies, extreme haste in our preparation was urgent. We were called upon to make up in a few months for the neglect of years during which self-satisfied provincialism and smug complacency had prevented the most elementary efforts toward a reasonable precaution to meet such an emergency.

In an attempt to provide the thousands of additional officers needed for the first 500,000 troops tentatively considered necessary under the War College plan, the Secretary of War about the middle of April directed the establishment of training camps, one for each of the proposed sixteen infantry divisions that were to form such a force. Noncommissioned officers from the Regular Army and the National Guard, augmented by graduates of schools and colleges where military instruction was given, were put through a three months' course of instruction in these camps.

Early in April, before the declaration of war, I had sent the following telegram from Fort Sam Houston to The Adjutant General of the Army:

"Have inaugurated intensive training along lines of European war experience, with a view to prompt preparation regular regiments for foreign service if needed. Suggest early announcement that all cavalry and infantry regiments this department are to be increased to war strength. Many regiments have already received recruits considerably beyond peace strength. If new increments are to be added to Regular Army in near future recommend corresponding number recruits in addition to above be attached as rapidly as enlisted so that advantage may be taken of training now in progress."

On May 12th, after waiting more than a month, orders were issued directing the recruitment of all line organizations to war strength.

Among other subjects considered with the Secretary was the assembly for training of the National Guard and the men to come in under the draft. The organization of our Army had never been based upon the tactical requirements of battle, but we still maintained our troops at small posts, as in the days of Indian warfare. Some of these posts, although they lacked sufficient barracks and training areas for units as large as a division, could have been advantageously used in the earlier stages of training up to the limits of their accommodations.

In lieu of any previous plans, the Secretary contemplated the construction of cantonments in different parts of the country, and on May 7th the Commanding Generals of the several departments were directed to select sites for that purpose. Under the circumstances, the proposed plan seemed to be the only alternative for training the larger units, provided this building program could be carried out without delay; but it should have been possible to obtain enough tentage for the Regular Army and the National Guard at once so that training for the necessary additional drafts to fill them could have been started in their respective localities. Time was the most important factor to be considered.

The actual construction of cantonments was not begun until nearly three months after we had entered the war, and even though the task of erecting them was accomplished in record time, some ninety days more had elapsed before they were ready to receive troops. Thus, it was, with some exceptions, practically six months before the training of our new army was under way. Even then several of these camps were not favorably located and training was seriously handicapped on this account during the fall and winter months.

About this time the Allies brought up the question of utilizing our men to build up their armies. As we shall see, the subject arose from time to time in one form or another and we had to fight against it until the end of the war.

Both the French and British Missions, under M. Viviani and Mr. Balfour respectively, then in our country, were very keen to have American recruits to fill up the ranks of their armies. The French really wanted us to send small, untrained units for incorporation in their divisions. Their views were clearly set forth in a memorandum by the French General Staff which was presented by their Military Attaché. Marshal Joffre, of the French Mission, however, evidently learned that such a proposal would not appeal to us, so he suggested that we also organize our own divisions, and urged that one division be sent over immediately to stimulate French morale, which he frankly confessed was then at low ebb. In addition, he asked for 50,000 trained men for service on their railways, in the shops, and with their medical units.

The following is quoted from the French memorandum:

"We cannot expect to see American armies, entirely organized with staffs and artillery, which are indispensable to the service of large forces, before the expiration of a period of preparation the duration of which it is impossible to estimate.

"On the other hand it seems possible to obtain from America within a brief period of time a portion of the great resources of that nation in combatant and noncombatant personnel which is available."

Speaking of maintaining the strength of existing French formations, they proposed:

"Voluntary enlistment in French armies, using French depots, centers of instruction and instruction units. With this system of intensive training we could utilize men with the least delay. This is a solution which divides American effort, but which has the advantage of furnishing us immediate aid and of hastening the victory.

"It could be understood that these volunteers could be withdrawn from the French Army and placed at the disposal of the American Commandant when the regularly organized forces arrive."

Another proposal, known as the "General Nivelle Scheme," requested that we send 80,000 men to perform various kinds of work. The following quotations will indicate the French attitude as to command, as well as their view regarding the urgency of their requirements:

"In order that there may not be any officers of higher rank than the French officers with whom these auxiliary troops will be called upon to work it is preferable that in the different units there should not be for the present any officer above the rank of captain. When the units will become sufficiently numerous to require superior officers these can be chosen from the captains of existing units.

"The important thing is to act quickly and to send groups or units of the character asked for as rapidly as possible. However small the first expeditions may be it is of capital importance that there should be no hesitation in sending them at once, even half units will be welcome."

A definite proposal that our men should be drafted into the British Army was also pressed by the military representative with the British Mission, Major General G. T. M. Bridges. His suggestions were set forth in the following letter to Major General Scott and also mentioned in conversation with me:

"Dear General:

"You asked me to write you my views as to the coöperation of your military forces in Europe. They are as follows:

"1. If you ask me how your force could most quickly make itself felt in Europe, I would say by sending 500,000 untrained men at once to our depots in England to be trained there, and drafted into our armies in France. This is the view alike of our Commander-in-Chief in France and the Chief of the Imperial General Staff (Sir Douglas Haig and Sir W. Robertson), their reasons being that we are short of men, the war is at a critical stage, when we may yet be able to turn the scale and force a decision during the summer, and *every day* counts. Our recruits are put into the field after 9 weeks' training in England, and 9 days in France, and give a good account of themselves. With your intelligent men under our system and instruction this would be found ample. In no other way could those 500,000 men make their presence felt before what we call the fighting season is over for the year. Both Sir Douglas Haig and Sir William Robertson, however, recognize the difficulties attending such a course in view of the fact that you are engaged in raising a national army. However, I put it forward for your consideration whether in view of your enormous manpower you cannot do both, in which case the drafts sent to us could eventually be drafted back into the U. S. Army and would be a good leavening of seasoned men. * * *

" * * * In view of the large armies now engaged, a few divisions would have to come under command of either the British or French Commander-in-Chief. * * * "

Speaking then of armament, he advocated the adoption of the British Enfield and their 18-pounder in preference to the French Lebel rifle and 75-millimeter field gun. Going on, he said:

"9. It appears to me that the above considerations may have some weight in the decision of your Government as to whether your initial forces are directed to the care of our army or to the French. The French may be able to promise a separate line of supply for a small force. I understand they are extremely anxious to have your army with them, and they are probably willing to sacrifice a good deal to this end. I feel certain that Sir D. Haig could not promise this, but would stipulate that your divisions would have to come into line with ours as regards ammunition supply. If with the French you would probably want your own food supply also.

"A few other points occur to me in this connection. You will have the language difficulty to contend with if your divisions go to the French. The French have very few English-speaking officers; not so many as they think. A good instructor can indeed seldom speak English, and men will soon get tired of being instructed through interpreters.

"We have been told that the sentiment in this country is in favor of fighting with and for the French. We understand this sentiment. * * * I think I have made it clear there are serious military disadvantages, and you will be sacrificing some of your efficiency for this sentiment, and making, in my opinion, the task of your commanders and staff more difficult in the field. Once you had a sufficient force in France, however, it would be quite feasible to place your army between the French and ourselves, where it could, if so desired, be under French direction, and supplied by us. * * *

"10. We would be glad if you would consider the question of allowing recruiting of American citizens for the British, Canadian and French Armies, from the surplus you will have over your requirements. We are all going to suffer from a shortage after this summer's fighting. * * * "

General Bridges requested that, in the event we could not see our way clear to draft men as individuals, then minor units, such as battalions and regiments, should be incorporated in British divisions.

I was decidedly against our becoming a recruiting agency for either the French or British and at that time this was the attitude of the War Department also. While fully realizing the difficulties, it was definitely understood between the Secretary of War and myself that we should proceed to organize our own units from top to bottom and build a distinctive army of our own as rapidly as possible.

The evident rivalry between the British and French for control and use of our forces, even before we had an army in the field, bore out my impression that those two Governments were not working entirely in harmony. It had been apparent for some time that there was a lack of coöperation between their armies. Their efforts were often separate and distinct. First one and then the other would attack, each apparently without reference to the other. Generally speaking, such methods could not seriously affect the enemy, who would thus be at liberty to utilize his reserves against them in turn. I had often remarked that the Allies would never win the war until they secured unity of action under some form of coördinated control.

History is replete with the failures of coalitions and seemed to be repeating itself in the World War. Marlborough, in the War of the Spanish Succession, complained of the lack of coöperation among the armies. His plans were impeded by the jealousies of the allied commanders and it required all his gifts of diplomacy to secure concerted action. Napoleon said that it was not difficult to beat a coalition. The lack of unity in military operations conducted jointly by allied armies often results from divergence of war aims. In the pursuit of these aims, governments may seek to place part of their forces in a position that would be advantageous after the war is over and lose sight of the fact that complete victory can only be achieved by beating the enemy's army. The success of such operations depends upon complete military coöperation. The absence of entire united effort between the Allied armies on the Western Front during the earlier years of the war was probably due merely to lack of understanding between the commanders, but its continuance would have undoubtedly led to their defeat.

My first meeting with Marshal Joffre was during his farewell call on the Secretary of War late in May. I entered just as he and his party were leaving. He spoke of the serious situation in France and expressed the hope of seeing American troops on the Western Front very soon. Here was a Marshal of France who, as Commander-in-Chief of the French Army for nearly three years, had made his name immortal, apparently appealing for military assistance from a man recently designated to be commander-in-chief of an army not yet in existence. I have often wondered what must have been his thoughts under the circumstances, but whatever he may have felt as to the new commander himself, the totally unready situation that he found in America could not have been very encouraging. It is a pleasure to say that this great soldier became my loyal and consistent personal friend.

While I was in Washington the American Red Cross had assembled some hundreds of business and professional men and women from all parts of the country to consider plans and devise ways and means of raising funds. The Red Cross had already been active in France, but now that we were in the war the time had come for extraordinary effort.

One day during the conference Mr. Henry P. Davison, President of the Red Cross, Mr. Eliot Wadsworth and Mr. John J. O'Connell burst into my office and insisted that I should go before the meeting and speak. I protested vigorously, but it was of no use, as they literally dragged me off then and there. When we reached the hall, Mr. Herbert Hoover had the floor and was describing his experience in Belgium as director of relief provided by America for the needy inhabitants. Mr. Hoover was speaking in a low voice as if quite embarrassed and this gave me some courage, although when the chairman, the late ex-President Taft, introduced me he very vividly expressed my feelings by saying he was sure that I would rather face a battery of artillery than face that gathering. Among other things, I said in substance:

"Now that we are in the war, the Red Cross has new obligations. Its great work is to help the Allies. The people of France especially are in sore straits. The losses they have suffered have reduced their power to fight and to produce. We must supply their needs. It is our duty to assist them to rehabilitate themselves so that they can continue in the war. We must help their widows and orphans. We must help the French people in every way possible. The Red Cross will not fail."

The announcement was made by Mr. Davison that $100,000,000 would be needed to carry on the work with our own and the Allied armies. I did not think it would be possible to raise such an enormous sum through subscription and could hardly believe that so much money would be necessary. But the men handling the affairs of the society had large vision, as the contribution in that first drive was more than $114,000,000, and between June, 1917, and February, 1919, the total amount subscribed was over $400,000,000.   This response to Red Cross needs was a striking example of the generous spirit of our people.   How happy it would have made Clara Barton, whom I knew in Cuba during the Spanish-American War, if she could have been similarly supported, but the Red Cross was not then considered of such importance.   I recall that after the surrender of Santiago, when she was helping to feed the more needy Cubans, I gave her a lot of surplus rations that had been accumulated by my regiment, the 10th Cavalry, for which she was very grateful.

About the middle of May arrangements were made for me and my staff to sail, but on account of prowling German submarines sailings were uncertain and our departure was postponed from time to time until May 28th.   While important that we should get off, yet the extra time was well employed, especially by the members of the staff, in studying conditions and requirements and in placing advance requisitions for supplies in so far as our needs could be foreseen.   The details of organization for the 1st Division were worked out under my direction and orders for its concentration and embarkation prepared before we left.

The last few days included several formal calls on diplomatic representatives, with a semi-official luncheon or dinner thrown in here and there.   The French Ambassador and Madame Jusserand gave a luncheon at the Embassy that was memorable for its cordiality and charm.   She was American by birth and was most enthusiastic over our entry into the war.   With tears in her eyes, she said, "I always thought you would come in, and now I can be proud of my native country, for with America and France again fighting side by side I know we shall win."   Another similar occasion was an informal luncheon with Mr. Balfour, the cultured head of the British Mission, where, instead of books and politics, the conversation turned to the more practical phases of Allied coöperation.   The Secretary of State and Mrs. Lansing also entertained at dinner several members of the special missions then in Washington, among whom was the Prince of Udine, the Chief of the Italian Mission. In meeting the members of these various missions one could not help being impressed by their extreme anxiety for the future.

On the afternoon of May 24th, the Secretary of War and I called on President Wilson for my first and only meeting with him until he came to France after the Armistice. After engaging in conversation with Mr. Baker for a few minutes on the subject of shipping, he turned to me and said, "General, we are giving you some very difficult tasks these days," to which I replied, "Perhaps so, Mr. President, but that is what we are trained to expect." Mr. Wilson spoke of my recent expedition into Mexico and inquired about my acquaintance with France. I had naturally thought that he would say something about the part our Army should play in the war in coöperation with the Allied armies, but he said nothing.

Upon leaving, I said, "Mr. President, I appreciate the honor you have conferred upon me by the assignment you have given me and realize the responsibilities it entails, but you can count upon the best that is in me." His reply was, "General, you were chosen entirely upon your record and I have every confidence that you will succeed; you shall have my full support." The President then asked me to convey to His Majesty the King of Great Britain and to the President of France his greetings and best wishes. His manner was cordial and simple and I was impressed with his poise and his air of determination. His assurance of confidence in me was gratifying, but in the difficult situation that arose later regarding the manner of giving military aid to the Allies he was inclined to yield to the persistent importunities of the Allied representatives in Washington. In the actual conduct of operations I was given entire freedom and in this respect was to enjoy an experience unique in our history.

On May 27th, the day before I was to sail, the Secretary of War sent me a letter of instructions concerning my command, authority and duties in Europe, which is quoted here in full:

"War Department
"Washington

"May 26, 1917.

"Secret
"From: The Secretary of War.
"To: Major General J. J. Pershing, U. S. Army.
"Subject: Command, Authority and Duties in Europe.

"The President directs me to communicate to you the following:

"1. The President designates you to command all the land forces of the United States operating in Continental Europe and in the United Kingdom of Great Britain and Ireland, including any part of the Marine Corps which may be detached for service there with the Army. From your command are excepted the Military Attachés and others of the Army who may be on duty directly with our several embassies.

"2. You will proceed with your staff to Europe. Upon arrival in Great Britain, France or any other of the countries at war with the Imperial German Government, you will at once place yourself in communication with the American Embassy and through its agency with the authorities of any country to which the forces of the United States may be sent.

"3. You are invested with the authority and duties devolved by the laws, regulations, orders and customs of the United States upon the commander of an army in the field in time of war and with the authority and duties in like manner devolved upon department commanders in peace and war, including the special authorities and duties assigned to the commander of the Philippine Department in so far as the same are applicable to the particular circumstances of your command.

"4. You will establish, after consultation with the French War Office, all necessary bases, lines of communication, depots, etc., and make all the incidental arrangements essential to active participation at the front.

"5. In military operations against the Imperial German Government, you are directed to coöperate with the forces of the other countries employed against that enemy; but in so doing the underlying idea must be kept in view that the forces of the United States are a separate and distinct component of the combined forces, the identity of which must be preserved. This fundamental rule is subject to such minor exceptions in particular circumstances as your judgment may approve. The decision as to when your command, or any of its parts, is ready for action is confided to you, and you will exercise full discretion in determining the manner of coöperation. But, until the forces of the United States are in your judgment sufficiently strong to warrant operations as an independent command, it is understood that you will coöperate as a component of whatever army you may be assigned to by the French Government.

"6. You will keep the Department fully advised of all that concerns your command, and will communicate your recommendations freely and directly to the Department. And in general you are vested with all necessary authority to carry on the war vigorously in harmony with the spirit of these instructions and towards a victorious conclusion.

"NEWTON D. BAKER."

At the same time, the Chief of Staff handed me a letter, which is also quoted in full:

"WAR DEPARTMENT
"Office of the Chief of Staff

"Washington, D. C.,
"May 26, 1917.

"SECRET

"MAJOR GENERAL JOHN J. PERSHING, U. S. A.,

"WASHINGTON, D. C.,

"DEAR GENERAL PERSHING:

"In compliance with the orders of the President assigning you to the command of the United States forces in France, the Secretary of War directs that you proceed, with the necessary staff, to Paris, France, via England.

"The Secretary of War further directs that, upon your arrival in France, you establish such relations with the French Government and the military representatives of the British Government now serving in France as will enable you effectively to plan and conduct active operations in conjunction and in coöperation with the French armies operating in France against Germany and her allies.

"As a preliminary step, the Secretary of War deems it desirable that you have a thorough study made of the available bases, lines of communication and camps of instruction, so that you may direct preparations for the arrival of successive contingents of our troops in France. The equipment and training for active service of the troops under your command in the trenches or on the firing line should be carried on as rapidly as possible. While the entrance of our forces into the theater of active operations will be left entirely to your judgment, it should not be unduly hastened. Yet it is believed that the purpose of your presence in France will be materially advanced by the appearance of our troops upon the firing line.

"The Secretary of War desires that you keep the department fully advised of all questions of importance concerning the operations of your troops and that you submit your views from time to time upon such questions, as well as upon matters pertaining to the general situation in Europe.   He also expects that, as the superior military representative of the United States in France, you will exercise such general authority as will best contribute to the fulfillment of your mission in France.

"Very sincerely,
"TASKER H. BLISS,
"Major General,
"Acting Chief of Staff."

I have never understood why there should have been two letters of instructions emanating from the same authority.   However, they are both admirable examples of the powers that should be vested in a commander in the field and were never changed or amplified in any essential.   The insertion of the directions contained in paragraph five of the Secretary's letter regarding the identity of our forces was prompted by the efforts which had been made by both the British and French Missions to have the United States utilize her manpower as replacements for the Allies.   But the policy of building up eventually an independent American army had been discussed and was fully understood by the Secretary of War and myself.

As to coöperation, the instructions contained in the two letters are apparently in conflict.   According to the Secretary's letter it might be that our armies would actually serve in conjunction with any of the Allied armies.   According to the letter of the Chief of Staff it would be limited to service in coöperation with the French Army.   However, the general character of our mission was such as to indicate clearly that our forces should operate in combination with any of the Allied armies in France, according to circumstances.

MY party assembled at Governors Island on the date of sailing and we left from there to go aboard the British steamship *Baltic*. Upon my arrival at his headquarters, Major General J. Franklin Bell, then in command of the Eastern Department, most warmly extended his greetings and congratulations and presented the officers of his staff. After a brief conversation, he drove with me to the pier and reminded me of his letter in which he had asked for an active command. Knowing his physical condition, I was forced to remain noncommittal to this very dear friend. Though several years senior to me in rank and service, he would have served loyally, and I should have been fortunate to have had him, as his experience would have made him invaluable.

Despite persistent and powerful opposition in and out of the Army, General Bell, while Chief of Staff, had succeeded in developing through our service schools an effective system of training a limited number of officers for command and staff duty, and for this contribution to our success he deserves high praise. It was a source of keenest regret to me later that his failing health made it impossible to permit him to undertake arduous service in the field. His last days were filled with sadness and disappointment at not being allowed again to lead American soldiers in battle. It can be said of Franklin Bell that our army has never produced a finer type of officer and gentleman.

All of my party had been directed to proceed with the utmost secrecy, even to the extent of wearing civilian clothes until we reached the ship. Although we stole silently aboard the tender that carried us out through the fog and down the bay, the large number of quartermaster and other officers stationed near New York dashing about in uniform rather ostentatiously that day really gave notice that something out of the ordinary was happening. As if this were not sufficient notice the large number of boxes and crates piled up on the dock, addressed to various chiefs of supply departments, A.E.F., in my care, and the artillery salute fired from the batteries on Governors Island made the announcement of our departure complete. It can be said to the credit of the representatives of the press, however, that they were most discreet, as the newspapers in general published nothing about us until after we had landed in Europe.

It was the purpose of the British Admiralty, from which all their ships received sailing orders, to transfer my party to another vessel at Halifax, but after lying off that port in thick weather for about forty-eight hours the *Baltic* was directed to steer her course to a designated rendezvous.

Among the passengers were several British and Canadian officers with distinguished service at the front to their credit. They kindly consented to answer questions on the subjects of organization, training, and fighting. The conferences thus held and a study of confidential reports from the British and French helped to put us more closely in touch with many details which could not have been learned otherwise except through experience. The study of the French language was also taken up by many of the officers and refresher classes were in session at all hours under direction of those who had sufficient knowledge to become teachers.

One evening was given over to the customary entertainment for the benefit of British seamen's families, in which several of us took part as speakers, including one of the British officers; Mr. Frederick Palmer, the war correspondent; Mr. Charles H. Grasty, of the *New York Times;* and myself. The national anthems of the Allies and our own *Star Spangled Banner* were sung with enthusiasm, and on the whole the evening was given a pronounced inter-allied flavor.

During the voyage most of my time was spent in discussion with the heads of staff departments regarding their respective duties and plans. Major Harbord and I considered an organization for the General Staff, and the skeleton outline of principles then approved became the basis of the larger organization later adopted after a study of French and British general staff systems. Arrangements were made and officers designated to initiate immediately upon arrival in England and later to carry on in France the necessary investigations concerning ports, railways, and possible lines of communications. It was on board the *Baltic* that I tentatively decided that as a beginning we should plan for an army of at least 1,000,000 men to reach France as early as possible. Preliminary consideration was also given to such important subjects as the composition and organization of our forces; where they could best operate for decisive action; their relation to the Allied armies; and the availability of shipping for the transportation and supply of our troops.

The commander of the *Baltic,* Captain Finch, was a typical British sea-dog, who inspired every one with confidence in his efficiency. He very properly insisted that all should attend boat drills and each one become familiar with his assignment in case it should be necessary to abandon ship. In passing through the danger zone we all wore civilian clothing as it was certain that in the event of a successful attack by a German submarine its crew would fire upon any small boat carrying men in uniform.

On June 5th the *Baltic* began to zigzag on her course and we then realized that we were actually in the danger zone. The next morning the sight of an escort of two American destroyers, the *Tucker* and the *Rowan,* steaming well out on our flanks gave all on board somewhat of a thrill and fully restored confidence. Although there were many rumors and occasional alarms, no submarines were observed. The weather was perfect throughout the voyage except for the fog about Halifax, and if we had been going over for pleasure it would have been a delightful trip. But we were all very busy and kept at work without interference except by our medical officers, who, not to be remiss in their immediate obligations, vaccinated us every day or so against all the diseases that might be prevented by such measures.

(Diary) London, Sunday, June 10, 1917. Arrived at Liverpool on Friday morning and London that afternoon. Attended dinner given by the officials of the British War Office.

On Saturday paid a visit to Buckingham Palace, accompanied by my staff, and went from there to our Embassy. Called on the Duke of Connaught.

Attended divine services to-day at Westminster Abbey with several members of my staff. I accompanied Ambassador and Mrs. Walter Hines Page to the country for luncheon with Major and Lady Astor, and returned after dining with General Sir Arthur and Lady Paget.

We reached our anchorage in the Mersey River on the evening of June 7th and steamed into Liverpool the next morning under a clear sky. I had been in Europe twice before, my first visit being in September, 1899, en route to the Philippine Islands, as a bachelor, and the next in the autumn of 1908, on leave of absence, en route home from a second tour in the Islands, accompanied by my wife and two small children. The sojourn in France with my family had been filled with delightful visits to friends and with motor trips to historic places. The recollection of those happy days often came back to me very vividly in striking contrast with the troublous days of the war.

The *Baltic* reached the dock at 9:30 A.M., and a cordial reception awaited us. Rear Admiral Stileman, of the British Navy, and Sir Pitcairne Campbell, K.C.B., commanding the Western District of Home Defense, with the Lord Mayor and Lady Mayoress, came on board at once. After formal introductions, I went ashore with our hosts, accompanied by the principal members of my staff, to return the salute and walk through the ranks of the guard of honor. As we stepped off the gangplank onto British soil, the band struck up the *Star Spangled Banner* to welcome us, this being the first time in history that an American Army contingent was ever officially received in England.

The very smart-looking guard of honor was from the 3d Battalion, Royal Welch Fusiliers, and most of the men in ranks had seen service in France, many of them proudly wearing wound chevrons. Not the least picturesque member of the detachment was the thoroughly groomed, ribbon-bedecked goat, the regimental mascot, which strode up and down with an air of considerable importance.

The selection of the Royal Welch Fusiliers as guard of honor had a sentimental significance in that the regiment not only fought against us at Bunker Hill but it fought beside us during the Boxer Rebellion in China. An interesting feature of the uniform of the Royal Welch was a black patch on the neck and upper part of the back of the tunic. During our Revolutionary War they wore the periwig with its queue, and while serving in Nova Scotia after having fought in the British Army from Bunker Hill to Yorktown they learned that it had been discontinued. As the last regiment to wear the queue, they took the ribbons with which it had been tied and sewed them on their tunics. This "flash" was later recognized officially as a distinctive mark of their uniform. The preservation of this badge of former service struck all of us as a characteristic example of the conservatism of the British that served so well during the World War to hold the people to their traditional obligations.

Following the reception on the wharf, we returned on board and stood along the rail at the salute while the band played *God Save the King*. The formalities being over, about fifty British and American newspaper men assembled in the lounging room for an interview. My natural aversion to that sort of thing was strongly reënforced by the conviction that this was not the time to do much talking. After evading several questions, I finally yielded to their insistence and said:

"Speaking for myself personally, the officers of my staff, and the members of my command, we are very glad indeed to be the standard bearers of our country in this great war for civilization. To land on British soil and to receive the welcome accorded us seems very significant and is deeply appreciated. We expect in course of time to be playing our part, and we hope it will be a very large part, on the Western Front."

The royal coach was attached to a special train for our use and after leave-taking we pulled out for London. En route Captain Charles de Marenches, of the French Army, who had been sent by General Pétain, reported for duty as a member of my personal staff, in which position he rendered invaluable service throughout the war.

Within a few hours our train reached Euston Station, where we were heartily welcomed by Lord Derby, Secretary of State for War; Field Marshal Sir John French; Lieutenant General Sir Francis Lloyd; Brigadier General Lord Brooke; Mr. Walter H. Page, the American Ambassador; Admiral William S. Sims, U.S.N., and many others. We were escorted to the Savoy Hotel and became guests of the British Government. There was nothing unusual to mark our arrival except the cordial reception at the station and a few complimentary notices in the press. Our appearance on the streets attracted little attention, as many of our military men had passed through England on one mission or another and the American uniform had become a common sight in London.

That evening the senior members of my party were tendered a dinner at the Savoy by members of the British War Office and we had an excellent opportunity to meet and get acquainted with many officials who were later on to be of material assistance to us. Brigadier General Lord Brooke was assigned as my aide while in England and Major Maitland Kersey kindly acted as guide about London. It was on one of my visits with the latter to a tailor shop that I first met Field Marshal, then General, Lord Allenby, who later achieved fame in the campaign in Palestine. Several officers were detailed to look out for members of the staff and arrange for them to meet the heads of the British staff departments whom they wished to consult.

Together with my senior staff officers, I was invited to visit the King at Buckingham Palace on the morning of June 9th. His Majesty, smartly dressed in the uniform of a Field Marshal, received me in democratic fashion for a few minutes before the others were presented. I gave him the President's message, to which he replied with high praise of Mr. Wilson, commenting upon the very large war powers of our Chief Executive. His Majesty was pleased that America had come into the war and dwelt upon the fact that Anglo-Saxon peoples were at last united in a common cause. He mentioned the great cost of the war, the large numbers of men Great Britain had already furnished the Army and Navy, and the tremendous losses they had suffered. He severely condemned the German submarine atrocities and told of the recent sinking of several vessels with the loss of practically all on board. He was not optimistic over the outlook and expressed the hope that we "would send over a large number of destroyers." As to aviation, he had heard through the dispatches the extravagant claims of certain boastful Americans and he asked me whether we really expected soon to have 50,000 airplanes in the field. I had to acknowledge that such reports were extremely exaggerated and that we should not be sending over any planes for some time to come.

He inquired particularly regarding the organization of our Army and the prospects of our bringing a large force to France. I explained the Draft Act and what I thought would be the plans of the War Department, but it turned out that my views were rather optimistic, at least as to the immediate future. He mentioned with satisfaction the successful explosion on June 7th of extensive mines under an important German position on Messines Ridge, which was subsequently captured by the British. Incidentally, I visited this spot after the close of the war and found that the craters had become large lakes, one of which was being used at the moment as a bathing pool by hundreds of German prisoners employed in clearing the débris from the battlefields. His Majesty was exceedingly well informed, interesting and earnest, and his informal manner made one feel quite at ease.

When I presented my staff he spoke a few words of welcome, and among other things said:

"It has always been my dream that the two English-speaking nations should some day be united in a great cause, and to-day my dream is realized. Together we are fighting for the greatest cause for which peoples could fight. The Anglo-Saxon race must save civilization."

Leaving the palace, we went to our Embassy and the members of my staff were presented to the Ambassador by my old friend, Irwin Laughlin, the Counselor, with whom I had served at our Legation in Tokyo when I was there as Military Attaché. During the conversation which followed, Mr. Page remarked how happy he was that America was at last in the war, and added, "Now I am able to hold up my head and look people squarely in the eye." He said he had always believed it our duty to help the Allies and that many times in trying to maintain cordial relations between the two Governments he had been tremendously handicapped, but now his task would be less difficult. He was very modest and unassuming, but his courage, his broad knowledge of affairs and his practical common sense enabled him to render distinguished service to our country during a distressing period. Throughout his career as ambassador he was beloved and honored by the British people, who admired his virile personality. Many Americans, however, did not approve of his rather apologetic attitude toward his own country prior to our entry into the war.

I had a talk with Admiral Sims, who was not in personal command of our fleet serving with the British Navy, but remained in London with an office at our Embassy and directed the movements of our naval vessels, especially destroyers, from there. He was not satisfied with the support given him from home and complained that the Navy Department had not sent all the destroyers asked for. He said the Department seemed to fear attacks along our coast and did not realize the danger to the cause in the enormous destruction of merchant shipping going on in European waters. His report of these losses was nothing short of startling, but he thought they might be checked if he could have a sufficient number of destroyers. Without more of this class of vessels, Sims was not sanguine over the prospects of protecting our transports. However, he made it clear that every possible effort would be made to that end. This conversation increased my anxiety about getting the American forces to France in time to beat the German armies before they could gain a decision over the Allies.

Our objective was well defined and we could not delay for the possible destruction of the German submarine fleet. The war could not be ended until the German land forces were beaten. Troop movements overseas had been conducted in previous wars while hostile fleets were intact. I was with the Shafter Expedition in 1898, and sailed from Tampa, Florida, for Santiago, Cuba, while the Spanish fleet was still in being, and had seen Japanese transports cross the China Sea en route for Manchuria while Russian fleets were in existence. Irrespective of the outcome of the warfare being waged against submarines, we had to assume the risks and put our armies into the battle at the earliest moment if the Allies were to have the superiority which was necessary to defeat the Germans.

After the usual visits of courtesy to the houses of the other members of the royal family, I called by appointment on Field Marshal the Duke of Connaught. His intimate knowledge of American affairs in general, acquired, no doubt, while he was Governor General of Canada, and of our military history in particular, made the call most interesting. As a soldier of experience, the Field Marshal, more than any other official in England with whom I talked, seemed to realize the difficulties that lay before us and the time it would take to overcome them.

Nothing that occurred while we were in London left me with a deeper impression of British stamina than the religious services at Westminster. The Archbishop of Canterbury spoke feelingly of the nation's sacrifices and, referring to our presence, expressed confidence in the successful issue of the war. I had visited the Abbey before, but this joint meeting there with the British, high and low, amidst the old things, the traditions, the history, seemed to symbolize the unity of aims and purposes of our two peoples, through which, fighting shoulder to shoulder, we should one day achieve the victory.

The drive with the Pages from London to Cliveden through the well-kept countryside was delightful. The Ambassador told me that Lady Astor and her husband had been very helpful to him since he had been in England and he wanted us to meet them. When we arrived, they greeted us cordially, introduced their four children and made us feel entirely at home. Lady Astor, a native of Virginia, whom everybody called Nancy, was quite as informal as she ever could have been as Miss Langhorne back where she was born. We soon found ourselves seated with some twenty people at the luncheon table, over which she presided with simple dignity.

In the afternoon we strolled through the estate and presently came to the Canadian hospital nearby, where Lady Astor was hailed with affection. As we went through the wards she seemed to know every man by name and had a cheerful word for each one. My visit to this hospital was my first contact with the tragic side of the war. At her request, I was glad to speak to a group of convalescent soldiers assembled on the lawn, who accepted my remarks, no doubt, as coming from a neighbor who spoke their dialect. It was altogether an interesting afternoon, made so particularly by our charming hostess who had adapted herself to British surroundings without sacrifice of the dominant American traits so evident in her character.

In the evening several of us, including Harbord, Alvord and Brewster of my staff, had dinner with General Sir Arthur and Lady Paget, in company with Ambassador and Mrs. Page, Lady Drogheda and Mrs. Leeds. Lady Paget, formerly Miss Stevens, of New York, was very happy at the news that one of her sons had been promoted to the grade of Brigadier General. Sir Arthur had passed the age for active service and at the moment was in command of Home Defense Forces.

(Diary) London, Monday, June 11, 1917. In company with the Pages had luncheon with the King and Queen and Princess Mary.

In the afternoon called on General Robertson and visited Parliament
House. Attended dinner given by the American Ambassador.

There was an air of charm and simplicity at Buckingham
Palace that permitted a freedom in the conversation more or less
intimate. The plain fare was quite in keeping with the food
situation throughout England. All were enthusiastic over our
entry into the war and hopeful that we might soon participate
actively. After leaving the luncheon table, the King, the Ambassador and I stood near a window overlooking the garden,
which, as his Majesty explained, instead of growing flowers as
usual was producing a crop of potatoes. He told of the visit of
the Kaiser to London a few years before and how he had brought
his Chief of Secret Service along and put him up at one of the
hotels to learn all he could, while the Kaiser himself was, of
course, a guest at the Palace.

His Majesty spoke bitterly of the inhumanity of the Germans
and dwelt especially on the night bombing of London. Pointing
to the beautiful statue of Queen Victoria, just outside of the
window, he said, with a solemn expression of profound indigna-
tion, "The Kaiser has even tried to destroy the statue of his own
grandmother." If the resentment of King George at the air
raids over London reflected the feelings of his people, then the
German Government made a very serious blunder in carrying
on this hideous form of warfare against the unarmed masses, of
whom the greater part were women and children. There is no
doubt that these attacks served to strengthen British determination to fight to the last man.

After leaving the Palace, I called on General Sir William
Robertson, Chief of the Imperial General Staff. He was a rugged,
heavy-set, blunt soldier, of Scottish descent, whose record in the
army had been exceptional in that he had risen from the grade
of private to his high position. As he sipped his tea, I explained
our plan for the organization of our armies by raising the small
Regular force and the National Guard to war strength and
training additional units besides. As the British themselves had
gone through the same experience about two years before, I

stressed the fact that the latter process would take considerable time. Like all the British officials, he was much in favor of having our army serve with or near their forces. He pointed out that we were both Anglo-Saxons, spoke the same language, and gave other reasons to support his views. It seemed necessary to explain in detail that as the American Navy was working in conjunction with the British Navy we should probably plan to place our land forces beside the French if there were to be any preference. It appeared logical that we should do this as we were to operate on French soil and use French ports, railways and matériel. The main thing, I went on to say, was to form our own army as soon as possible and use it to the best advantage in beating the Germans.

I emphasized our lack of tonnage and told him that we must have additional shipping if we were to bring over an army worth while, but his reaction to this was not encouraging. He said he thought that it was entirely out of the question for the British to provide us with any shipping since they were already in sore straits to find vessels for their own national necessities.

At Parliament House I met several of the members and had tea on the terrace overlooking the Thames with Mr. Winston Churchill, then Minister of Munitions. Unusually well informed on American affairs, he showed the keenest interest in our plans and prospects. The equipment of our armies was naturally one of mutual concern and I found him ready to provide British artillery if necessary. We had, however, already practically decided to adopt the French types of artillery.

In the evening a few of us were entertained at dinner [1] by the American Ambassador. I had suggested to him that I much preferred not to have a formal dinner, as we had come on a

---

[1] Among those present were Mr. Lloyd George, Prime Minister; Mr. Arthur Balfour, Minister of Foreign Affairs; M. Paul Cambon, French Ambassador; Lord Derby, Minister for War; Lord Robert Cecil; Admiral Jellicoe; Admiral W. R. Hall; General Sir William Robertson; General Macdonogh; General Sir John Cowans, Quartermaster General; General Sir Francis Lloyd; Field Marshal Viscount French; Mr. W. H. Page, American Ambassador; Admiral Sims; General Smuts, of Boer War fame; Mr. Irwin Laughlin, Counselor of the Embassy; Col. Wm. Lassiter, Military Attaché; and Mr. Edward Bell, First Secretary.

serious mission, but he was so elated that our country was in the war that he insisted on our meeting some of his British friends in this way. It was a notable company of men in official life, civil, military and naval. Our activity as participants in the war was to bring us into contact with every one of them during the succeeding two years.

(Diary) London, Tuesday, June 12, 1917. Spent a most interesting forenoon visiting the training center of General Paget's command, where recruits are given a nine weeks' course before going to the front. Returned to the city for luncheon with Lord and Lady Derby and later called on Mr. Lloyd George. Attended State dinner.

At the training camp we witnessed an interesting demonstration of British methods of making an attack, including the tactical formations of successive thin lines, the employment of special weapons incident to trench fighting, and defense against gas. With the use of trench mortars and hand grenades the exercise was more realistic than anything we had so far seen in our own service. Most of the men engaged were unfit for active duty at the front, many of them having been wounded or sent home ill and only sufficiently convalescent to be useful for home defense or for training new drafts. Many British officers realized that the period of nine weeks' training for recruits was insufficient, but such preparation was for trench warfare only. Much to my surprise they gave little thought to the possibilities of open warfare in the near future, if at all.

On our return to London a few of us were guests at an informal luncheon given by the Secretary of State for War and Lady Derby. Their hospitality was only equalled by Lord Derby's very earnest desire in his official capacity to be of service to us. He was more than courteous and during my short stay we formed a friendship that later made coöperation easy wherever his authority was concerned. According to arrangements which he kindly made, his assistants took a personal interest in giving the members of my staff every facility for the study of British combat formations, tactical training, supply and replacement systems, and for consultation with their experienced staff officers on all subjects that would aid us in completing our staff and line organizations.

Mr. Lloyd George, the Prime Minister, when I met him, went right to the point and inquired as to when our troops would be organized and trained and the numbers we expected to send over. He was affable and expressed a desire to help us in every possible manner, but when I stressed our need of assistance to transport our troops he did not seem to be particularly interested and gave little hope that the British would be able to furnish us any shipping whatever.

In the evening a State dinner [1] was given at Lancaster House to the senior members of my party. It was official without being either stiff or formal and was intended not only as a social welcome tendered us by about twenty of the leading officials of the Government but as a gathering for friendly discussion. The British, of course, wanted to show their satisfaction that we were in the war, although I feared that they were building too high their hopes of early American aid.

Much to my gratification, the speeches were limited to toasts to the King and the President. Mr. Lloyd George, who presided, was in excellent humor and frequently joked with his confrères at his own and other tables. Lord Curzon was late in arriving, which the Prime Minister said was no doubt due to the fact that he had lately taken a young American wife. And he added that the delay reminded him of French officials, who were proverbially late. The various social functions which we attended in England and France occupied considerable time, but they were the means of establishing good feeling and understanding, so important for a beginning.

Underneath the surface of the seeming cheerfulness there was

[1] Attended by Mr. G. N. Barnes, M.P.; General Lord Brooke; Sir Edward Carson; Lord Robert Cecil; Major Spender Clay; Mr. H. J. Creedy; Earl Curzon; Lt. Gen. Sir F. Davies; Sir M. de Bunsen; The Earl of Derby; The Hon. Sir Eric Drummond; Mr. H. W. Forster; General Furse; Lord Hardinge of Penhurst; Gen. Sir D. Henderson; Col. James; Major Maitland Kersey; Sir Guy Laking; Col. Lassiter, U.S.A.; Gen. Macdonogh; Capt. MacDougall; Mr. J. I. MacPherson; Viscount Milner; Mr. W. H. Page, the United States Ambassador; Admiral Sims, U. S. Navy; Mr. R. F. Synge; Mr. Andrew Weir.

more than a suggestion of serious apprehension. U-boat activities were spoken of almost in whispers. At the dinner, we were again told of the total losses, which, including April, had reached 3,000,000 tons, and during April and May amounted to 1,500,000 tons. It was an appalling increase. The figures could not be given out, of course, for fear the knowledge would hearten the enemy and frighten the Allied peoples, and the public did not know until long afterward just how grave the situation was. From a rough calculation, it was easy to conclude that if the destruction of British shipping continued at that rate there would soon be none left either to help transport an American army to Europe or to supply it after arrival.

Under the circumstances, the apparent unconcern of the British as to our need of shipping is not difficult to understand. They were seriously alarmed regarding their own food situation. It seemed to me, however, that they had allowed their pessimism to carry them too far, but at the moment they could see no relief for the future and hence no prospect of aiding us in tonnage.

In the bearing and attitude of the people in general there was little to indicate the uneasiness which they felt regarding the outcome of the war, although one frequently caught a troubled expression among the faces of people in the streets. There was, naturally, considerable military activity to be seen, but the people went about their business apparently in the usual fashion. The shortage of food and the continuous air raids at night had a depressing effect. From nearly every family some member was numbered among the dead, but there were few women in mourning. In the seacoast towns there was said to be considerable fear of invasion, much the same, no doubt, as existed along our Atlantic seaboard during the Spanish-American War, so that probably larger forces than necessary were held for home defenses to satisfy coast residents. The burden of three years of war, with no end in sight, bore heavily upon the people and hidden forebodings filled many a heart. Still underneath all this there was an unflinching courage and dogged determination that held the man at the front up to his task and the people at home solidly behind him. London was the objective for men on leave for a few days and individuals or groups of the various units were easily identified, from the "Tommy," smart in his plain uniform of dark khaki, and the bare-kneed Highlander in checkered kilts, to the Canadian and Australian in campaign hats much like our own. They were over from France for a change and rest, newcomers constantly taking the places of others as the brief period of vacation expired. Under the surface these soldiers perhaps saw more of depression than the casual observer and most of them were glad to get back to the front, where "things were different," they said.

Early on the morning of June 13th we were off for France, and after taking leave of our hosts or their representatives we boarded a special train for Folkestone, where we took the Channel boat to Boulogne. We left with the feeling that our stay in London had been pleasant, in spite of war conditions, and above all, that it had been profitable. Much detailed information was obtained while in England that was to be of the greatest value to us later on.

CHAPTER V

AFTER an exceptionally smooth passage our cross-Channel boat reached Boulogne about 10 A.M., and there, lined up at present arms under the covered dock, stood a guard of honor of French Territorials in field uniform, while the band played the American and French national anthems. Then both civil and military representatives came on board with enthusiastic greetings. As we stepped on shore with our new hosts, we were made doubly welcome in words that expressed both gratitude and hope. It was a significant and solemn moment and I am sure that each one of us silently wished that our Army might have been more nearly ready to fulfill the mission that loomed so large before us. The French troops, together with the assembled men, women, and children from the town in the background, presented a colorful picture, and as we walked along the ranks of the guard of honor it was observed that their stripes and decorations indicated that every man had seen service at the front.

Among those who came to greet us were the Under-Secretary of War, M. Besnard; Colonel Jacques Aldebert de Chambrun, who later became one of my aides; Brigadier General Peltier, a one-armed veteran, who was to be liaison officer at my head-quarters; Brigadier General Duport, representing Major General Pétain; Major Thouzellier, representing Marshal Joffre; Admiral Ronarc'h, representing the Navy; Major General Dumas, commanding troops in the North; the Prefect and other local French officials; and Lieutenant General Fowke, Adjutant General of the British Expeditionary Force.[1]

There was some delay in our departure for Paris, and to pass the time we were taken to see the old sixteenth century fort overlooking the harbor, which it formerly protected. Although the railway to Paris runs through an attractive part of France, our five days in London had been so strenuous that I retired to my compartment for a rest and did not see much of the country. The journey, as I afterwards learned, was regulated so that we should arrive about the close of business hours in the evening in order that the French people might take part in an impromptu welcome, the idea being to give them visual evidence that Americans were actually coming.

The officials who met us at the station included M. Painlevé, Minister of War;[2] Marshal Joffre; M. Viviani; Major General Foch, then Chief of Staff; Ambassador William G. Sharp, and many others. There was nothing formal about our reception, in fact it was cordially informal, simple and brief, with no speechmaking, and consisted merely of introductions all around. The station was packed with people and the atmosphere seemed electrical with pent-up enthusiasm. In the assignment to automobiles, M. Painlevé and I were placed together and took the lead, followed by the members of my staff, each with a distinguished French companion.

The acclaim that greeted us as we drove through the streets en route to the hotel was to me a complete surprise. Dense masses of people lined the boulevards and filled the squares. It was said that never before in the history of Paris had there been such an outpouring of people. Men, women, and children absolutely packed every foot of space, even to the windows and

[1] In the French armies there are two grades of general officer: Brigadier General and Major General, the next and highest rank being Marshal. In the British armies the grades are Brigadier General, Major General, Lieutenant General, and General, then Field Marshal. In our service we follow the British except that General is the highest rank.

[2] M. Painlevé became Prime Minister in September, 1917, but continued to hold the portfolio of Minister of War.

housetops. Cheers and tears were mingled together and shouts of enthusiasm fairly rent the air. Women climbed into our automobiles screaming, "Vive l'Amérique," and threw flowers until we were literally buried. Everybody waved flags and banners. At several points the masses surged into the streets, entirely beyond control of the police.

In every possible manner the French gave full sway to their emotions. It is not easy to imagine that any people could be so wildly demonstrative. It was most touching and in a sense most pathetic. It brought home to us as nothing else could have done a full appreciation of the war-weary state of the nation and stirred within us a deep sense of the responsibility resting upon America. After our arrival at the Crillon Hotel I was again and again forced to appear on the portico of my apartment to greet the dense crowds that lingered in the Place de la Concorde. The acclaim by the people of Paris was in no sense a personal tribute to me like that given to Marshal Joffre in America. It was simply a spontaneous outburst of joy over the evidence of support from a nation whose traditional friendship was sincere and unselfish. I was to see its parallel when the Armistice was signed and on two other occasions, once when President Wilson arrived, and later when the Victory Parade took place on July 14, 1919.

A group of press representatives, largely French, called later for an interview and my knowledge of their language was immediately put to the test. After a sentence or two I concluded in my mother tongue and for some time thereafter limited further attempts to an occasional familiar phrase. Former Ambassador, "Uncle Bob" Bacon, as he was informally known at my headquarters, used to tell how Mr. Roosevelt "murdered" the language in his speech before the French Institute, and this gave me courage to try again in an address here and there.

On the evening of our arrival Ambassador and Mrs. Sharp gave a dinner for me and the principal officers of my staff, which was attended by many distinguished French civil and military officials and several members of the American colony. No one could have been more elated than the Ambassador, who no doubt expressed the sentiments of all Americans in France when, with trembling voice, he said: "You cannot realize the satisfaction I feel that we are in the war and that you are here to prepare for our participation. It is a great day for America and for France. The civilian now gives way to the soldier," and he added, "I hope you have not arrived too late." That same thought was in everybody's mind, so low was the morale of Allied peoples and their armies.

(Diary) Paris, Thursday, June 14, 1917. There never could have been another welcome such as that given us yesterday by the populace of Paris. Difficult to see how we are to meet the expectations of the French. To-day I visited Les Invalides, including Napoleon's tomb. Called on President Poincaré and had luncheon with him and Madame Poincaré at the Palace. Afterwards went to the Chamber of Deputies, thence to Le Bourget aviation field. Later called on the Minister of Marine. Dined with the Minister of War.

Although I was very anxious to get to work, it was necessary for me to make certain official calls and attend a few entertainments that had been planned for us. The French suggested that we should first go to visit Napoleon's tomb in Les Invalides. Founded in the reign of Louis XIV as a hospital for disabled veterans, the building has become the great French war museum and now contains, as every one knows, many beautiful works of art, together with relics that cover the history of French wars for generations.

We were taken to the tomb of Napoleon and down to the crypt, where I was handed the great key and was asked to unlock the heavy wrought iron entrance door. We were shown the uniforms and the baton that belonged to Napoleon and then his sword. Our veteran escort reverently removed the sword from the case and offered it to me as if to transmit some of the genius of the great captain. So much of French sentiment and tradition are associated with this tomb and its treasures that every one who visits there with Frenchmen must share their feelings of profound emotion. This incident, more than any other connected with my reception, impressed me with the martial spirit of the French people.

I called next to pay my respects to President Poincaré and to present greetings from President Wilson. "The French people are very happy," he said, "that America is in the war. Your coming is a great satisfaction to us." He inquired generally about our plans, seeking, as they all did, some assurance that we should soon be in the trenches. His attitude was rather formal and reserved, but he at once impressed me as a man of ability and force.

The President and Madame Poincaré invited me and several members of the staff to the Élysée Palace to luncheon, which was delightful in every particular. Nowhere are such things done so well as in Paris at the palace of the President. The plate, the silver, the linen are models of taste, while the menu and service find no parallel elsewhere. M. and Mme. Poincaré both understand English thoroughly and she speaks it perfectly. From her account, and that of many others, of the deplorable conditions and the sorrow throughout France, I seriously wondered whether the morale of the people could be restored. She felt certain that it could be and cheerfully added that our presence had already heartened them.

In the afternoon I visited the Chamber of Deputies in company with our Ambassador and heard a speech by M. Viviani in which he referred with much feeling to his reception in the United States and mentioned his having been privileged to deliver an address before Congress. His eloquence over America's entrance into the war and what it meant to France caused prolonged cheering and an enthusiastic recognition of our presence by the Deputies.

Later on several of us went to the aviation field at Le Bourget, where we saw numbers of airplanes always held in readiness to take the air against raids by enemy aircraft. The defense system also included the latest developments in anti-aircraft guns, both at Le Bourget and in the suburbs. The exhibition of attack and pursuit formations and of other expert flying left us with the painful thought that our aviation had a long way to go to attain similar efficiency.

Incidentally, I must mention our wild automobile ride to Le Bourget. Not to be outdone by aviators, the Prefect of Police directed our car through the crowded streets of Paris at not less than sixty miles an hour, all the while yelling and swinging his arms and scattering traffic right and left as though we were going to a fire. Every block furnished a new sensation, each hair-breadth escape from a crash being more narrow than the one before. This was far too dangerous for me, so, yielding to my protests, the Prefect on the return trip broke no more records for speed.

I next called on the Minister of Marine, M. Lacaze, who dwelt on the gravity of the losses by submarines and the consequent menace of food shortage. France was actually dependent for her food supply upon some 1,200,000 tons of British shipping that had been allotted to her use. Although the Minister claimed that the food situation was becoming serious, the British held that the French Government failed to limit the consumption of food by the people to the same extent they did.

In the evening the Minister of War gave us a dinner, where we met several members of the Cabinet and made some new and important acquaintances. The dinner was held at the Ministry in a room fitted up for the occasion with rich tapestries and other decorations. It was a sort of get-together party that marked the real starting point of our association with the various French bureaus and their chiefs.

(Diary) Paris, Saturday, June 16, 1917. Lunched yesterday with Marshal and Madame Joffre at the Military Club. He and I were called to the veranda several times to greet the crowds. Visited the Senate and met its President, M. Dubost, and other Senators. In company with the Marquis de Chambrun and his brother, Colonel de Chambrun, descendants of Lafayette, drove to Picpus Cemetery and placed a wreath on Lafayette's tomb.

Harbord and I visited the French General Headquarters at Compiègne to-day and had luncheon with Major General Pétain. Went to front lines near Saint Quentin with Major General d'Espérey and got our first glimpse of enemy positions.

Attended special performance at the Opéra Comique this evening in my honor.

The visit to French General Headquarters was primarily to meet General Pétain and the officers of his staff. Pétain is above medium height and weight, he wore a full mustache, slightly gray, and was then about sixty. He has a kindly expression, is most agreeable, but not especially talkative. His keen sense of humor became apparent from the jokes he told at the expense of some of his staff. Our conversation after luncheon was almost entirely on military affairs, including America's probable part in the war, which, as matters stood, gave little promise of becoming effective until the following spring.

My impression of Pétain was favorable and it remained unchanged throughout the war. Our friendship, which I highly treasure, had its beginning at this meeting. Complete coöperation is difficult even under the most favorable conditions and is rarely attained between men or peoples of different nationalities, but it seemed probable that Pétain's breadth of vision, his common sense and his sound judgment would make for understanding, and this proved to be the case.

At the luncheon there were several general officers, among whom was Major General Franchet d'Espérey, then in command of a group of armies under Pétain. He was considered one of the ablest and most aggressive officers in the French Army and was very popular with his men. He was short and stout, of ruddy complexion, and somewhat quick tempered, but a most agreeable companion. As we wished to get a glimpse of the actual front, he took us by motor as near as possible without drawing the fire of the enemy's artillery, although at the time there was little activity on that part of the front. The point of observation that we reached was opposite Saint Quentin, which was then within the enemy's lines, and which was later near the center of the great German drive of 1918 against the British. On the return trip the chauffeur, after being cautioned several times, continued to drive at a somewhat dangerous speed, which so exasperated the General that he finally threatened the chauffeur with violence, whereupon the speed was greatly reduced.

(Diary) Paris, Monday, June 18, 1917. Our headquarters are temporarily at 27 and 31 rue Constantine. We have scanty accommodations but sufficient for our probable brief stay in Paris.

Harjes, of Morgan, Harjes Bank, called to-day. I spent the afternoon in conference with the staff.

Basically the Allied situation appears to be worse than reported.

As we were now ready to begin the foundations of our great military structure, it seems pertinent to give a brief summary of what had happened in Europe during the war up to that time.

1914. Although the Germans in 1914 had failed in their immediate purpose, their armies were in almost complete possession of Belgium and occupied rich industrial regions of northern France, embracing one-fourteenth of her population and about three-fourths of her coal and iron. They held a strongly fortified line 468 miles in length, stretching from the Swiss border to Nieuport on the North Sea. They were within forty-eight miles of Paris and the initiative remained in their hands. The close of 1914 found the Russian armies ejected from East Prussia and driven back on Warsaw.

The entry of Turkey into the war, because of the moral effect upon the Moslem world and the immediate and constant threat created against Allied communications with the Far East, led to an effort by the Allies in the direction of the Dardanelles.

1915. Italy joined the Allies in May, 1915, and gave their cause new strength, but the effect was more or less offset when Bulgaria entered on the side of the Central Powers.

The threatening situation on the Russian front and in the Balkans was still such that Germany was compelled to exert an immediate offensive effort in those directions and to maintain only a defensive attitude on the Western Front. German arms achieved a striking series of successes in the vicinity of the Mazurian Lakes and in Galicia, capturing Warsaw, Brest-Litovsk and Vilna. The Central Powers overran Serbia and Montenegro.

Meanwhile, the Italian armies forced Austria to use approximately one-half of her strength against them.

In the west the French and British launched offensives but the objectives were limited and the results unimportant.

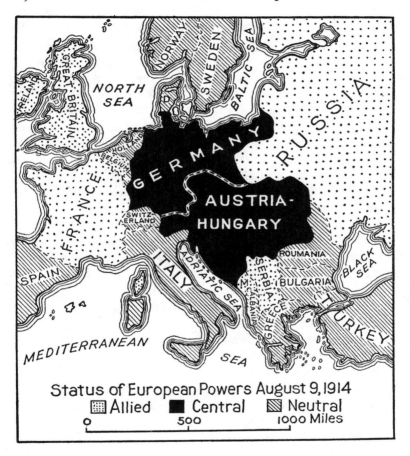

Status of European Powers August 9, 1914
Allied   Central   Neutral
0   500   1000 Miles

The Dardanelles expedition, having failed in its mission, was withdrawn in January, 1916. In Mesopotamia the Allied operations had not been wholly successful. Although the British fleet had established its superiority on the sea, the German submarine blockade had developed into a serious menace to Allied shipping.

1916. Germany no doubt believed that her advantage on the Eastern Front again warranted an offensive in the West and her attack against Verdun was accordingly launched in the spring of 1916. Every preparation by the Germans was made in the most thorough manner. Although unprepared for the attack, the French met it with great courage. There followed probably the most severe battle of the war, which was only ended the following summer by the successful offensive of the British and French armies along the Somme, which forced Germany to return to the defensive in the West. Russia was not yet beaten and early in June, aided at the same time by the threat of the Italians in the West, she began a great drive in Galicia that proved disastrous to Austria. Roumania, having entered on the side of the Allies, undertook a promising offensive against Austria. In September, Germany initiated a campaign in the East which, before the close of the year, was calamitous for Russia as well as Roumania.

1917. Germany, retaining on the Eastern Front the forces considered sufficient for the final conquest of Russia, was prepared to aid Austria in an offensive against Italy. The relatively low strength of the German forces in the West and the successful defense of Verdun by the French, however, led them, with much confidence, to attempt a decision on this front in April, known as the Nivelle Offensive. Their casualties were very heavy and the effort signally failed. Meanwhile, the revolution in Russia forecast the final collapse of the Czarist régime.

Financial problems of the Allies were becoming more difficult, supplies were being exhausted, all of which added to their tremendous losses caused discouragement, not only among the civil populations but throughout the armies as well. Allied resources in manpower were low and there was little prospect of materially increasing their armed strength, even in the face of the probability of having practically the entire military force of the Central Powers against them in the spring of 1918.

Thus, during three years Germany had seen practically all her offensives excepting that at Verdun crowned with success. Her battle lines were held on foreign soil and she had withstood every Allied attack since the Marne. The German General Staff could now foresee the complete elimination of Russia, the possibility of defeating Italy before the end of the year, and, finally, the campaign of 1918 against the French and British on the Western Front which might terminate the war. With the results of the submarine campaign in her favor, it cannot be said that German hopes of final victory were extravagant, either as viewed at that time or as seen in the light of history.

The Nivelle defeat, previously referred to, well-nigh blasted Allied hopes. Naturally enough, the successful defense of Verdun in 1916 and the British gains along the Somme seemed to revive the spirit of determination and confidence of the Allies, especially the French, who were encouraged to undertake this offensive in the following spring. The superiority of the Allies over the Germans on the Western Front at the time was more than 20 per cent, or, as measured in divisions, it was 190 to 154.

Under the circumstances, it was decided in November, 1916, while Marshal Joffre was still Commander-in-Chief, that the Allies should attempt to break through the German lines on a broad front between Soissons and Reims. In December, General Nivelle, of Verdun fame, succeeded to the high command, and a change in the ministry in March brought in M. Painlevé as Minister of War. Although some opposition had developed to the plan, the new French commander determined to carry it out with some modifications.[1]

By agreement between the two Allies, the British were to assist by making a subsidiary attack on the Arras front, and preliminary attacks were to be made on other portions of the French and British front to draw German divisions to those fronts. After this the French were to assault the weakened German lines on the Aisne and overwhelm them. In order to insure the coöperation

[1] See Painlevé's "How I Appointed Foch and Pétain," in which he states: "In January, 1917, three months before opening his offensive movement, General Nivelle declared, 'We shall break the German front at will, provided we do not attack it at its strongest point, and provided we carry out our operations by means of surprise and sudden attack, in from twenty-four to forty-eight hours.' "

of the two armies, it was understood between the British War Cabinet and Government and the French Government that except in so far as he might consider that this would endanger the safety of his army, Marshal Haig should conform his preparations to the views of the Commander-in-Chief of the French Army (General Nivelle). It was further agreed that during the operations Marshal Haig should carry out the orders of General

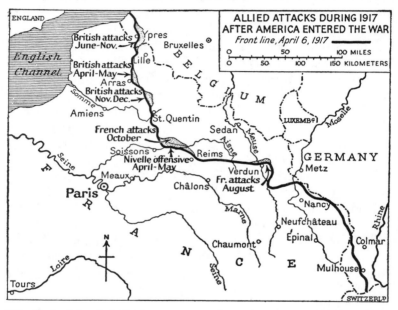

Nivelle.[1] Marshal Haig was not pleased with the arrangement and insisted on such modification as would insure his retaining control of his own forces.

The French had assembled a strong mobile force close in rear of their assaulting divisions, ready to pass through the gap they expected to make in the enemy's lines, believing that they could thus carry the battle into the open and by pressing strongly compel a retirement along the whole front. Unfortunately, the Germans had obtained from captured documents complete details

---

[1] See Charteris' "Field Marshal Earl Haig."

of the French plan of attack and had made complete preparations accordingly. In fact there seems to have been so little secrecy observed regarding the intentions of the French that it was a matter of common gossip.

The British, on April 9th, began operations by an advance in the region of Arras, and this was followed, on April 16th, by the French attack between Soissons and Reims. The initial assault of the French was made with great dash and the fighting continued violently for two days. Suddenly on the third day, according to the Minister of War, the attack was thrown into such confusion that it was halted without important gains.[1] However, the responsibility for the abrupt termination of the action was charged to political interference to stop excessive losses on the one hand and military failure on the other.

The unexpected withdrawal of the enemy in March from the line of the Somme contributed to his advantage as it shortened the line and left him a number of extra divisions available for defense against the threatened point. It also caused delay in Allied plans that gave the enemy further time for preparation.

[1] See Painlevé's "How I Appointed Foch and Pétain," in which he says: "After preliminary attacks by the British along the Scarpe, huge masses of French and French Colonial troops, in the early morning of April 16, 1917, poured over the top and surged toward the line of German trenches stretching from Soissons to Reims. The Nivelle offensive was on; the Verdun school of warfare was pitted against the Somme school. It was one of the most brilliant military onslaughts in the whole history of the war.

"Less than one hour elapsed. Then—

"On the plateau of Craonne, on that of Vauclerc, our infantry whirled backward and forward, caught by the cross fire of innumerable machine guns hidden in hollows or concrete shelters. At the end of the day we had advanced 500 meters instead of the 10 kilometers demanded by the schedule of the attack. Before Brimont in the east, before the Laffaux Mill in the west, our attack had been stopped with a like brutal completeness; and even though, in the region of Juvincourt, we smashed the enemy's first position, his massed counterattacks, launched with powerful artillery support, annihilated our shock troops. The plain of Juvincourt became a cemetery for our tanks.

"On the whole vast battlefield there was one point upon which passionately eager attention had been fixed—the historic Hurtebise Farm, at the junction of the Craonne and Vauclerc plateaus. There, it was said, the black troops of Mangin would crush all enemy resistance and begin their overwhelming march on Laon. Yet that was one of the places where fighting was most furious, where our attack was most promptly stopped."

The result was a disastrous defeat for the French, in which they suffered the tremendous loss of over 100,000 men.

Having heard a great deal about what was to be accomplished by this offensive, and having such high hopes of its success, the disappointment of the people was bitter. The reaction in the army itself became grave indeed and disaffection in the ranks was widespread, amounting in places to open mutiny. An officer who served at French G.H.Q. says that "the revolt broke out in most perfect order, as if rigorous orders were applied. There was no spilling of blood, however. The officers, although disobeyed, were respected except on very rare occasions. 'You are abused in the same manner as we. We will not harm you but we have had enough.' Thus they spoke to the officers. 'The war must come to an end.' These scenes sprang up in sixteen army corps all at one time or at very short intervals." [1] This was the situation in the French armies when General Nivelle was replaced by General Pétain.

The morale of the British armies held up well, notwithstanding the French defeat. The British continued their attacks intermittently for several weeks with local successes here and there. But their losses were altogether out of proportion to the results, amounting to nearly 177,000 from April 9th to June 6th.

The collapse of the French offensive indefinitely suspended further attempts to carry out combined operations. This adverse situation after three years of struggle was so depressing that the prospects of Allied victory probably never before looked less hopeful. This was the situation that confronted us upon our arrival in France in June, 1917.

[1] Jean de Pierrefeu's "Three Years at the Great General Headquarters." Chapter 3, Vol. II.

CHAPTER VI

Joffre Heads Liaison Group—Red Cross Relief for French—Allied Morale
Low—Pétain's Clear Statement of Why the War Should Continue—
My Comment—Non-Existence of Plans—Study of Port and Rail
Facilities—Logical Front for American Effort—Agreement with
Pétain

(Diary) Paris, Tuesday, June 19, 1917. Held conference on Sunday with Major Grayson M. P. Murphy, head of the Red Cross in France, and his assistant, Mr. James H. Perkins, on coöperation with the Army.

Marshal Joffre and aide came for conference this morning. Thirty-four French officers requested as instructors by War Department reported ready to sail. Have prescribed Sam Browne belt for our officers.

AS soon as the formalities incident to our arrival were over, and I made them as brief as possible, we got down to work, as it was urgent that we should begin at once to lay the foundation for the development and employment of the American Army. The size of the army, its organization, its place on the front, and the selection of lines of communication all had to be determined as far as practicable before our troops in any numbers should arrive. In connection with our supply system, preliminary consideration had to be given to improvements in facilities at ports, the erection of storehouses and shelter, arrangements for logging and sawing lumber in French forests, the procurement of animals, the purchase of guns and munitions, shipment from home of raw material for their manufacture, agreements for the early supply of airplanes, increases in trackage and rolling stock for French railways, and numerous other matters which came along in the natural course of events. Under the title "Line of Communications," the great business organization for receiving, transporting and supplying our forces was to be built up.

In order to expedite handling the many questions that must arise, especially in our relations with the French War Office, which controlled practically all industrial facilities and transportation, it was M. Painlevé's idea that there should be a group of French officers placed at our disposal. He thought that an agency familiar with the French organization, authorized to communicate directly with the bureaus involved and through which we could make our wants known, would aid us in matters of procurement.

Marshal Joffre was designated as the head of this liaison group and his first visit was to explain how the proposed system was to work. The instructions received by him from the Minister of War were transmitted to me in a polite note which set forth his conception of the duties of the mission. Naturally, it was pleasing to think of being associated with Marshal Joffre, but I thought that the adoption of the plan at this time would only add an extra channel through which requests must pass and that this would complicate rather than simplify matters. The scheme indicated that a sort of tutelage was contemplated, which also made it objectionable.

In my opinion it would be more expeditious to utilize the French officers then on duty at my headquarters and to develop a workable system through experience. I explained my views to M. Painlevé and readily arranged for the officers of our supply departments to confer directly with the chiefs of the corresponding bureaus of the French organization. In the beginning it looked as though we should have easy sailing but we soon found that we had much to learn in dealing with French bureaus, either directly or indirectly.

During the three years preceding our entry into the war several charitable organizations from home, each independent of the others, had become engaged in aiding the Allied armies and peoples, and now that we were in France these societies began to appeal for some kind of official recognition. While most of them were doing excellent and necessary service, there was considerable overlapping, and it was desirable that their efforts should be coördinated. As the Red Cross was our principal agency for such work, I requested this organization to undertake the general direction of American charitable endeavor. We decided also that it could best handle the task if given a semi-official status. Therefore, Major Murphy, the head of the Red Cross in France, was attached to my headquarters. My cable a few days later informed the Secretary of War of the plan, as follows:

"June 23, 1917.

"Have had several conferences with Red Cross management in order to coördinate work with American Army, French Army and civilian population. Aid for latter two classes especially important. Assistance now and during coming winter will have great influence upon morale of French Army. Major G. M. P. Murphy, head of Red Cross in Europe, has complete confidence of Davison. * * * He will control and direct all Red Cross activities among Allies. * * * "

The French situation gave me the gravest concern. Pacifist sentiment was prevalent in France and in many quarters there was talk of a peace parley. Old political feuds were revived and the influence of defeatism was openly charged against the ministry. This pessimistic and despondent mood of the people further depressed the morale of their armies as men at the front contemplated another winter of suffering and distress for their families. To help meet these conditions, I suggested to Major Murphy that the first duty of the Red Cross should be to aid needy French people. As a result, he and his assistant, Mr. Perkins, proposed that funds be distributed to soldiers' families wherever necessary.

When the idea was presented to General Pétain he expressed the keenest appreciation and at once undertook through his military organization to obtain the necessary data. The Red Cross arranged to make 5,000,000 francs (nearly $1,000,000) available to be distributed by local charitable agencies as rapidly as the information could be furnished as to where funds should be sent. This gift, to which a like amount was added later, proved to be most valuable during the ensuing months in building up French morale. Our Red Cross did not stop there, but extended help to the British by contributing £200,000 (approximately $1,000,000) to the British Red Cross. These appropriations for immediate use were merely the beginning of extensive and generous aid given in many ways to the peoples and the armies of the French, British, Belgian, Italian, and other Allied nations.

(Diary) Paris, Friday, June 22, 1917. Purchase of horses and mules in France taken up with War Department. Prices high but payment justified by tonnage saved.

Dorothy Canfield, the novelist, took breakfast with me yesterday. We talked of earlier days in Lincoln, Nebraska, where her father was Chancellor of the University and she my star pupil in mathematics.[1] Dr. John Finley called and was surprised to find that we had met before, when he spoke on "Slang" at Wellesley College, where I was present, with my wife and 500 other alumnæ.

Dined with the Harjes' last night to meet General Pétain, who gave a disquieting report on French morale.

Lunched to-day with Prime Minister and Madame Ribot. Having been American before her marriage, she was very frank in speaking of the depression among the people.

The opinions of Pétain and the Ribots made conditions look more gloomy than ever. There was no question that, underneath the great enthusiasm shown by the people on the afternoon of our arrival, there existed serious despondency among all classes. The terrible strain of the previous years of continuous fighting, with heavy losses, was telling against both the French and the British. Temporary successes in different theaters of war had brought small comfort, followed as they had been all too frequently by disastrous reverses.

With the actual conditions in mind, one could fully understand why the Allies had been so insistent that a contingent of American troops be immediately sent to France to bolster Allied morale. While not yet prepared to do any fighting, we could

[1] I was Commandant of Cadets at the University of Nebraska from 1891 to 1895, and during the first two years I was also instructor in mathematics.

and did furnish men for service behind the lines. We also provided raw material and certain manufactured supplies as rapidly as possible and gave financial aid without stint.

The following significant statement made by Mr. Lloyd George at a meeting of the Allies at the Quai d'Orsay on May 4, 1917, showed that the Allies expected little real military aid from us and doubted whether the shortage in tonnage would enable us to maintain large American forces:

> "It is upon the shoulders of France and Great Britain that the whole burden of the war rests. * * * America is still an unknown. We must not count upon her aid in a military way for a long time to come. Five hundred thousand Americans brought to this side of the water would be useful to us, if the war lasts so long, but we must live while awaiting them, and we do not know whether we will have next year the tonnage necessary to maintain such considerable forces transported from the other side of the Atlantic."

The possibility of our being able to send a completely trained and equipped army within a reasonable time, even though there had been sufficient shipping, was remote because of our woeful state of unpreparedness. We had no such army and could not have one for several months to come. Allied hopes were still centered on our sending individual recruits or companies to maintain the strength of their armies, and if a military crisis had arisen at this time our condition would have compelled us to comply with their wishes. It was most fortunate that the Central Powers did not then have the necessary forces on the Western Front to assume a vigorous offensive.

In our after-dinner conversation at the Harjes', speaking confidentially, General Pétain confirmed the reports of the very low morale of the French, both in and out of the army, and suggested the possibility of having President Wilson use his influence to strengthen the resolution of those in control of the French Government. He also spoke of a statement he intended to give out and asked if I would write something for publication to support it. What he said so clearly set forth the facts as we saw them at the time that I must quote some extracts from it, as published under the title of "Why We Are Fighting":

"We are fighting in order to drive the enemy from our territory and, by a firm and complete peace, to prevent such an unprovoked assault from ever being repeated.

"We are fighting because by a cowardly withdrawal we would criminally betray both our dead and our posterity.

"We are fighting so that peace may restore to our country a freedom of action and inspire a responsibility which, were the war to have a bad ending, would be much worse than what our people suffer to-day. * * *

"As early as July 29 Nicholas had, by a personal dispatch to William, offered to submit the problem to the Hague tribunal. William rejected the offer, but, doubtless being conscious of the crime he had committed, suppressed this very important dispatch in the German White Book.

"That is confession. When Vienna was, perhaps, on the point of negotiating, William hastened to force the conflict by declaring war on Russia before Austria could even act and to the despair of the entire world.

"It is, indeed, true that for many years Germany had wished to make war on Russia and France. For a long time she had been preparing to the smallest detail for a simultaneous invasion of both countries by the organization of a spy service, entirely unprecedented, and by the most complete military preparation. * * *

"Germany had the hope to crush us in a few months. Traitorously attacking through Belgium, and with formidable forces, she believed she could certainly be in Paris long before England could send anything but a 'miserable little army.'

"What Germany desired, the Pan-Germanists demonstrated. In particular she desired, besides our departments of Nord and Est, Flanders, Artois, Lorraine, our most valuable mineral, industrial, and agricultural resources, and to extract from us ten times the gold that she got in 1871.

"Beaten on the Marne and Yser, stopped at Verdun, obliged by many defeats to yield ground, besieged by almost all Europe, has Germany renounced this odious dream?

"Not in the least. The more we have inflicted severe losses upon her, the more does she desire compensations.

"Doubtless humiliated by her defeats, starved by the blockade, bleeding ever in her battles, does she desire peace?

"But she wants it full of honor, as they say; that is to say, full of profits. It is such a peace she has pretended to offer us—a peace of prey.

"Proof of Germany's bad faith is in her reply to President Wilson when she refused to set forth her aims in the war—proof that they could not be revealed.

"That is to say, because Germany does not dare to lay them before the world to-day. She maintains all her pretensions. She desired war in order to realize them. The only one in Europe prepared for it, she alone desired it, brought it about, precipitated it, decreed it, and rendered it inexplicable by her procedure, atrocious by her methods.

"By keeping secret and having no honest desire to declare her pretensions for domination, she stands as the sole obstacle to peace."

My press comment on General Pétain's article, published the next day, was as follows:

"I have read General Pétain's article with the deepest interest. His answer to the question is complete and logical. The facts set forth should convince the world of the justice of our great cause.

"I cannot think it possible that any one should hold a different view of why we are in the war. It is quite beyond reason that any one, knowing the truth, should fail to condemn the course pursued by the German Government, and the truth has been clearly pointed out by the distinguished Commander-in-Chief of the French Army.

"There must be no peace except a lasting peace. The ideals for which the Allies are contending must be held sacred. France will continue her splendid fight for human rights and human liberties, and fresh examples of heroism by her valiant armies will still further inspire those fighting by her side."

The more serious the situation in France, the more deplorable the loss of time by our inaction at home appeared. It is true that a committee at the War College in February had presented a brief outline report on the organization of a limited force, yet no comprehensive general plan had been considered for the formation or employment of such a force, much less for a larger one. In an indorsement on a War College memorandum dated May 28, 1917, which referred to a recommendation by the French that administrative, engineer, quartermaster, sanitary, and dock personnel be sent first, to be followed by combatant troops, the Acting Chief of Staff, Major General Tasker H. Bliss, said:

"* * * General Pershing's expedition is being sent abroad on the urgent insistence of Marshal Joffre and the French Mission that a force, however small, be sent to produce a *moral effect*. We have yielded to this view and a force is being sent *solely to produce a moral effect*. If all necessary arrangements are not made on the other side, it is the fault of the French General Staff and not of ourselves, since their officers were and are fully cognizant of our unprepared state for sending a *serious* expedition for *serious* business. Our General Staff had made no plan (so far as known to the Secretary of War) for prompt dispatch of reënforcements to General Pershing, nor the prompt dispatch of considerable forces to France. * * * But it seems evident that what the French General Staff is now concerned about is the establishment of the important base and line of communications for a much larger force than General Pershing will have. They evidently think that having yielded to the demand for a small force for *moral* effect, it is quite soon to be followed by a large force for *physical* effect. Thus far we have no plans for this. * * * "

Figuratively speaking, then, when the Acting Chief of Staff went to look in the secret files where the plans to meet the situation that confronted us should have been found, the pigeonhole was empty. In other words, the War Department was face to face with the question of sending an army to Europe and found that the General Staff had never considered such a thing. No one in authority had any definite idea how many men might be needed, how they should be organized and equipped, or where the tonnage to transport and supply them was to come from.

As already noted, both the Joffre and Balfour Missions did not hesitate to make proposals regarding the employment of Americans, and each had expressed the hope that our men, either as individuals or in small units, might be assigned for training and service with their respective forces. Their suggestions were no doubt prompted to some extent by the belief that we would be unable within a reasonable time to build up a separate army capable of operating independently, although it was suspected that this was not the only reason and that the Allies were not keen for us to have an independent combat army. There was certainly a sentiment among them in some quarters that while our entry into the war was necessary to bring victory, we had come in late and therefore could not expect much credit for what we should do. The thought found some basis in the attitude of the leading Allies regarding one or two other nations, whose entry into the war was often openly attributed in Allied circles to the selfish desire of being found on the winning side at the end of the war. Of course it was never even hinted that our action was prompted by such motives, but there is little doubt that the formation of an American army was not looked upon with favor. Our belief in the existence of such an attitude on the part of the Allies naturally stirred in our minds a feeling of distrust, which was emphasized by their later efforts to dominate, and which, therefore, continued to be a factor in all our relations up to the end.

In the midst of the various opposing opinions and schemes of the Allies, the idea remained fixed in my mind that the morale of our troops, their proper training, and their best strategical use all demanded their concentration into an American army instead of being allotted beyond our control as replacements in the ranks of the Allied armies. In fact, every consideration dictated that our army should in no sense be in a subordinate relation to the others, but that we should plan from the start to build up our own independent organization.

(Diary) Paris, Tuesday, June 26, 1917. The question of quarters in Paris for myself and my personal staff most satisfactorily settled through the kindness of Mr. Ogden Mills, who has placed his residence at 73 rue de Varenne, with its beautiful garden, at my disposal.[1]

Went to Compiègne to-day, accompanied by Major James A. Logan and Captain de Marenches, to confer with General Pétain. We tentatively agreed on the American front and the use of certain ports and lines of communication and the sector for our first offensive.

[1] The building and the magnificent garden, with century old trees, date from the early part of the reign of Louis XV. The house was greatly improved during the reign of the first Napoleon. It was once owned by the widow of Marshal Lannes. Mr. Mills restored the grounds to their former beauty and fitted up the mansion with all modern conveniences.

Although we were generally committed to operate with or near the French when our army should be ready, it was necessary to consider the different possibilities of the problem as a whole before making the final decision. We realized that the selection of the actual front must be strategically sound to permit the American Army to strike at a point where a successful offensive would operate to defeat decisively the German Army.

After our forces were organized, equipped and trained at home, they must be sent from different parts of the United States for distances varying from 3,000 to 6,000 miles to reach the battle front. Our merchant marine had never recovered from the great loss in ships during the Civil War, and we were now confronted with the question of transporting our armies across the sea in the face of the serious menace of submarines.

Granting that shipping would be found, we must select terminal ports in France available for our use and reasonably free from submarine dangers, and consider the construction of additional berths. Railway lines must be designated and repaired, new lines must be built and increased rolling stock provided in order that the system should be ready to transport our troops to the front upon their arrival and debarkation. Then came the question of handling the enormous quantities of munitions and supplies that would have to be furnished in order to maintain our forces once they should engage in active operations.

These were some of the problems that confronted us. Their solution demanded prompt action in making plans and persistence in carrying them out. Much of the necessary material for docks, railways, and storehouses must come from home, together with labor to utilize it. Without the utmost effort it would have been impossible to have the army and its supply system ready when the time came for decisive achievement.

Soon after our arrival in London several members of my staff [1] were sent to study the availability of the various ports of France

---

[1] Col. D. E. McCarthy, Q.M. Corps; Col. H. Taylor, Corps of Engineers; Lt. Col. M. W. Ireland, Medical Corps; Maj. H. A. Drum, Gen. Staff; Capt. H. B. Moore, Q.M. Corps.

and to examine the rail facilities leading to the Western Front. In doing so, we had to consider the unprecedented quantities of munitions, railroad rolling stock and other means of transportation incident to the conduct of trench warfare required by the Allied armies, which then numbered more than 5,000,000 men.

The British wanted our army to operate with or near their forces and presented the argument that instead of undertaking the improvement of French ports and railways elsewhere we could use those behind their lines. But we could not be dependent upon facilities already heavily taxed to serve another army. The imposition of the additional burden upon Channel ports and upon railroads leading to the British front would have created a complicated situation with the risk of a breakdown under great stress. The American Army could not occupy a portion of the line between the British and the French without restricting its sphere of activity. Moreover we would have largely displaced the French armies, whose location was based on the defense of Paris, to which above all things they were committed. Also, we might have found ourselves in a position that would have made it difficult to avoid amalgamation and service under a foreign flag, and that possibility alone was sufficient to preclude consideration of the Channel ports.

As to the French systems, all lines running from the base at Paris to the front were bearing their maximum burden. If we were to have independent and flexible lines of communication, our army could not be tied down to the railways they were using. Our rail communications must be carefully chosen to avoid any increase in the load that had to be carried by the systems already in use by the two great Allied armies. But an additional reason for not accepting any of these suggestions was that we could not take the chance of the disastrous effect that German success against the Allies would have upon us if our lines of supply were coextensive with theirs.

The only ports on the west coast of France that would accommodate vessels of more than moderate draft, and that were otherwise free, were St. Nazaire, Bassens and La Pallice, while

Nantes, Bordeaux and Pauillac were capable of taking light draft shipping. These ports had the advantage also of being

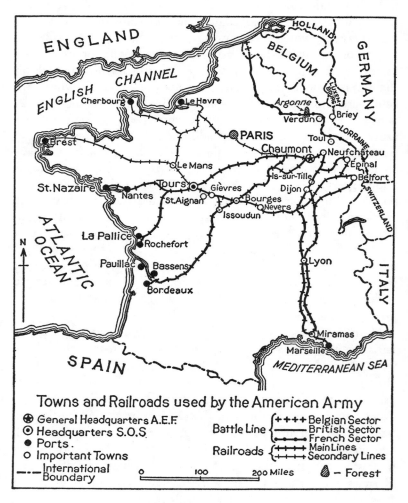

Towns and Railroads used by the American Army

⊕ General Headquarters A.E.F.
⊙ Headquarters S.O.S.
● Ports.
○ Important Towns
–··– International Boundary

Battle Line { ++++ Belgian Sector
——— British Sector
——— French Sector }

Railroads { +++ Main Lines
++++ Secondary Lines }

0   100   200 Miles

🝁 – Forest

somewhat beyond the patrolling area of German submarines trying to blockade the British Isles. In 1914, after the Germans had overrun northern France and were almost at the gates of

Paris, the British temporarily occupied St. Nazaire as a base for their then relatively small force.

The main railroad routes from these ports toward northeastern France were not included in the service of the rear for either of the Allied armies, and hence, as compared with routes farther north, they were more available for handling material and supplies for our armies. The double-track railways from St. Nazaire and Bordeaux united at Bourges, running thence to Nevers, Dijon and Neufchâteau, with radiating lines extending from the latter point toward the Lorraine sector. It was estimated that these lines, with the collateral routes available, could be improved to meet all our needs, but in case another port and auxiliary line should be necessary we had in reserve the port of Marseille and the railroad leading north.

After all, the principal thing was to determine the sector of the front where our forces, fighting as a unit, would be most effective. Without doubt our mission would eventually lead to large aggressive operations instead of the limited offensive attitude of the French and British. In other words, it was essential that we should prepare to strike the enemy where a definite military decision could be forced.

The sphere of activities of each of the armies in the West had been necessarily restricted, because, as we have seen, the British were committed to operations covering the channel ports, and the French had to consider the safety of Paris. Each of these Governments was very sensitive to the national obligations involved and neither army had sufficient strength to extend operations to other fronts. Therefore, on the active front anywhere west of the Argonne Forest there would have been little space or opportunity for the strategical employment of our army.

On the battlefront from the Argonne Forest to the Vosges Mountains a chance for the decisive use of our army was clearly presented. The enemy's positions covered not only the coal fields of the Saar but also the important Longwy-Briey iron-ore region. Moreover, behind this front lay the vital portion of his rail communications connecting the garrison at Metz with the armies of the West. A deep Allied advance on this front and the seizure of the Longwy-Briey section would deprive the enemy of an indispensable supply of ore for the manufacture of munitions. It might also lead to the invasion of enemy territory in the Moselle valley and endanger the supply of coal in the

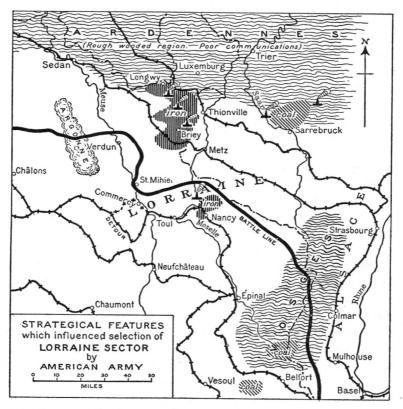

armies of the West. A deep Allied advance on this front and the seizure of the Longwy-Briey section would deprive the enemy of an indispensable supply of ore for the manufacture of munitions. It might also lead to the invasion of enemy territory in the Moselle valley and endanger the supply of coal in the

STRATEGICAL FEATURES
which influenced selection of
LORRAINE SECTOR
by
AMERICAN ARMY

Saar basin. Allied success here would also cut his line of communications between the east and west and compel his withdrawal from northern France or force his surrender.

Under the circumstances, the enemy could but regard the Verdun salient as threatening this sensitive area in the event that the Allies should find themselves capable of taking the offensive on that front.   It was the desire to improve his position and also his prestige that prompted his violent and persistent attacks in the attempt in 1916 to capture Verdun.

Another point was that northeastern France afforded accommodations for billeting and training troops not found elsewhere within striking distance of the front.   Few troops had been located in that section and certain classes of supplies not yet exhausted could be obtained locally.

As to our main depots, it was important that they should be easily accessible and also be at a safe distance from the front, because we were to engage a determined enemy who would possibly soon be capable of conducting successful offensives in more than one direction.   The area through which the lines under consideration passed embraced Tours, Orléans, Montargis, Nevers and Châteauroux, which were available for the relatively safe location of depots, hospitals and training centers and at the same time were centrally situated with regard to practically all points on the Western Front.

The low morale and the worn condition of the Allied armies suggested that they might be unable to protect their communications and, therefore, it was essential that we should have our own independent system, even though the greater distance from the western ports to the northeast would somewhat increase transportation difficulties.   Moreover, this line possessed advantages that would permit us to operate with our bases and depots of supply reasonably secure in case the burden of defense should eventually fall upon us.

In view of the availability of these western ports and the railway lines leading to northeastern France, it was logical to conclude that, from the purely military standpoint, the employment of the American armies on the Lorraine front would prove the most beneficial to the Allies.   Accordingly in conference with Pétain, the tentative understanding was reached as to the region for our activities and the location of the line of communications indicated.   However, instead of an indefinite front in Lorraine, it was necessary to have a particular sector in mind in order to plan and construct the requisite rail and distributing facilities. From a glance at the map it will be seen that before any decisive operation could be carried out, either on the Verdun or the Nancy fronts, the reduction of the St. Mihiel Salient would be necessary because of its flank position with regard to either, and also because it controlled the railroad, through Commercy, essential to the supply of an army operating in the vicinity of Verdun or Nancy.

Looking forward to the active employment of our armies, it was virtually understood between Pétain and myself that the American sector should include St. Mihiel. I suggested that our first offensive would naturally be the elimination of the salient, with which he fully agreed. The strategical advantages and the moral effect of an initial American success there were so evident that even then we entered into a more or less detailed discussion of the proposal. A few weeks later I formally approved a provisional plan for our activities in Lorraine, which, at that time, we calculated could be carried out in the following spring or summer, with an operation against the St. Mihiel salient as a preliminary move.

CHAPTER VII

Arrival 1st Division—Censorship—Inspection of Ports—American Troops in Paris—Enthusiastic Reception—Fourth of July—Urgency for Haste —Cable for 1,000,000 Men—Problem of Their Supply—Letter to Secretary of War

(Diary) St. Nazaire, Thursday, June 28, 1917. A group of Alsatians, regarding me of Alsatian ancestry, called yesterday to express the hope that the American armies might restore their province to France.

Arrived at St. Nazaire to-day to meet the advance elements of the 1st Division and to inspect the port. Had lunch with Admiral Gleaves on flagship *Seattle*.

THE first section of the 1st Division convoy had brought to St. Nazaire the division headquarters, the 16th Infantry, two battalions of the 28th Infantry, one battalion of the 5th Marines, some motor transport troops, and some stevedores. To see the naval vessels and transports flying the American flag in the harbor gave us all a thrill of pride. It was a pleasure to meet the naval commander, Rear Admiral Albert Gleaves, who was to have general charge of the convoy system. The Admiral very kindly invited me and the senior officers of the division to take luncheon with him on board his flagship, the *Seattle,* where he explained some of the problems that lay ahead of him. The convoy, which totaled fourteen vessels,[1] was divided into four sections, each being escorted by one cruiser and four or five destroyers. The number of troops in this convoy, including one regiment of marines, was about 14,500.

The regiments of the 1st Division had all served under my command at one time or another. They were now, however,

[1] Admiral Gleaves in his "History of the Transport Service," (p. 33) says: "Looking back to the first expedition of June, 1917, it seems indeed that the hand of Providence must have been held over those arks or the task never could have been accomplished."

composed of a large percentage of recruits and would have to go through a long period of training. After a few days spent in the cantonment at St. Nazaire, the infantry of the division was sent to the training area of Gondrecourt, north of Neufchâteau, and the artillery to Valdahon, near Belfort.

Major General William L. Sibert, who had won distinction as an engineer in the construction of the Panama Canal, was in command of the 1st Division. The two infantry brigades were commanded by Brigadier Generals R. L. Bullard and Omar Bundy, both of whom had many years of line service behind them. I had known all three of these officers for many years, as we had been cadets together at West Point, although all belonged to classes ahead of mine.

The general officers and the regimental and battalion commanders who had arrived were assembled and I gave them a brief outline of the Allied situation and explained the tentative plans for the training and employment of our troops. I also cautioned them regarding the observance of censorship rules and directed that, except officially, under no circumstances should the discussion of military affairs with people either in or out of the service be permitted.

The importance of strict censorship was emphasized by the unauthorized publicity given the next day to the arrival of these first troops. It had been understood that the regulations restricting reference to the Allied armies by the press should apply to the American forces. But to my utter surprise the French and British papers, in their eagerness to let their people know that the elements of the American Army had really reached France, carried full accounts of the arrival of this convoy, giving the port of debarkation, the designation of units and the number of men. The publication of this piece of news was in open contravention of the censorship rules and called for immediate steps to prevent further infractions. I directed Major Frederick Palmer, who was in charge of the press correspondents with our army, to take up the question with the French at once. He entered a vigorous protest to the authorities, and arranged to place in the French Press Bureau an American representative to whom all matters regarding our army was to be submitted for approval.

The special purpose of censorship and other precautions to prevent the publication of military information was to keep the enemy from learning of our plans and movements. Secrecy gives a commander the possibility of surprising his opponent and the surest road to defeat would be to let the enemy know all about one's plans and preparations. The operations of an army cannot be successfully conducted under any such open methods. It was impressed upon our forces and upon the correspondents that every person who, either willfully or inadvertently, disclosed facts of military value thus gave the enemy an advantage, and that such person, if in the army, might actually be responsible for the unnecessary sacrifice of his own comrades.

The rules of censorship were prescribed in considerable detail, but they were not always wisely applied, as no two censors ever construed them alike. In order to be on the safe side, the censor oftentimes eliminated from press dispatches and personal correspondence information that was harmless, but in the main few errors were made. In the enforcement of the regulations it was a question of deciding between giving our anxious people at home facts which they had every right to know and the necessity of keeping the enemy in the dark regarding our numbers, plans and movements. There is no doubt, however, that the suppression of news prevented our people from obtaining a clear and contemporaneous conception of the great and oftentimes brilliant achievements of our armies and left such knowledge to be gleaned from meager accounts by participants or from the later writings of historians. It was unfortunate that such rules had to be enforced, as otherwise much that might have been published at the time may never be known; however, there was nothing else to be done without serious risk.

During my stay at St. Nazaire I further investigated the conditions of the port. It is a typical seaport town. The descendants of its ancient Celtic population, though now of a decided mixture, still retain the old customs and peculiarities. It was one of the principal shipbuilding ports of France, with two deep-water channels leading to the sea. There was a locked, double basin capable of taking ships drawing twenty-eight feet. In this basin were a limited number of berths, of which at first we were assigned five. The shore arrangements for handling cargo were almost archaic and the storage space was practically confined to the dock sheds. Railway cars in order to be spotted had to be shunted one at a time by means of a turn-table worked by hand. The rail connections with the main lines and the dock yard accommodations were entirely inadequate. Although the facilities were then above the average of French ports, it was evident that radical changes in the system of handling cargo would be necessary to obtain the maximum of efficiency that would eventually be required.

Neither the local official personnel nor the port employees at St. Nazaire appeared fully to realize that their country was in the throes of a great war. They seemed to accept our arrival as a routine matter, and longshoremen continued to handle the supplies of rations and other stores in their customary deliberate and easy-going fashion. The people of the town showed some curiosity and French Army officials began to offer assistance to the troops once they were ashore. Our officers related some of the difficulties already encountered in attempting to expedite the handling of cargo, but all of us were destined to experience many discouragements before the end of the war in our efforts to improve conditions, both here and elsewhere.

I also visited Nantes, a city of 200,000 inhabitants, some thirty miles inland from the mouth of the Loire. The city boasts a fine modern cathedral, an excellent museum of art, an ancient château, then used as a prison, and many fine old buildings occupied by factories and shops. The people of this city have always been loyal to the principles of liberty and the officials were very gracious in their desire to aid us. As a port, however, only vessels of light draft could be accommodated and the facilities were very much out of date.

(Diary) Paris, Wednesday, July 4, 1917. Dined the 1st with Marshal and Madame Joffre. She told an amusing story of their courtship and how he was in love with her when she was a girl. She did not want to marry a fat major then, she said, but accepted him later when she became a widow. It is a charming household.

Two of the Roosevelt boys, Theodore, Jr., and Archie, reported yesterday. Unable himself to participate, their father's fine spirit is represented by his sons.

The Garde Républicaine Band serenaded me early this morning and I had to appear on the balcony, partially dressed. In an impressive ceremony this forenoon at Les Invalides, a battalion of our 16th and one of French troops were paraded together. The American battalion then marched to Lafayette's tomb and was loudly cheered by crowds of people along the route.

Lunched at Chamber of Commerce, visited our Embassy in the afternoon, and attended banquet in the evening given by General Foch, the Chief of Staff.

The French wished to honor our Independence Day, and suggested that some of our troops should participate with theirs in its appropriate observance. The people of Paris had not yet seen any American troops and the authorities felt also that their actual appearance on the streets would have a good effect on French morale. A battalion of the 16th Infantry was brought from St. Nazaire for the occasion. Although these troops were from a Regular regiment, we were not prepared to make much of an impression from the military point of view as the unit had recently been raised to war strength and about two-thirds of the men were recruits. The untrained, awkward appearance of this unit, which was regarded by French officers as representing our Regular Army, could not have escaped their critical observation. However, if they could have foreseen the triumph of this same battalion and of others that took part in the second battle of the Marne, we might have been spared many delays and difficulties in carrying out our plans.

The ceremony held in the Court of Honor at Les Invalides was a fine gesture in recognition of our entry into the war. The President of the Republic, M. Poincaré, presided and was accom-

Note: Total strength of the A.E.F. on June 30th, 523 officers, 13,836 enlisted men.

panied by Marshal Joffre and other high officers and a group of French veterans of former wars. The impressive formalities were carried out with studied precision. A stand of our national colors was presented by the President to our battalion and a pair of guidons to me. There in this national shrine, sacred to the memory of the glorious past of the French people, where Napoleon assembled his cabinet to do honor to the immortal Washington when he died, and where Napoleon himself lies buried, an official welcome was extended on Independence Day to America's first contingent of troops. No other occasion that I recall was more significant or more clearly indicated the depth of French sentiment and affection for their old ally.

This first appearance of American combat troops in Paris brought forth joyful acclaim from the people. On the march to Lafayette's tomb at Picpus Cemetery the battalion was joined by a great crowd, many women forcing their way into the ranks and swinging along arm in arm with the men. With wreaths about their necks and bouquets in their hats and rifles, the column looked like a moving flower garden. With only a semblance of military formation, the animated throng pushed its way through avenues of people to the martial strains of the French band and the still more thrilling music of cheering voices. By taking parallel streets, I was able to gain several successive vantage points from which to watch this unique procession pass. The humbler folk of Paris seemed to look upon these few hundred of our stalwart fighting men as their real deliverance. Many people dropped on their knees in reverence as the column went by. These stirring scenes conveyed vividly the emotions of a people to whom the outcome of the war had seemed all but hopeless.

The exercises at the cemetery consisted of a few speeches, the principal speaker being Mr. Brand Whitlock, our Ambassador to Belgium. I had been previously asked to deliver an address but had designated Colonel C. E. Stanton, of my staff, an old army friend of mine and somewhat of an orator, to speak in my place.

M. Painlevé, Ambassador Sharp and I were standing together listening to the various speeches and as the exercises were drawing to a close Painlevé said to me, "Aren't you going to speak?" I said, "No, Colonel Stanton is speaking for me." "But," he said, "you must speak," and Sharp backed him up, so I was ushered to the stand and spoke entirely extemporaneously. As the day was filled with inspiring incidents, I found no difficulty in saying a few words regarding their significance.

It was on this occasion and upon this spot that utterance was given to an expression that could have been born only of inspiration, one that will live long in history—*"Lafayette, we are here!"* Many have attributed this striking utterance to me and I have often wished that it could have been mine. But I have no recollection of saying anything so splendid. I am sure that those words were spoken by Colonel Stanton and to him must go the credit for coining so happy and felicitous a phrase.

The annual luncheon of the American Chamber of Commerce, which I attended, really took the form of a celebration of our entry into the war. All the speakers naturally adopted our participation as their theme. Many high French and American officials were present, including Marshal Joffre and M. Viviani, who were given an ovation by the Americans.

In the afternoon the usual Fourth of July reception at the Embassy became almost a gala occasion. It gave me an opportunity to meet nearly all of our countrymen then in Paris, and I was overwhelmed with the warmth of their greetings.

This eventful day was brought to a fitting close with a dinner given by General Foch, where we fraternized with representative officers of the French Army, both from the front and from the War Office. The evening was enlivened by the presence of several opera singers, whose appropriate patriotic selections appealed to the sentiments of both the French and ourselves.

(Diary) Paris, Monday, July 9, 1917. Had conference on Thursday with Colonel Thornton, British Army, regarding transportation problems.

Cabled Washington Friday asking for 1,000,000 men by May.
Wrote Secretary of War to-day giving résumé of situation.

The parade of our troops through Paris doubtless fortified the morale of the people to a certain extent, but we all knew that eventually something very much more effective would have to be done. While it was important to consider the temporary state of mind of the Allies, yet after all, the outcome of the war would depend upon the size of the force we could bring to their aid. In order to get at the real situation before advising the War Department of what we should undertake to do, a thorough study was made of the actual and potential strength on both sides. The low state of Allied morale was already well understood. While the full extent of defection in the Russian armies was not realized at this time, enough was known to lead to the conclusion that they could not be counted on to give much further assistance to the Allies.

In that event, of course, Germany would be relatively stronger than before and would probably be capable of transferring a large proportion of her eastern armies to France. Although the Allies were at the moment superior on the Western Front, the advantage in general, both as to manpower and morale, was decidedly in favor of the Central Powers. The real question, then, was whether the Allies could hold out until we were ready. It was clear that no half-way measures on our part would answer and that Allied hopes lay in American military assistance on a vast scale at the earliest moment.

The Allies thought an American force of 500,000 men the maximum that we could have in France in 1918, but it was my opinion that this number would not be enough to meet the situation. Although this would aid, we could not be content merely to lend a helping hand but we must prepare to strike a decisive blow. While the appearance on the front of any American force was still months away, there was little doubt that if we could induce Allied coöperation we should be able to give much greater assistance than they believed possible. Our study having confirmed the correctness of my tentative estimate made on the *Baltic,* I therefore cabled Washington on July 6th, as follows:

"Plans should contemplate sending over at least 1,000,000 men by next May. * * * This estimate would give practically half million men for trenches. Inasmuch as question affects all Allies whose common interests demand that we exert maximum military power consistent with transport problem, suggest early agreement be reached among Allies which would provide requisite transportation * * * and limit sea transportation to food and military supplies and the exclusion of every kind of luxury as well as other supplies in excess of immediate needs of countries dependent upon oversea supplies."

The question, in its finality, was, therefore, one of sea transportation, but so far all efforts to get the Allies, especially the British, to consider giving help to bring over men and supplies had been futile. They did not seem to realize that America would be practically negligible from a military standpoint unless the Allies could provide some shipping. Nor did they seem to appreciate that time was a vital factor. But the spirit of full cooperation among the Allies did not then exist. They seemed to regard the transportation of an American army overseas as entirely our affair. This apparent indifference also gave further color to the suspicion that perhaps an American army as such was not wanted. The situation from our standpoint was grave and embarrassing, for it looked as though it might not be possible for us to save either the Allies or ourselves.

A careful calculation, with a minimum factor of safety, showed that to maintain an army of 1,000,000 men with all kinds of supplies, including munitions (guns, ammunition and aviation), would call for the daily delivery in France of at least 25,000 tons of freight and continuous berthing capacity for 20 or 25 vessels. As a matter of course we expected that the use of certain facilities such as ports, railways and storehouses would be granted us by the French Government, but even with the most generous attitude on their part an extensive program of new construction would be necessary in order to accommodate the large amount of tonnage required. Many new berths would have to be built outright, the railway rolling stock and personnel would have to be greatly expanded, and considerable additional trackage laid. The estimated area on which storehouses would have to be erected for the shelter and care of supplies amounted to many square miles. As we expected eventually to expand our forces to at least 2,000,-000 men in France, the great task that lay before us can well be imagined. To achieve these results in time to be of any real assistance to the Allies was to test our resourcefulness and energy to the limit.

I recall an after-dinner discussion of this problem with Admiral Sims, during which I stated that according to our plans we should eventually need ships, port and rail facilities, and personnel to handle 50,000 tons of freight per day from home for the 2,000,000 men we expected to have. It was somewhat of a surprise to find that Sims apparently regarded this as very much of an exaggeration or else as just an army joke. Although I insisted that it was a positive and serious statement based upon our preliminary study, I doubt whether he was convinced until the time came in 1918 when we had that number of men in France and were actually discharging daily and sending to the front over 45,000 tons of munitions and other supplies.

The following letter to the Secretary of War gives a résumé of the situation as to morale as viewed at that time:

"July 9, 1917.

"DEAR MR. SECRETARY:

"I feel it important that I should write you confidentially something of the general situation in France as it appears from certain facts that have come to me since my arrival in Paris. Sometime before our arrival, as you know, the French Army had been badly hammered, so much so that its morale dropped to a very low ebb. As a consequence also the people themselves became very much disheartened and gave voice to rather severe criticism of the army management in general. The result of all this was that Nivelle was replaced by Pétain as commander-in-chief.

"Dissatisfaction in the army has rather continued to grow and has probably been encouraged by the French civil socialistic element, no doubt influenced by German socialists. It is generally known that several instances of mutiny have occurred among the troops, and that it became necessary recently to execute some of the ringleaders, variously reported to number from thirty to one hundred and twenty.[1] The socialistic element of the Chamber of Deputies itself has subjected the army to criticism that still further served to unsettle the minds of the people, and add to the discontent of the army.

"The fact is that France is very tired of this war. The common people openly complain of the heavy taxes, and protest that they are being ground down to enrich government contractors, and possibly officials well up in government service. Prices of food are high, so that the general cost of living weighs heavily upon the civil population. Coal costs from $80.00 to $90.00 per ton and the supply is very limited. Complaints from families have their effect on the men in the ranks, so that the fighting ability of the troops may be seriously impaired by their discontent. The army authorities seem to be gravely concerned, as is indicated by the fact that General Pétain, last week, asked me to meet him at the home of a mutual friend for conference.

"At this meeting, he told me frankly that affairs were not going well in France, and that unless the Government and the people would stand by the army and assist at home, instead of undermining its morale by criticism and fault-finding, he felt that something bordering on revolution might result. Such an outcome, he said, would permit the Germans to dictate the terms of peace instead of the Allies. He, of course, feels that our entering the war has brought courage to the nation, but, realizing as he does that we shall not be in a position to render any material assistance before next spring, he thinks that, in addition to that, some outside pressure might be brought that would check political intrigue among government officials and prevent a further loss of confidence among the people at large.

"As you know, of course, politics ordinarily play a very important part in every act of the average French public official who is very much inclined to over-play the game. Of course anything like a revolution in France at this time might not be easy to stop, and the final burden of the war might thus fall upon our shoulders. Realizing the low spirits of the people, I have taken advantage of an occasional opportunity, without appearing to meddle and without talking too much, to speak encouragingly of the splendid stamina of the French people and of the army, and have endeavored to inspire confidence among them in their military organization and its commander.

"With this same idea of bolstering up French morale, General Pétain has issued a public statement setting forth the reasons why

[1] It is now known that only twelve of the ringleaders were executed.

the French are fighting. Before giving it out, he asked me if I would do something to back it up after it was published. I am enclosing a translation of General Pétain's article, and my brief comment published the following day.[1]

"General Pétain believes that perhaps there may come a time when President Wilson, for whom the whole French nation have a sublime admiration, might take some action through the French Ambassador at Washington, or otherwise, that would stiffen the French Government into a full realization of the seriousness of these matters and of their responsibility in the premises. By this I mean the civil end of the Government in whose hands rests so much obligation to support their army commanders.

"On the other side of this general view of the subject, our Ambassador here holds the opinion, which I have gained from general conversation with him, that all factions in France are working together harmoniously. I should add also that many others hold this same view. Of course they all know of the general complaints and all that, but they do not regard them as indicating anything serious. I have the very highest regard for Mr. Sharp, and for what he says, and what I say is in no way a criticism of him. He is in every sense a high-minded and, I believe, efficient and conscientious official. But I am writing in order that you may also have the viewpoint of the French Commander-in-Chief, whose views I could not safely mention to any one else.

"It must be stated that our Fourth of July celebration with troops participating has stirred all France; also that yesterday the Government and the Chamber of Deputies seem to have had a very satisfactory understanding, and the French people are in much better spirits than when General Pétain made the above comments on the situation. General Pétain himself now says that the morale of the army has improved lately. So for the present things look better.

"My own opinion is that the army, as it stands to-day, can hold on until spring against any probable effort of the enemy, but that poverty and discontent, magnified by the socialistic press, especially should the Government fail to continue to back up the army, may so dishearten the people and the army that the latter will lose its morale and disaster follow.

"I shall do everything consistent with my position to encourage and hearten both people and soldiery. With the Red Cross now under an organization that is working practically under my very general control, much can be done to cheer up the soldier in the

[1] These enclosures have already been set forth in Chapter VI.

trenches and to help his family at home during the coming winter. The Y.M.C.A. is also working with us in its own field toward the same end.

"I should very much prefer that all this be held as entirely confidential in so far as my conference with General Pétain and my remarks about the Ambassador are concerned. For General Pétain's sake, as well as my own, no suggestion or recommendation should be made connecting him or me in any way with whatever course that may be considered advisable, should future events seem to suggest action along the lines indicated.

"I trust, Mr. Secretary, that you will understand that I am writing you only because I feel that in no other way could I place before you a view of the situation and its possibilities. In conclusion, I would add that I have the utmost confidence in General Pétain, and believe that he is a loyal patriot, whose sole aim is to serve and save France.

"With high personal esteem and respect, I remain,

"Yours very sincerely,

"JOHN J. PERSHING."

CHAPTER VIII

Organization for First Million Men—Expansion of Supply Service—
General Headquarters Staff—Shortage General Staff Officers—Experts
in Business, Industry and Transportation Required—Timber and
Lumber Procurement—Forestry Service—Troops Requested for Italy
—Artillery Procurement Arranged—Welfare Organizations—Organi-
zation of Line of Communications

(Diary) Paris, Wednesday, July 11, 1917. Called last night on
Ambassador Sharp, who thinks French morale is rather better.
Neither of us believes that anything can come of peace talk.

Completed conference to-day on organization of combat units. Indications are that railway situation is worse than early reports show.
Immediate shipment engineers and material for dock construction,
also men and equipment for Forestry Service, urged on Department.
1500 locomotives reported allocated to Russia by Council of National
Defense. Have cabled for priority on 600. Took up question of
winter clothing with War Department. James Gordon Bennett, who
called, has complete faith in Allies.

AS plans for the manufacture of many of our supplies at
home, especially munitions and equipment, were largely
dependent upon early decisions by me as to the tactical
organization, armament and equipment of troops, all of which
should have been settled months before by the War Department
itself, it was very essential that the outline of organization for
the first million men should be determined without delay. After
my departure for France a board of officers [1] was sent over by the
War Department to look into these questions, and this group,
acting upon my suggestion, very wisely concluded to work in
conjunction with the Operations Section [2] of my staff, already

[1] This board consisted of Col. Chauncey B. Baker, Col. W. S. Graves, Col. C. P.
Summerall, Col. D. E. Aultman, Col. M. L. Hersey, Lt. Col. H. E. Ely, Lt. Col. E. D.
Anderson, Lt. Col. K. Walker, Lt. Col. S. A. Cheney, Maj. M. E. Locke, Maj. G. S.
Simonds, Maj. F. A. Ellison and Capt. J. G. Quekemeyer.

[2] The principal members of the Operations Section at this time were: Lt. Cols. John
McA. Palmer and Fox Conner and Majors A. B. Barber and H. A. Drum.

engaged in similar studies. To evolve and perfect a complete scheme of organization and armament for all combat units from the platoon and company on up through the battalion, regiment, division, and army corps, and for the necessary special troops, was an enormous task, particularly in view of the urgency for prompt action, and the realization that the recommendations would have a far-reaching effect upon the operations of our army.[1] As these studies approached completion, the War Department board and my staff were called together at my quarters in joint session, over which I presided, and after deciding certain points of difference the plan which became known as the General Organization Project was adopted and forwarded to Washington on July 11th, with the following statement:

"It is evident that a force of about 1,000,000 is the smallest unit which in modern war will be a complete, well-balanced, and independent fighting organization. However, it must be equally clear that the adoption of this size force as a basis of study should not be construed as representing the maximum force which will be needed in France. It is taken as the force which may be expected to reach France in time for an offensive in 1918, and as a unit and basis of organization. Plans for the future should be based, especially in reference to the manufacture, etc., of artillery, aviation, and other material, on three times this force—*i.e.,* at least 3,000,000 men."

The fact that when we entered the war our Government had done little or nothing toward the organization or equipment

[1] The infantry units of the A.E.F. were organized and commanded generally as follows:

Platoon, 58 men, commanded by 2d or 1st lieutenant.

Company, 6 officers and 250 men, by a captain.

Battalion, 4 companies, by a major.

Regiment, 3 battalions and a machine gun company, 112 officers and 3,720 men, by a colonel.

Brigade, 2 regiments and a machine gun battalion, 258 officers and 8,211 men, by a brigadier general.

The organization of the field artillery, engineers, signal corps, air service, and other arms and services was along lines similar to the infantry.

Division, 2 infantry and 1 field artillery brigades, 1 engineer regiment, 1 machine gun battalion, 1 signal battalion, and trains; 72 guns, 260 machine guns, 17,666 rifles; 979 officers, 27,082 men; by a major general.

Corps, 2 to 6 divisions, by a major general.

Army, 3 to 5 corps, by a lieutenant general or major general.

Group of Armies, 2 or 3 armies, by a general, lieutenant general or major general.

of an army, not to mention its transportation beyond the sea, was a tremendous handicap which few of our people realized then and which is not generally understood even as this is written, thirteen years later.

As a necessary preliminary step in building up the supply service, early consideration was given to plans for the expansion of railroads, the building of docks, and the erection of storehouses, for which the procurement of the necessary material was the first essential. Washington had been advised of the requirements in rolling stock to increase the efficiency of French railroads, but to indicate the urgency of early action the following cable was sent:

> "July 11, 1917.
>
> "The further our investigations proceed as to general conditions and the state of the French resources, the greater appear their deficiencies and the smaller their abilities to aid us in material and labor. Therefore deem it of the utmost importance that this be realized at home. Dock facilities available for our use will be very cramped when we begin to send over continuous convoys of troops and supplies. Therefore construction of additional dock accommodations should be pushed. The railroads we are to use are also deficient in equipment and need repair. Material and rolling stock should be shipped without delay. The French have practically no material available so that both material and labor must come from the United States. * * * "

Coincident with other immediate questions, the development of a satisfactory general staff system to meet the demands of modern warfare required my special attention. The history of our Army offered no guide to the organization and duties of the general staff under conditions involving the handling of millions of men in a great war. After Congress had created the General Staff in 1903, considerable hostility grew up against it in both Houses. Moreover, there existed no little opposition to it within the Army itself, especially in the entrenched supply departments and bureaus at Washington. A certain limited class of line officers who regarded their commissions as sufficient evidence of superior qualifications and as carrying a vested right to live at the expense of the Government with a minimum of exertion, also decried it. But the main thing that retarded its evolution was the lack by the successive Chiefs of Staff, of a clear conception of its proper functions and the consequent centralization of details in their hands.

It required no genius to see that the coördination and direction of the combat branches and the numerous services of large forces could be secured only through the medium of a well-constituted general staff, and I determined to construct it on the sound basis of actual experience in war of our own and other armies.

Our most highly trained officers as a rule came from the Staff College at Fort Leavenworth and from the Army War College, but the majority of the relatively small number of graduates from these schools were scattered throughout the United States and our overseas possessions. During the first two months in France the work imposed upon the few staff officers who had accompanied me was very heavy. However, after urgent and repeated requests, I was fortunate in having at my disposal later in the summer a small group of men which included some of the most efficient and highly educated officers in our Army.[1] After selecting the best features of the French and British staff systems, a general staff organization was created with this nucleus of officers, which effectively met every demand made upon it throughout the war and which remains to-day as a model for present and future guidance.

Not only did G.H.Q. need an efficient general staff to work

---

[1] In addition to those already with me, the officers included in the following cable I regarded as especially fitted for the duties for which they were desired:

"Request Robert C. Davis, Adjutant General, be sent these hdqrs. earliest date. Request Frank Moorman or J. O. Mauborgne be sent these hdqrs. earliest date for duty as code expert. Request Samuel T. Hubbard, Jr., Signal Corps, now here, be called to active service and ordered report to me. Request ten of following named officers be sent to report to me by second convoy for General Staff duty: Frank R. McCoy, George Van Horn Moseley, Malin Craig, Alfred W. Bjornstad, H. B. Fiske, Allen J. Greer, Paul B. Malone, Edgar T. Collins, Samuel R. Gleaves, Laurence Halstead, Nicholas W. Campanole, Aristides Moreno, Preston Brown, LeRoy Eltinge, W. B. Burtt, Frank T. Hines, Edward L. King, J. P. McAdams, W. C. Sweeney, J. B. Barnes, Kerr T. Riggs, W. H. Winters, Wait C. Johnson, Stuart Heintzelman, Upton Birnie, Jr., Kirby Walker, Berkeley Enochs. * * * "

out plans and exercise direction in their execution under the Commander-in-Chief, but combat units and the various services also required qualified staff officers. In order to provide some training without awaiting the establishment of our own schools of instruction, the French and British kindly offered to admit our officers to their schools or attach them to their units until we could get our own courses started. The urgency of sending officers to France for instruction and experience in staff duty was presented to the War Department in July in a cable recommending that 200 graduates of the School of the Line or the Staff School be sent over, or if such number could not at once be spared that selected officers of the National Guard and Reserves be substituted, but the Department only partially complied with the request.

As the details of our mission abroad developed, it soon became evident that in all that pertained to the maintenance and supply of our armies as distinguished from the purely military task, men with expert knowledge and broad experience in business, industry and transportation would be necessary. In the technical branches of the Army were many officers with theoretical training in special lines, but, with some notable exceptions, they generally lacked broad constructive or administrative training. The more important activities requiring special knowledge included the management of railways, the handling of shipping, the direction of forestry and lumbering, the use of radio and wire communications, and the development of aviation and chemical warfare. From the start I decided to obtain the best talent available and was fortunate in practically every field to find able men who were anxious to do their part.

The earliest application of the principle came in connection with timber and lumber procurement. We naturally expected to obtain in France much of the enormous quantity of lumber for barracks and timber for piles, telegraph poles, and fuel, especially as it would be impossible with our limited tonnage to bring a great amount across the Atlantic. The British were being allowed to cut in certain French forests and had installed sawmills here and there, and we sought similar permission, realizing that the French did not have the men to turn out timber and lumber for us and that we must do the work ourselves. Both the French and British Missions to Washington had obtained promises of American forestry engineers, but our needs took precedence and theirs had to be deferred. The French somewhat reluctantly granted us the privilege of cutting timber, but we encountered considerable delay in the allotment of forests.

A cable to the War Department early in July recommended the immediate organization of a forestry service consisting of sawmill units to be composed of experienced lumbermen, and eight to ten thousand unskilled laborers to build roads and to handle lumber. Special request was made for the appointment of Professor Henry Graves, Chief of the United States Forestry Service, then on the ground, as the man to take charge of lumber operations. A number of other specially qualified men were asked for as lumber operators, logging engineers, forest examiners, and organization experts. This being the first intimation given the War Department that such a force would be needed, naturally some time elapsed before it could be organized, brought over and put to work.

(Diary) Paris, Tuesday, July 17, 1917. Dined on Friday with Thomas Nelson Page, our Ambassador to Italy, who praised Italian armies and wants us to send them troops.

On the morning of the 14th, as guest of President Poincaré, witnessed near the Bastile the presentation of Legion of Honor insignia. The review of 11,000 veterans, including squads bearing colors of all regiments from the First Empire down, was an inspiring sight. Attended a Franco-American manifestation in the afternoon at the Trocadéro, where national anthems were sung and the famous composer, Saint-Saens, played selections from his own compositions.

Visited Red Cross building and Y.M.C.A. headquarters to-day with Colonel Bradley. Both associations are progressing in organization and extending their activities.

Sent cable urging manufacture of artillery. Have requested that passports to visit France be refused to officers' families.[1]

[1] This recommendation was approved by the Secretary of War with the concurrence of the Secretary of State. It was construed to apply to wives and sisters.

The suggestion from Ambassador Page that we send a few divisions to aid the Italians indicated that they were about to enter the lists with the other Allies to contend for an allotment of American reënforcements. The Ambassador seemed disappointed to find me strongly opposed to the use of our troops anywhere except on the Western Front and as components of our own army.

The question of artillery procurement caused me much concern. The almost negligible amount on hand when we went to war consisted mostly of field guns of the 3-inch type, then largely in the hands of troops, in the Philippine Islands or elsewhere, and unavailable for issue. Moreover, for calibers heavier than the 3-inch type our Ordnance Department had adopted nothing which was really up to date.

When George Washington was once asked which arm of the combat service he would increase if he could have the choice, he replied that it would be the artillery. Since his day its ratio to infantry in all armies has gradually grown. The most striking change in our time developed in the Russo-Japanese War, when the proportionate increase, especially by the Japanese, became greater than ever before. Our American observers in Manchuria fully reported to the War Department the increased employment of artillery, but in those days it was idle for any military man to talk of more guns for our Army, and the Government made no attempt to keep pace with this tendency in modern armies. On the other hand, Germany quickly realized the growing importance of artillery and so effectively did she develop this arm that during the first years of the World War the Central Powers had a decided superiority over the Allies. It is hardly believable that the Allies should have failed to appreciate their disadvantage in the face of the significant demonstration by the Germans in Belgium in 1914, of the value of heavy artillery, yet apparently not until its further prodigious use against the Russians did the Allies fully appreciate its necessity.

A board of officers [1] from my staff, appointed while on the

[1] The members of this board were Col. C. C. Williams, Lt. Col. Fox Conner and Capt. J. B. Taylor.

Baltic to study this subject, made a preliminary calculation, based upon the immediate organization on a war footing of an army of 500,000 men. It was estimated that we should have, as an initial requirement, 2,524 guns with a possibility of obtaining only 80 in September and 40 in October from our own foundries, and with no prospect of further deliveries until June, 1918. The enormous proportion of both light and heavy guns used by both sides, the knowledge of our deficiency and the realization of the length of time that must elapse before we could manufacture and deliver them made it imperative that we seek other sources than our own to help equip our armies.

Following up an intimation, it was learned definitely that, although not fully supplied themselves, the French could increase the output of their factories provided they could get steel from the United States. As it seemed probable that we should operate in proximity to their armies, we adopted the French types for the usual calibers and sought their assistance in obtaining the guns needed, at least for the first two years. We secured an agreement that our troops, as they came along, would be provided with French guns and ammunition, including not only the 75's and 155's but 37-millimeter guns and 58-millimeter trench mortars as well. In advising the War Department by cable of the arrangement, late in June, it was insisted that nothing should diminish our efforts at home, not only to produce these types, but also those of the 4.7-inch and 6-inch mobile types. In my cable of July 14th, the expedition of the 8-inch and 9.5-inch howitzers then under manufacture was also urged. It was most fortunate that we were able to get these guns from the French, as up to the end of the war no guns manufactured at home for our army, of the types used, except 24 8-inch mortars and 6 14-inch naval guns, were fired in battle. Trench guns of the 3-inch and 6-inch mortar types, with ammunition, were purchased from the British.

The Red Cross reported excellent progress, especially in its first efforts to assist the French, as agreed upon with General Pétain. Its organization by Major Grayson M. P. Murphy for war work with our own armies was now about completed. The establishment of canteens and huts at the ports and other important points had already begun and the numbers increased as fast as needed. These centers of service later maintained dispensaries and provided beds and bathing facilities for men traveling under orders or on leave. When the necessity arose the Red Crosᵉ actively coöperated with the Medical Corps in the field, contributing large quantities of supplies and oftentimes additional nurses. The work of the society, directed from a central office in Paris, eventually embraced practically every endeavor touching the health of the armies.

The Y.M.C.A., with Mr. E. C. Carter in charge, was equally earnest, its principal field of activities being that of recreation and entertainment. Through bureaus of information it also undertook to provide personal services for officers and men, both in France and England. It supplied athletic equipment and encouraged sports; conducted clubs and hotels, furnishing reading matter and writing material; cared for the women of the Y.W.C.A., and made a beginning at educational work wherever possible. Later on, at my request, the Y.M.C.A. also undertook to conduct our regimental and regional canteens in which they carried certain supplies for sale to troops. Although handicapped at all times by lack of tonnage, land transportation and efficient personnel, this enormous task was creditably performed.

In addition to these two societies, the Knights of Columbus engaged in welfare work without material interference with the organizations above mentioned. It also grew to be a most helpful agency. The Salvation Army came, and filled a place all its own, leaving on the armies a distinct impression of sincere and unselfish service. Later came the Jewish Welfare Board, which gave especial attention to Jewish soldiers. All these organizations rendered valuable service to our troops.

(Diary) Paris, Thursday, July 19, 1917. Held conference yesterday with General Staff on details of organization of Line of Communications and location of sections pertaining to the rear.

To-day, accompanied by de Chambrun, called on M. Jules Cambon, of the Foreign Office. Visited American Hospital for French army patients at Neuilly.

The Line of Communications, under one chief, with headquarters first at Paris and later at Tours, included all supply activities and installations up to the Zone of Operations. For convenience in administration, it was subdivided territorially into sections, each being a unit in itself bearing a certain relation to others, and all subject to the same directing authority. It required efficient organization in order to function as a whole in maintaining a constant flow of supplies to our forces. Each base section embraced at least one important port for the discharge of munitions, equipment and other supplies from home. A certain percentage of subsistence elements was stored [1] near the ports and the balance sent forward to plants in the Intermediate Section for storage and assortment by classes or components. Munitions and equipment went to special depots toward the front. The Advance Section embraced stations from which the distribution of supplies was made direct to the troops as needed. Along the Line of Communications the Medical Department located its principal hospitals for the care of the sick and wounded. Many of its units were installed in buildings borrowed from the French and others in hospitals we ourselves constructed. The Line of Communications, through which the enormous demands of our armies were handled successfully, became known later as the Services of Supply.

As to ports, St. Nazaire, La Pallice and Bassens were designated for permanent use, while Nantes, Bordeaux and Pauillac were tentatively chosen for emergencies. We arranged that Le Havre and Cherbourg could also be used if necessary, while

[1] Our largest storage plants were:
Base
  St. Sulpice, with eventually 2,627,000 sq. ft. of covered storage.
  Montoir-de-Bretagne, with 3,447,000 sq. ft.
Intermediate
  Gièvres, with 3,839,000 sq. ft.
  Montierchaume, with 1,214,000 sq. ft.
Advance
  Is-sur-Tille, with 1,355,000 sq. ft.

several smaller ports became available, chiefly for the discharge of coal from England. When our tonnage increased, Marseille and Toulon were used to relieve the pressure on other ports and Brest became a port of debarkation for troops.

To all intents and purposes our forces were based on the American continent. With enemy submarines menacing our shipping and the quantity of available tonnage yet unknown, and with a line of communications by land stretching from three to four hundred miles from the French ports to our probable front, the organization had to overcome many difficulties which the Allies could hardly understand or appreciate, least of all many of the higher commanders upon whose coöperation success depended. It was a large military undertaking, quite distinct in character from the conduct of armies on the battlefields, but which, to be successful, required coördinating direction by the same authority.

In order that the estimates and plans regarding our participation should be realized, this organization behind the lines would have to become a great army in itself. But it would be one organized simply as a great business enterprise to receive and transport not only the combatant troops but every conceivable requirement shipped from home or obtained abroad for their maintenance. Concisely stated, the establishment behind the Zone of Operations would practically require the organization in France on an unprecedented scale of another War Department, and this is precisely what it became.

CHAPTER IX

Visit Field Marshal Haig—Study British Organization—Meeting of Allied Leaders—Conference of Commanders—War Department Program of Troop Shipments—Tonnage Inadequate—Need of Replacements— Allies Adopt Defensive Rôle—Submarine Losses Decreasing—Loose Handling of Secret Information at Home—Suggested Importation of Farmers for France—Request Prompt Action Forest Allotments

(Diary) Paris, Tuesday, July 24, 1917. Have just concluded four-day visit to British G.H.Q. Made detailed inspection of systems and methods in offices of the Adjutant General, Chief of Artillery and the General Staff.

Called Saturday at headquarters of the British Second Army, commanded by General Plumer. Visited flying fields and shops on Sunday with General Trenchard, who is most enthusiastic over aviation. German planes attacked British G.H.Q. Sunday night but did no damage.

On Monday visited the British Fifth Army, General Gough. Saw troops there studying miniature enemy trenches preparatory to attack. Had an instructive forenoon to-day at Railway Transportation Offices, returning to Paris this evening.

IT had been my intention to pay an earlier visit to Field Marshal Sir Douglas Haig, the British Commander-in-Chief, in response to his cordial invitation, but the many important questions to be considered had made it necessary to defer that pleasure longer than I had wished.

Accompanied by Colonel Harbord, Colonel Alvord and Captain Geo. S. Patton, Jr., I left Paris on July 20th and motored northward over a well-kept highway through Beauvais and Montreuil. It was harvest time, and as we sped along the beautiful avenues of tall shade trees, the succession of cultivated fields, farm houses, woods and small villages which unfolded before our eyes in sunlight and shadow, presented a wonderful panorama. Our reverie was soon interrupted, as the presence of British troops here and there indicated that we had reached their zone of operations.

Our first stop was to call on Lieutenant General Fowke, the Adjutant General of the British armies, at Montreuil. Here a very smart-looking guard of honor, from the Ancient and Honorable Company of Artillery, was drawn up in the courtyard and gave a military touch to the hearty personal welcome extended by the General himself. After a few minutes' survey of the offices, we drove with General Fowke to his quarters, where we had luncheon. It was a pleasure to be with him again, as I had not seen him, except for a moment at Boulogne, since we were together in Manchuria twelve years before, when, as observers with the Japanese forces, both of us had been attached to Kuroki's army. Naturally, we rather monopolized the luncheon conversation recalling old times.

Going through the various branches of his department in the afternoon, we found some one at each office ready to give us information. We delved into the organization, the system of recruitment, and the routine method of handling correspondence and records in the British Army. Although our military system had been practically copied from the British a century and a half earlier, it was surprising to find so few points of difference after this lapse of time.

It was almost dusk when we arrived at an old château, half-hidden in a magnificent grove of chestnut trees at Blendecques, which was occupied by the Field Marshal. His cordial greeting and that of the members of his household at once made us feel very much at home. There was nothing to disturb the quiet of the place save the sound of distant guns wafted in from the front by the evening breeze.

At dinner the conversation naturally turned to the situation in the various armies. All were keen to know about our organization and the prospect of our putting troops in the field; but as our active participation depended on many factors, such as training, equipment, and shipping, my replies were necessarily indefinite and no doubt disappointing. In turn, we asked many questions, and it was especially interesting to hear the importance of artillery emphasized by its Chief, Major General Birch, who spoke of the difficulties they had experienced in supplying themselves with guns that matched the enemy's. Referring to the British lack of artillery at the beginning of the war, he said there was reason to believe that they had finally attained a superiority over the Germans. A glance at the chart, seen later at his office, showed that the British then had 3,712 field guns and howitzers and 2,258 guns of other calibers, which gave them a sufficient number of guns of all calibers to average one to every twenty-five yards of their more than eighty miles of front. These figures were transmitted to the War Department to support my cable urging the haste in gun construction at home.

Sir Douglas told me some of the details of Nivelle's attack in the spring, how it was known far and wide beforehand, and spoke particularly of the serious discontent among the French troops which had resulted from their defeat. Although he had placed himself under Nivelle's command for these operations, he had felt, he said, little confidence in the outcome from the start. He also commented on the failure of the French to coöperate fully on various occasions. His remarks entirely confirmed the belief that I had long since held that real teamwork between the two armies was almost totally absent.

During my visit General Robertson happened to be there and we had a detailed discussion of the question of manpower. The British casualties in the Arras Offensive [1] during April and May had amounted to nearly 175,000 officers and men, and preparations were under way at that moment for another attack soon to be made on Passchendaele Ridge. This was the beginning of the operations that lasted until late in the autumn, with casualties which increased the total for the year to about 500,000 officers and men. The British High Command, however, claimed that they had inflicted heavy losses on the enemy, and it was obvious that the serious aspect of the general situation had not noticeably dampened their aggressive spirit or weakened the purpose of the British War Office to continue.

[1] The British losses up to the middle of June were almost twice as great as Nivelle's in April, although they did advance their lines somewhat.

There was considerable criticism by certain officials of the British Government regarding the excessive loss of men in these offensives, which, it was alleged, could not materially affect the final outcome. The superiority of the Allies during the first half of 1917 would, no doubt, have produced greater results if there had been unity in the conduct of operations, but the Allies did not appear to realize that without it there could be little prospect of gaining more than a local advantage. The theory of winning by attrition, with isolated attacks on limited fronts, which was evidently the idea of the British General Staff, did not appeal to me in principle. Moreover, their army could not afford the losses in view of the shortage of men which they, themselves, admitted.

Sir Douglas discussed the difficulties that he had encountered in handling rail transportation. He said that at first he had army engineers in control and later specially selected officers, but that in neither case were the results satisfactory. Finally, Sir Eric Geddes, an experienced general manager of railways, consented to take charge, and he in turn selected expert railroad men as assistants, with almost immediate improvement. I visited the headquarters of the Transportation Corps at Nashville, humorously named for General Nash, who had succeeded Major General Geddes, after whom the place had previously been called Geddesburg. The organization was patterned after the railway systems in England, but in addition to rail construction, transportation and management, it also had control of docks, debarkation, and the handling of supplies. This general plan of organization and of selecting experts for the task was later adopted for our armies.

Probably the most important thing we did on this visit was to study the organization of the Headquarters General Staff, in which we were graciously aided by Major General Butler, Assistant Chief of Staff. He and his subordinates were most patient in explaining the details of the several staff sections and the relations of each one to the others. We also examined the organization of the general staff of a field army, visiting the Second Army for this purpose. Unfortunately, General Plumer, the Army Commander, was absent—although I met him later—but every courtesy was shown by his Chief of Staff, Major General Harington. At the headquarters of Lieutenant General Morland's Corps, we had a talk on corps organization, after which the usual five o'clock tea was served.

Scarcely anything during this visit more strikingly impressed upon me our unpreparedness than what I saw during a few hours spent with Major General Trenchard at the flying field. Here we witnessed expert fliers doing every imaginable stunt, saw planes of all classes, and inspected the thoroughly equipped repair shops. The incomparable spirit of the young officers and the enlisted personnel especially impressed me, as it did later in our own aviation service. Every man seemed to be disappointed when a flight of planes departed for the front without him. Trenchard himself was an expert flier and one of the most progressive officers of aviation in any army. He was a very strong advocate of bombing and the British were doing a great deal of it at that time. It is interesting to note that a year later General Trenchard brought the British Independent Bombing Corps to our front, where it served with our air forces for the St. Mihiel operation.

Our visit to the Fifth Army Headquarters brought us more closely in touch with the active part of the front. After a general inspection, during which we saw immense quantities of engineering material and equipment accumulated in preparation for the coming offensive, we went to a small area nearby, where the plan of the German front to be attacked had been reproduced in miniature. All the details of the terrain had been worked out from air photographs and were shown in relief. The plan was large enough so that the men could actually study the approaches and walk through the various trenches of the successive lines.

We returned to have luncheon with General Gough, the Army Commander, whom we found in good spirits and, true to his Irish blood, most hospitable, jolly, and friendly. He gave us the rare treat of seeing and hearing his band of Irish bagpipes, which played many lively and familiar airs. The effect was such that I think any of us, with small encouragement, would have tried a jig or a clog dance. Their playing on the march was unique, in fact they played best while marching and the drum major seemed then to be happier.

Our visit to the British General Headquarters was most instructive as every opportunity was given us to study intimately the details of the British wartime organization. After similar studies of the French system, we selected from each those features best suited to perfect a well-balanced staff for our own army. The cordial relations and good understanding established between Sir Douglas Haig and myself and between the members of our staffs later proved very advantageous to us. In London, long after the Armistice, Sir Douglas, in an after-dinner speech, referred to this visit, which happened during a period of depression, and said that our timely appearance at his headquarters had aroused in them a strong feeling of hopefulness for the future.

(Diary) Paris, Thursday, July 26, 1917. Had breakfast yesterday at the Crillon with Mr. Lloyd George. He is alert and energetic and has a clear conception of Allied problems. Took lunch with Mr. Balfour, who thinks we have reason to feel easier regarding submarines. Representatives of the various Allies met for conference on general situation. In the evening, M. Ribot, Prime Minister, gave a State dinner to officials attending conference.

To-day attended luncheon to Allied representatives given by the President and Madame Poincaré at the Elysée Palace. In conference this afternoon with Pétain, Cadorna, Robertson, and Foch at latter's office. Discussed military plans, talked about tonnage possibilities and shortage of personnel. All pessimistic and reserved. Had dinner with Minister of War.

Mr. James Stillman, just returned from a tour of France, confirms reports of serious depression.

The conference referred to in the diary was one of those periodical meetings held to discuss the situation, both political and military, and to decide upon policies and programs. The French were anxious that we should participate, and M. Ribot had requested Washington to designate our Ambassador and me to attend. M. Jules Cambon, of the Foreign Office, whom I had known many years before when he was Ambassador at Washington, asked me also to urge that we should be represented. Speaking for the French Government, he felt that we should begin to take part in Allied councils and have a voice in directing policies.

It seemed to me, after full consideration and consultation with Ambassador Sharp, that if we participated in the conference our discussions should be limited to military questions in which we were immediately interested and that it would be wiser not to discuss any other subjects at the time. But as our participation, even in this limited way, might be misunderstood by the Allies, a possibility which the President wished to avoid, arrangements were made for a separate meeting of the military leaders.

During breakfast with Mr. Lloyd George, he pointed out the grave consequences of continued German success against Russia, his conclusions concerning the outlook being, like those of almost every one else, that Russia could no longer be relied upon for much help in a military way. He said the existing situation made it especially important that America should assume part of the responsibility of deciding the course to be followed by the Allies. In reply to this I explained the reasons why the President felt that for the present we should join only in the consideration of the military aspects of the general situation.

This meeting with the Allied military leaders, which was my first, brought out little that was hopeful. The political relations of the Allies were touched upon in a general way, but only so far as they might affect the military situation. The most significant recent event, of course, had been the crisis in Russia. Kerensky had succeeded in reviving the spirits of the Russian armies in Galicia and for a short time they were able to make considerable gains against the Austro-Germans. In the end, however, they had been badly beaten and reports indicated that great demoralization existed throughout the nation. Although lacking in complete information, the opinion prevailed in the conference that Russia was practically eliminated as a military factor. The general idea seemed to be that the Germans, with the men they could take from the Russian front, would be able to renew offensive activities on the Western Front in the spring at the latest.

With reference to American assistance, I gave in detail the situation as to the strength, immediate and prospective, of our army, especially in the light of the latest plans of the War Department, and laid special emphasis on the necessity for additional shipping. A cablegram had just been received in response to mine of July 6th, in which I had requested that at least a million men reach France by the following spring. This message, indicating that the War Department foresaw small chance of securing the necessary tonnage, was read to the conference:

> "By using all shipping which is now in sight for the purpose and which will be available after month of November, the plan proposes to transport to France by June 15, 1918, 21 divisions, comprising about 420,000 men, together with auxiliary troops and replacement troops, line of communication troops, and others, amounting to 214,975 men, making a total of 634,975 men. These will be in addition to the second half of General Sibert's division now preparing to go. The plan proposes the following number of troops to be sent on or about the given dates: August 15th, 5,500 auxiliary and replacement troops; September 1st, 13,000 auxiliary and replacement troops; October 1st, two divisions or 41,750 men; November 1st, two divisions or 39,250 men; November 15th, one division or 20,500 men; December 1st, 13,000 auxiliary and replacement troops; January 1st, three divisions or 59,750 men; January 15th, one division or 28,000 men and 8,000 auxiliary troops; February 1st, two divisions or 39,250 men; February 15th, one division or 20,500 men; March 1st, 13,000 auxiliary and replacement troops; April 1st, three divisions or 59,750 men; May 1st, two divisions or 39,250 men; May 15th, one division or 20,500 men; June 1st, 13,000 auxiliary and replacement troops; June 15th, two divisions or 54,250 men and 14,250 auxiliary and replacement troops."

Although short of my recommendations, even this schedule could be carried out only by a very large increase in tonnage. The other members of the conference were of the opinion that if new adjustments could be made there might be shipping for nine or ten of our divisions before spring. So, for the moment, there did not seem to be the slightest chance of transporting a million men to France by the following June.

As to the state of their respective armies, Robertson pointed out that the British casualties had been heavy during the year and their manpower greatly reduced. Pétain mentioned their severe losses and said that the French could only slightly augment their strength. Cadorna said that the Italian Army was little, if any, better off. The depletion of their resources in men caused considerable anxiety among the Allies in the face of the probability of having to meet the full force of the Central Powers in the spring.

After canvassing the whole situation, the conference expressed the unanimous opinion that a defensive rôle should be adopted on all secondary fronts. The British and French representatives hoped that the surplus troops resulting from this course might be available to strengthen their armies in France, and General Cadorna, of course, thought the Italian armies should have their share. The following cable conveyed to Washington the conclusions of the conference:

"Informal conference Commanders-in-Chief Allied armies held Paris July twenty-sixth, present Generals Robertson, Pétain, Foch, Cadorna, Pershing. Steps to be taken in case Russia should be forced out of war considered. Various movements troops to and from different fronts to meet possible contingencies discussed. Conference also weighed political, economic and moral effect both upon Central and Allied Powers under most unfavorable aspect from Allied point of view. General conclusions reached were necessity for adoption of purely defensive attitude on all secondary fronts and withdrawal surplus troops for duty on Western Front. By thus strengthening Western Front believed Allies could hold until American forces in sufficient numbers arrive to gain ascendancy. To accelerate participation American forces and provide necessary transport for American army and movement of armies from secondary fronts conference recommends that question of shipping be immediately taken up by Inter-Allied Commission. However, consensus of opinion was that steps should be taken by Allies to determine part to be played by America, Great Britain, France and possibly Japan to support Russia with a view to avoiding extreme eventualities."

About this time further disturbing reports were submitted to me confidentially by one of our naval officers sent by Admiral Sims. They were based upon tonnage losses for May, June and July, and seemed to confirm the conclusions of a month previous that there would soon be insufficient Allied shipping left to bring over an American army of the strength required, and that the Allies would find it difficult to keep up their supply of food from overseas and provide matériel necessary to carry on the war. The data presented appeared to prove that if the rate of destruction of shipping could not be reduced, the war would be lost before we could fire a shot.

This report was certainly most pessimistic, but it did not dispel my confidence in the success of the plan which had been tested and was about to be inaugurated of sending ships over in convoys under the protection of naval vessels. Additional destroyers requested by Admiral Sims had by this time increased such craft in European waters and as a result the activities of submarines had been somewhat diminished for July as compared with April. Submarines could not afford to take great risk in the presence of cruisers and they were especially fearful of destroyers. They had learned of the disastrous effect of depth bombs used by destroyers and trawlers and also that detection would be almost certain in operating against a convoy. Yet for the time being, ship construction in British yards continued below losses and our Shipping Board at home had scarcely stopped wrangling over materials and types. All these facts caused everybody to realize the extreme urgency of speed, and that in turn gave some hope that the prospects might soon become brighter.

It was my belief, even in the face of the heavy losses, that with complete coöperation under expert management and distribution the shipping would be ample for all purposes. This would require, of course, that it be placed under some central authority, but the governments, especially the British, that controlled most of it, while apparently desirous of helping, did not seem inclined to think they could make any concessions. They had entered into arrangements to assist each other with shipping for foodstuffs, but there was no such thing as the pooling of Allied tonnage for general purposes.

Although the Allied authorities at this stage were concerned over the question of tonnage, on which the success of Allied military effort really hinged, their doubt of the possibility of any considerable numbers of our troops being ready at an early date to operate as a distinct American force probably made them less active in trying to find shipping for our purpose. At the same time, one could not help thinking that with our consent to feed men into the various armies, the governments concerned would find it possible to send over vessels to bring their respective allotments across.

However, the discouraging reports on the situation did make such an impression on the military leaders that, as reported in my cable, they suggested the possibility of pooling all available shipping and accordingly recommended a commission to consider the question, with special reference to the transportation of the American Army. In order to reach a solution, it was necessary, in the first place, to ascertain as nearly as possible what the requirements in shipping would be and then investigate the various sources from which ships might be obtained. In any such survey it was essential that we should be represented by men with expert knowledge to present our case before this commission.

The success of submarine warfare had been largely dependent upon advance knowledge concerning movements of vessels. As there was no doubt that the sailing dates of much of our shipping reached Germany through spies, one way to reduce the danger would be to close their sources of information. In the beginning the practice of our War Department in transmitting secret intelligence was extremely loose. The data regarding sailings were, of course, sent to my headquarters, but at the same time, or often before, they were given to both French and British Military and Naval Attachés and Missions in Washington. These officials immediately transmitted the news by cable to their respective Governments, with the result that it usually became almost common knowledge. Frequently, in the early days of troop movements, word regarding sailings reached us first through civilian channels in Paris.   Finally, after consultation with Admiral Sims, through his representative, I recommended that all data regarding movements of transports be given only to our naval authorities, to be transmitted by their secret code.   This precaution largely, if not entirely, checked the leakage through the channels named.   Yet persistent protests had to be made before the War Department could be induced to discontinue its careless methods.

But there were other means possessed by the enemy of finding out about our movements.   One message, intercepted by the French, sent from some wireless station in Spain to the German General Staff, announced the arrival of several American vessels at Nantes and of 10,000 American soldiers at St. Nazaire, and also gave the routes taken by our transports.   Another, evidently intended for submarines, reported the departure of a convoy from New York.   These and similar facts that came to my knowledge were cabled at once to Admiral Sims and to Washington.

The War Department was also advised of the probability that certain favorably located Portuguese and Spanish ports were being used by German submarines.   Wireless messages intercepted in France indicated that enemy agents located at such ports had established a regular system for obtaining valuable information regarding Allied movements at sea.   While it was said that Spain sympathized with the Allies, still some anxiety was manifest on account of the reports of the activities there of German interests.   It being important that Spain should remain neutral, the whole situation was cabled to Washington and presumably diplomatic representations of protest were made to the Spanish Government.

At the time of this gloomy outlook regarding tonnage losses, the question of supplies appeared precarious enough for Washington to send to me for comment a suggestion that had been received regarding the possibility of augmenting the food supply for our armies through increased cultivation of the soil in France and northern Spain by American farmers.   Armies in the past in that part of the world had often subsisted themselves and such a possibility had already been discussed at my headquarters. But in my opinion, as cabled to the War Department, it would be wiser to increase our military forces more rapidly and then, if necessary, relieve the older classes of French soldiers from the front to enable them to return to their farms.

(Diary) Paris, Saturday, July 28, 1917. Had luncheon with James Gordon Bennett and found him more aggressive than ever. Called on M. Painlevé, with Major Graves of the Forestry Service, to urge immediate permission to cut timber.

Notwithstanding previous promises of forest concessions, granted, it is true, with some hesitation, the French officials were slow to designate areas for our use. As a regiment of forestry engineers stood ready to go to work and the necessity for large quantities of lumber had become urgent, I called at the War Office and laid the matter before M. Painlevé, who never failed to do all he could do to expedite our business. He was surprised to find that nothing had been done, and at once gave positive instructions that action should be taken immediately. Eventually, at my suggestion, the requisition system of obtaining forest concessions was adopted and we had no further trouble.

This was only one of numerous instances in which delay compelled me to go direct to the supreme authority to get decisions on matters of recognized importance. It should not be inferred from this instance, however, that there existed any inherent disinclination on the part of the French to aid us, but it often required considerable personal effort to overcome the inertia in the various bureaus. In this instance and in others the question of authority between officials also entered as a factor.

CHAPTER X

Leadership for Higher Units—Visit 1st Division Billeting Area—Relations between Troops and Peasants—G.H.Q. Located at Chaumont—Order to Troops on Attitude Toward People and Property—Calling of National Army Delayed by Lack of Equipment—French Furnish Machine Guns and Automatic Rifles—Organization of Military Police—Railway Problem

P ROBABLY the most important factor in building up an aggressive army is the selection of leaders. Without efficient leadership the finest of troops may suffer defeat by inferior forces skillfully led. During my experience, covering a considerable period of years, many otherwise able and conscientious officers had been seen to fail for want of initiative, one of the important requisites of a successful leader. The lack of leadership by a number of officers of high rank in the French and British Armies in the early days of the war afforded an immediate object lesson for us on the necessity of selecting capable officers for important positions.

In our Regular Army in time of peace, the system of promotion by seniority, instead of by selection, deprives many capable and energetic officers of the opportunity to command the larger units, which would help to prepare them for higher places in time of war. The same comment applies with equal or greater force to our National Guard, in which politics adds another factor often adverse to efficiency in the higher grades.

Inasmuch as our success would depend upon the offensive spirit among combat troops, it was essential that vigorous and intelligent leadership should, if possible, be assured at the outset. I therefore urged the choice of relatively young and alert officers for the active command of higher units. It was especially desirable that this be done early in order that they might gain experience and also have the chance to prove themselves worthy. The following were my recommendations on the subject to the Secretary of War:

"My observation of British and French Armies and most exacting arduous service conditions at the front fully convinces me that only officers in full mental and physical vigor should be sent here. Contrary course means certain inefficiency in our service and possible later humiliation of officers concerned. General officers must undergo extreme effort in personal supervision of operations in trenches. Very few British or French division commanders over forty-five or brigadiers over forty. We have too much at stake to risk inefficiency through mental or physical defects. Strongly recommend conditions be fully considered in making high appointments and suggest that no officer of whatever rank be sent here for active service who is not strong and robust in every particular. Officers selected for appointment general officer of line should be those with experience in actively commanding troops. Officers not fulfilling above conditions can be usefully employed at home training troops."

These recommendations were not altogether followed at home, in fact very little effort seems to have been made at selection, so that some officers without ambition or initiative, whose inefficiency should have been well known, and others whose age and physical condition were such as to disqualify them for strenuous service, were given important assignments. Generally speaking the policy of the War Department from the beginning to the end of the war seemed to be to appoint officers to the higher grades according to seniority with the intention of weeding out the inefficient later on. It was not a sound policy and it caused no end of trouble in France, because after the appointment of such officers it was a slow process to eliminate them. Presumably the method of appointing according to rank was suggested by the successive Chiefs of Staff.

Of course there were difficulties in applying the principle of selection, which I thoroughly understood. But a process of elimination of officers known to be inactive could have been applied easily enough. The records of all officers were kept in the Adjutant General's office and a careful study of these would have enabled the Chief of Staff and his assistants to cross off those in the grade of colonel or lieutenant colonel whose records showed them lacking in enterprise and activity. Selection could then have been invoked and a list of relatively young and vigorous general officers would probably have been the result.

Most of the general officers appointed were known to me and not a few, who under the rule of seniority had been commanders of regiments and departments, had lacked the energy even to train their commands or themselves in battle exercises where favorable opportunity had been afforded. However, those appointees who were unprepared professionally for the duties of modern war eventually fell by the wayside as victims of a system that had failed to stimulate activity of mind or body in times of peace.

(Diary) Paris, Friday, August 3, 1917. Left Tuesday for St. Dizier and Ligny-en-Barrois, accompanied by Harbord, Colonel de Chambrun and Captain Patton, mainly to examine possible locations for headquarters.

Went to Menaucourt and Naix on Wednesday, saw Marines under Colonel C. A. Doyen; then to the 28th Infantry, Colonel B. B. Buck, at Saint Amand and Tréveray; the 26th, Colonel G. B. Duncan, at Saint Joire; thence to the 16th Infantry, Colonel W. H. Allaire, at Abainville; and the 18th Infantry, Colonel U. G. McAlexander, at Houdelaincourt. All troops well turned out, billets reasonably comfortable. The French 47th Infantry Division detailed to assist in training our 1st Division. The French troops made a fine appearance.

At Neufchâteau in the afternoon saw sixteen American newspaper correspondents under charge of Major Frederick Palmer. Regret we cannot permit them to tell what we are doing. At Mirecourt later met Major General de Castelnau, commanding the Eastern Group of French Armies. He is of the old school, very courteous, about seventy, short and sturdy. Spent the night at Vittel. Accommodations ample, surroundings beautiful, but rail communications inconvenient and social attractions objectionable.

Inspected Chaumont yesterday, where French commander, Major General Wirbel, pointed out disadvantages while the Mayor, M. Lévy-Alphandéry, favored its selection as our headquarters. Afterwards continued on to Paris.

Held conference with Ambassador this evening.

In driving through those areas nearest the front, one could not help being depressed by their deserted appearance. As the limited crops of grain had been mostly harvested, little work of any kind was going on in the fields. Few people were seen even in the villages, except old men and women, with now and then some small children. We noticed but few animals, either along the roads or in the pastures. It was almost as though the population had disappeared with their flocks and herds. Many families had moved away, and, of course, most of the able-bodied men were in the armies. There were no ruins, for the reason that no fighting had taken place in that section. The country simply had an abandoned look.

It would have been out of the question to supply barracks or tentage for all our troops in France and we had adopted the billeting system, whereby the troops of a division as they arrived in their training area were spread around by regiments, battalions or companies in the various towns and villages. Regardless of accommodations the billets were usually preferable in winter to either barracks or tents.

The smaller French villages, which consist merely of groups of farmhouses, were not generally sanitary from our point of view, as the residue from the stables, regarded as invaluable fertilizer, was usually stored in the streets, where the unsightly heaps, with their pungent odors, reminded one of a country barnyard. At the expense of considerable labor on the part of troops, with such help from the French as could be impressed, most of these dumps had to be removed before our men were content to settle down to work. Where there was not enough spare room in the dwelling houses of the inhabitants, which was usually the case, the barn or stable lofts were quickly converted into fairly comfortable quarters, with hay or fodder in lieu of barrack beds or cots. On account of the danger, no fires were allowed in these billets and even smoking had to be prohibited.

My inspection of the 1st Division showed that it was well settled in its training area in the region of Gondrecourt, south of Bar-le-

Note: Total strength of the A.E.F. on July 31st, 726 officers, 16,022 enlisted men.

Duc. The troops of the division had already established friendly relations with the French peasantry and had quickly adapted themselves to their new mode of life. The training of the division was proceeding and the officers and men were eager for the day when they could test their strength against the enemy.

As the natural consequence of the financial condition of the frugal French provincial, he was wont to profit unduly by the presence of the British and ourselves, and the open-handed pay-day habits of the Americans served to give some encouragement to this inclination. As a result, some coolness grew up later between our men and their early friends. While one can appreciate the temptation to take advantage of such an opportunity, yet the average American soldier, quite overlooking the great inconvenience our troops caused the people and their kindness in general, could not quite bring himself to understand this attitude. As a matter of truth, the liberal spending indulged in by our men was a source of difficulty to the French themselves, as the resulting higher levels of prices for commodities imposed hardships on those who did not enjoy the profits flowing from sales to the Americans.

At the conclusion of my inspection of various places, Chaumont was selected as the best site for my General Headquarters. It was on our line of communications to the front and centrally placed as to probable sectors of our operations. The fine regimental barracks there furnished office space for our headquarters and we were able to obtain ample billeting accommodations in private houses for all except the enlisted men, who were provided with temporary barracks.

This old town of some 15,000 inhabitants is situated near the upper Marne, on a plateau that dominates the wooded hills and cultivated valleys of the surrounding country. Of historical interest is the fact that in 1814 Chaumont was the scene of the conference between the sovereigns of Great Britain, Austria, Russia and Prussia to decide the fate of Napoleon. The house in which this meeting of emperors and kings occurred became in our day a club where the younger French and American officers no doubt frequently discussed the form of punishment that the Allies should eventually impose upon the Kaiser. The people of the town were very hospitable and soon became our warm friends. When the end arrived, we were loath to leave behind us a community so generous and open-hearted and for whom we felt such affection and esteem. Americans who had the good fortune to live in Chaumont will always cherish their association with its charming people.

The extreme patience and fortitude of the French, their industry and their frugality, made all the more necessary through the hardships of war, demanded that we should not by any avoidable act render their situation more onerous or reduce their capacity to produce by any disregard of their interests. That all our forces might understand these obligations, an order was published, from which the following is quoted:

"For the first time in history the American Army finds itself in European territory. The good name of the United States and the maintenance of cordial relations require perfect deportment of each member of this command. It is of the greatest importance that the soldiers of the American Army shall at all times treat the people of France, especially the women, with the greatest courtesy and consideration. The valiant deeds of the French Armies and those of their Allies by which they have together successfully maintained their common cause for three years, and the sacrifices of the civil population of France in support of their armies command our profound respect. This can best be expressed on the part of our forces by uniform courtesy to all the French people and by faithful consideration of their laws and customs. * * *

"The intense cultivation of the soil in France and the conditions caused by the war make it necessary that extreme care be taken to do no damage to private property. The entire French manhood capable of bearing arms is in the field fighting the enemy. Only old men, women and children remain to cultivate the soil. It should therefore be a point of honor with each member of the American Army to avoid doing the least damage to any property in France."

It was hardly necessary to issue such a proclamation as it was noticeable from the beginning that the attitude of the men toward the inhabitants and their property was most commendable. I do not believe that in all history there has ever been an army on foreign soil so considerate and observant of the rights and interests of the people. The peasant class made a strong appeal to every man in the army. Their simplicity, their love of the soil, and the long hours of work in the fields by the old men and women and the young boys and girls remained the constant admiration of our soldiers. I am inclined to think, however, that the excellent behavior of our soldiers, the rather unmilitary appearance of the earlier contingents in ill-fitting uniforms, and their apparent lack of formal discipline created at first the impression in the minds of the French officials that such men were not likely to become aggressive fighting troops.

(Diary) Paris, Monday, August 6, 1917. Had conference on Saturday with M. Albert Claveille, head of Bureau of Transportation, regarding railway matters. Washington says lack of equipment will delay call for National Army.

Colonel Williams reports French behind in delivery machine guns and automatic rifles. Conferred with Harjes today about services of Norton-Harjes Volunteer Ambulance Unit.[1] Had an interesting evening with Pétain as dinner guest. He spoke confidentially of plans for an offensive; wants me present.

In the organization of our armies for the World War it was evident that if any considerable numbers were to be sent abroad, an additional force would be needed over and above the Regular Army and the National Guard. The War Department therefore established what was called the National Army, to be composed principally of men who were to come into the service through the draft. Most of the divisions of the National Army were organized in August and September and some men were then assigned to them. As the time approached to begin the training of the smaller units, it was found that after equipping the special troops urgently needed in France there was little equipment left even for the additional men required to fill up the National

---

[1] Harjes had established and was supporting a volunteer ambulance unit for service with the French.

Guard. Unfortunately, this made it necessary to delay calling out more drafts for the units of the National Army. However, considerable numbers were called into service and proceeded with preliminary instruction, but the lack of equipment seriously delayed their progress.

The development of the machine gun as an infantry weapon, following the experience of the Russo-Japanese War, had been carried to a high degree of perfection, especially in the German Army, where its value was more fully appreciated than among the Allies. In this, as in every other line of preparation, we were far behind all others. The question of adopting new types of machine guns and automatic rifles for our army had been discussed at home for years and test after test had been made, but the nearest approach to a decision was an acrimonious discussion in and out of the press between the Ordnance Department and certain inventors. The result was that when we entered the war no conclusion regarding the best make of gun had been reached that, in the opinion of the War Department, would warrant its manufacture in quantity. Not only were we without sufficient machine guns, but our organization tables did not anticipate their use in anything like the numbers employed by the enemy.

To equip our advance divisions, especially in view of the possibility of an emergency requiring prompt entry into the line, arrangements were made to purchase Hotchkiss machine guns and Chauchat automatics from the French. But, on account of delay in deliveries, instruction of our troops in the handling of these weapons was slowed down considerably. Notwithstanding these handicaps, the most modern conception of the use of machine guns was taught in our schools, and our machine gunners eventually reached a high degree of proficiency.

At this time the production of the Vickers machine gun was proceeding slowly. Soon after the adoption of the Browning automatic weapons, following the tests in May, the manufacture of both the heavy gun for ground work and the light gun as an automatic rifle was begun, although none of these became available for use in battle until September, 1918. The Lewis machine gun, about which there had been so much controversy involving the Ordnance Department, was not considered suitable as an automatic rifle but was recommended for airplanes.

Our earlier divisions were seriously handicapped in their preparation at home by lack of machine guns for training, many units not receiving this arm until after their arrival in France. When it is recalled that each division at the beginning of the war was allowed only 92 machine guns and no automatic rifles, and that under our war organization 260 machine guns and 768 automatic rifles were required, the result of delay in providing these guns needs no further comment.

(Diary) Paris, Tuesday, August 14, 1917. Had M. Painlevé, M. Viviani and M. Claveille to luncheon on Thursday, hoping to make coöperation easier. Took dinner with General Nash and Colonel Thornton, British Army, Manager and Assistant, respectively, for their rail transportation in France.

General Hornwood, British Provost Marshal General, called to-day with Colonel Ely to discuss military police. Visited Mrs. Whitelaw Reid's hospital, which she wishes us to take for officers.

Department recommends Mr. Atterbury for railway chief; have requested that he be sent over.

The maintenance of good order among our troops under the peculiar conditions of service in France was most important and for this purpose a military police was essential. Such a force, under the control of the Provost Marshal General, corresponded to the police department in a well-organized city, except that its jurisdiction included only those in the military service. The British, whose situation was similar to our own, gave us helpful information regarding their system, which, with slight modification, was adopted for our armies. In our previous wars, the Provost Guard, so called, usually consisted of troops of the line detailed for the purpose but without any special training for such duty.

Colonel Hanson E. Ely was selected to organize the police corps and made a good beginning in laying the foundation, but, at his own request, he was shortly relieved and sent to regimental duty. His successor, Colonel W. H. Allaire, became Provost Marshal General until the following July, when he was relieved by Colonel J. C. Groome. In September, 1918, Brigadier General H. H. Bandholtz, on account of his special fitness for such work from his experience as Chief of Constabulary in the Philippine Islands, became the permanent head of the corps. Due credit must be given to each of these officers but particularly to Bandholtz for the smart appearance and the high efficiency of the military police. Its services were indispensable in directing and handling traffic during combat activities, in preventing straggling and in maintaining order among scattered groups of our armies both before and after the Armistice. The organization on November 1, 1918, numbered 463 officers and 15,912 men, spread practically over the whole of France.

The use of railways for the movement of troops and supplies had never before attained any such proportions as in the World War and there was no service, except sea transportation, upon which we placed greater dependence for our success. The long haul from our ports to the front made it highly important that the rail system be organized according to the most modern methods and managed by experienced personnel.

The first study of railway conditions in France was made by a Board of Engineers chosen by the War Department headed by Major Wm. Barclay Parsons, afterward Colonel 11th Engineers. This board submitted an exhaustive report of its investigations and conclusions, which fully agreed with the opinion of Colonel Taylor, my Chief of Engineers, and his assistants. These independent investigations showed that the French railways, especially those that we planned to use, were sadly in need of physical rehabilitation and that the additional burden to be placed on them would require on our part an immense program of construction of new yards, terminals, multiple tracks, cut-offs, regulating stations and other additions. Both groups of engineers felt also that the methods of the French would have to be greatly improved to meet the extraordinary demands that would arise in handling our traffic. It was apparent that we could not depend entirely on the French without great risk of failure at a critical moment, and it was evident that if we expected the maximum efficiency in this service we must provide our own personnel as well as additional locomotives and cars, all to be as far as practicable under American management. Differences in language, customs and methods combined to make this one of our most delicate and trying problems, as any one who has traveled on French railroads can readily imagine.

A separate transportation corps had never been provided in our army; in fact, no department had been specifically charged with the management of railroads. In the Quartermaster Corps a bureau issued transportation requests, routed personnel and freight and settled the accounts, and it was the understanding that in time of war the army engineers would step in and take charge when railway operation should become necessary. With this plan in view, commendable progress had been made toward both procurement and organization by Colonel Taylor. Complete estimates for rolling stock and construction at ports, terminals and yards, including an accurate survey of building and equipment requirements, had been made under his direction by Major W. J. Wilgus, formerly Vice President of the New York Central, afterwards Colonel, a clever and brilliant man of vision who had been a member of the Parsons Board. These estimates without change served as a permanent guide for railway construction plans and material.

Coördinate with the procurement and maintenance of railway material and equipment, we were confronted with the vital question of organization for operation and management. We had no officers in the Regular service of sufficient experience in railway administration to insure success. Therefore, the evident course to pursue, to which the precedent of both the British and French pointed the way, was to create a transportation corps, immediately under the direction of some man of outstanding reputation in the railroad world. In accordance with the principle of obtaining the most competent men for important positions, the following cable was sent on July 29th:

"Have made thorough study of railroad situation and am convinced that operation of railroads must be under man with large experience in managing commercial railroads at home. Successful handling our railroad lines so important that ablest man in country should be selected. After almost disastrous results with inexperienced military men running railroads British selected ablest man could find to have charge transportation. Question here mainly one of physical operation and management in intimate relation with French who retain general control which is necessary to handle ordinary commercial traffic. Question of railroad transportation of course involves equipment maintenance and new construction at front as army advances and should be practically independent department although nominally under engineers. Railroad man chosen should be sent here without delay together with three or four able assistants of his own selection. Later on it is believed these men should be given appropriate military rank."

This elicited the reply mentioned in the diary recommending Mr. W. W. Atterbury, General Manager of the Pennsylvania Railroad, for the place.

CHAPTER XI

Visit French and American Troops with Pétain—Inspection French Regulating Station—Witness Successful French Attack—Recommend Production Powder and Explosives at Home—Difficulties of Coördination with Allies and War Department Bureaus—Purchasing Agency Established

(Diary) Paris, Tuesday, August 21, 1917. Visited billeting areas of French 47th Division and our 1st Division with General Pétain on Sunday.

Inspected St. Dizier Regulating Station and witnessed French attack near Verdun yesterday. Visited French hospital at Souilly.

Returned this morning with M. Painlevé, Minister of War, on his train.

AS I had accepted General Pétain's invitation to see the French offensive that was to take place on the 20th, I motored to French G.H.Q. on Saturday afternoon, the 18th, accompanied by Colonel Palmer and Captain Carl Boyd, and after dinner left with General Pétain and two or three members of his staff on his train for an inspection of French and American troops. We reached Gondrecourt the next morning and began with a review of the French 47th Infantry Division, which was paraded on a prominent plateau near Houdelaincourt. Before the march past, several officers and men, drawn up in front of the center of the lines, were decorated by Pétain for gallantry. It was a proud moment for each one to have his badge of courage pinned on his breast by the distinguished Commander-in-Chief of the French Army. Indeed, while awards were bestowed upon but a few outstanding individuals, the whole division shared in this recognition of its splendid services. The ceremony could hardly have been more impressive. With not a soul in sight save those in uniform, the stillness was like that which follows a battle, leaving the distinct feeling that these brave men were being decorated on the field of honor.

To the stirring strains of the famous *Sambre et Meuse,* the division swung past in review in almost perfect lines and with the élan characteristic of French troops. General Pétain then had the officers assembled by Major General de Pouydraguin, the division commander, and in a brief talk praised their appearance and especially their record. He encouraged them to promote the morale and efficiency of their men in preparation for arduous work yet to come. This division had been in every serious engagement of the war and its losses had been very heavy, as could be easily surmised from the youthful appearance of the officers, most of whom had risen from the ranks to replace casualties among their seniors. General Pétain told them that because of its fine record the division had been given the special honor of assisting in the instruction of the American 1st Division.

Accompanied by Brigadier General Bundy, Colonel William M. Cruikshank, and others, I took Pétain to see some of our troops being trained in throwing grenades, and in the use of the French automatic rifle. An amusing story was told us in connection with the grenade instruction. It seems that one of the men insisted on throwing his grenade immediately after setting the fuse instead of waiting till he slowly counted seven, which was necessary so that the explosion would occur as the grenade reached its destination. After being cautioned several times by his officer, the man said, "Captain, I just can't hold these grenades any longer because I can feel them swelling in my hand."

We visited several villages occupied by French and American troops. As we passed through our billets and inspected the kitchens, Pétain inquired particularly about the components of our ration and the manner of cooking and serving meals. The French soldiers were furnished wine in place of coffee provided for our men, and the allowances differed in other respects, ours containing a larger meat component. But when it came to cooking, the French were ahead of us, although our men preferred our own to either the French or British ration.

In going around with General Pétain it was significant that every honor which the scant population could show was paid to him. All the villages were decorated and the people appeared in gala dress. At each place some young girl especially selected for her good looks presented the General with flowers, for which she expected and proudly received the customary acknowledgment of a chaste kiss on each cheek.

In many places we had to climb ladders to reach the American billets in the hay mows. In one loft I happened to stand apart near a neatly made bunk and in the dim light Pétain mistook me for the sergeant in charge. He asked me how we liked our billets and a number of other questions about our life in France, which I answered respectfully, playing the part the best I could. He did not know the difference until he was told by some of the amused members of his staff after we had descended.

Motoring to Souilly, the headquarters of the French Second Army, we met Major General Fayolle, commanding the Group of Armies of the Center, and Major General Guillaumat, Commander of the Second Army, whose Chief of Staff explained in detail the plan of the battle that was to take place the next day. We had luncheon with Fayolle, whom later I came to regard as one of the ablest of the French generals. In appearance he was rather frail, no longer young, but active and alert.

On our visit to the military hospital at Souilly, Pétain presented Mlle. de Baye, a nurse, with the Croix de Guerre, as she lay on a cot suffering from a severe wound inflicted by a piece of shell two days before. When he told her who I was, she said, "I am glad you are here, General, to see how a French woman can suffer for her country." She was so happy over her decoration, however, that I am sure that for the moment she had entirely forgotten her pain.

The following morning, at my suggestion, we went to St. Dizier, to inspect the regulating station. There we met M. Painlevé, the Minister of War, who had come to the front to witness the battle, in company with M. Albert Thomas, the Minister of Munitions. I spent a most instructive forenoon studying the method of distributing supplies to units at the front.

The regulating station was essentially a development of the World War. All rations, clothing, fuel, ammunition and other supplies came in bulk from depots in the rear to one of these stations, and from there the trains, one each day or so, for each division or corresponding group went forward as far as safety would permit, carrying everything needed for the period. The supplies were then sent by the light railway to the railhead, thence by divisional trucks or wagons to the proper organizations. The system seemed simple enough but to make it work successfully thorough organization and expert management were necessary. This was especially true when it had to serve large forces, as was the case during the St. Mihiel battle the following year, when we handled through this station the greater part of the supplies for the more than half a million Americans on that front.

In the afternoon I had a most agreeable surprise. Motoring to the command post of the XVI Corps, which conducted this offensive, I found an old friend of Russo-Japanese War days, Major General Corvisart, in command. As viewed from his post, with the sun at our backs, the battlefield lay before us like a panorama, and we could easily follow the advancing French lines, one particular unit under observation being the famous Foreign Legion, in which I had become interested many years before from reading Ouida's tale, "Under Two Flags."

Being entirely assured regarding the outcome of the battle, Corvisart and I dropped into reminiscence of our former service together in Manchuria. We had been military attachés in Japan at the same time, both of us being assigned to General Kuroki's army as observers. I inquired about Major Caviglia, the Italian attaché, and learned that he was then a lieutenant general commanding an army in northern Italy. We recalled that when we were with the Japanese Army, Caviglia used to wake us every morning singing Italian opera. Corvisart said that the Austrian attaché had been advanced to the same rank and position as Caviglia. Sir Ian Hamilton, of Gallipoli fame, already held the rank of major general when he was observer with the Japanese.

Colonel Fowke had become lieutenant general and adjutant general of the British forces. And so we ran through the list up to the German attachés. Colonel, then Captain, Hoffmann had but recently succeeded Ludendorff as chief of staff on the Russian front and later became a general. He was a jolly sort and was quite popular among the group attached to Kuroki's army. I then asked about Major von Etzel, the senior German attaché, and it was easy to anticipate the reply as Corvisart, with a smile of satisfaction, pointed to the battlefield and said, "I have just beaten him to-day. He is commanding a division opposite me."

This attack of the French Second Army, although made astride the Meuse River, was directed principally against Le Mort Homme hill and Hill 304, both famous in the struggle of 1916. In order to destroy the wire entanglement and other obstacles, as a precaution against heavy losses, the infantry assault was preceded by four days' continuous bombardment, and relatively the amount of artillery ammunition expended exceeded that of any previous engagement, its value being, as I was informed, $75,-000,000. The proportion of the artillery force as compared to the infantry in this battle was as eleven to ten. The firing attained such precision and volume that the German troops in the forward positions were submerged and the attacking infantry reached most of its objectives by nightfall the first day, making an advance of three miles and capturing 6,000 prisoners.

The sector where the French attack took place was to have a peculiar interest for me before the end of the war. My headquarters as commander of the First Army one year later occupied the building in Souilly, then used by Major General Guillaumat, and the line reached by Corvisart's troops in this battle became our jump-off line in the Meuse-Argonne battle. In fact, every foot of the ground covered in this inspection with General Pétain became associated with America's greatest effort in the war. After visiting the French installations and the manifold activities carried on behind this front, with the shifting masses of combat troops and the thousands engaged in the services of supply and transportation, it seemed quite improbable that we should be able to marshal a sufficient army in time to replace the French on this front until late in 1918.

I found it most agreeable as well as instructive to be with Pétain in this intimate way and have an opportunity to hear something of his experience. His discussion of the defense of Verdun, in which, as French commander, he served with such marked distinction, was especially entertaining. As we drove about, he spoke of the courage of his men and of the tremendous losses they had sustained. He pointed out the vast amount of road work, including the Voie Sacrée from Bar-le-Duc to Verdun, rebuilt under his directions for the constant movements of large bodies of troops and supplies necessary to maintain the defense.

In lighter vein, his comments on French politicians during this trip were amusing, if not always complimentary, and he congratulated me many times on being so far removed from political interference. One afternoon the conversation drifted to painting and he asked me how many times I had sat for my portrait. "Several times already," I said. "The last one, which I thought very good, was done by a distinguished artist by the name of Jonas (English, Jonah) for *l'Illustration.*" Immediately he said, "Don't let them publish it! Don't do it! Every officer whose portrait by Jonas has appeared in that journal has been relieved from his command." Not that I am superstitious, quite the contrary, but I immediately forbade the publication of the portrait, and to this day it has never appeared.

From the time of Nivelle's failure in April, the depression in the French armies had been so great that Pétain, who succeeded him, had been content simply to hold the trenches, and no French offensive operation of consequence until this one had been attempted. From the moment of his assignment, Pétain began to build up the shattered morale of his armies, and probably no other officer in France could have performed the task so well. His immense success in the defense of Verdun had won for him the confidence of the army and the country, and yet he remained the same modest, unassuming character, consistent and conservative. He, perhaps better than any other, understood the temperament of the French soldier, whom he handled with infinite patience and tact. Without flourish of trumpets, he went among the disaffected regiments with counsel and advice. The recalcitrant element he severely disciplined, even to the execution of several leaders. In establishing a Department of Morale, he took steps to counteract defeatist propaganda among the men on leave. During his visits of inspection he mingled with the troops and listened to stories of abuses, which, as far as possible, he corrected on the spot.

Pétain had visited some ninety divisions and impressed them with his personality and prestige. As his efforts began to bear fruit, he concluded to try a limited operation, to be carried out by specially selected units. The plans for the attack, which we had just witnessed, were worked out in minute detail and with the utmost secrecy in order to insure success, its avowed purpose being to stimulate the morale of both the army and the people. Pétain himself and the Ministry were much pleased with the result.

It is my opinion that, under the circumstances, Painlevé's selection of Pétain to be Commander-in-Chief of the French armies had as important an effect on the outcome of the war as the later appointment of a supreme commander for the Allied armies.

(Diary) Paris, Thursday, August 23, 1917. Held conference yesterday with General Blatchford.[1] Continued lack of construction material emphasizes imperative need of shipping. Conferred with Major Murphy regarding coördination Red Cross work and shipments of supplies. Discussed airplane types with Colonel R. C. Bolling, who is efficiently working out details to send home. Ambassador and Mrs. Henry Morgenthau, Major and Mrs. Robert R. McCormick, and a few others dined with us last evening.

After careful consideration of the subject of powders and explosives, it is certain that we must undertake their manufacture ourselves.

[1] Brig. Gen. (later Maj. Gen.) Richard M. Blatchford was then Commanding General of the Line of Communications, which included the ports.

It was highly important that the gravity of our tonnage situation be brought forcibly to the attention of the Allies. Apropos of the approaching conference on shipping, I sent the following cable to Washington:

"August 23, 1917.

"Reference proposed meeting of shipping representatives Allied powers London, American representative will be confronted with question of shipping required by United States and should be strongly supported in demand upon Allies for sufficient commercial shipping to carry out army program * * * any consideration of less tonnage should be opposed by our representative. * * * The British, and especially the French, have reached absolute limit of manpower and any augmentation their military forces cannot be expected. Imperative hasten our organization and training so that we will have the troops contemplated your project in Europe for active service by May or June. Military activities of Allies on land should be strongly reënforced by combined navies and destruction U-boat bases accomplished if possible. High British army officers confidentially condemn waiting policy British Admiralty. * * * In view of gravity of shipping question recommend our Government insist upon aggressive policy by combined British and American Navies. * * * Our position in this war very strong. * * * Allies now fully recognize dependence upon our coöperation and we need not hesitate demand both aggressive naval policy and full share Allied commercial shipping. Recommend American representative shipping conference be instructed accordingly."

Numbers of officers of all Allied armies felt very strongly that in order to check the losses by submarines the two navies should take some risk and attempt to destroy the bases from which these boats operated. I do not know, however, whether any steps were ever taken to convey this suggestion to the combined navies.

A study by a joint French and American commission of the question of production of powders and explosives in France showed that the greater part of the raw materials for their manufacture must be imported, and that, due to the shipping situation, France in December would produce only about half of the current output. It was apparent, therefore, that to avoid calamity the United States must not only furnish powder and explosives for all of its own forces but must supply about half the French requirements, and the War Department was so advised. By this arrangement a large saving of tonnage would be effected, as the weight of raw materials was ten to twenty times that of the finished product. As nitrates for the manufacture of powder and explosives had to be imported mostly from Chile, the hazard to shipping would be reduced by avoiding the long haul to France. Millions of dollars were expended in the construction of plants at home in an attempt to produce nitrates, but none had been turned out before the end of the war. In view of these costly experiments, it would seem wise during peace to make some provision for the future.

Our efforts to arrange for the procurement in France of munitions, aviation, various classes of equipment and supply, and the use of facilities, brought our officers in close contact with bureaus of the French Government. In the beginning we were largely dependent upon these bureaus to make up deficiencies in many things necessary to complete our preparations. The failure of the French to realize the necessity of hearty coöperation became evident very early in our relations with them. The higher authorities apparently understood, and promises of assistance were readily given, but when we got down to actual details we encountered difficulties. This was true especially as to the granting of docking facilities, the allotment of rail transportation, and the assignment of forests for lumber procurement.

One confusing thing we encountered was the lack of a clear division of authority between bureaus and departments. Even after three years of war there remained considerable question between the Zone of Operations and the Service of the Rear as to the control of munitions and transportation. The Commander-in-Chief claimed to have the final voice in the allotment of artillery, aviation, and railroad rolling stock, but his authority behind the Zone of the Armies was not conceded by the bureaus of the War Office, and was especially contested as to rail transportation. In actual practice, he was not really vested with control of material except that in the possession of the armies, but his influence as commander-in-chief was such that his approval was usually necessary to insure definite action.

In our dealings with French bureaus we had to overcome many obstacles. The subordinate one might happen to encounter at the start was usually impressed with his own importance and would undertake to make a decision, which would lead one to think the matter practically settled, only to find that this official had little if any authority and that his action was not approved by the senior next above him. Then, having already lost much time, it would be learned that this was not the proper office after all. At last reaching the responsible bureau, one was likely to be told that the thing could not be done, no reason being apparent except that it never had been done. So, frequently throughout the war, it was necessary for me to make a personal appeal to the Minister concerned that orders be given for supplies or services already promised and which, therefore, we had every reason to expect should be furnished. Although our own departments at home were considered rather adept in the use of red tape, yet, to use an apt though inelegant comparison, the art of tying things up in official routine was in swaddling clothes in America as compared to its development in France.

After a few contacts with their system one marveled that the French had managed to get along so well in supplying their armies during three years of war. The French are very intelligent and they have a highly organized government, but from the practical viewpoint they often become deeply involved in nonessential details and lose sight of the main objective. I always likened the average French bureau official to a certain narrow type of quartermaster who held sway at an earlier period in our army and who regarded all government property under his charge as his own, and when he finally issued it always made the recipient feel that he was being especially favored.

However, such difficulties were not confined to dealings with the French. While not entirely disadvantageous to be 3,000 miles from base, it was often very much of a handicap. Our War Department officials could not always understand conditions as we did and some of them were often none too willing to accept our views. A few of the chiefs of supply departments seemed to have the notion that it was their duty to negotiate our purchases abroad. Without notice, they frequently placed orders with the French or British Governments that duplicated those already given by my staff, and they did so even after having full information that we had ordered the same things. So independent of control or suggestion had some bureaus of our War Department become that it was a long time before their chiefs would consent to leave such matters to their representatives at my headquarters acting under my authority.

Another source of confusion arose, especially in the beginning, through our War Department seeking the opinion of Allied representatives in Washington on my requests. After we had made an exhaustive study and sent specific recommendations to Washington it was not uncommon for the Chief of Staff or the head of a supply department to refer the matter to a foreign representative for his views or those of his Government. This official would naturally refer the matter back to his home office and eventually it would reach me through French channels with a request for my opinion. Such procedure discredited my recommendations and placed my entire staff in an embarrassing position in the eyes of the foreign Government concerned, to say nothing of the delay in complying with our requests, which, in many cases, were of immediate and almost vital importance. The following protest was cabled to Washington, but, as will be seen later, the practice of interference was not at once discontinued:

"The Chief of Staff, Washington.
"Inquiry comes from * * * through French War Office as to my views on this subject (organization of our units recommended three months before). Have replied that my views would always be sent my own superiors through proper channels. Seems unwise that our General Staff should permit such inquiries to be made, at least through a Civil Commissioner."

This sort of thing also suggested to the French the idea, at least temporarily, of handling our business directly with Washington.

An example is recalled in connection with procurement of horses. We had obtained from the French a definite promise to furnish us with 7,000 animals per month beginning September 1st. Some ten days after this arrangement was made, the French War Office cabled the French Commissioner at Washington, who in turn transmitted it as a sort of dictum to our War Department, that it would be impossible for the French to furnish us any horses or mules and that our Government should begin at once to supply them, although the French offered to lend us 4,000 animals with the understanding that they would be replaced by November 1st. This news was cabled to me and it was the first notice we had that the French did not expect to fulfill their promise.

(Diary)   Paris, Wednesday, August 29, 1917.   The correspondents called on Saturday and were given confidentially a general outline of plans.

Had dinner on Sunday with Mr. and Mrs. Edward Tuck, in company with Ambassador Sharp, Ridgeway Knight [1] and others.

Representative Medill McCormick has come to make a study of conditions. Have detailed Lieutenant Colonel Dawes as Chief of Purchasing Board. He tried to beg off, but when its importance was explained he gracefully accepted.

In view of the uncertainty of obtaining more than a limited amount of ocean tonnage, it was natural that we should procure abroad as large a proportion of supplies as possible, and our supply departments began at once to make inquiries to meet the demands for construction material, subsistence stores and engineering equipment. Many sources of general supply had been developed by the French and we soon found ourselves not only in competition with them, but also with the British; then, too, our own different departments had begun to bid against each other. The principal article that caused rivalry was lumber, the Corps of Engineers and the Quartermaster Corps having entered into a lively contest for advantage, with a consequent elevation of prices. This condition, involving immense quantities of lumber required at once for barracks, hospitals, docks and wharves, was not only

[1] Mr. Ridgeway Knight was one of the well-known American artists in France.

annoying to us but it gave the French much concern. They very soon, and naturally, imposed restrictions upon sales that made it difficult for us to meet even our most urgent requirements until the whole question was readjusted.

In our Army at home it had long been the custom for each department to make its own contracts without regard to the others, except that the quartermaster was supposed to purchase and distribute certain military stores and other things that were in common use by the entire Army. Our sources of supply at home during the years of peace had been so great and the needs of the Army relatively so small that it had not been necessary to consider the possibility of shortage. In France, however, it was imperative to regulate purchases in order to prevent a rise in prices that would add to the financial burdens, especially of the Allies, who were much less able to pay than we were. Besides that, quantities of all kinds of supplies were limited, which was the principal reason why it became necessary to arrive at some understanding for a just allotment.

In an effort to reach a solution, I appointed a board of officers to study the question of purchases, and suggested that some agency might be created that would supervise procurement in general, and by coördinating our own and Allied needs check the scramble for supplies. In a rather extended discussion, the board came to the conclusion that a centralized agency to control purchases would be illegal and unanimously recommended the continuance of existing methods. But an emergency confronted us and it was no time to discuss technicalities. Some business-like method had to be adopted to meet the situation. In other words, a remedy for an approaching chaotic condition resulting from the independent, uncontrolled action of the several services must be found. To my mind the solution seemed to be merely a matter of coördination. Therefore, I tore up the recommendation and established a Purchasing Board to consist of one or more representatives of each service making purchases of any sort, including the Red Cross and the Y.M.C.A. Lieutenant Colonel Dawes, 17th Engineers, well known as a man of large business experience, was appointed as the head of this Board, the members of which were to meet together and make known their respective needs and then agree among themselves as to where and by which department each purchase was to be made, thus mutually assisting instead of competing with each other. Under the arrangement, coöperation with the French was established and the agency became increasingly effective in handling our procurement activities.

CHAPTER XII

THE most important question that confronted us in the preparation of our forces of citizen soldiery for efficient service was training. Except for the Spanish-American War, nearly twenty years before, actual combat experience of the Regular Army had been limited to the independent action of minor commands in the Philippines and to two expeditions into Mexico, each with forces smaller than a modern American division. The World War involved the handling of masses where even a division was relatively a small unit. It was one thing to call one or two million men to the colors, and quite another thing to transform them into an organized, instructed army capable of meeting and holding its own in the battle against the best trained force in Europe with three years of actual war experience to its credit.

Few people can realize what a stupendous undertaking it was to teach these vast numbers their various duties when such a large percentage of them were ignorant of practically everything pertaining to the business of the soldier in war. First of all, most of the officer personnel available had little or no military experience, and had to be trained in the manifold duties of commanders. They had to learn the interior economy of their units— messing, housing, clothing, and, in general, caring for their men—as well as methods of instruction and the art of leading them in battle. This great task was, of course, under the direction of the War Department.

To supplement the instruction at home, a general scheme of schools for the A.E.F. was prepared by the Operations and Training Section of my General Staff, but in order that this instruction should be as complete and uniform as possible and at the same time be coördinated with other activities, I decided that training should be handled by officers who could devote their entire time to it. An additional section of the Headquarters General Staff was, therefore, established, called the Training Section, to function under my personal direction. As chief of this section Colonel Paul B. Malone was chosen, with Colonel H. B. Fiske as his assistant.

In the preparation of a course of training a special study had been made not only of the basic principles taught by the Allies but also of the methods employed to give these principles practical application. The British and French were not entirely in accord in their ideas of organization or of battle tactics and each sought to impress us with the superiority of their respective systems. Our officers engaged in this duty were directed to keep in view the development of the most efficient fighting machine as quickly as possible and as a means to this end to adopt only sound doctrines of training and make them essentially our own.

The British methods of teaching trench warfare appealed to me very strongly. They taught their men to be aggressive and undertook to perfect them in hand-to-hand fighting with bayonet, grenade and dagger. A certain amount of this kind of training was necessary to prepare the troops for trench warfare. Moreover it served to stimulate their morale by giving them confidence in their own personal prowess. Through the kindness of Sir Douglas Haig, we were fortunate early in our experience to have assigned to us Lieutenant General R. H. K. Butler and other officers of the British Army in addition to French officers to assist in this individual training. Later, several French and British officers also came to lecture at a number of our schools.

We found difficulty, however, in using these Allied instructors, in that the French and, to a large extent, the British, had practically settled down to the conviction that developments since 1914 had changed the principles of warfare. Both held that new conditions imposed by trench fighting had rendered previous conceptions of training more or less obsolete and that preparation for open warfare was no longer necessary. French publications and manuals were generally in accord with this theory. It was, perhaps, logical to expect that the French should take this view as, nationally, unlike the Germans, they had been on the defensive, at least in thought, during the previous half century. It is true that on occasions the French assumed the offensive, but the defensive idea was ever in mind.

In the situation that followed the first battle of the Marne, the great armies on the Western Front were entrenched against each other and neither had been able to make more than local gains. The long period during which this condition had prevailed, with its resultant psychological effect, together with the natural leaning of the French toward the defensive, to which should be added the adverse effect of their recent spring experience, had apparently combined to obscure the principles of open warfare.

If the French doctrine had prevailed our instruction would have been limited to a brief period of training for trench fighting. A new army brought up entirely on such principles would have been seriously handicapped without the protection of the trenches. It would probably have lacked the aggressiveness to break through the enemy's lines and the knowledge of how to carry on thereafter. It was my opinion that the victory could not be won by the costly process of attrition, but it must be won by driving the enemy out into the open and engaging him in a war of movement. Instruction in this kind of warfare was based upon individual and group initiative, resourcefulness and tactical judgment, which were also of great advantage in trench warfare. Therefore, we took decided issue with the Allies and, without neglecting thorough preparation for trench fighting, undertook to train mainly for open combat, with the object from the start of vigorously forcing the offensive.

Our units then in training were nearly all recruits and many of the officers and noncommissioned officers were easily influenced by the ideas of the French designated to assist us. In order to avoid the effect of the French teaching it became necessary gradually to take over and direct all instruction ourselves. For the purpose of impressing our own doctrine upon officers, a training program was issued which laid great stress on open warfare methods and offensive action. The following is a pertinent extract from my instructions on this point:

> "The above methods to be employed must remain and become distinctly our own. All instruction must contemplate the assumption of a vigorous offensive. This purpose will be emphasized in every phase of training until it becomes a settled habit of thought."

Intimately connected with the question of training for open warfare was the matter of rifle practice. The earliest of my cablegrams on this subject was in August, in which it was urged that thorough instruction in rifle practice should be carried on at home because of the difficulty of giving it in France:

> "Study here shows value and desirability of retaining our existing small arms target practice course. In view of great difficulty in securing ranges in France due to density of the population and cultivation recommend as far as practicable the complete course be given in the United States before troops embark. Special emphasis should be placed on rapid fire."

The armies on the Western Front in the recent battles that I had witnessed had all but given up the use of the rifle. Machine guns, grenades, Stokes mortars, and one-pounders had become the main reliance of the average Allied soldier. These were all valuable weapons for specific purposes but they could not replace the combination of an efficient soldier and his rifle. Numerous instances were reported in the Allied armies of men chasing an individual enemy throwing grenades at him instead of using the rifle. Such was the effect of association that continuous effort was necessary to counteract this tendency among our own officers and men and inspire them with confidence in the efficacy of rifle fire. Ultimately, we had the satisfaction of hearing the French admit that we were right, both in emphasizing training for open warfare and insisting upon proficiency in the use of the rifle.

My view was that the rifle and bayonet still remained the essential weapons of the infantry, and my cables, stressing the fact that the basic principles of warfare had not changed, were sent in an endeavor to influence the courses of training at home. Unfortunately, however, no fixed policy of instruction in the various arms, under a single authority, was ever carried out there. Unresponsive to my advice, the inclination was to accept the views of French specialists and to limit training to the narrow field of trench warfare. Therefore, in large measure, the fundamentals so thoroughly taught at West Point for a century were more or less neglected. The responsibility for the failure at home to take positive action on my recommendations in such matters must fall upon the War Department General Staff.

There were other causes, as we shall see later, that led to confusion and irregularity in training to such an extent that we were often compelled during the last stages of the war to send men into battle with little knowledge of warfare and sometimes with no rifle practice at all.

In the system of schools established in the A.E.F. there were centers of instruction for all units up to divisions, including the training centers for replacements; and corps schools for unit commanders and noncommissioned officers of all arms. Under the supervision of General Headquarters were the General Staff College; the schools to train instructors for corps schools; others for candidates for commissions; schools for recruits; and schools for specialists of every staff and supply department and every other branch of the service.

A school system would have been desirable in the best of armies, but it was indispensable in an army which had to be created almost wholly from raw material. The training of troops for combat was, of course, the primary objective, and schools for instructors were merely a means to that end. In order to give troops the advantage of the latest tactical and technical developments and to make up for the defects of training at home, the plans contemplated an additional period of training for divisions of about three months after reaching France. This gave us an opportunity to secure a certain uniformity in standards, and was especially valuable in affording the newly arrived troops the benefit of experience in the immediate atmosphere of war.

The very limited number of General Staff officers at my disposal had been able to outline basic plans, but as our forces grew increasing numbers were needed, especially to aid in the direction of troops in battle. My cables had failed to make much impression on the War Department as to the difference in functions between staff officers with an army in the field conducting operations and those on duty at the War Department, where they were charged mainly with preliminary organization and training and with directing the procurement and shipment of supplies and equipment. In our army abroad, staff experts were necessary in administration, intelligence, tactical training, and especially in operations, as well as in directing the supply and transportation of the active armies. The following cable expressed my views:

"Urgency training general staff officers for particular duty at army headquarters cannot be overestimated. Their services are needed now to study details in connection with operations and other duties. Our staff officers generally have little conception of problems involved in directing armies * * * or of strategic questions involved. * * * We are now planning for spring campaign and success not possible without thoroughly efficient General Staff. Limited number of officers brought in June much overworked and unable to handle and fully consider many subjects requiring immediate action. Impossible to make this appeal and recommendation too strong and urgently request matter be taken up with Secretary of War without delay."

To help meet this lack of experienced general staff officers with our armies, the General Staff College established at Langres, a few miles south of Chaumont, provided an intensive course of three months, which, though brief, covered instruction in the details of our own staff organization and administration, our system of supply, and the coördination and employment of our forces in combat. While the student officers were selected for their aptitude, it was not possible to graduate thoroughly trained staff officers in such a short time, but the urgency was so great that the course could not be made longer. Having been taught a common doctrine, with a loyal sense of coöperation well accentuated, they were fairly well grounded in theory and had to trust to the costly school of experience for the rest.

(Diary)   Paris, Saturday, September 1, 1917.   Held conference with Atterbury, who has just reported.

As French continue to urge trench warfare, went to Compiègne for conference with Pétain; made clear the necessity for basic elementary training of our troops.   We also considered procurement within Zone of Armies.   Headquarters transferred to Chaumont to-day.

As has been previously stated, in response to my request for an experienced railroad man, Mr. Atterbury, of the Pennsylvania Railroad, was selected and sent to report to me.   In our first brief conversation we merely ran over the problem in a general way. Considerable headway in the organization of our railroad system had already been made by the Corps of Engineers.   Much to my surprise, Atterbury seemed to be very familiar with the situation, and his personality, his force, his grasp of the difficulties of the task and his willingness to undertake it appealed to me at once.   So, without hesitation, and with a feeling that undoubtedly the right man had been found, I told him that he would be placed in charge of railroad transportation.   A few days later, in consultation with Colonels Taylor and Wilgus, we determined the details of readjustment required.   An independent transportation department was created to operate and maintain the broad and narrow gauge railways and the canals in American use, and to construct roads and wharves, shops and other buildings for railway purposes.   It was found necessary, however, to leave construction under the Corps of Engineers.

Upon Atterbury's suggestion, a cable was sent requesting certain men to fill important positions in the organization.   The list included J. A. McCrea, General Manager of the Long Island Railroad, for general manager, with C. M. Bunting as business manager, H. C. Booz as engineer for construction, and J. G. Rogers as deputy, the last three of whom were then with the Pennsylvania

NOTE: Total strength of the A.E.F. on August 31st, 1,616 officers, 35,042 enlisted men.

Railroad. The railway problem was far from easy and many were the obstacles to be overcome, both in our own and in the French services. Successful management would have been very doubtful under a leader without Atterbury's patience, ability, and force of character.

(Diary) Paris, Monday, September 3, 1917. Called on General Foch, Chief of Staff, yesterday on routine of procurement, but his office has no control. Afterward talked with Minister of War on the same subject. De Chambrun, de Ferronay, and my own staff working for better liaison with French bureaus.

Conferred with Atterbury this morning, also with Colonel Bolling. Took Colonel Dawes this afternoon to call on Minister of War and explained purpose of our purchasing agency. Went with Brigadier General William L. Kenly to call on the Minister of Munitions, hoping to expedite manufacture of airplanes for our service.

Frequent conferences with heads of our various activities enable me to give direction and impetus and promote coördination.

It was foreseen that with the removal of my headquarters to Chaumont our supply officers would find it difficult to keep in close touch with the corresponding French bureaus in Paris, and that since we were to be within the Zone of the Armies, coöperation with French Army Headquarters would assume greater importance. Inasmuch as the line of authority separating this zone from the rear was not distinctly defined, it was evident that procurement in general, especially regarding the use of facilities, might become complicated. In my discussion with M. Painlevé he stated that he thought that with intelligent liaison officers there should be no difficulty, and promised to expedite our business with the bureaus.

Visits to our training areas by the French, official and otherwise, had become rather frequent. One of the visitors, M. Clemenceau, who was always a power, called at the headquarters of the 1st Division, accompanied by General de Castelnau, the commander of the Group of Armies with which this division was serving. In the course of the conversation with General Sibert, the division commander, M. Clemenceau, with considerable emphasis, urged that our troops be put into the line without delay. It was explained to him by General de Castelnau that as soon as they were sufficiently advanced the troops of the division were to be placed by brigades with the French in a quiet sector near Lunéville.

Although there was nothing threatening in the situation and no immediate probability of a serious German offensive, M. Clemenceau wished to know why they could not go in at once. General Sibert told him that the division had been in the area but a short time and had only recently begun training, and that the American Commander-in-Chief must determine when and where the division should be employed. M. Clemenceau went on to say that America had now been in the war several months and the French people were wondering when they expected to take an active part. He said that the French Army was exhausted by the war and that its morale was poor. He insisted then, as he did with even greater vehemence later in an official capacity, that it was not so much a question of troops being ready as it was of giving relief to the Allies.

Although the division was only partially trained, it could have been used in case of necessity, but no emergency existed at this time and no suggestion had been made that the division should go into the line for serious work. It was obviously quite out of place for M. Clemenceau to make any such demand, yet there is little doubt that he gave expression to a very general sentiment among the French people at that moment. They simply wanted to see American troops in the trenches.

I could well understand this attitude of the French Army and the people, and realized that their morale was none too high. However, the censorship of private letters of soldiers in their Army showed that it was gradually growing better, based largely upon the hope of considerable aid from America. Quite apart from sentiment, however, it was a question of having the Division in fair shape before placing it even in a quiet sector, as the Germans would certainly take advantage of our first appearance in the line to strike a blow at American prestige.

From another point of view, M. Clemenceau's visit left the

impression that the French were inclined to dictate what disposition we should make of our units.   In many of their suggestions it was easy to see the possibility of amalgamation lurking in the background.   Another circumstance that suggested the same thought, the knowledge of which came to me about this time, was that the French High Commissioner at Washington had reported difficulty in persuading the Secretary of War to divert tonnage to send over units other than those designated for our army.   It was difficult to construe his move in any other light than as further evidence of the none too well concealed opposition of the French to our building up an army.   Such methods were, of course, irregular, but nevertheless similar pressure to alter our program was repeatedly used by both French and British before the end of the war.   There can be little doubt that the Allies, especially the French, entertained the hope that we would provide them not only with replacements, but with laborers and technical troops as well.

In looking back over the period immediately prior to our entry into the war, the very primitive state of our aviation still gives me a feeling of humiliation.   The Punitive Expedition of 1916 went into Mexico with eight of the thirteen antiquated tactical planes which constituted our all in aviation.   In a country almost uninhabited, save for a few villages scattered here and there, where the difficulties of obtaining information were almost insurmountable, a well-trained, up-to-date fleet of airplanes would have been invaluable.   These old planes were not in any sense properly equipped as compared with those being used by other nations even then, and with no adequate facilities for repair work they were constantly in danger of going to pieces, yet the services of our aviators in Mexico stood out strongly as an indication of what American fliers were to accomplish in the World War.

The daring and the courage of men like Townsend Dodd,[1]

[1] Colonel Dodd served through the World War but was killed in an airplane accident on October 5, 1919.   The fliers who were with me in Mexico, with their rank at that time, were: Captains B. D. Foulois and T. F. Dodd, and Lieutenants C. G. Chapman, J. E. Carberry, H. A. Dargue, T. S. Bowen, R. H. Willis, W. G. Kilner, E. S. Gorrell, A. R. Christie, and I. A. Rader.

Foulois, Dargue and others who were with that expedition aroused my most enthusiastic admiration. While there were many hairbreadth escapes in Mexico, fortunately all our fliers were spared to form the nucleus of our World War aviation corps, in which they all served with distinction. Although at the date of our entry into the war more than a year had elapsed since the beginning of the Mexican Campaign, there were still only thirty-five trained fliers and about one thousand men in aviation, with only a few training planes, none of which were suitable for anything else.

An extensive program following cabled recommendations from the French Premier after we entered the war [1] seems to have been adopted at home as the basis of our efforts. Upon the recommendation of the Chief Signal Officer, Brigadier General George O. Squier, Congress made an appropriation of $640,000,000 in July, 1917, in an effort to overcome past negligence. There followed many extravagant claims by prominent civil officials connected with aviation and by the press, that we would soon have large fleets of airplanes in operation and that we would end the war at once with a preponderance of aircraft. But Congressional action, even though generous, furnished no magical power to transform our Air Service from a mere skeleton into a real fighting force in an instant. Everybody who stopped a moment to think knew that time would be necessary and that it was idle to count upon airplanes from our own factories within a year, or perhaps longer.

The failure of our aviation bureau to keep abreast of airplane development in the contending armies cost us serious delay. With a lack of data in the beginning, little progress had been made at home on our aviation program at the end of five months. Fruitless efforts to describe mechanical construction, give definite information concerning production, and otherwise reach decisions, by cable, prompted Washington to send to France a special mission of which Major R. C. Bolling [2] was the head. Through

[1] Chapter III, page 28.

[2] Major Bolling, then Colonel, was killed during the German advance on Amiens in March, 1918, while on a special mission in that region.

his ability and expert knowledge he rendered exceptional service in coöperating with aviation officials of the Allies and in obtaining the necessary technical information upon which to base action at home. The investigations made by his mission confirmed the view that our manufacturers could not begin to furnish airplanes before the summer of 1918. At this time it looked as though we should not have even sufficient airplanes for training, and much less be able to furnish them for our troops as they went into the line. With my mind filled with these impressions, and realizing the vital importance of aviation, my efforts were unceasing to overcome the deficiency.

After inquiry as to French capacity to turn out airplanes, I made a contract with the Air Ministry late in August committing us to an expenditure of $60,000,000 for 5,000 planes and 8,500 engines to be delivered as rapidly as possible at intervals before the first of June, 1918, on condition that we should provide certain tools and raw materials. To make a contract to pay such an amount appeared somewhat bold, but under the circumstances some one had to take the initiative in providing planes needed at once for the development of our air force.

As aviation was in no sense a logical branch of the Signal Corps, the two were separated in the A.E.F. as soon as practicable and an air corps was organized and maintained as a distinct force. In order to coördinate our training with that at home, Brigadier General William L. Kenly was sent over the latter part of August and was appointed Chief of Aviation in the A.E.F. Colonel William Mitchell, who had succeeded Major Dodd, the first Chief of Aviation, was given jurisdiction in the Zone of the Advance. Colonel Bolling was placed in charge in the Zone of the Interior and soon succeeded in securing better coöperation through an Inter-Allied Aircraft Board.

The next essential step was the training of airplane pilots, and accordingly arrangements were made for our men to enter flying schools in England, France, and Italy, after they had passed their preliminary tests at home. Vacancies were held for us in the Allied schools but we were unable to take full advantage of this opportunity because of the delay in sending over fliers. However, we proceeded with the establishment of our own training centers, the first of which, located at Issoudun, was planned for a capacity of 900 pilots by spring. Other school facilities offered by the French were utilized later, such as those at Clermont-Ferrand and Tours.

Before we entered the war, a number of young American aviators enlisted in the French air service and later, after persistent efforts on the part of a few leading spirits, the French Minister of War granted them permission to form an organization to be known as the American squadron. This unit was placed under a French captain and later still became known as the Lafayette Escadrille. Fortunately, some ninety of these experienced American fliers who had thus volunteered in the French Army from 1914 to 1917 joined our aviation, and their services as instructors and in combat proved of inestimable value to us.

Our matériel was to come from both American and European sources. We established an acceptance park at Orly to receive and distribute matériel obtained abroad, and a production center at Romorantin where all airplanes and engines from home were handled. Other plans in progress contemplated the extension at the front of our air and ground organization, of which we shall see more later.

CHAPTER XIII

(Diary) Chaumont, Thursday, September 6, 1917. Left Paris yesterday morning for Chaumont, stopping at Troyes for lunch. Headquarters offices duly installed here in regimental barracks. Surroundings give relief from depression of Paris. On my invitation, President Poincaré came this morning to inspect 1st Division. Colonel Wagstaff reported as head of British Mission.

DRIVING to Gondrecourt with my Chief of Staff and aides, we found General Pétain, his staff and an escort of French troops drawn up at the station, where President Poincaré and his party, including the Minister of War, were received with due formality. The President and I led the way by motor to Houdelaincourt, where the ceremony of inspecting the 1st Division was held.

It was a compliment to the Division to have a visit from the head of the French Republic and every man was on his mettle. The troops were already assembled when we arrived. As the President and I walked through the ranks he commented very favorably on the appearance of the men and was quite struck with their size and their youth and vigor. After the command had marched in review, the President asked to meet the officers and made them a very happy speech. Upon the conclusion of his talk they showed their appreciation by promptly giving him three rousing cheers, which pleased him very much.

From the purely military point of view, the impression gained by the President at this review could not have been particularly favorable, as at least two-thirds of the men were recruits and over one-half of the officers had been but recently commissioned. Moreover, the men had been hard at work on combat training and this, together with the uneven ground of the muddy hillside where the review was held, made military precision difficult. However, he was a very keen observer and no doubt drew great satisfaction from the thought that many other Americans were coming and that with a few more months of training this group of 25,000 Americans would make a fine addition to the forces of the war-worn Allies.

(Diary) Chaumont, Saturday, September 8, 1917. Have seen various officers of Missions [1] at my headquarters. General Ragueneau, as Chief of the French Mission, becomes General Pétain's representative.

Miss Elizabeth Hoyt, Secretary of the Red Cross, took luncheon with us and gave an interesting account of recent Red Cross activities. Governor Henry J. Allen, of Kansas, and William Allen White, also of the Red Cross, came to call.

Saw Malone and Fiske, of Training Section, and cabled urgent request for instructors for army schools and staff college. Brigadier General William Lassiter dined with me this evening.

In order to maintain closer relations among the Allied armies and to keep each Commander-in-Chief advised regarding the morale, proposed operations, and movements of troops of other armies, and in fact all matters that might affect the general situation, a system had grown up whereby the army of each nation was represented at the headquarters of the others by a group of officers called a mission. Consequently, when we definitely established headquarters at Chaumont we exchanged missions with the British, French, Italian, and Belgian armies. That of the French naturally became the largest and most important, as

[1] The Chiefs of Missions were:

French: Brig. Gen. C. M. Ragueneau until August, 1918, when Col. J. L. A. Linard succeeded him.

British: Lt. Col. C. M. Wagstaff (later Brig. Gen.) until late 1918, when he was succeeded by Lt. Col. F. K. Puckle.

Italian: Brig. Gen. Ippolito Perelli from June, 1918.

Belgian: Major J. Th. Tinant.

it was entrusted with handling most of the questions that arose in our relations with the French.

The missions with us, especially those of the French and British, did not always confine their activities to normal lines, but often took occasion to advance their ideas regarding the training and use of our army. The French continually argued that we would contribute more to the Allied cause by helping to strengthen French and British units than by building up an independent army of our own, and the British were not far behind in their efforts along this line. Knowing this attitude, it was necessary to be on the lookout to avoid commitments to suggestions that might eventually involve the question of amalgamation. Apart from this, however, and considering their services as a whole, it should be said that the fine spirit of helpfulness and coöperation shown always by the members of these missions appealed to us, and many close friendships grew out of our association with them.

(Diary) Chaumont, Tuesday, September 11, 1917. On Sunday, saw representative of Postal Department sent to organize service for the armies. Conferred with several staff officers. Dr. Woods Hutchinson called. Chemical Warfare department, known as "Gas Service," established in A.E.F. System of schools for our forces completed.

Conferred yesterday with Brigadier General Williams; prospect of obtaining tanks not hopeful unless they can be produced at home. Project for upbuilding services of rear adopted.

The use of poisonous gases in warfare had been discussed at the Hague Conference in 1899 with the result that several nations pledged themselves against the employment of projectiles whose only object was to give forth suffocating or poisonous gases. This action had created a feeling of security regarding such a possibility. Germany had subscribed to the agreement, and when her armies disregarded this pledge and became the first to use gas shells, the impression was that the Germans had now thrown every consideration of humanity to the winds. The first gas attack occurred on April 22, 1915, against the French in the northern part of the Ypres salient. It came as a complete surprise and caused great consternation among the troops. Its effect on the

French was vividly described later by Sir John French in his report to Lord Kitchener as follows:

"Following a heavy bombardment, the enemy attacked the French Division at about 5 P.M., using asphyxiating gases for the first time. Aircraft reported that at about 5 P.M. thick yellow smoke had been seen issuing from the German trenches between Langemarck and Bixschoote. The French reported that two simultaneous attacks had been made east of the Ypres-Staden Railway, in which these asphyxiating gases had been employed.

"What followed almost defies description. The effect of these poisonous gases was so virulent as to render the whole of the line held by the French Division mentioned above practically incapable of any action at all. It was at first impossible for any one to realize what had actually happened. The smoke and fumes hid everything from sight, and hundreds of men were thrown into a comatose or dying condition, and within an hour the whole position had to be abandoned, together with about 50 guns."

This action by the enemy forced the Allies to adopt the use of gas themselves as a matter of retaliation. From that time on its employment became common to all combatants.

On July 12-13, 1917, the Germans used a new gas against the British, called "mustard gas," the effect of which I reported to our War Department by cablegram:

"Following with regard to the new gas called 'Mustard Gas' used by the Germans sent for your information. Since July 18th the British have suffered 20,000 casualties from this gas alone. Five per cent have been fatal, 14 per cent have been serious, while the balance have been mild. This so-called gas is really a liquid carried in shells which scatter the liquid on the ground. There is a slight odor of mustard of which men nearby are sensible. One can remain in this odor for five minutes or so without suffering any harm. The action is not noticeable for four or five hours after exposure. Then the soldier feels a burning of the eyes and a dryness and parched condition of the skin. He then becomes blind and the respiratory passages develop a condition similar to that in diphtheria. There are usually exterior burns on the exposed parts of the skin, hands, back of neck, and tender parts, as gas attacks the skin regardless of clothing. In mild cases the subject is blind and incapacitated for duty for about three weeks. In serious cases for a considerably longer period. The only defense is prompt use of gas mask and even this only guarantees a reduction in losses."

The use of gas in warfare presented an entirely new problem to us and the organization of a service to handle it demanded immediate attention. The first plan of the War Department provided that the Engineers should devise and handle the mechanical features and the Medical Department the chemical, but this soon proved to be impractical and it became evident that, as we had maintained at the beginning, a separate service would be necessary. Meanwhile application was made for a complete chemical laboratory to be shipped to France for use mainly in investigation, supplementing similar work in the United States.

Considerable information concerning gases and the organization of gas service troops had been gathered by my staff. Lieutenant Colonel Amos A. Fries, who was designated as Chief of the Gas Service, made some further investigation in the British and French armies, and as a result an order issued on September 3d established a department known at that time as the Gas Service. It was charged with the organization of personnel, the supply of material, and the general direction of the service, offensive as well as defensive. Other branches of the army assisted in providing material and appliances.

Experiments were at once begun to discover new gases and devise improvements in gas masks. In order to save tonnage and avoid the dangers of explosion in transit, it was decided, after consultation with the Allied services, to request the shipment from the States of the basic elements and manufacture the chemical products in France. After making thorough tests of different types of masks, we adopted the box respirator used by the British, and a preliminary purchase of 100,000 was made to meet immediate demands for training.

With the development of trench weapons and special tactical methods of defense, never had the offensive been more costly in human life than in this war. The ingenuity of the Allies was put to the test to devise new engines of war that would make the attack possible without excessive losses.

While the tank, which was simply an armored caterpillar-traction motor car, was favored by many officers as an aid to infantry in the attack, this opinion was by no means unanimous. Our investigations, however, led to the conclusion that we should accept Allied experience and also adopt the tank as a weapon. As to types, both the French (light) Renault, weighing six tons, and the British (heavy) Mark VI, a tank of thirty tons, appeared to be useful according to circumstances, and it was estimated that we ought to have at least 1,200 of the former and 600 of the latter. They were to be variously armed with machine guns, 6-pounders and 3-inch guns, with a proportionate number especially built to carry twenty-five men each and others to carry supplies. Negotiations for their procurement were begun with the respective Governments and it was found that the French wanted us to manufacture 2,000 Renaults for them. As there was little or no prospect of our obtaining tanks abroad, their manufacture at home was recommended and full details of requirements were accordingly cabled to Washington.

The World War was a struggle involving all national resources, and that fact was particularly emphasized by a close-range study of the many requirements for preparation. Every industry and every art, beginning with the farms and mines, must contribute its full share, and every citizen must fulfill his obligation to serve. America's part in the contest could be successful only by the combined efforts of the armies and the people. The man with the rifle was merely the privileged representative of a thousand others who were as deeply concerned in the result as he was. Thus while the people at home were hurriedly trying to overcome the heavy handicap of past neglect in providing men and equipment, we in France were equally strenuous in doing our part to prepare units for battle and to perfect arrangements to insure the required flow of material and supplies of every nature toward the front.

To discharge cargo and handle it along the Line of Communications and to assist in the more pressing work of construction, we had already been compelled to use incoming combat troops. One regiment of marines, and other troops, had been detained in the rear several weeks for these purposes, but makeshifts of this sort could not solve the problem and would only increase the danger of a breakdown in the end.

In order to provide supply troops as they were needed to correspond with the growth of our combat armies in France, a general scheme was prepared and sent to Washington on September 18th as a guide for the War Department. This project embraced the great body of specialists and laborers that would be necessary to run railroads, construct wharves and storehouses, saw lumber, and receive, store, and transport systematically the immense volume of supplies and material that would be consumed by our armies. Thorough organization and training for such work were as essential as tactical training for the fighting man. It was desirable that the quotas for these purposes should arrive progressively along with corresponding increments of material and supplies so that a balanced development could be maintained.

This outline of personnel, known as the Service of the Rear Project and the Organization Project for combat troops, formed the basis of our personnel structure in France. From the combination of these projects, a statement was prepared prescribing the order in which the troops and services enumerated should arrive. This schedule of priority, forwarded to the War Department on October 7th, divided the initial force called for into six phases, each including a combatant army corps of six divisions, with the service of the rear troops to correspond. With this schedule, Washington was provided almost from the start with a clear-cut program.

But we went still further than that. The supply departments worked out an automatic system for the shipment of the various classes of supplies and equipment, corresponding to the phase schedule of combat and service troops. It was intended to obviate the necessity for frequent cables under the old peacetime monthly requisition method to which the War Department was wedded. This automatic schedule contemplated the accumulation and maintenance in France of a certain quantity of supplies in reserve storehouses, with an equal amount distributed at accessible points farther toward the front. When it became apparent that the submarine danger was growing less, the total amount was limited to forty-five days' supply.

These outlines of our requirements in men, equipment, supplies, and material gave Washington something definite to follow. But the lack of a central control in actual procurement, during the early months of our participation in the war, resulted in unlimited competition among our supply departments at home, and the situation became one of almost overwhelming confusion. Later on threatened military crises led to frightened importunities of the Allies for immediate aid, from manpower to steel ingots, and the combination of swiftly moving events wellnigh wrecked the whole supply scheme at several points before we were to see the end of the war.

(Diary) Chaumont, Thursday, September 13, 1917. Unusually busy to-day with details of administration. Many reminders of another birthday [1] have been received, including a surprise party by the staff this evening.

As this was exactly three months after I had reached France, the time seemed to be passing very rapidly with little apparent progress against the day when an American army should be on the front line. Winter was approaching, with the prospect of increasing hardships for the troops and the people. These thoughts were not particularly cheerful, but there was a lighter side. The wishes for good fortune that came from all parts of our country on my birthday showed a widespread solicitude in our behalf and revealed anew the sincerity of the patriotic sentiments that so strongly supported us. Although we could but look forward to the service ahead of us as being full of difficulties, yet, with the nation behind us, there was much of encouragement to be garnered from the messages received at this time.

(Diary) Chaumont, Saturday, September 15, 1917. Transportation Department created, with Atterbury as Director General.

Had luncheon to-day with General Wirbel, the local French commander, at which General de Castelnau and General Hellet, his

[1] The St. Mihiel victory came precisely one year later.

Chief of Staff, leading civil officials, Harbord, Bacon and others of my staff were present. It was a sentimental occasion, showing that the people really feel grateful to us.

Received letter from General Robertson on shipping. Conferred with General Staff and approved priority schemes for shipment of supplies.

The luncheon given by General Wirbel indicated an attitude of good will in the community toward Americans. As Madame Wirbel and her daughters received us, I was attracted by the youngest, a beautiful child of six, and undertook to chat with her in French. As she did not reply to my questions, I said, "Comprenez-vous?" With childish frankness, she replied, "Non," much to the amusement of several of the less respectful members of my staff. This occasion was opportune, as it brought together officers of the two armies who were to be closely allied in service. In a brief speech, General Wirbel referred with much feeling to the aid America was bringing to France and to the fraternal relations among us. My response, I fear, was considerably below the high plane that he reached. General de Castelnau was even less oratorical than I, and merely said that he hoped we should all soon have the chance to water our horses in the Rhine.

The importance of shipping for the American Army was beginning to receive attention in Allied circles as indicated by personal discussions and correspondence. In a letter General Robertson spoke of their increasing losses in men and of his anxiety regarding the voyage of our troops across the Atlantic. He said the tonnage question was entirely between Great Britain and ourselves, as none of the other Allies could furnish any shipping to speak of. He suggested that Admiral Mayo and I should go to London to consider with the Admiralty shipping arrangements needed for American troops the following year. His letter showed the possibility of coöperation in the future when it should have been immediate. On top of this, in conference a few days later with Lord Derby, the British Minister of War, I was told that his Government could not be counted on to furnish us ships as transports.

The substance of General Robertson's letter was cabled to Washington suggesting the importance of taking advantage of the opportunity offered to obtain additional shipping. A few days later we were told that arrangements for trans-atlantic transports were being made by the Shipping Board. This information was contained in the following cable:

> "President of the United States says question of shipping is being looked after from here and that arrangements now being made would be confused by such a conference as you suggest. Our shipping must necessarily be supplied by ourselves and Shipping Board here is in direct conference with British authorities controlling their shipping."

The question of greatest importance to the Allies and ourselves was to get American troops across at an early date. As no advice was received beyond the above cable, it was presumed that arrangements were being made by the Shipping Board for all necessary tonnage.

There was little in the general situation to give comfort to the Allies. Losses by the British through continued operations were still growing. There no longer remained any doubt as to Russia's fate, and it was consequently certain that German troops on that front would be released for service in the west. Under the circumstances, the tired Allied peoples were easily influenced by rumors. The Pope's proposal, issued in August, started some talk of peace, but because it failed to condemn Germany's violation of treaties and her inhumane submarine warfare the note did not make a favorable impression on the Allies. In fact, it was criticized in terms that were not at all moderate. The various replies from the different Governments did, however, arouse some hope, which was altogether unwarranted by the real attitude of the authorities of the belligerent powers on either side. The discussion of the proposal was unfortunate because the French people, not realizing that peace was improbable, lost some of their courage, and the depression from this and other factors caused uneasiness among both civil and military leaders.

From our sources of information, which included the Intelligence Bureaus of the Allied armies, we got the impression that

Austria, Bulgaria, and Turkey would make peace on any reasonable terms if they could do so. But the German Government dominated the policy of all the Central Powers and it was certain that any peace less favorable to them than the *status quo ante* would not be entertained. The German military leaders thought they would eventually win and did not believe that the blockade would produce serious discontent in their country. In fact, the German people themselves, as well as their Government, feeling that with Russia now practically out of the war they would have an enormous advantage which the Americans would not be able to overbalance, firmly believed in ultimate victory.

My cable to the Secretary of War will show our estimate of the situation at the moment, as far as the French were concerned:

"September 15, 1917.
"There is considerable talk of possibilities of peace this winter and discussion is heard among people of all classes, including those high in military rank. Failure to stop German armies and revolt among Russian troops have had depressing effect upon Allies. Present French Cabinet believed to be strongly in favor of continuation of war, but French people in state of mind to accept any favorable proposition. Believe that withdrawal of Germans from Belgium with concessions as to Alsace and Lorraine and return to antebellum status in Balkans would be hard for French to resist, especially with the prospect of giving Germany satisfaction from Russia. * * * Recent British attacks beginning with latter part of July have been very costly and British morale not as high as two months ago."

(Diary) Chaumont, Tuesday, September 18, 1917. Visited artillery school at Le Valdahon on Sunday with Harbord, de Chambrun, Boyd, and Collins. Progress of artillery and the instruction of 100 young officers very satisfactory.

Colonel Russel called yesterday to urge cabling for telegraph and telephone material ordered before leaving Washington.

Examined Medical Department's plans to-day with Colonel Bradley and find good progress. There will be no repetition of experience of '98.

The military post of Le Valdahon, near the Swiss border, used by us as a school for our field artillery, was one of several which had been kindly set apart for Americans in different parts of

France. The others were at Coëtquidan and Meucon, near St. Nazaire, and at Souge and Le Courneau, near Bordeaux, and also at Montmorillon, Saumur, and Angers, with a school for heavy artillery at Mailly, southeast of Reims. The extensive artillery ranges and the large aviation field at Le Valdahon afforded exceptional facilities for coöperation between the artillery and the air service and for the instruction of officers of both services as airplane observers. This school was then under the direction of Brigadier General P. C. March, an energetic and alert commander. At the time of my visit, the field artillery brigade of the 1st Division was there for training.

Concerning the Signal Corps and its progress, before leaving Washington Colonel Russel had ordered a large consignment of material for both telegraph and telephone lines, but so far none had been received, except what was sent with us on the *Baltic*. Finding it necessary to establish our own telephone system in Paris, where the city service was almost useless, we were fortunately able at once to obtain enough material for the purpose in England and France.

The lines throughout France were so inefficient and unreliable, as government-owned utilities usually are, that in order to provide unfailing connections it was necessary for us to put in much new construction along our channels of supply, from base ports to headquarters. In addition to rebuilding entirely some of the more important lines, we were able to utilize others by replacing the old wire. As a rule, efficient telegraph and telephone service in the zones of our activities was obtained only by superimposing our system on that of the French, and using our own officers, operators, and maintenance. We soon completed direct connections from Chaumont to our offices in Paris, and later to the Headquarters of the Services of Supply at Tours, and also to London.

The Signal Corps had, of course, to anticipate the communications necessary in battle. Therefore, definite decisions were required some time in advance as to spheres of operations. Tons of material, the most of which, except wire, was obtained in

France, and a great amount of labor were used in the actual installations. The main telephone and telegraph lines in proximity to the battle areas were, when practicable, laid underground to prevent destruction. Wire communication within smaller units was handled by their own personnel with Signal Corps matériel.

Besides a thorough network of wire connections, it was considered advisable also to have wireless apparatus available for use if necessary between important points. The employment of radio in airplanes also was essential to the successful coöperation of aviation with artillery.

The perfection of our communication system in the A.E.F. demanded the most modern terminal, station, and line equipment. In order to assist the efficient, though limited, personnel of the Regular Army Signal Corps, the ablest men available to help plan and build, as well as to operate, were called into service from civil life as emergency officers.

One of the crying needs, when we once began to use our own lines, was for experienced operators. Instead of trying to train men of the Signal Corps, I requested that a number of experienced telephone girls who could speak French be sent over, and eventually we had about 200 girls on this duty. Some doubt existed among the members of the staff as to the wisdom of this step, but it soon vanished as the increased efficiency of our telephone system became apparent. No civil telephone service that ever came under my observation excelled the perfection of ours after it was well established. The telephone girls in the A.E.F. took great pains and pride in their work and did it with satisfaction to all.

The Medical Department's plans constantly received my careful attention through frequent conferences with the Chief Surgeon, Colonel Bradley, and his assistant, Colonel Ireland. Most of the older officers remembered with something akin to horror the unsanitary condition of our camps at Chickamauga and elsewhere, and the resulting high death rate from disease during the Spanish-American War, and all concerned, especially the medical men, were resolved that nothing like that should be repeated in our armies in the World War.

Our problem of handling the sick and wounded was more difficult than that of any of the Allies because we had no civil hospitals of our own available. Full provision, therefore, had to be made for hospital accommodations in France, as only convalescents manifestly unfit for further service could be sent home. The early estimates submitted in August, based upon a small force of 300,000 men, called for 73,000 beds in permanent, semi-permanent, or temporary hospitals, and plans for expansion were on hand to keep pace with the expected requirements of our armies once they should become engaged. While this beginning appeared quite liberal, it was calculated to meet further demands of the immediate future.

All the facilities throughout France were available for the French, but they had so many sick and wounded that their hospital resources were pretty well exhausted. As there seemed to be only a few suitable buildings that could be assigned to us, we had to plan a great deal of new construction. This called for additional labor and material, both of which were scarce, and although there was some delay we managed by persistent effort to keep pace with requirements.

While the medical personnel must bear a certain ratio to the size of the army, yet as we did not expect to be actively engaged until spring, and the demands for men for every other purpose were pressing, the allowance of medical personnel had to be restricted temporarily.

The French used the ordinary railroad facilities for the transportation of their wounded, but the distances from our probable front to the zone of available hospital accommodations, and thence to our base ports made it advisable to have the most approved rail equipment. Negotiations were at once started in England to obtain hospital trains, which began to arrive early in February. The ward cars were of the Pullman passenger type, with double tiers of berths. Each train had, in addition, a kitchen and dispensary, with an operating car, a dining car, and sleeping cars for medical officers and nurses. Nineteen trains of fifteen cars each were in operation at the time of the Armistice.

One of the important duties of the Medical Department was the prevention and cure of venereal disease, which in all other wars had caused serious reductions in effectives. Its prevalence in the Allied armies presented no exception to previous experience. From the purely practical standpoint of difficulty in replacing men, the possibility of having large numbers of ineffectives from this cause could not be contemplated without making every effort to prevent it. Among the first measures taken to restrict the evil was the promulgation of very stringent regulations in which medical officers and all others were enjoined to impress continence upon our troops, not only as a military obligation but as a patriotic duty. Commanding officers were directed to encourage and promote high moral standards of living among the members of their commands. General orders placed the responsibility for good conduct directly upon the soldier himself and prescribed that where men became unfit for duty through misconduct summary punishment would follow. This question was destined to give us considerable concern because of the difference between the French attitude and our own regarding the suppression of the sources of infection, but our efforts on the whole were remarkably successful. The percentage of ineffectives in our army from this cause was much lower than that of the Allies and surpassed any previous record in the history of wars.

(Diary) Paris, Thursday, September 20, 1917. Arrived from Chaumont by motor on Tuesday and have spent two busy days here. Coal shortage so serious that we are borrowing for current needs. In conference with Lord Derby and Major General Sir Frederick Maurice yesterday found they can furnish some coal but no tonnage to carry it. Lord Derby offered any supplies England can spare.

Admiral Mayo, Atterbury, Dawes, and Commander Sayles, naval attaché, lunched with us to-day to discuss coal situation. Mayo agrees that Navy and Army interests should be considered together.

Orders issued to-day directing strictest economy in use of fuel and oil.

The capture or destruction by the German Army of many of the mines of northern France had forced the importation from

England of a large proportion of the coal needed for various purposes in both France and Italy. Lack of cross-Channel tonnage had produced a serious situation for the French and ourselves, and the danger of a coal shortage during the approaching winter gave us much concern. Italy was even worse off owing to her greater distance from the sources of supply. The continuous manufacture of munitions in France demanded a constant inflow of coal, the railroads needed an assured amount, while the troops and civil populations had to have their proportion. The French foresaw the gravest consequences unless increased quantities could be brought regularly from England, and our necessities were tied up with theirs. Although the French themselves were not working their remaining mines to the fullest extent, yet when it was proposed that American miners be sent to assist them, the suggestion was not favored because of internal labor conditions.

We needed some 40,000 tons of Channel shipping to keep us going at this time and we would require an even larger amount as our activities increased. In an endeavor to make independent provision for our Army on the same basis as the Navy, which was being supplied from British sources, Colonel Dawes was sent to confer with Admiral Sims, only to be told that our Navy in European waters could not furnish us any tonnage. A statement of the situation was cabled to Washington with the request that steamers, possibly from the Great Lakes, be sent.

As satisfactory arrangements could not be made through Admiral Sims, an appeal was made to Admiral Mayo, who was already fully alive to needs of the American Army. He suggested the possibility of shipping coal from America in naval colliers, or as ballast for our transports. The following cable was sent as a result of this conference:

"Situation in both Italy and France reference coal regarded * * * as very serious. England has plenty of coal but cannot furnish transportation, although possible obtain some British assistance to carry coal across Channel for ourselves. * * * Question of transportation should be considered as a whole and entire problem of coal for

American forces including both Army and Navy be coördinated and obtained from nearest sources. When not otherwise employed full use should be made of available navy colliers and army freight transports to supply coal for our army and help France."

The outcome of our efforts, with the very effective assistance of Admiral Mayo, was that some colliers, one of which was already at Brest, were ordered into service for immediate use and these were supplemented later by vessels from the Shipping Board. The organization of the cross-Channel service was completed under the control of our Quartermaster Corps and later transferred to the Transportation Department. Although the coal question became more or less critical at various times during the winter, in the main we were fairly well supplied.

CHAPTER XIV

French Mission to Aid in Procurement—Importance of Rifle Again Emphasized—More Ordnance Indecision—Inefficiency in Loading Transports—Urgent Need of Labor—Weekly Summary of Events—Over 1,000,000 Tons Shipping Needed—Letter to Secretary on Vigor of Officers, Training, and Promotions—Visit to 1st Division—French Appeal for Mechanics—Ladies of Chaumont Present Flag

(Diary) Chaumont, Monday, September 24, 1917.   Held conference Saturday with Atterbury, Wilgus, Harry L. Rogers and William D. Connor on readjustment of staff relations in S.O.S. Pétain designates Ragueneau, Chief of Mission, as representative of Minister of War and French G.H.Q. in procurement.

To-day discussed Gas Service organization with Colonel Fries. Sent positive cable to War Department on training.

Work at office very strenuous,[1] but riding every day keeps me fit.

IN negotiating with the French for supplies and material, the understanding was that we should deal with the French Mission at my headquarters in regard to such as were controlled by the Zone of the Armies, and directly with the bureaus of the War Office as to those under control of the Services of the Rear. But in practice this plan proved quite too complicated. So, after considerable discussion, it was agreed by the Minister of War, General Pétain, and myself that procurement in general should be handled through the French Mission. While this plan held in principle, yet our purchasing officers, in ordnance and aviation especially, usually found it necessary to conduct negotiations directly with the corresponding French ministers and bureaus in the War Office, and in these matters my personal intervention and assistance were frequently required.

Having learned that despite recommendations little or no

[1] My diary shows conferences of more or less importance with some twenty-five different officials from the 21st to the 24th inclusive. This was about the average of those early days of organization.

attention was being given at home to the importance of teaching our men the use of the rifle, it seemed necessary again to emphasize my views, especially after further knowledge of the neglect of rifle training in Allied armies. The infantry soldier, well-trained in stealthy approach and in the art of taking cover, makes a small target, and if he is an expert rifleman there is nothing that can take his place on the battlefield. The following quotation from one of my cables will suffice to show my attitude:

"Sept. 24, 1917.
" * * * Strongly renew my previous recommendation that all troops be given complete course in rifle practice. * * * Specialties of trench warfare instruction at home should not be allowed to interfere with rifle practice or with intensive preliminary training in our schools of soldier, company and battalion."

On this latter point the following, which was dwelt upon in the A.E.F. with all vigor, was added:

"I cannot too strongly impress upon the War Department the absolute necessity of rigid insistence that all men be thoroughly grounded in the school of soldier. Salutes should be rendered by both officers and men in most military manner. * * * The loyalty, readiness and alertness indicated by strictest adherence to this principle will immensely increase the pride and fighting spirit of our troops. The slovenly, unmilitary, careless habits that have grown up in times of peace in our Army are seriously detrimental to the aggressive attitude that must prevail from highest to lowest in our forces. Strict methods used at West Point in training new cadets in these elementary principles have given the Academy its superior excellence. These methods should be applied vigorously and completely in the forces we are now organizing."

(Diary) Chaumont, Wednesday, September 26, 1917. The French agree that we should retain exclusive jurisdiction over American soldiers in France. Find Captain R. B. Owens, the head of Electrics, University of Nebraska, when I was there, now Russel's assistant.

Chief of Ordnance at Washington delays storehouse construction by requesting views of French Commissioner regarding our necessities. Colonel Jefferson R. Kean, Medical Corps, just arrived, assigned to command medical units with British. Frederick Palmer spent last night with us.

Have again cabled relative to carelessness and delay in loading of transports.

The War Department had brought up the question of civil jurisdiction over the members of our forces in France and had inquired regarding the attitude of the French. A committee of the American Bar Association, being of the opinion that counsel and advice might be needed, had offered the free services of several of its members familiar with French laws and language. My Judge Advocate, Colonel W. A. Bethel, presented our opinion to the French authorities, which was that according to the principles of international law and in view of the conditions under which the American Army was serving in France its members should not be subject to criminal prosecution in French courts but should be answerable only to our own military tribunals. This view was readily accepted by the French and very properly the jurisdiction over our forces, both civil and military, remained in our hands.

With reference to storage for ordnance, a very careful calculation had been made of our requirements by my Chief of Ordnance, Colonel Williams, and sites for three large depots and shops were selected at Gièvres, Méhun and Foëcy, besides storage depots at the ports of St. Nazaire and Bordeaux, and in the forward area at Is-sur-Tille and Jonchery. There were also many smaller plants at various points in the S.O.S. With the exception of special repair shops it had been requested that the matter of construction be left in the hands of my Chief of Ordnance. Satisfactory types of buildings had been developed by the French and British and the organization of our Ordnance Department was such that the work could be done by men on the ground. However, the Chief of Ordnance in Washington was apparently unwilling to accept our calculation and asked the French Commission at Washington to obtain the views of the French on the subject. The Commissioner transmitted the request to his Government and the Government sent it to General Pétain, who, of course, referred the question to me. My reply, which went direct to Washington, naturally supported the original recommendation. At times it seemed that the last refinement was being invoked to cause delay. The following cable regarding the incident was sent to the Chief of Staff:

"* * * This endless chain should clearly indicate the necessity of handling such matters direct with my headquarters. Ordnance officers here capable of managing this construction work, thus leaving to Chief of Ordnance more important duties and decentralizing his office as to details that should be handled here. Request approval of my recommendation and reply by cable.

"* * * Again recommend that all requests for information required by our War Department be sent direct to these headquarters as invariably such matters are referred here by French either directly or indirectly."

It appeared to be difficult for some of the bureaus of the War Department to think in terms of a world war and they naturally hesitated to make decisions on questions involving the large requirements in supply, construction, and material. If they had only realized the pressing necessity for early preparation and had accepted the views of the men on the spot, it would have saved time and patience.

As a matter of fact, my cables were too often regarded merely as recommendations which the bureaus might approve or not, as they chose. This conception of their functions by the bureaus was entirely erroneous in that there had been no previous study of these questions made at home and they could not, from that distance, know what we needed as well as we ourselves knew. Moreover, in principle it was simply their duty to furnish the army overseas what it asked for, if possible, as otherwise we could not be held responsible for results.

As pertinent to this disregard of my requests in some quarters of the War Department, we received on a certain date confidential cable advice of sailings that were to take place from New York. This information had been furnished the French representative nine days earlier. After protesting once more against the dangerous practice of giving this sort of advance information to the French, the Chief of Staff at Washington finally stated that it would be discontinued entirely.

(Diary) Chaumont, Friday, September 28, 1917. Infantry Officers' Schools established at Valbonne and Valréas with General Bullard as Commandant of both.

Washington promises every effort to load vessels promptly and shorten round trip. Many complaints coming in of labor shortage.

General Kenly and Colonel Mitchell came to discuss aviation. Approved their recommendation for location air parks, depots, and receiving stations.

Approval of organization project for army in France, submitted early in July, just received from Washington nearly three months later.

Up to this time we were not getting the full use of even the limited shipping at our disposal, as the average time for a round trip of our transports, estimated to be forty days, was being exceeded considerably. The delay was partly due to our inability to discharge rapidly at French ports on account of meager dock facilities and shortage of labor, but that loss of time occurred at ports of departure was shown by the fact that the average time of the first twelve transports to make the round trip from St. Nazaire was over fifty-five days. These facts were cabled the War Department and the reply was as follows:

"Future estimates cannot be based on past performance of present transport fleet. In taking over and outfitting first transports, many necessary repairs and alterations were not originally made. Installation of additional ventilation and heating systems all require time, necessitating delays on this side. Installation of necessary armaments, modification of emplacements, all of which must necessarily be done here, are largely responsible for excessive turn-around up to date. Transports must be self-sustaining which requires large additional amount of coal. Some labor difficulties have been encountered to date. Greater fleet when turned over will be absolutely ready for service. Estimates this office that turn-around for fast vessels of fleet will not exceed three weeks, for slower vessels five weeks, for cargo transports six weeks. Time of dispatching troop transports abroad at present seems to this office excessive, especially with reference to last fleet. Every effort is being made to expedite sailing of vessels, bearing in mind necessity for every precaution being taken which entails some delay on account of convoys."

There was ample evidence of great confusion at home due to lack of efficient supervision, even in New York harbor, where experts should have been easy to find. Ships were seldom loaded to their full capacity; supplies greatly needed were often left behind; nonessentials were being sent over; many things were broken due to careless loading; and troops were often shipped to one port and their equipment to another. The Washington bureaus oftentimes followed blindly some out-of-date supply table perhaps drawn up under a former régime by an antiquated desk soldier long since retired and forgotten. As an illustration, I recall a bill of lading from one of our transports that was presented to me about this time as a curiosity. It listed a number of articles quite useless to an army in the field and provoked the following cable:

"For all departments. Recommend no further shipments be made of following articles * * * bath bricks, book cases, bath tubs, cabinets for blanks, chairs except folding chairs, cuspidors, office desks, floor wax, hose except fire hose, step ladders, lawn mowers, refrigerators, safes except iron field safes, settees, sickles, stools, window shades. Further stop orders will follow soon."

I have often wondered what manner of man was responsible for shipping such things, whether on supply tables or not, thereby wasting tonnage, when winter clothing, building material, steel and any number of real necessities were being delayed.

All of these facts suggested a condition of affairs during those earlier months that must have paralleled the inefficiency displayed in the management of our transport system in the Spanish-American War, a comparison that was frankly stated in the following cable:

"October 10, 1917.

" * * * Assignment of Medical Department with troops heretofore arriving indicates lack of supervision. The field hospital ambulance company that came with 26th Division arrived without any except personnel equipment and without transportation of any kind. Regimental detachments came with combat equipment only. Medical officers report their equipment was loaded on ships on which they sailed but prior to sailing it was taken off and sent on other ships.

Manner in which these regiments came to France does not indicate much improvement over conditions Spanish-American War. ✴ ✴ ✴ ”

It was then six months after we had entered the war and little system at points of embarkation was apparent.

We were short-handed, both at depots and along the Line of Communications, in all classes of labor that should have been sent over long before. The Quartermaster Corps in France was seriously handicapped in handling, caring for, and issuing stores and supplies. The engineers had laid out many projects of construction and made a beginning on those most necessary, but it looked as though we should be unable to keep up with the demands for facilities and accommodations.

The need for stevedores had become most urgent. Combat troops were still being used to unload cargo and thus much time was lost by the employment of labor that was entirely unsuited for this sort of work. Moreover, it was important that the combat troops should be sent inland to receive their battle instruction. The French, although short of labor themselves, had lent us a few prisoners and also some women, to help out, but neither class was satisfactory. Under these conditions, there was danger that our ports would become hopelessly congested. About the middle of October, fifteen weeks after I made my initial request, which had been followed by further urgent appeals, the War Department promised to send stevedores at once.

From our point of view it was not understood why any number of laborers, both skilled and unskilled, should not have been sent to France promptly. It may be stated, however, that it was hinted that there remained in Administration circles a lingering hope that after all it might not be necessary to send a large army abroad. The slowness in beginning the preparation of cantonments at home and in organizing the ports of embarkation, the delay in sending over both labor and combat troops, and material for the construction of docks and railways, and the apparent failure to utilize available tonnage or to obtain an additional amount elsewhere, could all be explained on the above hypothesis. Otherwise, even granting our deplorable want of preparation, it must be conceded that there existed at home either a lack of comprehension of the importance, the urgency, and the immensity of the task, or of competent leadership in handling it.

The French now came forward with a strong plea for mechanics for airplane construction, claiming that we had promised to furnish them. Whatever the understanding may have been, it was manifest that we should not be likely to get many airplanes unless we made an effort to provide the French additional help. Accordingly the matter was fully explained to the War Department and a request made for 3,000 mechanics in November, a like number in December, and 6,000 in January. The French offered some of their slow ships to carry them across, but it was not regarded as safe at that time to employ transports of less than sixteen knots speed, as they could not be sent with the regular convoys. The War Department agreed to provide mechanics, but concluded that our shipping could transport them as fast as they were ready.

A weekly summary of events was started in order to keep Washington advised of the general situation as it appeared at my headquarters. These reports were based mainly upon information gathered by the Intelligence Section of the General Staff from every available source, and in addition to the résumé of facts, it is remarkable how accurate they were in drawing conclusions and in forecasting conditions. The following is an extract from the report for the week ending September 30th:

"German Army consists of 146 divisions on Western Front and 91 on Eastern Front. Western armies have suffered since July 31st by British and French attacks * * * but their fighting efficiency not seriously impaired. * * * The object is to keep Germany to the strategic defensive rôle and diminish her manpower and secure important local objectives in preparation for greater successes when U. S. is ready.

* * * * * * *

"Politically the power of the War party in Germany and the morale of the German people have been considerably strengthened by the military success at Riga and by the disorganization in Russian Army and Government. * * * Germany's iron supply is adequate for the moment * * * but manufacturing problem one of increasing difficulty. * * *

"Conflicting war aims and interests among Germany's allies have brought increasing friction. * * * The abandonment of Bagdad to the British has caused the Turks to grumble, while the failure to send troops to attack Salonika has brought unrest to the Bulgarians. Austria's dissatisfaction over the abandonment of the Roumanian campaign for operations at Riga has been mentioned, yet those disaffections have not reached a magnitude where * * * a political detachment appears diplomatically feasible.

"Finally, the war still retains a character such that continuous hard blows offer the only path to success."

(Diary) Chaumont, Monday, October 1, 1917.   Received authority to discharge officers for inefficiency, which will help to maintain high standards.   British steel situation reported critical and they demand shipments as offset to coal.   Lassiter recommends securing Austrian vessels interned in Spain.

It was natural to expect that our continuous demands on the Allies for munitions and supplies of all sorts, including such items as artillery, airplanes, ammunition, horses, coal, and lumber, should be met by requests that we furnish American skilled labor and raw material.   The immense proportion of artillery ammunition required called for large quantities of steel and explosives, and the prospect of increased expenditure could be foreseen in the certainty of general activities the following year.   The British were urgently demanding steel, and asked that we send over 50,000 tons in our own ships, suggesting this be considered as balancing our request for coal.   The War Department thought our tonnage was not equal to any such burden and advised us that shipping for England was being handled through the British Shipping Board.

Estimates of tonnage necessary to carry out the War Department program [1] indicated that the amount of shipping then employed would have to be increased to over 1,000,000 tons and that

---

[1] See cablegram quoted on page 118, Chapter IX.

NOTE: Total strength of A.E.F. on September 30th, 4,406 officers, 57,125 enlisted men. Divisional units arriving in September included the first elements of the 26th Division (National Guard from New England), Major General C. R. Edwards.

to maintain the forces overseas thereafter would require the constant use of 800,000 tons. The possibility of acquiring the Austrian fleet, consisting of twenty-one vessels, was suggested to the War Department. The actual tonnage of vessels we had in service on October 1st was only 255,228 tons, and so far there was no indication as to when the "Greater Fleet" already mentioned would be ready.

One of my periodical letters to the Secretary of War gives a brief résumé of several matters of interest at the moment:

"France, October 4, 1917.

"*Personal and Confidential.*

"Dear Mr. Secretary:

"I wish to express my sincere appreciation of your note of August fifteenth regarding the handling of our affairs in France. Things have not always gone to my own satisfaction, but it has been, and will continue to be, my whole endeavor to carry out, with a broad view, the purpose for which we entered the war, and to do so in accordance with the wishes of the President and yourself.

"The details of a thorough staff organization, and the studies on construction, including railroads and docks, and the estimates for material therefor, have entailed a great amount of labor. The scarcity of trained officers to assist in working out these problems has been severely felt. Of course I realize the need for trained officers at home, and have not lost sight of the many knotty problems you have had to solve. In turn, I wish to congratulate you warmly upon the way you have handled them.

"Our relations with the French and British have been very cordial. Both Allies fully appreciate our difficulties and have given assistance accordingly. Our requests of the French, of course, have been many, and they have occasionally seemed a little restless that we have not moved faster in our preparations, but I have asked them to be patient and hold on until we could get our stride.

"A tentative system of instruction and training has been outlined, based upon the best information obtainable, and schools of instruction have been organized to provide instructors. The French have helped us train the First Division, while the British are taking as many young officers as they can accommodate in their schools. Our impression is that the French rather favor defensive tactics, while the British incline more to the offensive. I am making every effort to inculcate a strong, aggressive, fighting spirit among our forces, and to overcome a more or less perfunctory attitude engendered by years of peace.

"My earnest thought has been devoted to organization, and it is believed that the general system evolved will, in a short time, become more or less automatic, especially as to the services of the rear. The administrative staffs and my General Staff have been brought into thorough accord. The new railway transportation department, under Mr. Atterbury, as material and personnel arrive, will soon be able to meet our transportation requirements. But the delay in the arrival of forestry troops and dock material will postpone construction and may result in some congestion. The purchasing agency, under Colonel Dawes, is coördinating American purchases in Europe in conjunction with the French and British control, and will bring a great saving in the cost of supplies and economy in transportation.

"Training our troops for this new and exacting service is exceedingly important, and relatively difficult because of the large proportion of young officers who are generally able enough, but without experience. It may be added that there are older officers also who are not up to this work. Planning and directing individual training and instructing new officers in the tactical handling of our units require not only activity, but experience in such work as well, together with ability to grasp and apply the technical developments of the war.

"I hope you will permit me to speak very frankly and quite confidentially, but I fear that we have some general officers who have neither the experience, the energy, nor the aggressive spirit to prepare their units or to handle them under battle conditions as they exist to-day. I shall comment in an enclosure [1] on the individuals to whom I refer particularly. Both the British and French higher officers emphasize in the strongest terms the necessity of assigning younger and more active and more impressionable men to command brigades and divisions. We would commit a grave error if we fail to profit by their experience. A division commander must get down into the trenches with his men, and is at all times subject to severe hardships. I regret that I did not write you fully on this subject, but I only partially realized the difficulty you would have in making these assignments and contented myself with sending a cablegram relative to the activity required of brigade and division commanders.

"None of these classes of officers have the vigor and alertness to inspire our men with confidence, and our soldiers deserve the best

[1] Remarks in this paragraph refer to certain officers, listed confidentially, who were considered unfit physically and professionally.

leaders we can give them. The French Army was filled with dead timber at the beginning of the war, and many French failures are due to this fact. General officers must be fitted physically and mentally, must have experience and must have the go and initiative if they are to fill positions fraught with such momentous consequences to the nation and which involve the lives of thousands, perhaps hundreds of thousands of our men. All the officers referred to are friends of mine, but that should count for nothing. There are so many active, energetic, able men for selection that I strongly recommend that no general officers who are in any way physically inactive or unsound be sent here to command units. I deemed it my duty to you and to the President to give you my very best judgment in such matters, regardless of individuals.

"There is one thing more, if you will pardon me. An army is a better fighting unit if it is a contented army. All other things being equal, this can best be produced by giving the most efficient officers merited recognition. Always having high efficiency as a guide, I believe promotions could safely be made from various arms on a basis of length of service and experience.[1] The French Army has adopted this principle and efficient officers have been promoted and assigned without very much regard to the arm of the service. Any high class officer who has made good with troops in one arm very soon grasps the duties of another arm.

"Perhaps some declaration or expression announcing this principle for future selections might go far to allay some feeling of discontent found both here and at home among very capable officers who have been passed by juniors selected from another arm. Of course I realize that for special corps, like Railway Transportation and Aviation, the plan for selecting men with particular qualifications must be followed. Nor have I any doubt that all sides of this promotion question have been considered, but simply give you this as an observation.

*   *   *   *   *   *   *

"The Russian situation looks gloomy from our point of view, but appears to have had a stimulating effect upon German morale. As to complete Allied success next year, much depends upon what Russia may do, and Russia's failure may prolong the war through 1919. Germany seems confident that Russia is no longer much of a factor. However, six months of winter may make a change in the situation.

*   *   *   *   *   *   *

[1] This refers to a rule in making promotions to the grade of brigadier general by which vacancies were filled proportionately from the different (combat) arms.

"Again renewing my purpose to do everything within my power and ability for our success, I remain, Mr. Secretary, with highest esteem and warm personal regards,
"Yours faithfully,
"JOHN J. PERSHING."

(Diary) Chaumont, Thursday, October 4, 1917. General de Castelnau called on Tuesday to discuss entry of 1st Division into the line.

Witnessed attack maneuver of the division yesterday and conducted critique. Took luncheon with General Sibert and his staff.

Ambassador Sharp came to-day with M. Joseph Reinach for a visit and had lunch with us. Have cabled appeal for officers fitted for General Staff.

The French, always solicitous regarding the progress of our training, were anxious that our most advanced American unit take its place in a quiet sector for the experience. The main reason they advanced for suggesting front-line training at this time, with which I fully agreed, was that it would give new encouragement to their armies and through them to the people. The 1st Division itself was keen to take a more active part and was soon to have the opportunity.

This division had been billeted in the training area since July 15th and had begun to show the excellent effects of the system of training we had prescribed. At the maneuver which I attended the officers handled their units with considerable skill, particularly Major F. H. Burr, who directed an attack with his battalion of the 28th Infantry, and Major Theodore Roosevelt, Jr., who conducted a similar problem with a battalion of the 26th Infantry. At the division school the bayonet exercises, special rifle practice, firing with trench mortars, grenade throwing, and other trench training activities were well carried out. I returned much pleased with the evidences of efficiency in this organization, which was later to become famous among the armies on the Western Front.

When Ambassador Sharp and M. Reinach, a noted French journalist, lunched with us, the latter proved to be an entertaining guest, with his running comments on public men, their ages, peculiarities and shortcomings. Replying to some remark concerning his youthful outlook at the age of sixty, he said in English, with a pronounced French accent, "You know, when one is born young, one remains young always." Ambassador Sharp came just to pay a visit to "the boys," as did many other Americans in France in those days. Such visitors always left apparently in better spirits after contact with our men, and the Ambassador was especially buoyant. While we had only a handful of troops, their energy and enthusiasm were really an inspiration.

(Diary) Paris, Wednesday, October 10, 1917. Spent Sunday at Gondrecourt. Attended 1st Division Field Meet, with General Harbord, General Ragueneau and Representative Medill McCormick. We lunched with Bullard.

Yesterday evening the officers at G.H.Q. called to extend congratulations on confirmation of my appointment as General. All heads of permanent staff departments appointed to grade of Brigadier General.[1]

A group of Major Generals are over on tour of inspection.[2] Delivery of airplanes by French doubtful.

Division commanders from the States and their chiefs of staff were being sent over to visit the battlefields, armies, and schools in order to become acquainted with conditions and to experience the atmosphere of war. It was important that they should appreciate the realities and the urgency of thorough preparation of their commands. It was thought they would be impressed with the aggressive spirit that characterized our training in France by coming into close touch with our methods. These officers were sent to visit the Allied fronts and to see exercises at our own training fields and schools and were also escorted along the Line of Communications. I took occasion to give them personally my conception of the course of training that should

[1] The following were so appointed: J. G. Harbord, Chief of Staff; Benj. Alvord, Adjutant General; H. L. Rogers, Quartermaster General; W. A. Bethel, Judge Advocate General; Edgar Russel, Chief Signal Officer; C. C. Williams, Chief of Ordnance; and A. E. Bradley, Chief Surgeon.

[2] Major Generals F. J. *Kernan*, A. P. Blocksom, W. M. *Wright*, C. G. *Morton*, W. H. Sage, C. G. *Treat*, E. St. J. Greble, G. *Bell*, Jr., H. *Liggett*, J. F. Morrison, F. S. *Strong*, J. Parker, C. M. Clement, J. F. *O'Ryan*. Those whose names are in italics afterwards served in the A.E.F. Major General Morrison unfortunately became ill in France and much to my regret was unable to come over with his division.

be followed at home, making a special point of rigid discipline, rifle practice, and the instruction of junior officers in open warfare. Quite a number of the division commanders who came over as observers were either physically unfit or had reached the age when new ideas fail to make much of an impression and consequently I recommended that both classes be left at home for other duty or be retired.

All contending nations were finding themselves hard pressed to meet the demands for matériel, although according to reports the Allies were worse off than the Central Powers. The French had agreed to furnish us 5,000 airplanes but they were encountering difficulty in expanding their production, the alleged reason being the non-arrival of raw material and skilled labor from the United States, to which I have referred. My frequent appeals did not bring us the men and material and our contract for airplanes hung in the balance. The fact is that we never did catch up with our own or French requirements in labor, either skilled or unskilled, or in raw materials.

But there were also demands at home for mechanics, and as the supply was by no means unlimited, to provide them both at home and abroad was not an easy matter. Nevertheless our situation was growing more serious and it was important that we should furnish the French as many mechanics as we could without further delay. I therefore clearly presented the situation to Washington and recommended that these men be sent in civilian clothes, with brassards and overalls, if uniforms were not available.

(Diary) Chaumont, Sunday, October 14, 1917. Received approval of my suggestion that soldiers be permitted to subscribe to Second Liberty Loan.

Representatives of Aero Club, Mr. Harold E. Porter and Mr. Sidney Veit, called yesterday at Paris office to offer coöperation. Sent strong cable requesting motor transportation be expedited.

A touching ceremony took place to-day at the Hôtel de Ville, where I was presented with a beautiful American flag embroidered by the ladies of Chaumont. Took luncheon with Mayor.

The event which occurred in Chaumont on October 14th I shall ever recall with pleasant memories. I had been invited to appear at the Hôtel de Ville, and my party and I went there at the appointed hour. I was surprised to find a large crowd of townsfolk gathered in the main square, and the neighboring houses bedecked with flags. As we entered the hall, the Mayor, much to my surprise, pointed out a marble slab on which there was an inscription recording the establishment of our headquarters in Chaumont. Following introductions to the assembled guests the Mayor, in a moving speech, presented me with a flag in the name of the ladies of the city, as a souvenir of their appreciation of America's aid in the war. As usual, I had not anticipated that there was to be any speech-making and could hardly find words to express my feelings. Toasts were drunk, friendly sentiments expressed, and altogether the ceremony was very delightful. A number of us went to the Mayor's residence for luncheon and were delighted by the charm of the home and the cordiality of our host and hostess. I keep this flag as one of my most highly prized souvenirs, recalling, as it does, my sojourn among the hospitable people of that community.

I cannot resist commenting on their Mayor. He was one of those Frenchmen, of whom there are not a few, who, like the corresponding American species, can grow eloquent on almost any subject. They often rise to unwonted heights of oratory and make a profound impression whether one happens to understand the language or not. From this point of view the Mayor quite surpassed all his previous efforts. As Mayor he was most efficient and the people evidently so regarded him, which is proved by the fact that he had been the municipal head of that quiet little town on the upper Marne a number of times and was afterwards sent to the Assembly.

(Diary) Chaumont, Monday, October 15, 1917. Marshal Joffre came yesterday, upon my invitation, to visit our troops. He reviewed 1st Division to-day near Tréveray and spoke to the officers. We lunched at Neufchâteau, then inspected other troops and billets.

Am gratified that Major General Morrison, upon my recommendation, has been appointed Director of Training at home.

WHEN Marshal Joffre came to Chaumont, the French military officials were anxious to show their respect and it was arranged to have both an American and a French guard of honor drawn up to salute him upon his arrival at my residence. These two small guards vied with each other and both seemed to get a great thrill out of the ceremony. After an interesting evening with the Marshal and his staff as our guests, we left the next morning by motor car for Tréveray, accompanied by Generals Ragueneau and Alvord, Colonels de Chambrun and McCoy, and Captain Boyd. The troops of the 1st Division were drawn up in line ready to receive us and presented a much better appearance than at the review by President Poincaré. The men were especially keen to be inspected by a Marshal of France and their pride was clearly evident by their perfect lines as they swung by in the march past. The Marshal in turn was enthusiastic over their vigorous appearance and military bearing.

One incident occurred that was not on the program. On the way to the field for the ceremony a well-groomed mule that happened to be running loose, pricked up his ears, looked us over and decided to trot along with us. One of my staff wagered that this wise animal knew what was going on and would be present to witness the review. Sure enough, when we reached our position this Missouri product had preceded us. Cautiously approaching, he displayed the greatest curiosity in the guest of honor. As all efforts to drive him away were futile, he hovered near as an interested spectator of the proceedings, much to the amusement of Marshal Joffre.

I gave a luncheon at Neufchâteau for the Marshal's party and the senior officers of the 1st Division. After that we saw the training conducted by the First Corps School and visited the American and French billets at the village of St. Blin, where the 101st Infantry, 26th Division, and the French 69th Division passed in review in excellent form. As we started toward Chaumont, other American and French units were drawn up by the roadside in honor of the Marshal. It was rather late and darkness overtook us while passing on foot through the lines. The trumpets of each regiment sounded as we approached and with the lights from our automobiles close behind us illuminating the trees that bordered the highway and the faces that peered through the shadows to catch a glimpse of the Marshal, the scene suggested some legendary painting. Finally we halted, and the troops, including the French 151st Infantry, which had made a remarkable record at Verdun, marched past us. As the regiments came out of the darkness into the spotlight of our autos they made a moving picture never to be forgotten.

The political unrest in France at that time found expression in frequent criticism of the Government under M. Painlevé. It was whispered in some circles that there might be a *coup d'état* led by an outstanding military figure. The removal of the Marshal as Commander-in-Chief of the French armies had not dimmed his popularity as the idol of the people and he might easily have been selected as the leader of such a movement had it been seriously projected. In speaking of its possibility as we drove back, he said, confidentially, that it had been discussed and that it might occur under certain circumstances. But, much to his credit, he hastened emphatically, and I think very sincerely, to disclaim any ambition in that direction. If the idea was ever really considered among the opposition to the Government, it never got beyond a very small coterie. In fact, there existed no actual crisis that was likely to precipitate a change in the form of government. The Republic had stood firmly for three years under the extreme stress of war and there seemed little probability of its being overturned at this time by such a stroke.

On October 17th the following summary was sent to Washington showing the estimate of the situation in Europe:

" * * * The Germans on Western Front have been reënforced by four divisions from the Russian front, giving a present total of 150 divisions.

"Persistent reports from widely separated sources of an (early) offensive by Germany and Austria against Italy. * * *

"Manifest that Germany is making determined effort to use present economic difficulties of Switzerland to excite Swiss people against Allies * * * French report activity on part of Swiss in construction of fortifications on French border.

"Reports indicate that after the failure of the Peace Conference asked for in Pope's peace proposal the German Government began active efforts to stiffen the spirit of the country * * * in support of new Pan-Germanist party whose platform is a victorious peace. * * * "

(Diary) Paris, Saturday, October 20, 1917. General Charteris, Chief of British Intelligence, visited G.H.Q. on Thursday.

Arrived in Paris from Chaumont last night. Called this morning on Ambassador Sharp, who thinks Painlevé Ministry will not last much longer. Dined with M. Painlevé this evening but saw no indications of uneasiness on his part. Among the guests were Marshal Joffre and General Foch.

Just heard that dispatch from Berlin to *New York Times* represents me as saying that German lines are impregnable. Have cabled that our shortage of winter clothing is critical. Have again insisted by cable on special training with rifle and bayonet.

The reported statement attributed to me that the German lines were impregnable might have been idle gossip, but it was more probably circulated to create the impression that our armies were starting on a forlorn hope. While not in the habit of taking notice of statements that appeared in the press, this was so far from the truth that I cabled the Secretary of War that the report was absolutely false and without any foundation whatever. In every reference to our future operations I had strongly maintained that it was not only possible to break the German lines but that it would be done. The very system of training that we were persistently following was based on the determination to force the Germans out of their trenches and beat them in the open. On no other theory could they have been defeated.

Yet without question there were not a few among our Allies and probably some in our own army who thought the task impossible, supporting their view by citing the failures of the previous three years, especially that of the spring of 1917. It was none the less a surprise, however, when a report came directly to me that such views had actually been expressed in the presence of civilian visitors by officers of rank in our army. I was indignant to learn of that kind of talk and in commenting on it to the Americans who had heard such statements made, I said that "the German lines can be broken, they must be broken, and they will be broken," and those present will recall that it was said with considerable emphasis. Positive steps were taken at once to eradicate such notions, or at least to prevent them from being openly stated, and I was determined to relieve immediately any officer, without regard to rank, who should express any such opinion. The following letter, couched in no uncertain language, was sent to the several division and other commanders:

"1. Americans recently visiting our training areas and coming in contact with officers in high command have received a note of deep pessimism, including apprehension of undue hardships to be undergone, of the disadvantages of billeting as compared to field conditions that have prevailed in our own country, of the great numbers of the enemy, and a belief in the impregnability of his lines, mingled with some comment on the peculiarities of our Allies, and generally have come away with an impression that the war is already well along toward defeat for our arms. It is especially to be regretted that such an impression has been derived mainly from general officers who, if prompted by considerations of soldierly duty, of leadership, of patriotism, fortitude and ambition, should maintain quite an opposite attitude.

"2. While realizing that optimism cannot be created by order, it should be unnecessary to point out that such a state of mind on the part of officers in responsible positions is at once reflected among their troops, and it is not an overstatement to say no officer worthy of command would give expression to thoughts of depression, much less communicate to untutored civilians false ideas of the morale of our troops.   A conservative firmness and faith in our cause is not inconsistent with a serious estimate of an enemy's forces or even of a grave strategic or tactical situation, but I hardly need add that a temperament which gives way to weak complainings, which views with apprehension the contact with the enemy, which carps at the individuality of our Allies, and querulously protests at hardships such as all soldiers must expect to endure, marks an unfitness for command of such an officer, and indicates his practical defeat before he goes to battle.

"3. The officer who cannot read hope in the conditions that confront us; who is not inspired and uplifted by the knowledge that under the leadership of our Chief Executive, the heart of our nation is in this war; who shrinks from hardship; who does not exert his own personal influence to encourage his men, and who fails in the lofty attitude which should characterize the General that expects to succeed, should yield his position to others with more of our national courage. The consciousness of such an attitude should in honor dictate an application for relief.   Whenever the visible effects of it on the command of such an officer reach me in future, it will constitute grounds for his removal without application.

"JOHN J. PERSHING."

Nothing more was heard of the existence of such sentiments within our army, if, indeed, they had ever found more than a temporary lodgment in the minds of a few naturally timid or critically inclined souls. The mere suggestion that such views might be held only made it all the more imperative to emphasize and develop an aggressive spirit among our troops.

(Diary) Paris, Wednesday, October 24, 1917. General situation on the Western Front not encouraging.   The 1st Division entered trenches in quiet sector the night of the 21st.   At the start each regiment will be assigned to a French division.

Shipment of troops through England and use of Brest under discussion.

Went to French front Monday, accompanied by Harbord, de Chambrun, Logan and Boyd.   Spent the night at Compiègne with Col.

Frank Parker, head of our Mission. Witnessed successful offensive at Chemin des Dames yesterday.

Conferred with a number of officers to-day. Saw Cornelius Bliss and Charles H. Grasty and lunched with Atterbury. German offensive against Italians began this morning.

Chartered transport *Antilles* torpedoed and sunk the 17th.[1]

My general impression of the situation at this time was set forth in a cable to Washington sent on October 21st:

"During the past week the water-soaked ground in Flanders and on the Western Front generally has prevented further development of offensive movements. Summing up wastage of German Army in this year's campaign, a single offensive, such as the Anglo-French in Flanders in progress since July 31st, is insufficient materially to weaken Germany's manpower. Next year must see two offensives, continuously maintained throughout summer, if decisive result is to be obtained. This can only be secured through aid of effective United States Army on this side. * * * The troops on the Western Front have been reënforced by one German division from the Russian front. * * * "

As the training of the 1st Division had now progressed sufficiently, it was put into line in the quiet sector northeast of Lunéville, under the supervision of the French, for actual trench experience. The division was under-officered and short of horses, clothing and many other things, especially rolling kitchens, of which a few had only recently been received from home, and trucks, which were being borrowed from the French.

My repeated cables, beginning in July, for winter clothing had received scant attention and with the coming of colder weather the shortage became critical. The initial stock requested was disallowed, the monthly allotments were totally inadequate and the depots were practically empty. The explanation received from the Quartermaster General's office, that our requests could not be granted on account of the needs at home, showed a total

[1] The *Antilles* left Brest as a part of a convoy on October 15th, returning to the United States. On the morning of the 17th she was struck by a torpedo and sank within six minutes. Sixty-seven lives were lost, sixteen being enlisted men of the Army. The survivors were picked up by vessels of the escort and returned to Brest, from which point the message was telephoned to my headquarters. This was the first transport lost in our service.

lack of appreciation of the necessity of properly clothing the fighting man actually at the front in preference to all others.

Notwithstanding all these handicaps, the men were highly enthusiastic over the prospects of contact with the enemy and the rest of us were gratified that at last we were to be represented on the front. Thirty days were allotted for this preliminary training, one battalion of each regiment occupying the line for periods of ten days at a time. The sector had been inactive and uneventful since the stormy days of 1914, when General de Castelnau halted the German advance on the Grande Couronne de Nancy.

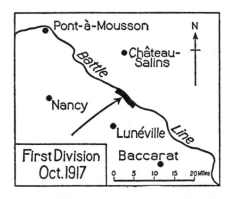

A few of the French peasants remained in their homes in advance of our support positions, while on the German side people continued to live near enough to the front lines to be seen going to church on Sundays. This presented to the men an odd contrast to the pictures of war which they had built up in their imaginations.

The offensive by the French on the Chemin des Dames was the second since Nivelle's failure in April. I went to the front upon the invitation of General Pétain, arriving by motor at the headquarters of General d'Espérey, Commander of the Group of Armies of the North, in time for dinner on the evening of the 22d. The plans for the attack were explained to us and, from the extreme care taken in working out the details and from their accurate knowledge of the enemy's force and his position, there seemed to be little doubt of success.

Soon after their victory near Verdun in August, the French began to prepare for this offensive, in which they could not well afford to fail. The advance was made by eight divisions of the Sixth Army on a front of only seven and one-half miles, extending along the Aisne, with the object of gaining a more advantageous position for the winter and also still further building up French morale. General Maistre, the Army Commander, gave the operation his personal attention, prescribing an artillery preparation covering six days, during which the expenditure of ammunition was even greater than in the offensive of August 20th. The long period of artillery fire was considered necessary, as the Germans were strongly fortified along the chalky bluffs of the Aisne, where numerous caverns afforded cover for large garrisons held near the front.

The assaulting lines of infantry, accompanied by numerous tanks, succeeded without difficulty in reaching the limited objectives. Fort Malmaison, the key point, was reduced to a heap of rubbish by the very heavy artillery fire concentrated upon it. The capture of this dominant position by the French caused the immediate withdrawal of the Germans on the right and left, and during the succeeding fortnight they retired behind the Ailette.

As we drove toward the front in the forenoon we met German prisoners being taken to the rear and received reports that progress was very satisfactory. The day was foggy, with rain at intervals, so that aviators were unable to be of much service, and the advance, except at the start, was quite hidden from our view, even from old Fort Condé, a commanding position that had been selected as our observation point.

When the luncheon hour came General d'Espérey asked us into a chamber of the fort, where we sat down and enjoyed a menu that would have done credit to any restaurant in Paris. During the meal the General told us that, several years before, he had crossed America while returning from service in the Orient and his journey through Iowa happened during one of those periods when prohibition was in force in that State. If there is any one thing that a Frenchman cannot understand it is that any people should deliberately enact a law to deprive themselves of the privilege of taking a glass of wine. To have heard him describe how he suffered while in Iowa one would have thought he was telling of a trip across the Sahara Desert.

During the afternoon he took us to visit the headquarters of one of the attacking divisions, the 27th, and after its infantry had penetrated the main German defenses we went by auto to what had been no-man's-land and thence on foot to the enemy's second position. The artillery and machine gun fire were still frequent over that part of the field, which was strewn with the bodies of many gallant Frenchmen whose courage had made the victory possible. Gangs of laborers and truckloads of material which had been held in readiness behind the attacking army had already been brought forward to rebuild the roads across the shell-torn area. From the respect shown General d'Espérey as he passed along, speaking cheerfully to the men, frequently addressing them affectionately as "Mes Enfants," there could be no doubt of his popularity. This was my second contact with one of the most picturesque and delightful personalities in the French Army.

This achievement of the French in capturing positions against which the April offensive by Nivelle dashed itself to pieces had a very stimulating effect upon their morale, but it would have been more lasting had it not been followed so soon by the serious defeat of the Italians at Caporetto. In any event, there was every reason for Generals d'Espérey and Maistre to be proud of the victory, which still further increased their prestige.

After extending thanks to our host, we left for Compiègne, literally covered with mud, stopping there to congratulate General Pétain on the success of the day. While at Compiègne we dropped in at the dispensary where some American women under Miss Elsie de Wolfe maintained a clinic for badly burned gas cases. We also made a brief call at the hospital nearby to see Colonel Bunau-Varilla, of Panama Canal fame, who had lost a leg in the recent French offensive near Verdun. From his cheerful mood he seemed to be rather proud of his wound. It was he who organized and developed the system of water supply and purification for the French armies. In 1927 I took part in the dedication of the Ossuary near Verdun, at which Colonel Bunau-Varilla was present. On the rounds to inspect this fine monument we passed the many bays which contain the bones of men who lost their lives in the great battle. When we came to the bay corresponding to the sector in which he fought, he jovially remarked that he thought his leg must be in there.

Following closely on the heels of this limited French success came a tremendous counterstroke by the Austrians and Germans against the Italians. During preceding months, beginning in May, the Italian armies had made a series of attacks which at first met with considerable success. The Italians made progress in the Julian Alps, causing Austrian losses of some 30,000 prisoners, but the timely arrival of Austrian reënforcements enabled them to prevent serious dislodgment.

Meanwhile, the situation on the Russian front permitted the withdrawal of troops of the Central Powers to an extent that enabled them to assume the offensive against the Italians. Continuous rumors had reached the ears of the Allies that an attack was impending, but they were given little credence, especially by the Italian Commander-in-Chief, who professed every confidence in the strength of his armies.

The Germans had come to realize that operations with limited objectives, involving days of violent preliminary artillery fire, were far too costly when measured by results. They had adopted a new system based on a few hours of heavy bombardment, principally with gas shells, followed by a violent assault on the forward positions by picked battalions supported by an unusually heavy concentration of machine guns and other portable weapons. The defense once broken, fresh troops held close in rear poured through the lines of the leading troops and, increasing the momentum of the attack, rapidly carried the fight beyond the entrenched positions. This plan had already been tested in the battle of Riga, where a complete rupture of the opposing fortified lines was accomplished and the fighting successfully carried on in the open.

The demonstration at Riga by General von Hutier's army was convincing proof of the soundness of the plan and of the correctness of the doctrine of training for open warfare that we were so persistently following in France and so continuously trying to impress upon the War Department at home. It simply proved that nothing in the great war had changed this age-old principle of the art of war. Thenceforth this method was to characterize German attacks, and the capture of Riga was only the precursor of Caporetto and the series of strokes by the Central Powers later on, which were more or less uniformly successful.

The most delicate phase of the system was the secret concentration close to the front of the large force necessary. This was usually accomplished by a series of night marches, the troops being concealed by day in villages and woods. Under German control and reënforced by seven picked German divisions, the Austrian forces, following out this plan, completely surprised the Italian Army on a nineteen-mile front near Caporetto on October 24th during a heavy fog and succeeded in breaking entirely through their lines on the first morning, rapidly forcing the Italians into the open. The advance crossed the Isonzo River and German troops were over the frontier by the 25th.

The feeble resistance of the Italian Second Army, which stood the brunt of the attack, has been attributed to well-organized propaganda on the part of the Austrians, who were said to have fraternized with the Italians on the theory that they were brothers and if they declined to fight each other the war would end. But the inherent weakness of the Italian position was not overlooked by the Germans. It appears, entirely from Italian sources, that there was actually a gap in the Italian lines between their Second and Third Armies at Tolmein, where the Austrian outposts held a commanding position on the high ground in the interval. The Italian reserves were insufficient, few defensive positions had been prepared in the rear, the bridges across the Isonzo were in-

The official portrait of General John J. Pershing. (National Archives photograph)

General Pershing and his staff in Mexico during the Punitive Expedition campaign.(The photograph is a reproduction from the collections of the Library of Congress.)

General Pershing and his staff arrive in Europe in 1917. (The Signal Corps, U.S.A., photograph is a reproduction from the collections of the Library of Congress.)

On November 18, 1917, in Chaumont, France, General Pershing inspects American troops. (National Archives photograph)

General Pershing was very popular with the French people. He is seen here taking a moment to chat with a little French girl. (National Archives photograph)

General Pershing (left) with his aide, Colonel George C. Marshall, Jr., in France in 1917. Pershing met Marshall shortly after his arrival in France and made him his chief staff officer until Pershing retired in 1924. (National Archives photograph)

adequate, and the supply depots, which were in front of the Tagliamento, were too far forward. At any rate, the Third Army was left in a critically exposed position from which it barely escaped by a rapid retreat.

Before the operation ended on November 10th the enemy had advanced some 60-odd miles and was confronting General Cadorna's men on the Piave. More than 300,000 prisoners, 3,000 pieces of artillery and immense quantities of supplies were captured by the enemy. All the Italian gains in the war were wiped out during the first thirty-six hours of this battle. Seemingly in an instant the cause of the Allies had been dealt a master blow and five British and six French divisions were rushed to Italy to save the situation. This victory tremendously strengthened the hands of the German Government.

One gleam of light was revealed in this dilemma. The magnitude of the disaster and its immediate effect on all the Allies forced a realization of the necessity of better understanding and closer coöperation. They soon after made a really determined effort to secure unity of command through the Rapallo Agreement, though a later disaster still more serious was necessary before this ideal could be finally accomplished.

(Diary) Paris, Wednesday, October 31, 1917. Reached St. Nazaire from Paris on Thursday with Harbord, de Chambrun and Nolan and went to artillery camps at Coëtquidan and Meucon. The following day visited St. Nazaire docks, shops and storehouses with Colonels Samuel D. Rockenbach and Louis H. Bash; thence to the new depot at Montoir with Colonel John S. Sewell, and to the hospital at Savenay with Colonel Jos. F. Siler.

On Saturday, with Brigadier Generals R. M. Blatchford, commanding Line of Communications, and Mason M. Patrick, and Colonels Charles R. Krauthoff and David S. Stanley, inspected labor camps at Bordeaux, new docks at Bassens and camp at Souge.

Sunday visited Russian detention camp at Le Courneau, the vilest and most unsanitary place I have ever seen.

Monday inspected hospital at Châteauroux, the aviation center at Issoudun, the great supply depot at Gièvres, and the ordnance depot at Méhun. Took train at Nevers; arrived Paris yesterday.

Received gratifying cable that large consignment of lumber, piles and crossties are en route. Heavy artillery school established at Camp Mailly under Brigadier General Frank W. Coe. Brigadier General Patrick assigned temporarily to command the Line of Communications; Major General Bundy to command the 2d Division.[1] Have requested French Mission to procure authority for entry of Spanish laborers. Had a group of visiting Congressmen [2] to dinner this evening.

This trip of inspection to Coëtquidan and Meucon was made by motor and the route ran through a portion of Brittany, picturesque with the autumn foliage of forests, orchards and hedges. The quiet countryside, the quaint houses with their thatched roofs, the people in old-time costumes, all suggested happiness and contentment regardless of the war.

At Coëtquidan, a French artillery station, we found the artillery of our 26th Division in training under General Lassiter, but the camp was very much crowded, as a regiment of French artillery had been left to assist in the instruction of our men. We then went to Meucon, which was to be another artillery camp, although not yet occupied by any of our troops. En route we passed through the "Landes de la Lanvaux," a sort of lowland covered with scrub pines. We stopped a few minutes at the ancient Château Josselin, where the young Duchess, whose husband, the Duke of Rohan,[3] had been killed in battle a short time before, showed us over the château. The defiant rise of this medieval structure above the cliff, at whose base flows the Oust River, is most striking, while the beautiful façade and the charming interior filled with family paintings and other souvenirs of past glory leave a lasting picture in the mind.

The port of St. Nazaire was found more or less congested, due to several causes. One was that we had not been able to expand the facilities fast enough to keep pace with requirements; an-

---

[1] This division was organized in France and was composed of one brigade of Regular troops and one of Marines.

[2] The following Congressmen constituted the party: C. C. Dill, F. C. Hicks, W. S. Goodwin, R. W. Parker, C. B. Timberlake, D. V. Stephens, J. F. Miller, S. M. Taylor, P. H. Dale and A. Johnson.

[3] This gallant officer, holding the rank of major, was three times severely wounded and sent to the rear, each time returning still convalescent, and was finally killed while leading his unit in battle.

other, that the French insisted on assuming the right to control movements of our transports in and out of the harbor; and, a third, that too many vessels were sent there, owing to the disinclination of our naval authorities in European waters to escort a due proportion of them to Bordeaux. The routing by the Navy of supply ships from home ports and coal boats from England and their disposition at French ports bore no relation whatever at this time to port accommodations available. The Navy pleaded the increased danger from submarines and a shortage of destroyers as the reason, and it was only after earnest and repeated representations and considerable further delay that there was much improvement in this annoying state of affairs.

The stevedore situation was worse even than had been reported and the inability to discharge vessels with rapidity was another cause of their slow turn-around at French ports. In a certain regiment of stevedores, especially recruited for that work, there were only eleven officers with previous experience, out of a total of about thirty, all the rest being absolutely without any knowledge whatever of handling cargo.

The construction of storehouses at Montoir, just out of the city limits, and the necessary rail connections were proceeding very slowly, with the result that valuable property had to be piled up on the docks or be left in the open at the warehouse sites. With adequate railway facilities all supplies could have been forwarded to our main centers, but sufficient rolling stock had not arrived and the French could furnish only a limited number of trains. At that moment the Allies had been called upon to meet the Italian crisis, which required the exclusive use of many trains to transport French and British troops, munitions and supplies to that front. If any further evidence had been needed, the situation thus created proved conclusively that we must develop and control our port accommodations and our own means of land transportation to the fullest extent possible.

The next objective on our trip was Bordeaux, sixty miles up the Gironde River. The city itself has real charm, with its broad proportions, public gardens, quaint old houses along the quays, its modern cathedral and old churches built a thousand years ago. It is the fourth city in France, especially noted for the large quantity and fine quality of its wines, in which it carries on a world-wide commerce.

The larger vessels could not enter the port except at high tide. As the port facilities were sufficient to accommodate only a limited amount of additional medium-draft shipping, we had started the construction of new docks at Bassens, six miles below, where the deep water would permit vessels to come alongside. Although considerable quantities of material had been sent over, this new construction was delayed principally because of lack of long piling which the engineers had planned to have brought from the Pacific Coast.

It became evident that this was impracticable within a reasonable time and that we must obtain as much piling as possible from forests in France. The French authorities were loath to yield to such demands, protesting that they had no standing timber of the necessary dimensions. Having driven through the forest reserves in the Vosges Mountains, I was able from personal observation to assure them that we should have no trouble in finding just what we wanted. Our foresters confirmed my assertion and logging companies were soon turning out quantities of piling. Our forestry service supplied the engineers with a total of 39,000 piles, 15,000 of which were long piles, thereby saving several shiploads, to say nothing of the strain on rolling stock of hauling this amount of material across the continent. Even with piling obtained from French sources, it was necessary to procure an additional quantity from the Pacific Coast.

An incident happened in connection with the shipments of piling from home that would have been amusing if it had not been so serious. One cargo reached Bordeaux that was supposed to consist of especially long piling, but upon inspection the engineers found it much shorter than prescribed. It was learned later that in order to get the piles in between bulkheads the supercargo had sawed the ends off, making them useless for the purpose intended. While speaking of forest products, another example of inefficiency that occurred soon after might be mentioned. One ship from home came over loaded by the Quartermaster Corps with shavings for our cold storage plants, when tons of sawdust and shavings could have been obtained from the logging districts in France.

Continuing the inspection, we went on Sunday to Le Courneau, about forty miles from Bordeaux, thinking it might possibly be available for our use later on. It was then occupied by a brigade of disaffected Russians who, like most of their fellows, had defied their officers and refused to participate further in the war. After being withdrawn from the line, they had given the French so much trouble, even to committing depredations on the people, that they had to be sent out of the Zone of the Armies to this rather remote camp, where they were held practically as prisoners. There was no transportation to carry them back to Russia and as they had been allowed to keep their arms it was difficult to enforce discipline among them. I spoke to two colonels and commented on the lack of sanitation, but it was evident that they were unable to compel the men to work, even to the extent of cleaning out stables, latrines or drains, and the conditions may better be imagined than described. The men were a heavy, stupid-looking lot, who, in their new estate, apparently did not care how bad things were so long as the French continued to feed and clothe them.

We then drove to Arcachon, a well-known watering place on the coast, for luncheon, and returned to Bordeaux through Souge, which later became the site of a hospital and also an artillery camp and remount station. Again boarding the train, the next morning found us at Châteauroux, where we had already begun the construction of a large base hospital, and where we were planning to establish a great depot of supplies similar to the one farther toward the front at Gièvres. At the largest aviation center, Issoudun, our next destination, we found the construction of quarters and the aviation field well under way, with several hundred aviators already receiving instruction, although handicapped by a very limited number of airplanes.

Gièvres, which lies 100 miles directly south of Paris, became the site of our principal supply depot in France. Under Colonel C. J. Symmonds' able and energetic direction, construction to cover an area of twelve square miles was going forward with all possible speed. He was gradually putting order and system into the place. The engineers were building storehouses for rations and a cold storage plant to hold hundreds of tons of fresh meats, and the Transportation Department was rapidly laying the mile upon mile of sidings that would be required. During this period of construction, which had only recently been started, the force at Gièvres was already receiving, classifying and either storing or forwarding supplies in amounts that eventually reached thousands of tons daily.

The ordnance depot at Méhun took but a few minutes, as building was hardly begun. Leaving there about dusk, en route to my train at Nevers, we motored through Bourges and saw the magnificent cathedral as it stood out in all its glory under the full moon. The view of this wonderful example of 12th Century architecture under the circumstances was one of the most impressive sights I have ever seen.

Regardless of the many drawbacks against which the Line of Communications was laboring, there was everywhere a fine spirit among the officers and men, who were generally cheerful and optimistic. After all, considering the lack of men and material, we were making progress on the physical side of the organization that would feed, clothe and furnish munitions for the great army we hoped to have. One of the obstacles was to be found in the number of independent bureaus represented at the ports and the larger centers of activity, not only in our own system, but especially in that of the French, and the consequent difficulty of securing teamwork among them. As a remedy, I sent to each base section a competent general officer with an organized staff to coordinate and systematize the management of affairs, and in a brief time considerable improvement was noticeable in methods of handling troop arrivals and cargo and in the increased progress of construction.

CHAPTER XVI

Conference with Mr. Lloyd George—Allied Ministers Meet at Rapallo—
Supreme War Council Formed—Enemy Raid on 1st Division Trenches
—Political Undercurrents—Aims of Different Allies—Ammunition
Question Acute—Letter from Secretary of War on Preparation, Selec-
tion of Commanders and Morale—Letter to Secretary in Reply

(Diary) Paris, Sunday, November 4, 1917. Went to Chaumont
Friday, returned yesterday. Major Generals Liggett, Parker, O'Ryan,
Clement, and Strong, visiting A.E.F., came to Paris with me. Major
General Morrison left behind ill. Germans made raid on our lines,
killed three, wounded several.

Took breakfast with Mr. Lloyd George this morning. Generals
Sir Henry Wilson, Smuts, and Maurice were in the party. Discussed
the advisability of establishing Supreme War Council. Had luncheon
with Sir Douglas Haig, who does not favor the suggestion. Called
on M. Painlevé. Congratulations from Secretary on splendid total
subscribed by A.E.F. to Second Liberty Loan.

IN our conversation at breakfast, Mr. Lloyd George referred
to the Italian disaster as most serious and pointed out that
sending British and French divisions to Italy had materially
weakened the lines in France. He also spoke at some length on
the lack of concerted action among the Allied armies. I agreed
with him in this and added that in my opinion there never had
been real coöperation on the Western Front between the British
and French, that when one was attacking the other was usually
standing still, and that the Germans were thus left free to concentrate their reserves against the threatened point.

We were facing a grave crisis next year, if not sooner, Mr.
Lloyd George said, and no one knew how it was to be met. The
enemy might attack each one separately, with the same results
as in the case of Italy. He then asked what I thought of creat-

NOTE: Total strength of the A.E.F. on October 31st, 6,064 officers, 80,969 enlisted
men.

ing a Supreme War Council. Having in mind a council called together in the field to decide upon military operations, I told him that the advice of war councils was not usually of any great value and that the proposition did not appeal to me. I said that authority should be vested somewhere to coördinate the operations on the Western Front and suggested the possibility of having a supreme commander. He replied, in effect, that it was unlikely that the Allies could agree upon any one, as the French would object to any but a Frenchman and the British might not like that.

He expressed the opinion that in any event a permanent council would be useful primarily in bringing the heads of the Allied Governments together at intervals to consider general policies. I admitted that such an organization might serve to unite the Allies in common purpose but that the conduct of operations by the combined armies should be left entirely under military direction. I got the distinct impression that while he was seeking to secure greater unity of action, he also sought some means of controlling the activities of the British Army. During previous months that army had been engaged in an almost continuous offensive practically single-handed, and had suffered very heavy losses without compensating gains.

Mr. Lloyd George went on to say that there was to be a conference of the Prime Ministers at Rapallo, Italy, and that he hoped they might reach some agreement that would result in a council such as he had in mind. He thought that the United States ought to be represented at this meeting and suggested that I should attend. As the purpose of a council seemed to be more for political coördination than for purely military control, I told him that I considered it inadvisable for me to participate without some intimation from my Government to do so.

In the afternoon, I called on M. Painlevé, at his request, and he also told me of the proposal to form a Supreme War Council and wanted me to go to the conference in Italy. I gave him the same reply that I had given Mr. Lloyd George.

The result of the meeting at Rapallo was an agreement among

the Prime Ministers of the Governments participating, as shown by the following:

"Decisions of a Conference of Representatives of the British, French and Italian Governments Assembled at Rapallo on November 7, 1917

"I. The representatives of the British, French, and Italian Governments assembled at Rapallo on the 7th of November, 1917, have agreed on the scheme for the organization of a Supreme War Council with permanent military representation for each power contained in the following paragraph.

"II. (1) With a view to the better coördination of military action on the Western Front, a Supreme War Council is created composed of the Prime Minister and a member of the Government of each of the Great Powers whose armies are fighting on that front. The extension of the scope of the Council to other fronts is reserved for discussion with the other Great Powers.

"(2) The Supreme War Council has for its mission to watch over the general conduct of the war. It prepares recommendations for the decisions of the Governments, and keeps itself informed of their execution, and reports thereon to the respective Governments.

"(3) The General Staffs and Military Commands of the Armies of each power charged with the conduct of military operations remain responsible to their respective Governments.

"(4) The general war plans drawn up by the competent Military Authorities are submitted to the Supreme War Council, which, under the high authority of the Governments, insures their concordance, and submits, if need be, any necessary changes.

"(5) Each power delegates to the Supreme War Council one permanent military representative whose exclusive function is to act as technical adviser to the Council.

"(6) The Military Representatives receive from the Government and the competent military authorities of their country all the proposals, information, and documents relating to the conduct of the war.

"(7) The Military Representatives watch day by day the situation of the forces, and of the means of all kinds of which the Allied Armies and the enemy Armies dispose.

"(8) The Supreme War Council meets normally at Versailles, where the permanent Military Representatives and their staffs are assembled. It may meet at other places as may be agreed upon, according to circumstances. The meetings of the Supreme War Council will take place at least once a month.

"III. The permanent military representatives will be as follows:

"For France—General Foch

"For Great Britain—General Wilson

"For Italy—General Cadorna."

By the inclusion of sub-paragraph (4) it would seem that the Prime Ministers had it in mind to assume greater control of operations if such action should appear necessary. While the Commanders-in-Chief of the armies concerned were expected to attend meetings of the Council, and usually did so and freely expressed their views, they were not members and had no vote.

The creation of the Supreme War Council did not meet with universal approval. The commanders of the British and French Armies and many high officials in civil circles were opposed to it. Military commanders were afraid it would result in undue interference with the conduct of operations and it was often referred to in derision as the "Soviet." The British Army viewed it with considerable suspicion, thinking it might substitute politicians for professional soldiers as directors of the strategy of the war. A stronger central control by the French was advocated by influential French papers in the fear that their Government might not have so much to say in Allied affairs as theretofore. The formation of this Council indicated, however, a realization that Allied success in the future would depend upon better coördination of effort. The action of the Prime Ministers was a step in the direction of unified command, which was no doubt one reason why most British as well as French officers, and a considerable number of those in high civil positions, were lukewarm toward it; yet not a few who spoke against the Council at the time said later that they had always been in favor of unified control. The action taken at Rapallo was approved by President Wilson on November 17th and that fact appeared in the press a day or so later. The President's action strengthened the hands of those who favored the Council and probably became the influence that saved it.

It is probable that if the French and British army commanders, in a friendly spirit of coöperation, had made a joint study of the military problem on the Western Front as a whole and then had seriously undertaken to pull together, the Supreme War Council might never have been born. And yet, when one analyzed it, coöperation between the armies presented many difficulties with two peoples of such different points of view. For example, as we have seen, the offensive in the spring of 1917, which was under French leadership, received only half-hearted approval of the British. Then later, the British carried on their offensives during most of the summer, but the French conducted only two limited attacks. So they apparently made plans independently, and any advantage gained was purely local, with little material effect upon the final outcome.

The Supreme War Council made a favorable start at its first meeting and gave the impression that a wise and conservative exercise of its really unlimited powers would characterize its actions. It refrained from interfering directly with military commanders and operations and confined itself largely to questions of policy, such as the coördination of Allied resources, and the conservation and distribution of Allied strength. However, as time went on, the Supreme War Council undertook to exercise greater authority over military questions.

As indicated in the diary, our 1st Division had not been long in the quiet sector of the Vosges before the peaceful aspect of things was disturbed by a German raid on an isolated post of the 16th Infantry early in the morning of November 3d. A group was caught in a box barrage and although the men made a courageous resistance against the large raiding party three were killed,[1] five wounded, and twelve captured. These were the first casualties that had occurred in our army to units serving in the trenches. The French took charge of the funeral ceremony and turned out a formal guard in addition to our own. The services

[1] Corporal James B. Gresham, Co. F, 16th Infantry.
Private Thomas F. Enright, Co. F, 16th Infantry.
Private Merle D. Hay, Co. F, 16th Infantry.

were conducted by the French General, Bordeaux, who came with his full staff and delivered a beautiful oration over the graves. A large number of French troops also came informally to pay their final tribute. This joint homage to our dead, there under the fire of the guns, seemed to symbolize the common sacrifices our two peoples were to make in the same great cause. It seemed as though their death had sealed a new pact of understanding and comradeship between the two armies.

As to the political situation, the undercurrent at the moment, as nearly as could be learned, showed a continued lack of accord among the different nations, which were not at all in agreement with Mr. Wilson's ideals. Each nation had its own aspirations and each sought to gain some advantage over the others. Some of the divergent war aims had to do with territory distant from France, and troops sent there might have been more usefully employed on the Western Front.

A very reliable agent, an American, who was in close touch with the leading Allied statesmen, brought to me personally a memorandum which voiced the underlying sentiment, and which I at once enclosed in a letter to the Secretary of War:

"November 3, 1917.
"My dear Mr. Secretary:
   "I am enclosing you herewith a memorandum, marked 'A,' which I think well worth reading, giving as it does an estimate of the political situation since the Italian disaster.
   "Of course, only time will tell just how this Italian defeat is going to affect our allies. I am rather fearful, however, that it may be only the beginning of further successes in that direction by the Central Powers. In this event, there will have to be a more or less complete readjustment of military forces on what may become an extended Western Front.
   "I hope to be of some use to Colonel House when he arrives, and shall get in touch with him as to the military outlook at once.
   "I am also enclosing a memorandum, marked 'B,' which is a report of a conversation held by a man in my confidence with a British official high up in the councils of Great Britain. The date of this

was October 24th. Perhaps it should not be taken too seriously, but is an indication of the British attitude.

"With high esteem and warm personal regards, I am,
"Very sincerely yours,
"JOHN J. PERSHING.

"2 enclosures."

"Enclosure 'A'

"THE ITALIAN DISASTER,
ITS DIPLOMATIC CONSEQUENCES; THE 'PACT OF LONDON,'
AND THE UNITED STATES

"It is felt in the soberest political worlds of the Quai d'Orsay and Parliament that the military disaster that has befallen Italy will have among its inevitable consequences at all events one that is peculiarly opportune, and *perhaps indispensable at this hour.* It will have shown the Italians, who love 'waltzing alone,' that the interests of all the allies are identical. It will also have shown the Italians that a religious respect for the *Pact of London* is the sole condition of success in this war. The days of *Nostra Guerra* are numbered. * * * Italian Imperialistic pride has received a rude blow. When the British and French disembark in the Italian ports, Italian hearts will lose a certain cock-sureness; and this change of heart will be all to the good, both for the ultimate peace-negotiations and for the future of the balance of power in the Mediterranean. Italy, in a word, is once again reminded that she has become, in a night, only a humble little Latin Sister.

"On the other hand, this rapid disaster will be a much needed revelation for certain circles in London, Paris, and Washington as to the duplicity of the Austrians. The chief lesson *for statesmen* of this military disaster is that the Central Empires are a block, which only the impact of a more coherent, bigger block can shatter. While the Austro-German Governments were preparing their Italian offensive simple souls in the Parliaments of the world were fancying that their malicious proffers of peace were sincere! Candid victims of Boche blackmail and malice, socialists and radicals everywhere, extolled * * * a policy of seeking to disarm Germany and Austria by resonant declarations in favor of right, repudiating all unholy Imperialistic aims. The very way the Italian disaster has been brought about * * * is a magnificent object lesson."

"Enclosure 'B'

"Lord X.

" 'The European Allies and America are not fighting for the same thing. Mr. Wilson thinks a great deal more of his ideas of people governing themselves, of a friendly working arrangement among all the great powers after the war, than he does of territorial or specific things going to this or that country. What he wants is to smash the German military power and have a society of democratic nations afterwards. But to England, France, and Italy these things are phrases, useful perhaps, but of secondary interest. England wants to maintain her colonial possessions, to keep her position on the sea, and her commercial position in the world. We know what France wants —Alsace-Lorraine, as indemnity and security for the future. Italy has definite territorial claims; thus the governments of these countries think a great deal about what they want for themselves and less about ideals, unless these ideals are incidental to success. So there is no clear unity among the Allies in Europe and America.

" 'Suppose the European allies find themselves in a situation where they ought to make the best peace they can, what is the United States going to do? Russia has gone. Is Italy going to be able to stay? We are fresher than any of the other belligerents in Europe, but we cannot win the war alone.'

"A.

" 'The Allies ought certainly to be able to maintain the military equilibrium for another fifteen or eighteen months, until we (the Americans) are prepared to make a great effort.'

"Lord X.

" 'I am glad that you recognize that it will take you that much time. Looked at from this side, you seem to be very deliberate.'

"A.

" 'General Pershing is not going to put his army in the front line until we are ready.'

"Lord X.

" 'General Pershing is quite right, he ought not to go into the front line until he is ready to do something really effective. I wonder if your people are studying the Italian situation.'

"A.

" 'It has seemed, looking at Italy from Paris, that she is going strong, and will be capable of a vigorous campaign next spring.'

"Lord X.

" 'I don't know whether the Italian people will go on; it all depends on whether they have enough to eat this winter, upon whether there are such great disturbances over food and heating that the government would be greatly weakened in their pressing the war. Well, if Italy went out we couldn't go on. I think we must give considerable attention to Italy.' "

(Diary) Chaumont, Friday, November 9, 1917. Came back from Paris by train Tuesday morning; brought along Mr. Charles R. Crane and Mr. Joseph E. Willard, Ambassador to Spain. General Pétain and three staff officers stopped for dinner in the evening. His confidential reports indicate Italians lack schools of instruction for staff and line officers. He thinks the Italian line will hold on the Piave.

Major Generals Kernan, Wm. M. Wright, and George Bell, lunched with us yesterday.

As French are behind on ordnance deliveries, have again strongly recommended production at home. Have recommended the use of Brest for deep draft transports. Directed another urgent cable be sent for motor transportation. Major Generals Blocksom, Treat, Greble, Edwards, and Sage took luncheon with us to-day.

Experienced Allied officers in position to know from observation were of the opinion that the Italian Army, especially its artillery, was not so efficient as it ought to have been and that the training of officers especially had been neglected. It was suspected that the Italian armies had been somewhat affected by the same doctrines that ruined Russia and that this tended to obscure the presence and the intentions of the large increase in enemy forces on that front. At any rate, whether this view was entirely correct or not, there was sufficient reason for me to give warning to our War Department by cable that precaution should be taken in America through the Intelligence Division, General Staff, and through the Department of Justice, supplemented by counter-propaganda through pulpit and press, if feasible, in order to prevent attempts at this sort of propaganda among our people and in our Army.

The ammunition question again became acute despite our agreements with the French and their positive assurances that they would make prompt deliveries, but their explanation was that we had not furnished the full amount of raw material required. In previous references to the prospects of procuring artillery of 75- and 155-millimeter calibers and ammunition for its use, it had been expected that nothing should diminish our efforts at home in their manufacture. But when the probability of delay and possible failure of the French to furnish ammunition for these guns was reported to Washington my cable met with the complacent reply, much to my surprise, that "the French Government must furnish it, for there is no other way of getting it. At the present time there is not in this country any actual output of ammunition of the types mentioned. None has been expected."

As the French contracts covered only a part of the amount deemed necessary, it was not understood why the Ordnance Department had done nothing. In view of the Italian disaster and the certainty of serious German offensives in France in the spring, the possibility of shortage in ammunition caused some apprehension. We were already behind in steel deliveries to the French by over 20,000 tons; the supply of powder and explosives was still uncertain; and the prospect of placing further contracts or even of obtaining regular deliveries on those already placed seemed doubtful. The establishment of our own sources of supply at home appeared vital, and setting forth the above situation by cable I added, "I cannot too strongly urge the greatest expedition in the production of artillery matériel and ammunition in America."

The difficulty of providing the French with raw material was largely due to the lack of shipping and, of course, to the unscientific use of what we had. The fact is that the ports at home were overcrowded with all sorts of material and supplies awaiting vessels. The French had over 600,000 tons of supplies at our seaboard which they were unable to move and they were clamoring for 150,000 additional tons of steel rails. The War Department had purchased over 100,000 tons of rails for us but had been able so far to ship only 30,000 tons. The optimistic view of the Department of a month previous that there would be plenty of shipping now began to look visionary.

As the situation in which we found ourselves regarding artillery ammunition was approaching a crisis, it became necessary to lay the whole question before the Inter-Allied Munitions Board. After a full investigation of their resources, both the French and British concluded that they could undertake to meet our requirements, with the distinct understanding that their plants must be greatly increased in capacity and that we should furnish raw materials promptly. General Bliss, Chief of the War Department General Staff, who arrived about this time, brought the latest data from home and his knowledge enabled him to give valuable assistance to General Williams, my Chief of Ordnance, before the Allied conference in our efforts to find a solution to the difficult munitions problem. He urged the manufacture at home of heavy guns and ammunition and also strongly reënforced my appeals for motor transportation.

The following letter from the Secretary of War had only recently been received and gave me an idea of some of his problems:

"September 10, 1917.

"My dear General Pershing:

"Your confidential letters of July 9th and 27th reached me safely, the latter through Mr. Frankfurter, whose observations and comments have most helpfully supplemented my information about the conditions in France and particularly about some aspects of your problem about which it would be difficult to get information in any other way.

"At present it seems questionable whether I should come to France. If it were possible for me to go incognito and go over the situation with you on the ground without the interruptions which would be necessary were it known that I was in the country, * * * while if I undertook to visit both London and Paris, my trip would be deemed to have a diplomatic character, which would be inopportune if not embarrassing. Moreover, it seems important for me not to relax my personal supervision of the preparation of supplies and men to be forwarded just at this time. But I am hopeful that I can come a little later and, when our camps are thoroughly established and our preparation going forward as smoothly as I trust it soon will, an absence would be less difficult here and perhaps more helpful to you.

"Meanwhile I am sure you will understand my frankness when I

tell you that your course from the moment you landed in England
has given both the President and me the greatest satisfaction and
pleasure. As you know, you started with our full confidence, but we
feel happy to have our judgment justified as it has been at every
point by your discretion, tact, and effective activity.

"The work of preparing the Army here has gone forward with
remarkable smoothness and in a day or two the National Guard will
be in its camps. Already a substantial part of it is in camp and has
begun its preparatory work. Meantime, the sixteen National Army
cantonments are substantially completed and the first contingent of
drafted men are being received apparently without confusion or excitement. Early in October the entire number will be assembled
and the arrangements promise speedy training for them, as their
officers have already been assembled at the cantonments, a course
of instruction prepared and the usual preliminary preparations for
active work either begun or well under way.

"On this side we hear rather frequently of the work your men
are doing. Such French officers as have come to us and have seen
your troops in France are enthusiastic in praise of their alertness
and spirit and, as the larger forces begin to arrive, no doubt even
more impressive exhibitions will be given of what our people can do.

"There are three points about which I am especially concerned and
about which I would be glad to have your confidential observations
whenever a convenient means of communicating with me presents
itself.

"1. I am especially concerned that our troops should not be engaged
in actual fighting in France until they are there in such numbers
and have made such thorough preparation that their first appearance
will be encouraging both to their own morale and to the spirit of
our people here. I think it goes without saying that the Germans
will make a very special effort to strike swiftly and strongly against
any part of the line which we undertake to defend, in order to be
able to report to their people encouragingly about our participation
and also with the object of discouraging our soldiers and our people as
much as possible. I have no doubt this has all been present to your
mind and I refer to it only because I want you to know that we will
exercise all the patience necessary on this side and will not ask you
to put your troops into action until in your own judgment both
the time is opportune and the preparations thoroughly adequate.

"2. In the matter of selecting corps and division commanders, I
constantly feel that I ought to have your advice and judgment. You
realize of course the difficulty of selecting division commanders out
of our army, made up as it is of very zealous and fine men but

necessarily men who have had no experience with the sort of warfare now being waged and few if any of them having even had the experience of actually commanding a division of troops in maneuvers. From all that you have said, supplemented by all I have learned elsewhere, the need for young and physically strong men is apparent and I am perfectly willing to go any limit in meeting this requirement. It will, of course, necessitate passing over a substantial number of our older general officers who are very eager to go to France and who in their own ideas and that of the country have certain right to be preferred; but their occupation here in the training of troops is, of course, a valuable contribution to the cause and, whenever I can feel sure in the selection of the younger man that he actually has the capacity to develop to a sufficient extent to justify his being preferred to a man of greater experience, I shall not hesitate. But most of these younger officers present problems of judgment and foresight, and your advice on the subject would be most helpful. At present I am planning to send practically all of the general officers to France for a visit to the front, so that they will come back to their training camps with actual knowledge of the conditions of present methods of warfare. After they have been to France, they are to call on me individually to report and I hope in that way to have opportunity to make personal estimate of their vigor and alertness both of mind and body. In the meantime, you of course will see them all while they are in France and I would be grateful if you would let me have an estimate of the impressions they make on you while they are actually at the scene of war and studying the conditions at the front.

"3. In this country, we have been able to surround our camps with an environment far better than any soldiers in this country have ever had. The problem of drink is certainly under control and the problem of prostitution is in a better condition than we have ever had it. When our troops get to France, however, both of these problems present new and difficult aspects. The local police situation is, of course, difficult, and I have no notion what steps can be taken to minimize these two evils. I think, before very long, I shall ask Mr. Raymond Fosdick, chairman of our recreational committee, to visit France and see whether any helpful solution of these problems can be afforded by an extension of the recreational system which we are devising here to our camps in France. * * *

"There is a fourth subject upon which I want to say a confidential word. General Scott will retire on the 22d of this month. He will, of course, be called back into active service and put in charge of one of our training camps where his fine character and soldierly experience will be an inspiring example to the young men under him. General Bliss, who has three times acted as Chief of Staff, will succeed General Scott for the few months which intervene until his own retirement. But when General Bliss retires in November (December), it will be necessary to select a Chief of Staff and my strong desire is to have a young man who has had some months of experience in France. My mind has rather run in the direction of General March who, by the middle of November, will have had an excellent opportunity to become familiar with the whole situation abroad and whose experience in the War Department has been such that there would be no loss of time on his part in understanding the intricacies of bureau operation here. In addition to that, he is a man of positive and decided character. I realize, of course, that bringing General March away might be a serious loss to you and I have by no means decided upon him for the place, but I would like to have your judgment on this question. It seems to me that coöperation in Washington is of an importance impossible to overestimate and that we can assure it best by having a young, aggressive man who will realize from actual observation and participation your difficulties and be able to understand from the least hint just what is necessary for us to do to be of the maximum support to you.

"With cordial regards, believe me,
"Sincerely yours,
"NEWTON D. BAKER,
"Secretary of War."

In view of the emergency that was so clearly set forth by the Joffre (Viviani) and Balfour Missions when they visited the United States, and which was confirmed after my arrival in France and reported with all emphasis, I have never been able to understand the unnecessary delay due to waiting six months for the construction of large cantonments before calling out men and assembling them for training. Of course it was particularly urgent that the specialists and laborers needed in France to build up our facilities should have been provided as fast as they could be profitably employed, but nothing should have postponed the immediate mobilization of the combat units of the Regular Army and the National Guard. Each of these categories could have been brought to war strength with a proportion of its trained officers and men as a nucleus, reserving the rest for duty in training camps and for assignment to new units. In this way we could have put a greater number of trained units into battle much easier than we did, and without delaying the training of the new army. As it was, the services of most of these already partially trained organizations, especially those of the Regular Army, were not available abroad until it was all but too late.

The following was my reply to the Secretary:

"France, November 13, 1917.

"DEAR MR. SECRETARY:

"Your letter of September 10th was handed to me by General Treat. First of all, I wish to thank you most sincerely for your cordial expressions of approval for what has been done. It has not been easy at all times to determine the best course to pursue. The British and the French, as you know, are each watching out that the other does not receive too much attention from us. So far we have succeeded in steering fairly clear of breakers, as I have persistently tried to impress both allies that our whole purpose here is to assist in every possible way in beating our common enemy, without any thought of leaning toward one ally more than the other.

"With reference to our entering the trenches for active service, I have emphasized the necessity of thorough preparation, and have been following a logical program leading up to the important final training of artillery and infantry in coöperation. This has been accepted as sound by the military authorities, both French and English, so that unless something very threatening should occur, we should not go in until we are ready. Of course, even then there will be much to learn from actual experience.

"In all my conferences with General Pétain on this subject we have fully agreed that, when our troops go into their sector, they would be fully supported by the French artillery and be in close touch with their infantry. It is also our joint idea that every effort should be made to have the first clash, if possible, a victory for the Americans. Such a result would of course raise the morale of our allies and correspondingly depress the enemy. General Pétain is in full accord with this view, and I am sure that when the time comes he will coöperate to the fullest extent to bring about such a result.

"The venereal and the liquor problems are both extremely difficult. The greatest danger points seem to be our ports of entry. I have recommended to the Minister of War that he declare a 'state of siege' at both Bordeaux and Saint Nazaire, and he has promised to do it. Such a state practically exists in Saint Nazaire already. This corresponds to our martial law and the control of these questions would then be in the hands of the local French military commanders, who, in coöperation with our local commanders, under stringent orders, should be able to keep the ports comparatively clean. There is another serious question there, too, and that is the large number of spies that continuously infest these ports. Martial law should give us a much better control of that danger.

"In the training areas men are kept busy and as this region is entirely under army control the above problems are less difficult, although not easy there. I have established a series of medical aid stations in these areas for the sole benefit of the French people, in coöperation with the leading local French women. This effort is very much appreciated by the inhabitants who, for the most part, have been left almost without medical attention. It is also hoped that venereal cases among the women may eventually visit these dispensaries for treatment. The organization of these stations has been placed under Major Hugh H. Young, who is one of Johns Hopkins' most famous doctors, and who has made a specialty of this class of disease.

"By publishing in orders the ravages of venereal disease in Europe, and the constant dangers of uncontrolled sexual relations, and by encouraging Y.M.C.A. work, and demanding the interest of officers in the welfare of their men, an excellent foundation has been laid. I feel much pleased with the attitude of the army toward this question and am gratified at what is being accomplished toward morality. I shall be very glad to have Dr. Fosdick make a visit here to study the situation and give us the benefit of his experience and advice. We cannot do too much to protect our young men from immorality and consequent disease, to say nothing of its effect upon our fighting strength.

"With relation to the general officers, I wrote you in my letter of October 4th my views in general, and my opinion of several of these officers in particular. * * * I would emphasize my remarks with reference to the others mentioned in my former letter, and am adding some further comment in the enclosure herewith.

"Generally speaking, the young and active officers of a command look upon their division commander as their leader, and if he is inactive they lack the confidence in him necessary to his success. Such a man becomes more or less a figurehead instead of a soldier in whom they believe. The position of division commanders is so important that it may be very truly said the success of this war depends upon them. If a division commander does not know his work and is not up to the high standard found in the Allied armies, he has no place in our army here.

"The matter of recommending a Chief of Staff, and I may say of selecting men in general for important assignments, is the most difficult thing that has so far confronted me, and I can readily understand how puzzling it must be for you. * * * I am very favorably inclined toward General Biddle, and I think perhaps you will find him a broad-minded, energetic man who may measure up to your ideal. * * *

"Next to him, I have an idea that General March would make a good executive. I have always had a high opinion of March and had often thought of him as timber for Chief of Staff, even before I received your letter. I think March is a strong man and that he would be of great assistance to you, especially in the possible reorganization of the War Department, which I think you are going to find necessary. I should miss him here but consider your need the greater.

"I shall have General March come to my headquarters at an early date in order that he may make a study of the general staff organization that I have established here. All of the visiting general officers have been impressed with the plan and especially with the very complete coördination of all staff and supply departments under one control. It might be advisable to have a study made of it for application in the War Department.

"There may be other officers who would do better, but it would be a chance, so therefore I recommend to you the consideration of General Biddle as your Chief of Staff and General March as his assistant. You will then have two good men, and if General Biddle [1] should not turn out to be the man I think he is you would have General March there to take his place or to retain as assistant in case you should not be satisfied as to his qualifications for chief, and conclude to select some one else.

"Just a word as to the supply departments. The general officers sent over complain that their divisions are not being provided with equipment, especially transportation, and say they are told that their transportation and other things that are lacking will be furnished upon arrival in France. Of course there is no transportation here and little else that does not come from home, so that our organizations are now arriving without adequate transportation and generally with none. [2]

"It seems to me quite necessary that each division should be as-

[1] I had a high opinion of General John Biddle and thought that having been in France and England he would measure up to the position of Chief of Staff. Before leaving, however, he said to me that he did not consider himself fitted for the place.

[2] This was unquestionable proof of the inefficiency of the supply department responsible.

sembled at some point near the port of embarkation, where it can be fully equipped and the division commander be given an opportunity to see that he has everything in readiness. This would insure his being prepared to take care of himself upon arrival here, and would avoid confusion in issuing initial equipment at this end and possibly the more serious inconvenience of not having it at all. I send you this as I get it, as it may not have reached you in just this light.

"The War Department now has our complete project for troops and supplies, estimated on a basis of 1,200,000 men. It also has the priority schedule for both personnel and matériel. So there should be less difficulty in handling both when the personnel is organized, and if the supplies are available. In making these comments I do not fail, Mr. Secretary, to appreciate the enormity of your problems, but make them with a view to aiding you in their solution.

"General Bliss and the other members of the Allied conference are in London. I hope to have an opportunity to go over in detail many things with General Bliss before he returns. I am writing you in a separate letter a discussion of the general military situation.

"In conclusion, Mr. Secretary, permit me to congratulate you and the country in that we have you as a Secretary. You are doing a great work and doing it well. May I ask you, at your convenience, to extend to the President my most loyal greetings.

"Believe me, with sincere personal and official regard,
"Your humble servant,
"JOHN J. PERSHING."

Enclosure.

"COMMENTS ON GENERAL OFFICERS

"Confidential for the Secretary of War.

*   *   *   *   *   *   *

"As to other officers mentioned in my former memorandum * * * I am more thoroughly convinced than ever that none of them is alert or physically up to the requirements, and most of them are too old anyway to begin to learn the important duties that would be required of them. * * *

"With regard to sending officers over as observers to return to their divisions, I would suggest that only those known to be entirely fit should be sent, unless you want them especially to train troops at home later.

"Allow me to suggest, Mr. Secretary, that all division and brigade commanders be very closely observed at home, and their attitude, their activity and prowess in training these units be fully taken into consideration and reported upon before it is finally decided to send them over with their commands.

"J. J. P."

Soon after the receipt of the Secretary's letter of September 10th, which was handed to me early in November, it became necessary to report adversely on the fitness of a number of the Major Generals who had been sent over for a visit to the various armies as observers. My message read in part as follows:

"Earnestly request that only division commanders who have strong mental and physical vigor be sent here as observers. Division commanders who are in any way unable to stand continuous work actually in the trenches under conditions found on the Western Front are useless here. Consider it imposition on Allies to send officers not fit in every particular."

To this cable came the prompt reply:

"With reference to your * * * every effort will be made to send you suitable division commanders. * * * You will be thoroughly supported in the relief of any officers you care to relieve. * * *"

CHAPTER XVII

Tank Construction—Visit to 26th Division—Military Situation—Letter to
Secretary of War—Painlevé Ministry Overthrown—Clemenceau
Premier—Motor Transport Corps—Control of Shipping by British—
American Tonnage—Cambrai Offensive

(Diary) Chaumont, Wednesday, November 14, 1917. Held conference Saturday on tank question and authorized agreement with
British for manufacture of the heavy type.

On Sunday visited 26th Division in billets near Neufchâteau.

Senator Kendrick, an old friend from Wyoming, and Senator Kenyon, of Iowa, came to lunch to-day.

British insist on steel billets and lumber in return for steel products, coal and huts.

UP to this time our efforts to arrange with the Allies for the
tanks we should need had resulted only in half promises
for a limited number, with considerable doubt whether
in the end we should get any at all from either the French or
British. With no previous plans for their manufacture, the prospects of obtaining tanks from home by the time they should be
required for operations seemed so remote that it appeared best
to arrange, if possible, for their manufacture overseas. Meanwhile, an Inter-Allied Tank Commission was formed and Major
James G. Drain was appointed the American member. As the
French decided to take no active part, the British proposed that
we undertake the manufacture of heavy tanks jointly with them,
so, upon the conclusion of my conference with Major Drain and
Captain Sanderson, of the British Army, approval was given to
the plan. It was understood that the British would build the
hulls and we would furnish the motors and chassis, the assembling to be done in France.

The units of the 26th Division, Major General Clarence Edwards commanding, began to arrive during the latter part of

September, continued during October, and were now assembled in the billeting area near Neufchâteau. Meanwhile it was necessary to use a part of the division on the Line of Communications because of lack of labor troops. At my inspection, the various organizations presented a very creditable appearance, the officers seemed alert and military, and the personnel looked strong and vigorous. Their instruction had been carried out under the direction of Brigadier General Peter E. Traub, one of the brigade commanders, and was reported to be well advanced. As this division was composed of National Guard units from the New England States, whose troops had borne a fine reputation in all our wars, its preparation for active service was watched with great interest.

The Allies were much concerned over their probable situation in the spring with respect to manpower. The Germans had captured Riga in September. Kerensky's power was at an end and the Bolsheviki government was established, with Lenin and Trotsky in control, and there was no longer any doubt that Russia had become entirely negligible as far as assistance to the Allies was concerned.

An analysis of the probable relative strength of the contestants by early spring showed that Germany would be able to spare a considerable number of divisions from the Russian front. Careful study by my staff, in coöperation with the Allied staffs, had led to the conclusion that the total number of German divisions in the West might be as many as 217, not counting the rather remote possibility of the added strength of 48 divisions from Austria. The greatest number the Allies could muster, according to estimates, would be 169 divisions, or considering two American divisions as four because of their double strength, the number would be 171. Italy could not be counted on for some time to do more than barely hold her own, even with the help of the eleven Allied divisions then on the Italian front. Other American divisions might possibly be in Europe by May 1st, if they should arrive according to schedule, which was doubtful, but the later divisions would be too late to participate in the expected spring operations. At the slow rate of arrival, we should not have more than half of the twenty-one divisions promised by the War Department ready for service by June.

With these possibilities before me I wrote the Secretary of War, setting forth our estimate of the situation and urging that the utmost efforts be exerted to hasten the arrival of American forces. The main points of my letter are quoted as showing the situation as it appeared at the time:

"November 15, 1917.

"DEAR MR. SECRETARY:

"It seems advisable at this time to send you in this personal way a résumé of the situation here as it appears to me. I am sending a similar letter to General Biddle.[1]

"With reference to memorandum prepared by the Allied Council in August and forwarded to the War Department, recent events on the Russian and Italian fronts now require us to give careful consideration to the problem outlined in that memorandum. * * *

"At the outset it should be remembered that the Central Powers, while relying mainly upon their armies to secure favorable terms of peace, are using every possible means to stir up strife among the people of each of the Allied nations and to create dissension among the powers themselves. As viewed by the world at large, the success of the Central Powers by whatever means would be attributed solely to military prowess. It will therefore be necessary to break their military resistance if the Allies are to dictate the terms of peace. If possible, this ought to be done before the French and British are too weak to stand against the extreme efforts Germany will make to win before the United States seriously enters the war.

"As a result of the several British and French offensives, the German strength on the Western Front has been very much weakened during the past summer. Of the 150 divisions she now has on the Western Front, only 60 are able to take the offensive. Her regiments have suffered serious losses that will have to be made up from the 1920 class—the 18-year-old boys. It is estimated that she will have only about 500,000 of these to put in the lines for the spring campaign, and on the average these will not be of high fighting value. Her annual losses since the beginning have been about 800,000 estimated, so that her manpower will begin to run down about May or June. * * * Conceding this estimate of manpower as correct, we have another reason to believe that the supreme effort of the Central Powers will be exerted between now and midsummer of 1918.

[1] General Biddle was Acting Chief of Staff at Washington at that time.

" * * * The Allied forces cannot be materially increased on any front until America brings her strength into the war. To carry out an Allied offensive on any other than the Western Front with the forces now available would compel a defensive attitude in that theater. * * * The psychological effect on the French and Italian people and probably upon the British and our own people as well of such a defensive rôle would be as depressing to them as it would be encouraging to our enemies.

"Under probable conditions, an Allied offensive on the Western Front could not be carried on by the French or Italians without the British; and the strength of these three powers will probably be so low that the Americans will also be needed. It seems clear to me that the war must be won on the Western Front, and that the efforts of the Allies should continue as now in progress. * * *

" * * * Only a few German divisions have been brought from there (Russia) to the Western Front. * * * As long as Russia does not actually conclude a separate peace, Germany will have to keep a certain number of divisions there.

"Distribution of German Divisions

"It is estimated that there are 150 German divisions on the Western Front; 78 on the Eastern Front; 2 on the Macedonian Front; and 9 on the Italian Front. Of the 78 divisions on the Eastern Front, it is believed that only 36 are fit to take active place against the Allies in the West. Some 22 are capable only of defensive action, and 20 are new levies of Landwehr troops. * * * The 9 divisions in Italy are fit for the offensive anywhere, but the 2 divisions in Macedonia are not likely to be removed.

" * * * Three months would suffice to transfer these divisions to the West. Of 90 divisions on the Western Front not now considered fit to take the offensive, it is estimated that by February 1st 60 will be sufficiently rested to take their places in the line. These, plus the 45 good divisions from the East [1] and the 60 intact in the West, make 165. If we add the 22 Eastern defensive divisions and the remaining 30 in the West, we should have 217.

"Austro-Hungarian Divisions

"It is estimated that 25 Austrian divisions are on the Eastern Front, 2 divisions on the Albanian Front, and 49 divisions on the Italian Front. On the Eastern Front (cavalry excluded) 16 divisions are estimated as 1st class, and 9 as 2d class divisions.

[1] 36 from the Eastern Front and 9 from the Italian Front.

"In Italy, 34 divisions are 1st class and 15 divisions are 2d class. The two in Albania could not well be withdrawn. Of the total, 50 Austrian divisions are sufficiently good to be employed on the Western Front, and the rest would do for the defensive there or elsewhere.

"Seventy-four divisions would then be available if a separate peace were made with both Russia and Italy. If a separate peace were made with Russia only, the number of troops to be held in Italy would only depend upon the line. Assuming the line to be the Adige, and that it were held against Italian troops, 20 divisions on the line and 6 in reserve would probably make it sufficiently secure, so that with these 48 Austrian divisions, Germany might then bring her total number of disposal divisions on the Western Front from 217 to 265.

* * * * * * *

"The situation in Italy remains uncertain, but it would appear that she has awakened to the point of putting forth her entire strength, which should enable her to hold her defensive positions. * * *

"Relative Strength

"The number of British divisions on the Western Front is now 58; French, 102; American, 2; Portuguese, 1; and of Belgian, 6; making a total of 169 organized and suitable for offensive action, except the Americans.

* * * * * * *

"With their superiority of about 30 per cent, the Allies have been able to do nothing more on the offensive than to wear down German strength little by little. In turn, an approximate superiority by the Germans, while it would justify them in an offensive, would not necessarily mean a break of the Allies on the Western Front. * * *

"In artillery, still more in munition supply, and in aircraft, the Allies have a superiority with the power of increasing that superiority very greatly. In reserves of manpower the Allies, including America, of course, will soon have a still greater superiority.

"As to France, she cannot be counted on to increase the number or strength of her divisions, and the British will probably be able only to hold theirs at present strength. * * *

"Taking what appears now to be the most unfavorable view (always conceding that France herself will not give way), and considering Russia out of the war, and Italy holding on behind the Adige, it would be possible for the Central Powers to bring 265 divisions (German 217, and Austrian, 48) against 169 Allied divisions on the Western Front. Even under these adverse conditions, it is possible that the Allies would be able to hold their defensive, but it points clearly to the necessity for the utmost effort on our part.

"Other Powers

"The entry of Switzerland into the war has not been considered, but such action is a possibility, and every means should be exerted to bring her in on the side of the Allies, or keep her out altogether. * * *

"As to Spain, if she could be induced to enter on the side of the Allies, it would add considerable force for the defense of the Western Front, and would secure valuable sources of supply. It would guarantee the flow of metals to the Allies, as well as close the Spanish coast as a base for U-boat activities. * * *

"Japan's possible active participation has not been mentioned. Her shipping, at least, should be made available for us, and her arsenals as a source of ordnance supply ought to be given serious thought, not to mention her armies. My remarks on these three countries are presented as having urgent bearing on the general situation.

"General

"It may be accepted that German propaganda is always at work and should be met by counter-propaganda regardless of its cost. This especially applies to Russia, where no stone should be left unturned to counteract Germany's influence there and if possible place Russia again actively in the war.

"The utmost coöperation among the Allies must be secured. The recent endeavor to get the Allies to take a broad general view of the war as a whole shows an awakening. Hitherto, each nation has largely considered only its own interests, thus enabling Germany to beat her enemies in detail.

"It may not have been possible to avoid the Russian collapse or to have saved Roumania, but as has been pointed out, it does seem that with a unified control the Italian failure might have been avoided.

"Conclusions

"Viewed at its best, the situation is, of course, grave, and (this) should be fully realized. America must stand firmly behind the Allies, as any sign of weakness may cause the collapse of Allied resistance. The contingency must also be faced of Great Britain and ourselves being left to carry on the war without material aid from any other power. I have pointed out the dark side of the picture, but in war we must prepare to meet the worst.

"The conclusions, from the purely military standpoint, are evident, and are no doubt fully appreciated, but they cannot be over-emphasized in view of the German advantage that might confront us. It is therefore urged that—

"1. The most intense energy should be put into developing America's fighting forces for active service during the coming summer. Winning the war is vital to our future, and if humanly possible it ought to be done in 1918. There is no telling what might happen if we defer our utmost exertion until 1919.

"2. All available sources of supply of artillery and ammunition should be investigated and developed, having in mind Japan's resources in this regard. France may not be able to meet even our early requirements.

"3. Finally, every possible ton of shipping should be secured by purchase, construction, or otherwise, in the Orient or elsewhere, with the least delay for use in carrying our armies to France.

"It should be no longer a question of how much tonnage can be spared for military purposes, but only the most imperative necessity should permit its use for any other purpose. To secure this result the whole of our shipping ought to be under War Department control, and as much more obtained as possible from neutral or Allied sources.

"Please pardon the length of this note, and accept my high esteem and very sincere regards.

"Yours faithfully,

"John J. Pershing."

In this war, where the battle lines extended across entire countries, and in which the qualities of the opponents, man for man, were about equal, the outcome was largely a question as to the number and location of divisions on either side; hence the detailed discussion in my letter to the Secretary. In the end success would lie with the side which could provide the necessary superiority of force. In other words, it would depend upon the number of troops that America could send over.

All eyes were on the Eastern Front. To Allied statesmen the collapse of Russia meant possible grave political consequences; to the Allied commanders it forecast the release of approximately 100 divisions and the increase in the enemy's ranks in Belgium and northern France to a preponderance that would be difficult to resist. To us it indicated a race between America's best effort to pour our fighting men into France, and Germany's determination to crush the Allies before our soldiers could arrive in sufficient numbers to dominate the battlefield.

(Diary) Paris, Sunday, November 18, 1917. On Friday inspected trenches of 1st Division, still in sector northeast of Lunéville. Saw several men who were with me in Mexico. Went to headquarters French 18th Division, Major General Bordeaux. Visited graves of three American soldiers recently killed in trench raid.

Major General Morrison dined with us last night.

The Painlevé Ministry has fallen and M. Clemenceau succeeded in forming a new Ministry on Friday.

Reports from all quarters complain of shortage of trucks. Sent cable regarding British control of neutral shipping.

Motored from Chaumont and dined this evening at de Chambrun's with Tardieu.

During my visit to the 1st Division the officers of the French units serving with our regiments spoke with deep feeling of the first Americans to lose their lives at the front. They praised the bravery and courage of the detachment as though the men had been their own. The spirit of comradeship that prompted such sentiment naturally served to draw us closer together and stimulated coöperation as to material things.

A change in the ministry in France had been expected for some time and when M. Painlevé's Government fell on November 15th it occasioned no surprise. Among the reasons given for its unpopularity were the general disapproval of the Supreme War Council, the timidity of the Prime Minister in not pressing charges of disloyalty against high French officials, the cumulative opposition to the Government by many people looking for some one to blame for their misfortune, including Nivelle's failure, and the existence of pessimism in general. The main political fight against M. Painlevé was made by M. Clemenceau, who, as President of the Legislative War Committee, had attained an immense popularity because of his condemnation of the alleged pacifistic tendencies of some of the members of the Ministry. It was, therefore, logical from the French point of view, that he should be selected to form the new Ministry.

Once he became Prime Minister, M. Clemenceau lost no time

in attempting to clear the administrative offices of red tape. He took up energetically the whole question of scandals and vigorously attacked socialistic tendencies. He proclaimed that there were to be "no more pacifistic campaigns, no more German intrigues, and neither treason nor half treason." He tried to get into communication with Kerensky having in view the mobilization of what remained of disciplined forces in southern Russia, but his efforts were fruitless. All these steps demonstrated his activity and his aggressiveness.

By further reference to the diary, a shortage of trucks is noted, and my thoughts revert to our only experience in this field prior to the World War, when the expeditionary forces which I commanded in Mexico were supplied by truck trains managed from Columbus, New Mexico. Although the roads in northern Chihuahua were little more than cross-country trails used by mule teams in supplying the sparsely settled districts, our trucks operated at one time to a distance of more than two hundred miles from the border. The country was dry and the roads rarely muddy, but, with exceptional stretches where the surface was hard-pan or caliche, the soil was generally sandy and the roads required an excessive amount of repair by the engineers. As the distance from the border increased, the need for trucks became greater until altogether twenty-two companies of twenty-five trucks each were in operation, with complete repair shops and a large depot of spare parts at Columbus. Officers and men trained in the management of truck transportation under these adverse conditions became the nucleus of our motor truck organization in France.

The use of motor transport had become an absolute necessity, not only in the supply of troops but in transporting them from one field of activity to another, often in the emergency of battle. An army without such facility for ordinary purposes and without a reserve to meet the exigencies of operations could not be considered as prepared to engage successfully an adversary who was so equipped. It was estimated that our requirements, calculated from our own data and that of our Allies, would be some 50,000 motor vehicles, with an unlimited reserve of spare parts. Our priority schedules contemplated an increasing allowance of motor transportation to correspond to the growth of our forces, but despite my most urgent appeals and the resulting promises from Washington we had to borrow, even at this time, large numbers of trucks from the French.

It was evident almost from the first that the importance of this service demanded that it should have a separate organization. For the time being it was left under the Quartermaster Corps, but eventually it came under the Commanding General, Line of Communications.[1] In anticipation of a full equipment of motor vehicles for our armies, a skeleton organization was created, with extensive depots, repair shops, and the necessary schools for mechanics and chauffeurs.

With our country by far the greatest producer in the world of automobiles and trucks, it was surprising that we were so poorly equipped with them. Advices at one time indicated that the War Department was waiting for our allowance to be manufactured before sending any to France. This, of course, was quite out of the question, and I suggested that the cantonments at home might use horse-drawn vehicles and that their motor transportation be sent to us. It was also suspected that the transport bureau of the Quartermaster Corps at home, not realizing the extent to which motor vehicles were needed, thought our requests excessive.

As to ocean transportation, practically all neutral tonnage then considered available on time charter, was under the Norwegian flag. In attempting to obtain some of this shipping we learned that it was controlled by the Inter-Allied Chartering Executive, orginally organized with representatives of Great Britain, France and Italy, but reported to be dominated by the British Admiralty. The latter dictated the chartering of such tonnage by withholding bunker facilities if any charters were granted without its specific approval. Notification that bunker facilities would be thus with-

---

[1] Motor Transportation was placed under Lt. Col. F. H. Pope, of the Quartermaster Corps, in August, 1917. Col. Pope was succeeded by Brig. Gen. Meriwether Walker, July 9, 1918, when Motor Transportation was made an independent service.

held served on the Norwegian Association of Shipowners by the Chartering Executive was said to have brought about a law in Norway prohibiting charter without the consent of the Association, which practically resulted in placing control in the hands of the British. Even the French Government itself was unable to obtain vessels badly needed, despite the fact that it offered special premiums for direct charters.

In our own case, after signing a charter for eleven steamers, subject to approval of the Norwegian Association, our application was rejected. Knowledge of available shipping always reached London first and the British were at that time not seriously restrained by any sentiment for the Allies or generally speaking by considerations other than those which affected their immediate interests. This attitude in regard to granting the use of shipping to others was apparently little affected by their requirements, as the spirit of coöperation did not then prevail in any liberal sense either among Allied governments, or among their armies.

Our estimate of tonnage required to transport and supply the twenty-four combat divisions and S.O.S. troops which it was considered essential to have in France by the end of June showed that the amount then allotted to us would have to be increased up to May by 2,000,000 tons. No one seemed to know where we were to obtain this additional shipping. It appeared certain then that should disaster befall the Allied armies under these conditions we would be left in an almost hopeless situation.

Taken as a whole, the apparently slow progress of our preparation in Europe caused considerable adverse comment, if not dismay, among the Allies. Inquiries were made directly by the military and civil officials as to why we did not move more rapidly, to which the reply was always, "lack of shipping." It might have been added also that it was due partly to the backward state of our preparations. I always felt confident, however, that tonnage could be found for our purposes if the necessary pressure were exerted to force it into use. Appeals were made continuously and persistently in an effort to get action at home on this vital question, but several months elapsed and a crisis came before relief appeared.

About this time there were difficulties at our end of the line. The sea transport service, then under the Quartermaster Corps, claimed that the congestion of freight at St. Nazaire, and to a lesser degree at Bordeaux, was due to the failure of the railways to remove it promptly. The railway management contended that the Quartermaster Corps was interested only in clearing the ships and would do little to expedite the loading of cars directly therefrom. In order to remove this source of friction, the discharge of vessels was placed under the Transportation Department. As a result, there was much improvement both in the clearing of vessels and in the movement of freight. Another cause of delay in the turn-around of ships was the lack of ballast for returning transports, which had often to wait several days before the necessary quantity of sand, which was ordinarily used, could be obtained.

Regardless of the cause, these delays without doubt served to encourage Allied hopes that we might finally be forced to allow our men to be used as drafts, and made it more difficult to carry out in France the details of arrangements for equipping and organizing an independent army.

(Diary) Paris, Wednesday, November 21, 1917. By invitation, I arrived at British G.H.Q. Monday evening to observe Cambrai offensive. Went over plans with Chief of Staff, Lieutenant General Sir L. E. Kiggell, and the Operations Officer. Attack made yesterday. Returned to Paris. Called on M. Clemenceau this morning. He is well along in years, not strong physically, but vigorous of mind. He spoke in favor of an energetic war policy. Saw Atterbury and discussed continued shortage of freight cars. Am urging haste in sending over car erecting forces and cars.

Immobilized by the mud of Flanders, where British attacks had continued intermittently from the end of July to the middle of November, with rather excessive losses,[1] the British Commander-in-Chief turned to a more southerly portion of his line for the

[1]The casualties in the battle of Ypres, July 31-Nov. 10, were more than 270,000.

final offensive of the year. Choosing the Cambrai front on which to launch the effort, careful preparations, including the concentration of an unusual number of tanks, were made to insure success in overcoming the German defense. The tanks and the infantry were to break through the lines, after which the cavalry was to follow and assault the flanks of the enemy. The French troops held in readiness in the vicinity were to enter and assist. The command of these combined forces when both should become engaged was to be left to the senior general officer in the vicinity, who might be either French or British. In going over the plans, it seemed to me that their idea of securing coöperation after the French should go in was rather vague.

On the first day of the attack, I went to visit General Byng, commanding the British Third Army, who explained further details of the plans and the progress already made. He and his Chief of Staff were busy receiving news from the front and were confident that all was going well. General Byng is a large, fine-looking man and a high type of British soldier, vigorous, forceful, and efficient.

While awaiting the development of the attack, I expressed a wish to visit a field hospital in operation, to which General Byng readily assented, sending Major Watson, a medical officer, along as a guide. We motored towards the front, meeting many groups of prisoners, and shortly reached the hospital. Considerable numbers of the wounded were being brought in and many were there already awaiting their turn. I followed the handling of the patients from the time they arrived until they were tagged for further disposition. Most of the men seemed cheerful and were pleased over what was believed to be a victory. I spoke to several of the poor fellows, among them being a mere boy with the rank of captain, who told me that he received his wound as he was crawling through the wire entanglement. He was especially keen to learn how the battle was going, quite unconcerned that he would probably lose a leg. Noticing several men on cots at one end of the room not receiving attention, and inquiring the reason, I was told in whispers that they were moved aside as being quite beyond hope. I was impressed with the efficiency with which this hospital was managed.

The attack was made on a six-mile front and the British had the advantage from the outset. The sudden debouchment of the long line of tanks, closely followed by the infantry, all without the usual warning of a long preliminary artillery bombardment, completely surprised the Germans. The tanks broke wide gaps in the wire and subdued the machine gun nests, aiding the infantry through the defenses with a minimum of loss.

The front was rather narrow, considering the depth of the objectives. A maximum gain of some four and a half miles was secured the first day and a greater result was prevented, it was said, by a serious check to the tanks at Flesquières. I remained at cavalry headquarters most of the afternoon, hoping to see something of how they handled this arm, in which I had spent many happy years in our own service. It was reported later that a bridge over the Scheldt Canal at Masnières was blown up, so the cavalry was not sent forward. The French were not called into action, presumably because the British cavalry, which was to precede them, could not go forward as planned. The offensive continued for two or three days longer with varying success. It was, however, a decided victory and while not so great as the British expected, it gave encouragement to the Allies on the Western Front and no doubt helped to offset temporarily the depressing effect of the serious defeat recently sustained by the Italian Army.

CHAPTER XVIII

Allied Conference—General Situation—Talk with House—Urge Increased
Program—Twenty-four Divisions by June—Robertson and Foch Ap-
prove—Determined Attitude—Meeting Supreme War Council—
Lloyd George's Note to Mr. House on Use of American Troops—
Recommend Regular Divisions—Training—Criticism of Italians

(Diary) Paris, Sunday, November 25, 1917. Delegates are gathering
for an Inter-Allied conference.[1] Talked with Winston Churchill
Thursday and think we may get some tonnage to bring over steel.

On Friday took General Bliss to call on M. Clemenceau. Had House
and Bliss to luncheon.

Attended luncheon given yesterday by President Poincaré to conference delegates.

Mrs. Whitelaw Reid has transferred to A.E.F. her hospital complete with beds for fifty officers.

THE Inter-Allied conference had been planned before the
meeting of Prime Ministers at Rapallo which had brought
the Supreme War Council into existence. It was one of
the periodical assemblies of Allied representatives held for the
discussion of problems of common interest concerning the conduct
of the war. Its purpose in the present instance was to consider
the most effective means by which the resources in men and
matériel of Allied countries, including the United States, could
be utilized. In an early, informal discussion with Mr. House
and General Bliss I gave them an outline of our situation, our
relations with the Allies, and the progress of our plans, and
explained to them the urgency of our requirements.

At the time the representatives of the different nationalities

[1] The Americans were: Mr. Edward M. House, Head of Mission; Ambassador Wil-
liam G. Sharp; Admiral William S. Benson, U. S. Navy, Chief of Operations; General
Tasker H. Bliss, U. S. Army, Chief of Staff; Oscar T. Crosby, for U. S. Treasury;
Vance McCormick, Chairman War Trade Board; Bainbridge Colby, Shipping Board;
Alonzo E. Taylor, for Mr. Hoover; Thomas N. Perkins, War Industries; and Paul D.
Cravath.

gathered in Paris, the current reports of decreasing losses of ocean tonnage and greater destruction of German submarines, with still better prospects in the future had given more of hopefulness to the general situation and had somewhat revived the spirits of the Allies.

The British had won at Cambrai and were making satisfactory progress in their advance on Jerusalem, which, it was said, would be facilitated by the use of their new base at Jaffa. The Italians seemed to have recovered their morale to a limited extent with the stiffening of their lines by British and French divisions, and had successfully held their own against the Austrian attack on the Piave. Although the enemy had made some advances in the Trentino, he had not been able to force an entrance to the Venetian plains. In Switzerland the economic concessions by the United States as to cotton and credits were hailed with satisfaction, which, coupled with the exports by the French, made it practically certain that Switzerland would remain neutral, although there had been a noticeable increase in pro-German sentiment there following the Italian disaster, with talk of a possible German invasion of eastern France through Switzerland.

On the other hand, some rumors were heard of a German-Bulgarian offensive against Salonika, while the armistice on the Eastern Front confirmed the worst fears regarding Russia. The successes of the Germans in Italy had given rise to peace hopes in Germany which proved embarrassing to the new Chancellor, von Hertling, but he had apparently established an accord among the leaders of Prussia, South Germany, and Austro-Hungary.

Not the least hopeful event for the Allies was the step just taken toward unity of command by the creation of the Supreme War Council. The decisive factor in the whole situation, however, if it could be utilized in time, was the tremendous economic and physical power of the United States. To make that power available before it was too late was the problem upon the solution of which depended the success of the Allied cause. Would the Allies see the solution and would they work together to apply it? That was the question.

(Diary) Paris, Thursday, November 29, 1917. Had Major General H. L. Scott, observer, as guest on Tuesday; brought him to Paris last night. Have named Major General F. J. Kernan Commander of Line of Communications, relieving Brigadier General Patrick, who will direct all construction. Brigadier General B. D. Foulois appointed Chief of the Air Service, vice Kenly.

This morning, accompanied by Harbord, attended Inter-Allied conference held at the French Ministry of Foreign Affairs. Afterwards conferred with Foch, Robertson, Bliss, and Vance McCormick.

Took Thanksgiving-day lunch at Hotel Palais d'Orsay with American Club. Heard good speeches by Viviani, Lawrence Benét, Bainbridge Colby and Tardieu. Called at our Embassy and afterward on General Robertson.

Have cabled Washington that heavy guns, howitzers, and mortars absolutely essential in successful offensive.

Before the assembly for the conference,[1] the American delegates, known as the "House party," Harbord and I, met informally in order to have a general understanding regarding our part in the proceedings. Mr. House gave us his ideas on the subject, and we then proceeded to the Ministry of Foreign Affairs where the meeting was to be held.

When all were seated around the table in the assembly room at the Ministry, M. Clemenceau, who presided, spoke briefly, setting forth the importance of the gathering, and the necessity of translating the noble spirit of the alliance into action. No attempts at oratory were in evidence, nor was there prolonged discourse on any subject. Naturally, questions concerning available manpower, shipping, munitions and supplies were mentioned in a general way, but the conference did little more than to agree that the study of the various subjects should be left to committees composed of Inter-Allied representatives.

It was very clear that everybody was looking to America to provide the additional manpower needed to give the Allies su-

[1] The delegates to this conference consisted of the Prime Ministers, Ministers of Foreign Affairs, Commanders-in-Chief, Chiefs of Staff, and other special representatives of the more important Allied nations, and those of various ranks and titles representing the smaller nations, delegates from sixteen nations, in all, being present as follows: France, Great Britain, United States, Italy, Japan, Belgium, Serbia, Roumania, Greece, Portugal, Montenegro, Brazil, Cuba, Russia, Siam, and China.

periority, and none of them were more eager to increase our forces than ourselves. For some time past our reliance upon the Allies for any considerable amount of tonnage had seemed almost in vain, and it looked as though we should have to depend upon our own limited resources for most of it.[1]

At the end of the session I asked Generals Foch, Robertson, and Bliss to meet with me for an exchange of views regarding a definite program to be recommended concerning the number of American troops that should be sent over by spring. I thought that the larger the program that could be agreed upon as necessary and possible the more likely we should be to obtain tonnage concessions from our own and British authorities. After some discussion with the officers mentioned, we found ourselves in agreement upon the proposal I had submitted, which is set forth substantially in the following cablegram:

"December 2, 1917.

"For Secretary of War and Chief of Staff.
"Par. 1.
"With the apparent total collapse of Russia and the recent success of the Central Powers in Italy, German morale is undoubtedly much improved and the probability of a serious offensive against the Western Front is greatly increased. In fact, information indicates German concentration in the Vosges opposite Nancy and also near the Swiss frontier. It seems probable that such an offensive may begin this winter. French military authorities are of this opinion and are actually moving troops to meet further developments at both above points. While it is not probable that the Central Powers can concentrate their full strength on the Western Front for some months, yet their resumption of the offensive clearly points out their purpose to push the war here before the Americans can bring over a large force.
"Par. 2.
"With Russia out of the war it is possible for the Central Powers to concentrate 250 to 260 divisions on the Western Front and still have a certain number on the Eastern Front and 26 divisions to hold the Italians. They could do this without interfering

---

[1] The British were giving some assistance in the transportation of men, but not nearly enough. American ships had carried up to November 1st, 67,218 men and the British 54,751.

with the *status quo* at Salonika, and these estimates do not take into account the possibilities of using Bulgarian or Turkish troops on the Western Front. Against these German and Austrian divisions the Allies have 169 divisions, some of which are under orders for Italy. This relative strength would give the Central Powers about 60 per cent advantage and make it difficult to hold them. The Allies have had about 30 per cent advantage all summer. Details set forth in letter to Secretary of War now en route.

"Par. 3.

"In view of these conditions it is of the utmost importance to the Allied cause that we move swiftly. The minimum number of troops that we should plan to have in France by the end of June is four army corps, or twenty-four divisions, in addition to the troops for service of the rear. Have impressed the present emergency upon General Bliss and other members of the conference. Generals Robertson, Foch, and Bliss agree with me that this is the minimum that should be aimed at. This figure is given as the lowest we should think of, and is no higher because the limit of available transportation would not seem to warrant it.

"Par. 4.

"A study of transportation facilities shows sufficient American tonnage to bring over this number of troops, but to do so there must be a reduction in the amount allotted to other than army needs. It is estimated that the shipping needed will have to be rapidly increased up to two million tons by May, in addition to the amount already allotted. The use of shipping for commercial purposes must be curtailed as much as possible. The Allies are very weak and we must come to their relief this year (1918). The year after may be too late. It is very doubtful if they can hold on until 1919 unless we give them a lot of support this year. It is therefore strongly recommended that a complete readjustment of transportation be made and that the needs of the War Department as set forth above be regarded as immediate. Further details of these requirements will be sent later.

"Par. 5.

"As to heavy artillery and ammunition it is now probable, after full consideration and investigation, that the British and French will be able to make up our deficiencies.

"Par. 6.

"The questions of sea transportation and artillery are under further discussion by the Allies and full report and recommendations will be made in few days.

"PERSHING."

Grave doubt existed generally as to the ability of the Allies to hold on until we should be able to afford assistance that would turn the balance in their favor. Nevertheless, there was no diminution of the fighting spirit among the leaders, as indicated particularly by the recent inauguration of a very vigorous war policy by M. Clemenceau. However, it was well known that in England outside of Government circles there was a sentiment in certain quarters in favor of ending the war by negotiation. One did not hear so very much of it in France, but those who held this view presented the argument that the Germans, having put Russia and Roumania, and possibly Italy, out of the war, would now have to fight only on the Western Front. They feared that the large numbers of German and Austrian troops that could be relieved from the Eastern Front, together with released prisoners, would give the Central Powers a formidable if not an overwhelming advantage in effective strength before the Americans could be brought over.

The ideas of a "reasonable man's peace" and "no desire to crush Germany," although characterized by the British Government as "pro-German" and "pacifistic," were, nevertheless, supported by not a few influential men, and openly so by Lord Lansdowne. This sort of a peace was also favored by several British newspapers, as reported to me at the time, notably by the *Manchester Guardian,* the *Daily News,* the *Westminster Gazette,* and *The Nation.* The existence of such sentiments without doubt had a more or less depressing effect, for the time being, upon British morale, and it certainly set the rest of us thinking, although, being in close personal touch with all the civil and military leaders, I was not at all of the opinion that it was generally taken seriously.

(Diary) Paris, Wednesday, December 5, 1917. Gave a small dinner on Friday to the Houses, the Sharps, Admirals Benson and Sims, and others.

Supreme War Council met on Saturday. The reverses of the British at Cambrai surprised everybody.

On Monday the second and final session of the Inter-Allied conference was held. President and Madame Poincaré gave formal dinner for all delegates that evening.

A large party, including the American delegates, the Ambassador and his family, and Lord Northcliffe, went yesterday by special train at my invitation to our training area.

Saw M. Clemenceau to-day regarding certain criticisms. Talked with Atterbury on dock construction. After conference with Foulois, made agreement with British for training 15,000 Air Service enlisted personnel in England. Dawes has secured some locomotives from Belgium. Encouraging cables promise shipments some heavy artillery, machine guns, horses, automobile mechanics, car erection forces, and cars.

The results of the British success at Cambrai were not to be permanent, as the Germans quickly retaliated. General von der Marwitz [1] hastily assembled a force of some fifteen divisions and on the 30th suddenly launched a violent counterattack. The British were short of reserves and before von der Marwitz was stopped his troops had regained most of the ground lost during the British attack. This surprising reverse of the British, close on the heels of the success of ten days before, came as a sort of warning of what the Allies might expect when their opponents should seriously assume the offensive in the spring. The turn of the tables against the British served to emphasize the actual pessimism that existed, of which there was considerable evidence at the meeting of the Supreme War Council a day or two later.

It was in this operation that a detachment of our 11th Regiment of Engineers serving with the British became engaged. The men, to the number of 280, were at work in the Gouzeaucourt railway yards when the Germans attacked. There were six killed, one officer and twelve men wounded, eleven men taken prisoners. Various units of the regiment fought with the British until their lines were reëstablished.

[1] General von der Marwitz afterward commanded the German armies on our front in the Meuse-Argonne.

NOTE: Total strength of the A.E.F. on November 30th, 7,696 officers, 118,254 enlisted men.

Divisional units arriving in November included nearly all elements of the 42d Division (National Guard, from twenty-six States and the District of Columbia), Major General W. A. Mann.

The session of December 1st at Versailles was the second conference of the Supreme War Council, the first having been held at Rapallo when the Council was created. Our representatives, political and military, at this meeting were Mr. House and General Bliss, respectively. At the opening session, M. Clemenceau drew attention to the general situation, referring especially to the collapse of Russia, the probable release of enemy troops from the Russian front, the adverse situation in Italy, the depletion of Allied manpower, and the reliance of the Allies on American assistance. He enjoined the military representatives [1] "to bear in mind that their function is to advise the Supreme War Council as a body and not merely as representatives of their respective nations on the Council, and that they should view the problems confronting them not from a national standpoint but from that of the Allies as a whole." The military representatives at this conference were instructed to examine the military situation and report their recommendations as to the future plan of operations, to study the condition in Italy from the offensive as well as from the defensive point of view; and to report on the utilization of the Belgian Army.

It was evident that the Supreme War Council was to become a kind of super-parliament not only for the discussion of resources, aims, and purposes, but for the determination of policies looking to concert of action in support of military efforts. The spirit in which the problems were approached at this meeting indicated that the Supreme War Council would sensibly promote coöperation among the powers.

When the second meeting of the Inter-Allied conference closed its sessions on December 3d, none of the questions brought before the first session could be settled, but they were taken up by the more permanent body, the Supreme War Council, which, as time went on, undertook to coördinate the work of the various committees which had been formed to handle the problems involved.

---

[1] The military representatives were: For France, General Weygand, who had relieved General Foch; for Italy, General Cadorna; for Great Britain, General Sir Henry Wilson; for the United States, General T. H. Bliss.

During the war, dinners and luncheons, formal and otherwise, were indispensable official features of these Inter-Allied gatherings, and, although infrequent, they no doubt aided in promoting good will and understanding. The dinner given at the Élysée Palace, with Madame Poincaré so graciously presiding, was quite in keeping with the reputation of the French for hospitality. It was interesting and picturesque, with the display of the gold lace of the foreign statesmen's dress, and the polished boots, belts, and spurs of the field uniforms of the army officers.

The special visit to our troops gave our delegates and friends a breath of optimistic ozone which must have been a relief from the supercharged atmosphere of depression and apprehension of the French capital. They were taken to the corps schools at Gondrecourt where they saw the different exercises of the various courses of instruction for officers and men. The glimpse of our G.H.Q. suggested some idea of our organization and of how the problems connected with building up and directing a modern army are worked out.

I had an interesting talk on the train with Lord Northcliffe regarding the formation of an American army and the possibility of sea transportation to bring it across. He thought his Government should do more to help with shipping, but like most Englishmen he believed it best for us to send our men for service with the British. He argued in favor of the proposal that Mr. Lloyd George had recently made to Mr. House that we should incorporate in their units any infantry that we might not be able to organize immediately into complete divisions of our own. I said, "It is all very well to make such an appeal to us but it is impossible to ignore our national viewpoint. The people themselves would not approve, even though the President should lean that way. I am strongly opposed to it. We cannot permit our men to serve under another flag except in an extreme emergency and then only temporarily." I also insisted that we could contribute more largely to Allied success by the use of the American Army as a unit.

Continuing, I said that there was nothing vainglorious in our attitude, but no people with a grain of national pride would consent to furnish men to build up the army of another nation. I pointed out to him that misunderstandings and recriminations would inevitably follow any reverse by such a mixed force, and that his Government had used none of their Colonials in any such way. It is quite certain that Northcliffe had not considered the subject from our point of view, for, at the conclusion of the conversation, he very frankly said that we were perfectly right. After that, so far as I am aware, he became a consistent advocate of the formation of an American army.

In another conversation, Mr. House asked my views of the proposal which had been sent to him by Mr. Lloyd George. The memorandum in question had been forwarded to Lord Reading for delivery to Mr. House, with a note by Mr. Lloyd George scribbled in his own hand as follows:

"2nd December, 1917.

"My dear R.

* * * * * * *

"The C.I.G.S. [Chief of the Imperial General Staff] is very anxious you should place the enclosed [memorandum] before Colonel House. I entirely concur and urge its acceptance. We shall be hard pressed to hold our own and keep Italy standing during 1918. Our manpower is pretty well exhausted. We can only call up men of 45-50, and boys of 17. France is done. The American soldiers will not be ready to fight as an army until late in 1918. Our experience proves that meanwhile we must keep the fight going. Even half-trained American companies or battalions would fight well if mixed with 2 or 3 years' veterans.

"Beg H. to consider this favorably.

"Yours,

"D.L.G."

Enclosure

* * * * * * *

"Would America therefore be ready to help in another way, as a temporary measure? When she first came into the war we hoped she might send some men for inclusion in the British Armies, as being clearly the quickest way of helping, but for reasons we quite understand she preferred to retain her national identity. No doubt she still desires to do so, but over and above the preparation of her divisions, and without interfering with it, would it be possible for her to provide a company of infantry to replace a British company in such a number of British battalions as America could bring over men? Even 100 such companies would be of the greatest value. Every consideration would of course be given to the companies, and *if they desired they could later on be recalled and posted to the American divisions.* It is thought that this mingling of American and British troops would establish a close and cordial feeling between the two armies, and would also give the American troops useful training. If this system is not possible would America find a battalion to replace a British battalion in as many brigades as possible. There would be no insuperable difficulty in meeting American wishes in any such matters as discipline, rations, and general maintenance. The only difficulty is American national sentiment which we quite understand. On the other hand the system suggested is clearly one which would the most rapidly afford much needed help during, perhaps, the most critical period of the war."

I told Mr. House that Mr. Lloyd George's plan would not do at all and gave him reasons for my belief, and my opinion as to what the result would be. This was, in fact, a revival of the plan put forward by the Balfour Mission. It never received support from any Americans except a few individuals, including some officers who were disposed to criticize generally the management of our interests in France, and who, for their own ulterior purposes, sought to gain the favorable opinion and receive the acclaim of the Allies. But Mr. House and all other upstanding, loyal Americans were from the start strongly in favor of building up our own army.

About this time, Mr. House told me that Pétain had criticized the American ideas of training and also that M. Loucheur, Minister of Munitions, had spoken about the rise in prices caused by American purchases. Mr. House had wisely suggested to these gentlemen, he said, that matters of this kind were for me to settle. I called without delay on M. Clemenceau and told him of the reports and explained my understanding about training agreements with Pétain and also the steps that had previously been taken by our Purchasing Board, in coöperation with his own bureaus, to prevent the rise in prices. I also told him that French dealers were largely to blame if prices had risen, as we had eliminated competition among ourselves, and that our purchases were and had been for some time actually handled through French officials.

I objected to these back-door methods of lodging complaints and emphasized the necessity of frankness and directness in all our dealings. I asked M. Clemenceau to give instructions that if there was any fault to find with our methods it should be brought to my personal attention. He entirely agreed with me and expressed chagrin and surprise that any other course had been followed.

I took occasion a few days later to let Pétain know very politely what I thought of the impropriety of this sort of thing and also criticized him then and there for telling anybody, even Mr. House, as he had done, about our purpose to attack the St. Mihiel salient as the first offensive by the American Army. I was pleased with Pétain's apology and his statement that there would be no further action of this kind on his part.

On the face of it, there was no other conclusion, however, than that both complaints were made for the purpose of finding out just the extent of my independent authority. The French probably regarded Mr. House as a sort of special ambassador and thought that they might be able to lay the foundation for an approach through him to the question of amalgamation.

Just before his return to the States, Mr. House told me that he was convinced that the President and the Secretary of War would leave the whole question of the disposition of our troops to my judgment. Assurance on this point was scarcely necessary, as I had full confidence that this was the case. During his stay in France Mr. House and I formed a friendship which enabled us to discuss all matters most freely and frankly. Before he left for home we arranged for confidential communication by cable should it become necessary to reach either Mr. Baker or Mr. Wilson direct.

(Diary) Chaumont, Tuesday, December 11, 1917. Returned here the 7th; am glad to have horseback rides again.

Chief Surgeon Bradley reported yesterday that he is getting more buildings for hospitals. Talked with Atterbury regarding Army Transport Service and find discharge of transports going better.

British under Allenby captured Jerusalem the 9th.

To-day gave French correspondents general outline of progress which may be reassuring. Our training at home not going well. Serious shortage of winter clothing notwithstanding repeated urgent cables.

The difficulties of transatlantic transportation in general made it necessary to limit our demands to those things that could not possibly be obtained abroad within a reasonable time, and every effort was being made toward procurement in Europe. France was responding generously, but her supplies were not inexhaustible. Attention was now turned to the neutral countries of Switzerland and Spain, and also to Portugal. Through negotiations directed by the General Purchasing Agent, it was found that these countries were willing to open up their markets provided the United States would make concessions as to financial accommodations in some cases and remove the embargo in others. The prospects for a time seemed encouraging for obtaining horses, mules, railway ties, and other needed supplies, but the numbers and amounts proved to be limited, and the quality, especially of the animals, unsatisfactory.

The instruction of our troops at home at this time was far from being satisfactory, tests of newly-arrived units having shown that their work was not up to our standards. It was evident that my recommendations were being disregarded. This threw the extra burden upon us of training officers and men after their arrival. I had urged that we should follow our own conception of preparation, emphasizing the rifle and bayonet as the supreme weapons of the infantry soldier, and insisting upon training in all the details of open warfare. It will be pertinent to quote my cable criticizing the policy of the War Department as set forth in one of the training pamphlets sent to me:

"December 7, 1917.

"In my opinion this pamphlet is not in harmony with the recommendations contained in my cablegram in regard to the training of divisions in the United States. The first paragraph of War Department document announces that 'in all the military training of a division, under existing conditions training for trench warfare is of paramount importance.' The program for training contained in the document is prepared accordingly and subordinates all instruction to training for trench warfare. * * * I invite attention to my cablegram and repeat my recommendations contained therein that intensive training in all phases of open warfare be accepted as the principal mission of divisions before embarkation, trench warfare and the use of special arms being taught in connection with the assumption of an offensive from an entrenched position. It is urged that future programs of training for divisions in the United States be prepared accordingly."

The training of officers for the General Staff, which also necessarily had to be undertaken in France, was well under way at the General Staff School, established at Langres, forty miles south of Chaumont, under the able direction of Brigadier General J. W. McAndrew. The three-month course of instruction was based upon our staff organization and was conducted by our own instructors, with two or three French, and an equal number of British officers to assist as lecturers. The difficulty was the scarcity of officers available for detail as students. We were confronted with the task of building up an army of millions that would require as many trained staff officers as we had officers in the whole Regular Army at the beginning of the war. To meet this urgent demand, Washington was asked to send over in advance a small percentage of officers from each division for instruction, but only a few ever came.

The first class at the General Staff School was composed of about seventy-five officers, most of whom were taken from our meager forces then in France. Unfortunately, all the schools were short of student personnel and it was not until the eleventh hour, when new divisions began to come over under pressure late in the spring, that any considerable number of officers could be obtained from our forces for special staff instruction.

(Diary) Chaumont, Sunday, December 16, 1917. Several members of Food Administration [1] lunched with us on Friday and gave an impressive account of restrictions at home.

General Gourko, Russian Army, came yesterday to urge acceptance of their officers in our army, but was told that it is impracticable.

As surest means of having trained troops in the spring, have cabled request for Regular divisions. General Pétain came this evening for dinner, also Colonel de Chambrun, General Ragueneau and Colonel Cornélis DeW. Willcox. Late reports from Italy far from reassuring. Our Remount Service reports shortage of over 15,000 horses and mules.

In considering the composition of our expeditionary forces the question of how to utilize the Regular Army to the best advantage became important. Instead of breaking up its units entirely and allotting the officers and noncommissioned officers to National Guard and National Army units, it was deemed wiser to keep up the Regular units and detach from them such officers and noncommissioned officers as might be needed to leaven the other contingents.

At this moment the training of the first draft had begun, assignments from the Regular units had already been made, and the vacancies filled by new personnel, both officers and men. The basic organization of these Regular units still remained and this with their traditions of service made them the most valuable contingent of our army. It was my opinion, with which both Bliss and Harbord agreed, that the quickest way to provide sorely needed assistance to the Allies would be to hasten the training of the Regular divisions and send them to France as soon as possible.

I recommended that Regular regiments at Honolulu and elsewhere be relieved for this purpose by National Guard regiments. These Regular troops would more nearly approximate the standards of our Allies at the start, and, more important still, their use would diminish the chances of reverses during our first encounters with the enemy. The Acting Chief of Staff at home,

[1] The members present were: Roscoe R. Mitchell, Buffalo, N. Y.; Everett Colby, West Orange, N. J.; J. Bright Lord, New York; Edward F. Trefz, Chicago; Dr. Julius Lincoln, Jamestown, N. Y.; Daniel A. Reed, Flint, Mich.

Major General John Biddle, agreed with my suggestion, but thought that the widely separated locations of these regiments made their replacement impracticable, and only the 3d, 4th, and 5th Divisions came in time for service early in 1918, the 6th and 7th arriving to take part in the fall campaign.

Although the Italians had recently yielded ground west of the Brenta River their lines were then holding on the Piave. However, there was an undercurrent of misgiving among the Allies concerning them, the prevalent belief being that there had been a serious lack of training in their armies originally, and that too little had been done after Italy entered the war. The experience of the other Allies had shown that in order to achieve and maintain a high standard, thorough and continuous instruction was necessary. Especially was this true of staff officers, upon whom so much of the success of an army depends.

It was said that the Italian artillery was not abreast of modern methods and conducted its firing largely without definite data, which was a vital defect, if true, as artillery unable to fire with precision becomes really a menace. When in immediate support of infantry, the barrage must be laid down with such accuracy, just ahead of the advancing troops, as to inspire them with confidence. Liaison between these two arms and with aviation became more and more essential as the war progressed and it could only be perfected by training the three arms together. Officers especially must have specific knowledge of the importance and the technique of coöperation. Yet instruction and preparation in general are of little avail unless positions on the front are wisely selected and protected by well coördinated plans for defense, and unless the armies are trained for open warfare. The other Allies criticized the Italians in all these respects.

The opinion was expressed in certain French circles that the French should take charge of the Italian Army and reorganize it if there was to be anything effective expected on that front. Another suggestion was that a French chief of staff be appointed for the Italians, and that the President of the United States, as a distinguished friend, should put the proposition forward with the necessary pressure to accomplish it. But, of course, no such changes were necessary or even remotely possible.

Incidentally, it was noticeable that the Allies were quick to criticize each other and allege inefficiency in case of reverses. In due time the British and French also suffered disastrous defeats and their armies were also open to criticism. Before the end of the war the records of reverses of the respective armies in the West were about a stand-off. Hasty criticisms are likely to be unjust. Moreover, the injustice is often perpetuated by ill-advised or malicious repetition.

CHAPTER XIX

District of Paris—Phases of Training—Supply Question—Haig's Proposition—Visit Belgian Army—Allies Pressing for Amalgamation—Pétain Proposes New Method of Training Our Troops—Clemenceau Interferes—Situation December 31st

(Diary) Chaumont, Wednesday, December 19, 1917. Attended commemorative services Monday at Church of St. John, Chaumont. Conferred with the Inspector General, Brewster, and several other staff officers. General Zankevitch called to offer services of Russian officers. Went to Paris in the evening, taking Ragueneau, de Chambrun and Dawes.

Had discussion with M. Clemenceau yesterday on supply and other questions. Arthur Frazier, our observer on Supreme War Council, thinks with me that some outstanding civilian should represent us. Called on Brigadier General E. M. Lewis, commanding Paris District. Visited Atterbury's office and was impressed with businesslike system.

Returned to Chaumont this morning, bringing Tardieu and Ganne. Ordnance motor trucks promised after February.

OUR activities in Paris required that numbers of officers and men be stationed there and many members of the A.E.F. frequently passed through the city in traveling officially, or went there on short leaves of absence, making it necessary to establish some authority to whom they could go for orders or information. Paris was, therefore, made a military district in November, 1917, and upon the removal of the Headquarters Line of Communications, to Tours, in January, 1918, became a separate command. The District Commander, Brigadier General E. M. Lewis, was given jurisdiction over troops stationed in the city and over all casuals. The orders published by General Lewis in December prescribed rules of conduct for members of the A.E.F. while in the city. These regulations generally remained in force under his successors through difficult periods when Paris was full of men seeking recuperation and recreation, and for whose good behavior the district commander was responsible.

When Mr. House and General Bliss, who sat in at the second meeting of the Supreme War Council, returned to the United States, Mr. Arthur H. Frazier, First Secretary of our Embassy, was designated to attend the meetings, but merely as an observer and without any voice in the proceedings. Mr. Frazier felt that he was more or less handicapped from lack of knowledge of military affairs, and thought that we should be actively represented. I agreed with him, although it would have been impracticable for the President to designate any one and clothe him with authority comparable to that of the Prime Ministers. I recommended the appointment of Major General Hunter Liggett as the military representative on the Council, but shortly afterward General Bliss was named for the position, and his selection was very agreeable to me. In addition to his other duties, he performed the functions that might have fallen to a civilian, in that he kept the President advised of the actions of the Council and received instructions from him.

(Diary) Chaumont, Tuesday, December 25, 1917. The Archbishops of Langres and of Chaumont paid a formal call on Thursday.

Visited the 42d Division at Lafauche on Friday and saw a well-conducted simulated attack by its training companion, Major General Monroe's French 69th Division. General de Castelnau and Generals Bullard, Bundy, Edwards, and Traub were present.

Left for Paris Saturday and on Sunday drove to Compiègne, lunching with Pétain.

Lord Milner called yesterday to sound me out on the question of amalgamation. Colonel de Chambrun and I dined with M. Jules Cambon, recently designated to handle certain matters of procurement as head of the "Comité Central des Affaires de Guerre."

Returned to Chaumont to-day and had Christmas dinner at quarters with official family.

Our program of training in France had become fairly well established under the immediate direction and observation of the Training Section of the General Staff. Most of our officers were firm believers in the soundness of our doctrines, although a few continued to defer to the opinions of French instructors, who were generally committed to the theory that only trench training was necessary. Our schedule of instruction consisted of three periods. The first included practice in the use of the various weapons, with tactical exercises for units up to the division over such terrain as might be available. The second embraced a month's tour in the trenches by smaller units with French regiments, supported by French artillery. The third concluded the course with combined work of infantry, artillery, and aviation conducted in the training area, after which the division went again into the trenches under its own officers and as a unit in a French corps.

The plan adopted of training with a veteran division was fairly successful, considering the circumstances, and would have been ideal if the model division could have been American. The objection was that the French were inclined to be too paternal and as a rule they went little further in their instruction than trench fighting.

The fact that many of our own officers were not well grounded in first principles made instruction more difficult. Recent inspections had revealed many deficiencies on the part of our officers, and further confirmed reports regarding the inefficacy of the training at home. In my own experience of many years in training troops it was not uncommon to find field officers with little conception of the practical application of the lessons taught in our elementary text books on minor tactics, and it was not surprising to find such a situation in our new army. It was not sufficient merely to issue instructions or schedules, as some officers in the higher grades seemed to think, but it was necessary that they, themselves, should be competent to teach details of execution, especially in the matter of correct tactical method. The most exacting tests were instituted to bring to all concerned a full realization of its importance.

The following cable sent at this time will explain my point of view:

"December 22, 1917.

"Reference training of troops in States, deficiencies noted here indicate, first, great laxity on the part of division and brigade commanders in requiring officers to learn their duties or perform them efficiently; second, almost total failure to give any instruction in principles of minor tactics and their application to war conditions. Officers from colonels down and including some general officers are found ignorant of the handling of units in open warfare, including principles of reconnaissance, outposts, advance guards, solution of practical problems, and formation of attack; third, no training whatever has been given in musketry efficiency as distinguished from individual target practice on the range. Many officers of high rank are hopelessly ignorant of what this training consists."

I had suggested the establishment of a training branch of the War Department under Major General J. F. Morrison, with Brigadier General R. M. Blatchford as his assistant, two of the best equipped officers in our army for such work. The spirit of the recommendation was not carried out, however, as Morrison was not given the necessary independence and authority that a director should have, and as a result the training continued defective, being usually limited to trench warfare.

After all is said, however, the success of a military commander depends largely upon his practical turn of mind, whether it be in planning and directing military operations in the field or managing the business of transportation and supply. Military science is based on principles that have been deduced from the application of common sense in the conduct of military affairs. While high sounding terms and learned discussions of principles and maxims often enshroud campaigns and operations in mystery, military genius is really only the capacity to understand and apply simple principles founded on experience and sound reasoning.

Of course, theoretical training is invaluable, as in any profession, but, as in most others, it forms merely the groundwork, as no two military situations are ever exactly alike. The necessity of professional education should not be minimized in the slightest degree; it is too highly important; but the best informed theoretical soldier without practical comprehension will often find his plans go wrong. To complete the qualifications essential to the successful soldier, there must be added persistence, force, initiative, and personal leadership.

In so far as supplies were available in France, the system of procurement was working fairly well. There was some improvement in the relations between our different supply departments and those of the French. The procurement of many things pertaining to the special and technical services, such as airplanes and all sorts of artillery and ammunition; matters relating to railways and ports and their management; construction; and the quest of buildings for hospitals, were handled personally by the chiefs of the departments responsible, dealing either directly with the ministry concerned or through another agency recently established called the "Comité Central des Affaires de Guerre." It was in the procurement of more general supplies by the purchasing agency that the French Mission at my headquarters could more advantageously present our requirements to the proper authorities and arrange details of purchases.

The appointment of M. Jules Cambon as chairman of this committee placed him in position to represent us before the Council of Ministers. He invited me to dine with him to discuss the relation that his new office would bear to our officials and agencies on the one side and the French Government on the other. The plan for coördination did not look to be very feasible in the hands of such an elderly and rather inactive official, but later M. Maurice Ganne became Director and later still M. Tardieu, and under these men the committee became very important in coöperation with our purchasing agency and other departments in handling our requests before the Ministry.

(Diary) Chaumont, Wednesday, Jan. 2, 1918. Both French and British pressing us for amalgamation.

Went to Marshal Haig's headquarters Friday by rail, accompanied by Colonel Wagstaff, and spent the night. Motored through heavy snow drifts out from Étaples; gangs of "conscientious objectors" opening up roads. Discussed with Sir Douglas possible shipment by and training of American troops with British.

Visited King and Queen of Belgium and their army at Adinkerke on Saturday. Returned to Paris Sunday, visited Major General J. Franklin Bell in hospital, and later called on M. Clemenceau.

Came to Chaumont Monday. Dispensed with New Year's calls on account of work. Dawes came from Paris and spent the night. Generals Wirbel and Ragueneau called.

Our general situation as to arrival of troops and material far from encouraging.

As we have seen, there had been some talk of the British providing shipping to bring over American troops for training behind their lines. During the evening I spent with Sir Douglas Haig, he presented his plans for training our troops. His idea was to place the battalions as they arrived, one to the brigade, in selected British divisions, preferably those serving on the southern part of their front, and then gradually to increase the number of battalions until the divisions should become wholly American. He was willing to place each of these divisions under an American general as soon as the division should become partly Americanized; or do so from the outset if more desirable, retaining the British divisional staffs, and brigade commanders and staffs, until the divisions should be at least half American, after which our staff officers and brigadiers would gradually replace theirs. He thought the sentiment against our men serving under another army might be thus overcome.

His battalions, when released by Americans, would be broken up to fill depleted ranks elsewhere. In this way such units as they were unable to maintain could be replaced by ours and an American army built up to take its place alongside the British.

NOTE: Total strength of the A.E.F. on December 31st, 9,804 officers, 165,080 enlisted men.

Divisional units arriving in December included elements of the 41st Division (National Guard, Washington, Oregon, Montana, Idaho, Wyoming, North and South Dakota, Colorado, New Mexico, and the District of Columbia), Major General Hunter Liggett.

The 369th Infantry of the 93d Division (National Army, colored) arrived January 1st. The 93d Division was never fully organized and its infantry regiments served with the French.

His plan contemplated that the British and American armies would both be based on the northwest coast of France. His Chief of Rail Transportation, General Nash, thought he would be able to receive our troops at Le Havre and send them up country without disturbing his own arrangements. However, I thought that Nash was not very enthusiastic over his Commander-in-Chief's idea.

Sir Douglas used arguments such as common language and the fact that American hospital units were already with the British, as well as the simplicity and expedition with which the plan could be carried out. Any objections the French might offer he thought would be met by building up the American Army between the two. Besides, he said, this would provide for the extension of the British front and meet the demands of the French, who claimed that the French armies were holding too much of the line in proportion to their forces.

The appeal of this proposition was that we should be able to hasten our shipping program and bring to France a much larger number of men than would be possible with the tonnage then in operation. Hoping to commit the British definitely on the question of tonnage, which up to that time we had not succeeded in doing, I did not offer serious objection to the plan and even approved some of the features, especially those pertaining to the earlier part of the proposed training, and for the moment the question was left open for further conference. In all these discussions, the British were bargaining for men to fill their ranks and we were trying to get shipping to carry over our armies.

I left British headquarters the next morning en route to the Belgian front to pay my respects to the King and Queen of Belgium. As Sir Douglas was off to London, my car was attached to his train and we traveled together to Boulogne, where he boarded the Channel boat and I took a special consisting of my car and one other and proceeded on my way.

We were due at Adinkerke, my destination, at a fixed hour, but to my surprise the train pulled in ten minutes ahead of time. I was changing into my best uniform, in fact was just pulling on the right boot when my aide, Colonel Boyd, stuck his head in at the door of my compartment and breathlessly said, "General, we have arrived." I knew it only too well, as the train had stopped and the royal band outside was playing the *Star Spangled Banner* in the usual mournful cadence common to foreign bands. It was an embarrassing thought that I should be late. In another minute, when the orderly and I were struggling, this time with the left boot, Boyd again appeared and said in a stage whisper that was no doubt heard by the entire escort outside, "Sir, the King is out there standing at the salute."

That was too much, the humor of the situation overcame me, and for an instant all of us, including the orderly, who rarely smiled, were convulsed with laughter. That did not help matters, of course, and meanwhile the band outside, which had already played the national air through three times, was dolefully beginning on the fourth, when I hurriedly descended the steps of my car opposite His Majesty, buttoning my overcoat with one hand and saluting with the other. At my appearance the band started afresh and, as though they had just begun, ran through our national anthem rather more vigorously, cheered up no doubt at last to see me in evidence. A few months later I had the courage to relate the incident in all its details to Their Majesties and they both seemed to enjoy it immensely.

After inspecting the escort in company with the King, he and I drove to their residence, where the Queen, in her most gracious manner, received us at the entrance. We had a very enjoyable luncheon, which Boyd thought was quite gay, especially when I became bold enough to air my dreadful French. After luncheon, King Albert, much to my surprise, said he wished to bestow upon me the Order of the Grand Cordon of Leopold. Although not unappreciative, I hesitated, saying that we were not permitted to receive foreign decorations, but he insisted that I should accept it conditionally, which, of course, was the only thing to do. Boyd was decorated also.

In the afternoon, the King, with his Chief of Staff, took me to his G.H.Q. and then to the front-line trenches, explaining the disposition of the limited force with which their positions were held. It consisted of only the six divisions which had stubbornly retired in 1914 in the face of overwhelming odds. It was then being recruited by Belgians who had escaped from within the German lines at the risk of their lives. During my visit I got a much clearer notion of the spirit of the Belgian Army and of its tenacious resistance, which had been of such importance to the Allies by delaying the German advance.

While driving with King Albert he related with much amusement some incidents of a recent visit by a party of our Congressmen, and inquired whether it was customary in our country for them to be on familiar terms with the President. He said that some of them had called him Albert, and one had slapped him on the back, saying, "King, you're the right sort of a fellow and everybody in America admires you." I explained to him that our Congressmen were more or less privileged characters at home and that they only meant to be friendly. As a matter of fact, I do not think the King was in the least offended at their familiarity.

During my brief visit, I was particularly impressed by the extreme simplicity of the home life of the King and Queen, living there, as they were, in a very modest country place within sound of the enemy's guns and almost within range. The Queen often went into the trenches to cheer the troops, and the fine bearing of Their Majesties through it all made them outstanding heroic figures of the World War.

In view of the suggestions that had come to my headquarters regarding various plans for training our troops with the French and British, it was in no sense a surprise to receive the following cable from the Secretary of War, delivered on Christmas Day:

"Pershing, Amexforce,

"Both English and French are pressing upon the President their desires to have your forces amalgamated with theirs by regiments and companies, and both express the belief in impending heavy drive by Germans somewhere along the lines of the Western Front. We do not desire loss of identity of our forces *but regard that as secondary* to the meeting of any critical situation by the most helpful use possible of the troops at your command. The difficulty of course is to determine where the drive or drives of the enemy will take place; and in advance of some knowledge on that question, any redistribution of your forces would be difficult. The President, however, desires you to have full authority to use the forces at your command as you deem wise in consultation with the French and British Commanders-in-Chief. It is suggested for your consideration that possibly places might be selected for your forces nearer the junction of the British and French lines which would enable you to throw strength in whichever direction seemed most necessary. This suggestion is not, however, pressed beyond whatever merit it has in your judgment, the President's sole purpose being to acquaint you with the representations made here and to authorize you to act with entire freedom to accomplish the main purposes in mind. It is hoped that complete unity and coördination of action can be secured in this matter by any conferences you may have with French and British commanders and line of action that may be agreed upon.

"BAKER."

During my visit with General Pétain at his headquarters a few days before this we had taken up anew the question of training for our divisions then in France and also for those yet to come. On account of the imminence of a powerful offensive by the Germans on the Western Front, he said we must be prepared to utilize all possible resources, including the Americans, a statement to which I readily agreed as a matter of course. Instead of following the plan then in operation as to training step by step, beginning with the smaller units, he wanted to take a quicker method and have each of the four infantry regiments of each of our divisions, together with the proper proportion of the artillery, engineers and other troops, assigned to a French division at once. After two or three months of service these troops would be reassembled, he said, under their own divisional officers and take their places in line. It was not simply for instruction in quiet sectors that these units were to be used, but for whatever service might fall to the lot of the French divisions to which they were assigned.

This, of course, virtually meant the building up of French

divisions by American regiments and carried with it the probability that we should not be able to get them back without
actually reducing the French divisions to a point where they
would be much crippled for further line service. Again, the
training of our higher officers and their staffs was entirely ignored
under this plan. I spoke of that as an objection and also mentioned the difference in language as being an insuperable barrier
to any idea of active service under an assignment that might
become permanent.

It was evident that the adoption of such a plan would interrupt
our steady progress toward the preparation of our divisions, and
thus interfere with the formation of our army. I told the French
that it seemed to me better, if such a course became necessary,
that we should amalgamate with the British, who were still making overtures for our troops. The French did not then offer any
objection to this counter-suggestion and it looked as though there
was an understanding between them.

In my formal reply to a communication from Pétain embracing his proposal, I declined to agree to the assignment of our regiments as he had suggested, but said that I should be glad to
attach them to French divisions solely for training for a period
of one month in a quiet sector provided that opportunity should
also be given our officers to learn how to handle larger units by
actually exercising their proper functions. The Secretary's cable
indicated complete coöperation between the French Government
and the Army Commander in their endeavor to carry their point.
The same could be said of the British.

In the meantime, the following cable was received, showing
the means to which Clemenceau resorted to force the issue:

"Washington, January 3, 1918.

"The French Ambassador called on the Secretary of War to-day
and read him a dispatch from M. Clemenceau to the effect that
General Pershing and General Pétain had conferred as to the wisdom
of seasoning American troops by attaching their regimental units to
French divisions before committing a part of the line to an American
division made up of troops not (sic) accustomed to actual front conditions.

"M. Clemenceau's cablegram stated that General Pershing had reported himself and General Pétain in substantial agreement after conference on the subject but General Pétain conveyed to M. Clemenceau the opposite opinion. Apparently some misunderstanding has arisen which the Secretary of War will be glad to have General Pershing endeavor to clear up by placing himself in communication with M. Clemenceau and reporting the result of the interview.

"The French urge action as outlined above as being safer for American troops than it would be to give them at once an independent place in the line, and urge very strongly that the Secretary of War here accept their view and commend it to you. This the Secretary of War is not willing to do, desiring to leave the matter wholly within your discretion after full consideration of the important elements of the matter.

"The French Ambassador has been told that the Secretary of War would lay the matter before you and would communicate to him your conclusions when they are arrived at."

The following extract of my cable of January 8th conveys the main points of my reply:

" * * * The French have not been entirely frank, as unofficial information indicates they really want to incorporate our regiments into their divisions for such service in the trenches as they desire. As to our instruction, a certain amount of work with French troops is beneficial and this we are having and expect to have. * * * Have expressed a willingness to aid in any way in an emergency but do not think good reason yet exists for us to break up our divisions and scatter regiments for service among French and British, especially under the guise of instruction. * * * The integrity of our own forces should be preserved as far as possible. Shall see M. Clemenceau * * * and expect to hold joint conference with Field Marshal Haig and General Pétain within a few days. Shall have frank discussion of the whole subject. * * * "

It thus appeared quite clear that the French were so intent on their plan that M. Clemenceau presumed to cable Washington as to how our units were to be handled. Upon the receipt of the cable from Washington about the disagreement between Pétain and myself, I wrote at once to M. Clemenceau quoting the cable and adding:

"May I not suggest to you, Mr. President,[1] the inexpediency of communicating such matters to Washington by cable? These questions must all be settled here, eventually, on their merits, through friendly conferences between General Pétain and myself, and cables of this sort are very likely, I fear, to convey the impression of serious disagreement between us when such is not the case. * * * "

His reply, translated into English, was as follows:

"My dear General:

"I hasten, without losing a moment, to reply to your letter dated January 5, 1918. I found myself under the necessity of cabling to the Ambassador of France at Washington because the two contradictory responses which I had received from General Pétain and from yourself, when you did me the honor of calling on me, obliged me, in the interest of the common cause, to seek an arbitration between the two Commanders-in-Chief.

"I need not conceal the fact that I placed full confidence in this regard in the American Government. However, it was not to the American Government that I addressed myself. I cabled to the Ambassador of France, as was my right and duty, in order to give him directions for the conversations which might take place either with the Secretary of War or with the President of the United States.

"It might very well have happened that later on I should have addressed the American Government, but I insist on the point, that I have done nothing of the sort. I had not authorized the Ambassador of France to read all or part of my dispatch to the Secretary of War. I regret that he did so, but I do not disavow anything that I wrote.

"So I am giving you here the explanation which I owe you and I shall exercise all the patience of which I am capable in awaiting the good news that the American Commander and the French Commander have finally agreed on a question which may be vital to the outcome of the war.

"With the assurance of my feelings of high esteem and of respect for you personally, I beg you, my dear General, to believe me,

"Sincerely yours,

"CLEMENCEAU."

As the French were dead set on getting our troops under their control, it is very clear that the Prime Minister, feeling that their plans were not working out, sought to create some question in

---

[1] "Président du Conseil" corresponds to "Prime Minister."

the minds of our Administration at Washington regarding the wisdom of my management of things. He no doubt thought that my opposition to amalgamation could thus be overcome. However, at later meetings with Clemenceau and Pétain the alleged differences were seemingly settled amicably, as indicated in my cable which follows:

"January 14, 1918.

"Confidential, for Chief of Staff.
"Par. 1.

"With reference to your 558 and 588, and my cablegram 467, have had entirely frank conference with Prime Minister Clemenceau and General Pétain. Have now definite understanding with French satisfactory to them and to me that our divisions now in France shall complete their training as already begun. In the future, divisions arriving in Zone of French Armies are to have period of training with French, each regiment in a French division. When sufficiently experienced by training in a quiet sector with French, our divisions are to be united under their own commander and will be placed in the line in our own sector.

*   *   *   *   *   *   *

"Par. 3.

"Discussion with Prime Minister Clemenceau and General Pétain was characterized by utmost frankness on both sides and it is believed that we now have complete understanding.

*   *   *   *   *   *   *

"PERSHING."

The first few months we were in France were actively employed in working out basic plans and in completing our organization. We had been ready and waiting to assign units to areas and duties as fast as they should arrive and begin or continue their training as might be required. Each of the supply and staff departments had been broadened in scope and new services created and their relation to the whole under the new conditions definitely fixed.

However, our situation as to numbers of troops and as to supplies and construction at the close of the year was not what we had every reason to expect after having been at war nine months. We had not obtained full service from the limited amount of tonnage thus far made available for military use. The supply departments in Washington had failed to provide sufficient material for the construction at ports, which was still very much behind. Only a part of the railroad rolling stock needed had been sent. As we have seen, the Navy, until recently, instead of routing vessels to different ports had brought most of them to St. Nazaire for discharge, at times causing considerable congestion there. Only about 350,000 tons of freight had been received.

We had less than 175,000 men in France, including about 100,000 in four divisions in various stages of organization and training, while there should have been at least ten divisions of combat troops and other forces in proportion. It was a very unsatisfactory state of affairs that confronted us, with little promise of improvement. At home we had forty-five divisions organized, and part of their personnel had been assembled and started in training, but it would take time to assign and instruct the additional drafts and put these into shape.

Apropos of the delay in the shipment of troops and supplies, the following cable, sent December 20th, will show the situation and my appeal:

"Understood here that a shipping program based on tonnage in sight prepared in War College Division in September contemplated that entire First Corps with its corps troops and some 32,000 auxiliaries were to have been shipped by end of November, and that an additional program for December, January, and February contemplates that the shipment of the Second Corps with its corps troops and other auxiliaries should be practically completed by the end of February. (Twelve divisions in all.) Should such a program be carried out as per schedule and should shipments continue at corresponding rate, it would not succeed in placing even three complete corps, with proper proportion of Army troops and auxiliaries, in France by end of May. The actual facts are that shipments are not even keeping up to that schedule. It is now the middle of December and the First Corps (six divisions) is still incomplete by over two entire divisions and many corps troops. It cannot be too emphatically declared that we should be prepared to take the field with at least four corps (twenty-four divisions) by June 30. In view of past performances with tonnage heretofore available such a project is impossible of fulfillment, but only by most strenuous attempts to attain such a result will we be in a position to take a proper part in operations in 1918. In view of fact that as the number of our troops here increases, a correspondingly greater amount of tonnage must be provided for their supply, and also in view of the slow rate of shipment with tonnage now available, it is of the most urgent importance that more tonnage should be obtained at once as already recommended in my cables and by General Bliss."

It hardly need be recorded that we were occasioned much embarrassment in facing the Allies with such a poor showing of accomplishment. Up to this time, we had been handicapped in our efforts by lack of aggressive direction of affairs at home. Whether this was due to inefficiency or failure to appreciate the urgency of the situation, the War Department General Staff, as the superior coördinating agency, must take the greater part of the blame. This situation was an unwelcome confirmation of the opinion formed by me on my first visit to the War Department the previous May. Notwithstanding the lack of plans and experience, it has always been difficult for me to understand why our General Staff clung so long to the antiquated systems and faulty precedents which had guided its activities previous to our entry into the war. It should be observed that the present War Department General Staff as reorganized is and will continue to be efficient so long as it follows the principles developed in the American Expeditionary Forces, upon which its reorganization was based.

Messages of mutual good-will and best wishes for the new year were exchanged between the Commanders-in-Chief of the Allied armies and myself in the name of our respective commands. The following was also received from Washington:

"The President and the Secretary of War send to you and to the American Army in France the most cordial greetings and good wishes for this Christmas Season from the people of the United States. Your comrades in arms of every camp and cantonment send you greetings. From every home to-day goes a prayer for the welfare and success of our troops in France and personally for every man of them. The nation reposes in you and them its full confidence that in God's good time and with God's blessing its troops in France, side by side with their gallant Allies, will bring victory and an abiding peace to the world."

This beautiful message expressed the fine spirit of the American people as exemplified by our war President. Coming at a time when Allied morale was low and the outcome of the war in doubt, the courage, the faith and the prayers of our people at home gave a new impetus to our determination to win.

CHAPTER XX

The West Point Spirit—Liquor Question—Increase of Chaplains—Aviation—Recommendations for Improvement Port Situation—Robertson Offers Sea Transport Conditionally—In Agreement with Pétain—Forage Supply—Letter to Secretary of War, General Conditions Reported

(Diary) Chaumont, Saturday, January 5, 1918. Gave Edwin Marshall, the correspondent, an interview on Thursday and saw Grayson Murphy, who is giving up Red Cross for service with troops.

Accredited correspondents came yesterday to study our organization and had luncheon with us. Generals Headlam and Wagstaff, British Army, dined with us.

Had message to-day from General Robertson requesting conference at Paris the 9th. Considerable discussion in late home papers concerning my orders against drinking.

MAJOR Grayson M. P. Murphy, who had been in charge of the Red Cross work in France, was a graduate of West Point, and before resigning his commission to enter the banking business had seen service in the Regular Army Infantry in the Philippines and elsewhere. When we entered the war he was selected by Mr. Davison to take charge of the Red Cross work in France, but after spending about six months abroad he sought active service with the Army. Major Murphy showed the universal spirit of the men of West Point. Almost without exception those who had gone into civil life returned to the Army during the war and both in the United States and abroad did their part along with other graduates in upholding the high traditions of their Alma Mater.

The necessity for controlling the use of strong drink among our troops had been brought forcibly to my attention through the ease with which alcoholic beverages could be obtained. The use of light wines as a part of the French ration was simply the continuance in the army of the universal custom of the people of having wine with their meals. The wines and beer were not so objectionable, but strong alcoholic spirits were regarded by the French themselves as dangerous and were prohibited to their troops. The prohibition was not well enforced, however, outside the Zone of the Armies.

The problem of controlling the sale to our troops by the French of the stronger liquors was difficult, especially at the ports of entry. Efforts to obtain enforcement through conferences with local authorities and through agreements with the port and district officials were made from time to time, but with little result. I finally appealed to M. Clemenceau for support, but he would only counsel local officials, as he did not wish to declare a "state of siege." In the end it was necessary to take the matter into our own hands and declare every bar and restaurant where the heavy liquor was sold as "off limits" for our troops. Our officers were directed to give their personal attention to the enforcement of this order, which is quoted in part as follows:

> "Commanding officers at all places where our troops may be located will confer with the local French authorities and use every endeavor to limit to the lowest possible number the places where intoxicants are sold. It is desired that these authorities be assisted in locating non-licensed resorts, which should be reported immediately to the proper authority for necessary action.
>
> "Soldiers are forbidden either to buy or accept as gifts from inhabitants whiskey, brandy, champagne, liquors or other alcoholic beverages other than light wines or beer. The gift or retail of these (stronger beverages) by inhabitants in the zone of the army is forbidden by French law. Commanding officers will see that all drinking places where alcoholic liquors named above are sold are designated 'Off Limits' (for American troops) and the necessary means adopted to prevent soldiers visiting them."

My most earnest thought and attention were given to this subject early in our experience and throughout the war. The habit of drinking was not only detrimental to efficiency but it often led to other indiscretions. It is a question whether under ordinary circumstances in times of peace a healthy moral sentiment cannot be created as a safeguard against excesses, yet during the war when men were not surrounded by the restraining influences of home life limited prohibition was necessary. Even though it had been possible of enforcement, I should not have issued orders to our armies prohibiting the use of light wines or beer. Armies are simply a cross-section of the people whom they represent and their psychology is the same, and any attempt to enforce such an order would have led to difficulties. Furthermore, coöperation by the French to that extent would have been out of the question. There was in fact comparatively little drinking in our armies and what there was decreased noticeably after the prohibition of strong drink.

About this time a cable was received from Washington saying that some publication at home had made a sweeping charge of both immorality and drunkenness against our men. No such statement could be based on fact or could serve any purpose except to cause unnecessary anxiety to parents and relatives, and perhaps satisfy on the part of some one an unworthy desire for sensation. My reply, which showed the character of our army and the kind of lives the men were leading, was as follows:

"January 21, 1918.
"Reference your cablegram 643, paragraph 8, there has never been a similar body of men to lead as clean lives as our American soldiers in France. They have entered this war with the highest devotion to duty and with no other idea than to perform these duties in the most efficient manner possible. They fully realize their obligations to their own people, their friends, and the country. A rigid program of instruction is carried out daily with traditional American enthusiasm. Engaged in healthy, interesting exercises in the open air, with simple diet, officers and men like trained athletes are ready for their task. Forbidden the use of strong drink and protected by stringent regulations against sexual evils and supported by their own moral courage, their good behavior is the subject of most favorable comment, especially by our Allies. American mothers may rest assured that their sons are a credit to them and the nation, and they may well look forward to the proud day when on the battlefield these splendid men will shed a new luster on American manhood."

(Diary) Paris, Thursday, January 10, 1918. Have appointed Major Robert Bacon to be Colonel and A.D.C. on my staff. Bishop L. H. Gwynne, Deputy Chaplain General, British Army, and Bishop Charles H. Brent were my guests at Chaumont on Monday. Went over aviation matters with Foulois, Bolling, and Dodd.

On Tuesday Brent and I discussed increase in number of chaplains, which we both favor. Left for Paris same evening.

Began discussion with Robertson and Maclay [1] yesterday morning about shipment of troops. Robertson and I went with Atterbury, Nash, and Maclay for conference with Claveille in afternoon on use of certain ports for large liners. Had talk with M. Clemenceau, again urging concessions as to berths and port control. Cabled request for rapid shipment of railway cars, 30,000 short.

Resumed discussion with Robertson to-day. Talked with M. Maurice Ganne about his work with the Committee on Franco-American Relations.

Bishop Brent had been selected by me for appointment as Chaplain with a view to his being the Chief of the Chaplain Corps which it was planned to organize. The Bishop did not approve of this idea and in deference to his opinion, and upon his suggestion, a permanent executive committee of chaplains was appointed to study the problems involved and to make recommendations direct to me from time to time. To assist us in organizing the work of our chaplains, Bishop Gwynne, Deputy Chaplain General of the British forces, kindly visited us and explained their methods of control and direction of the chaplains' work, and from their system we adopted such features as were applicable to our service.

Custom in our army, arising from lack of proper appreciation of the important duties of chaplains, had often relegated them to the status of handy men who were detailed to write up boards of survey or operate libraries. It can be said, however, that most chaplains, even in the face of such discouragement, continued in their efforts to fulfill their religious functions. I recall a visit of inspection to one of the regimental camps on the Mexican border before the war, where a most worthy chaplain who had been with me in Mindanao was stationed. Remaining over Sunday, I went

[1] Sir Joseph Maclay was a British expert on shipping.

to the large tent where he was to hold services, expecting to find an audience such as formerly assembled to hear him. As he had been very popular in the Philippine Islands and was noted for his attentions to the sick and wounded during our campaigns, I was greatly surprised to find that my aide and I constituted his congregation. But this attitude changed during the World War and chaplains were generally highly respected, many of them winning the esteem and affection of their units.

In recommending an increase in the number of chaplains, my reason was that I regarded recognition of the value of religious influence among our troops during the war as of special importance. Many temptations confronted our soldiers abroad and it seemed to me that the presence, the example, and the counsel of chaplains of the right sort would exert an excellent moral effect, especially among men without experience away from home. In recommending the increase of chaplains, I sent the Secretary of War the following cablegram:

"January 17, 1918.
"In the fulfillment of its duty to the nation much is expected of our army and nothing should be left undone that will help in keeping it in the highest state of efficiency. I believe the personnel of the army has never been equalled and the conduct has been excellent, but to overcome entirely the conditions found here requires fortitude born of great moral courage and lofty spiritual ideals. Counting myself responsible for the welfare of our men in every respect, it is my desire to surround them with the best influences possible. In the fulfillment of this solemn trust, it seems wise to request the aid of churchmen from home. To this end it is recommended that the number of chaplains in the army be increased for the war to an average of three per regiment. * * * Men selected should be of the highest character with reputations well established as sensible, practical, active ministers or workers, accustomed to dealing with young men. * * * "

This recommendation was approved by the Secretary of War and later enacted into law.

Aviation questions demanded unremitting attention, for in no other service was unpreparedness so evident and so difficult to overcome. Apparently there was earnest effort at home, but it was too often misdirected. The manufacture of airplanes was very uncertain, partly because of indecision as to types, and largely through inexperience in construction. In the A.E.F., differences of opinion and the consequent lack of coöperation among aviation officers upon whom rested the task of organization and training caused confusion and loss of time. The Allies, especially the French, had received a setback in their production program due to the lack of mechanics and the delay in procuring motors and other material, notably spruce. On account of these conditions and their own increased programs, the French and the Italians would not take more than a small proportion of our 1,500 flying cadets who were on the ground, and who, under agreement, were to be instructed by them.

The French Government claimed to be unable to meet its obligations to us owing to the delay in receiving machine tools and raw materials, besides mechanics, motors and spruce. The contract made with us in August was therefore formally abrogated, a possibility which had been forecast in my cables to the War Department. In its stead we later made an agreement whereby the French would provide us with airplanes according to the number of divisions we might have in France.

It developed a few days later that General Pétain had something to do with the decision of the Minister of Munitions regarding airplanes for us. The French program was then being greatly enlarged due to the increased air activity on the part of the enemy. It also appeared that after three years and a half of war the combined aircraft production capacity of the Allies was behind that of the Germans. Pétain was afraid that his armies might run short of planes and had intervened.

He realized our situation, but said that it was necessary to consider the needs of his aviation, which was actually employed, before making provision for us. He thought that by the time we should be ready to put our troops in line the rate of production could be increased so that we might have our due proportion. I suggested that if the French manufacturers were allowed to fulfill their contract with us our aviation would then be ready for service with the French armies, if necessary. But Pétain thought the manufacturers had undertaken more than they could do and that the output should be held as available where most needed. He said that the destruction of French planes had been very great and that it would be a considerable strain on the production capacity of their factories to furnish replacements of losses during the coming year. As I recall it, the replacements were something like 25 per cent per month.

Thus it was impossible to obtain assurance of any fixed number of planes until later when the necessity for the assistance of our aviation became urgent.

Early in December I signed an agreement with Lord Northcliffe, of the British Air Board, that we should send 15,000 enlisted men to England and maintain that number in training in their aircraft factories and air service stations. This plan proved beneficial to both sides, so far as carried out, but especially to ourselves, in providing us with trained men, and saving us the necessity of establishing extra schools. Due to the non-arrival of air personnel from home we were unable to furnish the full number as planned. We still lacked 4,500 men when the need for line troops arose and prevented the completion of our part of the agreement.

The urgency of radical steps to improve the port situation impelled me to lay the whole matter in detail before M. Clemenceau. He promised to do everything possible to correct those things that depended upon his action and asked me for a memorandum of suggestions and recommendations. I sent him a letter including the following summary of remedial action needed, stating that the conditions had been presented to the Ministry of Public Works by myself and by my representatives on several occasions, and that the results so far were unsatisfactory:

"1. That the French Government turn over docks and warehouses at St. Nazaire to A.E.F.
"2. That every berth that can be spared at all ports be placed under control of A.E.F.

"3. That facilities be increased for the quick handling of cargo from transports.

"4. That all available storage space be set apart for our use.

"5. That the most competent and reliable French officers be selected for command of ports.

"6. That certain ports be placed under 'martial law' in order to enforce regulations that will expedite our work."

While no formal reply was received, the number of berths was increased, additional storage was provided, and several changes were made in the French officers on duty at the ports.

When General Robertson came for a conference regarding the shipment of troops for training with the British, he brought along General Nash and Sir Joseph Maclay. As a preliminary, we discussed the general subject of expediting shipments by the use of additional French ports of entry as a means of shortening the time for the round trip. The suggestion that we might send some of the deep-draft vessels to Southampton had been made by Sir Douglas Haig when I saw him at Montreuil, the idea being that ships had to go there for coal, anyway. If used as a port of debarkation our troops could be taken from there across the Channel by the British to ports they were using, and be billeted behind their lines. It was proposed that some shipping other than deep draft might also be sent to Southampton instead of Bordeaux and Brest. Cherbourg and Lorient were also considered as possible ports of debarkation.

Generals Robertson and Nash thought it would be safer to discharge our ships at French ports, and that such a plan would avoid transporting baggage as well as men across the Channel if extra ports, especially Brest, could be made available. So the three of us and General Atterbury called upon M. Claveille, the Minister of Public Works, and made the suggestion, only to find that in the opinion of the French the naval docks at Brest were not suitable for large liners, but that Cherbourg might be available. Later on, when shipments became heavy, necessity compelled the use of both Brest and Cherbourg.

When we began to discuss the details of the disposition to be made of American troops which might be brought over in British shipping, it was found that General Robertson's proposal was practically the same as the one submitted to Mr. House through Mr. Lloyd George. He wanted to bring our infantry and machine gun units by battalions only and pointed out how much more expeditiously this would meet the shortage of men in the British Army than to ship whole divisions with all their equipment and stores. He said he did not wish to interfere with our program of building up an independent army, but thought that if we would agree to let them have as many as 100,000 or 150,000 men in addition to the complete divisions necessary for our army they could find the shipping to carry them. He believed that the British Government would take the risk of releasing temporarily some shipping engaged in carrying food and raw materials if America could see her way to provide the men, although, he said, it could not well undertake the transportation of complete divisions, as not enough men would be brought over in this manner to justify the great risks involved.

The question of drafting our men as individuals was mentioned, but the difficulties of discipline and the total loss of their identity were insuperable objections. The British really proposed two plans: one, suggested by General Robertson, which contemplated that our battalions should be assigned to their divisions and be absorbed; and the other, by Field Marshal Haig, under which they should successively enter selected British units which would eventually become American. General Robertson said that unless we could furnish manpower to build up their divisions there was the possibility of the British reaching such an exhausted condition by the severe fighting in prospect that the Allies would have a very heavy task in winning the war.

The arguments General Robertson advanced clearly indicated that the British were playing for advantage to themselves in offering to transport our troops. In other words, they had the shipping to transport American battalions on condition that they would serve in the British armies. Their purpose was to build up their own units instead of aiding the cause in general by augmenting the number of complete combat divisions on the Western Front.

The question that naturally arose in my mind was that if tonnage was available for this purpose, why had it not been offered to us some time before, or, indeed, why not at that very moment. If the broad view had prevailed that our forces would add just that much to the strength of the Allies, they could have provided additional shipping quite as well before as after the crisis in March. We could then have brought several more divisions to France and had them prepared to go into the line much earlier than was otherwise possible. And it is conceivable that they might have been able to prevent the disasters that came to the British in March and to the French in May. But, of course, the British were not thinking in terms of an American army at all.

However, as General Robertson's proposal would enable us to increase our strength more rapidly, my preliminary cable to Washington reporting the conference recommended that it be given consideration and that if approved the plan should be regarded as a temporary measure to meet an emergency; that as soon as possible the remaining troops of our divisions should be brought over and the units reassembled; that division, brigade, and regimental commanders and their staffs be sent with their infantry for training with the corresponding British units, and that the infantry be taken from those divisions that would not otherwise be transported until after June.

The arrangement proposed by Robertson, if adopted, was not to interfere in any way with our program for bringing our troops in our own tonnage as already planned. My cable suggested we should insist that the British Government continue to provide as many men for their armies as possible, and that it would be pertinent for our Government to inquire just what the British proposed to do to keep up their own forces. I feared that should we make this concession the tendency would be for them to relax and let the burden of keeping up their strength fall on us, to the detriment of preparations for building up our own army later on.

In a telegram to General Robertson, I set forth the report of our conversation which I had cabled the War Department, and further stated that it was of the utmost importance that the British Government should exert every energy to keep up its own manpower. I requested a full statement from him as to British resources, including the men then available and to become so during the year, in order that we might have all the facts before making a final decision on his proposition. In reply, General Robertson sent me the following data in a letter dated January 17th:

> "The British Government has given the most anxious consideration to the question of the maintenance of the armies in the field during 1918 and, by making every effort, there will become available for service at the front 449,000 men now under training, plus 100,000 to be called up. In addition there will be called up 100,000 men of lower category who are not fit for the first line, plus 120,000 lads of 18 years of age, who will not be available for service at the front till 1919. Please keep these figures strictly secret."

Nothing further was done toward an agreement until a week or so later, when conversations were resumed.

(Diary) Chaumont, Tuesday, January 15, 1918. Visited Pétain on Friday to discuss further the details of putting divisions in line.

Went to Versailles Saturday and reviewed military situation with Generals Sir Henry Wilson, Cadorna, and Weygand, and Mr. Frazier.

Returned here Sunday, bringing Dawes, Harjes, and M. Van de Vyvere, the Belgian Minister of Finance. Belgians have agreed, upon Dawes' representations, to turn over 300 idle locomotives for the French and ourselves. Sent cable regarding the President's speech before Congress.

Shortage of forage causing serious loss of animals. Lord Derby, British War Minister, proposes conference on land transportation on Western Front. Liaison officers reorganized under Major H. H. Harjes. Had visiting Generals J. Franklin Bell and T. H. Barry to dinner this evening; also M. Charles de Chambrun, who goes to Washington for duty at French Embassy.

Have organized I Corps Headquarters under Major General Liggett, with Colonel Craig as Chief of Staff.

This meeting with Pétain was gratifying in its results, in view of the rather radical differences in our views during the verbal and written discussions of training, which have already been mentioned in a previous chapter. The assignment of our divisions for training with the French was settled as to time and place and it was agreed that our general officers and their staffs should have every opportunity for experience. It was also understood that toward April or May we should take over a portion of the front and occupy it as the American sector. When advised of the conversation with Robertson regarding the amalgamation of American troops with the British, he saw no objection, but regretted that it could not be done with the French also.

To meet the need for replacements in their units, I consented to send temporarily to the French four colored Infantry regiments of the 93d Division. Some of the units had arrived, and others were expected soon to be en route, but they did not have in France even the beginning of a brigade or divisional organization. One regiment was to go to each of four divisions, with the provision that they were to be returned for the formation of the 93d Division when called for. Unfortunately, they soon became identified with the French and there was no opportunity to assemble them as an American division. Very much to my regret these regiments never served with us, but it was gratifying later to hear of their being highly commended by the French.

Our forage supply at this time was entirely inadequate, even for the small number of animals, amounting to about 21,000, then in service. Over a month had passed since the Quartermaster General's office at Washington had promised that the shipment of ninety days' supply would commence at once and be completed within thirty days. The actual situation is set forth in the following extract from my cable:

"January 12, 1918.
"35 per cent of the animals have been on less than half rations of oats for 10 days and also on short rations of hay and some have died from starvation. This, combined with the severe winter weather * * * with the temperature frequently below zero, has caused con-

siderable suffering and decreased vitality among our animals, while, due to the extreme shortage, * * * all transportation has to be worked to its full capacity. French * * * say that their forage crop is short so that we are unable to purchase any forage from them and all that is borrowed must be replaced as rapidly as possible. Advise what shipments are now actually en route and whether the flow of forage can be depended upon."

The problem of Allied rail transportation on the Western Front was brought up in a letter from Lord Derby, who said that the British War Cabinet considered it advisable to review the question with special reference to probable future operations as affected by the mobility of the Allied armies in the field. The rail facilities in France constituted a vital factor in the military situation. The recent movement of French and British troops to Italy had interfered with the railroad service in France by temporarily using a considerable amount of rolling stock, and the possibilities of heavy demands in the spring were causing much concern. At the time no organization existed to which the Inter-Allied Military Staff at Versailles could refer for an opinion as to the feasibility of large movements of Allied troops. So a committee was formed to study the question, General Nash, representing the British, and General Atterbury the Americans.

It was a pleasure to meet both Generals Bell and Barry again and to find them so deeply interested in all they had seen. It was well known that General Bell was and had been for some years in poor health, in fact he spent some time in the hospital while in France. The Chief Surgeon reported him to be wholly unfit physically for active service, and later General Barry was found physically disqualified also. I regretted to lose their services, as both of them would have taken high positions in the A.E.F.

The speech of the President before Congress on January 8th created a profound impression in Europe and was the subject of discussion in all Allied circles. It was eagerly read and its commitment of the American people to the principles of justice was evidently its high inspiration. I tried to convey the sentiment of the A.E.F. in the following cablegram to the Secretary:

"Speaking for our armies in Europe, may I extend to the President our extreme satisfaction upon his masterly declaration of the great fundamental principles of justice in international relations for which our people stand and for which our army and the armies of the Allies must fight to the end. This clear presentation of those principles will be the army's inspiration and its guide. To battle for them is the highest privilege that could be accorded to men. We pledge him everything that is in us that we may see these ideals prevail. May Divine Providence give us direction and determination that our country may be proud of the sacrifices we are more than ever willing to make."

To keep the Secretary advised on conditions and possibly clear up certain questions, I sent him the following letter:

"January 17, 1918.

"Dear Mr. Secretary:

"There are several matters that have been the subject of cables that can be made clearer by writing. One of them is differences we have had with the French on the subject of training.

"When the 1st Division arrived in its training area, the French kindly placed a division nearby to aid in instruction. Through association, the French officers and soldiers and our own became cordial and the spirit of fraternity has been passed on to succeeding divisions. This training alongside the French was limited mainly to the specialties of trench warfare and, under the then division commander, it was left almost wholly to the direction of the French. Their method was mainly to give demonstrations: that is, they went over and over their trench exercises while our platoons, companies and battalions were usually only observers. They failed to realize that for us at least it was necessary that officers commanding their own units should work out problems for themselves instead of remaining mere imitators.

"Another point of difference was as to tactical value of open warfare. We have held that our young officers lacked experience in handling their units in the open, and that a knowledge of the methods of trench warfare was not enough to prepare them for the important duties of commanding units where there was a possibility of open warfare. I have spent much time myself explaining that our company officers must have training in handling units in open attack and defense, and that they must be thoroughly schooled in the principles of what we call 'minor tactics.' The French have taken the opposite view and have held that our officers did not need that training now. Notwithstanding that many instances in both British and French experience prove the contrary, the French are very firm in their view. They are just a little bit inclined to hold themselves superior in the art of war to both the British and ourselves, and that does not always set very well.

"So finally they criticized us, not only to their war office, but General Pétain commented on our methods rather hastily to Mr. House and also to General Bliss. I explained our position to both these gentlemen, adding that I myself had studied, and had required as thorough study as possible by our officers of both French and British methods and experience and had endeavored to select and adopt the best. Naturally it would be quite impossible for us to adopt French tactics throughout. That we must retain our basic principles is agreed to by all officers experienced in training our troops. As we have used the French example less, following more our own ideas of requiring men to think for themselves, and learn practically the principles applicable both to open and trench warfare, the French hastily concluded that we were not progressing.

"This was the main cause of the feeling. As M. Clemenceau was very anxious for harmony, he rather exaggerated the thing in his own mind. I later explained my view to him, as I did also to General Pétain, who saw the force of my position and frankly said so. However, in the course of these discussions and correspondence, it developed that the French were really hoping to have our units amalgamated for service with theirs, with the special object in mind of their not being compelled to reduce the number of their divisions. This was hidden away under the insistence upon taking over our training. Of course we realize that the French are short of men, but, except in a temporary emergency, differences in language and methods would make the combination for actual fighting quite out of the question. In my recent discussions with them, I have made that point clear, and they seemed to have accepted it, so we had but to settle the question of training.

"In the end, my conferences with M. Clemenceau and General Pétain have resulted in what now seems to be a very satisfactory understanding. It has been agreed, then, that we should go on as in the past, aided by French instructors and a more limited number of French units, following such courses of training as we should prescribe, and that later, our regiments should go into French divisions, posted in a quiet sector, for experience in the trenches, the generals and staff officers to have service with corresponding grades and commands in French units. This duty with the French divisions is to be for training only and when finished the elements of our divisions are to be reunited under our own officers. I think the plan is the very best that we could adopt and the French seem equally satisfied. A few days ago I had a very cordial telegram from M. Clemenceau expressing his gratification that an agreement had been reached.

"The question of getting our men over as rapidly as possible is being emphasized by both our allies in France. The British have, as you know, made an offer to transport a number of battalions for service with their divisions. This has already been made the subject of considerable cable correspondence with which you are familiar. Although in serving with the British we should not have differences in language to contend with, the sticking point of the thing is service under another flag. If human beings were pawns it would be different, but they are our own men and we should therefore study carefully our national sentiment and the attitude of our army and the people toward the proposition. Generally speaking the army would be opposed to it, officers and all, but really the question presented is, can we afford not to send over extra men to help our allies in what may be an emergency when the necessary extra sea transportation is offered and we have the spare men. As already cabled, there is less difficulty in sending over men than material, and men will probably be needed before the material can be obtained and men trained to use it. If we agree to this, we must insist upon our men being returned when called for, or at least when we get over the remainder of the organizations from which they may be taken, and, besides, we must insist that the British and French both do their utmost until we can come in with a well organized and well trained force large enough to count. We must look forward to bearing a very heavy part in this conflict before it ends, and our forces should not be dissipated except for a temporary emergency. Moreover, it is unnecessary to say, when the war ends, our position will be stronger if our army acting as such shall have played a distinct and definite part. I have set this out in more or less detail in the dispatches, so shall leave it.

"Just a word as to the railroad situation. As our forces increase, the shortage of freight cars becomes more serious. The French management of railroads is very badly demoralized. They lack men in responsible positions and are very short of operators and laborers. For these reasons we have had trouble in getting men and supplies forward, but these conditions are now improving. With the Belgian locomotives now being put into shape, and an increase in the number of men to repair cars we shall be able to keep ahead of transportation requirements. There are thousands of cars in France that are out of repair, and to repair these and put them in operation will not only expedite matters, but will save much tonnage that can be devoted to something else.

"As stated in my cables, port conditions are much confused, accommodations are limited, material for construction arrives slowly and the procurement of ballast has been difficult. The lack of rail facilities has added to the difficulties, as has the inability of the Navy to convoy vessels to ports where they could find accommodations. All this has caused very great delay in getting transports back. The Navy now agrees to send vessels where we want them, and we have solved the ballast question for the time being. The French still hold control of the ports, notwithstanding their agreement (made by a former ministry) to give us increased, if not absolute control. This was once promised as to St. Nazaire, but has not been carried out. There are so many petty French officers, * * * and we find ourselves often interfered with and delayed by them. I have recently again represented the situation plainly in a strong appeal to M. Clemenceau, and I believe we are in a fair way to get it straightened out. So the situation is improving and promises to improve still further.

"According to cables, there has been some move made in Washington by the Engineer Corps to put the engineers back in control of our railroads here. This would be the greatest kind of a mistake. We now have experienced railroad men in charge of the Railway Transportation Department, and to my mind it would be next to fatal to give it over to engineers to run. None of them has ever had experience in railroading, and all would have to learn the business from the bottom up. As this ordinarily takes a lifetime, I should not think of changing back to their management.

"Coming back to Allied relations, I have succeeded in bringing about a meeting between Sir Douglas Haig, General Pétain and myself. We shall be at Compiègne, French General Headquarters, on Saturday night of the 19th instant. It would be unfair to say that there has been any lack of cordiality between us, or any disinclination to meet together, but it has rather been because each has had his hands full, which all have understood. But the fact remains that we have never met together and observers among the Allies have been inclined to think there might be some other reason for it than the actual one.

"Prompted by my suggestion, no doubt, a meeting of the three commanders-in-chief, together with Generals Robertson and Foch, is planned for next week. In conversation with both M. Clemenceau and General Robertson I dwelt strongly upon the urgency of a complete and harmonious military understanding among the Allied armies on the Western Front, especially as to plans of operation for the spring and summer, and am gratified to record the above as an indication of full accord with this view. I have asked General Foch to hold this meeting here at my headquarters, and think this will be done.

"It is to be noted that General Bliss is to be continued on the active list. I presume you have found his visit here made him very valuable. Moreover, I am not so sure that it would be safe to change now anyway. If you should decide to keep him there, as I think possible, then may I again mention General Liggett as a possibility for the Supreme War Council, if he should be available when the time comes? He once had the War College and I think would be able to give a good account of himself and render valuable assistance to us. I shall be glad if General March can be allowed to remain here to handle the army artillery.

"The Supreme War Council seems to be busy at work on various studies, although its status as yet is not very clearly defined. The opinion generally prevails that its function is only that of an advisory body, although it is credited with having a certain political aspect. There seems little probability of a Supreme War Commander being selected, nor, as I am informed, is it generally favored, especially by members of the Council. All the Allies want concerted action, of course, but for the present thorough understanding and close liaison between the high commands appear to be the only solution.

"May I again, Mr. Secretary, suggest to you the advisability of making a visit to France. Beside being profitable to see the procedure from this point of view, it would give a new inspiration to the Allies and would especially encourage our own forces.

"Begging your pardon for the length of this letter, and extending to you renewed expressions of high esteem and sincere regard, I remain

> "Very faithfully yours,
> "JOHN J. PERSHING."

With the growth of our armies and the consequent greater need for port and rail accommodations, our situation threatened an early crisis not entirely indicated in my letter to the Secretary.

CHAPTER XXI

Difficulties with Railways—Poor French Management—Conference Commanders-in-Chief and Chiefs of Staff—Defensive Attitude Decided—Joffre against Amalgamation—British Accept my Plan—Meeting Supreme War Council—Outlook and Conclusions—Supreme War Council Decides on Reserve—Letter to Secretary of War—Winter in France

(Diary) Paris, Monday, January 21, 1918. Discussed the whole subject of schools and training on Friday with Training Section. Left Chaumont that night for Paris.

Went to Compiègne Saturday to meet General Pétain and Field Marshal Haig. We dined with Pétain; discussion general.

Reports of conference with Sims' office yesterday indicate more rapid provision of escort for returning transports.

Went with Atterbury again to-day to see M. Claveille about rail transportation. Called with Foulois on Minister of Munitions. As the French fear shortage in artillery ammunition, have given authority for them to draw on our stock.

THE control of French rail transportation was so thoroughly centered in M. Claveille, that he had become autocratic in his methods and in his attitude toward all with whom he had to deal. He was unwilling to permit us any freedom in the operation of trains or turn over to us any fixed amount of rolling stock, or promise that any given amount would be placed at our disposal, even under French management. The British had met with the same difficulty, although by persistent effort they had eventually received satisfactory concessions as to operation.

Up to this time only a limited number of trains had been allotted to our use and these at such irregular intervals that our service was more or less haphazard. We were confronted with an increasing demand for rail transportation which the French did not seem to appreciate. In their own way they appeared to be making an effort to aid us, but Claveille undertook to keep track of every detail of operation, even to the allotment of each piece of transportation to this or that use, and we were left in a continuous state of uncertainty. He would not believe that there could be any method better than that of the French, which we regarded as antiquated. As there were nearly enough damaged or lost cars and engines here and there throughout France to supply our needs if they could only be located and put in order, I offered to send experts to assist in finding them.

With the object of obtaining control over our own movements of trains, with our own railway organization, General Atterbury and I had already made several visits to M. Claveille's office. On the visit mentioned in the diary, I asked that authority at ports, in so far as rail transportation and port management were concerned, be concentrated in one official, to which he agreed, although it was not done for some time. He also promised, as he had done before, better coöperation in furnishing cars. We proposed that the French should turn over to us a fixed number of engines and cars, and let us run them ourselves, but Claveille was obdurate and would not make this concession. It finally became necessary to take the matter up with M. Clemenceau himself before we got any consideration of this suggestion, but some time elapsed before our men were running trains, except a daily train between Chaumont and Tours.

(Diary) Paris, Thursday, January 24, 1918. Went to Chaumont on Tuesday. Made arrangements yesterday for 26th Division to go into quiet sector with the French near Soissons on February 5th.

Returned to Paris this morning. Conference looking to better understanding and closer coöperation held at Compiègne to-day. Field Marshal Haig, Generals Pétain, Foch, Robertson, Pershing, and Chiefs of Staff in the field, Generals Lawrence and Anthoine, and Colonel Boyd were present. Had dinner with General Bliss, who has returned from Washington to be our military representative on the Supreme War Council.

Every one in authority realized that all resources the Allies could muster would be required to meet successfully the great offensive of the Central Powers expected in the spring, but to use them effectively close coöperation among commanders would be imperative. It was with this in mind that I proposed to M. Clemenceau that the Commanders-in-Chief and Chiefs of Staff should get together to examine the situation and if possible determine a general program of combined action. He thought that would be a good thing to do and at once approved the suggestion. It was also favorably received by General Foch, who, it will be recalled, was Chief of the French General Staff. I proposed that the meeting be held at my headquarters, but the French selected Compiègne, Pétain's G.H.Q.

At the meeting, Robertson spoke first and suggested that we ought to have a general statement on the following points: (1) Mutual support between Allied armies; (2) Situation as to reserves; (3) Question of troops in Italy; (4) Situation as to the transportation of the American Army and facilities given it in France.

Pétain thought that for the present the Allies would be forced to remain on the defensive on account of lack of men. He said that the French Army had ninety-seven divisions with an infantry strength of from 5,000 to 6,000 men each, some thirty-odd of these divisions being in reserve and the rest in the trenches; besides eight cavalry divisions, two of which were dismounted and six mounted. All divisions, he thought, could be kept up until April if there should be no fighting, but later on, even without a battle, he would have to break up five divisions in order to maintain the others. The six mounted cavalry divisions would have to be reduced to four, and before the end of the year the total force would have to be reduced by twenty divisions.

Assuming that the Allies must remain on the defensive, he was prepared, he said, to retire to successive lines. He explained that the French had organized counteroffensive operations on four army fronts, to be utilized according to circumstances, with a force of about fifteen divisions in each one, and that he would be ready to transport available reserves by rail either to relieve tired troops or assist in the defense of any threatened front. The French reserves would be at the disposition of Sir Douglas Haig and he expected a similar arrangement to be made by the British.

The reserves, he said, were so located that they could be started in any direction within twelve hours.

Sir Douglas said the British had adopted the same policy as the French, one-third of their divisions being in reserve and the rest in line; that he had three lines of resistance; and that he had prepared three different localities for offensive actions of about five divisions each, one in the direction of Gonnelieu, the second toward Lens, and the third in the vicinity of Gheluvelt-Becelaere.

Foch declared that the best means of halting a strong and persistent offensive was a powerful counteroffensive and he thought that we should draw some lessons from the experience of 1916. At that time, he said, an offensive had been prepared by the Allies on the Somme, which was delayed by the unexpected German attack on Verdun. He added, "The German offensive at Verdun was stopped not by our resistance there but by our offensive on the Somme. Such an operation is possible only when foreseen and prepared beforehand. * * * In planning for the counteroffensive, I think," he continued, "that the entire front must be considered as a whole and not the French as one part and the British as another. The plan must envisage them together preparing for offensive action on a common battlefield with all the forces at their disposal."

Pétain said the situation was different from what it was at the time of the battle of Verdun and that there "the Germans attacked only at one point, with only 125 divisions at their disposal; now they will have 170, 180, or possibly 200 divisions, and they can attack at three points at once or successively, and at each point the attack can be more violent than at Verdun. * * * When they attack at one point," he asked, "should we then launch a counterattack?" Answering his own question, he said, "We cannot prepare such a counterattack because we shall not know where the enemy is going to strike and we must be ready with some reserves to meet it. We must be very prudent."

Foch remarked that one could not fix the moment of attack beforehand and declared that the counteroffensive launched on the Somme, to which he had referred, had been prepared long before, otherwise it could not have taken place. He did not favor these small counterattacks but thought we should look forward to a grand offensive action with all possible force,—French, British, and American. Pétain stated that he agreed in principle, but added that the suppression of twenty divisions would leave them without available troops for an offensive.

Robertson declared that it was not certain that the enemy would attack in so many places at once and that it did not seem possible to do more than prepare to support the army that might be attacked, and be ready to counterattack. "Anyway," he said, "one could not win the war by remaining on the defensive," and he then inquired of Foch how and where one ought to prepare for this counteroffensive.

Foch said he had not been charged with studying a combined counteroffensive and could not tell where the principle would be applicable, but it would be necessary for us to prepare for a great offensive together. Robertson expressed accord with Foch, but he did not see where or with what means such an offensive could be executed, and again stated that the war could not be won by remaining on the defensive.

Haig said, "Give us back the troops from Salonika and we will commence offensives." Foch replied, "We were not speaking of offensives but of counteroffensives." Robertson remarked that of course the French and British could reënforce each other and make counterattacks, and then asked, "Could they do more than that?" Pétain spoke up and said, "Not without the Americans." Robertson then said, "I think our only hope lies in American reserves," and he wanted to hear from me.

I stated that but few of the Allied authorities seemed to realize that our participation would depend upon the amount of shipping available for the transportation of our troops, and that the time when Americans would be needed was near at hand. As there had been some reference to amalgamation, I also took occasion to emphasize the point that we expected as a matter of course that the American Army would have its own front as an independent force and would not be used merely as a reserve to be sent here and there. One insuperable reason, I said, why we could not amalgamate with the French was the difference in language, and added that we would not use our troops in that way at all unless it became absolutely necessary.

I then discussed our problems, calling attention to the delays at the French ports and our shortage of rail transportation, and touched on the backward state of procurement of equipment, munitions, and airplanes. They all appeared surprised to learn of our difficulties, especially General Foch, although, even as Chief of the General Staff, he apparently could not interfere in matters handled directly by the Ministry. It was astonishing to find how little comprehension any of them had of the enormous task that confronted us.

Foch said, "None of these questions has been referred to me," whereupon Pétain retorted that, "One should not wait until such things are brought to his attention but should look around and find them." Pétain added at once that he would send an official to study our situation. Haig later sent one of his officers, who offered many suggestions out of the British experience.

It was the sense of the conference that every assistance should be given us in getting our troops across, and all seemed fully to realize that no successful offensive could be undertaken without us.

The declarations of the French and British Commanders-in-Chief that the reserves of each were available for the use of the other could mean much or it could mean nothing, depending upon the conception of the situation that might confront each of them and also upon the relations that might exist between them at the time. In the light of their previous experience, it should have been apparent that the difficulties of securing the necessary close coöperation between these two Allied armies might lead to disaster. While the meeting was perhaps worth while, if only for an exchange of views and the conclusion that the Allies must remain on the defensive, yet no definite understanding was reached as to real unity of action and the conference had little more effect than the one held in the preceding August.

(Diary) Paris, Saturday, January 26, 1918. Prince Arthur of Connaught called on Friday and referred to our having met in 1906 in Tokyo, where he took part in the Fourth of July celebration at the American Legation. Conversations with Robertson continued, with Bliss present.

This afternoon Harbord, Boyd, and I called on Marshal Joffre. Have requested 2,400 men to repair cars and same number to repair locomotives. Tank Corps created with Colonel S. D. Rockenbach as Chief. Additional motor mechanics, stevedores, and material for port construction promised by War Department.

This meeting with Robertson took place in the evening at the Crillon Hotel. The same arguments were repeated in favor of incorporating American units into British divisions. My immediate interest lay mainly in getting additional tonnage for the transportation of our men to form our own army and it was not my intention at any time to agree to amalgamation in any permanent sense with either of the Allies. So far we were not committed to any such plan, but Bliss, who came into the conference under instructions from the Secretary of War, was much impressed with the British point of view and almost out of a clear sky frankly expressed himself in favor of the Robertson plan.

Of course, American troops behind the British Army, even temporarily, would be an encouragement to its morale, and if the emergency should arise they could actually be put into the fighting line, but to agree to the transfer of American battalions to build up British divisions could not be thought of. When Bliss spoke in favor of it, I was forced to declare myself then and there. My stand was not quite what Robertson had expected and the meeting was adjourned with the position of all concerned no longer in doubt.

General Bliss and I met later by appointment to talk the matter over between ourselves and if possible come to an understanding. After some discussion, he suggested that each of us cable his views to Washington and ask for a decision. It was not my policy then or at any other time to put anything up to Washington that I could possibly decide myself. This would have been the last thing to do in this case, especially as the Secretary had left in my hands the determination as to how our troops should be employed. For two men in our positions to have appealed in this way would have indicated a clash, and Washington had enough trouble; besides, the Secretary could not possibly have been in touch with the undercurrent of these negotiations. So I said, "Well, Bliss, do you know what would happen if we should do that? We would both be relieved from further duty in France and that is exactly what we should deserve." We then spent some time examining the question from all angles, until finally he came around to my view and said, "I think you are right and I shall back you up in the position you have taken."

During an informal visit to Marshal Joffre, on the 26th, I was gratified to hear him confirm my objections to amalgamation. He observed that with all the conferences that were being held I must be quite well occupied. In due course, the conversation drifted to military matters and, speaking of the French Army, he said the class of 1918 recruits was available and the class of 1919 would soon be called. He said the French were combing the country for what he called "Embusques," or slackers, all of which taken together he thought would obviate the necessity of reducing the French Army by more than three or four divisions, and then not until late in the year.

The view of Marshal Joffre was that the British were not in such good shape, and, as we knew, they were under the necessity of reducing the number of battalions in each division from twelve to nine. He said: "The British plan to bring over 150 battalions of Americans is no doubt for the purpose of building up their weakened divisions."

Launching into the question of amalgamation, and speaking as a friend of mine and also in the interests of the Allies, Marshal Joffre said, "It would be a mistake to incorporate American battalions in British divisions, as it would adversely affect the divisions," and that "orders might be given by a British general or his staff that would be resented by Americans, but the same orders would be accepted without question if given by an

American commander. In case of a reverse, there would be the tendency to place the blame on the Americans.

"Furthermore," he went on to say, "in case of an attack, your infantry would have to be supported by British artillery, and here again there might be differences." He did not believe it possible that there could exist between them that perfect confidence and liaison that was absolutely necessary between the infantry and artillery. As an indication that it was not a policy suggested by good practice and experience, he pointed out that during the whole course of the war the British had never found it advisable to incorporate Canadians, Australians, New Zealanders, Indians, Portuguese, or even Scotch, in the same divisions with English. "Then," he said, "you must consider the American people at home and their interest in and their support of the war, which would be adversely affected by amalgamation." He said that of course his views were given to me confidentially as an act of friendship. Here, then, was a distinguished French soldier who could see these questions in their true perspective without prejudice or bias.

In speaking of the threatened German offensive against the Western Front, Marshal Joffre said there were those who thought that the defection of Russia would enable the Germans to bring as many as 230 divisions against approximately 170 Allied divisions, but he did not agree with them. Such talk, he said, was causing much uneasiness among the French people not under arms, and he felt that it was a mistake to allow such statements to appear in the press. Some people thought that the Allies were going to be overwhelmed, but he was morally certain that such a thing could not happen.

As between 230 and 170 divisions, of course the discrepancy was great, but he thought that the Allies could hold, and anyway he did not believe such a discrepancy would exist. He expressed the view that the enemy would have not more than 190 divisions on the Western Front at the outside, and allowing the Allies 168 instead of 170 the difference was not enough to cause any doubt in our ability to hold them. He said that in 1914 the Germans had an excess of 300,000 men over the Allied 700,000 and a great preponderance of artillery, and they did not break the line, and he thought their chances less favorable now. He was discussing, he said, the probabilities as they existed at the moment, and although he mentioned the prospective arrival of two American divisions per month and evidently had them in mind, he did not include them in his estimate as to relative numbers on both sides.[1] In all this he said he did not want to appear as criticizing his Government, but he deprecated its attitude in permitting the people to be frightened by the stories of a heavy German offensive.

It was about this time that I met a distinguished Englishman, who took occasion to discuss the same subject, saying practically just what Marshal Joffre had said, and advising strongly against mixing nationalities. Not that there was a shadow of doubt in my mind as to the soundness of my attitude, yet coming as did these independent views just at the moment of apparently greatest pressure by nearly all of official France and Great Britain to force our hand on this question, they had considerable significance.

There were Allied officers very closely in touch with my headquarters who, although very careful in our presence, secretly advised their superiors to make every concession in order to get control of American units, with the idea that they would then be in position to use them in any manner they saw fit. Among these there was one British officer who suggested to his superiors that they should aid us ostentatiously in building up a corps, which he thought would quiet the American people, especially if we were permitted to wave the flag hard enough. Of course any such idea of domination as this, the existence of which we were well aware, only served to stiffen our attitude. It is probable that many of those who were in favor of amalgamation believed it best purely from the standpoint of haste in preparation. But there were also many who no doubt advocated the principle

---

[1] We then had five divisions in France, numerically equal to ten Allied divisions, but they were not all sufficiently trained for offensive action.

in order to prevent the ultimate formation of an independent American army.

(Diary) Paris, Wednesday, January 30, 1918. Accidental explosion of trench mortar the 27th at demonstration near French front injured Major General Leonard Wood and Lieutenant Colonel Charles E. Kilbourne slightly, Major Kenyon A. Joyce severely, and killed several French officers and soldiers.

Had a pleasant call by Captain Amundsen, the Arctic explorer, who is visiting our army. Saw Atterbury; urged him to insist on better railway service from French.

Talked over with Kernan on Monday reorganization of Line of Communications and pressed him to hasten construction of port facilities. Cabled request of French for forage, which is running low.

Bliss and I held conference at Versailles yesterday with Mr. Lloyd George, Lord Milner, Field Marshal Haig, General Robertson, and General Wilson on transportation and use of American troops.

Went to Versailles again to-day in fog extremely dense; lunched with Lloyd George, who accepted my proposal of yesterday.

Supreme War Council began its third session to-day.

Once General Bliss and I had reached an understanding as to what our attitude should be toward amalgamation, he gave me his support in later conferences. When we met the British representatives as indicated in the diary, they presented their case, reiterating previous arguments. Mr. Lloyd George then asked Bliss for his views, to which he replied, "Pershing will speak for us and whatever he says with regard to the disposition of the American forces will have my approval." I submitted a compromise program which Bliss had already seen and the British concluded to take it under advisement.

The following day, while we were en route to Versailles together, Bliss expressed some doubt whether they would accept. At the meeting, Mr. Lloyd George acknowledged that my objections to amalgamation were sound and told me that he had said so to his confrères the day before. An agreement was then signed by Mr. Lloyd George, General Maurice, and myself as set forth in the following copy of the memorandum submitted and later cabled to Washington:

"CONFIDENTIAL.   "January 30, 1918.

*   *   *   *   *   *   *

"Following memorandum of our position was presented in conference between ourselves and British and was agreed upon. Memorandum has approval of General Bliss.

"A.—This memorandum refers to the request made by General Sir William Robertson, representing the British War Office, that the American Government send by British shipping to France 150 battalions of infantry for service in British divisions on the Western Front. Replying to this proposal, the following objections appear: 1st.—The national sentiment in the United States against service under a foreign flag; 2d.—The probability that such action by the United States would excite serious political opposition to the Administration in the conduct of the war; 3d.—The certainty of its being used by German propagandists to stir up public opinion (in the U.S.) against the war; 4th.—It would dissipate the direction and effort of the American Army; 5th.—Differences in national characteristics and military training of troops and consequent failure of complete coöperation would undoubtedly lead to friction and eventual misunderstanding between the two countries; 6th.—Additional manpower on the Western Front could be provided as quickly by some plan not involving amalgamation.

"B.—In order to meet the situation as presented by Sir William Robertson and hasten the arrival and training of troops, it is therefore proposed that the British Government use the available sea transportation in question for bringing over the personnel of entire divisions under the following conditions:—

"1. That the infantry and auxiliary troops of these divisions be trained with British divisions by battalions, under such plan as may be agreed upon.

"2. That the artillery be trained under American direction in the use of French matériel as at present.

"3. That the higher commanders and staff officers be assigned for training and experience with corresponding units of the British Army.

"4. That when sufficiently trained, these battalions be reformed into regiments and that when the artillery is fully trained, all the units comprising each division be united under their own officers for service.

"5. That the above plan be carried out without interference with the plans now in operation for bringing over American forces.

"6. That question of supply be arranged by agreement between the British and American Commanders-in-Chief.

"7. That question of arms and equipment be settled in similar manner."

A few days later the Secretary replied stating his views, as follows:

"We have no objections to the program which you suggested by the way of substitute in subparagraph of your 555 but in our judgment it would be wiser for the British to undertake to transport six complete divisions across the sea to be disposed of and trained as you direct, in conference of course with the commanding officers of the other forces."

Of course this was in accord with my views as stated in the proposal I made to the British and to which they agreed, except that the artillery pertaining to the divisions was not to be sent to the British but was to be trained under our own supervision. However, the fortunes of war intervened more than once to prevent adherence to plans and agreements.

(Diary) Paris, Saturday, February 2, 1918. The Supreme War Council in session the past three days.

Sir John Asser called on Thursday, sent by Haig; his experience on British lines of communication will enable him to give us valuable suggestions.

Called yesterday evening on Ambassador Sharp.

Have sent Colonel Logan, General Staff, G.H.Q., on special inspection of the Line of Communications to get better coöperation.

At the opening of the session of the Supreme War Council, Mr. Lloyd George spoke in some detail of the situation on the Allied fronts. He mentioned the large number of casualties the Allies had suffered during 1917 and in a very pointed manner declared that the costly offensives had produced no tangible results. Moreover, he said, the Allies now found themselves short of manpower at a crucial period of the war. His sharp criticism was evidently directed at Sir Douglas Haig and General Robertson, but neither was given an opportunity to reply.

NOTE: Total strength of the A.E.F. on January 31st, 12,785 officers, 203,003 enlisted men.

The Military Representatives presented a joint note with reference to military policy, as directed at the December meeting, and the opinion given was practically the same as that of the conference at Compiègne, on January 24th, and of the meeting in Paris in August. The note held the view that the campaign under General Allenby then in progress in Palestine should be continued. It will be recalled that these two informal conferences of Commanders-in-Chief had concluded that the Allies should remain on the defensive on all fronts until the Americans should arrive in sufficient force to warrant the offensive. The joint note was approved as the decision of the Council, with the understanding, as suggested by the French, that no white troops should be sent from France to Palestine. It was decidedly the opinion of M. Clemenceau, and of all others present who expressed themselves, that the war could not be ended until 1919, when the American Army, it was thought, would reach its maximum power.

Of our five divisions then in France, none would be ready for active service for two or three months. However, the prospect was that in addition to these we should have a few others ready by June, and by September possibly seventeen, or the equivalent of thirty-four French divisions. The danger on the Western Front lay in the continuous increase of the German armies and in their ability to concentrate in turn against the French and British, and as neither had sufficient reserves of their own, it was clear that some arrangement must be made for better coördination and support.

The Military Representatives submitted another joint note which proposed the organization of a General Allied Reserve. The plan provided that the British, French, and Italian armies should each set apart a certain number of divisions to constitute this reserve, which would be called into action only in a great emergency. The discussion of this question became rather acrimonious. Haig and Pétain, also Robertson, were against such a reserve. They pointed out how they would be short of divisions very soon in case of severe fighting and presented figures on the subject that were very disturbing.

But the Council's scheme was cut and dried. The recommendations set forth in the note were adopted then and there. A General Reserve was prescribed and its control was placed under an Executive War Board to consist of Generals Foch, representing the French, Chairman; Bliss, the Americans; Cadorna, the Italians; and a British general officer to be named. At this same meeting of the Council, Mr. Lloyd George designated General Sir Henry Wilson as the British representative, to the very evident disappointment of General Robertson, who was present at the session. The selection of Wilson was regarded by the British High Command and the War Office as an open disapproval of their conduct of the war.

In accordance with the decision, the Executive War Board, as the administrative authority of the Supreme War Council, sent out instructions directing the French and British Commanders-in-Chief each to select a certain number of divisions to form a part of the General Reserve. The number was finally fixed at thirty in all; ten British, thirteen French, and seven Italian.

The use of these reserves appeared somewhat indefinite, but the idea as brought out in the discussion seemed to be that the divisions designated as constituting the General Reserve would be so situated that they could be moved expeditiously to the support of the army seriously attacked. Their use was to be determined after consultation between the Executive War Board and the Commander-in-Chief of the army affected. This plan of the Supreme War Council did not meet with the approval of the armies, especially the British, who apparently regarded it merely as an indirect means of assuming supreme command.

One other matter somewhat linked up with this question of a general reserve was the proportion of line that should be held by the French and British armies. The French occupied about 340 miles of front, with their right on the Swiss border, while the British had only about 110 miles, extending from the French left near St. Quentin to the right of the Belgian army. The French argued that they were holding a greater proportion of line than the British, but the latter contended that a large part of the French front was inactive and did not require many troops, while the British front was active. After considerable discussion, the question was referred to the Military Representatives on the Council for an opinion. Their recommendation was not acceptable to the French, so the matter was finally decided by agreement between General Pétain and Field Marshal Haig, under which the British were to extend their front some twenty-eight miles, to a point near Barisis. This concession was used later by Sir Douglas Haig as one reason why he could not spare divisions for the General Reserve.

The following letter to the Secretary of War covers matters of interest as viewed at that time.

"France, February 4, 1918.

"Dear Mr. Secretary:

"I am sending this letter by General March, giving a brief report of the negotiations concerning the troops to be brought over by the British and trained with their divisions.

"After fully considering the matter, I am quite convinced that it would be unwise for us to break up divisions by turning over infantry battalions, as such, for extended service with the British. The main reasons are set forth in my memorandum cabled to the Department, copy of which is enclosed herewith.

"As to the question of obtaining extra shipping from the British, it does not look favorable from this end of the line, but I hope we may increase our tonnage by every possible means.

"I am also enclosing two other memoranda, one a conversation with Marshal Joffre, which I would request be held in the strictest confidence, and another giving a synopsis of a conference held between ourselves and the British on the subject of their request for men. From the former it will be seen that the Marshal takes the same view that I do regarding service with the British. He further does not look upon the situation on the Western Front with quite so much alarm as is indicated in statements by Marshal Haig and General Pétain.

"One more word regarding this discussion. General Bliss, upon his arrival, was inclined to accede to the British request, basing his action upon the cable he received from the Chief of Staff, which stated that the proposition had my approval, although I had not intended to convey that impression. So, after further conference with him, in which I set forth the views of Marshal Joffre and similar views of a British officer of high rank, given me in confidence, General Bliss agreed with me, and we [later] appeared before Mr. Lloyd George in full accord. My views were then fully set forth and were afterward declared by Mr. Lloyd George to be entirely sound.

"The Supreme War Council has been in session since last Wednesday, during which time the whole subject of the conduct of the war has been discussed in its different phases. The establishment of a general reserve was determined upon and its control was placed in the hands of an executive committee consisting of General Foch and the following-named military advisers on the Supreme Council:— General Sir Henry Wilson, British; General Cadorna, Italian; and General Bliss, American. I think the arrangement for unity of command all that could be desired without one supreme commander, which ideal is apparently considered by all concerned as impossible.

"Generally speaking, the meeting of the Supreme Council was a success, and the utmost harmony finally prevailed. Personally, I am pleased with the outlook for military coöperation. We are at some disadvantage on the diplomatic side in the Council. I stated to Mr. House when he was here that I thought he should be our representative. He undoubtedly has the confidence of the Allied governments and would add great strength to the Supreme Council. I see by the dispatches that Mr. Lane [1] has also been suggested.

"Among the enclosures, I am sending you a copy of a compilation made for the Supreme War Council, showing the strength of both the Allies and the Central Powers on the date mentioned. It puts the matter in condensed form and will enable you to get a better idea of the manpower on both sides than any other statement yet sent you.

"Conditions at our ports are improving, and I am pushing the turn-around of transports with all possible speed. The Navy is giving us better service of late in convoying transports as requested. The shortage of railway cars is easing up, and will grow better as the number of repaired cars to be obtained from the Belgians increases.

"General March is returning to America as you requested. He will be difficult to replace, but I feel that you need the best man we can find, so I cheerfully let him go. He is in touch with plans, organization, and progress here and understands the situation very well.

[1] Mr. Franklin K. Lane, then Secretary of the Interior in Mr. Wilson's Cabinet.

"I shall not take up more of your time. Please accept my very sincere regards, and renewed congratulations upon your success.
"Yours faithfully,
"JOHN J. PERSHING."

The winter of 1917-18 was the most severe of the war. The cold was at times so intense as to make the generally unheated houses, barns and lofts used as billets nearly uninhabitable. The gloom of short days and long nights in the isolated and largely depopulated French villages can hardly be described. The snow was unusually heavy in eastern France, and periodical thaws, with consequent mud and slush in the trenches and dugouts, greatly added to the hardships of the men of all armies. Training in the open was often impossible for days, and under the conditions even the regular supply of necessary food for men in the trenches became a formidable task. Restricted areas in village streets were kept cleared for daily exercises only by the constant work of troops. The northeastern part of France, while beautiful in summer, is certainly somber and unattractive in winter.

The natural tendency of all troops, but especially Americans, under such conditions was to use an excessive amount of fuel. Nothing delights our soldiers more than to gather around a rousing fire either in or out of doors. But the allowance of firewood was limited and there was no such thing in France as stealing the top rail from fences, as our troops did in the Civil War. Many units had to go into the forests and cut their own wood, and the winter was well along before our forestry troops got to the point of keeping up the supply.

Then, the shortage of heavy winter clothing from home had not been met. The demands were no doubt greater than the Quartermaster Corps could supply. Much of the clothing that we received for our troops was reported to be shoddy. I saw numbers of men wearing uniforms which were light and thin and which, of course, offered insufficient protection. The lack of clothing had been met in part by purchases from the British. Our troops did not take kindly to the idea of wearing the uniform of another nation, and it was with considerable protest and chagrin that they did so.

I recall an incident that occurred in one of the regiments which was composed largely of Irish-Americans. This organization had received British uniforms on which the buttons had not been changed to our own. When the uniforms were issued a wave of opposition swept through the outfit against wearing buttons with the British coat of arms. In order to pacify the objectors, an automobile was sent post haste with American buttons, the changes were made, and the regiment then turned out looking both smart and serene.

The necessity for haste in preparation and for the maintenance of morale required that our program of training be carried out almost regardless of the weather, and even though it entailed some discomfort the constant outdoor life kept the troops in good health and hardened them for the work ahead. To the credit of our officers and men, be it said that they generally ignored adverse conditions and, barring some irritation at French methods and occasionally at our own, they kept at their tasks with commendable determination. Looking back over the different phases of the war, I regard that winter, with its difficulties, anxieties, and apprehension for the future, as the most trying period of them all.

CHAPTER XXII

Stars and Stripes—Tuscania Torpedoed—Labor Procurement—Shipping Improvement—2d Division—Reorganization Line of Communications —G.H.Q. General Staff—Visit from Foch—Aircraft Needs—Port Situation—Letter to Secretary.

(Diary) Chaumont, Friday, February 8, 1918. Dawes called Sunday in Paris with Captain Dean Jay, his assistant; Captain Cutcheon, who will head board on Contracts and Adjustments; and Major Jackson, Labor Procurement.[1]

Called Monday on M. Clemenceau and General Foch taking with me General March, who will be Chief of Staff in Washington.

Returned from Paris on Tuesday. Conforming to efforts at home, have issued strict orders on conservation of food. British fear invasion and their request that any of our troops in England should stand ready to aid approved by the Secretary of War. Arrangements made for coöperation between General Trenchard, British Air Service, and General Foulois, our Chief of Aviation.

Visited Intelligence Section to-day, under Colonel Nolan; find it well organized. Military Mission[2] being sent to Italian G.H.Q. First number of *Stars and Stripes* issued to-day. *Tuscania,* carrying American troops, reported torpedoed off Irish Coast, 166 missing. Went to Langres with Harbord and Boyd and found schools making excellent progress. January reports show increased rate of arrival of men and material.

WE were always concerned that the morale of our troops should be kept up to a high pitch. As an aid in this direction, it seemed to me that a publication of some sort that would be available to all the troops would be useful. By my direction, the question was taken up by Colonel Nolan and

[1] Major J. P. Jackson had been formerly Labor Commissioner of the State of Pennsylvania; Captain F. W. M. Cutcheon was a prominent lawyer in New York; and Captain Dean Jay had been Vice President of the Guaranty Trust Company of New York.

[2] The Mission consisted of Maj. Gen. Eben Swift, Col. John McA. Palmer, General Staff, Lt. Col. R. U. Patterson, Medical Corps, and later Capt. F. H. LaGuardia, Air Service.

317

the result was the *Stars and Stripes*—the official newspaper of the A.E.F. This publication was under the management of Lieutenant G. T. Viskniskki, who assembled as editors of the various departments a remarkable group taken entirely from the enlisted personnel of the Army. From the start, no official control was ever exercised over the matter which went into the paper —it was entirely for and by the soldier. The first number was issued on February 8, 1918, and its success was immediate. Before the Armistice its circulation grew to more than 500,000. I do not believe that any one factor could have done more to sustain the morale of the A.E.F. than the *Stars and Stripes*.

At dusk on the evening of February 5th, off the Irish Coast, a torpedo launched from an enemy submarine struck the British convoyed liner *Tuscania,* having on board American troops, causing a loss later reported to be 113 men. The fine discipline of the men and the efficient handling of a difficult situation by those in command, together with the splendid work of the British Navy, contributed to account for relatively light casualties. We were filled with profound appreciation of the devoted conduct of the British destroyers, which, notwithstanding the fact that hostile submarines were lurking in the vicinity, rendered every assistance and remained on the scene until all survivors were brought safely ashore. At the small ports of Ireland and Scotland where our men were landed they met with a warmhearted reception on the part of the people, who gave them every possible comfort and care.

In seeking to obtain additional labor abroad, a request was made for Italians from among those employed by the French, but it was found that none could be spared from the important work of constructing new lines of defense behind the French front. As we needed some 50,000 laborers, I started an inquiry as to the possibility of obtaining part of them direct from Italy. But as the American Ambassador at Rome had reported that the Italian Government was opposed to sending any more men out of the country, on the ground that they were needed at home, this plan did not appear very promising. Our need for laborers was pressing and a bureau for labor procurement was therefore created under the Purchasing Board, and the question was taken up with M. Ganne, of the Cambon Mission, to see what could be done.

At the ports the amount of freight received in January was somewhat encouraging, being about two-fifths as much as during the preceding seven months. The rate of discharge was accelerated to some extent through a better distribution of our transports by the Navy to the different ports. More construction material, including piles, was being delivered where it was most needed, and the future was somewhat clarified in this respect by the arrival of additional logging machinery.

During the month there was also an increase in troop arrivals, including divisional troops and 20,000 men for the Line of Communications. By the end of January approximately 120,000 combat troops, 34,000 engineer troops, and 61,000 for other services were in France. Although promising, that was, of course, only a beginning, as we were still far behind our schedule, and the shipments of men and material from home remained haphazard and not in the proportions needed. We were rapidly approaching the time when we were expected to be of some help to the Allied cause and it was necessary that our forces should be balanced to make them as independent as possible. Coöperation by the General Staff at home was needed.

In the absence of any preparation for war beforehand, the principle can hardly be questioned that the commander at the front and not the staff departments in Washington should decide what he needs. The employment of our armies in Europe had been fully covered by general instructions and there were no problems of strategy or questions concerning operations that devolved upon the War Department staff. These were matters for the Commander-in-Chief of the A.E.F. to determine. It remained, then, for the War Department simply and without cavil to support our efforts to the fullest extent by promptly forwarding men and supplies as requested. The Secretary of War was completely in accord with this conception, but it was evident that the staff departments had not grasped it or else the disorganization and confusion were such that it could not be carried out.

The increase in our tonnage appeared very small in the face of the demands from both the French and British for raw material, most of which we had promised for their manufacturing programs and upon which we must largely depend for munitions. Briefly, the French needed 120,000 tons of steel, 30,000 tons of copper and brass, 6,000 tons of tin, lead, and antimony, 9,000 tons of spelter, 31,000 tons of cast iron, and 30,000 tons of powder and explosives. The British required 165,000 tons of steel, 23,000 tons of copper and brass, 1,200 tons of tin, lead, and antimony, and 36,000 tons of explosives and powder, making a total of over 400,000 tons of material due the Allies from America. The manner of meeting these requirements now presented a most difficult problem, both of tonnage and priority.

Due, no doubt, to their anxiety, there was a tendency among our Allies, especially the French, to exaggerate the urgency of their requests for material. Oftentimes after investigation it turned out that their estimates could be substantially reduced and in some instances ignored altogether. So faulty was the organization and management of the Government's business that at times the French lost track of considerable amounts of raw materials they had actually received from abroad. Confusion was not entirely limited to America.

(Diary) Chaumont, Wednesday, February 13, 1918. Inspected 2d Division last Sunday in Bourmont area.

Met committee on staff reorganization to-day and decided important points for better administration. Saw Murphy, Perkins, and Eliot Wadsworth on Red Cross matters. Had E. H. Sothern and Mr. and Mrs. Winthrop Ames to luncheon.

Have received assurance of increased shipments of subsistence, forage, and clothing, to be followed by locomotives and cars. Weekly reports by Medical Department of health conditions continue favorable.

The 2d Division, commanded by Major General Bundy, which had been organized in France in October, was composed of an infantry brigade, with artillery and auxiliary troops of the Regular Army, and one brigade of Marines. The 9th and 23d Regiments, forming the brigade of Regulars, were of the old army and their experience and the traditions behind them, even with the large accession of recruits in their ranks, gave ample assurance of what they would do. The 5th and 6th Regiments of Marines had become a part of our forces at the suggestion of Major General George Barnett, then Commandant of the Marine Corps, and with my approval. These troops united with the brigade of infantry, formed a division of relatively well-trained troops; and with such an advantage at the start, this division was destined soon to take its place among the best on the Western Front.

In the process of development abroad of our great military machine, certain changes in the original organization were indicated. The probable early increase in our combatant strength made it necessary to plan for the rapid expansion in all activities, the development of which had been delayed for causes which have already been mentioned. As a great commercial concern, the Services of Supply [1] was charged with the reception, transportation, storage and distribution of everything the army had to have, and also with hospitalization of the sick and wounded. Without sound business administration it could not be successful. Its commander must have broad discretionary powers and the territorial or section commanders under him must also have certain independence of action. Wise and efficient management of an organization embracing so many interests and spread over such an extent of territory demanded decentralization in all matters on which a policy could be fixed.

In the new organization the chiefs of the supply departments of the A.E.F., respectively, acting under their titles and authority as members of the staff of the Commander-in-Chief, were to exercise all their functions of procurement, supply, transportation, and construction under the direction of the Commanding General, Services of Supply. The Judge Advocate General, the Adjutant General, and the Inspector General, whose duties did not pertain to supply but to general administration, remained at G.H.Q. The

[1] Heretofore referred to as the Line of Communications.

Transportation Department, the Motor Transport, and the Forestry Service, were placed under a Chief of Utilities, through whom their activities were coördinated under the Services of Supply. Although these technical staff and supply services were subject to the orders of the Commanding General, Services of Supply, a representative or group of each was attached to the General Staff at G.H.Q. to maintain the close liaison necessary for prompt service in the Zone of Operations.

In the successful command of an army such as ours eventually became, it was necessary to bring the supervision of all elements of the administrative and technical departments under the control of the Headquarters General Staff. None of the departments entered upon their duties with any experience in war, nor had they in any real sense been trained even theoretically to solve the problems that urgently demanded solution. During times of peace each department had grown relatively independent of the others, and each chief had directed the affairs of his department with little control, except of a very general character.

With reference to the General Staff, the same thing may be said as to experience in war or real preparation for it. In fact, so faulty had been the training of the General Staff as members of a great directive group that both the individuals and the group lacked initiative and purpose for want of a clear conception of their tasks. It was to overcome this inertia that I vested in the General Staff well-defined powers to give such direction, by my authority, as might become necessary to coördinate the different parts of the organization. This assumption of directive control did not reduce or affect the efficiency of the administrative or technical department chiefs or their assistants, because they too, under supervision, were given independent rôles, encouraged and moderated at the same time by the one requirement—success. Such was the broad conception of the organization built up as the G.H.Q., A.E.F.

(Diary) Chaumont, Monday, February 18, 1918. General Foch and General Weygand visited headquarters on Thursday, had luncheon with us, and examined the general staff organization. Captain

Todd, Director of Naval Construction, came to confer regarding wireless station at Bordeaux. Colonel Henry L. Stimson, former Secretary of War, now an efficient Colonel of Artillery, called and asked to be left with troops. Cable says Major General March appointed Chief of Staff at Washington, relieving Major General Biddle, ordered to England.

Left Friday, spent Saturday and Sunday with 1st Division in Ansauville sector; inspected infantry in front line trenches and the artillery. Saw General Debeney, commanding French First Army, under whom 1st Division is serving.

Returned to Chaumont to-day, stopping at aviation park, Colombey-les-Belles. Camouflage work exceptionally well done. Passed through Mirecourt to see General de Castelnau, who speaks highly of our troops. Went to Vittel and Contrexéville where newly arrived hospitals were found in poor condition; thence to Bourbonne-les-Bains and Montigny-le-Roi to inspect 3d Cavalry and engineer detachments and found discipline lax.

As General Foch had shown some surprise when, at the meeting at Compiègne in January, I told of the delays and difficulties we were having at the ports and in the operation of railways, I invited him to make a visit to my headquarters, hoping to put him in touch with our activities. We had already reached a state of development that confirmed the soundness of our organization and could forecast its ability to meet all requirements. I went with him to the various sections of the General Staff and while he expressed no opinion about what he saw, his aide and spokesman, General Weygand,[1] a staff officer of experience, was very complimentary. Foch never seemed interested when I talked with him of our problems and I doubt whether at the time he ever thought, knew, or cared much about our organization, or our questions of transportation and supply. He was essentially a student and teacher of history and strategy.

The very extensive and intricate organization necessary to handle a modern army engaged in war beyond the seas was not

[1] On one occasion during his visit to the United States Marshal Foch and I were speaking of our respective war-time staffs, and he referred particularly to Major General Weygand and Colonel Desticker, who, he said, were very close to him and who always thought as he did on any military subject. According to the Marshal, what either of these officers said was as though he, himself, had said it.

easy to grasp. Indeed, the details were not entirely understood in our own army except by a limited number of officers charged with the functions of direction and coördination.

One way to get an idea of the difficulties that had to be met would be to imagine that the 500,000 people residing in the city of Washington, D.C., were all capable of bearing arms and were sent to France and provided with clothing, food, arms, equipment, medical attention, and there trained for war. Then imagine that about the time they had been located in various towns and villages in France, the entire population, 1,500,000 people, of the city of Detroit, were also sent over, at the rate of 250,000 per month, to be handled under the same conditions and with the same object in view. This would be only a part of the problem, as the greater proportion of this multitude would then have to be moved to the battle front, or to its vicinity, and eventually engage the enemy in battle, in a coördinated effort involving infantry, supported by artillery, aviation, tanks, and all other auxiliary forces, controlled and moving toward a designated enemy position against all the opposition and violence the enemy could bring to bear. As to numbers and general description this is exactly what eventually happened. This comparison may assist the lay reader to obtain a better notion of our problem.

As to wireless communications, the possibility of interference by the enemy with our cables had caused some concern and the projected radio station at Bordeaux was a precautionary measure to meet such a contingency. Very properly, it was a naval proposal and plan, as the navy system had charge of the transmission of our confidential messages and was especially interested in those relating to the movements of transports. Although the Navy undertook the construction of this station at once, it was not completed until after the Armistice, and has since been turned over to the French as a link in their radio system.

In aviation development a crisis had been reached in raw materials, especially spruce and fir. Owing to the delay in furnishing these things, our aviation program abroad, which depended largely upon Allied production, was very much retarded. According to the Inter-Allied Aviation Commission, of which General Foulois was the American member, there was not enough spruce and fir in France to keep the French factories going more than a month longer, when they would require something like a million feet. The British and Italian factories were in about the same predicament. Our aviation control at home had made an allocation by which they had retained from 30 to 40 per cent of the production of these woods, although it was apparent that no such quantity could be utilized in the manufacture of American airplanes in time to be of use to the Allied cause. Questions of details of construction were still under discussion between our aircraft board at home and that abroad. The fact is that with us the industry had to be built from the ground up, and it had to be done with no experience to guide us.

A recommendation was cabled requesting that the three other countries involved be given a larger share of materials which they needed in building airplanes for themselves, and for us also, until our output could meet our own requirements. It has never been clear to me just why we should not have given full assistance and preference to factories [1] abroad that were already turning out planes of approved pattern, instead of clinging to the exaggerated claim of our airplane manufacturers that they could supply our armies within a reasonable time. That such a delusion still clouded the issue is shown by the promise made by Washington about the middle of February that by March 31st there would be something over 300 planes ready for shipment, and by May 1st a total of 1,600 would be completed, the numbers increasing monthly to a grand total of nearly 12,000 by the 1st of November. The first thousand planes were to reach the army in France by July 15th. We shall see in later chapters how much these promises lacked of being fulfilled.

At this moment there were several hundred of our men await-

[1] Orders were placed with the Italian Government for 700 planes and 2,400 engines, but our failure to deliver sufficient raw material, and the Italian reverses in the fall of 1917 prevented their fulfillment.

My contract with the French in August, 1917, for 5,000 planes and 8,500 engines was abrogated mainly on account of our non-delivery of raw material.

ing training, the French and Italian schools were full, and we had an insufficient number of planes to train them ourselves. Only nine squadrons[1] out of the sixty that we should require by June 30th for front line service could be considered at this time as anywhere near ready, and the prospects were that even this small number would have to use inferior types of planes purchased from the French, unless the receipt of raw material from the States and consequently the production in France could be materially hastened.   In the face of our failure to produce planes at home or to fulfill our engagements to furnish raw material for their manufacture in France, it was small wonder that the French found themselves in a situation that would only warrant a promise of planes as our divisions arrived.

I had recently inspected several stations like Vittel and Bourbonne-les-Bains, which were commanded by Regular officers, of whom, naturally, much was expected, and had found the personnel there careless in dress and none too strict in discipline. The conditions of service in France demanded serious attention to these essentials, not only as a matter of pride but because of the general effect upon morale and efficiency.   Good discipline is the first requisite to successful military effort and the degree of its enforcement in a command is an almost certain index of the character of performance in battle.   Likewise, an officer or soldier who takes no pride in his personal appearance is usually found careless in other respects, and to that extent less reliable in time of stress.   It need hardly be added that those of this class who came under my observation and who did not immediately respond to suggestion were very soon replaced by others of different attitude.

(Diary) Chaumont, Saturday, February 23, 1918.   Saw Maurice Ganne, M. Cambon's successor, who is earnestly helping in procurement.

Had conference yesterday with Atterbury, Taylor, Harbord, and

[1] Each monoplane pursuit squadron consisted of 31 officers, 181 enlisted men, and 25 planes.   The number of officers for biplane squadrons was 34, and for observation squadrons 43.   We were to have 120 squadrons at the front by December, 1918.

Connor on port and rail situation. Prepared detailed report for Secretary of War. Have cabled Washington important report by Inter-Allied Metals Committee.[1] Just learned that there has been some criticism in Congress of French management of ports.

Since last entry Generals Swift, Bell, Crozier, and Wood have been guests at various times.

Although there had been some improvement in the rapidity of discharge of freight, we were still handicapped by lack of modern mechanical appliances, the receipt and installation of which had been considerably delayed. This applied particularly to gantry cranes. A difference of opinion had arisen between engineers of the construction corps and those in the rail transportation as to the advisability of using them on the new docks. After several attempts to bring about an understanding between the agencies concerned, I ordered these cranes brought over for employment. Their use was made possible by strengthening the docks in question.

The continued shortage of railway cars to move freight from the docks aggravated the situation. It was true that some 30,000 damaged cars still lay on side-tracks here and there, but little or no attempt was made by the French to repair them. Repair personnel from home could not be obtained and we were able only partially to carry out our proposals to undertake the task. At this time 8,000 tons were discharged daily at all ports, but only 3,000 tons were being removed, although we should have reached a point by this time where it would have been possible to handle three or four times that much. Additional storage might answer temporarily, but it was easy to see that congestion could become serious.

Washington was naturally solicitous and even expressed hesitation about making further shipments, instead of complying with our requests and rushing over the personnel and matériel that would have permitted us to overcome the difficulties. In order

---

[1] The Inter-Allied Metals Committee undertook to adjust the requirements of various Allied Governments in products peculiarly necessary in the manufacture of metals for munitions and other purposes. These products were tungsten, chrome, zinc, spelter, tin, retort carbon, cryolite and emery.

to put before the Secretary of War a complete statement of conditions and causes, an analysis of immediate requirements was cabled in detail and also sent to him by letter. It was estimated that we must have sufficient tonnage, with accommodations and personnel, to have in France 287,000 men by April, and 771,000 by September. To correspond to this inflow, 8,700 tons of cargo must arrive daily in April, rising to 21,000 in September.

We had at this time ten berths at St. Nazaire, four at Nantes, three at La Pallice, four at Rochefort, six at Bassens, and four in prospect at Brest. The construction of berths at Bassens, ten in number, was well under way, and some were already in use. However, all berths could not be kept occupied, as ships, very properly, were still brought over in groups under convoy. Therefore, it was necessary to have an increased number of berths to accommodate several ships at once. With this provision at various ports and the completion of cargo-handling facilities, Atterbury and his associates in the Transportation Department, and W. D. Connor, of the general staff section, in charge, felt every assurance that the tonnage estimates could be promptly handled.

Concerning this question, it was explicitly stated in my cables as imperative that we must increase our storage space by rapid construction, and our rail facilities by a large accession of engines and cars, new and repaired. In addition, we had to have material to carry on the progressive laying of main-line tracks and 125 miles per month of sidings. It was equally pressing that we should have more rail and stevedore personnel without delay. With the fulfillment of these requirements, I insisted that there should be no hesitation in sending over troops, emphasizing the point that the exigencies of the military situation in France should govern, and that no obstacle, imaginary or otherwise, should prevent the full use of every available ton of shipping.

There continued to be considerable cause to find fault with the attitude and methods of French bureau officials. They had been repeatedly urged to turn over certain docks and facilities for our exclusive use, and while some concessions had been made, it was always grudgingly and by piecemeal, and we were never certain of more than temporary occupancy. Under the circumstances, I did not hesitate to call M. Clemenceau's attention to the remarks made in our House of Representatives criticizing the French attitude toward affording us port accommodations. While this resulted in a somewhat more liberal policy, it did not remove the necessity for constant pressure on our part.

In the S.O.S. a true spirit of coöperation was often absent among subordinate French officials, who seemed to make little attempt to understand our problems. Among the higher officials the desire was usually there, but only by dint of constant urging could we obtain the meager and insufficient facilities that we had to put up with. In all our relations with them throughout the Services of Supply, at the ports and in railway traffic, it was an ever recurring matter of surprise to me how our officers in direct daily contact with the many obstacles remained hopeful instead of becoming pessimistic. It must be said, however, that the French officers of the liaison group as individuals attached to various organizations were always found anxious to make things go smoothly, though in many instances they clung to the notion that we should adopt French ideas and methods. It can also be said that the services of our American liaison officers with the French at various offices and organizations in the Services of Supply were almost without exception praised by the French.

Apropos of the experience of many of our officers, I recall that one of the most efficient officers on duty at a very important port once said to me, "General, the trouble is that these subordinate French officials in immediate charge are either so hide-bound or else so conceited that it would be as easy to convince a Greek statue as to make one of them understand. How in the world it happens, Sir, that we do so well I do not see. Here we have come 3,000 miles to help them and yet we are treated like mendicants on the street corner holding a tin cup for passing pennies. I know, Sir, that coöperation is necessary if we hope to win the war, but it requires an excessive effort on our part, with more failures than successes to our credit." This was harsh comment, but there were times in the experience of most officers when it seemed to fit the case fairly well.

The following letter was sent to the Secretary of War in the hope of reaching him before he should sail on his contemplated visit to the armies:

"February 24, 1918.

"Dear Mr. Secretary:

"I hope this letter will reach you before you start for Europe, as I am sending a brief outline of the work that has been accomplished here by the various departments, in order to give you a view of the situation as a whole. Enclosure 'A' will give you a sketch of the projects, and the chart marked 'B' will show the progress that has been made in each. The other enclosures are a copy of my new general staff organization just adopted, and a small map showing the location of our troops in the line.

"I am having a résumé made up of our immediate needs as to material and labor, which I shall cable in a day or two and which should receive attention at once. The prospective early increase in the number of vessels available for transport and the consequent large increase in cargo and personnel will require increased accommodations without delay. As you know, * * * material and labor for these purposes are very much behind or we should have been in better shape. We must now push port work to the utmost. In this connection, the next most vital improvement necessary are the railroads, and I am sending in a condensed cable to-day covering that also. Both ports and railways, however, should go along together.

"I presume General Bliss has reported the results of the last meeting of the Supreme Council at Versailles, so I shall not go into that further than to say that the plan of operations on the Western Front meets with my entire approval and I think that the lines can be held in case the Germans carry out their much heralded offensive. But we must lose no time in getting ready for our part as the necessity for our aid may come very soon.

"Since my last letter on the subject of training and service of our units with the French and British armies, there has been much discussion, with the final result as cabled you. I think both the British and French now fully understand that we must look forward to the upbuilding of a distinctly American force instead of feeding our units into their organizations. Your decision on that point has settled all thought of our doing anything else.[1]

[1] This did not prove to be correct.

"I want to say that General Bliss is a most excellent choice for the post he now holds, and that our relations are most harmonious and I feel sure must remain so. He is an able man, as square as a die, and loyal to the core. I do not think you could have found any one to fill the place with greater credit to us all. He is very much occupied and has not been to my headquarters as yet, but I expect him shortly.

"In accordance with a tentative agreement made by General Pétain and myself, we shall in time have a sector of our own as soon as our divisions are able to act independently. It will probably begin where the 1st Division is now finishing its training, between St. Mihiel and Pont-a-Mousson, from which base we shall likely extend both to the west and east. I hope that the work they will be called upon to do may not at first be too severe, but one cannot always tell what is going to happen in war.

"It takes a long time to get troops in shape because the officers require so much practice and experience. This applies particularly to higher officers and officers of the staff. The multitude of detail that they have to grasp and prepare for can only be learned finally and thoroughly by application in the front lines.

"The particular sector selected, being one side of a German salient, is least likely to be the point of great German pressure, and it will afford, on the other hand, a better opportunity for offensive action than most other places within reach of our front. Of course, it should be understood that our divisions, when ready, even though in the line, should be considered available to go anywhere in an emergency.

"With reference to the enclosed memorandum on general officers, I think we must follow the experience of our Allies in that as in other lessons the war has taught. The ineptitude of the older officers so far tried completely bears out the experience of both British and French. It will not be profitable to spend any time trying to teach such men. In time we are going to develop a capable lot of younger men for higher commands.

"As to the General Staff, the work of all sections has been excellent under the former organization and designations, but in the new draft I have been able to correct defects that became apparent. The new designations for sections is an improvement. I must mention the work of G-4 (Coördination), as I think it very essential to have some such body who shall have a large view of the problem as a whole and be able to give directions that relieve me and the Chief of Staff of many details. I would suggest the application of this principle in the General

Staff at Washington if you have not already inaugurated it. * * *

"May I extend to you, Mr. Secretary, my sincerest good wishes for your success, and add that I have no sympathy with all this political fault-finding, which is serving no good purpose but which only tends to shake the confidence of our own people and give our enemy encouragement.

"With very warm personal regard, I remain, as always,

"Yours very faithfully,

"JOHN J. PERSHING."

CHAPTER XXIII

Air Service Difficulties—Extravagant Claims of Press at Home—Procurement Abroad—A.E.F. Gardens—Tonnage Situation Improving—M. Clemenceau Visits 1st Division—French Praise—Make Inspection of Troops—Cooking in Our Army—Casualty Lists—Decorations Authorized—Secretary Baker Arrives—Usual Calls—Visits Principal Activities

(Diary) Chaumont, Thursday, February 28, 1918. Held conference Monday with senior aviation officers, Foulois and W. B. Burtt, and later Mitchell. Newspaper clippings from home proclaim thousands of American airplanes in France. Have cabled protest.

Had call Tuesday from Mr. J. J. Davis and ex-Congressman Lentz, here in interests of Order of the Moose. Conferred with Brewster; troops making progress. Appealed for more Regular officers as instructors staff college and schools.

Bishops Brent and J. N. McCormick called yesterday and dined with us. Held conference with our members of Allied Maritime Transport Council, who lunched with us to-day. War Department has appointed representatives on various Committees of Supreme War Council.[1]

IT will be recalled that aviation was separated from the Signal Corps early in the history of the A.E.F. The difficulties of its organization were naturally inherent to those of any newly formed unit. The lack of a well-considered scheme worked out in time of peace was sorely felt. Differences in the views of the senior officers of the corps were not easily reconciled. Jealousies existed among them, no one had the confidence of all the others, and it was not easy to select from among the officers of the corps any outstanding executive. However, the questions of training and supply were fairly well worked out, but the handicap of shortage in both personnel and matériel was not readily overcome.

A number of excellent officers had been transferred from both

[1] Brig. Gen. B. D. Foulois, Aviation; Col. A. D. Andrews, Transportation; and Col. S. D. Rockenbach, Tanks.

line and staff to aviation, but their lack of technical knowledge reduced their usefulness in helping to build up this service. The whole subject gave me serious concern. However, the latest conference, mentioned in the diary, was somewhat more encouraging.

Meanwhile, some of the more sensational newspapers at home were making extravagant claims about the large number of American planes then actively engaged in France when in fact up to this moment there was not a single plane of American make on the Western Front. Of course unfounded reports of this sort were very harmful and their appearance led me to make a strong protest against its being permitted, as will be shown by the following cablegram:

"February 28, 1918.

"Newspaper clipping from United States received here to effect that United States has thousands of fliers in France and that thousands of American airplanes are flying above the American forces in Europe to-day. As a matter of fact there is not to-day a single American-made plane in Europe. In my opinion the result of such bombastic claims in the American press has had the effect of materially stiffening German production. Some sane statement might be given the press at home to counteract these exaggerations. These statements are grossly exaggerated and are extremely detrimental to the future efficiency and expectations of the Air Service, American Expeditionary Forces. Emphatically protest against newspaper publicity of this nature and urgently recommend drastic steps be taken to stop publication of such articles. One clipping in question is being returned by mail to-day. Suggest this matter be brought to the attention of Mr. Howard Coffin."

The frequent German raids and renewed activity all along the front indicated that the great German offensive might start at any time. The French General Staff thought the Allies would be able to hold without serious difficulty until we could help, but it was doubtful enough to cause considerable apprehension. It was depressing to think that ten months had elapsed since our entry into the war and we were just barely ready with one division of 25,000 men. With all our wealth, our manpower and our ability, this was the net result of our efforts up to the moment; all because our people had been deceived by a false and fatuous theory that it was unnecessary in time of peace to make even preliminary preparations for war. Here we were likely to be confronted by the mightiest military offensive that the world had ever known and it looked as though we should be compelled to stand by almost helpless and see the Allies again suffer losses of hundreds of thousands of men in their struggle against defeat. In spite of these reflections, there was the hope that with the utmost effort we should yet be able to develop our latent power in time to save our friends. At least, now that we were about to face the crisis, it was vital that America should exert herself to the utmost to complete what she had so leisurely begun.

It was evident to all that every available ton of shipping would have to be used to insure the fulfillment of our program. Hence, the saving in tonnage was becoming more and more important. The Allies were more alive than ever to the necessity of our obtaining as many things abroad as possible. The French had held out the promise to do their best to help us with horses and there was some hope that negotiations then in progress for 20,000 mules from Spain would be successful. With these prospects in view for obtaining animals, it was recommended that shipments from home could be postponed four or five months.

Our Forestry Department was in better shape than ever and gave every assurance that most of the timber and lumber for docks, wharves, and other construction would be obtained in France. Efforts were being made to improve the rail situation by securing more complete coöperation among the Allies in the matter of use of rolling stock, by urging the French to repair the thousands of damaged freight cars, and, in general, by keeping cars moving instead of allowing both loaded and empty cars to stand on sidetracks for days and even weeks at a time.[1] There was no doubt that the French railroads were very much run down and it was our task to help relieve this condition as soon

[1] This question of idle and damaged cars was taken up by letter addressed to the Chief of the French Mission, and in reply General Ragueneau explained, in substance, that all the 35,000 cars provided by the British were in use by their armies, and that 26,000 cars had to be employed by France in service for Italy, besides those required

as possible. Urgent cables were again sent asking that the shipment of rolling stock be hastened. Our agencies were vigorously at work trying to obtain labor from Italy, Spain, England and Norway for use on the railways and elsewhere. And as to procurement, no source, however limited, was overlooked.

As a means of relieving the burden on tonnage, it will be recalled that the suggestion had been made to bring farmers to France from the States to help increase agricultural production. Although that did not seem practicable, approval was given to the suggestion that suitable land left unproductive by the French who had gone to the front might be cultivated by and under supervision of our troops. To this end the Quartermaster Corps started a central garden at Versailles under a general superintendent of gardens who was to provide tools and distribute seeds to various units. Each division was instructed to begin a garden wherever practicable in its area and if transferred elsewhere to pass it on to the unit that followed. If successful, fresh vegetables that could not be obtained in any other way except in small quantities might thus become available. However, changes of units from place to place came in such rapid succession during the following months that the scheme did not reach expectations. But during the spring and summer, wherever they had an opportunity, our men aided the French on the farms near their billeting areas, with results that often accrued to our benefit.

As we have seen, a committee was appointed at the Inter-Allied conference in November to consider the question of Allied shipping, out of which developed the Allied Maritime Transport Council. At my request, several of our members [1] of the Maritime Council came to my headquarters to study the subject of our requirements and to continue their investigations regarding tonnage, both Allied and neutral, available for the use of our armies.

for the Americans, who had so far furnished only a limited number themselves; also, that their needs had been met by a great reduction in civilian traffic, but the tremendous wear and tear on rolling stock had made it difficult to keep it repaired with the limited amount of labor available.

[1] Dwight W. Morrow, R. B. Stevens, L. H. Dow, and George Rublee.

So far, there had been no definite or dependable allotment for our purposes, and commercial demands had been all too often given precedence over those of the army. The prospects of early relief by construction at home were not promising as only one vessel had been turned out in almost a year. Our members of the Council had given considerable study to the question of shipping and the information they had obtained enabled me to make a very strong appeal to the War Department for a greater allotment. The result was a reasonable increase in the number of vessels under our own flag to be assigned as transports and also the accession of some captured tonnage, which, together with that obtained by charter from the British, gave some promise that we should be able to carry out the estimates set forth in a preceding chapter. We were still much concerned, however, over the large requirements in tonnage necessary to meet our commitments in raw materials and supplies to the Allies and the considerable amounts of wheat, oats, and flour promised to the Swiss.

The heartening news of these additions to our passenger and cargo fleet stimulated activity in the various supply and equipment agencies both at home and abroad. It looked as though confusion and delay might give way to promptness and cooperation, or in any event this was the hope of those of us who had impatiently waited for such a turn of affairs.

(Diary) Chaumont, Wednesday, March 6, 1918. Heavy German raid repulsed by 1st Division on Friday morning. The enemy also raided the 26th Division lines and were driven off.

Had meeting Saturday with Colonels Johnson Hagood and Andrews on S.O.S. organization. Lord Brooke and Frazier house guests. Some American women journalists visited me that afternoon.

Went to Ligny-en-Barrois Sunday to meet M. Clemenceau, who came to congratulate the 1st Division on success repulsing raid. Met General Debeney, who was enthusiastic over conduct of our men. Spent the night at 1st Division Headquarters.

Motored to Langres with Harbord Monday to speak at opening of second session of General Staff College. Germans made raid on 42d Division that morning.

Yesterday, with de Chambrun and Boyd, went to Baccarat to see 42d Division.

Visited hospital this morning and found men wounded during raid in fine spirits. Also visited the 165th, 167th, and 168th Regiments; all making progress. Conferred with Generals C. T. Menoher, M. J. Lenihan and R. A. Brown. Experienced an air raid during dinner at Nancy and drove to Chaumont afterwards.

Upon conclusion of this inspection of the 1st Division I considered it ready to take the offensive at any time. It had been in France eight months, with varied experiences in training, had occupied an independent position in the St. Mihiel sector, and had made several successful trench raids. Duncan and Buck had their infantry brigades in efficient shape and Summerall had carried the training of the artillery brigade to a high degree. As to the 42d, 26th and 2d Divisions, the first two being then with the French in quiet sectors, and the 2d about to enter, each had yet to serve in line as an independent division to complete its training. In view of the certainty of determined German action at an early date, the quality and condition of our units were studied with solicitude by the French no less than by ourselves.

It was M. Clemenceau's custom while Prime Minister to spend Sundays visiting different portions of the front. As mentioned in my diary, he came especially to congratulate the 1st Division on its success in repulsing the raid and was enthusiastic over the conduct of the troops on that occasion. The vigor and the aggressive spirit he displayed, notwithstanding his age, were contagious. On these visits, he wanted to talk with the men right up at the front, and while it was not always convenient to humor him, one had to admire his attitude.

I wished especially to be present at the opening of the General Staff School in order to emphasize the importance of staff training. My speaking during the war was entirely extemporaneous, but it seemed more effective than if read from manuscript. In

NOTE: Total strength of the A.E.F. on February 28th, 16,547 officers, 235,342 enlisted men.

Divisional units arriving during February included elements of the 32d Division (National Guard, Michigan and Wisconsin), Major General William G. Haan.

this talk I stressed the necessity of preparation for duties that were expected of staff officers and dwelt on their obligations and their relation to the line. The new class for the second three-month session consisted, as usual, of officers selected from the various units of staff and line. The course of instruction had been carefully laid out by Brigadier General McAndrew and his assistants, all graduates of our Fort Leavenworth school, and consisted of an intensive study of lectures, specially prepared texts, and practical problems.

On the visit to the 42d Division we spent the night at Baccarat as guests of M. and Mme. Michaut. At dinner, with all the children and grandchildren present, the family formed a most charming group. The town had been partially destroyed early in the war and now that the Germans were again active because of the presence of Americans it looked as though they might make the destruction complete. I recall that when the possibility of putting an end to war was mentioned during the conversation at dinner, the grandmother of the household said, "No, that is not likely. We have had war here in this part of Europe every fifty years during the last thousand." That is the view of nine out of ten people and still they go about the work of reconstruction as though such a thing as war could never happen again.

The front occupied by the 42d Division, near Badonviller, had been under a severe artillery attack on the 4th and a trench mortar platoon had been almost completely destroyed. The French Army Commander congratulated General Menoher on the way in which our troops repulsed this raid. After an inspection of the different regiments of the division and a visit to the scene of this action, I went to the hospital to see the wounded. They were all very cheerful, especially a young officer, Lieutenant A. W. Terrell, 151st Field Artillery, who had lost one of his legs. He said that he wanted to stay through to the end of the war and hoped he could find something to do as a clerk. All these first contacts with the enemy were relatively small affairs, of course, but they furnished many examples of what we could expect of the American soldier.

(Diary) Paris, Sunday, March 10, 1918. Spent Thursday morning with Kernan, W. C. Langfitt and Atterbury and made adjustments in port and railway construction and management. Visited Camp de Mailly, where seacoast artillery is having splendid training under Brigadier General Frank W. Coe. Put up that night at a quaint little tavern in Montmirail.

On Friday visited Edwards' 26th Division, serving on Chemin des Dames under General de Maud'huy, the French Corps Commander. Lunched at headquarters with General Edwards and visited brigades under Traub and C. H. Cole. Arrived in Paris late at night during airplane attack. Branch of Judge Advocate General's Office established at my headquarters.

Upon Colonel Bradley's report of only thirty-day medical supplies on hand, sent urgent cable requesting immediate shipments. Cabled disapproval of suggestion by Mr. Paderewski for organization of division of men with Polish antecedents. Secretary of War landed at Brest to-day.

Major General de Maud'huy spoke with considerable enthusiasm of the men and of the officers of the 26th Division below regimental commanders, and especially praised their conduct of trench raids. He complimented Traub, one of the brigade commanders, but was of the opinion that the higher officers, generally, needed more experience to make them efficient. American troops that served with Maud'huy held him in high esteem. He was scrupulous regarding their instruction, to which he gave special attention.

He was very solicitous of the welfare of our troops, even going so far as to interest himself in the preparation of their food by detailing French cooks to teach ours the art. When I expressed my appreciation of his action, he said, "You know we are a nation of cooks and we delight in preparing good things to eat." After their instruction, the cooks in these units did better, thanks to the initiative of this fine old French general.

The cooks in our new units lacked experience in preparing the field ration, and in the beginning the men did not fare so well as our troops of the Regular Army on the frontier, where many cooks became experts. Personal supervision by officers and the establishment of cooking schools in the A.E.F brought improvement in due course of time. However, there is little doubt that much of the intestinal trouble among our men during the first months of their service abroad was caused by poorly cooked food.

As soon as our troops began serving in the front line in quiet sectors, we were faced with the problem of handling casualty lists. The solution reached was to defer cabling the lists until some time after the engagement and then to send them in groups, to be given out by the War Department, so that the particular battle in which the casualty occurred could not be identified. If we had given the names to the press at home immediately, it would have been equivalent to telling the enemy the engagement in which they occurred. The French published no lists, but the information was sent to the local mayor, who in turn notified the family of the soldier, at the same time extending them his condolences. Contrasted with this quiet, sympathetic way of giving such news to relatives, the method of publishing column after column of killed and wounded in the papers which people would eagerly scan day after day seemed inconsiderate and cruel.

The problem of decorations in our army had long been a knotty one, and except for the Medal of Honor and Certificate of Merit we had only campaign badges and those given for marksmanship. The Allies desired to confer their decorations on our men who served with distinction under them, but we were not permitted to accept foreign decorations without permission from Congress. There is no doubt that some sort of visible evidence of exceptional military service arouses pride and stimulates effort. The generous bestowal of decorations in each Allied army by its Commander-in-Chief was unquestionably an important factor in maintaining the morale of their troops. Our own Medal of Honor had inspired many an heroic act.

As it was a matter of importance to our officers and men, the whole question of decorations was taken up by the War Department on my suggestion with the result that Congressional action established certain medals of our own and authorized our soldiers to receive those of foreign governments. The medals created by Congress at this time were the Distinguished Service Cross for extraordinary heroism in connection with military operations against an armed enemy, and the Distinguished Service Medal for exceptionally meritorious service in a position of great responsibility. These were in addition to the Medal of Honor, our highest decoration, established in 1862, for gallantry and intrepidity at the risk of life above and beyond the call of duty. The award of the Certificate of Merit was discontinued.

Authority was also eventually given the War Department to confer our decorations on Allied officers and men who had rendered deserving service with our armies. The different grades of medals in the various countries were not entirely the same as ours. We had none that corresponded to the French or Belgian Croix de Guerre. There ought to have been one for gallantry in action somewhat less conspicuous than that covered by the Medal of Honor or the Distinguished Service Cross. I made a recommendation to this effect, but nothing came of it. There were thousands of instances in our armies where a medal of this class should have been bestowed. We were as liberal in decorating Allied officers and men as the provisions of our law would permit, and there is no doubt that the exchange of decorations helped materially to promote friendly relations.

(Diary) Chaumont, Sunday, March 17, 1918. This has been a busy week. Early Monday morning I met the Secretary of War upon his arrival in Paris and escorted him to Hotel Crillon. Later he and I called on Ambassador Sharp, M. Clemenceau and Marshal Joffre. The party,[1] together with the Ambassador and Secretaries Bliss and Frazier, lunched with me. There was a severe air raid that night, several bombs dropping near my quarters.

The Ambassador gave a dinner for the Secretary on Tuesday evening, after which we left by rail to visit the Services of Supply.

Returned to-day, having inspected our most important ports, depots, hospitals, regulating stations, aviation centers, motor parks and schools.

Word received of selection for shipment of six divisions for training

[1] The Secretary's party consisted of Maj. Gen. W. M. Black, Chief of Engineers; Lt. Col. M. L. Brett; Comdr. R. D. White, of the Navy; and Mr. Ralph Hayes, his secretary.

with British—28th, 30th, 77th, 78th, 80th and 82d. Successful trench raids by our troops continue.

It was essential that the Secretary of War be given every opportunity to inspect our whole system, from the Services of Supply to the trenches, in order that he might become familiar with our plans, observe the progress toward their completion, and obtain first-hand information of our requirements, all of which he was especially anxious to do.

Leaving Paris on the 12th, our first stop was Bordeaux. Spending a few minutes for an informal welcome at the station by the French commander, and the representative of the Base Section Commander, Brigadier General W. S. Scott, who was ill, we went at once to inspect the permanent port works. The next thing was a visit to Bassens, six miles down the Gironde, where we were using six berths turned over to us by the French. Since my last visit, much progress had been made on our own project of ten new berths. Then came the St. Sulpice storage area, just out of Bordeaux, where a network of railway sidings led to row after row of new storehouses being filled with property that required cover, while other classes were being accumulated in the open storage space. We concluded the morning with a walk through the base hospital, which had accommodations for 1,000 patients, and then went to one of the leading restaurants, the Chapeau Rouge, for luncheon.

The inspection of other activities a few miles out occupied the afternoon, and included the artillery camp of instruction at Souge, under Brigadier General Ernest Hinds, where several regiments at a time could be trained; the large hospital at Beau Desert, all ready for convalescents; and the principal remount depot, with a few hundred horses and mules.

On the following morning we reached St. Nazaire, omitting the smaller ports such as La Rochelle and La Pallice mainly used for special purposes. We were met by the section commander, Brigadier General R. D. Walsh, accompanied by the French Admiral de Marguery and by the Sous-Préfect, who, with unfailing adherence to the hospitable custom, was there to read his couplet of welcome, doing so with quaking voice and trembling knees.

After the formalities we inspected docks at which ten berths were to be assigned to us and found several ships discharging cargo while others were awaiting their turn. At all ports, according to reports we received, thirteen vessels were being unloaded that day, which was somewhat encouraging, as it set a new record. The dock facilities at St. Nazaire were to be augmented by construction of piers on the Loire, at Montoir, but lack of material had delayed the beginning of that work. An engine erecting plant was established at this port in February and a car erecting plant was located at La Rochelle. The motor parks, which came next, contained relatively few of the thousands of cars and trucks needed.

After luncheon we motored to Montoir, in the suburbs, where we boarded a flat car arranged with seats and were taken by rail over miles of sidetracks through the immense storage yard covering acres. We passed rows of warehouses, finished and unfinished, being filled with perishable supplies, while out in the open were quantities of various classes of material for which cover was not necessary. We then inspected the well-ordered base hospital located in the central school building at Savenay. It had accommodations for several hundred patients and was already filled. Mr. Baker had a cheerful word for each man as we walked through the wards. The nurses looked especially neat and military. We also saw the large dam at Savenay and the reservoirs at St. Nazaire which had been constructed by our engineers to augment the meager water supply for the various camps and other installations in the vicinity.

As we were making something of a flying trip, the same evening found us under way for Saumur, where we arrived the following morning, to visit our artillery school for officers. It occupied the accommodations of the famous French cavalry school and had capacity for handling 600 students. The commanding officer, accompanied by the French artillery instructors, escorted us through the classrooms and gave us a practical exhibition on the drill ground, all of which left in our minds a good impression of efficiency. During an examination of one of the 75-millimeter field guns, a French officer described its mechanism but omitted the details of the recoil system. When asked to explain it to the Secretary, the officer, faithful to his early instructions, replied that it was a military secret. Although the same guns were being made at factories in the States and every artillery officer of our Army was familiar with the principle, the young Frenchman admirably stood his ground and declined to take the chance of betraying his trust.

Our next destination was Tours, the headquarters of the S.O.S., Major General Kernan commanding. We glanced through the offices and the Secretary spoke briefly to the assembled officers and complimented them on their evident efficiency. We then saw the large salvage plant, under Captain F. D'Olier of the Quartermaster Corps, which was receiving, renovating and repairing uniforms, shoes and equipment of every kind and description from all parts of the A.E.F.

When a unit was relieved from the trenches every man was required to cast off his entire outfit of clothing and his equipment also, if badly worn, take a bath, go through the delousing process, and then draw a fresh outfit complete. All this was prescribed in orders for sanitary reasons and to save time. The clothing and unserviceable articles of equipment left behind were gathered up by the Salvage Service, Quartermaster Corps, and shipped to salvage depots by trains that would otherwise have returned empty. The system, by making most of these things available for reissue to the troops, saved many millions of dollars' worth of property during the war, to say nothing of the corresponding economy in tonnage.

Midday found us making a three-hour run to the small town of Gièvres, about 125 miles directly south of Paris, on our main line of supply running to the front. Here 20,000 men were employed in managing our largest interior depot. It conveys only a vague impression of the magnitude of this plant to say that it eventually covered twelve square miles, had 165 storehouses, with nearly 4,000,000 square feet of storage space, connected by 143 miles of sidetracks. It had storage for 2,000,000 gallons of gasoline, refrigerator capacity for 6,500 tons of fresh meat, and warehouse space for clothing and food for 30 days' supply of 2,000,000 men, not to mention the thousands of tons of medical, signal, engineering, and ordnance supplies, excepting ammunition.

To illustrate the celerity with which the system operated, we need take but one example, which later occurred when everything in the depot was in full swing. At 8:15 one morning in August a telegram was received ordering exactly 4,596 tons of supplies, including 1,250,000 cans of tomatoes, 1,000,000 pounds of sugar, 600,000 cans of corned beef, 750,000 pounds of tinned hash, and 150,000 pounds of dry beans. At 6:15 o'clock in the evening, or just ten hours later, this colossal requisition, which required 457 cars for transport, was loaded and on its way to the advance depot.

No other place gave such an impression of the tremendous task of supplying our armies and of the perfection of organization necessary to do it efficiently. We spent almost two hours going about on a flat car following the labyrinth of tracks and sidings in looking over this plant.

It was necessary for the Secretary, because of lack of time, to omit a number of stations, depots, repair shops, and aviation centers, including the large ordnance shops at Méhun for rebuilding heavy artillery, the ammunition depot at Jonchery, and the hospitals along the line of communications representing a total of beds and equipment for 50,000 sick and wounded.

The main Air Service School, at Issoudun, Lieutenant Colonel W. G. Kilner commanding, which we visited the following day, was a hive of activity, being one of the fifteen schools where early instruction in flying was given. General Foulois went with us through the school, the shops and the Red Cross and Y.M.C.A. buildings. I was pleased that the Secretary should see the really expert flying considered necessary to prepare aviators for their hazardous life at the front. I was able to draw a comparison between the British and French aviators on the one hand and ours on the other, and found that ours, even at that time, were fully up to the highest standards of either.

It was said that opposing aviators during the early days of the war often saluted each other as they passed on flights of observation. But they soon took another attitude and enemy planes became immediate objects of attack. By the time we entered the war aviation was an important auxiliary arm. Airplanes were built and classified for different missions and training was based upon certain principles of attack and defense. Our aviators had these things to learn, but they were remarkably quick in doing so. The aerial photography of the air service became the main source of information regarding the enemy's trenches, his movements and his positions, upon which firing data for the artillery was largely based.

From Issoudun our party went to Nevers, Colonel A. Johnson commanding, in the vicinity of which were extensive hospitals, the main railroad shops, where most of the relatively small French engines and cars were repaired, and the principal motor, machine and construction shops, virtually a large automobile factory. Several of our new hospital trains were also held at Nevers in readiness for service.

The most interesting point we visited, probably because of its intimate relation to the battle front, was the regulating station at Is-sur-Tille, southeast of Chaumont, under Colonel Milosh R. Hilgard. Supplies were received in bulk from the main storage plants in the rear, segregated, and sent forward to the railheads by the trainload, each division usually receiving one trainload a day. All the details were explained to the Secretary, who took pains to understand the mechanism of the system.

We next motored to Langres, where the great central group of schools was located, with hundreds of officers and men undergoing instruction. The Secretary and I had luncheon with Brigadier General W. R. Sample, commanding the Advance Section, S.O.S. Then, beginning with the General Staff School, we looked over the schools for infantry officers, and those for machine gun and tank instruction and several others. It was gratifying to see the interest shown by the students. A more earnest lot was never assembled together and they exemplified fully the fine spirit that prevailed throughout the A.E.F.

We completed the rounds of the Services of Supply on March 17th, reaching the headquarters at Chaumont that evening by motor. The Secretary had been given a bird's-eye view of the general plan of handling supplies for an army of 2,000,000 men which, with additional construction, would enable us to meet the demands of an army twice that size. Yet he had seen only the main features or types of activities. The entire system extended over almost the whole of that part of France contiguous to the ports and to our main lines of communication. It was estimated that construction, generally speaking, was nearly half completed at that time, although all activities were going concerns and practically fulfilling the demands made upon them notwithstanding the constant shortage of labor and transport facilities.

The vast institution, the Services of Supply, which we had inspected, functioned according to the system shown on the accompanying diagram. This system assured to the troops a con-

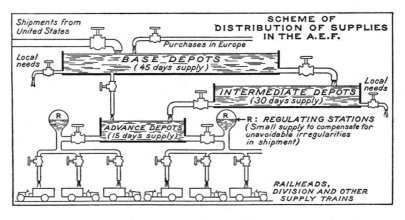

stant and adequate flow of supplies, while, at the same time, as a measure of safety against submarine and other losses, there was maintained in France a sufficient reserve.

Shipments from the United States, augmented by such supplies as were purchased in Europe, were placed in the warehouses within the Base Sections. From these base depots there was a constant flow of shipments to the storage depots in the Intermediate Section, so controlled as to maintain therein a large, fixed reserve of all supplies needed by the troops. These storage depots themselves served as a reservoir from which the depots of the Advance Section were stocked and in which a reserve adequate for fifteen days' needs of the troops was held. Emergency shortages were filled direct from base depots. The function of these advance depots was to fill the bulk requisitions of the regulating stations in the forward areas, sending the shipments in trainloads to the proper stations. At these, the supplies for each division were made up into trains and sent forward to the railheads, where they were received by the units to which they were consigned. Each combat division required the equivalent of twenty-five carloads of supplies daily, and these supplies had to be delivered promptly and regularly to points within short truck-haul of the location of the troops.

(Diary) Chaumont, Wednesday, March 20, 1918. On Monday handled several matters observed during inspection. Cabled request that locomotives and cars be sent complete to save trouble of erecting them here. Have asked for light-draft vessels that enter shallow ports. Sent cable about shortage of nitrate in France. Mr. Baker was shown through headquarters and later spoke to General Staff officers in complimentary terms. We went to Langres in the afternoon to witness a tactical demonstration, after which the Secretary left with Harbord for the front.

To-day Henry P. Davison, Perkins and Wadsworth took luncheon with us and Davison explained the world-wide activities of the Red Cross. This afternoon went to Tréveray, where Mr. Baker reviewed John L. Hines' brigade of the 1st Division. Returned by way of the birthplace of Joan of Arc. To-night we leave by special train for French G.H.Q.

When the Secretary of War visited the headquarters and spoke to the assembled officers of the General Staff, he said that his conception of the tremendous task was very different since his coming to France. He appreciated, he said, the complexities of the problem and affirmed the determination of the administration at home to support the A.E.F. in its great work. He was agreeably pleased with the organization and thanked the General Staff officers for their loyalty and devotion to the sacred cause.

I brought to the attention of the Secretary our serious handicap due to an insufficient number of general staff officers and urged that more should be sent over in view of the approaching German offensive. We discussed the exchange between general staff officers at home and abroad, which had been suggested by the Chief of Staff in order that he might have more officers at home familiar with our difficulties in France. The idea would have been carried out later, but events of such importance followed one after another that our officers could not be spared and the principle never found regular application.

Secretary Baker and I talked over the subject of promotions, which had already been the occasion of considerable cabled correspondence. The point was that many officers had received advancement in the States ahead of others in France whose experience and abilities had shown them especially qualified for promotion. In order to do justice to all, I proposed that rank should attach to the position and not necessarily to the individual. With the Secretary's approval and his expressed desire that it should receive consideration by Congress at an early date, a cable was sent to the Department embracing the idea, as follows:

"An officer assigned to the command of troops or to a staff position in the American Expeditionary Forces by orders from competent authority shall, during such assignment, have rank and be entitled to the pay and allowances appropriate to the command so exercised or the staff position so occupied as shown in approved organization tables. An officer so assigned to command shall take rank over all officers in the command to which he is assigned."

The recommendation was never enacted into law, but such a provision would have been entirely fair and would have made it less embarrassing to replace officers who did not prove efficient. If the tenure of office in time of war were made to depend upon the character of performance, an officer could be continued if satisfactory or if not he could be relieved and could not claim consideration simply on account of his rank. There were many instances both in France and at home where officers of high rank had to be replaced and there was no appropriate duty commensurate with their permanent rank to which they could be assigned. Permanent rank should be made to depend upon the efficiency shown while holding the temporary rank.

CHAPTER XXIV

German Offensive Begins—British Driven Thirty-seven Miles—Confer with Pétain—British Proposals to the Secretary of War—Italians Appeal for American Troops—Supreme War Council Requests Accelerated Shipment of Infantry and Machine Gun Units—Foch Selected to Coordinate Allied Action—Visit to Clermont to Offer Foch American Troops—German and Allied Tactics in March Offensive

(Diary) Chaumont, Monday, March 25, 1918. Arrived Compiègne on Thursday with Secretary Baker, took luncheon with General Pétain, who afterward explained the military situation. We could hear heavy artillery firing which proved the beginning of the German attack, although no definite news had then been received. The Secretary, with Colonel Palmer and Major Collins, left to call on Field Marshal Haig on their way to London and I returned with Boyd to Paris.

Drove to Versailles on Friday to see Bliss, and later saw Atterbury on shortage of rolling stock caused by large number of trains now moving troops.

Returned by auto to Chaumont Saturday. Received reports on Sunday of long-range German gun [1] firing on Paris the day before.

Went to Compiègne this afternoon to offer Pétain all our available divisions as needed. Am urging Washington that State and Treasury insist on our getting 15,000 laborers from Italy in return for loan of $30,000,000. Think we must replace 9,000 tons of foodstuff and forage we have purchased from French.

IT will be recalled that the plan of the Supreme War Council, adopted in February, was to form a general reserve to be composed of thirteen French, ten British, and seven Italian divisions. The British Commander-in-Chief claimed, however, that in taking over from the French Army the additional front

---

[1] This gun was afterwards known as "Big Bertha." It was 120 feet long, caliber 8¼ inches, and used a shell weighing 264 pounds. It was fired from different positions, at ranges varying from 56 to 75 miles, and at intervals from March 23d to August 9th, using 367 shells, killing 250 people and wounding 640. Seven of these guns were manufactured. The life of each gun was but 50 rounds, when it had to be rebored to a somewhat larger caliber. *The Paris Gun*, by Col. Henry W. Miller.

from opposite St. Quentin to Barisis in January he had to put in divisions that might otherwise have been available, and that he had none left for the general reserve. The directions regarding the reserves were not carried out, and an agreement between Haig and Pétain as to mutual support was substituted in its stead.

When these facts were made known to the Supreme War Council by the British Commander-in-Chief they occasioned much surprise. But the lack of divisions on the part of the British was explained to the Supreme War Council on March 14th at its meeting in London, and the Haig-Pétain arrangement was accepted by the Council as satisfactory. The agreement was in substance the confirmation of the understanding between Haig and Pétain as explained at the military conference held in Compiègne in January. The time had now come for the fulfillment of this agreement.[1]

On March 21st the great German offensive began against the British armies between the Oise and the Scarpe, near the junction of the French and British lines, on a front about fifty miles in length, extending from near La Fère to Arras. Near the center of the attack was General Gough's Fifth Army, with the Third Army under General Byng on its left. The artillery bombardment preceding the infantry advance was of short duration but of great intensity, with an unusually high proportion of gas shells. Following a heavy barrage, the German infantry, using the same tactical methods that had been so successful at Riga and Caporetto, delivered its blow. The weather favored the enemy, as a heavy fog continued intermittently for three days, much to the disadvantage of the defense. The overwhelming force of sixty-four specially trained German divisions out of their 192 then on the Western Front [2] compelled the British lines to yield. Although at the end of the first day the Fifth Army had not entirely given away, its losses had reached several thousands

---

[1] Discussed in Chapter XXI.

[2] The relative strength of the two sides on the Western Front on April 1st was estimated by my own and Allied Intelligence Sections: German rifles 1,569,000 and Allied rifles 1,245,000, giving the Germans a superiority of 324,000 rifles.

and there was no question that the Germans were making a serious attempt to separate the British and French armies.

While there seemed to be every confidence before the attack that the lines could hold, full consideration had not been given to the certain use of open warfare tactics by the Germans, in which neither the British nor the French had been sufficiently trained. Adherence by the Allies on the Western Front to trench

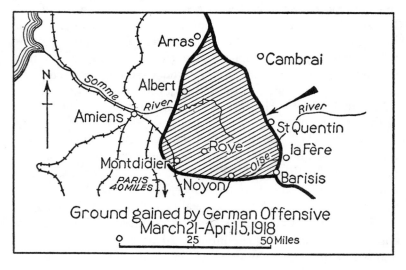

Ground gained by German Offensive March 21-April 5, 1918

warfare methods proved advantageous to the Germans. Except for the Verdun affair of 1916, Germany had been on the defensive in the West while completing the conquest of Russia and the Near East. As expected, the collapse of Russia and the total defeat of Roumania released a large number of German divisions for the 1918 offensive in the West, where the Germans gained numerical superiority for the first time since 1914. With this advantage, they promptly began training for open warfare with the object of forcing their adversaries out of the trenches and beating them in the open.[1] In this sort of warfare the British

[1] During the winter 1917-18, German divisions were given intensive instruction and training in mobile warfare with unceasing drill from morning until night. By February 10th, 58 divisions had completed a four weeks' course.

were seriously handicapped on account of their long adherence to stabilized warfare. Their officers said that when the men had to leave the trenches they acted as though something were radically wrong in that there was not another trench somewhere for them to get into.

On the second day of the battle the last of Gough's reserves were put in, yet he received no support to stop the widening gap in the British front until the following day, when one French infantry division and one French dismounted cavalry division arrived. On the 24th four other French divisions got into position. These divisions and others that came in the next two or three days were put into battle by General Fayolle without regard to the integrity of units or the order of their entry, some of them being very short of ammunition.

The British Fifth Army was evidently sorely pressed from the start, yet no British reënforcements were sent to Gough until the 24th, and then only one division, no others arriving during the first week. By the end of the fifth day the German forces had driven a salient into the British front some thirty-seven miles deep and were threatening the important railway center of Amiens, the capture of which would probably have made a complete breach between the French and British armies.

A small American unit participated in the defense against the German attack. Several companies of the 6th Engineers, which were on duty behind the British Fifth Army on railway repair work, were furnished arms and engaged in the operation until after the lines were established.

In view of the agreement for mutual support, it is not clear why the British and French should not have had a greater number of reserve divisions within easy reach of the point of juncture. Certainly it seemed logical that the enemy would endeavor to separate the two armies by attacking at that point. In fact, our information for some time previous indicated that he intended to do so. In the extension of the British front, the French had gained several divisions for their reserves, but when the blow came few of them were near enough to be of immediate service.

The French staff seemed to fear that their front might be the German objective, and this might account for the lack of French reserves near the junction of the two armies. Whether the general reserve would have been adequate or not, there is no doubt that the substitute agreement for mutual support did not fully meet the situation.

In the moment of greatest stress, when it seemed very doubtful whether the German advance could be stopped, General Pétain sent the following order to his armies:

> "The enemy has hurled himself upon us in a supreme effort.
> "He hopes to separate us from the English so as to open the way to Paris. Cost what it may he must be stopped.
> "Hold your ground! Stand firm! Our (American) comrades are arriving. All together you will throw yourselves upon the invader.
> "The battle is on. Soldiers of the Marne, of the Yser and of Verdun, I call upon you. The fate of France hangs in the balance."

British losses were reported to have been not less than 150,000. Lord Northcliffe, whom I recall meeting on the 24th, was almost unable to speak of it, so many of his friends had lost relatives. The depression among their people was probably worse than at any other period of the war. Among the French there was much anxiety as to the safety of Paris, and there was talk of moving the Government to Bordeaux again, as was done in 1914.

The reports from the front gave an extremely dark picture of disaster and I felt that we should do everything possible to render assistance. It was to offer General Pétain such of our troops as could be used that I went to Compiègne on the 25th. I arrived about 10:00 P.M., to find him and his Chief of Staff, General Anthoine, waiting for me, but ready to leave for Chantilly, which had been selected as their G.H.Q. when the German advance had endangered Compiègne.

The General's customary confident and nonchalant attitude was entirely gone and he wore a very worried expression. Our conference was necessarily limited to a hurried discussion of the situation. We went over the maps of the latest positions, which he thought could be held, but he had few reserves left. I told him that for the moment I should waive the idea of forming our I Corps and that any of our divisions that could be of service were at his disposal, but with the qualifying remark that of course we should look forward eventually to their assembly under their own commander.

Pétain thought that certain of our units might be placed in the battle line but he hesitated to give us at once a portion of the front that might become active, preferring to have them sent into quiet sectors to release French divisions, which amounted to the same thing so far as it affected numbers in the battle line. He suggested that if the action continued it might be necessary to straighten out his line either at Verdun or in the vicinity of Nancy and Toul in order to obtain extra French divisions for service elsewhere. In that event he would have to execute a maneuver which could be entrusted only to experienced staffs.

We discussed briefly the general subject of handling new units as they should arrive, and finally I left with the understanding that American units would be used as circumstances might demand. As the reënforcement of the British was a vital necessity, I was willing to accept any arrangement that would release French divisions for that purpose, or put our divisions into the battle if thought best. I gave orders at once that our units should be held in readiness for any eventuality.

(Diary) Paris, Wednesday, March 27, 1918. Telegram from Mr. Baker in London renews Mr. Lloyd George's plea for infantry.

Talked yesterday with General Rawlinson and General Giardino, who replaces Cadorna at Versailles, and both urge American troops for their armies. In evening met Secretary and party, just back from London. Gare du Nord was packed with French refugees from the front.

American mechanics reported en route to repair French locomotives and cars. Saw Mr. Oscar T. Crosby and Mr. Paul D. Cravath this morning and discussed the possibility of getting laborers from Italy. Mr. Winston Churchill in letter suggests formation of an Inter-Allied Commission for Chemical Warfare Supply. Chief Surgeon reports non-effective rate for the week at 4.41 per hundred, the lowest this year.

Mr. Baker went to London to discuss with the British authorities the prospects for additional shipping and also the general subject of munitions. While there he sent me the following telegram embodying suggestions from the Prime Minister which showed the deep anxiety of the British:

"London, March 25th.

"I have just had a long talk with the Prime Minister. He urges three proposals for your consideration: First, that our divisions in France be placed immediately in line to relieve French divisions for service elsewhere, quiet sectors being chosen for troops with least training. Second, that all available engineer troops be taken from Lines of Communication work and sent to aid of British engineers preparing positions back of present lines. It is urged that suspension of our work would be but temporary and that the work suggested is imperative. Third, that infantry be sent first of the entire six divisions to be transported by British in view of present acute needs of that Army. No answer to the foregoing is necessary until I see you to-morrow when we can discuss the suggestions fully. If railroads in France are too fully occupied to make the Italian trip possible I should abandon it. At any rate we should not permit diversion of engines and cars if they can be used in present emergency. We leave here to-morrow, Tuesday, at 7:30, for Paris.

"BAKER."

Meanwhile, Sir Douglas Haig had asked for engineers and heavy artillery, of which three regiments of the former were placed at his disposal at once and the personnel of two regiments of the latter about to arrive were offered.

During my visit to Versailles on March 26th, General Giardino made an appeal for an allotment of our troops. He argued that their presence would be tangible proof of the intense feeling of coöperation that inspired the American nation, that it would encourage those Italian working people who had been in America, that it would increase their confidence in the successful outcome of the war, and that, above all, they needed help. No doubt much of this was true, but it would have opened the way for similar concessions to the other Allies and in the end our forces would have been frittered away probably to little or no purpose. These appeals by the Allies, presented anew from time to time, only served to fix in our minds the idea that each was thinking in terms of its own army rather than of benefit to the Allies as a whole.

The railroad station at Paris on the evening I met the Secretary presented a scene that was most pathetic. The terror-stricken crowds from threatened villages and farms were fleeing they knew not whither, many of them for the second time during this war, from an enemy whose invasion of their country in days gone by had perhaps driven out their fathers and mothers before them. War in its effects upon the armies themselves is frightful enough, but the terror and the suffering that it causes women and children are incomparably worse. These thousands were leaving everything behind them, going to some distant part of their country to become, many of them, dependent upon their friends, others, perchance friendless and penniless, to live by charity as a burden to the community or to beg from door to door. There was even then hope that they might return later and through the help of the Government rebuild their homes. But will the shadow of this dreadful experience ever pass, or will war come again to cause like suffering to their posterity? No one can answer, but all can strive to the end that such ill fortune, which is the heritage of lands where the embers of hatred and jealousy are kept alive at the fireside, may come no more.

(Diary) Chaumont, Friday, March 29, 1918. Held conference with the Secretary of War and General Bliss yesterday morning on joint recommendation of Military Representatives of the War Council, after which the Secretary left for Chaumont by motor. I then went to Clermont-sur-Oise to offer Foch our troops. Roads very congested as we approached the front.

Left Paris this morning by way of Fontainebleau and reached Chaumont in four hours and twelve minutes, distance 155 miles. At Pétain's request, the 1st Division ordered to battle line, which Mr. Baker said people at home would enthusiastically approve. Mr. Cravath dined with us this evening, and, speaking of unity, favored placing control in the hands of a committee composed of Marshal Haig, General Pétain, and myself.

The situation was considered so serious that the Military Representatives seemed to think it necessary to recommend that all previous plans for the shipment of American troops be disregarded and that nothing but infantry and machine gun units be shipped until otherwise directed by the Supreme War Council. This they did in the form of a joint (or unanimous) note, which was, of course, approved by the Supreme War Council. I was very much surprised at the attitude of General Bliss, our military representative with the Council, as without his consent the joint note could not have been submitted to the Council.

The presence of the Secretary of War fortunately afforded me the opportunity to discuss with him not only the demands of the particular situation existing at that time but the general attitude of our Allies regarding the manner in which Americans should be employed. When the joint note was presented to Secretary Baker, I pointed out to him and General Bliss that the proposal, if approved by the President, would place the disposition of American units entirely in the hands of the Supreme War Council and take them quite out of our control, even for training, and would without doubt destroy all possibility of our forming an American army. The Secretary was as strongly opposed to any such outcome as I was and after some discussion he dictated his views in a cable to the President, explicitly recommending that the control of our forces should be retained by our Commander-in-Chief and that the joint note be approved only in that sense, as follows:

"March 28, 1918.

"Paragraph 1. The Secretary of War this morning directed this telegram be sent direct to the President with copy for Secretary of State and Secretary of War and Chief of Staff. Following Joint Note 18 of the Permanent Military Representatives with the Supreme War Council is transmitted for the action of the President. Following the text of the Joint Note are the recommendations of the Secretary of War dictated by him this morning.

"Paragraph 2. The following Joint Note 18 was adopted by the Permanent Military Representatives March 28, 1918, quote:

"(1) In paragraph four of Joint Note No. 12, dated 12th of January, 1918, the Military Representatives agreed as follows:

"After the most careful and searching inquiry they were agreed on the point that the security of France could also be assured. But in view of the strength of the attack which the enemy is able to develop on this front, an attack which, in the opinion of the Military Representatives, could reach a strength of 96 divisions (excluding reënforcements by roulement), they feel compelled to add that France will be safe during 1918 only under certain conditions, namely:

"(a) That the strength of the British and French troops in France are continuously kept up to their present total strength, and that they receive the expected reënforcements of not less than two American divisions per month.

"(2) The battle which is developing at the present moment in France and which can extend to the other theaters of operations may very quickly place the Allied armies in a serious situation from the point of view of effectives, and the Military Representatives are from this moment of opinion that the above detailed condition (a) can no longer be maintained and they consider as a general proposition that the new situation requires new decisions.

"The Military Representatives are of opinion that it is highly desirable that the American Government should assist the Allied armies as soon as possible by permitting, in principle, the temporary service of American units in Allied army corps and divisions, such reënforcements must however be obtained from other units than those American divisions which are now operating with the French, and the units so temporarily employed must eventually be returned to the American Army.

"(3) The Military Representatives are of opinion that, for the present time, in execution of the foregoing, and until otherwise directed by the Supreme War Council, only American infantry and machine gun units, organized as that Government may decide, be brought to France, and that all agreements or conventions hitherto made in conflict with this decision be modified accordingly.

"Paragraph 3. The following is the action recommended by the Secretary of War:

"To the President:

"The foregoing resolutions were considered by General Bliss, General Pershing, and me. Paragraph (3) proposes a change in the order of shipment of American troops to France and necessarily postpones the organization and training of complete American divisions as parts of an independent American army. This ought to be conceded only in view of the present critical situation and continued only so long as that situation necessarily demands it. The question of replacements will continue to embarrass the British and French Governments, and efforts to satisfy that need by retaining American units assigned to them must be anticipated, but we must keep in mind the formation of an American army, while, at the same time, we must not seem to sacrifice joint efficiency at a critical moment to that object. Therefore, I recommend that you express your approval of the Joint Note in the following sense:

"The purpose of the American Government is to render the fullest coöperation and aid, and therefore the recommendation of the Military Representatives with regard to the preferential transportation of American infantry and machine gun units in the present emergency is approved. Such units when transported will be under the direction of the Commander-in-Chief of the American Expeditionary Forces and will be assigned for training and use by him in his discretion. He will use these and all other military forces of the United States under his command in such manner as to render the greatest military assistance, keeping in mind always the determination of this Government to have its various military forces collected, as speedily as their training and the military situation will permit, into an independent American army, acting in concert with the armies of Great Britain and France, and all arrangements made by him for their temporary training and service will be made with that end in view.

"BAKER."

This action by the Military Representatives just at this crisis was intended to put the weight of the Supreme War Council behind the idea of maintaining the strength of Allied units by American replacements as a policy. The text of the joint note made it entirely plain that this was their purpose.

Returning to the battle then going on, it had developed on March 24th that the French divisions on the left of their line had received instructions that if the enemy continued his drive in the direction of Amiens they were to fall back so as to cover Paris. Marshal Haig, apprehensive that such action would result in separating the two armies, at once communicated his fears to his Government. This brought about the important conference at Doullens on the 26th between members of the British and French

Governments to consider the question of better coöperation between the two armies.

President Poincaré presided at the conference, which was attended by M. Clemenceau, M. Loucheur, Lord Milner, Marshal Haig, General Sir Henry Wilson, and General Foch. According to information received by General Bliss, and transmitted to the Secretary and me, there was much difference of opinion concerning what should be done. One suggestion made prior to the formal meeting was that M. Clemenceau be selected as the Allied Commander-in-Chief, with General Foch as his Chief of Staff. Finally it was decided that General Foch, as the senior military member of the Executive War Board, should be charged with coördinating the action of the Allied armies on the Western Front. General Foch immediately took command of the situation and under his direction the French lines were extended to the left as far as the Luce River.

As soon as I learned of the action of the Doullens Conference I decided that General Foch himself should know of our desire to do whatever we could to strengthen the Allies. Although I had offered our troops to Pétain on the 25th, it seemed to me that it might be better to make it emphatic by letting Foch know that I was prepared to put into the battle every man that we could muster. I had often thought of the possibility of a crisis that would require such a step and I wished Foch to know our attitude.

After my important conference with Mr. Baker and Bliss on the morning of the 28th, I motored in the afternoon to Clermont-sur-Oise to see Foch. As we approached his temporary field headquarters, the continuous columns of motor trucks, slowly working their way forward with troops and supplies, blocked the road here and there and it took much time to make the journey. At the headquarters of the French Third Army, in the town, every one professed ignorance of the General's whereabouts until a staff officer, an old friend of Captain de Marenches, my aide, put a French soldier in the car who directed the chauffeur around the edge of town, thence through a lane of tall poplars to a small, typically French farmhouse well off the road, and hidden among the trees.

We waited outside for a few minutes among the shrubbery and spring flowers and especially admired a beautiful cherry tree in full bloom that stood on the lawn. The place was quaintly picturesque and quiet, entirely undisturbed by the sound or sight of anything suggestive of war. Yet only a few miles to the northeast the French were at that moment making a furious counterattack against the enemy at Montdidier in one of the critical battles of the war. As we entered the house, Clemenceau, Foch, Pétain, and Loucheur were intently studying a map spread on the table. The situation was pointed out to me, showing that already the British had used thirty divisions and the French seventeen against the Germans' seventy-eight. It seemed to be the opinion that the British Fifth Army was getting back on its feet and that the lines would hold for the time being.

Intimating that I had come to see General Foch, the others withdrew into the yard, leaving us alone. I told him that the Americans were ready and anxious to do their part in this crisis, and that I was willing to send him any troops we had. I asked him for suggestions as to how we might help. He was evidently very much touched and in his enthusiasm took me by the arm and without hesitation rushed me out across the lawn to where the others stood and asked me to repeat what I had said to him. They, of course, showed keen interest, especially M. Clemenceau, as I told them what I had said to General Foch. Colonel Boyd, my aide, was kind enough to say that, under the inspiration of the moment, my French was spoken with a fluency that I could not have mustered ten minutes before or after. It appeared in the French papers the next morning, although I feel certain that it was written up in much better French than I actually used.

"Je viens pour vous dire que le peuple américain tiendrait à grand honneur que nos troupes fussent engagées dans la présent bataille.

"Je vous le demande en mon nom et au sien.

"Il n'y a pas en ce moment d'autres questions que de combattre.

"Infanterie, artillerie, aviation, tout ce que nous avons est à vous.

"Disposez-en comme il vous plaira.

"Il en viendra encore d'autres, aussi nombreux qu'il sera nécessaire.

"Je suis venu tout exprès pour vous dire que le peuple américain serait fier d'être engagé dans la plus grande bataille de l'historie." [1]

At the conclusion of my visit, the details of making use of our troops were left to be arranged with Pétain, who remarked that he and I had already discussed their employment. If the responsibility had been mine, I should not have hesitated a moment to put into the battle any or all of our five divisions then in France. The 1st Division was the only one used for the time being, the others being placed in quiet sectors, each to relieve two French divisions. As our divisions were more than twice as large as theirs, it amounted to almost immediate reënforcement of ten divisions.

It was the prevalent British view that General Foch was simply a liaison officer between the two armies, with advisory and coordinating authority only. Although inadequate to meet all circumstances, even this concession was a stride in the right direction, and his position was soon to be more clearly defined. In fact, President Wilson sent General Foch the following message on March 29th:

"May I not convey to you my sincere congratulations on your new authority. Such unity of command is a most hopeful augury of ultimate success. We are following with profound interest the bold and brilliant action of your forces.

"WOODROW WILSON."

The following telegram, received at my headquarters on April 1st and cabled to Washington, is General Foch's reply to President Wilson's message of congratulations:

[1] "I have come to tell you that the American people would consider it a great honor for our troops to be engaged in the present battle. I ask you for this in their name and my own.

"At this moment there are no other questions but of fighting.

"Infantry, artillery, aviation, all that we have are yours; use them as you wish. More will come, in numbers equal to requirements.

"I have come especially to tell you that the American people will be proud to take part in the greatest battle of history."

"A Monsieur le Président de la
    République des Etats-Unis.

"En pleine confiance grace à la parfaite Union des Alliés et en particulier au noble élan de l'Armée Américaine demandant a entrer immediatement dans la bataille, je vous addresse mes vifs remerciements pour votre télégramme de félicitations.

"Foch." [1]

Mr. Cravath's idea that command of the Allied forces be vested in a committee was never seriously considered by any one in authority, and it fell short of absolute unity of command, but it would more likely have met the situation than the plan adopted by the Supreme War Council. In theory, the plan for a general reserve appeared to be a reasonable method of avoiding the difficulties inherent in any plan for mutual support between the French and British armies. Upon analysis, however, one could not escape the conclusion that its application would result in the senior officer of the Executive Board assuming supreme control of the joint action of the two armies, at least on the defensive. With thirty reserve divisions at his command, he would be in position to dictate what should be done. The failure of the plan to become operative for lack of divisions to constitute the General Reserve fortunately led to the selection of an Allied Commander-in-Chief, which was probably the object sought by some of its far-sighted advocates.

Mr. Baker's message of March 28th to the President, forwarding the joint note with his recommendation was answered on the 30th as follows:

"The President concurs in the Joint Note of the Permanent Military Representatives of the Supreme War Council in the sense formulated in your number 67, March 28th, and wishes you to regard yourself authorized to decide questions of immediate coöperation or replacement."

It was thought that this statement, coming from the President, would check, at least for the time being, the demands of the Allies

[1] "To the President of the United States.

"In full confidence, thanks to the perfect union of the Allies and especially to the noble spirit of the American Army requesting to enter immediately into the battle, I extend to you my sincere thanks for your telegram of congratulations. Foch."

that we provide units for building up their divisions, but, as we shall see later, their insistence continued.

The President's message was followed on March 30th by a cable from the War Department, which stated: "The recommendations of Secretary of War to President * * * that preferential transportation be given to American infantry and machine gun units in present emergency understood and will be followed." It went on to say that these units pertaining to three divisions, the 3d, 5th, and 77th, would be sent at once and those of three other divisions about May 1st.

Replying on April 3d to the Department's cable, the fact was emphasized that it was "not intended that our units shall replace the losses of British or French organizations and therefore our artillery should be held in readiness to follow when called for," although it was possible that the situation might become "so serious that some of our infantry units will be forced to serve with British temporarily." My intentions were further indicated by saying that "Americans must not lose sight of the purpose to build up divisions and corps of their own," and also that "we must avoid our tendency to incorporate our infantry into British divisions where it will be used up and never relieved." My cable recommended that the infantry of two divisions should be sent by British shipping and two by our own, but that present plans should go no further than this. It was my purpose not to become too deeply involved in an agreement that would make it impossible later to form our own independent force under our own officers.

The German offensive which created such great concern in the ranks of the Allies was the first serious effort the enemy had undertaken since his costly attacks at Verdun in 1916. During the whole of 1917 he was outnumbered on the Western Front but in this recent attack he had a decided advantage both in strength and position. From a selected concentration zone within the great salient that projected into France, the enemy could strike with superior force to the west against the British or to the south against the French. He was doubly favored, for he had the advantages not only of the initiative but also of interior lines of communication, and was thereby enabled to keep the Allies in doubt as to the appropriate points for their concentrations of reserves.

The precise methods employed by the enemy at Riga and Caporetto were definitely known, as already mentioned, and information had been obtained prior to the spring offensive which clearly indicated that his forces in France were being carefully trained in the same system of attack. This "maneuver of rupture," as it was called, contemplated a penetration of six to eight miles the first day and a much more rapid exploitation thereafter. The attack was to penetrate quickly by infiltration and turn the successive positions by striking them in rear. A weak resistance by one group, or its demoralization by artillery fire or by the enemy infantry, would naturally involve adjacent groups and possibly force the whole to give way.

To meet this form of attack the French had, as far as possible, prepared a defensive system of great depth, and the British had adopted somewhat the same idea. In theory such distribution of forces was tactically correct, but when this German offensive began there was a lack of reserves near the line where the principal resistance was to be made. As both of the Allied armies were almost completely wedded to trench fighting and their troops had been given little or no training in open warfare, they were at great disadvantage once they were forced out of the trenches.

Although experience had actually demonstrated that instead of placing too many troops out in the front lines a carefully selected position of resistance, not too far forward, should be strongly held behind a thin outpost zone well in advance, the principle was often neglected. It may be noted in passing that this was exactly the system laid down in our own tactical regulations before the war.

In carrying out our plans for the organization of an American army on the Lorraine front, with the reduction of the St. Mihiel salient planned as the initial operation, the volume of construction necessary along our line of communications had been pushed as fast as conditions permitted. The establishment of advance depots and other installations in Lorraine were well under way.

On January 16th the 1st Division (Bullard) had entered the line north of Toul, with the understanding that other divisions would follow as they became sufficiently trained, and that when four divisions were available an American army corps would be formed and the sector would pass definitely under American control. The 26th Division (Edwards) had been withdrawn

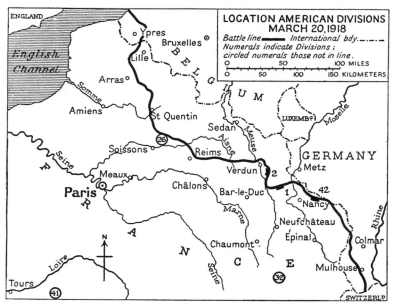

LOCATION AMERICAN DIVISIONS
MARCH 20, 1918
Battle line ▬▬▬▬ International bdy.▬∙▬∙▬
Numerals indicate Divisions ;
circled numerals those not in line.

from the Chemin des Dames on March 21st, and the 42d Division (Menoher) from east of Lunéville two days later, and both were prepared to take their places beside the 1st. These were to be followed by the 2d Division (Bundy) then in line for preliminary experience at Sommedieue, south of Verdun, while the 32d Division (Haan), which had only recently arrived, would come in later.

The headquarters of the I Corps (Liggett), which had been organized at Neufchâteau in January, was to move up to Toul as soon as there were three divisions in the line. It could be said that an important step in organizing an American army would then be taken. But just as our hopes were about to be realized the storm broke, the situation on the British front created a grave crisis, and the concentration of our troops in an American sector, much to my regret, was voluntarily and indefinitely postponed.

CHAPTER XXV

Conference at Beauvais—Foch Chosen Allied Commander—President Wilson Approves—Limits of Authority—Lack of Training—Inspection of Divisions—Troops for Training with British—Letters to and from Secretary—Mr. Baker Departs for Home

(Diary) Paris, Thursday, April 4, 1918. The Secretary left for Italy on Saturday. Ex-Senator Percy, Y.M.C.A., dropped in on Monday. Conference Tuesday with Colonel Fox Conner, Chief of Operations, regarding disposition new divisions. Reports indicate that they seriously lack instruction, especially the replacements.

Left Chaumont yesterday morning and went to Beauvais for conference. War Council decided on General Foch as Allied Commander-in-Chief.

Advised Elmer Roberts, Associated Press, this morning of action of conference. The Secretary and party returned from Italy to-day and are stopping with us. Visit of the Prince of Wales planned for to-day has been postponed. Two French and one British divisions and four brigades of British field artillery being withdrawn from Italian front. Labor situation improving; 6,000 on hand with 12,000 possible from Italy. Sent cable to help Third Liberty Loan.[1] Brigadier General Williams, my Chief of Ordnance, ordered to Washington to be Chief.

M R. BAKER felt that he should pay a visit to Italy while in Europe and left Paris on the 30th for that purpose, accompanied by Colonel T. Bentley Mott, who was entirely familiar with the Italian situation. Before his departure, he and I took up the question of a supreme commander, which

[1] "For Secretary McAdoo: Every dollar subscribed to the Liberty Loan is a dollar invested in American manhood. Every dollar subscribed as the result of self-denial means partnership in the hardships and risks of our men in the trenches. Every dollar subscribed will confirm the determination of our people at home to stand by the army to a victorious end. An overwhelming subscription to the Third Liberty Loan will be a patriotic expression of confidence in our ability as a nation to maintain all that we hold dear in civilization."

Facilities were provided in the army in France for making subscriptions to this loan but no active campaign was instituted.

we had discussed before and were ready to accept in principle when proposed. Apropos of its probability, he sent the President the following cable:

"March 30, 1918.

"I have just been shown a copy of a message from Lloyd George to you with regard to General Foch and American troops. The situation seems to be that Lloyd George is personally in favor of a Supreme Commander but fears British opinion will be the other way because such a Commander could sacrifice the Channel ports to the defense of Paris. The arrangement therefore is that General Foch is to be supreme enough to coördinate but without being called Supreme Commander. General Pershing will, of course, act under General Foch as Pétain and Haig have agreed to do. I venture to suggest that in replying to that part of Lloyd George's message you might go further than he asks and say that we are willing to accept a general Supreme Command whenever the French and British are. Perhaps the relative smallness of our present forces and our having no immediate defensive object in France would make it unwise for us to urge the point though the present events would seem to have demonstrated the need. * * * General Pershing's prompt and fine action with regard to the use of our troops and facilities here in the emergency has won enthusiastic commendation from French and British. Our 1st Division will shortly be withdrawn from trenches and used in battle.

"BAKER."

The main points of Mr. Lloyd George's message to President Wilson are contained in a message, dated March 29th, received by General Bliss and sent by him to the Secretary of War and me, as given below:

"The following has been handed to me by the military representative of Great Britain and is transmitted for the information of the Secretary of War and General Pershing:

"Secret. From the Prime Minister.

"Subparagraph A.

"Please communicate to General Bliss that I have cabled to President Wilson asking him to approve of Foch exercising the same * * * authority over the American Army as he is exercising over the British and French; to send men over to France with the utmost possible speed to make good losses; and to agree to arrangements made by General Pershing to their being brigaded as they become available with French and British divisions for the duration of the crisis.

"Subparagraph B

"The Prime Minister thinks that before this fighting is over, every man may count, and he can see no other way of making splendid American material available in this crisis of the war.

"BLISS."

In response to a notice from M. Clemenceau, I went on April 3d to Beauvais, about forty-five miles north of Paris, to meet with the Supreme War Council. This curious old town, not far from the active front, has much of historical interest. Arriving early, Colonel Boyd and I strolled about and visited the cathedral, a fine specimen of Gothic architecture of the 13th Century, and then had to wait an hour at the Hôtel de Ville before M. Clemenceau and Lloyd George came into the conference room. Marshal Haig and Generals Foch, Pétain, Sir Henry Wilson, Bliss, Weygand, and I were the others participating. Brigadier General Spiers acted as interpreter and Lieutenant Colonel Sir Maurice Hankey, who usually accompanied Mr. Lloyd George, acted as recorder. The meeting was finally called to order by M. Clemenceau, who stated its purpose, saying in substance:

"We have come together to settle a very simple question regarding the functions of General Foch. I think we are all in agreement as to the coördination of Allied action, but there is some difference in the understanding of General Foch's powers as conferred upon him at the Doullens conference of March 26th. General Foch will explain his difficulties."

General Foch then set forth briefly his situation, about as follows:

"The powers conferred by the Doullens conference were limited to the coördination of action between the Allies. They were conferred while the action was on. The power to coördinate has been construed to be limited to the time the Allies were in action. That was March 26th at Doullens. It is now April 3d. Now that the two op-

NOTE: Total strength of the A.E.F. on March 31st, 18,966 officers, 299,655 enlisted men.

Divisional units arriving in March included elements of the 3d Division (Regular Army), Major General Joseph T. Dickman, and 5th Division (Regular Army), Major General John E. McMahon. The major portion of the 5th Division did not arrive until May.

posing armies are no longer in action but have stopped and are facing each other, there is nothing to coördinate. There should be authority to prepare for action and direct it. So that we are right back where we were before, and nothing can be done until an action starts again."

Mr. Lloyd George then entered the discussion, saying substantially:

"We have had more than three years of this war, and we have not had unity of action during that time. During the last year we have had two kinds of strategy, one by Haig and another by Pétain, both different, and nothing has been gained. The only thing that was accomplished was by General Nivelle when he was in supreme command. The Germans have done exactly what General Nivelle tried to do. The Supreme War Council that met in February adopted a plan for handling a general reserve, but through the action of those concerned nothing has come of it. It is a nullity. What has happened recently has stirred the British people very much and must not happen again, as the people will demand why it has happened, and somebody will be called to account. They want some sort of unity of command. General Foch is now empowered to coördinate the action of the Allied armies, but this does not go far enough as he has no authority to control except by conferring with the respective Commanders-in-Chief. He wants authority to prepare for action. I think the resolution made at Doullens should be modified so that we may have a better understanding. I should like to hear what General Bliss and General Pershing have to say."

General Bliss read the Doullens resolution, which was as follows:

"General Foch is charged by the British and French Governments to coördinate the action of the Allied armies on the Western Front. To this end he will come to an understanding with the Commanders-in-Chief, who are to furnish him all the information necessary." [1]

He interpreted it to mean, first, that General Foch was given no authority to act except in conference with the two Commanders-in-Chief; second, that they should furnish him certain information regarding the situation of their respective forces. He went

[1] Le général Foch est chargé par les gouvernements britannique et français de coördonner l'action des armées alliées sur le front ouest. Il s'entendra à cet effet avec les généraux en chef, qui sont à lui fournir tous les renseignements nécéssaires.

into some further analysis of the resolution to the effect that in order to meet all situations the powers conferred upon General Foch should be enlarged.

I then gave my view, which was set forth in a brief memorandum prepared in pencil after the discussion began, as follows:

"The principle of unity of command is undoubtedly the correct one for the Allies to follow. I do not believe that it is possible to have unity of action without a supreme commander. We have already had experience enough in trying to coördinate the operations of the Allied armies without success. There has never been real unity of action. Such coördination between two or three armies is impossible no matter who the commanders-in-chief may be. Each commander-in-chief is interested in his own army, and cannot get the other commander's point of view or grasp the problem as a whole. I am in favor of a supreme commander and believe that the success of the Allied cause depends upon it. I think the necessary action should be taken by this council at once. I am in favor of conferring the supreme command upon General Foch."

When I had finished reading it, Mr. Lloyd George came over to where I sat, took me by the hand, and said:

"I agree fully with General Pershing. This is well put."

Mr. Lloyd George then asked for the views of Marshal Haig, who said:

"We have had practically complete unity of action. I have always coöperated with the French, whom I regard as in control of the strategical questions of the war. I was placed directly under the command of General Nivelle, and General Pétain and I have always worked well together. I agree with General Pershing's general idea that there should be unity of command, but I think we have had it."

The views expressed by General Pétain were practically the same as Marshal Haig's, although I think they both realized the necessity of some definite coördinating control.

As a result, after some further informal discussion, a draft of a resolution was submitted which omitted reference to the American Army. Whereupon I called attention to the oversight, saying:

"I think this resolution should include the American Army. The arrangement is to be in force, as I understand it, from now on, and the American Army will soon be ready to function as such and should be included as an entity like the British and French armies."

General Pétain remarked:

"There is no American army as such, as its units are either in training or are amalgamated with the British and French."

To which I replied:

"There may not be an American army in force functioning now but there soon will be, and I want this resolution to apply to it when it becomes a fact. The American Government is represented here at this conference and in the war, and any action as to the supreme command that includes the British and French armies should also include the American Army."

The foregoing account of the conference may not be an exact record of the language used, but is given as my aide took it down at the time.

The following resolution was then read and adopted:

French

BEAUVAIS, le 3 Avril 1918.

Le Général FOCH est chargé par les Gouvernements Britannique, Français et Américain de coordonner l'action des Armées Alliées sur le front occidental; il lui est conféré à cet effet tous les pouvoirs nécessaires en vue d'une réalisation effective. Dans ce but, les Gouvernements Britannique, Français et Américain confient au Général FOCH la direction stratégique des opérations militaires.

Les Commandants en Chef des Armées Britannique, Française et Américaine exercent dans sa plénitude la conduite tactique de leur Armée. Chaque Commandant en Chef aura le droit d'en appeler à son

English

BEAUVAIS, April 3, 1918.

General FOCH is charged by the British, French and American Governments with the coördination of the action of the Allied Armies on the Western Front; to this end there is conferred on him all the powers necessary for its effective realization. To the same end, the British, French and American Governments confide in General FOCH the strategic direction of military operations.

The Commanders-in-Chief of the British, French and American Armies will exercise to the fullest extent the tactical direction of their armies. Each Commander-in-Chief will have the right to appeal to his Government, if in his opinion his

Gouvernement, si dans son opinion, son Armée se trouve mise en danger par toute instruction reçue du Général Foch.

> G. Clemenceau
> Pétain
> F. Foch
> D. Lloyd George
> D. Haig, F.M.
> Henry Wilson, General, 3.4.18.
> Tasker H. Bliss, General and Chief of Staff.
> John J. Pershing, General, U.S.A.

Army is placed in danger by the instructions received from General Foch.

> G. Clemenceau
> Pétain
> F. Foch
> D. Lloyd George
> D. Haig, F.M.
> Henry Wilson, General, 3.4.18.
> Tasker H. Bliss, General and Chief of Staff.
> John J. Pershing, General, U.S.A.

While the momentous events of the previous two weeks had been in progress, it had become increasingly evident that the lack of coördination between the Allies had prevented the best use to be made of their combined strength. The conclusion was inevitable to any one conversant with the facts that some arrangement for better teamwork must be found. The idea of an Allied commander-in-chief had been suggested and discussed many times unofficially, but for various reasons, political and otherwise, it had never been adopted by the Supreme War Council. With the distrust that existed among the Allies, it was not easy to bring about the decision in favor of a supreme commander and it was only made possible by the extreme emergency of the situation.

It was natural that the position of supreme commander should fall either to a French or a British officer. An American could hardly have been considered for the one reason, if for no other, that we then occupied no front of our own and our force was still relatively small. While the two Allies should have realized the necessity for closer coöperation, yet the sentiment in the armies and among noncombatants of each against selecting any one from the army of the other was difficult to overcome. The British held that the Channel ports must be defended at all costs and feared that this might not be fully appreciated by a French supreme commander. The French were compelled to protect their capital and were uncertain of the attitude in that regard that a British supreme commander might take. These obligations were, of course, important, and each was considered vital by the Government concerned. The common objective of their combined forces, however, was the German Army, though this fact was apparently often obscured by the individual point of view of each of the Allies. Previous to this crisis they did not seem to realize fully that the success of their common cause demanded complete unity of action, both on the offensive and defensive, and that without it they could not win.

Human nature is the same whether it be regarded as affecting the actions of individuals or of nations. The subordination of a national undertaking of any kind to the authority of another nation can hardly be thought of except under the most pressing necessity. In this case national pride entered to an unusual degree. Although we were face to face with the greatest crisis of the war, none of the Governments concerned was willing to place its army under control of a supreme commander chosen from another army. This was shown in the Beauvais resolution by the limitations placed upon the authority of the Allied Commander-in-Chief. He could coördinate the action of the armies and determine the strategy, but each Commander-in-Chief was alone responsible for the tactical direction of his own army. The right was given each one to appeal to his Government in case there should be any interference with this prerogative. It was the safeguard against the identity of any of the armies being disregarded. While the powers of the Allied Commander-in-Chief were thus defined, yet, under the agreement as adopted, unity of action was secured as far as was necessary, and the independence and initiative of the respective armies were protected.

It was proposed by the French that the title of Commander-in-Chief of the Allied Armies in France should be given to General Foch. On April 15th I received a letter from M. Clemenceau advising me that Mr. Lloyd George had approved the suggestion, and asked if I agreed. I replied in a personal note expressing my approval, subject to the confirmation of the President, which came on the 17th.

Once the question of supreme command was settled, the co-ordinated energies of the Allied armies could be directed with maximum effect toward a common end. Although dark days were still ahead, we were spared the chagrin of inefficiency through lack of teamwork. With unity of command and the still more important fact of almost unlimited American reënforcements looming on the horizon, the chances of Allied success were much improved.

Yet, scarcely had the appointment of Foch been announced than considerable outspoken dissatisfaction among the British began to appear. One newspaper, *The Globe,* supposed at that time to represent the views of the British High Command in the field, said:

> "Our objections to a Generalissimo (which we believe to be shared by our readers and by practically all Englishmen outside the war cabinet and its press) remain. They are not so much military as political. Any Generalissimo is the servant of the state that appoints him. Consequently such an office involves (the possibility) that the Allied Army passes under the control of foreign politicians. * * * Indeed the feeling on this side of the Channel is so strong that we may safely assume that the appointment of that honored soldier, General Foch, as Generalissimo is a temporary arrangement for the present operations, and as such it is as welcome in London as it is understood to be at G.H.Q."

Now that the supreme effort must be made on our part, and when units were sorely needed for active service, it was all the more deplorable that the divisions then coming to France contained a large percentage of untrained men. This condition, mainly the result of a very grievous lack of appreciation by the War Department of the urgency of continuous and thorough training of complete units must, as already pointed out, be blamed upon the General Staff. It failed to provide men for special services and relied upon taking them from combat divisions instead of anticipating such requirements and segregating these specialists from the start and training them as such.

This was a most vicious continuance in time of war of a very objectionable habit that had grown up in our Army in time of peace. The practice was carried to such an extent that divisions of 25,000 men, which should have been held intact, and each one perfected as an organized team, were constantly called upon to send large groups of their trained soldiers to other duties. The numbers taken aggregated from 15,000 to 40,000 men for each division. As green men were substituted, the result was that training had to be practically started all over again with each such reduction. Although the War Department eventually established a replacement system, as urgently recommended by me, it was done too late to be of material benefit even to the last divisions that came over in the fall of 1918.

Although the thirty-four National Guard and National Army divisions that eventually came to France were, with two exceptions, organized in August and September, 1917, they did not receive training as complete units from that time on. They were filled gradually and by piecemeal, weeks and even months usually elapsing before they reached full strength, and, as we have seen, the personnel was constantly changing.

Therefore, when the time came for service abroad, a very large proportion of the men in these divisions had little or no experience, and the training of the unit as a whole had been seriously delayed. Moreover, training methods at home had not improved, as preparation for trench warfare still predominated. All this was discouraging to their officers, disastrous to morale, threw upon the A.E.F. an extra burden of training, and resulted in our having a number of divisions only partially trained when the time came to use them.

The indications were that incoming units would soon have to be put in the front lines, with no time to carry out a complete course of training in France for units composed largely of recruits. I therefore sent a vigorous protest against the practice of taking men out of the units in training and emphasized again the necessity of open warfare exercises for all organizations including the division. The urgency of target practice and musketry training of platoons and companies was especially stressed and it was requested that no men be sent over without four months of intensive training.

This condition of things signalized the failure on the part of the General Staff at home to realize that their most important function was to supervise the organization and training of complete divisions for combat and provide them with equipment and supplies. Their obligations to the armies in the field were not fulfilled by merely sending units carelessly prepared and with an undue proportion of green officers and men to fight against trained veterans.

Only 300,000 men had joined the colors in France up to April 1st, and of the latest group a sizable proportion of the men had been in training only a few days. In order to provide the men and give them as much time to train as possible, I laid before the Secretary of War while he was in France the urgency of calling out all the men that we should be likely to need by fall and putting them in training at once. He seemed willing to do so but pointed out that this would probably cause a shortage of labor for planting and harvesting the crops. I thought that this demand ought to be met in some other way and that the military needs, under the circumstances, were of first importance.

(Diary) Paris, Sunday, April 7, 1918. Went to Chaumont on Friday, accompanied by Colonel Boyd and Lieutenant G. E. Adamson, my secretary. Mr. Baker remained in Paris.

Yesterday saw part of 1st Division at Toul entraining for the Somme. Found General Bullard ill in hospital. Visited 26th Division, in quiet sector but anxious for active employment. Saw 2d, in line south of Verdun, equally keen. At Souilly called on Major General Hirschauer, Commanding French Second Army, who spoke in high praise of our soldiers. Conferred with Harbord, Fox Conner, and Fiske in evening about use of our divisions.

Came to Paris this afternoon, where Mr. Baker and I conferred with Generals Whigham and Hutchinson, British War Office, on shipment and use of American troops. Discussed with Generals Ford and Dawney from British G.H.Q. the training of our troops with British. The Secretary left this evening for Brest, en route home.

In view of their possible early employment, I wanted especially to look into the general state of efficiency of our available divisions and give some personal instructions about training. On going the rounds, I met General Hirschauer, who was one of the able French generals, and found him very enthusiastic about the 2d Division, which had been in line at Sommedieue under his command. He said that without doubt it was then as efficient as any of his French divisions, confirming my own opinion formed from observation and reports. The 1st Division was further advanced than any of the others and its morale was high at the prospect of going into the battle line.

Recent developments had brought into immediate consideration the question of the employment of American troops. The President's qualified approval of the recommendation of the Supreme War Council, as embodied in Joint Note No. 18, was seized upon by the Allies and construed as a concession for the unlimited absorption of our troops in their armies. No doubt my offer to Foch lent encouragement to the Allied view. At the conclusion of the Beauvais conference, Mr. Lloyd George told me that a cable had been received from Lord Reading, the British Ambassador at Washington, stating that he had approached President Wilson with the view of obtaining the dispatch to Europe of 120,000 infantry and machine gun units per month, beginning with April, provided the necessary shipping could be obtained.

On the following day a cable came from the War Department, quoting information received through British shipping channels, as follows:

"We have informed War Cabinet that in shipping provided by Great Britain we shall be able to embark in America in April some 60,000 men. Admiral Sims' estimate of carrying power of American troop fleet is 52,000 per month. In addition there is certain Dutch tonnage available for use by America and we are obtaining use of certain Italian tonnage. In total it is considered that 120,000 American troops can be embarked in April and if anything rather more in following months. In view of urgent military needs Lord Reading has approached the President with the view of obtaining dispatch of

120,000 infantry per month to Europe between now and July, infantry and machine gun units only. Men to be brigaded with British and French divisions on the same basis as in case of six-division plan. This means using all troop-carrying ships to carry American infantry without reference to recent controversy. The President agrees that all possible measures must be taken to insure maximum use of troop tonnage."

The receipt of this plan from British sources evidently created something like consternation in the War Department, judging from its cabled comments, in which it was stated that "this program would practically stop all shipments of artillery, technical units, service of rear, army, and corps troops."

On the day of the Secretary's departure Generals Whigham and Hutchinson came over from the British War Office to discuss arrangements for the transportation of American troops, in accordance with the provisions of Joint Note No. 18. The conversation indicated that the British understood that we were to send 60,000 men per month to train with them and that they were to bring over the same number, making a total of 120,000 per month beginning with April. They held that the President's approval of Joint Note No. 18 had superseded agreements previously made, including the six-division plan. General Whigham said:

"The interpretation of the British War Office is that the Versailles agreement (Joint Note No. 18) wipes out all previous agreements and it is now a question of sending infantry and machine gun units to be trained by British, French, and Americans, the proportion to go to each to be decided later."

The whole tenor of the conversation showed that the British then regarded it as certain that our troops were to be used to build up the French and British armies. But neither Mr. Baker nor I had received any intimation that the President had agreed to the British proposal mentioned in the above cable, and his qualified approval of Joint Note No. 18 did not commit us to any such program as the British claimed. Moreover, I was opposed to any commitment that would tie our hands and make it impossible to form an American army. My attitude toward the pro-

posal was made perfectly clear. Mr. Baker knew nothing more
than the declaration contained in the joint note, which stated no
figures.

The British conferees entirely ignored the specific condition
that the final arrangements as to training and disposition of all
our units were to be left in my hands. Their error was pointed
out and Mr. Baker then said:

> "What is pertinent to the present discussion is that American
> troops are going to the British for training. I don't want the British
> public or army, or the French public or army, to get an exaggerated
> idea that this scheme provides or will provide a means by which their
> losses will be made up in the future. I want no feeling of disillu-
> sionment when General Pershing calls for the troops entrusted to
> them for training."

The conference ended with the understanding that 60,000
American infantry and machine gun units to be brought over by
the British in April should go to them for training. It was also
understood that the disposition of other troops would be left for
later decision. Certain deficiencies in land transportation, clothing and machine guns were to be provided by the British. While
they accepted this at the moment and declared that they thoroughly understood, that was not to be the last of it, as the whole
question was taken up again in conference in London later in
the month.

Mr. Baker's visit to our armies during this critical period was
fortunate as he could thus see the problems that confronted us
in their true perspective. He had an opportunity to meet the
Allied leaders, both civil and military, and to get in touch with
conditions in the different countries. Of still greater importance,
he saw with his own eyes the building of our organization. He
was a keen observer, with clear understanding and a logical mind,
and obtained in a short time an accurate conception of our task
and its difficulties. As to our relations, he gave me from the start
that strong and sympathetic support which means so much to
a military commander in the field, and I undertook to keep him

and the President at all times in confidential touch with our armies and the plans for supplying and handling them.

When Mr. Baker left, it was felt that the result of his visit would be that under his direction the War Department would function with a better understanding of our task and therefore with greatly increased efficiency and energy. Before sailing, he sent the following letter, which was published to the command:

"General Orders⎫   "American Expeditionary Forces,
    "No. 57 ⎭   "France, April 15, 1918.

"1. The Commander-in-Chief takes pleasure in publishing the following letter from the Secretary of War:

                                " 'France, April 7, 1918.

" 'To the Officers and Men of the American Expeditionary Forces in France:

" 'After a thorough inspection of the American Expeditionary Forces, I am returning to the United States with fresh enthusiasm to speed the transportation of the remainder of the great Army of which you are the vanguard. What I have seen here gives the comfortable assurance that plans for the effectiveness of our fighting forces and for the comfort and welfare of the men have been broadly made and vigorously executed. Our schools and systems of instruction are adding to the general soldier training the specialized knowledge which developed among our French and British associates during the four years of heroic action which they have displayed from the beginning of the war.

" 'Fortunately, the relations between our soldiers and those of the British and French are uniformly cordial and happy, and the welcome of the civil population of France has been met by our soldiers with chivalrous appreciation and return.

" 'We are building a great army to vindicate a great cause, and the spirit which you are showing, the courage, the resourcefulness and the zeal for the performance of duty both as soldiers and as men is not only promising of success, but it is worthy of the traditions of America and of the Allied Armies with which we are associated. Press on!

                        " 'NEWTON D. BAKER,
                            " 'Secretary of War.'

"In adding his own high appreciation of the splendid spirit of our army, the Commander-in-Chief wishes to impress upon officers and men of all ranks a keen sense of the serious obligations which rest upon them, while at the same time giving fresh assurance of his complete confidence in their loyalty, their courage, and their sincere devotion to duty.

"2. This order will be read to each company and separate detachment at its first assembly after the receipt of the order.

"By command of General Pershing:

"JAMES G. HARBORD,

"Chief of Staff."

Fearing that I would not see Mr. Baker again before he sailed for home, I sent him the letter quoted below, and although we later discussed its contents briefly, it is given as showing the reaction of at least part of the British press at the time:

"April 5, 1918.

"DEAR MR. SECRETARY:

"I noticed the other day that one of the British papers, in referring to the fact that plans had been made to send American troops to the assistance of the Allies, stated that this would relieve the British of the necessity of depleting the strength of the forces kept at home for defensive purposes.

"This suggests to my mind a certain political phase of the British situation which may give us additional explanation as to why Mr. Lloyd George and British representatives are so urgent in their appeals for assistance from America. The train of thought leads me to conceive the existence of a condition that may be fraught with danger to the cause, in that it indicates a serious lack of coöperation between the civil and military authorities of Great Britain, as was also indicated to you in some of the things I repeated to you yesterday. * * *

"Following this further, may I suggest that you give the matter serious thought. There is so very much at stake for us that it seems to me that very frank representations should be made to the British Government as to the urgency of their putting into the army every possible man that can be mustered to meet the immediate emergency. It need not be pointed out that there is a limit to the rapidity with which our troops can be brought over, and there seems to me to be a very real danger of the British political world allowing itself to be lulled into inaction upon the theory that the Americans are in a position to meet all possible contingencies that may arrive.

"It may be that you would think it advisable to go to London, or else to intimate to the President by cable the urgency of Great Britain's putting into the ranks every possible man to withstand the present German onslaught, even if they have to promise to withdraw them in six months, and of their doing so without waiting on us or counting on us in the slightest degree. There will be few enough men even with the best we all can do. It will be time enough for Great Britain to consider the defense of England after she has put forth every possible energy on the continent. Here is the place to beat Germany, and not on British soil. In writing this I have in mind what you told me regarding available men in England.

"I give you the following from General Sir William Robertson in a letter to me dated January 17th:

" ' * * * The British Government has given the most anxious consideration to the question of the maintenance of the armies in the field during 1918 and, by making every effort, there will become available for service at the front 449,000 men now under training, plus 100,000 men to be called up. In addition, there will be called up 100,000 men of lower category who are not fit for the first line, plus 120,000 lads of 18 years of age, who will not be available for service at the front till 1919. Please keep these figures strictly secret.'

"It may be that some of these have already been called out, but I am informed that large numbers of men are held for home defense.

"Believe me, with very sincere regard and high esteem,
                    "Yours faithfully,
                                "JOHN J. PERSHING."

CHAPTER XXVI

Awakening of Allies—Greater Activity Necessary—Airplane Situation—
Liberty Motor—Water Supply—New Burdens on S.O.S.—1st Division
in Picardy—Talk to its Officers—Visit to Foch—Marshal Haig's Order
of April 11th—Letter to Clemenceau on Unified Supply—President's
Liberty Day Proclamation

(Diary) Chaumont, Friday, April 12, 1918. Washington reports
140,000 increase in cargo tonnage by use of Dutch ships. Infantry
and machine gun personnel of four divisions promised this month.
Brest selected as terminal of *Leviathan,* formerly the German *Vater-
land.* Expansion of all activities necessary.

Conferred on Monday with Generals Kernan, as to ports, Rogers on
quartermaster supplies, Williams about ordnance, and Foulois as to
aviation. Talked yesterday with General Hinds, who will be Chief
of Artillery.

THE Allies were at last thoroughly alive to the urgency of
making an extraordinary effort to provide tonnage for the
transportation of our troops. After months of delay and
discussion, they now realized fully that the superiority of forces
vitally necessary to avert defeat must come from across the
Atlantic. America was their reliance. Early aid was imperative.

Mr. Baker's first-hand knowledge of the situation in France
enabled him to give a fresh impetus to the efforts of the War
Department. With General Peyton C. March as Chief of Staff,
the General Staff and the supply departments began to exert more
energy. The War Industries Board, under the leadership of
Mr. B. M. Baruch, had taken definite steps toward the control of
the Nation's industries for war purposes. During the preceding
year, through lack of authority and organization, there had been
much confusion and little progress.

Acting under the direct authority of the President, the object
of the Board was to mobilize the country's resources and coördi-

nate the demands of the fighting forces with those of the civilian population. It undertook to stimulate production of war materials and limit that of war non-essentials. The Board controlled and harmonized output and determined priority. It made allotments to the different departments of the Government and to the Allies of necessary raw materials and manufactured products. The remarkable success of its efforts points to the wisdom of invoking a similar civilian super-agency in case of any future major war emergency.

In the face of the crisis, our hope for an improvement in methods and a more competent coördination of effort seemed about to be realized. If a similar awakening had taken place in the previous autumn, we should probably have had at least one-half million combat troops in France ready for the spring campaign and they would have been better trained than those who were arriving. Moreover, we would have been in position to answer more effectively the Allied arguments for amalgamation.

The larger program of shipments contemplated that twice the number of troops previously considered possible would be sent to France. Realizing the enormous problem that now confronted us, every element of the A.E.F. concerned attacked it vigorously. Fortunately, the larger ports of Brest and Cherbourg were available for the debarkation of personnel, leaving our regular ports to handle the increase of cargo. Meanwhile, we had secured a a few more berths and had gradually improved our port facilities, even with shortage in labor and material. At the same time, considerable progress had been made in expanding rail transportation. New engines and cars were arriving from the States, the repair of cars was progressing steadily, and the construction of additional storage was under way to meet the new requirements. Consequently when inquiry came from Washington again indicating some apprehensions regarding our ability to take care of the increasing arrivals of troops and cargo there was no hesitancy in replying: "Send over everything you have ready as fast as you can. The responsibility for failure will be ours."

The aviation question began to look more promising at this time. According to recent cables the shipments of airplanes from the States were expected to begin in May and increase to 600 per month by October. The manufacture of planes by the French had slowed down for want of mechanics and spruce, but we had given them considerable assistance and there was a possibility that agreements might be partially fulfilled. The combined programs promised to approximate the numbers that we should need for divisions that were likely soon to be engaged.

During the preceding months the War Department had made every effort to secure quantity production of an improved airplane motor, to be called the "Liberty." The design had been finally determined, and the manufacture was under way. The introduction of a new type of our own seemed the only way out of the bewildering confusion of this problem, even though it somewhat retarded the schedule of airplane manufacture. In the end, this superior motor proved to have been essential to meet an urgent demand, both by the Allies and ourselves.

New training and billeting areas for the increased numbers of divisions and detachments in prospect were none too easy to find within the already crowded space near the front, and it became necessary to open up new territory near the ports to provide temporary accommodations for incoming troops until the pressure could be relieved by readjustment and by the entry of the more advanced units into the lines.

Water supply was comparatively simple as long as our troops occupied areas that had previously been used, but when they were assigned to other localities it was often difficult to procure the necessary quantity and quality. The problem varied depending upon the region and the activity and size of the forces to be supplied. The systems of towns were utilized wherever possible, but frequently new wells had to be dug, pumps installed, and pipe lines laid. Water was often obtained from streams and lakes. Water carts were employed, especially by troops at the front, and chemical treatment was applied wherever necessary. This duty of providing water for our units in various parts of France was performed by the engineers.

The burden upon our staff and supply organizations in France became exceedingly heavy. The rapidly increasing numbers of men and the precipitate rush of supplies would be of no avail unless they could be mustered in orderly fashion. The crisis had found us with less than 320,000 officers and men in France, of which about 100,000 were necessarily engaged in the Services of Supply. There was great danger that the enemy would be able to defeat the French and British armies before substantial aid could be brought from America. If our forces could not be put into the lines in sufficient numbers within the next few months it might be too late. The war was up to America to win or lose.

No army was ever thoroughly trained or fully organized; in fact, there is no such thing except in theory. Governments or commanders who wait for absolute perfection in organization and training, or who expect every detail of equipment and supply to be complete before they act, are likely to lose opportunities and risk possible defeat at the hands of a more daring opponent. Vigorous action is necessary when the hour comes whether everything is entirely ready or not. It is a question of balance between opportunity and preparation.

(Diary) Paris, Tuesday, April 16, 1918. Bradley called at Chaumont Sunday, reporting again slow arrival of field hospitals, personnel and medical supplies. Discussed with Atterbury the rail situation; efficiency improving, but operating personnel needed to replace shortage of French. Left for Paris in afternoon.

Went to Chaumont-en-Vexin yesterday to witness practice maneuver of the 1st Division. Bullard back to duty. Met the Duke of Connaught in Paris and chatted a few minutes.

Visited 1st Division again this morning and spoke to the assembled officers. Went to Sarcus to confer with Foch, who looked tired and careworn. Arranged to send Colonel Mott to his headquarters as liaison officer.

At Pétain's request, the 1st Division was withdrawn from the line near Toul and sent to Chaumont-en-Vexin, northwest of Paris, to go into an active sector. The occasion of my visit was to witness the division's final maneuver in open warfare. Both officers and men were in splendid condition, notwithstanding their long rail journey, and all were ready for the test of actual battle. General Micheler, who commanded the French Fifth Army, to which the 1st Division had been assigned, came also to witness the maneuver. He spoke highly of the condition of the troops and their efficiency. The weather was clear but rather sharp. The countryside was radiant with its green meadows and early flowers and one could not help thinking how different would be those other fields on which this unit was soon to be engaged.

This division, composed as it was of Regular units with a nucleus of trained soldiers, did not present the difficulties to be met in organizing our new units. It is relatively easy to absorb partially trained recruits in veteran organizations, but it is quite another matter to create new organizations entirely of raw material. There were not enough officers in the Regular Army to furnish an adequate number to our new units. Even in the Regular regiments the percentage of Regular officers was low, and this applied to staff organizations as well. The I Corps had only seven per cent of officers from the Regular Army. Less than one per cent of all captains of the line in the A.E.F. at that time had been in the service a year. However, the 1st Division had been under training in France for several months and even with a large proportion of new officers there was no doubt that it would do well.

It was a source of real regret to me not to command the division in person and this coupled with the fact that its entry into the battle was of considerable moment led me to speak a word of confidence and encouragement. When the officers, about 900 in all, were assembled in the grounds of the château occupied as division headquarters, they formed a rare group. These splendid looking men, hardened by the strenuous work of the fall and by two months in winter trenches, fairly radiated the spirit of courage and gave promise that America's effort would prove her sons the equals of their forefathers.

I shall lay aside modesty and record my remarks, spoken under the inspiration of the moment:

"General Bullard and Officers of the 1st Division:

"It has not been convenient for me to meet the assembled officers of the 1st Division before, but I did not want you to enter into real participation in this war without my having said a word to you as a body.

"You have now been on French soil ten months, and you have carried out a progressive system of instruction under varied circumstances. You have lived in billets according to the custom of European armies; you have served in different sections of the trenches as a part of your training and have taken on a military complexion akin to that of our Allies. Officers of the Allies, in passing judgment upon your work, have expressed themselves as completely satisfied. I, myself, having witnessed your maneuvers, and closely followed the progress of your work in the trenches and elsewhere, now express myself as well satisfied. I believe that you are well prepared to take your place along with the seasoned troops of our Allies.

"But let us not for a moment forget that, while study and preparation are necessary, war itself is the real school where the art of war is learned. Whatever your previous instruction may have been, you must learn, in the actual experience of war, the practical application of the tactical principles that you have been taught during your preliminary training. Those principles are as absolute as they are immutable. Whatever may be the changing conditions of this war, those principles remain practically the same, and you should constantly bear them in mind. Now that you are going to take a place in the line of battle, you will be called upon to meet conditions that have never been presented to you before. When confronted with a new situation, do not try to recall examples given in any particular book on the subject; do not try to remember what your instructor has said in discussing some special problem; do not try to carry in your minds patterns of particular exercises or battles, thinking they will fit new cases, because no two sets of circumstances are alike; but bear in mind constantly, revolve in your thoughts frequently, and review at every opportunity, those well-established general principles, so that you may apply them when the time comes.

"While it is necessary to know how to apply the general principles of military tactics to the problems of actual battle, yet the main reliance after all must be upon your own determination, upon the aggressiveness of your men, upon their stamina, upon their character and upon their will to win. It is this will to win, more than anything else, that will carry you over the trying periods that you are soon to meet.

"You should always have the interests of the individual soldier at heart, for he is the principal part of the machine upon which you are to rely to carry you to success. His morale must be kept up to the highest pitch. That morale is affected by his confidence in his officers, by a realizing sense that they are his example. They should really be an example in everything that personifies the true soldier, in dress, in military bearing, in general conduct, and especially an example on the battlefield.

"To get the best out of your men they must feel that you are their real leader and must know that they can depend upon you. They must have confidence in you. Do not hold yourself aloof from your men, but keep in close touch with them. Let them feel that you are doing the very best you can for them under all circumstances, not only in providing their personal wants, in looking forward to a regular supply of food, and clothing, but that, as their leader, you are directing them wisely in the trying conditions of battle. On the other hand, you should always endeavor to make them realize their own responsibility and that you, in turn, rely fully upon them, and that when the occasion demands it they must make the supreme sacrifice.

"I did not come here to make a speech, I am not given to speech-making, so only a word more. I have every confidence in the 1st Division. You are about to enter this great battle of the greatest war in history, and in that battle you will represent the mightiest nation engaged. That thought itself must be to you a very appealing thought and one that should call forth the best and the noblest that is in you. Centuries of military tradition and of military and civil history are now looking toward this first contingent of the American Army as it enters this great battle. You have behind you your own national traditions that should make you the finest soldiers in Europe to-day. We come from a young and aggressive nation. We come from a nation that for one hundred and fifty years has stood before the world as the champion of the sacred principles of human liberty. We now return to Europe, the home of our ancestors, to help defend those same principles upon European soil. Could there be a more stimulating sentiment as you go from here to your commands, and from there to the battlefield?

"Our people to-day are hanging expectant upon your deeds. Our future part in this conflict depends upon your action. You are going forward and your conduct will be an example for succeeding units of our army. I hope the standard you set will be high—I know it will be high. You are taking with you the sincerest good wishes and the highest hopes of the President and all of our people at home. I assure you in their behalf and in my own of our strong belief in your success and of our confidence in your courage and in your loyalty, with a feeling of certainty in our hearts that you are going to make a record of which your country will be proud."

That afternoon I motored to Sarcus to see General Foch and sound him out regarding the prospects of uniting our divisions in a sector of our own. I told him that the Secretary of War, when in France, had expressed an earnest desire to hasten the formation of an American army and that this was also the wish of the President. It was my opinion, I said, that early action would be of great importance in stimulating the morale of our troops and our people. Now that the 1st Division was to go into line, the people at home would expect soon to hear that an American army was engaged on its own front. I suggested the possibility that the I Corps might be assembled near the 1st Division as a beginning.

General Foch agreed in principle to the suggestion, but was uncertain when the other divisions could be spared, which I, of course, fully appreciated. He remarked that the enemy was very aggressive and referred to his severe attack against the British on the Lys between Lens and Ypres which began on the 9th and was still in progress. But looking beyond, I insisted that the 26th and 42d Divisions might be withdrawn at any time from quiet sectors, to be followed by the 2d and the 32d and also the 3d a few days later. I pointed out that this force of six divisions, including the 1st would equal twelve French divisions and gave it as my opinion that it would be better to use this American group for active operations than to detain the units in quiet sectors and send French divisions to the battle front. My understanding after this discussion was very definite that the plan would soon be carried out, leaving the exact time and place to be determined. It was immaterial to me just where it should occur, the point being to get it done.

The German offensive on the Lys was another formidable attempt to break the British lines. The attack was made to the north and south of Armentières on a front of twenty-four miles by twenty-seven German divisions. The exhausted British, though they fought with most commendable courage and skill, were forced again to yield, with heavy losses to themselves and the division of Portuguese that was with them. It was in this ex-

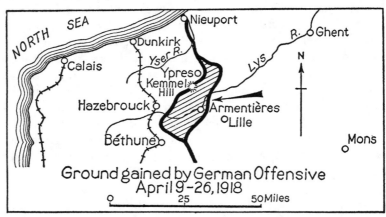

Ground gained by German Offensive
April 9–26, 1918

tremity that Marshal Haig's famous order to his armies dated April 11th was issued:

"Three weeks ago to-day the enemy began his terrific attacks against us on a 50-mile front. His objects are to separate us from the French, to take the Channel ports and destroy the British Army.

"In spite of throwing already 106 divisions into the battle and enduring the most reckless sacrifice of human life, he has as yet made little progress towards his goals.

"We owe this to the determined fighting and self-sacrifice of our troops. Words fail me to express the admiration which I feel for the splendid resistance offered by all ranks of our Army under the most trying circumstances.

"Many amongst us now are tired. To those I would say that victory will belong to the side which holds out the longest. The French Army is moving rapidly and in great force to our support.

"There is no other course open to us but to fight it out! Every position must be held to the last man; there must be no retirement. With our backs to the wall, and believing in the justice of our cause, each one of us must fight on to the end. The safety of our homes and the freedom of mankind alike depend upon the conduct of each one of us at this critical moment."

Although several French divisions were hurried to the Lys front, it was a week after the attack began before they were put into the line. They then relieved British divisions at the famous Kemmel Hill, only to be surprised and defeated themselves on April 25th, much to their chagrin. The battle was practically ended by the last of the month with a gain by the Germans of ten or eleven miles, but they failed in their effort to capture the important objective of Hazebrouck.

(Diary) Paris, Thursday, April 18, 1918. Had a call yesterday from Major General Sackville-West, who is with Supreme War Council.

Lord Milner, recently appointed British Minister for War, came to-day to suggest conference on shipment of our troops. Went to see M. Clemenceau to discuss Inter-Allied supply control.

Washington cables Ordnance Department will furnish some 600 guns army and navy heavy artillery, but delivery far off. Another brigade infantry and machine gun units of marines to be sent by naval shipping. Sixth Engineers receive high praise from British for conduct in battle March 21-April 3. Covered space for storage at ports now practically amounts to 2,250,000 square feet.

One effect of unified control of the combatant forces was to emphasize the desirability of applying the same principle to the question of supplies. In practice, the French and ourselves had been slowly moving in that direction for several months. A fairly good working basis had already been established through the efforts of our General Purchasing Board in conjunction with the French Mission attached to my headquarters. The principle was already applied to certain classes of supplies, but there was no assurance of its larger application under stress of circumstances when it might possibly be vital to success.

The expansion of its scope was particularly important to us, as we were short of many supplies, and if they could be procured from the Allies it would save tonnage. Unless coöperation should become more general there might be some doubt of our obtaining needful equipment and munitions to enable our increasing armies fully to do their part.   On the other hand, the Allies were seeking in our markets raw material for their factories, and much tonnage might be saved if they could be induced to pool their demands. Such action appeared reasonable and it had often been discussed, yet, like the unity of command, it looked as though only a crisis in the question of procurement, resulting especially from lack of tonnage, could bring the supply agencies of the different governments to give the question serious consideration.

When I visited M. Clemenceau's office and explained the idea to him, he was quick to see the advantages of such a plan and asked me to present my views in writing so that he could have it studied.   This was done in the letter quoted below:

"France, April 19, 1918.

"Dear Mr. Clemenceau:

"Referring to our conversation of yesterday, permit me to confirm my suggestion that all supplies and war materials that are used in common by the Allied armies be pooled and that the principle be extended as far as possible to the civil populations of the Allies in Europe.

*   *   *   *   *   *   *

"The defects of present methods of handling supplies have long been recognized * * * but each of the Allied armies continues to think only in terms of its own requirements independently of the other armies.   While it is fully realized that there are many classes of supplies that are used by all the Allies which could be pooled and issued to a particular army as required, a practical solution to the problem has not yet been reached.

" * * * The A.E.F. has recently reduced or postponed its requirements in tonnage to the lowest limit to save sea transportation, and a study of the subject leads to the conclusion that our Allies could do much more than is now being done.

"While some attempt has been made through coördinating Allied committees, including the Supreme War Council, these bodies are only advisory. * * * The authority to order the allotment and distribution of supplies to the different armies does not exist. * * *

" * * * The following classes of supplies, naturally, would be included: Aviation material, munitions as far as practicable, horses, oats, hay, meat, flour, coal, gasoline, wagons, harness, motor transport, depots, warehouses, lumber and timber.   Such concentration or control of supplies would probably result in economy of port construction and especially in storage facilities.

"To meet the situation in question, I propose to you the designation of one occupying a position as to supplies and material similar to that of General Foch, as to military operations, who shall have authority to decide just what supplies and material should be brought to France by the Allies and determine their disposition.

"May I urge that this matter be given early attention? Permit me to suggest that Colonel Dawes, Purchasing Agent of the A.E.F., be called into consultation with such officers of the French Army as you may designate to discuss this important subject.

"I remain, with high personal and official esteem,
                    "Your obedient servant,
                                        "JOHN J. PERSHING."

This subject was also taken up with Washington and with the British, but the question of pooling in general and of having any single individual determine the allotment of supplies to various armies did not meet with entire approval. M. Clemenceau became much interested in the idea involved and met with an Inter-Allied committee charged with its consideration. He approved the plan in principle, which gave us hope that some definite understanding would eventually be reached. Naturally, the success of the plan would have required a joint board of Allied officers to canvass the supply situation and make recommendations to the controlling authority. Later an eminently satisfactory arrangement was perfected whereby the coördination of supplies was placed in the hands of such a board.

The Third Liberty Loan was getting under way, as indicated by the cable conveying the President's Liberty Day Proclamation, which was such a patriotic utterance that it must be quoted in full:

"An enemy who has grossly abused the power of organized government and who seeks to dominate the world by the might of the sword, challenges the right of America and the liberty and life of all the free nations of the earth. Our brave sons are facing the fire of battle in defense of the honor and rank of America and the liberty of nations. To sustain them and to assist our gallant soldiers in the war, a generous and patriotic people have been called upon to subscribe to the

Third Liberty Loan. Now, therefore, I, Woodrow Wilson, President of the United States of America, do appoint Friday, the 26th day of April, 1918, as Liberty Day. On the afternoon of that day, I request the people of the United States to assemble in their respective communities and liberally pledge anew their financial support to sustain the Nation's cause. A patriotic demonstration will be held in every city, town, and hamlet throughout the land under the general direction of the Secretary of the Treasury and the immediate direction of the Liberty Loan committees organized by the Federal Reserve Bank. Let the Nation's response to the Third Liberty Loan express in unmistakable terms the determination of America to fight for peace, the permanent peace of justice. For the purpose of participating in Liberty Day celebrations all employees of the Federal Government throughout the country whose services can be spared may be excused at 12 o'clock noon on Friday, April 26th."

The following instructions were received from the Secretary of War:

"Liberty Day will be observed by the troops in your command to the extent that you deem wise, but wherever patriotic programs are presented, public reading of the President's proclamation will be included."

Volume II

CHAPTER XXVII

Visit British Front—Inspection of 77th Division—Agreement on Training with British—Conference in England—London Agreement—Discussion with Foch on Shipment American Troops—Shipping Situation—Recommend Call for 1,500,000 Men—Seicheprey—French and British Propose Limiting our Production Airplanes—Italians and Unity of Command—Foch's Authority Extended to Include Italian Army.

(Diary) British G.H.Q., Saturday, April 20, 1918. Washington disturbed over German propaganda.[1] Came here yesterday at Sir Douglas Haig's invitation to discuss training of our troops and study operations in progress.

Stopped at our II Corps Headquarters at Fruges to-day and find organization well handled by Chief of Staff, Colonel G. S. Simonds. Saw some of 77th Division, now arriving in British area. Visited General Currie's headquarters at Chamblain l'Abbé.

WE were always made welcome at British headquarters. It so happened that on the day of our arrival Lord Derby, who had just been replaced as Minister of War by Lord Milner, was there en route to Paris as British Ambassador. During dinner the conversation ran along freely as though we were members of the official family. At length, Lord Derby and

---

[1] The following cable was sent on April 19th: "For Chief of Staff. With reference to your cablegram, German propaganda has used such stories persistently in effort to stir up distrust and dissension among Allies. In some cases facts have been distorted as, for example, the capture of unarmed American working parties being played up as capture of combat troops. In most cases stories are completely false. Following are examples from German wireless news: 'March 5th—The Americans recently captured had been placed with French troops in the front lines for training purposes. * * * They are strong young fellows but do not seem to have much desire to fight. They have no understanding of the war. To them it is an enterprise undertaken by New York financiers. They hate but respect the English. With the French they are on good terms. They have not the slightest idea of military operations and seem stupid and fatalistic in comparison with the war-accustomed Frenchmen. * * * They were glad

Sir Douglas drifted to the subject of British politicians. It would betray no confidence to say that during this conversation there was considerable criticism of some who held prominent places. The coalition Government came in for its share because of its attitude toward the military High Command. Lord Derby was well known to be a warm supporter of the British Commander-in-Chief, and from what I knew of the relations between the civil and the military authorities of Great Britain it is fair to presume that this might have been the reason he relinquished his post as Minister for War. He asked why all parties were not represented in our Cabinet, but I did not undertake to give any explanation, although I had often asked myself the same question. It need hardly be recalled that in so far as the Americans were concerned Lord Derby was always most helpful.

The operations on the Lys were still active and the Germans were showing their usual persistence. Marshal Haig spoke in high terms of the fine conduct of his divisions against the enemy's offensive. They deserved high praise, as they were not at all fresh, and generally occupied a much wider front than safety demanded. Sir Douglas seemed to be confident that the offensive would soon spend itself.

It was stimulating to morale to visit the headquarters of the Canadians, where one soon caught the fine spirit of that superb corps. We talked with the Corps Commander, Lieutenant General Sir Arthur Currie, his Chief of Staff, and others, and had tea with them. The alertness and confidence of these neighbors of ours were admirable, and the excellent record they had made and were still making gave us as much gratification as though they had been our own countrymen. I remember this visit with much pleasure and recall the prediction of the Canadians that Americans would soon play an important part in the war.

to escape further fighting. March 29th—French officers do not conceal their disillusionment over the value of the veteran American troops and are using them by battalions and larger units among the English and French infantry. They are entirely incapable of carrying out independent operations.' Distribution of propaganda is attempted by small balloons sent across with favoring wind; also printing of cleverly imitated Italian papers for distribution back of Italian front; also circulation of stories by enemy agents. These efforts having scant success."

General Currie deplored the fact that the British had so easily given up Passchendaele Ridge, which the year before he had been told must be taken at all cost, and for which the Canadians made the tremendous sacrifice of 16,000 casualties. His divisions were then holding 9,000 yards each, or a little over five miles of front, as compared with from 4,500 to 7,000 yards per division held by Gough's and Byng's armies in March. Currie considered that his extension would be excessive in the face of a determined and powerful offensive using shock tactics. Whatever the disadvantages were, it did show the British Commander-in-Chief's confidence in the Canadians.

I took advantage of the opportunity while on the British front to visit the Nordausques area to inspect the advance elements of the 77th Division, which was one of the divisions selected for training with the British. We took luncheon with Brigadier General Evan M. Johnson, then temporarily in command, and his staff officers. He praised the soldierly qualities of the men, but said they were very much behind in their training. This division had suffered severely from the practice followed by the War Department of taking men who had been under training for some time and sending them elsewhere for special purposes. A total of 30,000 men had been selected from time to time from this division and their places filled with recruits, with the result that the infantry and machine gun units, numbering about 17,000 men, that reported in France were composed largely of untrained or partially trained troops.

While at Sir Douglas' headquarters, he and I reached an understanding as to the training and administration of American troops that were to be temporarily with the British. In the first place, they were to be allocated by regiments to British skeleton divisions under such a schedule as might be agreed upon. The training staffs of British divisions were to be at the disposal of these regiments, especially for instruction in the use of the rifle and machine gun, and in the handling of gas. After that, and with the approval of their American division commander, each regiment was to be attached to a British division in line, so that each of its three battalions would have the opportunity of serving with one of the British brigades. Our battalions were to be commanded by our own officers, and our regimental staffs were to be attached to those of British brigades. In the next stage, each of our regiments, with its three battalions united under the regimental commander, was to act as a brigade in a British division. The final stage would find the four American regiments reunited to form the division under its own officers, with British artillery until the arrival of its own artillery brigade.

In carrying out this scheme, the tendency at first was for British officers actually to assume command of our units in training. Our officers in most cases permitted this to be done until it was checked by my orders, which directed that "American units must be commanded in training by the officers and noncommissioned officers who are to command them in battle," and, further, that American troops would in all cases be commanded in battle only by Americans.

The program probably expedited preparation in some respects, but questions of food, transport, and methods of instruction arose which demonstrated that any attempt at permanent amalgamation would have surely led to friction and inefficiency. Because they were needed elsewhere, none of the divisions sent to train with the British, except the 27th and 30th, remained long enough to carry out the prescribed course.

The subject of coördination of the supply systems of the armies on the Western Front was also taken up with Sir Douglas. I explained my idea of pooling supplies, and pointed out that he was already committed to the principle, as illustrated by his providing certain equipment and transportation for our divisions that were to serve behind his lines for training. But the proposition of relinquishing control of his supplies, even partially, did not appeal to him. He was afraid that if it should be given general application it would be a one-sided affair. To a certain extent this might have been the result, as we would probably have been the greatest beneficiaries. But if by pooling certain things common to all armies, more tonnage could have been saved to transport our troops and supplies, it would have meant that much more aid to the Allied cause.

(Diary) London, Wednesday, April 24, 1918. Left British G.H.Q. for London on Sunday, with Harbord, Boyd, and Adamson. Were met at Folkestone by Biddle and Rethers.[1] Also met Stevens and L. H. Shearman at Folkestone, both anxious about coal supply. Little evidence of food shortage at the Savoy Hotel, where we are stopping.

Called Monday on Ambassador Page, who said my offer to Foch had greatly pleased the British. Saw Admiral Sims and find he thinks decreased danger from submarines warrants sending troops by smaller ships. Started conference with Lord Milner and Sir Henry Wilson.

On Tuesday Winston Churchill told me that as the German attack was a month later than expected they had plenty of artillery and ammunition, notwithstanding recent losses. Called on Mr. Lloyd George and discussed Allied supply with him but got little encouragement.

Resumed conference this morning and agreed on details of troop shipments. Had luncheon with Major and Lady Astor. Dined informally at St. James' Palace with the Duke of Connaught, who does not share the gloomy outlook, although he deplores the severe losses.

Following the suggestion of Lord Milner, I went to London to consider further the shipment of American troops. At our first meeting there were present Lord Milner and General Sir Henry Wilson, who had succeeded General Robertson as the Chief of the General Staff, Harbord, and myself. The main point of difference that had developed in previous conferences as to just how far the Americans should be committed to serve in active operations was again considered. I stated that the principal thing was to get our units trained, and that while I was opposed to amalgamation, yet if during the period of instruction the British units with which they were serving should be attacked, or if another great emergency should arise, of course our men would go in. Naturally, the British wanted unlimited infantry and machine gun units, but I could not go further than to consider a limited extension of the six-division plan.

During the conference, a cable from Lord Reading to the Prime

[1] Maj. Gen. John Biddle was in command of the Base Section comprising England and Col. Harry Rethers was Chief Quartermaster of the section.

Minister was brought forth which stated that the President had agreed to the amalgamation of Americans with the British. I had nothing official at hand later than the President's conditional approval of Joint Note No. 18 as suggested by Mr. Baker, so I promptly said that it could not be possible that any such concession had been made, and that the classes of our troops to be shipped over and their disposition must be left to me. Of course, we knew that the British were pressing this point by constant appeals to the President and that they were insisting that he should agree to the shipment of 120,000 infantry and machine gun units per month for four months, to the exclusion of all other personnel. While the British conferees had concluded from Lord Reading's cable that their case was won, I took quite another view and declined to consider the information as conclusive.

As a result of these discussions, we reached an agreement which provided for the shipment in the month of May, by British and American tonnage, of the infantry, machine gun, engineer, and signal troops, together with the various unit headquarters, of six divisions for training with the British Army. It was provided that any shipping in excess of the amount required for this number of troops should be utilized to transport the artillery of these divisions, and that such personnel as might be required to build up corps organizations should then follow; it being understood that the artillery regiments would train with the French and join their proper divisions when the training of the infantry was completed.

In order to meet any emergency which might require an excess of infantry after the completion of this program, it was agreed that all the American and British shipping available for the transportation of troops was to be used under such arrangement as would insure immediate aid to the Allies, and thereafter as far as possible provide other units necessary to complete the organization of our divisions and corps. It was further agreed that the combatant troops mentioned in connection with May shipments should be followed by such service of supply troops and other contingents as we ourselves might consider necessary, inasmuch as the shipment of such troops had been postponed; and that all these troops should be utilized at my discretion, except that the six divisions which the British were to transport would be trained with them.

Upon reaching Chaumont, I found a cablegram, dated April 26th, transmitting a memorandum, dated April 19th, that had been sent by direction of the President to the British Ambassador at Washington in conformity with his approval of Joint Note No. 18 of the Supreme War Council. In this memorandum the shipment of only infantry and machine gun units for four months was conceded, and it was hoped and believed that the number would be 120,000 per month. Their assignment for training and use was to be left to my discretion. The memorandum went on to say that the United States, until the situation changed, had no intention of departing from as full compliance with the recommendation of the Permanent Military Representatives as the nature of the case would permit.

This was the first official information I had received that the Administration had agreed to send any specific numbers of infantry and machine gun units to France.

The following quotation is a continuation of the memorandum:

"It being also understood that this statement is not to be regarded as a commitment from which the Government of the United States is not free to depart when the exigencies no longer require it; and also that the preferential transportation of infantry and machine gun units here set forth as a policy and principle is not to be regarded as so exclusive as to prevent the Government of the United States from including in the troops carried by its own tonnage from time to time relatively small numbers of personnel of other arms as may be deemed wise by the United States as replacements and either to make possible the use of a maximum capacity of ships or the most efficient use of the infantry and machine gun units as such transported, or the maintenance of the services of supply already organized and in process of construction for the American Army already in France."

This concession went further than it was necessary to go and much further than I had expected. Realizing the complications that might arise from commitments so far in the future and the delay in forming an American army that would follow, I did not agree in later discussions at the Supreme War Council with all that the Allies now felt justified in demanding. I was opposed to the action of the Council in assuming the power to dispose of American troops under any circumstances. Moreover, it was not in any sense a prerogative of this body.

There can be little doubt that even before the President's memorandum was issued Lord Reading received the distinct impression that infantry and machine gun units would be sent to France at the rate of 120,000 men per month for four months, beginning with April. That the President agreed to this "in principle" is practically certain. It need not be further emphasized that such a concession, even though prompted by the most generous impulse, could only add to the difficulties of our task of building up an army of our own. It is probable that Lord Reading, skilled advocate that he was, did more while Ambassador at Washington to influence the Administration to grant Allied requests than any other individual.

The Secretary of War upon his return caused the Administration's position to be somewhat more clearly defined through the President's memorandum, but the statement still left much to be desired in the way of a positive declaration of our purpose to have our own army. It left a very definite notion in the minds of the Allies that the Administration at Washington was favorable to amalgamation and that the main obstacle to be overcome was the military head of the American forces in France. This is doubtless the reason why all the Allied verbal "heavy artillery" was often turned in my direction.

The agreement made in London, as actually drawn, while insuring the shipment of largely increased numbers of troops did not commit us to sending infantry and machine gun units exclusively beyond June 1st. It provided a reserve of the classes of troops that might be needed by the British until their new drafts should be available, and offered the possibility of our getting other classes of troops to complete our plans of organization for the auxiliary arms and Services of Supply. The British thought that this program could be very much exceeded and believed it might be possible to transport entire divisions besides a number of corps and S.O.S. troops. The concession we made for May was a radical departure from the wise policy of bringing over balanced forces in complete organizations, but the clamor was so great and the danger of the absolute defeat of the Allies seemed so imminent that it was thought to be warranted as a temporary expedient.

The question of applying conscription to Ireland was then under consideration by the British and it appeared probable, according to views expressed more or less guardedly, that British troops would be required to enforce it. Inasmuch as such a measure would more than likely have affected the attitude of American troops of Irish origin toward service with the British, our argument was strengthened regarding the desirability of keeping our own troops together and organizing them into an American army at the earliest possible date.

(Diary) Paris, Saturday, April 27, 1918. Left London Thursday by automobile, boarded a British destroyer at Folkestone, reaching Boulogne about four in the afternoon. Colonel Mott was there with request from General Foch for me to come to Sarcus. Held conference and went to Paris that night.

Yesterday morning met with Stevens, Morrow, Rublee, and Shearman of Allied Maritime Transport Council. Saw Colonel Percy L. Jones regarding relations with French of our ambulance companies under his supervision. Discussed coal situation with Loucheur, also heavy artillery and airplanes.

Cabled recommendation that call be made for 1,500,000 men.[1] Rumors thought reliable indicate that Germans contemplate building up armies with Russians. The enemy attacked the 26th Division at Seicheprey on the night of 20th-21st and inflicted considerable loss. 1st Division began entering line on the 24th and to-day assumed command of front opposite Cantigny.

[1] See page 381, volume I, for discussion of the subject of calling out men for training.

Arriving at General Foch's headquarters, we found Generals Bliss and Weygand, and after dinner we entered into a general discussion about American troop shipments:

Foch:

"On March 28th you came to offer the services of American troops. I have a vivid recollection of the occasion. As to the American divisions, in what order do you think they should be employed?"

Pershing:

"The order would be the 26th, 42d, 2d. (The 1st had already been sent to an active front near Amiens.) The regiments of the 32d will be ready by May 1st."

Foch:

"I do not think they can be used before May 5th, but the more we put into the line the better it will be. Your 77th Division has arrived, I see. What about the 3d and 5th?"

Pershing:

"The infantry of the 3d has arrived, and that of the 5th will soon follow."

Foch:

"What we need now is infantry, especially the British, on account of the present crisis. That is why the Supreme War Council at Versailles recommended that all tonnage be devoted to that purpose for the time being. I hope that America may send over as much infantry as possible during the next three months. The other arms to complete your divisions can come afterwards. What do you think of that plan?"

Pershing:

"I cannot commit myself to such a proposition. If nothing but infantry and machine gunners are brought over to the total of 360,000, it will be October or November before the artillery and auxiliary troops could arrive and we could not foresee the formation of an American army until next spring."

Foch:

"I think your calculation is rather pessimistic, for we could begin bringing your other troops in August, but, without considering that point, we can furnish you with artillery and its personnel, and you can have your divisions reconstituted beginning with October. What would you propose in this connection?"

Pershing:

"I think we should limit the transportation of infantry to the month of May, and that the artillery and auxiliary troops should come in June. They should not arrive more than a month later than the infantry."

General Foch then made some calculations based upon 100,000 men per month for three months and continued:

Foch:

"If we could bring 120,000 in May, that would still leave us 100,-000 below British losses."

Pershing:

"Under what conditions would you employ the American infantry units?"

Foch:

"What proposition have you to offer on that subject? To begin with, I would not split up your regiments."

Pershing:

"When would these regiments be grouped into brigades and the brigades into divisions?"

Foch:

"A final decision cannot be made on that subject. That will evidently depend upon the degree of instruction of the units. In the crisis that actually confronts the Allied armies, it is effectives that we lack. The method of employing these units is a question to be handled in due course and according to their efficiency."

Pershing:

"I would like to have the conditions under which these units are to be employed determined now and to fix the time during which the regiments and brigades will be used separately."

Foch:

"Make your proposition on that subject."

I then explained to him the details of the system that was being followed where our divisions were in training with the French, and the plan agreed upon with the British. I added that it was fully understood that if an emergency should arise while our troops were in training, they would go into battle as part of the divisions with which they were serving. He seemed to approve the method, but returned once more to the decision taken by the Supreme War Council with reference to the shipment of American infantry and machine gun units, upon which the following conversation ensued:

Foch:

"I do not doubt the excellency of the method, but in the crisis through which we are passing I return to the decision of the Supreme War Council and I ask you to transport during the months of May, June, and July, only infantry and machine gun units. Will you consent?"

Pershing:

"No, I do not consent. I propose for one month to ship nothing but infantry and machine gun units and after that the other arms and service of the rear troops to correspond."

Foch:

"If you adopt the plan I propose you would have by July 31st, 300,000 more American infantry."

Pershing:

"You said just now that you would furnish the artillery and even artillerymen, which would be joined with our infantry to complete our divisions. Then why not consent to transport our artillery personnel along with our infantry?"

Foch:

"I repeat that it is the infantry of which we have the greatest need at this time. I would like to have General Bliss tell us what were the considerations which led to the decision taken by the Supreme War Council at Versailles."

Bliss:

"The collective note recommended to the United States to send only infantry until the Supreme War Council should give instructions to the contrary. The Government of the United States in conformity with this note and with the recommendations of Mr. Baker consented to this plan. As far as the employment of the units on the front is concerned, the question should be decided by General Pershing according to agreement with the Commander-in-Chief to whose army they may be attached."

Pershing:

"I have been discussing this question of training our units for the last eight months, first with General Pétain and then with Marshal Haig. The method agreed upon leads naturally to the formation of constituted American divisions."

General Foch stated that he wished to see American divisions constituted and an American army formed as large as possible, but the policy he was advocating would have made it impossible to form an American army without serious delay, if ever. Continuing, he said:

"But do not forget that we are in the midst of a hard battle. If we do not take steps to prevent the disaster which is threatened at present the American Army may arrive in France to find the British pushed into the sea and the French driven back behind the Loire, while it tries in vain to organize on lost battlefields over the graves of Allied soldiers."

He was assured that it was fully understood that if an emergency should arise while our troops were in training with the British or French, they would go into the battle and do their part. I then gave him the numbers to be shipped during May and told him that it had been agreed between the British and ourselves to consider the question for June later. I informed him that the British shipping authorities now thought that it would be possible within the next three months to transport to France 750,000 men.

He was surprised to learn that enough shipping had been found to bring over so many, and, while insisting that we continue the May program into June, said that if it was possible to transport any such numbers he saw no reason why whole divisions should not soon be transported. Nevertheless, a few days later he made a still stronger demand for special shipments of infantry and machine gun units.

The shipping situation as brought out in conference with the American members of the Maritime Transport Council did not appear so favorable as we had been led to believe. Only two of our newly built vessels had been delivered and our shipbuilding program was not yet far enough along to count as an important factor, although prospects were that the rate would soon begin to increase. A full study made by our delegates to the Council of the demands to be made upon Allied and neutral tonnage for military, naval, and general needs showed an estimated shortage of nearly 2,000,000 tons. It was obvious that the program for strengthening the Western Front must be carried out if possible. Therefore, all practicable measures for the economical employment of every available ton of shipping, especially for freight, were given consideration at our conference.

It was thought, in the first place, that the Allied navies could reduce their requirements of merchant tonnage by a joint examination of the naval programs; second, that considerable shipping could be saved by suspending or reducing military and naval activities in theaters of war other than the Western Front; third, that further reductions in Allied civilian imports might be made temporarily; and, finally, that insistence upon the adoption of unified action in the supply services by the Allies on the Western Front, already suggested, would result in a material saving of tonnage.

I heartily approved of the above recommendations and sent a cable to Washington to that effect, of which the following is an extract:

"April 30, 1918.

"I therefore heartily approve the recommendation made by the Allied Maritime Transport Council (which, it is important to note, is a body upon which French and British ministers are sitting) that all of the military programs of the Allies be brought under joint review by the appropriate military authorities to the end that effort may be concentrated on the Western Front. While this is of vital importance to the common cause, it is of peculiar and of almost supreme importance to our own rapidly growing army. If programs are allowed to remain in effect which call for more tonnage than is in existence, the calls for diversion of our ships for food supplies, coal, nitrates, and other things essential to our Allies will become more and more insistent. They will tend to converge more and more upon our program because our program is rapidly expanding and the others are comparatively rigid. Therefore a cutting down of all military programs that do not directly contribute to the common cause and a greater unity in the prosecution of those plans that do contribute to the common cause are essential during the next few months if we are to avoid the disaster that will come from haphazard curtailments of absolute essentials at the eleventh hour."

Of course, certain agreements as to raw materials had to be maintained in order to keep production of ammunition and airplanes going and these required at least 30,000 tons monthly. In general, as with the question of unity of supply, to which all agreed in principle, so it was with sea transportation, but action in the latter case presented serious difficulties. As a matter of fact, in the broad sense the two were intimately connected. It seemed to me that the control of Allied supplies could well be vested in a board (with executive powers) consisting of a representative from each Government. It appeared logical that this board, in consultation with the Allied Maritime Council, should be authorized to allot Allied tonnage. This was fully stated in my cables, but Washington did not wholly accept my views.

Confronted as we were by the lack of trained men at this time, it was evident that we should within a few months find ourselves facing a still more serious situation unless increased numbers were put in training without delay. Supplementing the suggestion I had made verbally to the Secretary, a cable was sent on April 27th, which included also a reference to the numbers of partially trained men in divisions then arriving, as follows:

"Regard it most imperative that there be no delay in calling out a new draft and the entire summer season devoted to instruction and training so that new troops may be thoroughly and systematically trained without disturbing organizations when formed. Believe German offensive will be stopped but Allied aggressive must be undertaken as early as possible thereafter and American forces must be in position to throw in their full weight. Recommend that a call be issued at once for at least one million and a half men. Having in mind large replacements of losses that are sure to occur and the delays of organization and equipment of new drafts, this is the smallest number that should be considered."

In reply to this the following was received, dated May 7th:

"With reference to paragraph 1 your 990, troops sent you have been best available. Divisions became depleted during the winter on account large numbers being taken for staff corps and other unavoidable causes, and lack of equipment for replacements. Conditions will improve early in July so that eventually only those divisions with at least six months training will be sent. * * *

"With reference to paragraph 3 your 990, 643,198 white, and 73,326 colored men, total 716,524, have been drafted since January 1st, including May draft. Draft will be continued monthly to maximum capacity. Impracticable to draft one million and a half at one time. Draft already called will fill all divisions now organized and all other troops for second and third phases. Question of organizing new divisions under consideration. We now have troops of all classes under training in replacement camps."

On the night of April 20th-21st, the Germans made a raid on the 26th Division in the vicinity of Seicheprey. The attack covered a two-mile front extending west from the Bois de Remières. It came during a heavy fog and was a complete surprise to our troops, who were considerably outnumbered. The fighting in Seicheprey was violent, causing heavy losses on both sides. The town was taken by the enemy. The success of the raid may be attributed largely to the destruction by the German artillery of the divisional system of communications, which naturally resulted in some confusion in the division. Although coöperation among the units was difficult under the circumstances, it was finally established and the original front was reoccupied the following day. [1]

(Diary) Paris, Tuesday, April 30, 1918. Congress has wisely passed an act providing for indemnity to Allies for damage by our troops abroad.

On Sunday took up with Colonel H. B. Jordan, of the Ordnance, the subject of heavy guns from French, and with Foulois their production of airplanes. General Crozier, back from Italy, favors sending American troops there. Left for Chaumont that evening.

Generals John L. Hines and Brewster called yesterday, and Martin

[1] In this affair we lost 1 officer, 80 enlisted men, killed; 11 officers, 176 enlisted men, wounded; 3 officers, 211 enlisted men, gassed; and 5 officers, 182 enlisted men, missing and prisoners. The losses of the enemy in killed and wounded were reported as even greater.

Egan [1] came for confidential conference. General Liggett, I Corps,[2] reports good progress in his divisions. Censors of letters of French report very favorable comment on Americans in trenches. Returned to Paris to-day.

Under the provisions of the Act of Congress mentioned in the diary, authority was granted for the settlement of all claims "Of inhabitants of France or any other European country not an enemy or ally of an enemy" for injuries to persons or damage to property occasioned by our forces. The procedure followed was in accordance with the law and practice of the country in question. These claims were handled by the Renting, Requisition and Claims Service, which had been formed in March primarily to procure lands and buildings needed for our forces. The efficient administration of this Service in the prompt settlement of claims had an excellent effect upon the people of the European countries concerned.

We were never quite sure of obtaining airplanes from the Allies, as material and expert labor for their manufacture were never fully up to requirements. While advices from home and the frequent promises of the French kept us hopeful, the cancellation by the latter of our early contract for airplanes created an uncertainty that made it difficult to plan either for the training of our aviation personnel or their participation in operations. So far we had received no planes from home and none from the French except a few for training purposes.

My conference with General Foulois was to consider a proposition purporting to bring about closer coöperation with the French,

[1] Mr. Egan came to France about this time at my request and joined me as civilian aide. His experience in the newspaper and business worlds made him most valuable in this position. He was a keen observer and kept in touch with Allied sentiment and the attitude of the Allies toward Americans. The suggestions and advice he gave from time to time were of great assistance to me.

[2] This corps at the time of the report consisted of six divisions; the 1st (Bullard) with the French Fifth Army in line in vicinity of Gisors; the 2d (Bundy) with the French Tenth Army in line by small units between Verdun and St. Mihiel; the 26th (Edwards) in Toul Sector under French XXXII Corps; the 32d (Haan) in the 10th training area, headquarters at Prauthoy; the 42d (Menoher) in sector east of Baccarat under the French VII Corps; and the 41st (Alexander) depot division with headquarters at St. Aignan.

emanating from their Minister of Munitions, M. Loucheur. In a letter from the Undersecretary for Aeronautics, it was suggested that the French should increase their output of airplane bodies of various types and that we should confine ourselves to the production of Liberty engines, and possibly also undertake the manufacture of a particular type of engine which they recommended. Analysis of the proposal showed that, if adopted, we should have to abandon our plans for the manufacture of planes at home, and furnish the French additional raw material, and probably expert labor. We were always keen for coöperation that would advance the common cause, but production would not have been hastened under this plan. Our experience so far had not been such as to give confidence in their fulfillment of an agreement of this sort, so the suggestion was politely rejected.

A few days later a British air representative also sought joint coöperation with us. The proposal he made was that we should limit our construction, other than for training purposes, to long range strategic bombing aircraft and the manufacture of Liberty engines, and that the British would supply us aircraft for purely American operations. We were asked to send a small staff to London to coöperate along these lines and they would send a strong mission of experts to Washington. When the matter was presented to me along with a prepared telegram to be sent to Lord Reading stating that we and the French concurred, I inquired how it came that the French had agreed to this without consulting us, and it was found that the plan had not yet been taken up with them. I then told the British representative that when the air services of the Allied armies reached an agreement regarding this proposal I would consider it. This was the last we heard of it. Such incidents as these showed the tendency to gain particular advantage and caused us to doubt the sincerity of proposals for coöperation in such matters.

In discussing unity in general, the failure of the Italians to place their armies under the Supreme Command on the Western Front was frequently mentioned, and it was feared in high places that there might arise another dangerous situation similar to Caporetto, but all hesitated to take action. From the military standpoint the Western Front really extended to the Adriatic Sea, and support for the Italians in case of necessity would have to come, as before, from the armies in France.

The question was a delicate one, but it occurred to me to suggest to the Secretary of War that the President might intimate to the Italian Government the propriety of completing the unity of command by placing its armies under the same control as the others. It was believed that the Italian Cabinet might be willing to take the step if it could be done in such a way as to prevent hostile criticism among their own people. It was thought that if the suggestion should come from the British or the French, especially the latter, it would very likely be regarded with suspicion, whereas none could ascribe any but the highest motives to Mr. Wilson in making such a move. However, the question came up for discussion at the next meeting of the Supreme War Council, which was held at Abbeville, and the authority of General Foch was extended to include the Italian armies. This completed the unity of command from the North Sea to the Adriatic.

CHAPTER XXVIII

Conference at Abbeville—Allied Leaders Greatly Alarmed—Insistent on American Replacements—Infantry and Machine Gunners Urged—Heated Discussions—Lloyd George Makes More Tonnage Available—Agreement Reached—Some American Troops for Italy

(Diary) Paris, Thursday, May 2, 1918. Just returned with Colonel Le Roy Eltinge and Colonel Boyd from two-day conference of Supreme War Council at Abbeville.[1] Extreme pessimism prevailed regarding present crisis. Everybody at high tension. Allies persistent in urging unlimited shipment of our infantry and machine gun units. Discussion at times very lively. Have agreed to send a regiment to Italy. Informally discussed with Prime Ministers the pooling of supplies.

Swiss reported now favorable to us in view of allocation and shipment of wheat. War Department plans completion of shipment in May of infantry and machine gun units of twelve divisions.[2]

THE necessity for hastening the shipment of American troops was now fully realized and their allotment to the Allied armies had assumed great importance in the minds of the Allied leaders. They were urgently demanding that only infantry and machine gun units be sent to France as recommended by the Military Representatives of the Supreme War Council and approved with certain modifications by our Government. As we have seen, an agreement had just been concluded with the

[1] There were present for France, M. Clemenceau, General Foch, and General Pétain; for Great Britain, Mr. Lloyd George, Lord Milner, Marshal Haig, and General Lawrence; for Italy, Mr. Orlando and General di Robilant; while General Bliss and I represented the United States. Certain staff officers accompanied each group.

[2] These divisions were 77th (Johnson), 82d (Burnham), 35th (Wright), 28th (Muir), 4th (Cameron), 30th (Read), 3d (Dickman), 5th (McMahon), 27th (O'Ryan), 33d (Bell), 80th (Cronkhite), 78th (McRae).

Note: Total strength of the A.E.F. on April 30th, 23,548 officers, 406,111 enlisted men.

Divisional units arriving in April included elements of the 77th Division (National Army, New York), Brigadier General Evan M. Johnson, the first of the National Army divisions to reach France.

British for shipments in May, but, as foreshadowed in Foch's remarks during our recent conversation, the Council wanted that agreement extended to cover June. I was opposed to such commitment, as it was my expectation that in June we should bring over the artillery and auxiliary arms to correspond to the shipment of infantry in May. At this session of the Supreme War Council the discussion was prolonged and only the main points are given. M. Clemenceau, who presided, opened the meeting with the following statement:

"The military representatives expressed the opinion in their Joint Note Number 18 that only infantry and machine gun units should be sent to France for the present. Since then the agreement between Lord Milner and General Pershing, signed at London on April 24, 1918, has intervened. This agreement makes a change.

"It had been understood at Versailles [1] that America would send 120,000 men per month, which the French and British armies would share equally. Under the Milner-Pershing agreement, it appears none are to go to France. The French have not been consulted. We might suppose that in compensation the American troops arriving in June would be given to France. But it now appears they are also to join the British. I wish to protest that this is not satisfactory.

"I am not discussing the figure of 120,000 men; I am prepared to accept that these men go to the British in May. I am asking to receive the same number of troops in June. There are close to 400,000 Americans in France at present, but only five divisions, or about 125,000 men, can be considered as combatants. That is not a satisfactory proportion."

Lord Milner arose, much incensed at M. Clemenceau's statement, which he considered quite unjust. He said, in part:

"M. Clemenceau has intimated that there was something mysterious about the London agreement. I believe that an explanation is necessary. He appears to believe that the agreement we signed is a reversal of the Supreme War Council's decision. I know only of a Joint Note embodying the recommendations of the Military Representatives, but it is of no value without the approval of the Governments.

[1] This refers to the action of the Permanent Military Representatives on the Supreme War Council, who held their sessions at Versailles.

"Besides, M. Clemenceau seems to be under the impression that half of the American troops were to go to France and the other half to the British. I do not recollect any such decision. All that General Pershing and I have urged is that infantry and machine gunners should be sent to France. We had no intention of depriving France of any American troops. I do not know that anything has been said regarding their allotment on arrival in France. We simply wanted to hasten their coming."

I then said:

"In making the agreement with Lord Milner I had in mind bringing troops as rapidly as possible to meet the existing situation. Lord Milner is quite correct in stating that there was no agreement as to the allocation of American troops either to the British or French armies. There is no agreement between my Government and anybody else that a single American soldier shall be sent to either the British or French. There is in existence an agreement between Mr. Lloyd George and myself that six divisions should be brought to France. Mr. Clemenceau will remember that I spoke to him about going to London to arrange for the shipment of American troops to France and that he approved because it would expedite their arrival. I also spoke to General Pétain about it."

M. Clemenceau remembered my speaking of it, but disregarding his previous approval continued his objections, saying:

"We have been informed that nothing had been decided on at Versailles, but something has been decided on at London, and France was closely concerned in this. It was decided that six divisions should go to the British. Well, I will not argue about that. You announce to us that you want artillery for the month of June, but France is overflowing with it.

"Where four are in alliance, two of them cannot act independently. Nothing has been provided for France in June.

"The appointment of General Foch as Commander-in-Chief is not a mere decoration. * * * This post involves grave responsibilities; he must meet the present situation; he must provide for the future.

"I accept what has been done for May, but I want to know what is intended for June."

M. Clemenceau said further that the French had not received certain specialists they had asked for, and also quoted from the conversation I had held with General Foch with reference to sending over troops in May and June.

Mr. Lloyd George then spoke up and said:

"I am of M. Clemenceau's opinion. The interests of the Allies are identical; we must not lose sight of that, otherwise the unity of command has no meaning. We must consider what is best for the common cause.

"What is the situation to-day? The British Army has had heavy fighting and has suffered heavy losses. All available drafts have been sent to France and we shall send all who are available in May and June. This would be the case even if all the Americans who arrived in Europe during these months should be assigned to the British Army.

*   *   *   *   *   *   *

"At present certain British divisions have been so severely handled that they cannot be reconstituted. General Foch will remember the number."

General Foch:
"Yes, ten."

Lloyd George:
"As we cannot again put them in line, they must be replaced by new units. The Germans are now fighting with the object of using up our effectives. If they can do this without exhausting their own reserves they will, sometime, deal us a blow which we shall not be able to parry. In the meantime, I suggest that the decision for the allotment of the American troops for June be taken up when these troops arrive. In May, in fact, either of our two armies may be hard pressed. That is the one which should be reënforced. It is not desirable now to decide how troops arriving in June should be allotted."

Foch:
"It is undeniable that the British Army is now exhausted; so let it receive immediate reënforcement in May. But lately the French have had grave losses, notably at Montdidier, and both during the last few days have been fighting shoulder to shoulder. So American aid is now needed almost as much for France as for Great Britain. Above this question of aid to the French or to the British is aid to the Allies. We are agreed that the American Army is to reënforce the British Army at once; in June we too shall need infantry and machine gun units. So let us make the agreement for June at once by saying the same shipment of infantry and machine guns as for May. If there is

tonnage available, we shall devote it, after that, to the elements necessary for filling up the American divisions. I am sure that General Pershing, with his generosity and his breadth of view, will grant the fairness of this and will extend for June the agreement decided upon for May."

Whereupon Mr. Lloyd George gave support to the declaration of General Foch, saying that British recruits would not be available until August and he understood it was the same for France, when both would be able to furnish their own recruits. He then changed his previous suggestion and asked that the May program be extended over June, a request in which M. Clemenceau joined.

Noting Foch's special plea for France, I said:

"I do not suppose that we are to understand that the American Army is to be entirely at the disposal of the French and British commands."

M. Clemenceau:

"Of course this is not the intention."

Continuing I said:

"Speaking for my Government and myself, we must look forward to the time when we shall have our own army. I must insist on its being recognized. The principle of unity of command must prevail in our army. It must be complete under its own command. I should like to have a date fixed when this will be realized. I should like to make it clear that all American troops are not to be with the British, as there are five divisions with the French now and there will be two more in a short time.

"As to the extension of the May agreement to June, I am not prepared to accept it. The troops arriving in June will not be available for the front before the end of July or the middle of August. So we have the whole month of May ahead of us before deciding whether the emergency still exists. I have explained to Lord Milner and General Foch why I do not wish to commit the American Army so long in advance. If need be, I shall recommend the extension into June. I can see no reason for it now."

Mr. Lloyd George spoke again and said that as a representative of the British Government he fully approved of the principle of an American army. He continued:

"It would not be reasonable or even honorable to consider the American Army as a reservoir from which we can draw. It is to our advantage to have a powerful American army as soon as possible to fight beside us, and as head of the British Government I accept the principle. However, at the present time, we are engaged in what is perhaps the decisive battle of the war. If we lose this battle, we shall need tonnage to take home what there is left of the British and American armies.

"What is our best hope of winning this battle?

"The decisive months will perhaps be those of September, October, perhaps later. If the American Army could intervene at that time, it would suit us all. I have no reason to believe that these two opinions are incompatible, but we should not wait until the end of May to decide, for questions of tonnage are involved which we must go into now."

He then proposed that the question of continuing the May program into June be held in abeyance for two weeks. He also brought up the question of the use of the slower ships for the transportation of troops and thought 30,000 or 40,000 more men a month might be transported in these ships. Both Admiral Sims and I had already pressed that point with our Government. Mr. Lloyd George calculated that the British would be able to transport 150,000 per month as a maximum, and that we could bring over 40,000 to 50,000, which he thought would allow us to include the auxiliary services required to complete our divisions and organize our own army. But he asked that priority in embarkation be given to the infantry and machine gun units.

I approved this request up to six divisions and stated that toward the end of May we could decide whether the program was to be continued into June.

Then General Foch announced that he, too, favored the formation of an American army, saying:

"Nobody is more for the constitution of an American army than I, for I know how much more an army is worth when fighting under its own commander and under its own flag. But now the needs are immediate; there is a battle to be won or a battle to be lost. I ask for the continuation of the May program. General Pershing asks that we transport the elements necessary for the constitution of his army; I am told that the tonnage will allow this; all the better; but in two weeks we shall all be dispersed, so we ought to decide to-day to continue in June what was decided on for May. I ask Lord Milner, as well as General Pershing, to join me after the meeting to sign an agreement."

Replying that I was glad to hear General Foch express himself so strongly in favor of an American army and that no one more fully than I appreciated the present situation, I said that it did not appear necessary for the Council to decide to-day. Foch then continued:

"I am Commander-in-Chief of the Allied Armies in France and my appointment has been sanctioned not only by the British and French Governments, but also by the President of the United States. Hence, I believe it my duty to insist on my point of view. There is a program signed by Lord Milner and General Pershing at London. I ask to be made a party to this arrangement. If the Supreme Commander has nothing to say regarding such conventions, I should not hold the position.

"So I ask that an agreement be made this evening between Lord Milner, General Pershing and myself, extending to June what has been decided on for May."

Of course, we all knew that no authority to dictate regarding such matters had been conferred upon General Foch and his remarks only showed that the Allies had put him forward to force the kind of agreement they wanted. They were ready to go to almost any length to carry their point.

M. Clemenceau then said that he agreed with General Foch and favored an American army, but that the Germans were at Villers-Bretonneux and if the lines were broken there they might quickly arrive under the walls of Paris and liaison between the Allied armies might have to be established on the Loire, or if the lines were pierced at Hazebrouck the enemy could reach the sea. "What is important for the morale of our soldiers," he said, "is not to tell them that the American soldiers are arriving, but to show them that they have arrived." In other words, he wanted smaller American units to be put in French divisions. He referred to the help the French were giving the British,[1] who had to break up ten divisions, he said, and added, "It is essential both in May and June when we shall be short of drafts that we should have men." Continuing, he said, "We have no right to order the American Government to do as we wish, but what we want is to attract its attention to the gravity of the situation," and he did not think I would refuse to listen.

In my opinion, the plan proposed was entirely unsound, and I thought that the best and quickest way to help the Allies would be to build up an American army. Moreover, the implied presumption that the Council might dictate to us either as a Council or through the Allied Commander-in-Chief in the arbitrary manner indicated, set me more firmly than ever against American units serving in Allied armies. The day's discussion made it quite clear that both Allies intended to obtain our commitment to the proposed schedule as far into the future as possible.[2]

At M. Clemenceau's suggestion, the meeting of the Council was

[1] There was no instance during the World War that I know of where small units such as battalions and companies of one nation served in the armies of another. As to regiments, we had four that were assigned, one to each of four French divisions. Entire divisions, under their own officers, were often sent in an emergency from the army of one country to that of another.

[2] As indicating the efforts made by the Allies to carry their point, the following extract from one of many cables on this subject sent by the British Secretary of State for Foreign Affairs to Lord Reading, British Ambassador at Washington, is pertinent. Referring to the conference held in Paris between General Hutchinson (British) on one side, and Mr. Baker and myself on the other, the cable read: "It is evident from this brief account of the conversation that General Pershing's views are absolutely inconsistent with the broad policy which we believe the President has accepted. The main difference, of course, is that we interpret the promise as meaning that 480,000 infantry and machine gunners are to be brigaded with French and British troops in the course of four months. General Pershing admits no such obligation and does not conceal the fact that he disapproves of the policy.

"A second and minor difference is that, while the British Government quite agrees as to the propriety of ultimately withdrawing American troops brigaded with the French and British so as to form an American army, they do not think this process could or ought to be attempted until the season for active operations this year draws to its close, say in October or November.

"I am unwilling to embarrass the President, who has shown such a firm grasp of the situation, with criticisms of his officers. But the difference of opinion * * * is so fundamental and touches so nearly the issues of the whole war, that we are bound to have the matter cleared up."—(See pp. 124-125, "It Might Have Been Lost," by Thomas Clement Lonergan, formerly Lieutenant Colonel, General Staff, U.S.A.)

adjourned at this point in order that Foch, Milner, and I might meet and examine the question, and see if some agreement could be reached. Whereupon we repaired to an adjacent room and went over the whole subject again.

Milner, and especially Foch, insisted that the war would be lost unless their program was carried out. I repeated the arguments presented to the Council and added that I fully realized the military emergency but did not think that the plan to bring over untrained units to fight under British and French commands would either relieve the situation or end the war.[1] I pointed out that, regardless of the depressing conditions and the very urgent need of men by the Allies, their plan was not practicable and that even if sound in principle there was not time enough to prepare our men as individuals for efficient service under a new system, with the strange surroundings to be found in a foreign army. The very lowest limit ever thought of for training recruits under the most favorable circumstances, even for trench warfare, had been nine weeks devoted to strenuous work. Counting out the time that would be consumed in travel, the untrained arrivals could not be ready before August, when the trained contingents of the Allies for 1918 would become available.

Here Foch said: "You are willing to risk our being driven back to the Loire?"

I said: "Yes, I am willing to take the risk. Moreover, the time may come when the American Army will have to stand the brunt of this war, and it is not wise to fritter away our resources in this manner. The morale of the British, French and Italian armies is low, while, as you know, that of the American Army is very high. It would be a grave mistake to give up the idea of building an American army in all its details as rapidly as possible."

Then Foch again said that the war might be over before we were ready.

I said that the war could not, in my opinion, be saved by feed-

[1] While our units were to be brought for training as a part of larger British or French units, it was thoroughly understood that they were there to fight, in case they were needed.

ing untrained American recruits into the Allied armies, but that we must build up an American army, and concessions for the time being to meet the present emergency were all that I would approve.

At about this juncture, Mr. Lloyd George, M. Clemenceau, and Mr. Orlando, evidently becoming impatient, walked into the room. Milner met Lloyd George at the door and said in a stage whisper behind his hand, "You can't budge him an inch." Lloyd George then said, "Well, how is the committee getting along?"

Whereupon we all sat down and Lloyd George said to me, "Can't you see that the war will be lost unless we get this support?" which statement was echoed in turn by Clemenceau and Orlando. In fact, all five of the party attacked me with all the force and prestige of their high positions.

But I had already yielded to their demands as far as possible without disrupting the plans toward which we had been striving for over a year, and a continuance of May shipments into June, without any provision for transporting artillery and auxiliary and service of supply troops, could not be granted without making it practically impossible in the future to have an American army. After going over the whole situation again and stating my position, they still insisted, whereupon I said with the greatest possible emphasis, "Gentlemen, I have thought this program over very deliberately and will not be coerced." This ended the discussion in committee and when the Council reconvened M. Clemenceau stated that the question of American troops would be taken up again on the following day.

The Council then examined a number of other matters. Among them was that of breaking up divisions in distant theaters of the war in order to obtain extra men for the Western Front and thus save the tonnage required for their supply. A resolution was adopted providing that "a French and a British general officer should be dispatched forthwith to Salonika, where, in association with the general officer commanding the Italian forces at Salonika, they will confer with General Guillaumat[1]

---

[1] General Guillaumat was the French Commander of Allied Forces at Salonika.

on this question in order if possible to arrange with him for the immediate withdrawal of Allied battalions."

Then some one suggested that with an Allied Commander-in-Chief there seemed to be no need of the Executive War Board of the Supreme War Council which had been created in February to handle the general reserve, and after considerable discussion, action was postponed until the following day, when a resolution dissolving the committee was adopted.

The next question taken up was that of Italian reënforcements for France. Mr. Orlando spoke at some length on the critical situation on the Italian front and declared that the Austrians were well prepared and were about to attack again, and that Italy could not spare any troops for service in France. This brought up the question of General Foch's authority over the Italian Army. Mr. Orlando said that the Italian Commander-in-Chief would have to be consulted before Italian troops could be taken to reënforce Allied armies elsewhere.

He failed to recall that it was the prompt action of the French and British in sending troops to Italy after Caporetto that probably saved the Italian Army. However, in further conversation on the following day, he agreed that the Western Front should be considered as extending from the North Sea to the Adriatic and accepted the principle of unity of command, but he specifically reserved the right of the Italian Commander to appeal to his Government in case any orders from Foch should be inimical to the general interests of Italy.

When the Council met for the afternoon session of the second day, the discussion of shipments of American personnel was at once resumed. General Foch spoke at length, repeating previous arguments and giving a rather grandiose dissertation on the Allied situation and the dire things that would happen unless the Americans agreed to the proposal of the Council. In the course of his remarks he said:

"I have been selected as Commander-in-Chief of the Allied armies by the Governments of the United States of America, France, and Great Britain, and my command has been extended to embrace the Italian

Army. In that capacity it is impossible at the most perilous stage of the great battle of the war to withhold the expression of my views on the question of disposal of American troops.

"That is why, feeling the very heavy responsibility that rests upon me, at the time when the greatest German offensive is now threatening Paris and our communication with Great Britain through Calais and Boulogne, I expressly insist on each of the Governments taking, in its turn, its portion of responsibility."

In a dramatic way, he went on to say that he thought it absolutely necessary that 120,000, or more, if tonnage permitted, American infantrymen and machine gunners should reach France monthly, by right of priority, at least during the months of May, June, and July. Losses of the French and British had been greater, he said, than in any previous offensive of the war and could not be replaced, while on the other hand Germany could furnish from 500,000 to 600,000 replacements for her armies; and he most earnestly requested the Council to submit a statement to President Wilson on the subject. He fully appreciated my remarks, he said, but the situation would not warrant any delay, as the greatest of German armies was making the most determined offensive of the war against Amiens and Ypres and the issue of the war itself might depend upon the success of the enemy before either of these objectives.

Mr. Lloyd George in turn spoke at some length. He asserted that the Germans hoped to use up the British and French reserves before their own were exhausted, and that the British had already called up nearly 7,000,000 men for their army and navy and had extended their age limits to all men between 18 and 50 years of age. He continued:

"If the United States does not come to our aid, then perhaps the enemy's calculations will be correct. If France and Great Britain should have to yield, their defeat would be honorable, for they would have fought to their last man, while the United States would have to stop without having put into line more men than little Belgium."

Possibly realizing the unfairness of the comparison, he quickly went on to say that he was sure that I was doing my best to meet the emergency, and that:

"General Pershing desires that the aid brought to us by America should not be incompatible with the creation of the American army as rapidly as possible.

"I, too, am counting on the existence of that army, and I am counting on it this very year to deal the enemy the final blow. But to do that, the Allies will have to hold out until August."

He then took up my proposal that the May program, which called for 120,000 infantrymen and machine gunners, be extended into June, provided the British Government would furnish transportation for 130,000 men in May and 150,000 in June. After some further discussion, during which he offered to increase greatly the British tonnage, he said:

"I propose then that America give us 120,000 infantrymen and machine gunners in May—the same number in June, with a supplement of 50,000 infantrymen and machine gunners if we 'scrape together' the tonnage to transport them."

He further proposed that the situation be again examined in June before deciding whether there was reason to extend to July the program decided upon for May and June, and called on the Council for the acceptance of his plan.

I then made the following remarks:

"I am entirely in agreement with General Foch as to the gravity of the present situation. In fact, we are all agreed on that point.

"Speaking in the name of the American Army and in the name of the American people, I wish to express their earnest desire to take their full part in this battle, and to share the burden of the war to the fullest extent. We all desire the same thing, but our means of attaining it are different from yours.

"America declared war independently of the Allies and she must face it as soon as possible with a powerful army. There is one important point upon which I wish to lay stress, and that is that the morale of our soldiers depends upon their fighting under our own flag.

"America is already anxious to know where her army is. The Germans are once more circulating propaganda in the United States to the effect that the Allies have so little confidence in the American troops that they parcel them out among Allied divisions.

"The American soldier has his own pride, and the time will soon come when our troops, as well as our Government, will demand an autonomous army under the American High Command.

"I understand that in Mr. Lloyd George's proposal we shall have to examine the situation again in June before deciding for July.

"That is all I can agree to at present, and I think by this arrangement we are meeting the situation fairly and squarely."

My proposal contemplated a largely increased amount of British tonnage, which would permit the transportation of a greater number of artillery and auxiliary units, and a greater proportion of special troops for the Services of Supply than had been previously indicated. Upon consideration, it appeared that this would leave us with sufficient tonnage to provide at least 40,000 men by British shipping and all that could be transported by American shipping of the classes of troops we most desired. M. Clemenceau then read the resolution that I had submitted confirming the London agreement and including an understanding for June, which was agreed to substantially as set forth in the following cablegram to the Secretary of War:

"Following agreement adopted by Supreme War Council May 2d at Abbeville. Will cable more in detail later. It is the opinion of the Supreme War Council that, in order to carry the war to a successful conclusion, an American army should be formed as early as possible under its own commander and under its own flag.[1] In order to meet the present emergency it is agreed that American troops should be brought to France as rapidly as Allied transportation facilities will permit, and that, as far as consistent with the necessity of building up an American army, preference be given to infantry and machine gun units for training and service with French and British armies; with the understanding that such infantry and machine gun units are to be withdrawn and united with their own artillery and auxiliary troops into divisions and corps at the discretion of the American Commander-in-Chief after consultation with the Commander-in-Chief of the Allied Armies in France.

"Subparagraph A.

"It is also agreed that during the month of May preference should be given to the transportation of infantry and machine gun units of six divisions, and that any excess tonnage shall be devoted to bringing

[1] Then it was thought the war would continue to 1919.

over such troops as may be determined by the American Commander-in-Chief.

"Subparagraph B.

"It is further agreed that this program shall be continued during the month of June upon condition that the British Government shall furnish transportation for a minimum of 130,000 men in May and 150,000 men in June, with the understanding that the first six divisions of infantry shall go to the British for training and service, and that troops sent over in June shall be allocated for training and service as the American Commander-in-Chief may determine.

"Subparagraph C.

"It is also further agreed that if the British Government shall transport an excess of 150,000 men in June that such excess shall be infantry and machine gun units, and that early in June there shall be a new review of the situation to determine further action."

In his reply, the Secretary of War observed that this agreement provided less priority for infantry and machine gun units than was previously recommended by the Supreme War Council. This was true, as it was my intention to make it as favorable to the ultimate formation of an American army as possible, and it was more so than we had reason to expect in view of the recommendations contained in Joint Note No. 18 of the Military Representatives, which, as we have seen, had been practically approved by the President. The full purport of this commitment was not emphasized by the Allies during the discussion.

Nobody realized more than I that the military situation was most threatening. Following the powerful enemy offensive of March 21st had come that of April 9th, and another attack had been made by the enemy towards Amiens, while in the fighting farther east Villers-Bretonneux had been taken and retaken several times. As the British casualties since March 21st had been some 280,000, and those of the French 60,000 to 70,000, both Allies were prompted to make this urgent appeal for Americans to reconstitute their units not only physically but morally.

From the practical standpoint of increasing the efficiency of the Allied armies, the argument was against the unqualified acceptance of their proposals. The nationals of no country would willingly serve under a foreign flag in preference to their own.

The national sentiment involved was such that we could not possibly afford to enter into such an agreement, except in an extreme crisis. Moreover, the added strength of a distinct army would be much greater than to have its personnel parcelled out here and there. Another serious objection to our men serving in the Allied armies was the danger that the low morale and the pessimism in the Allied ranks would react adversely on our officers and men; in fact, this had already been the case to some extent, especially among our men with the British, where the contacts had been close.

As to personal relations, it was gratifying always to find that these discussions, though often heated, were largely regarded simply as official differences of opinion. There was at the same time a very distinct impression in my mind, and in the minds of many of our officers familiar with the arguments on both sides, that the Allies, while greatly in need of assistance, were especially inclined to press the plea for amalgamation as a means of keeping us in a subordinate rôle.

Yet, after these questions were settled, even temporarily, there was no ill-feeling in evidence, although, no doubt, at times each side thought the other difficult to deal with. Other proposals regarding the employment of American troops under Allied command were made from time to time, all of which I strongly opposed. Notwithstanding their attitude with respect to the use of our troops, I continued to maintain a high regard for my Allied associates, in consideration of their many acts of kindness and friendship.

After the decision at Abbeville, everybody seemed content, and General Foch, in parting with me, said, *"Mon Général, nous sommes toujours d'accord."* While this remark no doubt expressed satisfaction that an agreement had been reached, it did not mean that the Allies had at all given up their views as to how American troops should be trained or used.

The fact that neither the British nor French had trained their armies for open warfare, either offensive or defensive, was at least in part one cause of the tremendous success of the German drives with divisions trained expressly for that kind of warfare. That the French intended to impress their conception on us is indicated by a memorandum of instructions for the guidance of their officers on duty with American troops, emanating from the French General Headquarters, May 1st, that came to our attention. This memorandum shows also that the French still regarded the possibility of open warfare as more or less visionary. Speaking of Americans, it said:

"It should be borne in mind that they have an extremely highly developed sense of *amour-propre* based on their pride in belonging to one of the greatest nations of the world. Consequently an air of superiority over them should be assiduously avoided, a fact which in no way prevents the absolute subordination required by the service for carrying out the rules of hierarchy. * * * In case of necessity French officers should not hesitate to exercise their authority. * * * Americans dream of operating in open country after having broken through the front. This results in too much attention being devoted to this form of operations."

The attitude that the French assumed toward us in the World War was in marked contrast with the views held by them when their troops so generously came to America to aid us in the Revolution. The French Commander at that time received very explicit instructions from his Government on this subject, as the following sent to Rochambeau shortly before he sailed for America will show:

"It is His Majesty's desire and He hereby commands that, so far as circumstances will permit, the Count de Rochambeau shall maintain the integrity of the French troops which His Majesty has placed under his command, and that at the proper time he shall express to General Washington, Commander-in-Chief of the forces of the Congress, under whose orders the French troops are to serve, that it is the intention of the King that these shall not be dispersed in any manner, and that they shall serve at all times as a unit and under the French generals, except in the case of a temporary detachment which shall rejoin the main body without delay." [1]

[1] "Sa Majesté veut et ordonne au Sr. comte de Rochambeau de tenir, autant que les circonstances pourront le permettre, le corps des troupes françaises dont Sa Majesté lui a confié le commandement, rassemblé en un corps de troupes, et de représenter dans l'occasion au général Washington, généralissime des troupes du Congrès et aux ordres

After the sessions I spoke to M. Clemenceau and Mr. Lloyd George, suggesting that sending an American regiment might help to stimulate the Italian morale and asked their opinion. They both thought it would be a wise thing to do just at this time. I had opposed scattering our forces in this way, but the appeal of Italian officials and the recommendations of Americans who had visited Italy indicated that under the circumstances an exception could well be made for a small force.

When I told Mr. Orlando that this might be done, with the possibility of increasing the number up to a division later on, he was much pleased. Meanwhile, the President had been pressed by Italian representatives to send them troops, and word came by cable a few days later that he thought we might brigade some of our troops with the British and French divisions then in Italy. But to leave them independent was far preferable and the subject was not taken up with the Allies, my idea being that if we should find it necessary to send more troops to Italy it would be best to build up a division of our own.

Another matter taken up informally with the Prime Ministers after the conference was that of pooling Allied supplies. I explained its advantages and emphasized the saving in tonnage that would result. Mr. Lloyd George and Mr. Orlando did not commit themselves entirely, but accepted it in principle, as M. Clemenceau had done, and each of them agreed to designate an officer with business experience to meet with us at an early date to study the question. With this beginning, at least a step had been taken toward our objective, even though the principle might not be extended as far as we thought desirable. A few days later M. Clemenceau called a meeting of the representatives, in his office, General Sir Travers E. Clarke acting for the British, and Colonel Charles G. Dawes for the Americans.

duquel les troupes françaises doivent servir, que les intentions du Roi sont qu'il ne soit fait aucun dispersement des troupes françaises et qu'elles servent toujours en corps d'armée et sous les généraux français, sauf les cas de détachements momentanés et qui devront sous peu de jours rejoindre le corps principal. * * *

"Signé: Le Prince de Montbarey."

CHAPTER XXIX

Shipping Problems—British Request for Artillerymen—Venereal Question —British Object to Colored Troops—Résumé of Troops in France— Inspection of 2d Division—French and British Urging President for Further Priority Infantry and Machine Gun Units—Aviation—Duty at G.H.Q.

(Diary) Chaumont, Sunday, May 5, 1918. While in Paris saw Dwight Morrow and find prospects good for more shipping.

Returned to Chaumont yesterday. Have detailed Colonels Fox Conner, Nolan, Moseley, Fiske and Logan as Chiefs of Sections under revised General Staff organization. McAndrew appointed Chief of Staff to relieve Harbord, who will command Marine Brigade of the 2d Division. Regret my promise to let him serve with troops. Lieutenant Colonel Robert C. Davis made Adjutant General, succeeding Brigadier General Alvord, who has returned to States because of ill health. Branch of Judge Advocate General's office at Chaumont placed under Brigadier General E. A. Kreger.

OUR members of the Allied Maritime Transport Council were persistent in their search for additional tonnage. Mr. Dwight W. Morrow, of the Council's Executive Board of Shipping Control, had made an exhaustive study of shipping resources and was active in pointing out to his fellow members the urgency of our tonnage requirements. He reported to me prospects of some increase, besides calling attention to tonnage that was idle or not being used to the best advantage. The immense shipment of American troops contemplated the use of all available passenger-cargo carrying ships, British, American and neutral. As very little, if any, space would be left in such ships for freight, the demand would be greater than ever for cargo ships. Meanwhile, the amount of this class of Allied tonnage turned out during the preceding five months was scarcely equal to the losses, and the ships that we were building had only just begun to be available for service.[1]

It was at once evident that the large program of troop shipments would call for extraordinary concessions on the part of all concerned.   Indeed there was some doubt in shipping circles whether enough cargo ships could be provided for us without neglecting the requirements of other nations for food and supplies. However, the prospects of increased tonnage from American yards within the next few months enabled the Shipping Control to take some chances and permit the use of the accumulated supplies in various countries in the hope of replacing them later.

As the need for shipping increased, the necessity of saving every possible ton became more urgent.   Economy in the care of equipment and in the preparation of the ration was encouraged in every way.   The troops were reminded of the severe restrictions and the sacrifices of the people at home in my instructions issued on the prevention of waste, and the response was fully in accord with the fine spirit exhibited by our men in all the exacting requirements made of them.

The salvage section of the Quartermaster Corps had grown to be an extensive institution for the rehabilitation of unserviceable equipment of every class and description that would otherwise have required replacement by shipments from home.[2]   The economy in time, labor and transportation incident to the system was invaluable.

Labor procurement continued to be a difficult problem.   The demand for labor in all armies always exceeded the supply, but when the great emergency increased the necessity for combat

[1] Although hundreds of millions of dollars and the most strenuous efforts were expended, the tonnage built after we entered the war and in the service of the army by months was only as follows: February, 1918, 8,571 tons; March, 17,092 tons; April, 17,092 tons; May, 32,822 tons; June, 85,833 tons; July, 126,834 tons; August, 165,107 tons; September, 219,515 tons; October, 266,833 tons; November, 273,846 tons.

[2] In this class came shoes, rubber boots, belts, haversacks, coats, trousers, hats, field glasses, underclothing, rifles, periscopes, motorcycles; in fact everything that could possibly be repaired.   Artillery was salvaged by the Ordnance Department, and likewise the Signal Corps and the Medical Department each handled the salvage of its own special equipment.

troops we were able to prevail upon the Allies to furnish a considerable number of laborers, most of whom were French, to replace troops that we had previously been forced to detail as laborers. Through constant effort, the Labor Bureau had by this time obtained approximately 22,000 laborers, and an increase of 2,000 per week was expected.

The establishment of the European branch of the office of the Judge Advocate General expedited the final judicial review of records of trial in the expeditionary forces, as it saved the necessity of sending cases to the Judge Advocate General's office in Washington for review. The prompt action which resulted enabled commanding generals to carry into effect with the least possible delay all lawful sentences, thus preventing the detrimental effect that would have resulted had it been necessary to refer records of trial to the War Department prior to the execution of the sentences adjudged.

(Diary) Chaumont, Friday, May 10, 1918. Have had a very busy week in various conferences with staff, which is meeting new responsibilities in satisfactory manner. Majors Edward Bowditch, Jr., and John G. Quekemeyer have reported as aides. British object to taking colored troops for training.

Dr. John R. Mott and Mr. Carter, Y.M.C.A., came in Monday for conference on allotment of tonnage for canteens. Telegraphed all commanding officers about men writing home on Mother's Day, the 12th.[1]

Had request on Tuesday from Sir Douglas Haig for 10,000 artillerymen.

Several representatives of American Labor from home came to call yesterday.

Received letter from Foch to-day regarding early employment our divisions. Am sending committee to London for conference on venereal question. Marseille added to our ports; convoy in Mediterranean probably unnecessary.

---

[1] The following was my message to the command as indicated in the diary: "I wish that every officer and soldier of the American Expeditionary Forces would write a letter home on Mother's Day. This is a little thing for each one to do, but these letters will carry back our courage and our affection to the patriotic women whose love and prayers inspire us and cheer us on to victory."

On the heels of the clamor for nothing but infantry and machine gunners, I received a request from Marshal Haig for 10,000 artillerymen. The following are copies of letters from and to Marshal Haig:

"General Headquarters,
"British Armies in France.

"5 May, 1918.
"DEAR GENERAL PERSHING:

"I beg to enclose a note showing how I stand in the matter of Artillery Personnel. You will see that there is considerable shortage, and consequently if you could arrange to let me have 10,000 American Artillerymen, it would be of very great assistance to us.

"With kind regards,
"Believe me

"Yours very truly,

"D. HAIG."

"France, May 11, 1918.

"Confidential.
"MY DEAR SIR DOUGLAS:

"I am in receipt of your note of May 5th concerning the question of Artillery Personnel.

"Under the recent agreement the shipment from the United States of all Artillery Personnel other than that pertaining to divisions has been suspended, as you will recall, and infantry and machine gun units have a very considerable priority over even the divisional artillery.

"I regret to say that all divisional artillery units now in France have either joined their divisions at the front or are now on their way to do so, and, of course, will soon be in the line with their units to replace corresponding French divisions.

"As to heavy artillery, we have brought over only those units for which equipment was available at the time of embarkation or else promised for early delivery. But as the British War Office has been unable to deliver the heavy howitzers which had been promised for delivery in March and April, there are certain heavy artillery units which as yet I have been unable to equip or train.

"While under ordinary circumstances I would much prefer that the training be held at the usual centers, I would be glad to send a regiment of six batteries for temporary service, provided you have equipment available for them. In the event you desire these troops I should prefer that they be trained and employed by complete units.

I shall have the matter examined further and think I shall be able to increase this number.

"With high personal and official esteem, believe me
"Sincerely yours,
"JOHN J. PERSHING."

"General Headquarters,
"British Armies in France.
"15th May, 1918.

"MY DEAR GENERAL:

"I must express to you my sincere thanks for your kind offer of the services of a regiment of heavy artillery, conveyed in your letter of May 11th.

"I regret very much that no Field Artillery Personnel is available as my Heavy Artillery have not suffered to the same extent as the Field Artillery.

"I quite understand that you would of course prefer that the training of all your heavy batteries should be carried out at the usual centers, and I therefore appreciate all the more your generous readiness to assist me.

"Unfortunately, owing to our heavy expenditure of artillery material during the last two months' operations, I have only sufficient complete howitzer equipments to maintain British batteries in action and cannot hope to provide equipment for your six batteries under present conditions.

"I am, therefore, very sorry to say that I am unable to accept your kind offer.

"Yours very truly,
"D. HAIG."

The principle of coöperation among the Allies was being extended to many fields that affected the armies in common and it was now to be invoked for the promotion of morality. From the beginning, the prevention of social vices had given us serious concern, not only from the standpoint of effectives, but from that of morals. Large numbers of troops were soon to pass through England for service behind the British lines and it was deemed advisable that measures should be taken for collaboration in keeping our men clean. Bishop Brent was very active in this matter and had conferred with the Archbishop of Canterbury, who in turn suggested to the British War Office that a conference be held on the subject. Our representatives were Bishop Brent, Brigadier General Bethel and Colonel Ireland, who went with a definite plan of action to propose.

I wrote Lord Milner as follows:

"May 7, 1918.

"DEAR LORD MILNER:

"I am glad to respond to your call for the conference aimed at joint action by British and American authorities to handle the venereal situation as it affects the Allied troops in England and in France, and to our closer coöperation in measures that it may be deemed wise to take in the future. I am sending to represent the American Expeditionary Forces, General Walter A. Bethel, Judge Advocate of the Forces, Colonel Ireland, my Chief Medical Officer, and Bishop Brent, Senior G.H.Q. Chaplain, who are able to speak with authority on the general situation in America and France as regards the stand and measures our Government has taken to combat the venereal menace.

"The Allied military authorities have recognized the necessity of unity of purpose and coördination of effort in this fight in France. Three conferences on this matter have already been held between members of our medical corps and the French authorities with a very helpful outlook for concerted measures. The conference which you have called holds out the same promise as regards the coöperation of military and civil authorities in England, without which nothing we can say or do will help.

"I have heard also with great satisfaction of the recent decision of the British War Office that the licensed houses of prostitution are to be put out of bounds in the B.E.F. Many of us who have experimented with licensed prostitution or kindred measures, hoping thereby to minimize the physical evils, have been forced to the conclusion that they are really ineffective. Abraham Flexner has argued the case so convincingly that on the scientific side it seems to me there is no escape from the conclusion that what he terms 'abolition' as distinguished from 'regulation' is the only effective mode of combating this age-long evil.

"I have the greatest hope that the results of the conference which you have called will be far-reaching in their effect. This menace to the young manhood in the army forces and to the health and future well-being of our peoples cannot be met by the efforts of each Government working apart from the others. It is plain that every day it affects more and more all of the Allied nations now fighting on the Western Front in France. The question long since was an international one, and it is only by an internationalization of our aims and efforts that we can obtain the unity and coördination which will enable us to solve the problem. The gravest responsibility rests on those to whom the parents of our soldiers have entrusted their sons for the battle, and we fail if we neglect any effort to safeguard them in every way.

"We have the common ground of humanity, we have the well-considered conclusions of the best scientific minds on our side, and from the fact that, in this war of nations-in-arms the soldier is merely a citizen on war service, we have all the elements which will force coöperation between military and civil authorities. The army can do little unless the citizen at home plays his part in the big scheme. With our nations coöperating hand-in-hand, both in France and at home, we have the brightest prospects of winning the victory.

"I remain with high personal and official esteem,
"Faithfully yours,
"JOHN J. PERSHING."

This conference did not meet with the success that had been anticipated and little came out of it that was of practical value to us.

In fulfilling our part in military coöperation, we had already gone far beyond the mere recognition of the principle of unity of command and had begun to bring over hundreds of thousands of men almost regardless of the organizations to which they belonged in order that they might be available in the event of extreme necessity. This action was taken at the risk of our ever being able to form an American army. In conversation with Foch I had also offered several divisions for use anywhere on the Western Front. It was somewhat gratifying to realize that the Allies recognized our general attitude of coöperation, as indicated by the following extracts from a letter written by General Foch.

"During our conversation on April 25th you were most insistent that it was your desire that * * * American divisions should take part in the battle in which we are engaged, and you also suggested the order in which they should be employed.

"I am just as appreciative of this new evidence of your energetic and prompt coöperation as I was of the offer which you made with such generous impulse on March 28th."

A colored division, the 92d, had been selected by the War Department for temporary service and training with the British, armies, but their Military Attaché at Washington, acting under instructions from his Government, protested against it. I was surprised that they should take this attitude, inasmuch as the French were anxious to have colored troops assigned to their divisions, and, as has been mentioned, four regiments had been lent to them temporarily. In attempting to clear up the matter, I wrote to Marshal Haig, sending an identical letter to Lord Milner:

"May 5, 1918.

"MY DEAR SIR DOUGLAS:

"Some time ago, I received a cable from my Government to the effect that it was necessary to list one of our colored divisions for early shipment to France. As you know, all of our infantry and machine gun units to be embarked in the near future are destined for service, for the time being, with your forces. I accordingly replied to the cable * * * to the effect that the 92d (colored) Division could be included in the troops to be assigned to the forces under your command. It now appears, however, that the British Military Attaché in Washington has made a protest against including any colored battalions among the troops destined for service with your forces and that he has stated that this protest was made in behalf of your War Office.

"You will, of course, appreciate my position in this matter, which, in brief, is that these negroes are American citizens. My Government, for reasons which concern itself alone, has decided to organize colored combat divisions and now desires the early dispatch of one of these divisions to France. Naturally I cannot and will not discriminate against these soldiers.

"I am informed that the 92d Division is in a good state of training and I have no reason to believe that its employment under your command would be accompanied by any unusual difficulties.

"I am informing my Government of this letter to you. May I not hope that the inclusion of the 92d Division among the American troops to be placed under your command is acceptable to you and that you will be able to overcome the objections raised by your War Office?"

A few days later I received the following letter from Lord Milner, the British Minister of War:

"13 May, 1918.

"My dear General:

"Your letter of May 7th about the employment of colored Divisions with our British forces in France. I am rather hoping that this difficult question may not after all be going to trouble us, for I see, from a telegram received from General Wagstaff, that the Divisions so far arrived for training with the British do not include the 92d.

"I hope this is so, for, as a matter of fact, a good deal of administrative trouble would, I think, necessarily arise if the British Army had to undertake the training of a colored Division.

"Believe me,

"Yours very truly,

"Milner."

My cable to our War Department was to the effect that in the event the Secretary still desired to send this division to France I should adhere to my former recommendation that it be included among those to go to the British for training. However, the War Department evidently did not wish to insist upon it, as the division came over shortly afterwards and was not included among those assigned to the British.

(Diary) Chaumont, Tuesday, May 14, 1918. Report from Washington indicates that we have only limited number of trained men left. Spent three days last week inspecting units of the 2d Division, then under Major General Bundy. As division was just out of the trenches, the salvage dumps of this unit of about 25,000 men amounted to forty carloads of clothing and unserviceable equipment.

French and British Ambassadors are again asking the President for additional infantry and machine gun units. Washington cables that cavalry organized for A.E.F. now needed on Border.

To give a résumé of our strength on May 10th, it may be said that the number of men in the army at home and in Europe amounted approximately to 1,900,000, of whom more than 790,-000 were volunteers. In France and England we had 488,224.[1]

[1] The 1st, 2d, 3d, 26th, 32d, 41st, 42d and 77th Divisions were complete—the 5th, 28th, 35th, 82d and 93d incomplete. There were also 3 brigades of heavy coast artillery, the 30th regiment of gas and flame engineers, 4 regiments of cavalry and certain special troops. All divisions not in line were in training. With the British we had the 77th Division, 4 regiments of railway engineers, 1 regiment of pioneer engi-

Of these, there were eight complete divisions in France and five incomplete, which, with regiments and smaller units of auxiliary troops, made a total of 290,765 combat troops. Of the complete units, the 1st Division was with the French in line near Amiens, the 2d, 26th and 42d Divisions were occupying quiet

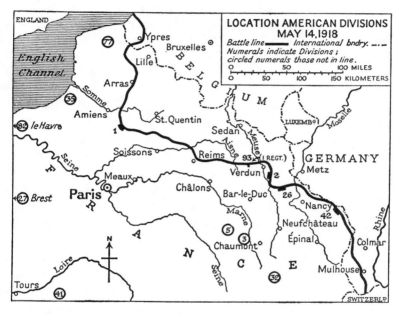

sectors, and the 32d Division was ready for that experience. With the troops then in line, we were holding an aggregate of thirty-five miles of front, or more than double that held by the Belgians.

Of those troops at home on May 10th, excluding three divisions at ports of embarkation, 263,852 were infantrymen of sufficient

neers, 1 telegraph battalion and 6 base hospitals; also 9,826 officers and men of the air service (4 squadrons being at the front). With the French were 4 regiments of colored troops in training, 5,500 motor mechanics, 6 machine shop truck units and 80 ambulance sections.

To recapitulate: (1) In service: in line in American sectors, 103,089; S. O. S. troops, 140,049; combatant troops used in S. O. S., 16,885; serving with British, 11,410; serving with French, 12,234; total in service, 283,667. (2) In training: in American training areas, 133,534; with British, 34,334; with French, 8,199; total, 176,067. (3) En route, 21,812; sick and detached, 6,678.

training for overseas service. It was therefore evident that the rapid rate at which they were being sent to France could not long continue without taking partially trained men.

It was my custom throughout the war, as both a duty and a pleasure, to visit the troops as frequently as possible in order to keep in touch with their state of efficiency and to help maintain the morale of officers and men. As Bundy's 2d Division was leaving the sector of the line south of Verdun where they had been for almost two months and was en route to the billeting and training area to finish preparation for battle, the moment was opportune to make an inspection.

I was pleased to find both infantry brigades, the regulars under Lewis and the marines commanded by Harbord and Cruikshank's artillery in very good shape. The trains of the division that were seen on the march did not look so well, due mainly to the appearance of the animals. This, however, was not entirely unexpected, as the care of animals is always difficult to teach and it was especially so in an army like ours in France. The entraining of that part of the division that I saw at Ancemont was being carried out in an orderly and systematic manner. I spent considerable time in talking with a number of different officers in command of smaller units and in discussing questions of supply with officers charged with that duty. On the whole my impression of the division was very favorable and this was soon to be confirmed on the battlefield, where it was to take its place among the best.

General Blondlat, in whose corps the 2d Division had been serving, spoke very highly of it, but, contrary to the view of most French officers, he thought that differences in language and temperament were serious handicaps to combined work and he was of the opinion that Americans should do their own training. It was exceptional to hear an expression from French sources that agreed so completely with our own.

Upon my return to Chaumont a cable from the Secretary of War was handed to me on the unwelcome subject of Allied demand for infantry and machine gun units. Extracts from it are given below.

"May 11, 1918.

"The President asked me to say to you that he has been very much impressed and disturbed by representations officially made to him by French and British Ambassadors showing the steady drain upon French and British replacements and the small number of replacement troops now available. He feels that you on the ground have full opportunity to know the situation and fully trusts your judgment as to how far we ought to give additional priority to infantry and machine gun units, in view of the fact that such troops seem to be the most immediately serviceable and urgently needed."

After saying that the Abbeville Agreement provided less priority than recommended by the Supreme War Council, it continued:

"It has been suggested to the President that General Foch may reopen this subject with you, and the President hopes you will approach any such interview as sympathetically as possible, particularly if the situation as to replacements which has been presented to him is as critical as it seems."

My reply set forth the principal arguments used at Abbeville against the unlimited shipment of the classes of troops the Allies requested. I pointed out that the statements made by Allied leaders at the conference indicated that possibly enough tonnage would be forthcoming to enable us to ship complete divisions, and that all concerned seemed to be satisfied with the concessions we made. I added further:

"I think we have fully and fairly met the situation. We have given the Supreme War Council all it asked at Abbeville. * * * It is believed that the action at Abbeville should be considered as the deliberate expression of the Supreme War Council's latest view. * * * Otherwise as long as there is the slightest hope of getting concessions there will be a continual clamor regardless of how it affects us. * * * Judging from what occurred at Abbeville and from the expressions of approval by General Foch, I think he cannot consistently reopen the subject until the question of July needs arises."

(Diary) Paris, Saturday, May 18, 1918. Saw a number of officers. Hamilton Holt and Judge Ben Lindsey came for luncheon and Irvin Cobb to dinner Wednesday at Chaumont.

Egan and Morrow called Thursday to talk over shipping. Talked with Eltinge, Deputy Chief of Staff, about reorganization of S.O.S. Headquarters. Left for Paris in evening.

Yesterday saw Patrick, who will be the new Chief of Air Service, and Foulois, and emphasized necessity for teamwork in aviation. Lunched with Ambassador Sharp, who says that Clemenceau, Cambon and others highly praise American troops.

Saw Foch at Versailles to-day and spoke again of building up an American sector, which he seems to approve. He expressed satisfaction with American aid and especially with the assignment of our aviators to the French. Had a talk with Bliss.

Brigadier General Foulois, at his own request and in order to assume charge of aviation in the First Army, was to be superseded by Brigadier General Patrick. Foulois' desire to secure general coöperation made him a valuable assistant and but for his experience and his efforts we might not have avoided so many of the pitfalls that lay in our way. In August he was relieved as Chief of Aviation First Army by Colonel Mitchell and became Assistant Chief of Air Service.

The demands of the Allies for material, for mechanics, for the adoption of this or that type of plane or engine, their efforts to secure preferential treatment from us or from each other, to say nothing of our own interior difficulties as to organization and manufacture, made accomplishment of definite results in preparation very difficult.

The Inter-Allied Aviation Committee, established in Paris in the fall of 1917 with the French Under-Secretary of Aeronautics as chairman, was presumably concerned with the requirements of the Allies in aircraft material, but it resulted in nothing practical in the way of coöperation. Meanwhile, in order to coördinate our own needs as well as assist the Allies, a Joint Army and Navy Aviation Committee in France was formed. Generally speaking, this committee did some effective work, but in the competition among the Allies for special advantage the interests of aviation as a whole were often overlooked. The French Aviation Control undertook, through the Inter-Allied Aviation Committee, to ignore the American Army and Navy Committee's action in allocating material by appealing to the Supreme War Council. As a consequence the Council established its own subcommittee, an outcome that really strengthened the American Army and Navy Committee and aided materially in bringing about better understanding among manufacturing interests.

Although conditions were unfavorable, training of aviators was being carried on, and our fliers were in demand for duty on the French front to fill their ranks. The services of these aviators were receiving commendation and General Foch seemed to be especially pleased with their work.

During the first few months at Chaumont I occupied quarters in the town, but later M. de Rouvre placed at my disposal his beautiful château some two miles away. My headquarters mess was limited to the few officers with whom I was most intimately associated and consisted of the Chief of Staff, the Adjutant General, my personal aides, and one or two others. Nearly always there were a few guests at meals invited from among the visitors, both French and American, who came to headquarters. Officers from French G.H.Q. were frequent guests and we were always glad to have them.

It was a welcome relief from the cares of the day when our dinner guests proved to be entertaining or interesting. If the guest was inclined to be more serious, he too was encouraged in his particular line. Irvin Cobb came along and in his inimitable character as an entertainer gave us an exceptional evening.

As a rule there was a ban on everything in the way of shop talk and the rule was rarely broken, and then only when we had special guests seeking enlightenment on some phase of the war, or information regarding our policies and activities. The members of the mess always looked forward to the occasion of meals as one of pleasure and relaxation. The mess was no place for one to pour out his woes or unnecessarily discuss the business of the day or the duties of the morrow.

There was one subject that would always start a discussion and that was the relative value of the different arms, each being represented by at least one officer, with an occasional guest from the staff to take sides according to his particular origin. The artilleryman would dispute honors with the infantryman, pointing out the helplessness of the foot-soldier without the support of the big guns, while the cavalryman would assert the superiority of his arm over either because he could fight on foot or on horseback and did not have to carry 110 pounds on his back over muddy roads day after day and night after night to get into battle.

Harbord and I were both from the cavalry and the member of the staff from that branch felt that he had at least a sympathetic audience. The infantry aide, however, with the support of Davis, who was originally a foot-soldier, always held his own in any discussion, for no matter how specious the arguments or perhaps the gibes at his expense we all knew that without the infantry the other arms would accomplish little. The associations of such a group are never forgotten and even a short period was enough to establish a permanent and affectionate relationship.

Rotation in office was early adopted as a principle to be applied to the staff in general and although it was never possible fully to carry it out, most of the officers of my staff got their chance at a tour with combat troops. Majors Collins and Shallenberger, two of the aides who went with me to France, were the first to go to other duty, being replaced by Majors Quekemeyer and Bowditch. Colonel Boyd, who joined me as aide shortly after my arrival in France, remained throughout the war. When General Harbord's turn came, his place as Chief of Staff was taken by General McAndrew. Several of the higher officers of the General Staff were given a tour with troops, not only that they might have the opportunity to serve at the front, which is every soldier's ambition, but because they would return to staff duty with a broader and more sympathetic understanding of the line officer's point of view and appreciate more fully the consideration that he deserves at the hands of the staff.

CHAPTER XXX

Visit Pétain at Chantilly—1st Division Preparing Offensive—Conference with S.O.S. Officials—Agreement Regarding Unified Supply—1st Division Attacks at Cantigny—Germans Drive French Beyond the Marne —2d and 3d Divisions Stop German Advance—Inspection of Divisions with British for Training—Call on Foch at Sarcus—Ragueneau on American Characteristics—Pétain's Instructions to French Liaison Officers

(Diary) Paris, Monday, May 20, 1918. Saw General Pétain at Chantilly yesterday. He says French must soon reduce twenty-five divisions to half strength and wants them filled up with American units. Went to 1st Division to discuss proposed offensive. Spent night with Bullard. To-day gave Bullard and his staff résumé of the general situation. Discussed tactical methods with Colonel George C. Marshall, Jr., Division Operations Officer. Saw Colonel B. T. Clayton, Division Quartermaster, on supply questions.

WHEN I called on General Pétain at Chantilly, he was found installed in a commodious private house hidden away in the forest, very near the residence that Marshal Joffre had occupied earlier in the war. The beauty and quiet of the surroundings on that Sunday morning seemed nature's protest against the horrors of other scenes and events of daily occurrence where the opposing armies were arrayed against each other.

The purpose of my visit was to discuss the possibility of assembling our divisions to form an American army. I recalled to Pétain that the earlier plans for their concentration in the vicinity of Toul had been postponed at my suggestion on account of the emergency that then confronted the Allies. He replied that he did not see how it could be done now, and that the matter of immediate concern to him was the reënforcement of his own divisions in such a way as to preserve both their number and

53

their strength. He was willing to accept our men by battalions, regiments, or brigades, but preferred the assignment of two American battalions to each of twenty-five divisions until October. Foch had asked for assignments of American troops only until August, when, it was said, the French 1919 class would be available for service. As fifty battalions of infantry would have been equivalent to that of at least four of our divisions, it would have compelled us to break up that number of incoming units, with little hope of reorganizing them. Of course, it was out of the question to consider such a possibility.

While his needs were appreciated, this was another request that could not be granted without yielding in my determination to bring about the formation of an American army. After some further discussion, we simply renewed the understanding previously reached that, for the present, American divisions with the French and not yet prepared for offensive action should occupy portions of the front in quiet sectors, relieving French divisions when the exigencies of the situation demanded that they should enter the battle. Thus for each partially trained division we would be able to free two French divisions. A few days later this arrangement received Foch's approval.

Although some weeks had passed since my offer of troops, so far none had been called upon to take part in active operations. The reason appeared to be that the Allies were skeptical as to the ability of our divisions, except for three or four of the best, to conduct an offensive. The opportunity soon came, however, to remove any reason for misgivings.

The 1st Division had now been in line for nearly a month opposite the town of Cantigny, near the point of farthest advance of the enemy in the Amiens salient. The French corps in which the 1st was serving had prepared a counterattack to be launched in that sector about the middle of May in case of another offensive by the enemy in Flanders, which it was believed would occur between May 15th and 20th. Since the enemy did not undertake the expected offensive, the proposed counterattack was not made.

It was then decided that the 1st Division should attempt to

improve its position. The Germans on its front continued to hold the advantage of higher ground, from which they were able to inflict constant losses on our troops while suffering little damage themselves. Another reason was that at this moment the morale of the Allies required that American troops make their appearance in battle. It was advisable also from the point of view that, if successful, it would demonstrate that we could best help the Allies by using our troops in larger units instead of adopting their plan of building up their forces. The high pitch of enthusiasm with which the 1st Division entered into the preparations for this attack gave us confidence that the result would be satisfactory.

(Diary) Chaumont, Thursday, May 23, 1918. Held a conference in Paris on Tuesday with Generals Kernan and Hagood on handling increase of men and supplies. Dr. Raymond Fosdick, under instructions from Mr. Baker, came to talk over welfare work.

Presented definite proposition yesterday to M. Clemenceau on Inter-Allied supply. Logan reported horse procurement more promising. Left for Chaumont in evening.

Went over aviation problems with Patrick and Foulois this morning and find organization difficulties are clearing up. Authority granted me to confer fifty Distinguished Service Medals on Allied officers. Local medical officers directed to assist mayors in carrying out law on epidemics. Have selected Grémévillers as casual advance headquarters because of its convenience to British front.

The matter of handling the rapidly growing business of the S.O.S. was one of constant concern. The expansion in shipments of men and material threw an increasing load on the inadequately manned system. Incoming freight was again accumulating at the ports somewhat faster than it could be removed. Still more berths had to be provided in order to prevent congestion. Although the submarine danger was passing, convoys were still necessary, and because they were composed of a larger number of ships, each individual vessel had to wait longer while the convoy was being assembled at ports of departure and before being docked at French ports. Therefore boats continued to be delayed at both ends of the voyage. Considerable new rolling stock was coming along and repairs were being made to the old, but yet the amount was not sufficient.

However, with anything like a normal or stable situation at the front and an economical allotment of railway resources, we should have been able to keep abreast of incoming tonnage. But conditions at the front were abnormal, as operations were in progress in several places at once. The constant shifting of troops from one end of France to the other to meet critical situations required an excess volume of rolling stock.[1] In order to be ready to move troops to meet emergencies, many trains had to be held in reserve behind the lines in the Zone of Operations, where they were beyond the control of the rail authorities in the rear. As we were dependent upon assignments from the French railway management, we were short of both engines and cars.

I called a joint conference of officials of the S.O.S., and the resulting improvement of methods relieved the congestion here and there and gave a more continuous flow of supplies toward the forward areas. The use of Marseille began to afford some relief to the port situation and although the voyage was longer it was offset by better accommodations for handling cargo. Moreover, as the railways from Marseille were not used in connection with operations, they could more easily carry the added burden. At all ports we had been able to obtain additional facilities, such as tugs, lighters, barges, troop tenders, and floating derricks, all of which increased our efficiency in unloading vessels, but we still lacked stevedores and other troops of the Services of Supply.

Coöperation in supply had been given a good start by the French and ourselves working together. As procurement abroad had a direct and important bearing on the tonnage question, efforts were renewed to extend organized coördination to Inter-Allied supply. At one period in our discussions, the control by a single authority had been proposed. But upon careful analysis, based upon the experience of the General Purchasing Board in negotiations with the French, it was concluded that an Inter-

---

[1] It required from twenty-five to thirty French trains to move one French division and twice as many for an American division.

Allied committee whose decisions should be unanimous would be the best solution to this difficult problem.

In further conference with M. Clemenceau an agreement was secured to broaden the scope of coöperation between our two armies, in the hope that later the other Allies might be induced to join. I presented the agreement given below, which became the basis of our understanding:

"It is hereby agreed among the Allied Governments subscribing hereto:

"1. That the principle of unification of military supplies and utilities for the use of the Allied armies is adopted.

"2. That in order to apply this principle and so far as possible coördinate the use of utilities and the distribution of supplies among the Allied armies a Board consisting of representatives of each of the Allied armies is to be constituted at once.

"3. That the unanimous decision of the Board regarding the allotment of material and supplies shall have the force of orders and be carried out by the respective supply agencies.

"4. That further details of the organization by which the above plan is to be carried out shall be left to the Board, subject to such approval by the respective Governments as may at any time seem advisable.

"We agree to the above and wish it to be submitted to the British and Italian Governments.

"G. CLEMENCEAU,
"JOHN J. PERSHING."

At first glance at this very general agreement, one could readily imagine many possible difficulties, such as indifference on the part of the supply departments of the armies or governments concerned, their inherent jealousies, the question of credit adjustments, as well as those of joint storage and transportation. But most of these were overcome in the actual application of the principles set forth and much duplication of effort was saved, with consequent reduction in transportation and expense. Certain supplies, light railways, and truck transportation that would not otherwise have been obtainable for our use, thus began to be available from the common pool.

The agreement was immediately invoked in the hope of meeting the horse situation. M. Clemenceau, in compliance with my request, and acting on information from his procurement agencies, promised to furnish us 100,000 horses, which was later reduced to 80,000.   But the plan did not work out and our representative who was conducting the negotiations ran into several obstacles, the principal one being the disinclination of the French farmers to dispose of their horses.   Only a limited number of owners could be tempted to present their serviceable animals for sale, even at the exorbitant prices offered, and the French Government so far had been loath to exert its powers of requisition.   At times the difficulties would appear less formidable, yet, notwithstanding constant pressure, our expectations were only partially realized.   The farmers in general simply would not sell, and one reason given us was that they had the idea that we would thus be compelled to make a large importation of horses, which would give them an opportunity to buy cheaply after the war.

(Diary) Grémévillers, Tuesday, May 28, 1918.   Spent Saturday with 3d Division (Dickman) at maneuvers.

Next day visited 5th Division (McMahon) in Bar-sur-Aube region. Lunched with McMahon and his brigadiers, Walter H. Gordon and Joseph C. Castner.   Reached Paris at 10 P.M. and had a talk with Atterbury, who was waiting to see me.   Will make readjustments to give him greater independence.   After year's delay, Department of Military Aeronautics has been established in the War Department.

Yesterday saw Major Lloyd C. Griscom,[1] who goes as Liaison Officer with Lord Milner.   Strong German offensive began yesterday against French on Chemin des Dames, with "Big Bertha" firing on Paris.

Have recommended that the following new services be created by Executive Order: Transportation Service, Motor Transport Service, and Gas Service.   Went to 1st Division (Bullard) and learned that attack on Cantigny to-day was completely successful.

The division maneuver in simulated attack, often repeated, such as that held by the 3d Division, was a valuable exercise in combat teamwork.   It was a test of the efficiency of the unit, especially that of higher officers and their staffs.   While the instruction of individual officers as leaders and the training of smaller units for open warfare were constantly stressed, particular emphasis was

---

[1] Lord Milner was anxious to have our relations work smoothly and suggested that I should send an officer to represent me at the British War Office.

given in the final preparation for line service to the importance of perfecting all means of communication throughout the division down to the smaller units in the trenches. No troops without considerable practice in this regard could be sent into battle with much hope of success.

The Cantigny sector at this time was very active, with artillery fire unusually heavy, and the preparations for the attack by the 1st Division were carried out under great difficulty. Many casualties occurred during the construction of jumping-off

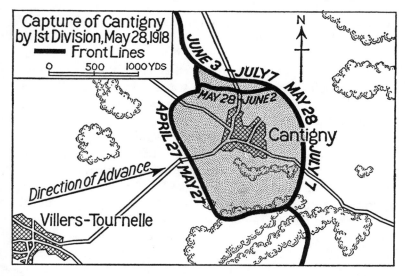

trenches, emplacements and advance command posts. The 28th Infantry, under Colonel Hanson E. Ely, designated for the assault, was reënforced by tanks, machine guns, engineers, and other special units. Additional French guns were sent to assist the artillery brigade of the division and particularly to suppress the hostile batteries that would attempt to interfere with the consolidation of the new position after it should be captured.

On the morning of May 28th, after a brief artillery preparation, the infantry advanced on a front of a mile and a quarter. The village of Cantigny and the adjacent heights were quickly taken, relatively heavy casualties inflicted on the enemy, and about 240 prisoners captured. Our troops behaved splendidly and suffered but slight loss in the actual attack.

Events then developing farther east, however, were seriously to complicate the success. The German assault in force against the French along the Chemin des Dames, between Soissons and Reims, began on the morning of the 27th and was making dangerous headway. By the morning of the 28th the gains of the enemy were such that the French High Command was compelled to relieve some of their artillery reënforcing the 1st Division and transfer it to the Chemin des Dames front. The enemy's artillery within range of Cantigny was increased soon after the assault and was thus able to concentrate a terrific fire on our troops in the captured position. His reaction against this attack was extremely violent as apparently he was determined at all cost to counteract the excellent effect the American success would produce upon the Allies.

Under cover of this bombardment, several counterattacks were made by the enemy, but our young infantrymen stood their ground and broke up every attempt to dislodge them. The 28th Infantry sustained severe casualties and had to be reënforced by a battalion each from the 18th and 26th Infantry regiments.

It was a matter of pride to the whole A.E.F. that the troops of this division, in their first battle, and in the unusually trying situation that followed, displayed the fortitude and courage of veterans, held their gains, and denied to the enemy the slightest advantage.[1]

(Diary) Paris, Friday, May 31, 1918. Went to British area Wednesday. Saw the 35th Division (Wright), its men above average size. Also the 82d (Burnham), which looks very promising. Took lunch with Wright and spent the night with Colonel Bacon, an admirable

[1] It is interesting to record that of the officers of the 1st Division to participate in this battle, Bullard was later to command an army; Summerall and Hines, corps; Buck, Ely, Parker and Bamford, divisions. Two members of the division staff, King and Marshall, were to become chiefs of staff of corps. Many other officers then with the division would have undoubtedly reached high positions of command had they not sacrificed their lives at Soissons and on other battle fields later on.

liaison officer. Our 2d and 3d Divisions ordered to reënforce the French.

Had breakfast yesterday with Sir Douglas Haig. He criticized the French and thought they should have foreseen this offensive, but added that his remarks were hardly warranted in view of recent British experience. Saw part of the 28th Division (Muir), the 77th (Duncan) and the 4th (Cameron) and am much pleased with them. All are apprehensive of being left with the British. Had luncheon with Muir and dined with General Foch at Sarcus.

Came to Paris to-day, held conference with McAndrew and Fox Conner, and saw M. Tardieu and Martin Egan. Have recommended training with British tanks at home. Tonnage allotments still short of requirements. Have cabled urgent request for trucks, also for 12,000 railway troops, badly needed.

The French situation is very serious. Our aviation doing well at the front.

The German attack of May 27th was made by thirty German divisions. It came as such a surprise that the French did not have time to destroy important bridges across the Aisne and the Vesle, over which their pursuers followed. By May 31st the enemy had captured Soissons and reached the Marne and Château-Thierry, a distance of thirty miles, driving the French in confusion toward Paris and inflicting upon them a loss of 60,000 prisoners, 650 guns, 2,000 machine guns, aviation material, and vast quantities of ammunition and other supplies.

I have heard this retirement referred to as a masterly, strategic retreat, but it was nothing of the kind and the French military authorities never made any such claim. The four French and three British divisions on the front of attack were completely overcome. The entire French reserve became engaged; in all, thirty-five French infantry and six cavalry divisions participating in the battle. In addition, two other British divisions which had been sent to that front to rest, two Italian, and two American divisions were called into action and suffered heavily.

Before the attack, it was the opinion of our Intelligence Section that the next blow would logically fall upon that part of the line and that view was expressed to the French by my Chief of Intelligence, Brigadier General Nolan. Yet on the day previous to the attack the French Army Headquarters on that front asserted that everything was quiet and that they did not expect an offensive there. This was indeed a compliment to the enemy as showing the secrecy with which his concentration was made, a precaution which we, ourselves, rather successfully followed later in preparing for both our major offensives.

The alarming situation had caused General Pétain to call on me on the 30th for American troops to be sent to the region

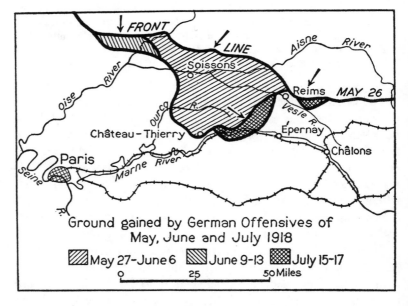

Ground gained by German Offensives of
May, June and July 1918

⬛ May 27–June 6   ⬛ June 9–13   ⬛ July 15–17

0   25   50 Miles

of Château-Thierry. The 3d Division (Dickman), then in training near Chaumont, being the only division within reach besides the 2d, was ordered to move north immediately. Dickman started his motorized machine gun battalion over the road on the afternoon of May 30th. The infantry and engineers entrained the same night and the division's supply trains marched overland.

The first element to reach Château-Thierry was the 7th Machine Gun Battalion, which arrived on the afternoon of May

31st and immediately went into action against the enemy, who then held the half of the town north of the Marne. By daylight on June 1st all available guns had been provided with cover and were in their positions, one company with eight guns defending the main wagon bridge and another with nine guns guarding the approaches to the railroad bridge. From these positions they repulsed all attempts by the Germans to cross the Marne. Meanwhile, as the infantry of the division came up on June 1st, its battalions were put into line to reënforce the French along the Marne for ten miles, from Château-Thierry east to Dormans. The conduct of the machine gun battalion in this operation was highly praised by General Pétain.

The 2d Division (Bundy) on May 30th was near Chaumont-en-Vexin and was preparing to move northward the next day for concentration near Beauvais to relieve the 1st Division at Cantigny. But its orders were changed late that night, and the division, moving by motor trucks, was rushed toward Meaux, which lies about twenty miles from Paris. On reaching there, the leading elements were hurried forward in the direction of Château-Thierry. The roads were crowded with French troops and refugees retreating in great confusion, many of the soldiers telling our men that all was lost. Definite information as to the location of the enemy and the disposition of the retiring French units in the vicinity was difficult to obtain.

The initial deployment of the infantry and marines of the division was made on June 1st, across the Paris highway near Lucy-le-Bocage, in support of two French divisions, which, however, had orders to fall back through the American lines. On June 4th, the French withdrew and that day the Germans began attacks against the American lines which were everywhere repulsed. On June 6th, the 2d Division began a series of local attacks which resulted in the retaking of important points from the enemy.

The sudden appearance and dramatic entrance of the 2d and 3d Divisions into the shattered and broken fighting lines and their dash and courage in battle produced a favorable effect upon the French *poilu*. Although in battle for the first time, our men maintained their positions and by their timely arrival effectively stopped the German advance on Paris. It must have been with a decided feeling of relief that the worn and tired French soldiers, retreating before vastly superior numbers, caught sight of Americans arriving in trucks at Meaux and marching thence on foot, hats off, eagerly hurrying forward to battle. And the Germans, who had been filled with propaganda depreciating the American effort and the quality of our training, must have been surprised and disconcerted by meeting strong resistance by Americans on different portions of this active battle front.

This defeat of the French furnished the second striking confirmation of the wisdom of training troops for open warfare. While the Germans had been practicing for a war of movement and concentrating their most aggressive personnel into shock divisions, preparatory to the spring campaign, the training of the Allies had been still limited generally to trench warfare. As our units were being trained for open warfare, this alone would have been sufficient reason why we could not allow them to be broken up and scattered among the Allies.

American divisions were arriving behind the British lines in increasing numbers without the artillery and other auxiliary components, but many of the infantry units were not up to strength and much of the personnel only partially trained. The late arrivals, like the earlier ones, complained of the vicious practice of the General Staff at home of frequently withdrawing large numbers of trained men and replacing them with recruits. It was, therefore, of the utmost importance to push their instruction, now fortunately beyond the possibility of such interruption. On visiting the new divisions, I impressed upon the officers the responsibility of putting their units in shape as quickly as possible and pointed out when practicable those features that should be especially stressed regardless of the type of instruction which the British might wish to undertake. There were many questions asked regarding their service with the British and all were given to understand that they were to be assembled as soon as possible to form an army of our own.

At British headquarters the officials were very anxious over the French situation and yet they expressed a feeling of relief that some of the adverse criticism which had been heaped upon them during the past few weeks could now perhaps be applied with the same force to their ally.

Returning from the British front, I stopped at Sarcus to see General Foch and took dinner with him and his staff. It would be difficult to imagine a more depressed group of officers. They sat through the meal scarcely speaking a word as they contemplated what was probably the most serious situation of the war. As we still had troops that were not actively engaged, I suggested personally to Foch, when we were alone after dinner, that an early counterattack be made against the new salient, offering him the use of these disengaged troops. Most confidentially, he said, that was what he had in mind. Speaking of the 2d and 3d Divisions, which had already been ordered to support the French, I told him that he could count on my doing everything possible in this crisis and that I was ready to exert the utmost effort to help meet it with all our forces then at hand, which he said of course he had never doubted. In further conversation, he seemed more than ever of the opinion that only infantry and machine gun units should be brought over from the States and still apparently could not see the advantage of having complete American combat units, or the urgency of bringing over men to relieve the extraordinary strain on our supply system.

After the success of our troops, we were in no mood to listen to unwarranted criticisms. Upon my return to Paris, M. Tardieu called and, no doubt with good intent, undertook to comment adversely on our staff and our organization. As these were subjects that he could not possibly know about, I replied that he had an entirely erroneous impression and that our General Staff was composed of men selected for their ability and efficiency. I intimated that we had had quite enough of this sort of thing from the French, either military or civilian, and suggested that if his people would cease troubling themselves so much about our affairs and attend more strictly to their own we should all get along much better. I fully appreciated M. Tardieu's ability and his eagerness to be helpful, and I really had a high regard for him, but the constant inclination on the part of a certain element among the French to assume a superiority that did not exist, then or at any later period, added to the attempts of some of them to dictate, had reached the limit of patience.

It must in fairness be said that a superior attitude was not assumed by the higher officers of the French Army and rarely by civilians, but was mainly noticeable among some bureau officials and others who, clothed with brief authority as instructors or otherwise, came in contact with our organizations. It is pertinent to mention here that the Chief of the French Mission made a full report to his superiors on the American characteristics, from which the following extracts are taken:

"The outstanding characteristics of Americans, taken as a people, are a highly developed national pride and a strong spirit of independence. * * * As a rule, these feelings of theirs are not openly expressed; they do not result in the slightest display of arrogance on their part in their dealings with us.

" * * * They have decided not to submit to any subordination whatsoever, and have made up their minds to be placed on a footing of complete equality.

"Now, we are sure to suffer a complete deception if we attempt to impose our opinions, or our advice, on Americans, even in matters of a strictly military nature. They are quite willing to recognize our true worth, and they appreciate our efforts. They are great admirers of France, of the achievements of her armies, and of the staunch bearing and the spirit of sacrifice displayed by her citizens. They are sincere in these feelings, but it does not follow that they are ready to take our advice blindly, or adopt our plans outright.

" * * * They argue that open warfare will regain all of its classic importance when the eventual break-through and its attendant exploitation takes place. This is bound to happen, in their opinion, when the American Army, as such, takes its place in line.

"Another consequence of this state of mind is that Americans are a unit in intending to organize an army which shall be wholly American and not have its components brigaded with the armies of the Allies. As to this point, they are unanimous, from their commander-in-chief down to the last officer who happens to give it any thought. The American officers will not listen to any talk of an amalgamation wherein the American Army would lose its distinctive character.

"At all events, it is my firm belief that, from now on, we should discard any idea of either systematically brigading entire American units with our own, or of systematically incorporating American soldiers with our troops.

"To sum up, we cannot flatter ourselves with the hope of forcing a complete and final adhesion to our way of thinking. The Americans are in the habit of listening to our views, and they often ask for them, when once we have gained their confidence; but they invariably reserve the right to make the final decision themselves, and they are accustomed, in the last analysis, to base their decision on their own reasoning.

" * * * It should not be forgotten that the leaders of the American forces actually in France enjoy President Wilson's entire confidence and that his powers are more extensive than those of any other ruler.

"Consequently, even if we cannot expect to realize all our aims, or secure the acceptance of all our views, this does not detract from the importance to us of American support, not only from the standpoint of financial backing and supplies of all kinds, but also with respect to military power. The first American troops to be organized as units are sturdy, eager, and well-disciplined, and have made rapid progress. Their officers, who are constantly subjected to a rigorous process of selection by elimination, already possess distinct qualities of character and leadership. The technical knowledge and the practical experience which they lack they can only acquire by degrees.

"We should therefore keep on working as we have begun. We should not indulge in pessimistic skepticism, nor should we pin our faith on results beyond reasonable expectation. By so doing, we can count on getting solid results. Our real and only danger lies in failure to make allowances for the spirit of the American people and for the idiosyncrasies of American mentality. In such case, we should proceed straight to defeat.

"I have reason to believe, on the contrary, that if we shall know how to give full play to the earnest craving of Americans to get into the fight with all of their resources, that we may then count implicitly on their joining hands with us in the spirit of utmost coöperation. * * * "

General Pétain himself was very particular in this regard and cautioned the French liaison officers in a letter of instructions which dwelt upon coöperation and friendly assistance:

"8 May, 1918.

"At the moment when the military assistance of our American allies assumes an importance which will make of it one of the decisive factors in the happy issue of the war, the General, Commander-in-Chief of the French Armies, believes it proper to recall to officers of every grade who are employed in connection with the American Army certain principles which should guide their action in the accomplishment of the important task which is confided to them.

"I. FRENCH OFFICERS SHOULD TAKE INTO CONSIDERATION THE IMPORTANCE OF THE MILITARY EFFORT MADE BY THE UNITED STATES.

"In April of 1917, at the moment of their entrance into the war, the United States did not have, properly speaking, an army.

"Within a year they have adopted universal and obligatory military service, raised, armed, equipped, and sent to France several hundred thousand men, and all of this is only the beginning. They have thus accomplished a task of military organization without precedent in history. They have accomplished and are now accomplishing within the interior of France various works of enormous importance (improvements of the ports of St. Nazaire and Bordeaux, storehouses and ice plants at Gièvres, etc.), which will remain after the war and will enable us to undertake the economic struggle under exceptionally favorable conditions as to equipment.

"The American Red Cross is placing at our disposition considerable sums, to relieve people who have met with all kinds of misfortunes.

"The General, Commander-in-Chief, desires that during their conversations with American officers the French officers prove to the American that the French fully appreciate the importance of the effort furnished by America and the grandeur of the service rendered to France.

"II. IN THEIR RELATIONS WITH AMERICAN OFFICERS THE FRENCH OFFICERS MUST ALWAYS USE THE GREATEST TACT.

"The Americans fully recognize the value of our military experience; for our part, we must not forget that America is a great nation, that the Americans have a national self-respect developed and justified by the breadth of vision which they bring to bear upon all the questions which they consider. French officers should treat the officers of their grade, or of a subordinate grade, as comrades who have arrived more recently than they upon the front, and should treat them as little as possible as a master does a scholar. As to officers who are of a higher grade than the French officers, the French should wait to give advice until such advice is requested.

"Finally, it is necessary, above all, to avoid giving advice, or to make criticisms in public.

"III. FRENCH OFFICERS SHOULD ENDEAVOR TO BE PERSONAL FRIENDS WITH AMERICAN OFFICERS.

"Between people who are living constantly side by side, official relations are necessarily very much influenced by personal relations.

"The French officers should, therefore, always endeavor to live with their American comrades under the best terms of friendship, and to gain their confidence by demonstrating to them that the advice which they give, and the criticisms which they make, have no other object than the general interest. Such relations are easily realized, for the American is by nature cordial and generous.

"It is important to ensure in the future as has been the case in the past close collaboration between the two Allied armies, a collaboration which constitutes the most certain guarantee of the final success of our common efforts.

"PÉTAIN."

CHAPTER XXXI

Animated Conference at Versailles—Allies Recommend 100 American Divisions—Allied Fear—Situation Reported to Washington—Refugees—British Partially Accept Principle of Coördination of Supply

(Diary) Paris, Sunday, June 2, 1918. Coördinated procurement established at home under principles in effect here since last August.

Supreme War Council met yesterday afternoon and again to-day. Heated discussion with Allied leaders over shipment of American troops. French and British now insist on unlimited infantry and machine gun units. Haig wants to retain our divisions that are with British and French wish them to relieve their divisions in the Vosges. All much pleased with efficiency of 1st, 2d, and 3d Divisions. News from French front less pessimistic.

THE sixth session of the Supreme War Council convened June 1st, and one of the first subjects to receive attention was the further shipment of American troops. As already clearly indicated, it was my opinion that neither the character of the troops we should send to France nor their disposition was within the province of the Council to decide. I thought that these questions should be determined by ourselves according to circumstances, perhaps after consultation with the Allies if required to meet an emergency. So I objected to their consideration by the Council, as such, and suggested a meeting outside the Council, which was approved.

Note: Total strength of the A.E.F. on May 31st, 32,642 officers, 618,642 enlisted men.

Divisional units arriving in May included elements of the following divisions: 4th Division (Regular Army), Maj. Gen. Geo. H. Cameron; 6th Division (Regular Army), Brig. Gen. James B. Erwin; 27th Division (National Guard, New York), Maj. Gen. John F. O'Ryan; 28th Division (National Guard, Pennsylvania), Maj. Gen. Chas. H. Muir; 30th Division (National Guard, Tennessee, North and South Carolina), Maj. Gen. Geo. W. Read; 33d Division (National Guard, Illinois), Maj. Gen. Geo. Bell, Jr.; 35th Division (National Guard, Missouri and Kansas), Maj. Gen. Wm. M. Wright; 80th Division (National Army, Virginia, West Virginia, and western Pennsylvania), Maj. Gen. Adelbert Cronkhite; 82d Division (National Army, Georgia, Alabama, and Tennessee), Maj. Gen. Wm. P. Burnham.

Accordingly, in the late afternoon, Lord Milner, General Foch, General Weygand and I, with Colonels Conner and Boyd, met in M. Clemenceau's office, the three Prime Ministers being, at the moment, engaged in closed session. General Foch began at once by stating the serious plight of the Allies and proposed the continued shipment from America of nothing but infantry and machine gun units in June and July, approximately 250,000 each month. Every one realized the gravity of the Allied situation, but there was a decided difference of opinion as to the best way to meet it. However, I was prepared to make some concessions, and stated them, with reasons for not entirely accepting Foch's view. But neither facts nor arguments seemed to make any impression. He was very positive and insistent and in fact became quite excited, waving his hands and repeating, "The battle, the battle, nothing else counts."

With equal emphasis I urged that we must build up our organization in order to carry on the battle to the end, and pointed out that our program had been seriously interrupted by the concessions already made. I called his attention to the fact that the railways all over France were breaking down for lack of efficient operators and of skilled workmen to repair rolling stock; that our ports would be hopelessly blocked unless we could improve the railways; that his plan would leave us 200,000 men short of enough to complete combat units and fill up special organizations that were absolutely necessary in the S.O.S.; and finally expressed the opinion that the restriction of our shipments to infantry and machine gun units would be a very dangerous and shortsighted policy. To much of this he paid little or no attention and replied that all these things could be postponed.

Mr. Graeme Thomson, the British expert on transportation and supply, came into the room at this point in company with Mr. Lloyd George and General Sir Henry Wilson and took part in the discussion. Mr. Thomson said with considerable emphasis that it would be a very serious mistake not to send over men to repair rolling stock and otherwise build up our rail transportation system and went on to describe the run-down condition of the railways. His views seemed to have no more effect on the French attitude than if they had not been uttered. This phase of the discussion further confirmed my opinion that none of the French officials had more than a vague conception of the tremendous difficulties of our problem.

At this point, I stated that it would be impossible for us to ship over as many infantry and machine gun troops as the Allies wished because on June 30th we should have left at home only 90,000 of such troops with the necessary training. General Foch used this as the basis for offhand criticism of our organization, asserting that we did not have enough infantry in proportion to other troops, failing entirely to appreciate our requirements for the services of supply and transportation, and for artillery, engineers, and other auxiliary arms.

It may be observed here that, notwithstanding my urgent recommendations for a large increase in the number of drafted men, the War Department had, up to May 1st, called out only an average of 116,000 men per month. Consequently, the supply of trained troops had run short in an emergency that required the shipment of 250,000 to 300,000 per month. During May, 373,000 men had been drafted, and of this number those who were being sent over had of course received but little training before their arrival in France, where it had to be completed oftentimes by costly experience in battle.

Continuing the conference, Mr. Lloyd George remarked that he thought President Wilson would be deeply interested to get General Foch's views. He then said that as America had no Prime Minister present he thought it would be inconvenient for us to make a decision, but that the question should be brought before the whole Council. I called attention to the cablegram from the Secretary of War, already quoted, showing that President Wilson had been very much embarrassed by representations made to him personally by the French and British Ambassadors and had suggested that the matter might be settled by a conference between General Foch and myself. I further pointed out that this cable did not mention the Supreme War Council and stated my opposition to making the subject one of general discussion by all Allied representatives and their staffs. I also mentioned the fact that the President was trusting to my judgment in this matter. As nothing was being accomplished, and hoping that the number of participants in the discussion might be limited, I proposed that we should adjourn until the following day.

The next afternoon, when we assembled, M. Clemenceau was waiting for the rest of us, and instead of there being fewer conferees the number had increased. Not unlike the situation at Abbeville a month before, everybody was keyed up, and, as we had anticipated, the battle had to be fought all over again. Foch, supported by Clemenceau and Lloyd George, reiterated his demand for exclusive shipments of infantry and machine gunners in June and in July. I was strongly opposed to this, and insisted that sufficient importance had not been attached to my reasons for the necessity of the auxiliary troops omitted in June. Foch resorted to his often-repeated question as to whether I was willing to take the risk, to which I replied very positively that I was ready to assume any responsibility that my proposal might entail, but that I must have a greater proportion of other troops to keep the American organization from going to smash.

Other objections, which the Allies apparently overlooked, and which I brought out, were that the drafts called in May could not possibly be ready for service until considerable time after arrival, and that neither the French nor the British could provide all the equipment and land transportation they would need. In accordance with my program, I was willing to agree to the reasonable shipments of fully trained infantry not needed for the instruction of recruits, but felt that this point should be left to the judgment of the Secretary of War.

Mr. Lloyd George then drew the conclusion that the month of July, as a consequence, would be a blank, and, in a rather dejected tone, said that the Allies were in a sense in the hands of the United States. He spoke of the generous and chivalrous attitude of President Wilson and said all they could do was to acquaint him with their needs and call upon him to come to their aid, more particularly to the aid of France at the period of the most terrible extremity that she had yet encountered. He proposed that we should bring over men that were partially instructed, as he thought they would learn faster in the atmosphere of war. I said we could not strip the country of every man with any sort of training as we should then be back where we had started in 1917, and argued that all men sent over should have at least three months' training if it were at all possible to give it. Whereupon M. Clemenceau asked what would become of the war in the interval.

I remarked that the discussion had become complicated, but that it was my hope that the greatest possible number of troops, including artillery and auxiliary combat troops and those required for railways and ports, should be transported. I tried to make our needs understood and appealed to Foch and Weygand, who, as soldiers, I said, could not fail to recognize the difficulties we had to surmount, not only in training our citizen army but in building up a complete system of supply in a foreign country. I well knew, however, that neither of them, in their extreme desire for American replacements, had given these questions serious thought, nor had they considered the deficiencies in our organization caused by concessions of the past few months. The British problems being similar to ours, though less difficult, the views of Mr. Thomson were more to the point. He had plainly said that it was impossible to assure the effective employment of our army without adequate rail and port facilities. Lord Milner agreed, and said he thought he fully understood our case.

M. Clemenceau reverted to the shortage of available men in the United States, saying he had thought our resources inexhaustible, and wanted to know when the shipments would be resumed. As he had evidently not followed the discussion, he was informed that in general they would of course be continued to the full capacity of tonnage and that the men we had called out in May would be available in August. He concurred with Mr. Lloyd George that President Wilson ought to be advised of the Allied situation.

Mr. Lloyd George then read a proposed message to the President suggesting that 170,000 infantry and machine gun units, without regard to training, be sent in each of the months of June and July out of a possible 250,000 in each month, leaving transportation for a total of 160,000 of the categories desired by me. Foch proposed that the message be sent and Lord Milner appealed for an agreement, but I objected to bringing troops with only one month's training.   I called attention to the fact that we were being importuned on the one hand to send over nothing but replacements for Allied divisions to the utter neglect of our own military establishment and on the other hand we were being pressed to furnish thousands of men for their technical services. Moreover, I said, it had already been demonstrated by the experience of our units serving with them that the Allies were not prepared to supply our men with either equipment or accustomed food.   I insisted that auxiliary and service troops be sent to build up our own organization in preference to the shipment of uninstructed men who would be of little use in the battle lines when they arrived.   I suggested that the July program might be postponed until August.   Clemenceau remarked that the German would not postpone his attacks, to which I replied that neither could we rely on untrained men in battle.

Here Mr. Lloyd George read a proposition which set forth the critical situation requiring the concentration of reserves in front of Paris and the urgent necessity of finding other troops to replace the French divisions taken from the British front.   He drew attention particularly to the opinion expressed by General Foch that the Allies would be defeated unless the number of British divisions could be maintained.   He then proposed that the British Commander-in-Chief should determine when the American troops with his armies had acquired sufficient training to be placed in the line.   This meant that such troops would become replacements, and, of course, it was impossible for me to agree to that.   I rather vigorously stated that this was a prerogative and a responsibility that I could not relinquish under any circumstances.   I said that this was not the Allies' business, but that should an emergency arise requiring immediate action every consideration would be given by me to any request from General Foch for our troops, trained or untrained.

Reading from notes, and appealing to me, Foch then proposed that a request be made on the United States for a total of 100 combat divisions to be sent over at the rate of 300,000 men per month. I said that in my opinion we would send as many divisions as possible and that our people would not fail to raise an army of the necessary size.

Transferring his attention to the British for the moment, M. Clemenceau asked how many divisions it would be possible for them to maintain in France, to which Mr. Lloyd George replied with some sarcasm that it would be best to postpone the question until the return of the French expert whom M. Clemenceau had proposed to send to England.[1]

Then General Foch took the cue and went on to say that we found ourselves with 150 Allied divisions opposed to 204 German divisions, and if the number were reduced then we should fail, and that whatever might be the report of the expert there ought to be the strongest resolve on the part of the British Government to keep up its divisions. Disaster would be inevitable, he said, if they were unable to maintain the fifty-three British divisions, and that it would be impossible to continue the war in the name of the Allies against an enemy whose effectives increased while ours diminished.

The whole discussion was very erratic, as one of the Allies would take exception to nearly every statement made by the other. Mr. Lloyd George said here that he could not understand why all the losses fell to the Allies and none to the Germans. Then came a lively tilt between the British and the French, Lord Milner taking direct issue as to the figures. He showed that the Allies really had 169 divisions and not 150 as General

[1] At one of the meetings of the Supreme War Council, during a discussion of reserve manpower, M. Clemenceau had suggested that an investigation of that question as to England might be made by a French expert.

Foch had declared.[1] He said that measures had been taken to increase their effectives through the application of a law of extreme severity, but that it would not bring results until the month of August. Nevertheless, he continued, it was not the intention of the British to reduce the number of their divisions.

Foch again spoke of Allied inferiority and asked for definite information of the British Government as to the number of divisions they would maintain. During the dialogue that followed between Milner and Wilson, who differed as to the number, Foch quietly asked me about the agreement regarding our divisions serving with the British. I told him the understanding was that the British would be able to fill their divisions by July or August, thus relieving the Americans who might be in their units, and that the question as to where our divisions would be used was in his hands until they should be required for our own corps and armies. I told him that Haig hoped to keep them, but I did not wish them to become absorbed in either the British or French army and as a consequence be unavailable later for the formation of an American army.

Further conversation showed the feeling of uncertainty in the minds of the Allies. Mr. Lloyd George came back to the question of losses and said that before the great battle he was informed positively that the Germans had only 400,000 replacements left, and now, after the most violent fighting, in which it was reported that the Germans had suffered very heavy losses, they still had more than 300,000 replacements. The Allies also had 300,000, but it was now claimed, he said, that the British Army was on the decline while that of the enemy was not. He asked if that could be cleared up, to which Foch replied that it was because the enemy managed better, and he went on to say that Germany, with a population of 68,000,000 people, could maintain 204 divisions, while Great Britain, with 46,000,000 inhabitants,

---

[1] Of the 169 divisions on the Western Front at this time, Lord Milner pointed out, 101 were French, 2 Italian, 4 American, 11 Belgian and 51 British, besides 2 British that were reduced to mere skeletons. These numbers had been variously stated according to which side was speaking.

could keep up only forty-three.[1]   Then, in response to a further question by Mr. Lloyd George, he said he could not pretend to say where Germany procured her replacements, possibly it might be from prisoners returned from Russia, for example, but all he knew was that they had 204 divisions to the Allies' 169. Then Mr. Lloyd George said that probably the real reason was that Allied losses were greater than those of the enemy.

After some further argument on discrepancies of the various figures and insistence on the part of Foch that the number of divisions be maintained, the question of shipment of American troops in June and July was resumed.   The discussion having reached an impasse, it was suggested that Lord Milner, General Foch and I should undertake to draw up a program.   In the consideration of the matter by the three of us, the point of my contention was won when Weygand, who was Foch's principal adviser, came forward with the remark that it would be as well to leave the new drafts to be trained at home for a month or so longer.   Although my arguments had failed to make any impression on Foch, he at once approved Weygand's suggestion. With this out of the way we soon drew up the agreement embodied in the following cablegram sent to Washington on June 2d:

"The following agreement has been concluded between General Foch, Lord Milner, and myself with reference to the transportation of American troops in the months of June and July.   The following recommendations are made on the assumption that at least 250,000 men can be transported in each of the months of June and July by the employment of British and American tonnage.   We recommend:

"A. For the month of June: 1st, absolute priority shall be given to the transportation of 170,000 combatant troops (viz., six divisions without artillery, ammunition trains or supply trains, amounting to 126,000 men and 44,000 replacements for combat troops); 2d, 25,400 men for the service of railways, of which 13,400 have been asked for by the French Minister of Transportation; 3d, the remainder to be troops of categories to be determined by the Commander-in-Chief, American Expeditionary Forces.

[1] It had been stated that the British counted on keeping up fifty-three divisions but that ten of them would be practically American.

"B. For the month of July: 1st, absolute priority for the shipment of 140,000 combatant troops of the nature defined above (4 divisions minus artillery, etc., etc., amounting to 84,000 men plus 56,000 replacements); 2d, the balance of the 250,000 to consist of troops to be designated by the Commander-in-Chief, American Expeditionary Forces.

"C. It is agreed that if available tonnage in either month allows of the transportation of a larger number of men than 250,000 the excess tonnage will be employed in the transportation of combat troops as defined above.

"D. We recognize that the combatant troops to be dispatched in July may have to include troops with insufficient training, but we consider the present emergency is such as to justify a temporary and exceptional departure by the United States from sound principles of training especially as a similar course is being followed by France and Great Britain.

"FOCH, MILNER, PERSHING."

The Prime Ministers at the same time sent a cable to the President expressing their "warmest thanks" for the remarkable promptness in sending American aid to meet the present emergency. They pointed out that General Foch had presented a statement of the "utmost gravity" showing the relative strength of the Allies and their adversaries with no possible increase in the number of Allied divisions in sight. While they declared that there was great danger of the war being lost unless the numerical inferiority of the Allies could soon be remedied by the addition of American replacements, their statement did not convey the extreme apprehension that prevailed. The cablegram as sent by the Prime Ministers is quoted in full, as follows:

"The Prime Ministers of France, Italy and Great Britain, now meeting at Versailles, desire to send the following message to the President of the United States:

"We desire to express our warmest thanks to President Wilson for the remarkable promptness with which American aid, in excess of what at one time seemed practicable, has been rendered to the Allies during the past month to meet a great emergency. The crisis, however, still continues. General Foch has presented to us a statement of the utmost gravity, which points out that the numerical superiority of the enemy in France, where 162 Allied divisions now oppose 200 German divisions, is very heavy, and that, as there is no possibility of the British and French increasing the number of their divisions (on the contrary, they are put to extreme straits to keep them up) there is a great danger of the war being lost unless the numerical inferiority of the Allies can be remedied as rapidly as possible by the advent of American troops. He, therefore, urges with the utmost insistence that the maximum possible number of infantry and machine gunners, in which respect the shortage of men on the side of the Allies is most marked, should continue to be shipped from America in the months of June and July to avert the immediate danger of an Allied defeat in the present campaign owing to the Allied reserves being exhausted before those of the enemy. In addition to this, and looking to the future, he represents that it is impossible to foresee ultimate victory in the war unless America is able to provide such an army as will enable the Allies ultimately to establish numerical superiority. He places the total American force required for this at no less than 100 divisions, and urges the continuous raising of fresh American levies, which, in his opinion, should not be less than 300,000 a month, with a view to establishing a total American force of 100 divisions at as early a date as this can possibly be done.[1]

"We are satisfied that Gen. Foch, who is conducting the present campaign with consummate ability, and on whose military judgment we continue to place the most absolute reliance, is not overestimating the needs of the case, and we feel confident that the Government of the United States will do everything that can be done, both to meet the needs of the immediate situation and to proceed with the continuous raising of fresh levies, calculated to provide, as soon as possible, the numerical superiority which the Commander-in-Chief of the Allied Armies regards as essential to ultimate victory.

"A separate telegram contains the arrangements which Gen. Foch, Gen. Pershing, and Lord Milner have agreed to recommend to the United States Government with regard to the dispatch of American troops for the months of June and July.

"CLEMENCEAU,
"D. LLOYD GEORGE,
"ORLANDO."

What a difference it would have made if the Allies had seen this a year or even six months earlier and had then given us as-

[1] In order to allow for a due proportion of corps and army troops, we roughly counted each combat division at 40,000 men. Thus 100 combat divisions would make 4,000,000 men in France.

sistance in shipping! Certainly, the situation had been clearly understood since the preceding August. It will be recalled that the commanders-in-chief and the chiefs of staff had at that time concluded that their dependence was upon America. The Governments, likewise, understood in August that the constitution of our army in France depended upon sea transportation, but they took no steps then to provide it. On the contrary their minds were centered on using America as a reservoir from which men could be drawn to serve under an alien flag. They failed to understand the psychology of the American people. They failed to foresee the results. They failed to do the only thing that good judgment dictated, and that was to assist by all possible means the organization of a powerful American army and to transport it to France at the earliest possible moment.

During this session of the Supreme War Council it was frequently asserted, and firmly believed in some circles, that there was real danger that Germany might recruit her manpower in Russia unless the Allied powers could counteract German influence. It was the opinion of several members of the Council that the Russians would look to the United States for advice and possible aid. But all believed that they would resent Japanese interference and might be inclined in this case to unite with the Germans. Apprehension of such a contingency possibly may have influenced the Supreme War Council to some extent in making such insistent demands on us, and no doubt prompted the Allies to send a mixed force into eastern Siberia.

It could not be questioned that the situation was decidedly serious, even though the German advance in the Marne salient had been held up for the time being. The French and British divisions which had occupied that front against the German attack had lost a large percentage of their personnel and practically all their matériel. Rested divisions had been sent to replace them, but the burden of aiding the British during the preceding two months had fallen heavily upon the French and their manpower was at a low ebb. The following cabled report, with recommendations, indicates the situation as seen at the time:

"June 3, 1918.

"Personal and confidential for the Chief of Staff and Secretary of War.

"Paragraph 1.

"Consider military situation very grave. The French line gave way before what was thought to be a secondary attack and the seven divisions that occupied that front have lost practically all their matériel and a large percentage of their personnel, although actual numbers of men and guns are yet unknown. The German advance seems to be stopped for the time being. The railroads in the area they have taken are not available for their use principally because of the destruction of the tunnel at Vauxaillon. As already reported, the infantry of our 3d Division is being used in Lorraine and the 5th along the Marne.[1] Our 2d Division entire is fighting north of Château-Thierry and has done exceedingly well. It is General Foch's plan to take the divisions from behind the British lines as needed and use them with French artillery in Lorraine to replace French divisions for the battle.

"Paragraph 2.

"The attitude of the Supreme War Council, which has been in session since Saturday, is one of depression. The Prime Ministers and General Foch appeal most urgently for trained or even untrained men, and notwithstanding my representations that the number of trained infantry in America would be practically exhausted by the middle of July, they still insisted on a program of infantry personnel. The agreement entered into, however, was not entirely satisfactory as to July, but instead of sending raw infantry troops it is believed wiser to send more of the classes we need for various services. I hope we shall be able to make heavy shipment of combat personnel in August and succeeding months.

"Paragraph 3.

"The utmost endeavor should be made to keep up a constant flow of personnel to the full capacity of tonnage, and I very strongly urge that divisions be organized as rapidly as possible and be sent over entire after July, and also that auxiliary troops of all kinds be shipped in due proportion. It should be most fully realized at home that the time has come for us to take up the brunt of the war and that France and England are not going to be able to keep their armies at present strength very much longer.

"Paragraph 4.

"I have pointed out to the Prime Ministers the necessity of both the French and British Governments utilizing every possible man at

[1] There was an error in the original cable. It should have read "Our 5th Division is being used in Lorraine and the 3d along the Marne."

this time, including 1919 drafts who still lack a month or so of completing their training. Attention is invited to general reference to this matter in the agreement which implies that both Governments are doing this, but I am not sure, however, that this is the fact. It might be wise to request the respective Ambassadors to urge their Governments to put in every available man to meet this crisis and hold on until our forces can be felt.

"Paragraph 5.

"In view of recent losses, the question of divisional artillery is also very serious. It is doubtful now whether the French will be able to supply us with the artillery we require. It is also reported that our program at home is very far behind. I most sincerely hope this is not so, as it is unlikely that France will be able to do more than meet her own requirements from now on. Will advise you more in detail later.

"Paragraph 6.

"The urgent cable sent by the three Prime Ministers giving General Foch's views as to Allied needs in troops and asking for an increased American program was read to me. I told them that America was fully alive to the necessity of doing everything possible and would do so. I can only add that our program should be laid out systematically and broadly, and men called out as fast as they can be handled.

"PERSHING."

This last request by the Allies for American troops was the climax of a succession of demands that must have created consternation at home. The first was based on my agreement with Mr. Lloyd George. Then came the one with Brigadier General Hutchinson, followed by that made in London. The Abbeville agreement came next and after that the one at Versailles. Each was an appeal to America for troops to build up the armies of the British and French, and each was greater and more pressing than the one before.

The difficulties that these successive demands presented can scarcely be imagined. Each of them made new calculations for shipment necessary. No sooner was one schedule determined upon than another had to be worked out. The selection of units, the transfers of available men from one unit to another, the movements of large bodies by rail to the seaports, and finally their embarkation, all constituted a task of tremendous proportions.   In its execution as a whole, the achievement stands out as a lasting monument to our War Department, marred only by the lack of foresight that made it necessary to send over untrained men and units in such precipitate haste.[1]

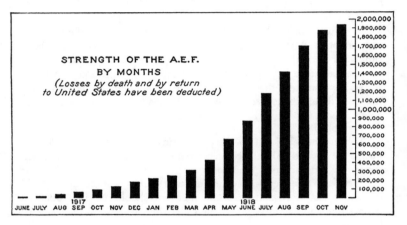

STRENGTH OF THE A.E.F.
BY MONTHS
(Losses by death and by return
to United States have been deducted)

(Diary) Chaumont, Thursday, June 6, 1918.   Lord Milner lunched with me on Monday.   He thinks they have been let down because Foch has requested five of our divisions from the British Front for service with the French.

While en route here on Tuesday, with McAndrew and Boyd, visited 2d Division, talked with brigade commanders, Harbord and Lewis, and also visited Dickman's 3d Division.   Both divisions with excellent morale.   Each has made successful counterattack against enemy attempt to advance.

Urged Ragueneau yesterday to visit Paris in aid of horse procurement.   French hope to furnish us 15,000 monthly.

Received letter of appreciation from Pétain for sending divisions to French Front.   War Department requested to rush construction of tanks and 3,000 additional Liberty engines.   Approved Major George Walker's request for publication in orders of my letter to Lord Milner on the venereal question.   British only partially approve suggestion regarding coördination of supplies.

[1] Of the men that came to France, 46.25 per cent were carried in American ships, 51.25 per cent in British owned or controlled, and 2.5 per cent in others.

The 2d and 3d Divisions, facing the Germans near Château-Thierry, had made their places in line secure, giving heart to the French, who were trying to stabilize their own positions around the newly formed salient. We shall hear more of these two divisions later. Although fully taken for granted by all of us, it was none the less gratifying to see these divisions for the first time in the line acquit themselves so well.

En route to Chaumont, we motored through Montmirail, passing long columns of French refugees fleeing from their homes, many on foot, men and women with bundles on their backs, leading the smaller children, driving their stock before them, and hauling in various types of conveyances the few remaining worldly goods they were able to take with them in their flight. Almost indescribable were many similar scenes as reported by our troops as they came up to reënforce the retiring French. It seemed to me then that if this picture of civilization engaged in the persecution of innocent and unarmed noncombatants could be brought home to all peoples, reason would be forced upon rulers and governments where too often their passions and ambitions assume control.

Serious inconvenience resulted from the crowding of these unfortunate people in our billeting areas. We wished to do everything possible for their comfort and were able by readjustments to increase the accommodations in towns by about 15 per cent to make room for them.

Although our experience in coördination of supply between ourselves and the French had already proved that it was distinctly economical as compared with the separate and independent systems, the British were slow to accept it. However, with the help of Martin Egan, Dwight Morrow, and Paul Cravath, a conference was arranged in London between Dawes and the Chief Supply Officer of the British, Lieutenant General Cowans, representing the army, which resulted in the following letter from Lord Milner definitely committing the British to the principle:

"War Office, Whitehall, SW.
"29 May, 1918.

"My dear General:

"Colonel Dawes has handed me the memorandum of May 22, 1918, signed by M. Clemenceau and yourself. We have all been in hearty accord with your aim to coördinate, so far as possible, the use of facilities and the distribution of supplies among the Allied Armies in France. Doubts, however, have been expressed by our Supply Departments as to the extent to which a unification of supplies and facilities would be practicable. I am glad to find that our hesitation, based on these doubts, has been due to a misunderstanding of the purpose and scope of your proposal.

"We now understand from your memorandum and Colonel Dawes' explanations:

"1. That your plan is intended to apply only to supplies and facilities of the Armies in France.

"2. That the avoidance of duplicate facilities in docks, warehouses, and railroads, and the proper distribution of labor supplies, are among the things of immediate importance. It is not intended that the Board shall interfere with the ration or with the distributing machinery of the respective armies, nor indeed with any other matters relating to their internal administration.

"3. That the requirement that the decision of the proposed Board shall be unanimous has been introduced in order to leave each army free to determine whether the principle of coördination is or is not applicable to any given case. For instance, your army might have what seemed like a surplus of foodstuffs on hand, but which was not a real surplus because of your distance from your base and the period that might elapse before further supplies arrive. The same might be true in the case of our army. The representative of each army on the proposed Board is therefore left free to exercise his own judgment in voting on such questions.

"4. That the decisions of the Board, when unanimous, are to be communicated, through proper military channels, to the Chiefs of the appropriate departments of the respective armies, and shall be given effect through them.

"If I am right in the above interpretation of your views, I shall be happy to give the proposed system an immediate trial and to nominate a representative on the Board. I assume that the Italians and the Belgians will also be invited to be represented on it.

"Yours sincerely,

"Milner."

The sphere of coöperation as expressed in the letter from Lord Milner, while indicating acquiescence in our proposal, did not entirely reach our conception of the possibilities. We believed that consideration of the control of supplies at the source would become necessary eventually. Although now the principle was made applicable only to supplies actually in military hands, yet it had received distinct recognition and its larger application was open to further discussion and correspondence. The coördination of many facilities and supplies in common use under direct charge of the respective armies was soon to become an established fact.

CHAPTER XXXII

Fears for Safety of Paris—Belleau Wood Taken—Pétain's Appreciation —Marne Counteroffensive Indicated—Visit Clemenceau and Foch— French Advance in Counterattack—Anniversary of Arrival in France —Discipline in Our Army—Italian Successes—Foch Requests American Regiments—Cables Regarding Promotions—Information to Press —Letter to Secretary of War

(Diary) Paris, Sunday, June 9, 1918. Conferred with staff on Friday regarding situation. The 2d Division is engaged in severe fighting in Belleau Wood. General Foch desires to leave five of our divisions with the British for the present. Hospital arrangements proceeding satisfactorily on 15 per cent bed status. Have recommended privileges of War Risk Insurance for war correspondents.

Colonel Groome lunched with us yesterday; also Mr. Otto Kahn, who referred to my position as embracing duties of the Secretaries of War, Treasury, and State combined. General Pétain has agreed to organization of American corps near Château-Thierry.

Arrived Paris last night; saw Clemenceau this morning. He spoke of new threat on Paris by the German attack on Montdidier-Noyon front. Went to Bombon for conference with General Foch. French communiqué highly compliments Americans in Château-Thierry region.[1]

MY position in France required the consideration of many questions of international importance, but as they all, either directly or indirectly, affected the formation, maintenance, and use of our army in coöperation with the Allied armies, it did not seem to me that the decisions involved could be made by any authority in France not under my control. Moreover, I could always count on the loyal aid of Ambassador Sharp when anything requiring his intervention came up, which was

[1] It said: "American infantry showed itself skilled in maneuvering. The courage of officers and men approached recklessness. * * * The courage of the combatant troops is equaled only by the superb coolness of some of their medical corps who, in a perfect hail of bullets, gave first aid to the wounded."

frequently the case. He was very helpful in the procurement of supplies outside of Allied countries, especially Spain and Switzerland. General Bliss, our Military Representative on the Supreme War Council, sat in a civil capacity also, in that he transmitted to Washington those questions of Allied policy that required the President's approval.

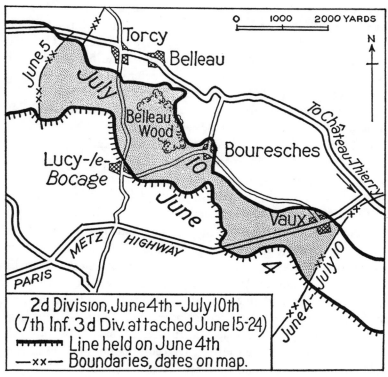

2d Division, June 4th – July 10th
(7th Inf. 3d Div. attached June 15-24)
▬▬▬ Line held on June 4th
—xx— Boundaries, dates on map.

As a result of the German successes against the French, something akin to a panic prevailed in Paris. Probably a million people left during the spring and there was grave apprehension among the officials lest the city be taken. Plans were made to remove the French government offices to Bordeaux and we were prepared to move those of our own that were in Paris. At the request of General Bliss, trucks were placed at his disposal for the removal, in case of necessity, of his offices and those of his British colleagues on the Supreme War Council. It was a matter of considerable satisfaction to feel that our base ports, lines of communication and supply areas were outside of the zone of the British armies and south of Paris, and hence comparatively safe.

The attacks begun on June 6th by the 2d Division culminated in the capture of the last German positions in Belleau Wood by its Marine Brigade and of Vaux by its Regular Infantry Brigade. The fighting during most of this period was intense. The German lines were favorably located on commanding ground and were made more formidable by the extensive use of machine guns, especially in Belleau Wood. The success of this division against an enemy determined to crush it was obtained with but little assistance from the tired French divisions on its flanks.

In the initial advance, the Marine Brigade (Harbord) captured Bouresches, and the Infantry Brigade (Lewis) made substantial gains. The progress during the next few days was slow but steady. On the 15th, the 7th Infantry, 3d Division, was attached to the 2d Division, relieving the Marines in the Wood, and holding the front there for a few days. The Marines then reëntered the line beginning on the night of the 21st. After an all-day artillery preparation on the 25th, they drove the enemy from his last position in Belleau Wood during the late afternoon and night. Meanwhile, the Infantry Brigade continued its attacks, and on July 1st, in a brilliantly executed operation, captured the village of Vaux. The division made no further advance. By July 9th, when it was relieved by the 26th Division, its lines had been consolidated on high ground captured from the enemy.[1]

Our first three divisions to participate in active operations had all distinguished themselves; the 1st at Cantigny, the 2d at Belleau Wood, and the 3d at Château-Thierry. Their achievements gave an indication of what trained American troops would do. Following, as it did, the crisis of May 27th, the conduct of these

[1] The casualties in the division were about 9,500. Over 1,600 prisoners were captured.

divisions was loudly acclaimed by the French, and, for the time being, it had a stimulating effect upon their morale.

With the transfer of activities to the French front northeast of Paris, our plan to build up an American corps near Amiens had become impracticable. It now appeared possible, however, to form at least a corps and perhaps an army somewhere along the Marne salient, preferably in the vicinity of Château-Thierry. I therefore suggested to General Pétain that we should bring other divisions to join with the 2d and 3d for that purpose, and accordingly the relief of the 26th and 42d from the inactive front was immediately ordered. The assembly of four American divisions on the Marne front would more than offset the recent French losses. General Pétain, in his letter accepting my offer, said in part:

"I must express my deep gratitude for the prompt and very important aid which you are bringing in the present crisis. The American troops already engaged in the battle have the unanimous admiration of the whole French Army. The power of the effort which your country is at present showing, as well as the resolute and generous spirit with which you enter the struggle are, for the Allies— and above all for France—a comfort in the grave times through which we are passing, and a pledge of hope for the future."

As the efficiency of certain units of our forces had been fully proved, it seemed to me that the time had arrived for us to utilize our troops to good advantage by combining them in an independent effort. It was a moment of depression for the Allies; but the large numbers of American troops arriving, and their success so far had helped Allied morale. The Germans had been stopped at the Marne, and their position in that salient was inherently weak. I felt that we should not give the enemy time to re-form and rest his forces, but should, if possible, take the initiative ourselves. It was with this thought especially in mind that I suggested to Pétain that we should assemble a number of American divisions in the Château-Thierry sector. I had already proposed to Foch that they should be utilized in a counterattack against the salient. It was obvious that a blow at the enemy's line south of Soissons, if successful, would compel him to retire. Such an attack would have the effect of threatening his rear, in so far as that part of his force in the vicinity of Château-Thierry was concerned. I was very eager that our troops should be allowed to undertake such an attack.

The German situation in the sector was set forth in my telegram to the War Department, as follows:

"June 11, 1918.

"The arrival of the enemy's troops on the Marne and their establishment from the vicinity of Château-Thierry to Verneuil on the night of May 29th to 30th definitely marks the end of the first phase of the Aisne Offensive. The enemy had secured by the first stroke a tactically important objective—a defensive flank on the Marne—and possessed a strategically important objective, the control of our main line of lateral communication with Verdun. Thus in about two and one-half days from the time of the original attack the reason for directing the axis of the attack straight south ceased to exist.

"Since the night of May 29th to 30th, the direction of the attack has changed pronouncedly to the southwest. To this must be added the operations to the northwest of Soissons which began on the night of May 30th-31st, the general direction of which is also southwest. It seems clearly established that so long as the enemy is allowed to retain the initiative his future operations will be directed on Paris. The situation in the salient Noyon to Reims is important. The keys to the transportation systems of the salient are the rail and road centers, Soissons and Reims. Without these the enemy will be confronted with difficult transportation problems, involving the use of motor trucks on the sixteen roads, for the most part cross-country roads, now available to him. The possession of Soissons has proved an enormous relief to the enemy since by means of it, from Rethel to Laon, he can reach every other sector of his new lines. Nevertheless, the enemy's transportation situation cannot be satisfactorily adjusted until he has taken Reims; hence the recent heavy attack on this important center."

On the morning of my call on M. Clemenceau the fourth great German offensive of the year had started between Montdidier and the Oise and reports indicated that it was meeting with considerable success. In our conversation, I asked him what he thought would be the result if Paris should fall. He said that he and Mr. Lloyd George had discussed that possibility and had reached the conclusion that of course they would do everything in their power to save Paris, but if it should be lost they would go on fighting, as "above Paris is France, and above France is civilization."

He expressed himself satisfied with the agreement reached at the special conference at Versailles and I recall distinctly his more than usual graciousness that day as he said, "You need never make an appointment with me at any time, but just come whenever you wish and you shall always see me." As I was leaving, he came to the door with me, and I said, "Well, Mr. President, it may not look encouraging just now but we are certain to win in the end." He clung to my hand and in a tone that showed the utmost solicitude, he replied, "Do you really think that? I am glad to hear you say it." This was the first and only time that I ever sensed any misgivings in his mind. Notwithstanding our occasional rather heated discussions on the use to be made of American troops, I admired him greatly. It always seemed to me that he typified the true spirit of confidence and courage of the French people.

I then motored, with Boyd, to General Foch's headquarters at Bombon, arriving just in time for luncheon. We took up my proposal to form an American corps near Château-Thierry, and he at once agreed to it. He spoke especially of the fine work of our troops. I asked him how a German drive which threatened or perhaps captured Paris would affect the armies and the people. His reply was almost word for word like M. Clemenceau's, showing that they had considered it together. He, too, was certain that the armies would go on with the war. Foch spoke so positively and with such evident feeling that I was moved to get up and vigorously shake his hand. I said that his attitude was gratifying and that the French people could be certain that the American Government and people would be with them to the last. Everybody was in an agreeable mood, and as I departed Foch asked me to come to see him oftener and talk over matters in general and to continue to let him know when anything turned up that I did not like.

Looking back to those days, one must say that although the French regard their country as the very keystone of the arch of civilization it might have been difficult to keep them in the war if Paris had fallen. While no one could have openly suggested any such thought at that time, some French officers felt that the loss of Paris would cause the Ministry to fall; to be replaced by a Ministry in favor of peace.

(Diary) Chaumont, Thursday, June 13, 1918. Lunched with General Bliss on Monday at Versailles. Saw General di Robilant [1] there and discussed transportation of our regiment to Italy. Recommended adoption of wound chevron. Approved request from Foch that 4th and 28th Divisions should be held near Villers-Cotterêts.[2]

Visited 1st Division on Tuesday. French Third Army gained one and a quarter miles in counterattack south of Noyon.

Returned to Chaumont yesterday. Saw General Liggett to-day about I Corps affairs. M. Jules Cambon spending the night with us. Many messages received this first anniversary of my arrival in France.

While the Italian Government was anxious to have American troops, yet so far they had found no sea transportation available to bring them over. Mr. Orlando, the Italian Prime Minister, wanted them sent direct from the States in order that they might go through Italy by rail to show the people that Americans were actually there. Moreover, he wanted them to be other than naturalized Italians for fear the people might doubt their nationality. When we came to consider the details, General di Robilant proposed that they should be transported from New York by Italian shipping, and entered into a lengthy discussion of their plan to send over three or four ships, to which I readily agreed. But it turned out later that the vessels he counted on were already included in the list of those which the British were going to use for carrying our troops. After a delay of about a month, and acting under instructions from Washington, I directed that the 332d Infantry Regiment of the 83d Division, which had recently arrived, should go to Italy by rail.

---

[1] General di Robilant was at that time the Italian Military Representative on the Supreme War Council.

[2] Villers-Cotterêts is located southwest of Soissons, convenient to the western face of the Château-Thierry salient.

The 4th and 28th Divisions, en route from the British area to the Vosges front, were halted in the vicinity of Villers-Cotterêts, the object being to concentrate several of our divisions on the west of the Marne salient, primarily as a precaution against another German movement toward Paris, but ultimately for possible use on the offensive. With the 2d, 3d, 26th, and 42d already in that general region, the 4th and 28th gave us a force equivalent to twelve French divisions, although the latter two were without their artillery.

An encouraging circumstance at the moment was the success of the French in holding von Hutier's attack on the Montdidier-Noyon front. This German offensive was an effort not only to widen the vulnerable Marne pocket but to secure the railway between Compiègne and Soissons and open the way to Paris. The French had anticipated this attack and fought desperately, yielding only under great pressure until the 11th, when, using tanks and quantities of mustard gas, they launched a series of local counterattacks, by which they were able to advance more than a mile on a seven-mile front. In view of their remarkable success in the preceding offensives, the defeat of the Germans and their heavy losses here materially encouraged the Allies. The credit for this brilliant operation by the French must go to General Mangin, one of France's greatest generals.

The anniversary of the arrival of our advance contingent in France was the occasion of many congratulations on the part of the French. It seems worth while to record some of these messages.

"The anniversary of your arrival in France furnishes a happy occasion to address my warmest congratulations to you and the valiant troops which you command and who have so admirably conducted themselves in the recent battles. I beg you to receive the assurance of my best wishes for the continuation of their success.

"RAYMOND POINCARÉ."

"On the anniversary of your arrival in France to take command of the American troops, I wish, my dear General, to express to you once more the greatest admiration for the powerful aid brought by your army to the cause of the Allies. With ever increasing numbers the

American troops cover themselves with glory under your orders in barring the route of the invader. The day is coming when, thanks to the support of your country and the valor of her sons, the enemy, losing the initiative of operations, will be forced to incline before the triumph of our ideals of justice and civilization.

"CLEMENCEAU."

"A year ago you brought us the American sword. To-day we have seen it strike. It is a pledge of certain victory. By it our hearts are more closely united than ever.

"FOCH."

"Your coming to French soil a year ago filled our country with enthusiasm and hope. Accept to-day the grateful homage of our soldiers for the daily increasing aid on the battlefield brought by their American brothers-in-arms. The last battles where the magnificent qualities of courage and military virtue of your troops were demonstrated in so brilliant a manner are a sure guarantee for the future. The day is not far off when the great American Army will play a decisive rôle, to which history calls this Army on the battlefields of Europe.

"Permit me, my dear General, to express to you on this anniversary my entire confidence and assure you of my feelings of affectionate comradeship.

"PÉTAIN."

(Diary) Chaumont, Monday, June 17, 1918. Frequent trench raids on our troops in quiet sectors indicate the enemy's anxiety. Our units, especially the 42d, which has been highly praised by French,[1] have made several successful raids.

---

[1] Although this division had so far served only in the quiet Baccarat sector, the Commanding General of the French VI Corps commended it highly in the following General Order, dated June 15th:

"GENERAL ORDER No. 50

"As the time has come when the 42d U.S.I.D. must leave the Lorraine front, the General commanding the VI Army Corps wishes to show his great appreciation of the excellent military qualities which this division has evidenced as well as the service which it has rendered in the Baccarat sector.

"Its fighting qualities, its ability to utilize and organize terrain, its appreciation of liaison, its systematic organization, the discipline shown by officers and men, and their initiative, all go to prove that this division will henceforth worthily fill its place on the new battle line.

"The General commanding the VI Army Corps wishes to express his sincere thanks to the 42d Division for its valuable coöperation. He especially expresses his gratitude to the distinguished Commander of this Division, General Menoher, to the General

On Saturday took up with General Bethel semi-monthly accumulation of court-martial cases. Brigadier General John A. Lejeune dined with us. Visited hostess house; found telephone girls comfortably situated.

Generals Foch and Weygand and Colonel Reboul lunched with us to-day. Foch had encouraging news from the Italian front, regarding attack begun on Saturday by Austrians on a twelve-mile front. Colonel William Hayward, 369th Regiment (colored),[1] called.

In a new army like ours, if discipline were lacking, the factor most essential to its efficiency would be missing. The army was composed of men representing every walk of life, from the educated professional and business men to those of the various trades and callings, and practically all were without military experience. In the beginning, our army was without the discipline that comes with training. The vast majority of both officers and men were unaccustomed to the restraints necessarily imposed, and unfamiliar with the rules and regulations required to insure good conduct and attention to duty. There existed, however, in general, a distinctly patriotic attitude of mind which made for self-discipline.

Yet, even after considerable military training, men were found in every command who, because of faulty bringing up or waywardness, could not be taught to realize the moral obligations of loyalty and obedience to constituted authority. It was from this class that usually came the offenders, relatively small in number, who gave the most trouble.

Officers under his orders, and to his Staff so brilliantly directed by Colonel MacArthur.

"It is with the deepest regret that the entire VI Army Corps views the departure of the 42d Division. But the affectionate bonds of comradeship which were formed here will not be broken. On our part, a faithful memory will be retained for both the living and the dead of the Rainbow Division; for those who are leaving to take part in other combats as well as for those who, having given their lives so nobly on the fields of the East, now remain there at rest, guarded with all sympathy by France.

"These expressions of highest esteem will surely be still further confirmed in coming battles, in which the future of the free people of the world will be decided.

"May our units, side by side, valiantly contribute to the triumph of Justice and Right.
"General Duport."

[1] Very naturally, the four infantry regiments of the 93d Division (colored), which had been assigned to four French divisions, were anxious to serve with our armies, and I made application for the organization and shipment of the rest of the division, but to no purpose and these regiments remained with the French to the end.

Minor delinquencies due to neglect or inexperience were handled by local commanders, but where moral turpitude and defiance of authority were in evidence trials by courts-martial were necessary. Such courts were ordered by division commanders and officers of that relative rank, who were also empowered in general to approve or disapprove the findings of the courts. Except in cases that originated in separate units not a part of a division or other similar organization, only those in which the penalty imposed was dismissal or death came to me for final action, or for recommendation before being forwarded to the President. In other words, as Commander-in-Chief of an army in the field, I was required to act personally upon, and was empowered to carry into execution, all sentences by courts-martial extending to the dismissal of any but general officers; and likewise, to take final action on all sentences of death adjudged after conviction for murder, rape, mutiny, desertion, and espionage.

At intervals of perhaps a week or two, the accumulated cases on which I had to act were brought before me by the Judge Advocate. There were forty-four sentences of death which reached me for confirmation and but eleven of these, all of them for murder or rape, were confirmed and executed. Of purely military offenses there were only four in which execution was recommended to the President, and none of these were approved by him.

When General Foch came to take luncheon with us on the 17th, he was much encouraged by the improved situation in Italy. The Austrians had attacked over a twelve-mile front on June 15th and succeeded in gaining certain crossings of the Piave, but in contrast to what had happened at Caporetto, the Italians had anticipated their opponents and vigorously confronted them with counter-artillery fire at each of the five main points of contact and had thus prevented more than small gains. Seizing the opportunity to counterattack, the Italians were able, by June 20th, to compel the Austrians to give up their gains. I sent General Diaz a cordial message of congratulations and it is presumed that he received many, as his success was very gratifying to the Allies, who were put at ease for the time being as to affairs on the Italian front.

In speaking of the numbers of Americans arriving, General Foch became a special pleader for the French and suggested that an American regiment be sent to each of their divisions. It would be especially desirable, he thought, thus to strengthen their exhausted units, at least during July. He said that many of the French soldiers had been asking where the Americans were, and this plan would have a beneficial effect on their morale. I could not see the question just as he did, as the effect on our troops would have been the other way, so I gave him no encouragement.

Evidently as an offset to this proposal, he said he was anxious to have an American army serving beside the French armies, to which I at once subscribed, saying that I hoped he would give us every assistance to this end. Due to previous concessions on our part regarding the shipments of infantry, we were already meeting with difficulty in providing auxiliary troops and armament necessary to complete even the more advanced divisions. These units were, nevertheless, rapidly increasing in efficiency, as shown by the complimentary orders and the general comment on their conduct after they had been tested in both quiet and active sectors.

In handling questions of policy it was not always easy to get my views before the Secretary of War in their proper light. This was especially true in attempting to cover important matters by cable. My experience led to the conclusion that the best way to reach him was through direct mail correspondence, as sometimes cabled requests were apparently acted on without his knowledge and in a manner adverse to our best interests. One of the questions involved was that of promotion to the grade of general officer. After frequent attempts to secure the promotion of several colonels whose abilities had been thoroughly tested in active service and having failed to get their names included in the list of promotions, I sent a cable asking for a reconsideration of my recommendations, suggesting that my cable be shown to the

Secretary in person. I also wrote him giving my point of view and explaining just what the promotion of tried officers with the armies would mean to the efficiency of my whole command. Referring to the matter in one of his letters, it was evident that he had not seen the full cable correspondence, as he replied in his usual cordial manner that it was his intention to give every consideration to the men of proved efficiency in France. Of course, this was all that I could ask but the principle was not altogether followed by his subordinates.

One subject that caused Secretary Baker some anxiety was that of giving the press news of our operations in a way that would meet the persistent demands, without disclosing the numbers or location of our forces, and which would "prevent the War Department from being regarded as suppressing and withholding news." Although necessarily never entirely satisfactory from either the news point of view or from that of morale building at home, this matter was adjusted as far as practicable through the distribution to the press by the War Department of material contained in the periodical communiqués published from my headquarters and cabled to the Secretary. These, and such information from my confidential cables on the situation as the War Department thought might be safely given out, furnished thereafter the basis of information to the press at home. It was, of course, fully recognized among the armies that communiqués rarely gave either fully or frankly all the facts. A complete statement in a communiqué might often have discouraged one's own people and encouraged the enemy. It was, therefore, natural that communiqués by opposing armies reporting the same engagement were often widely at variance.

A consideration of the question of supply for our forces, spread as they were over different parts of the battle line, led the Secretary of War to the same conclusion that I had reached. This was that there should be some coördination in the matter among the Allied armies. Mr. Baker wrote:

"* * * It looks as though an arrangement will ultimately have to be made either for a *common supply system* or else * * * the British will undertake to supply all the troops from the Channel up to a given point, the French from that point to another point, and the Americans the sector farthest east."

At that moment our forces were scattered all over France, some with the British and some with the French, the larger proportion being under our own command.

His inquiries and suggestions were taken up by letter, along with other matters uppermost at the time:

"June 18, 1918.

"Dear Mr. Secretary:

"Although I sent you a cablegram regarding the subjects discussed in your letter of May 13th, it does not seem to cover them quite fully enough, again illustrating the difficulties of expressing one's thoughts fully by cable.

"On the question of promotions, I feel sure that all concerned are prompted by the sole desire of selecting men who are best fitted for the work in hand. To make clear my purpose in writing you, permit me to say that in my recommendations of men in active service here it seemed to me that as their abilities to a certain extent have been tested in active service, we should be more likely to obtain efficiency in the new grades than if we should select men without such experience. I do not at all wish to intimate that promotions should be limited to men in France. Such a system would be manifestly impracticable and unfair, as well as discouraging to the hopes of good men still in the States. Yet, where you have men with experience available, it would be equally unfair to promote inexperienced men over their heads.

"As to establishing a 'Permanent Intelligence Department for the Signal Corps,' I quite agree with you that the difficulties of conducting aircraft construction by cable are well-nigh insuperable, and believe that the plan you suggest will help us over the difficulties. I need not assure you that any members of the aviation corps sent over by you for any purpose will always receive the very heartiest coöperation by their fellows on this side. I think the plan should enable us to speed up the aviation program, now very short of what was expected. A cable has just been received to-day regulating an exchange of officers for the very purpose of coördinating work between here and the States.

"With reference to the allotment of engines to the Navy, the correspondence between yourself and the Secretary of the Navy clears up my mind, as I cabled you a day or two ago, and we should be in a position to get harmonious coöperation between the Navy and Army Air Services from now on. General Patrick, the new head of our Air Service, is in London in conference with Admiral Sims regarding these questions and I have no doubt they will arrive at a satisfactory arrangement.

"In this connection, however, I wish to call attention to the fact that when the allotment of Liberty engines for the Navy was made, it was upon the theory that the production would reach certain estimates. We now find ourselves disappointed in that the supply of airplanes by the French has fallen off and we are face to face with a military crisis which demands the use of all airplanes possible. The enemy seems to have the advantage when he cares to use it and this adds to the odds he otherwise has over the Allies. We should meet this crisis on land as the success of the Allied Armies is at stake, and postpone the supply of engines for the Navy if necessary. The Naval program can have no effect upon the present emergency on the Western Front, and can only influence the final result. The situation is such as to warrant a reconsideration of the allotments, and I hope you may see your way to present the case to the Naval authorities and secure for us the Liberty engines we had expected.

"Regarding the distribution of news, I believe the matter has been placed on a satisfactory basis. Our newspaper men here have raised no protest against the plan of issuing our communiqué, as they understand that our cable is given out in Washington to the whole press.

"There have been requests here for the number of men we have in France, but I have in all cases declined to accede. The demands of the press at home are also insistent, and they are not so easy to decline. While we are exerting every possible effort to put trained men into action, there is indeed much to be said in favor of giving the people the facts. Just now it is very heartening to our Allies and has perhaps the opposite effect upon the enemy. But our Allies conceal their numbers and as our forces increase they will expect us to keep ours secret, and I think myself that, from a military standpoint, we must before long take the same view.

"I have taken up this matter of publication in the *Stars and Stripes* of certain military information and find that nothing has been published in that weekly recently that has not been either cabled home in our daily communiqués or by correspondents for publication in the daily press at home. The press men of course go much more into small details than we do in our cables. If any matter has escaped, it has been an oversight, as it is not the intention to publish in the

Stars and Stripes any exclusive matter or anything that has not been already published at home.

"As to the preferential shipment of infantry and machine gun units, I think that we have now reached the limit of those demands, although I thought the same thing last month. My reason for the conclusion is that both the French and British drafts will be available in August and September, so that after July they should not call upon us to supply infantry or machine gun units to fill up their divisions. I might add here on this subject that our men are almost universally against serving with the British or French and all clamor to serve under our own flag.

*   *   *   *   *   *   *

"With high esteem and warm personal regard, I remain, as always,
"Yours faithfully,

"JOHN J. PERSHING."

"P.S.

"With reference to sending over Mr. Stettinius as a member of the Munitions Board, the more I think of the proposal the more it appeals to me. Mr. Stettinius' broad acquaintance among Inter-Allied countries and his experience in handling just this line of work seems to me to fit him especially as your representative on the Munitions Board.

"This is a very broad subject which seems to me will become more and more complicated as time goes on. Board after board, and committee after committee are being piled one on top of the other and a state of confusion exists that only a man of Mr. Stettinius' abilities can straighten out, so far as we are concerned. I hope that you may send him over.

"His presence here would give great strength to our end of the program, which is destined to be a very important one. I have seen the telegrams sent by Mr. McFadden and Mr. Cravath, who were evidently brought into this by Mr. Loucheur. In the meantime, I have appointed General Wheeler as our representative until the question could be decided by you.

"Always sincerely,

"JOHN J. PERSHING."

CHAPTER XXXIII

Movements of Divisions—Allied Morale Dangerously Low—Sixty-six Division Program—Five Million Tons Shipping Required—Very Large Expansion Necessary—Progress of Services of Supply—Military Board of Allied Supply—Letter to Secretary of War on Urgency of Situation —Visit Troops in Vosges—Training with French and British of Slight Value—Physical Activity Required of General Officers—Colored Troops

(Diary) Chaumont, Tuesday, June 18, 1918. Called staff and supply officers together this morning and outlined plan to expand army to 3,000,000 men.

General Barnett, Chief of Marine Corps, recommends formation entire Marine division, but the 2d Division cannot be broken up after its fine record. The Navy will furnish a number of 14-inch guns, railway mounts and personnel. Shipment of 100 locomotives and 2,500 cars per month seems assured.

THE demands for American divisions were pressing. The 1st, 2d, and 3d had already become actively engaged, the 1st being slated to go to the reserve near the Château-Thierry salient when relieved from Cantigny. The 2d was still in line at Belleau Wood and the 3d south of the Marne. General Foch had asked for five of the recently arrived divisions that had been training with the British and I had agreed. While en route to the quiet Vosges sector to relieve French divisions, the 4th and 28th had been diverted to the reserve near the western face of the Marne salient. The 35th had moved to the vicinity of Épinal, and the 77th was about to enter the trenches in the Baccarat sector to replace the 42d, which was to reënforce Gouraud's Army east of Reims. The 82d was on its way to the Toul sector to relieve the 26th, which in turn was soon to replace the 2d. Thus there were three American divisions in quiet sectors and seven either in the battle line or held in readiness to meet any eventuality which might result from further activity of the Germans in the great wedge they had driven toward Paris.

The British were displeased at the transfer of our divisions from their area, claiming the right to retain them by reason of having brought them over. When Foch inquired of the conditions under which these troops were serving with the British, my reply made it clear that in the emergency he had entire authority to direct where they should go, as without it the supreme command would fail.

The rapid succession of German offensives had materially reduced the Allied powers of resistance, depressed their morale, and caused the darkest misgivings among them. They grew more and more fearful lest the enemy might still have untold reserves ready to swell his forces. Their low morale was shown in the conversation of many of their soldiers returning from the front to the rest areas. We have seen how the retiring French in the Marne sector expressed themselves concerning the situation. Reports from the British front were no better. Their troops continually told our men who were with them for training that we had come too late and that our entry into the battle would only postpone Allied defeat. This attitude seemed so alarming that I took steps to prevent such a spirit from affecting our army by promptly reporting the facts to Allied authorities. The prevalence of such sentiment was another important reason for opposition to any form of amalgamation.

We had fallen far short of the expectations of the preceding November when I had asked Foch and Robertson to join me in an appeal for twenty-four trained American divisions by the following June. It is small wonder that the Allies were now so insistent in urging increased and continuous shipments of men, trained or untrained. So serious was the Allied situation regarded that it was no longer a demand for twenty-four divisions but for one hundred. It is probable that the enormity of this request was not fully realized, or else the Allies had greatly exaggerated ideas of our power of accomplishment, surprising as it actually proved to be. A brief calculation of the demands of the Prime Ministers showed that they were asking for approximately 4,000,000 combatant troops by the following spring, which, augmented by those required for the Services of Supply, conservatively calculated for a well-balanced force campaigning in a foreign country under the circumstances that surrounded us, would increase the total to at least 5,000,000 men. The American combatant force would have equalled 200 divisions of the Allies, and their apprehension may be imagined when we realize that this was greater by one-fourth than the combined Allied army of 162 divisions then on the Western Front.

Although it is unlikely that this number could have been either transported, equipped, or supplied, it was imperative to lay plans for bringing over all we could. After giving the question careful study, it seemed to me that 3,000,000 men would be the limit we could hope to reach by the spring of 1919. Roughly speaking, this would provide at least sixty-six, or possibly seventy, combatant divisions. As we had hitherto made estimates for a total force of 2,000,000 men, it was necessary to make new calculations on the increased basis and begin the work of expansion everywhere in the A.E.F. accordingly.

In order to carry out such a program, the amount of passenger shipping then serving us would have to be retained and the cargo tonnage would have to be materially increased. Both Mr. Lloyd George and M. Clemenceau thought it would be possible to continue to aid us in shipping sufficiently to keep up the recent rate of troop arrivals, which was about 250,000 per month, and Mr. Graeme Thomson, the British shipping expert, also thought this could be done. In any event, the two Prime Ministers assured me that they would let us have all the shipping they could spare.

To supply the contemplated force of 3,000,000 men, the cargo tonnage would have to be augmented to at least 5,000,000 dead weight tons, and not less than 1,600,000 tons of cargo would have to be discharged monthly. At that moment there were only about 1,500,000 dead weight tons of American shipping in use, but our own yards were beginning to turn out ships more rapidly and it was presumed that construction would continue as long as necessary. However, it was certain that as much as possible of our cargo shipping engaged in commerce would have to be impressed.

The group of officers[1] to whom I outlined the enlarged program were those upon whom the additional burden would fall the heaviest. The spirit with which they accepted it was such as to inspire the utmost confidence in our ability to do our part. There was no word or hint of doubt expressed by any one present that it was excessive, but on the contrary every assurance was given by all that they could meet the new requirements. The ever-increasing demands made upon the various services of supply, transportation, and procurement in the A.E.F. had so far been taken care of in the most praiseworthy manner and the attitude of the entire personnel toward this vastly increased program was no exception. All staff and supply departments consequently instituted studies and investigations and at once began the preparation of new schedules for the guidance of the War Department and ourselves.

My cable sent three days later gave the reasons for fixing the program for the future definitely at 3,000,000 men as a minimum, and urged upon the War Department the utmost effort to meet our immediate needs for the expansion of port facilities and railroads. It also set forth in detail the numbers and classes of troops to be shipped each month from August, 1918, until May, 1919, inclusive. The situation as viewed at that time can perhaps be best shown by quoting part of my cable:

"June 21, 1918.
"The present state of the war under the continued German offensive makes it necessary to consider at once the largest possible military program for the United States. The morale of the French Government and of the High Command is believed to be good but it

[1] Those present at the conference were Maj. Gens. McAndrew, Chief of Staff; Kernan, Commanding Services of Supply; Langfitt, Chief of Utilities, S.O.S.; Brig. Gen. Atterbury, Chief of Transportation; Cols. and Assistant Chiefs of Staff Fox Conner, Operations; Logan, Administration; Moseley, Supply; Col. Dawes, General Purchasing Agent; and Mr. Shearman, Shipping Board.

is certain that the morale of the lower grades of the French Army is distinctly poor. Both the French and British people are extremely tired of the war and their troops are reflecting this attitude in their frequent inability to meet successfully the German attacks. It is the American soldiers now in France upon whom they rely. It is the moral as well as material aid given by the American soldier that is making the continuation of the war possible. Only the continual arrival of American troops and their judicious employment can restore the morale of our Allies and give them courage. The above represents the views of the Allied Military leaders as told me in person by General Foch himself, and I believe it is also the view of the civil leaders. We must start immediately on our plans for the future and be ready to strike this fall in order to tide us over till spring, when we should have a big army ready. The war can be brought to a successful conclusion next year if we only go at it now. From a purely military point of view it is essential that we make this effort, especially for the reasons above stated and on account of the grave possibility that the enemy will obtain supplies and men from Russia before next year.

"To meet the demands imposed by the above plan our minimum effort should be based on sending to France prior to May, 1919, a total force, including that already here, of 66 divisions (or better, if possible) together with the necessary corps and army troops, service of supply troops, and replacements. This plan would give an available force of about 3,000,000 soldiers for the summer campaign of 1919, and if this force were maintained, would in conjunction with our Allies give us every hope of concluding the war in 1919."

The organization of the S.O.S. was working at high pressure, the number of men in the various activities having grown from about 100,000 on March 1st to 175,000 on June 1st.[1] Every endeavor was being made to overcome the lack of men and material from which we constantly suffered. As to sea transport, we now had the exclusive use of thirty-nine berths at the most important ports, including ten of our own construction. An average of 244

[1] The chiefs of supply and transportation departments at this time were: Brig. Gens. Harry L. Rogers, Chief Quartermaster; Merritte W. Ireland, Chief Surgeon; Harry Taylor, Chief of Engineers; Charles B. Wheeler, Chief of Ordnance; Edgar Russel, Chief Signal Officer; Mason M. Patrick, Chief of Air Service; Maj. Gen. William C. Langfitt, Chief of Utilities; Brig. Gens. William W. Atterbury, Director General of Transportation; Edgar Jadwin, Director Construction and Forestry; Cols. Herbert Deakyne, Director Division of Light Railways and Roads; Francis H. Pope, Director Motor Transport Corps; Charles G. Dawes, General Purchasing Agent.

ships weekly were being discharged. The ports of St. Nazaire and Bordeaux were receiving 10,000 tons of supplies daily, principally consisting of armament, equipment, food, and some forage; while construction of trackage and shelter was slowly making progress.

The railways, employing the operators we had of our own both on the roads and in our principal railway shops at Tours and Nevers, were working with greater efficiency in conjunction with the French, although the demands for troop movements were creating an ever-increasing burden. The interior storage plants at Gièvres and Montierchaume had been expanded and were busy with the receipt and segregation of the accumulation of different classes of supplies provided by the Quartermaster Corps and Medical Department, not to mention the enormous quantities of Engineer and Signal Corps material.

Aviation had finally got started, though Liberty engines were not forthcoming in the numbers promised. Aviation centers at Romorantin and Issoudun, at the rear, and at Colombey-les-Belles, near the front, were busy places. Many of our aviators were in active service or ready for it and our mechanics were assembling and testing the D.H. planes that had begun to arrive in limited numbers from home.

The organization for the management of truck transportation was well under way, with main and subsidiary parks and extensive repair shops located at convenient points. Although only a small proportion of trucks, automobiles, and accessories had reached us, it was reported that the docks at Hoboken were crowded with them ready for shipment.

Some new construction and the adaptation of existing buildings for the Medical Department were gradually increasing hospital accommodations, about 40,000 beds then being available. The erection of great storehouses for the Ordnance Department was being hastened to meet the accumulation of ammunition of all calibers and extra equipment that would be necessary.

The activities of the Signal Corps were directed toward the extension and improvement of communications and the accumulation of material for use in our operations. The Forestry Department was extending its operations to almost every part of France, and even with the shortage of personnel was giving valuable aid in meeting our own and French requirements for heavy and light construction. The Chemical Warfare Service was energetically at work to discover new gases and to improve upon the British gas mask, which was never fully satisfactory. Its inadequate personnel was carrying on instruction throughout the A.E.F. in the use of gas, both in offensive and defensive operations.

In the establishment of the Military Board of Allied Supply, the principle of coöperation as to supplies in common use among the armies was recognized after prolonged debate and discussion. The Board consisted of one representative from each of the Allied armies. It was simply the representative body of the several supply departments of the respective armies and had nothing whatever to do with actual procurement. It was expected to study questions of supply and adopt proper measures for the coordination of Allied resources and utilities. Our supply officers were enjoined to utilize the services of the Board in seeking the equitable allotment of supplies and in coöperating with corresponding supply officers of the Allied armies. Colonel Dawes, who had charge in a more limited sphere of the coördination of our own supply departments, was detailed as the American member of the Board, and to him in coöperation with Colonel Payot, the French member, should largely go the credit for its success.

In order to emphasize further the urgency of beginning on the expanded plan and to put it before the Secretary of War directly, the following paragraphs were included in a letter which I wrote to him on June 18th:

"I now wish to take up a subject of very great importance. That is the burning one of getting troops over here and forming an army as rapidly as possible. I think it is imperative that our whole program for the next ten or twelve months be reconstructed. The Department's estimate of 91,000 men per month after August is not nearly as much as we must do. Mr. Secretary, I cannot emphasize this point too forcibly. We should have at least three million men in France by next April ready for the spring and summer campaign. To achieve this will involve the shipment of 250,000 men per month for the eight months ending April 1st. This is the smallest program that we should contemplate. The situation among our Allies is such that unless we can end the war next year we are likely to be left practically alone in the fight. If further serious reverses come to us this year it is going to be very difficult even to hold France in the war.

"The morale of both the French and British troops is not what it should be. The presence of our troops has braced them up very much but their staying powers are doubtful. Our 2d and 3d Divisions actually stopped the Germans. The French were not equal to it. I fear that I must put some of our regiments into the weaker French divisions, temporarily, to give them courage.

"After checking the German offensive, we must be prepared to strike as soon as possible. The German divisions are growing weaker and their manpower is running low. The German people would be inclined to make peace if they felt a few very heavy blows. We should be ready to give them. On the other hand, if we do not hasten, and the war is allowed to drag along during next year and the year after, we shall run a very great risk that Germany will recuperate by conscripting manpower from the Western Provinces of Russia. The British and French Governments are alarmed about this, as you know, and I consider it a real danger.

"Then, we must bear in mind the effect of a long war upon our own people. The idea seems prevalent at home that the war is going to be finished within a year and our people are wrought up and wish to see a big effort at once. But if we do not make ourselves strong enough on this front to assume the offensive and push the war to a finish, there is going to be criticism and dissatisfaction at home and a general letting down of our war spirit. Moreover, by using a large force and ending the war we shall avoid the large losses that have so dreadfully depleted our Allies. Let us take every advantage of the high tide of enthusiasm and win the war.

"I think that with proper representations as to the necessity for shipping, the British would do all they could to assist us. In fact, Sir Graeme Thomson said he thought the British would be able to continue the recent shipping schedule indefinitely. On our side, we should demand a greater amount of American tonnage than has hitherto been allotted to the army from the sum total of our available shipping, which is constantly increasing. Our shipping advisers here say that several hundred thousand tons can be added to the army allotment by proper paring.

"As to the preparation of this new army, may I not beg of you to consider a draft of 2,000,000 men by December 1st? My recent cable asking that 1,500,000 be called out should now be increased to 2,000,000. They should be called out, beginning now, at the rate of 400,000 per month for the next five months. We should not again be without trained men as we find ourselves now. Every possible means should be exhausted to train, clothe, and equip this force by the end of the year. These are strong words and the force looks large, but we are face to face with the most serious situation that has ever confronted a nation, and it must be met at any sacrifice and without any delay.

"I think we must bring women into our factories, transforming the whole country into an organization to push the war. The British could help on clothing. As to munitions, it matters little whether we have a particular kind of artillery; if we cannot get the French, we should take the British. The same can be said of small arms and personal equipment. If our ordnance cannot furnish them, the French and British have them. So in equipment and armament, there should be no delay.

"I am having a detailed study made of the supply and shipping questions involved, especially as to the amount of supplies that can be obtained in Europe. The pooling program will soon be in operation and I think we shall be able to obtain a greater amount of supplies here than we had anticipated. Spain is practically a virgin field for us which is as yet undeveloped and which, with diplomatic handling, should yield much more than she has hitherto yielded. I shall look into this further.

"The question of accommodations for our troops may have to be considered. If that stands in the way, then I am in favor of asking Congress to permit the billeting of troops. The French people are standing for it even by the forces of two foreign nations, why should not we at home be willing to billet our own troops among our own people?

"As to handling everything that must be sent over under this program, I stand ready now, without waiting for detailed study, to say that we can do it. The supply question will be less difficult as the pooling and the feeding of our troops by the Allies develop. The great port of Marseille is largely unused and will handle much additional tonnage. Our port construction and port facilities are progressing, the railroads are getting better and storage is becoming easier because the French are finding more and more room. The horse question will also probably be worked out here. So that there need be no hesitation in adopting the plan. We should do all that is humanly possible to carry it out.

"There is nothing so dreadfully important as winning this war and every possible resource should be made immediately available. Mr. Secretary, the question is so vital to our country, and the necessity of winning the war is so great, that there is no limit to which we should not go to carry out the plan I have outlined for the next ten months, and we must be prepared to carry it on still further after that at the same rate or maybe faster.

"I have outlined the plan as the least we should count upon to insure success, and I hope, with your strong support, that the President will approve it."

(Diary) Chaumont, Saturday, June 22, 1918. Recommendation for insurance privileges war correspondents disapproved. Orders published Thursday regarding Military Board of Allied Supply.

Have spent three days looking over divisions in the Vosges. 32d Division (Haan) is promising. Organization III Corps (Wright) going forward satisfactorily. Stopped at headquarters 42d Division (Menoher), at Châtel-sur-Moselle; also at Arches, headquarters of the 35th (McClure); and at Baccarat, 77th (Duncan). Found them making progress. Our officers insist that service with tired French divisions is of little benefit. Units now arriving much reduced in strength and deficient in training. Colored soldiers highly incensed that false stories of their mistreatment are being circulated at home.

The 32d, 35th, 42d, and 77th Divisions were engaged in training under the recently organized III Corps. Special effort was being made to hasten their preparation in both staff and line in anticipation of an early call for more serious service. My impressions of the troops inspected on this particular visit were favorable, although quite a number of officers were found unfamiliar with the principles of tactical leadership. In such hastily trained units this was hardly surprising, especially in view of the known defects of the instruction at home. Many were found with only slight appreciation of the natural defensive possibilities of a given position. Some battalion and even regimental commanders had not thought to ascertain the exact location of their front lines and of course had failed to work out the details of plans for defense.

My predilection for detailed instruction in minor tactics, growing out of my previous personal supervision of training in both small and large units, led me quickly to discover deficiencies. On all these visits, I emphasized the importance of understanding the basic principles of both offensive and defensive movements, laid emphasis on the question of mutual support among units, and above all stressed the importance of establishing every possible means of communication between the different elements of a command.

So much depends upon the leader of an organization that the process of selection of the more capable and the elimination of the unfit were constantly in operation. A competent leader can get efficient service from poor troops, while on the contrary an incapable leader can demoralize the best of troops.

Training in quiet sectors in association with French divisions, upon which the French laid so much stress, had proved disappointing during the past months, as their units coming out of the battle line, worn and weary, failed to set an example of the aggressiveness which we were striving to inculcate in our men. Of course our own officers were immediately responsible, but they were frequently handicapped by the lack of energy of tired French officers. After considerable experience, it was the inevitable conclusion that, except for the details of trench warfare, training under the French or British was of little value.

The adherence at home to the idea of concentrating on instruction in trench warfare, as advocated by the French instructors, placed practically the entire burden of training in open warfare upon us in France. This was not easy to accomplish under the circumstances in the brief time remaining after troops began to arrive in large numbers. In this regard the following extract from a cablegram sent to Washington seems pertinent:

"June 20, 1918.

"The reasons for sending men with insufficient instruction are fully appreciated in view of the large increase in number of troops sent over during past three months, and the inequalities in training are fully considered here. The plan of separating recently drafted men from divisions and giving them special training for a longer period than the others before being put in the line has already been adopted. It will, however, considerably reduce the fighting strength of several divisions to be ordered into the line.

"This situation emphasizes the importance of establishing the rule at home of keeping divisions intact, both as to officers and enlisted men, from the time they are organized until they are sent to France. The plan of using divisions through which to pass large numbers of men for instruction is very detrimental to thorough training of the divisions. It need not be pointed out that it takes much time to consolidate a division into a homogeneous fighting unit and build up its esprit de corps. Almost without exception, division commanders complain of the methods that have been followed. I recommend that in future the training of replacements and of special troops of all kinds be kept distinct from that of divisions.

"Our inspections of divisions recently arrived show that the training is uneven and varies much in different divisions. It appears superficial in many cases and generally lacks spirit and aggressiveness. In most of these divisions little attention has been given to training in open warfare, and in this regard younger officers are especially deficient. The training appears to have been carried on in a perfunctory way and without efficient supervision. The general impression is that division officers have leaned too heavily on French instructors, whose ideas are not ordinarily in accordance with our own."

In response to my objections regarding the practice of the War Department of taking from organized divisions large groups of trained men and replacing them with recruits, the Department cabled in July that the policy of keeping divisions intact would be followed. However, serious harm had already been done, as most of the divisions that served abroad had departed by that time or were sent soon afterwards.

After visits to units that had lately joined, further attention was given to the physical qualifications necessary in our higher officers. The British and French both had commented unfavorably upon the evident inactivity of many of them and even upon the infirmities of some of the division commanders who had been sent over during the preceding months to observe and study conditions at the front. It had been proved over and over again by the Allies that only the strongest could stand the continuous and nerve-racking strain of actual battle. Many of the disasters that had come to the Allies were due in a large part to the lack of energy and alertness of older commanders, who often failed to exercise that eternal personal supervision and tactical direction necessary to success. M. Clemenceau himself, then seventy-six years of age, said that the French had made a serious error in the beginning in retaining old officers in the service, and that later they had to be retired in considerable numbers.

It was a question not merely of being able to pass a perfunctory medical examination, but vigor, stamina, and leadership were demanded. The physical requirements were not fully appreciated by inexperienced medical boards at home. Inactive officers only threw extra burdens upon their staffs. We had long been accustomed in our service to regard a general officer's position as one that did not require activity. Not a few of the older officers, upon being called to high command, had occupied themselves with minor matters, to the neglect of personal supervision of instruction of their commands in battle tactics. It was the exception to find such men equal to the active command of troops. The advisability of selecting younger men to command brigades and divisions was no longer a theory in our service.

Cables from the War Department about this time stated that the colored people were being told that negro soldiers in France were always placed in the most dangerous positions, were being sacrificed to save white troops, and were often left on the field to die without medical attention. It was not difficult to guess the origin of this sort of propaganda. As a matter of fact, none of these troops had been in line except in quiet sectors. Those I had recently seen were in fine spirits and seemed keen for active service. The only colored combat troops in France were those of the 92d Division, then in a quiet sector in the Vosges, and the four infantry regiments of the 93d, each of which was attached to a French division. Several individuals in these units serving with the French had already received the Croix de Guerre for conduct in raids.

My earlier service with colored troops in the Regular Army had left a favorable impression on my mind. In the field on the frontier and elsewhere they were reliable and courageous, and the old 10th Cavalry (colored), with which I served in Cuba, made an enviable record there. Under capable white officers and with sufficient training, negro soldiers have always acquitted themselves creditably.

When told of these rumors, the colored troops were indignant, and later they did everything possible to counteract such false reports. It was gratifying to learn shortly afterward that Congress had passed very positive legislation against that sort of propaganda. The following paragraph from a cable sent at the time is pertinent:

"June 20, 1918.

"Exploit of two colored infantrymen some weeks ago in repelling much larger German patrol, killing and wounding several Germans and winning Croix de Guerre by their gallantry, has roused fine spirit of emulation among colored troops, all of whom are looking forward to more active service. Only regret expressed by colored troops is that they are not given more dangerous work to do. They are especially amused at the stories being circulated that the American colored troops are placed in the most dangerous positions and all are desirous of having more active service than has been permitted them so far."

CHAPTER XXXIV

Conference with Clemenceau and Foch at Chaumont—Relative Allied and
Enemy Strength—Eighty to One Hundred Divisions Recommended—
Foch Again Asks for American Regiments—Not Always Impartial—
Naval Aviation—Progress of Aviation in A.E.F.—Twenty-two Divi-
sions in France—New Corps Completed—Hospitalization for our Cas-
ualties at Château-Thierry Inadequate

(Diary) Chaumont, Sunday, June 23, 1918. M. Clemenceau, General Foch, and M. Tardieu, with Generals Weygand and Mordacq,
came to Chaumont to-day for conference on increase of American manpower. General McAndrew and Colonels Fox Conner and Boyd
were with me. Took Clemenceau to see some of our troops. Foch asks
for our regiments to strengthen French divisions.

M. CLEMENCEAU'S popularity in France was probably
at its height at this time. As this was his first visit to
Chaumont, the people turned out en masse, crowded
into the plaza and gave him a rousing welcome. His reception
within the Hôtel de Ville by the officials, both civil and military,
was marked by eloquent speeches of tribute to his service for
France. In his remarks, M. Clemenceau expressed confidence in
the future and gave the people every encouragement, referring
especially to the increasing forces of Americans.

As we were leaving, a widowed mother of a missing soldier,
her only son, came up in great distress and told M. Clemenceau of
her sorrow. He spoke very tenderly of her patriotic sacrifice,
put his arm gently around her and kissed her cheeks, mingling
his tears with hers. The pathos of this scene touched every heart.

As General Foch and the others were not to arrive until later,
M. Clemenceau and I, driving together, accompanied by Generals
Wirbel and Ragueneau in a separate automobile, went to the
headquarters of the 83d Division, Major General E. F. Glenn
commanding, which was billeted at Montigny, not far from

Chaumont. We saw a battalion at Essey and one at Mandres, the headquarters of Brigadier General T. W. Darrah. During the inspection, M. Clemenceau found in the ranks several men of foreign birth from various countries, which interested him very much. He afterwards chatted with the officers and made a short speech to them and the inhabitants of the village, who had gathered around him.

It was one of those beautiful days that leave a lasting impression, and as we motored along through the rolling country that rose toward the foothills of the Vosges Mountains we fell to discussing the probable situation of the different Allied countries and their relative standing after the war. He went to some length in his conjectures. He said, "Great Britain is finished, and in my opinion she has seen the zenith of her glory." I said, "What makes you think so, Mr. Prime Minister?" He replied, "First of all, the immense drain of the war will make it impossible for her to retain commercial supremacy and, second, the experience of her Colonial troops in this war will make their people more independent and she will lose her control over them." I could not entirely agree with M. Clemenceau's view and said, "Mr. Prime Minister, I think you are mistaken about the British and believe we shall see them fully recover from the effects of the war."

Continuing, I said, "What about France's future?" "Ah! she will once more be the leading power in Europe," he replied. "But you do not mention Germany," said I. He replied, "The Germans are a great people, but Germany will not regain her prestige and her influence for generations." He spoke of the others only casually and made no predictions about them. I remember one expression he used regarding the United States. "Ah! General," he said, "yours is a wonderful country with unlimited possibilities."

His view of the future of France was and is without doubt the dominant one among Frenchmen, especially those of the educated classes. There is no denying the fact that the French as a whole regard themselves as a superior people in many respects. One striking evidence of this is that they lose no opportunity to extol the achievements of their great men. The thought naturally ran through my mind that this attitude of dominance on the part of the French might in some measure account for their inclination to keep the American Army in a subordinate rôle. In any event they never gave up the idea of regarding us as only an associated power, that had come into the war late, to be used as they might dictate.

M. Clemenceau and I went on to discuss the immediate military outlook. I gave him my views regarding the probable situation of the German armies in the Marne salient and pointed out the chance we had for a successful counterattack on its western face. I spoke especially of the strategical effect of a successful blow just south of Soissons and the material results it would have, to say nothing of its stimulating effect on Allied morale. I suggested that we had at least six divisions, and possibly eight, that could be used in such an offensive. The idea that we could strengthen the French with an attacking force of fresh troops equal to sixteen Allied divisions seemed to surprise him, and as the idea made an appeal to his common sense he said he would call Foch's attention to it at once.

Later in the day I reminded General Foch of the suggestion which I had made to him at Sarcus regarding a counteroffensive. He had given instructions, he said, to have a study made, although there was no intimation as to when, where, or whether, it would be undertaken. That part of the German position to which I have referred offered every advantage for the successful outcome of such a move. It will be evident to any one who will glance at the map that once the line there was pierced the German rear would be threatened and their position within the salient would be untenable. The Allies could not have asked for a better chance than the Germans gave them.

Shortly after our return to the château, Generals Foch and Weygand arrived, and after lunch we all went into conference. This meeting was arranged for Sunday to give us plenty of time to go over the whole question of troop requirements. Its particular purpose was to discuss in detail the rate of shipments that would be necessary in order to give the Allies unquestioned superiority the following year. The continuation of shipments up to one hundred divisions, as already recommended by the Prime Ministers—Lloyd George, Clemenceau, and Orlando—formed the basis of French argument. M. Tardieu's estimate of the American problem was accurate, and doubting the possibility of our being able to reach the greater program, he favored reducing the immediate demands, but Clemenceau and Foch were for the 100-division program.

I did not think it possible, from our experience, that we could accomplish so much and gave the opinion that even a force of eighty divisions, or a total combat force of about 3,200,000 men, would probably overtax our facilities of transportation and supply. It was also a question in my mind whether either M. Clemenceau or General Foch really thought that a program calling for one hundred divisions, or even eighty, could be carried out within a reasonable time. At any rate, it was my opinion that the 80-division plan would serve as a goal toward which effort could be directed.

Moreover, it was clearly evident that if the war should be prolonged for any length of time the burden would fall more and more upon us. Hence, there was no question but that we should make a supreme effort to increase our manpower on the Western Front sufficiently to give the Allies superiority under any probable contingency. I was willing to ask for the greater numbers, feeling, however, that the War Department would do wonders if it could carry out even the 66-division [1] plan. In the course of our discussion, M. Clemenceau gave assurance that every possible effort to meet our deficiencies, including those in munitions and aviation, would be made by the French Government.

Germany was believed to have 3,534,000 men on the Western Front at the time, while the combined forces of the Allies in

[1] These estimates were rather general and the numbers stated depended upon the method of calculation. 3,000,000 men would probably have given us seventy divisions, so there was little difference between that total and the total that would have been necessary for an 80-division program.

France, exclusive of Americans, were estimated at 2,909,000, of whom Great Britain had 1,239,000, and France 1,670,000 men. The Germans were supposed to be still bringing troops from the Russian front, but according to Allied information they would not be able to muster more than 340,000 replacements from their own population. The British claimed that in providing 130,000 replacements for June they had reached their limit and said they would not be able to furnish any more until October; and the French said that their units at the front were short 80,000 men, with a reservoir of only 60,000 men to draw upon until the class of 1919 should become available, which would not be until September.

This matter of finding replacements for the Allied armies was not at all clear and many different statements were made about it from time to time. Whenever it came up for consideration the British and French locked horns, so to speak, and the discussion often became very pointed, each apparently doubting whether the other was doing everything possible to keep up its armies. The French claimed unofficially that the British were holding an excessive number of men in England and Ireland for home defense, but the British denied this vigorously. Of course it was a matter of common knowledge that the draft had never been enforced in Ireland and it was something of a bombshell thrown into the British camp when, at one of the sessions of the Supreme War Council, during a discussion of the subject, M. Clemenceau asked Mr. Lloyd George why he did not draft the Irish. Not to be forced into an explanation, Mr. Lloyd George replied, after some hesitation, and to the amusement of all present, "Mr. Prime Minister, you evidently do not know the Irish."

This was the situation when the conference met at my headquarters. The whole subject was thoroughly thrashed out and, considering the shortage of manpower claimed by the French and the British, to say nothing of the possible increase of the German armies from Russian sources, the main thought was to get over as many Americans as we could. It was finally agreed that we should propose an 80-division program to be completed by April,

1919, and aim at the larger program of one hundred divisions for July, 1919. These conclusions were conveyed to the War Department in the following cable:

"Val des Écoliers, June 23, 1918.

"To win the victory in 1919, it is necessary to have a numerical superiority which can only be obtained by our having in France in April 80 American divisions and in July 100 divisions. At Versailles on the 2d of June, 1918, the three Prime Ministers, in order to obtain this result, requested President Wilson to draft 300,000 men per month. This draft should be made up as follows: *First:* For the creation of six new divisions per month with the corresponding troops for Corps, Army, and Service of the Rear, 250,000 per month beginning with the 1st of July, 1918. *Second:* For replacements, which we determine according to the experience of the French Army at 20 per cent per year of the total strength, a figure which will vary from month to month, but which for the whole period considered would bring the monthly figure of 250,000 men mentioned above to 300,000 men.

"Subparagraph. By the measures indicated above we will assure the existence and the replacements in France of an army of 46 divisions in October, 64 in January, 80 in April, and 100 in July.

"F. Foch,
"John J. Pershing."

It was recommended that these numbers should replace those given in my dispatch of the 21st. The following paragraphs were included in the cable sent from Val des Écoliers:

"Paragraph 2. Recommend that above program be adopted in place of minimum outlined in our cable No. 1342. Am confident that with our tonnage liberally allotted for war purposes from now on, and augmented by available British and French shipping, we shall be able to handle both troops and supplies. M. Clemenceau, who was present at conference, gives assurance that every possible effort to supplement deficiencies in our supplies and equipment, including munitions and aviation, will be made by the French Government. No doubt British will do likewise.

"Paragraph 3. In working out details of cable No. 1342 we took into consideration our information regarding limited cantonment accommodations and lack of equipment, neither of which should enter as factors to delay immediate action on largest program possible. If cantonment facilities should be lacking, recommend that billeting be given consideration.   Will outline details of above extended plan in a day or so.

"PERSHING."

As a number of our divisions had won recognition and praise as offensive units, it was believed all concerned were convinced that our views on building up entire units and eventually an army were sound and that we should hear little more of amalgamation. Indeed, M. Clemenceau had recently said that while he had been opposed to the organization of a separate American army until later, he was now in favor of its being formed at an early date, as he thought it the best way to strengthen the Allied forces.

At this conference, consideration was given only to entire divisions and corps, and auxiliary combat and supply troops with which to round out our forces into an American army.   Yet after the agreement had been reached and M. Clemenceau had departed General Foch remained and again brought up the question of placing a few American regiments in French divisions.   I very frankly told him again that it could not be done.   This was but one of many suggestions made by Foch regarding the reënforcement of French divisions by American units.   His general inclination to aid the French at the expense of the other armies in France created the decided impression that he could not forget that he was a Frenchman and that he did not always act with the impartiality that the other Allies had a right to expect.

The visit of the party was in every way cordial and the discussions were carried on dispassionately, quite in contrast to some that had gone before and others that came afterwards.   M. Clemenceau interposed a witty story now and then, but Foch did not have that turn of mind.   During this visit I was more than ever impressed by M. Clemenceau's vitality and I asked him how he kept himself so vigorous.   He pointed out how little he ate and said he drank no wine.   He added that he took no violent exercise but that he had an expert put him through a course of bending and stretching exercises every morning followed by a massage before he got out of bed.

(Diary) Chaumont, Thursday, June 27, 1918. Captain Cone, of the Navy, came on Monday at Admiral Sims' direction to discuss coöperation in aviation. Conferred with Ireland; if Medical Department fails us it will not be his fault. Nineteen lake steamers coming over for port and cross-Channel service.

Held further conferences Tuesday with Staff on organization. Have directed completion of three corps headquarters and staffs.

General Gillain, Belgian Chief of Staff, came yesterday for a visit. Cabled Secretary McAdoo appreciation Government's measures reference insurance.[1]

In the question of coöperation between Army and Navy aviation, the Secretary of War had decided that the use of aviation against U-boat bases was entirely a naval matter. The original allotment of Liberty engines to the Navy was confirmed, but the output was not so great as expected and the Allies and our army were then far short of the number of engines required. While the use of naval airplanes against the submarine would have been of value in the long run, they possessed no advantages over destroyers, and such use was certainly of no immediate aid in meeting the crisis that confronted us on the Western Front, and that was the most important consideration.

Our aviators were appearing in increasing numbers over the front lines, where they were badly needed to reënforce the French, who were as short of fliers as they were of mechanics. We had already furnished 4,200 mechanics and had agreed to send a still greater number, especially to assist in the manufacture of planes. While on April 1st we had only one aero squadron in action— my old squadron of the Mexican Punitive Expedition—the number on May 15th had increased to eight but these were all equipped with French airplanes.

The usefulness of our Air Service during this period could hardly be overestimated, as previously the enemy had seemed to

[1] Upon receipt of information from Secretary McAdoo that nineteen billion dollars of insurance had been taken by service men, I sent him the following cable: "All ranks of the A.E.F. appreciate deeply the generous measures the Government has taken to provide insurance for their families, in proof of which more than 90 per cent of the men have taken out insurance. This wise provision for their loved ones heartens our men and strengthens the bonds that unite the army and people in our strong determination to triumph in our most righteous cause."

have the superiority whenever he cared to use it. That its importance was duly recognized is shown by a letter of June 11th from General Foch in which he said that the results obtained by the direct use in battle of Allied pursuit and bombardment aviation in the recent offensive had been without precedent. He also suggested that still greater concentration of aviation would be an essential factor in future operations. It was, therefore, desirable that all available air forces under our control be prepared for active service, not only to aid Allied endeavor at the moment but to qualify our aviators for early service with our own armies. When the German offensive began on July 15th the number of our squadrons had increased to twenty-one out of a total of sixty that we had expected to have at the front by this time.

Twelve of our infantry divisions were then either in line or in reserve behind the French, five were in training in French areas, and five were in training in rear of the British Army. Of those with the French, six were concentrated in the vicinity of Villers-Cotterêts and Château-Thierry between the French front and Paris. The British seemed to think that the French were unduly nervous about the safety of Paris and felt that Foch was holding a greater proportion of American troops behind the French lines than was necessary. They believed that there was a strong probability of another attack against their front and thought that Foch was not paying enough attention to their situation. However, they probably did not realize that a counter-offensive was contemplated against the Marne salient should the occasion present itself.

The I Corps Headquarters, organized in January under Major General Hunter Liggett, with Colonel Malin Craig as Chief of Staff, had become a smoothly working machine ready for active service anywhere, but events had moved so swiftly that there had been no opportunity for the assembly of divisions. With the increasing size of our army, it was evident that a greater number of divisions would be available to take part in operations at earlier dates than we had hitherto thought possible. Consequently, the organization of the II, III, and IV Corps Headquarters was at once completed.

The II Corps, Major General George W. Read commanding, with Colonel George S. Simonds as Chief of Staff, and a limited number of staff officers, was charged with matters of administration and command pertaining to the divisions behind the British front. The III Corps, temporarily under command of Major General William M. Wright, with Colonel Alfred W. Bjornstad, Chief of Staff, continued to supervise the training of divisions serving in the Vosges area. The IV Corps was temporarily under the corps Chief of Staff, Colonel Stuart Heintzelman, with headquarters at Toul. By the actual constitution of these corps they were expected soon to become efficient enough to handle units in operations. It was our policy throughout the war to make the basic corps organizations as permanent as possible. The corps commander and his staff and certain corps troops such as heavy artillery, signal and engineer contingents, and supply units thus formed a team that grew in efficiency with experience. Divisions were assigned to corps according to circumstances but were not attached with any idea of permanency.

When our troops became suddenly engaged in the Château-Thierry region we had to rely largely upon the assistance of the French to care for our wounded. Although they had given us every assurance that hospital arrangements for those operations would be complete, and without question they did their best, yet it was only through the mobile hospitals which we had organized that we were able to give our casualties proper attention.

In extenuation of the French failure to take care of our casualties properly, it must be said that when the Germans swept over the Chemin des Dames to Château-Thierry the French lost 45,000 beds included in some of their best equipped hospitals. We had no hospitals on that front and with limited transportation found it difficult to supplement the scant French facilities. In fact, our situation there as to hospital accommodations was about to reach a critical stage.

In this connection, a cablegram, which was scathing in its denunciation of our Medical Department, was actually submitted by Mr. Casper Whitney for the New York *Tribune*. The censor immediately informed the medical representatives at my headquarters, and General Ireland, the Chief Surgeon, requested an investigation, which was at once carried out by General Brewster, my Inspector General. Mr. Whitney was asked to be present at all the hearings and when the actual facts were brought out, showing the efficiency of the Medical Department, he was most apologetic and thereafter became an enthusiastic supporter of the wisdom of the censorship.

Our experience during these operations showed that we must depend on our own resources for the kind of hospitalization and treatment that we expected our sick and wounded to receive. Mobile hospitals could not always take the place of more permanent installations needed after a great battle. The important question of enlarged hospitalization, with ample accommodations and attendants for the sick and wounded, was, therefore, receiving very earnest attention. Although new problems were encountered here and there as our troops were sent to different parts of the front, they were all met in such a way as to reflect credit upon our Medical Department.

CHAPTER XXXV

Allotment of Liberty Engines to Allies—Horse Procurement—Chaplains—
Meeting Supreme War Council—Belgians and Unity of Command—
Fourth of July—Troops of 33d Division Attack with British—Reorganization of Services of Supply—American Troops Requested for
Balkan Front

(Diary) Paris, Tuesday, July 2, 1918. After busy days at Chaumont
came to Paris on Saturday, stopping at Orly to see new DH-4 with
Liberty engine. Saw General Langfitt on reorganization S.O.S., which
seems top-heavy.

On Sunday went to 1st Division and held first ceremony to confer
decorations. Camps in excellent condition. Motored to British
G.H.Q., stopping with Colonel Bacon. Called on Sir Douglas Haig.

Spent yesterday and to-day with General Read, II Corps, inspecting
new divisions, including the 80th, 78th, 30th, 33d, and 27th, and consider the personnel most promising.

Returned to Paris this evening. Have learned that French at last
have begun to enforce requisition for horses. Bishop Brent commissioned Major, National Army. Brigade of Regulars, 2d Division,
stormed Vaux this afternoon, capturing 500 prisoners.

IT was encouraging to see our own airplanes, even in limited
numbers, coming over at last. While some defects in manufacture had been observed in both the DH-4 plane and in
the Liberty engine, these had been pointed out to the War Department and were in course of correction.

Note: Total strength of the A.E.F. on June 30th, 40,487 officers, 833,204 enlisted men.
Divisional units arriving in June included elements of the following divisions: 29th
Division (National Guard, New Jersey, Delaware, Virginia, Maryland, and District of
Columbia), Maj. Gen. Charles G. Morton; 37th Division (National Guard, Ohio),
Maj. Gen. Charles S. Farnsworth; 78th Division (National Army, western New York,
New Jersey and Delaware), Maj. Gen. James H. McRae; 83d Division (National
Army, Ohio and western Pennsylvania), Maj. Gen. Edwin F. Glenn; 89th Division
(National Army, Kansas, Missouri, South Dakota, Nebraska, Arizona, New Mexico,
and Colorado), Brig. Gen. Frank L. Winn; 90th Division (National Army, Texas and
Oklahoma), Maj. Gen. Henry T. Allen; 92d Division (National Army, colored), Maj.
Gen. Charles C. Ballou.

Although the French manufacturers made many suggestions that we should adopt this motor or that, and had none too mildly opposed the adoption of the Liberty engine, its success was instantaneous and the Inter-Allied Committee soon found itself swamped with requests for allotments. In addition to the requirements of our own Army and Navy Air Services both at home and abroad, the British wanted over 5,000, the French over 3,300, and the Italians nearly 2,000, to cover their new construction for the next six months. The tonnage situation considerably restricted the shipment of planes from home, but for the time being France and England could furnish them, provided we could supply the engines. At all times the demand for both planes and Liberty engines was greater than the supply.

The horse question was one that gave us trouble continuously. On account of the lack of shipping and the scarcity of forage in France, and in view of the promise of the French to purchase and deliver to us 15,000 animals per month from April to August, both inclusive, we had, in March, recommended to the War Department that shipments from home be discontinued. But, as has been stated, the French farmers were reluctant to sell animals, even at the increased prices offered, and the climax came on May 31st, when the French advised that due to military developments on the Western Front the Government had issued orders suspending the purchase of any additional animals for the American forces.

I immediately took the matter up with M. Tardieu, of the Franco-American Committee, calling his attention to the extent to which the French failure to supply animals would immobilize a considerable portion of our forces. As a result, the French agreed to adopt a system of enforced requisition throughout France, commencing on June 20th and extending to August 1st. It was estimated that there were in France not in military service approximately 3,000,000 animals, of which from 300,000 to 400,000 were thought to be of suitable types. We were promised 80,000 of the 160,000 to be obtained through the requisition and in addition counted on approximately 14,000 from the British, in accordance with their promise to supply horses for the divisions behind their lines. Negotiations were also reopened for obtaining animals in Spain and it was thought that 25,000 could be obtained from that source.

These numbers, however, would still leave us with a large shortage on August 1st and the War Department was therefore requested on June 30th to resume shipments at the rate of 8,000 per month. It was realized that this number would not meet requirements, but it was hoped that we might obtain still further assistance from the Allies and thus avoid a greater demand on our already inadequate tonnage.

A few days later the success of the French requisition began to appear dubious, less than half as many animals as expected having been obtained. The question was taken up with General Foch at a conference on July 10th and Weygand explained that the requisition committee had not taken advantage of the prices authorized, principally because they did not think the animals worth such prices. He said, however, that we could count on the full delivery of 80,000 horses, but he was very positive that this would be the limit they could furnish.

About this time M. Tardieu took the initiative and, without consulting any one, sent a cable to the French Ambassador at Washington requesting that our War Department begin the shipment of horses for our armies at the rate of 35,000 per month, to be increased progressively to 60,000 per month. The Department was naturally alarmed, as the cable indicated a situation entirely at variance with what I had reported. This is mentioned as one of many incidents that illustrate the sort of uncoördinated activity often exercised by the French. It will be recalled that exactly the same thing had occurred in the fall of 1917 in connection with the shipment of horses, except that then M. Tardieu was on the receiving end in Washington. When his attention was called to the importance of coöperation he was much embarrassed and said that no differences in the future need be feared. M. Tardieu was most efficient and in the position of Chief of the Franco-

American Committee he aided us materially in procurement and in many other ways.

From my conference with Foch and from M. Tardieu's cablegram, it was apparent that we could expect no assistance from the French after the 80,000 requisitioned horses had been delivered and that there must be a large increase in the number to be shipped from home, which we had been trying to avoid. Making every allowance for the possibility of substituting motor traction for horses, still we should need for the 80-division plan something over 200,000, or 25,000 a month for the following eight months, a number that seemed prohibitive in view of the already enormous amount of tonnage required for everything else. These numbers were never reached and we were always approximately 50 per cent short of our requirements. The question continued to give us concern to the end. As to forage, the French gave every assurance that they would be able to feed our animals and told us that it would be unnecessary to ship any more forage from the States until the following spring.[1]

The appointment of Bishop Brent as an officer of the Army, made in response to my request, assured me of his services in the important capacity as Chief of the Board of Chaplains, which was the controlling body in that service, at my headquarters. At the same time, provision was made by Congress, according to my recommendation of several months previous, for an increase in the number of chaplains to one for each 1,200 officers and men in the service. That the significance of this addition to our forces might be understood and appreciated, an order was issued placing chaplains of our forces on the same footing, as regards the performance of their duties, as other officers of the service. In part the order read:

"The importance in wartime of the chaplain's work can hardly be overestimated. The chaplain should be the moral and spiritual leader of his organization. His continued effort should be the maintenance of high standards of life and conduct among officers and men.

[1] In my cable on the subject of horses and forage I said: "Like many other assurances given us, this may not turn out to be altogether true," and it was not so long after the cable was sent that our horses were short of forage.

* * * Though holding a military commission, it is on the basis of the supreme performance of his ministerial duties that he fulfills his fundamental obligations to the army. A sympathetic recognition of the chaplain's duties and responsibilities is expected of every officer. It is only through their ready coöperation that he can reach the entire army."

(Diary) Chaumont, Saturday, July 6, 1918. Conferred with Lord Milner Wednesday morning in Paris and later with Haig, giving my objections to our troops in training being taken for an offensive. Attended meeting Supreme War Council in the afternoon.

Reached Chaumont at noon the 4th and participated in celebration at Hôtel de Ville. French Mission also gave an entertainment, with movies of 1st Division at Cantigny. General de Castelnau called, and General Pétain, General Ragueneau, and de Chambrun dined with us and attended a troop entertainment. Received many telegrams. As a compliment to the French, issued orders yesterday making July 14th a holiday.[1]

Part of the 33d Division made an attack with the Australians on the 4th.

Held detailed discussion to-day with McAndrew, Hagood, and Eltinge on S.O.S. reorganization.

Lord Milner came in from Versailles and together we went over the problems of troop shipments and especially the question of continuing the tonnage then being used for the increased American program. He assured me that their plans contemplated the same help they were giving us at that time. He spoke of

[1] France, July 5, 1918.

General Orders } No. 109

July 14 is hereby declared a holiday for all troops in this command not actually engaged with enemy. It will be their duty and privilege to celebrate French Independence Day, which appeals alike to every citizen and soldier in France and America, with all the sympathetic interest and purpose that France celebrated our Independence Day. Living among the French people and sharing the comradeship-in-arms of their soldiers, we have the deeper consciousness that the two anniversaries are linked together in common principles and a common cause.

By command of General Pershing:

JAMES W. McANDREW,
Chief of Staff.

General Pétain embodied the text in an order which he issued to the French Army.

the American divisions behind the British lines and was very anxious that they should remain there. Somehow I felt that his assurance as to shipping might depend upon the number of divisions that would be held for service with their armies. Marshal Haig, who called later, was also solicitous as to the retention of our troops and said that he would be very much weakened if any more divisions were taken away. I told him that for the moment the question as to where they should serve would naturally depend upon where they were needed most. The principal scene of action had changed from the British to the French front, so the stronger demands for our forces now came from the latter source.

The Supreme War Council was holding a session at this time, but it had not been my intention to attend, until a telephone message was received from Mr. Lloyd George asking me to come. Although I had already written him a note, my attendance gave me the opportunity to thank him in person for the fine spirit that prompted the British desire to celebrate the Fourth of July with us. He had sent word through Major Griscom that he wished to visit some of our units, and I took this occasion to tell him that I sincerely hoped he would do so.

At this session of the Council there was an absence of the tension that had prevailed at the last two meetings. The only question discussed while I was present was whether the Belgian Army would be under the Allied Commander-in-Chief. The Belgian Chief of Staff objected to Foch on the ground that a King could not be placed under the command of a Major General. It did not appear to me that the point was well taken, as Haig and Pétain and I were senior in rank to Foch, who, after all, held his place by common agreement. Although this technical question of rank was raised, the Belgian authorities, as represented by the King, were strongly in favor of coöperation.

Once the portion of the line to be held by each of the Allies was distinctly defined and the operations to be undertaken by each were agreed upon, Foch's duties might have been considered as those of a chief coördinator. Each Commander-in-Chief was supreme in his own army, as he had been before, and Foch's task was to coördinate the operations of the armies in such manner as to make it impracticable for the enemy to concentrate against any one of them.   In effect, this was the rôle that he actually played under the provisions of his appointment.

The Fourth of July found me in Chaumont.   The French people there never missed an opportunity to show their pleasure at having us in their midst and their appreciation of American aid to the cause.   The principal ceremony of the day was a reception at the Hôtel de Ville tendered to the officers of my headquarters by the local French officials, both civil and military, and the prominent citizens.   The program included a series of suitable speeches, and the spirit of fraternity that prevailed made it easy to respond.   In fact, on this, as often on similar occasions, I found myself almost as enthusiastic as the French speakers, though perhaps less content with my effort.

Many Allied officials were kind enough to remember that it was our Independence Day, and messages came from Clemenceau, Foch, Haig, and others.   In order to record the friendly attitude that existed at the moment, several of them are quoted below:

"General Headquarters,
"British Armies in France,
"2d July, 1918.

"DEAR GENERAL PERSHING:

"On behalf of myself and the whole British Army in France and Flanders, I beg you to accept for yourself and the troops under your command the warmest greetings on American Independence Day.

"On the 4th of July of this year, the soldiers of America, France, and Great Britain will stand side by side for the first time in history in the defense of the great principle of Liberty, which is the proudest inheritance and most cherished possession of their several nations.

"That Liberty which British, Americans, and French have won for themselves they will not fail to hold, not only for themselves but for the world.

"With heartfelt good wishes to you and your gallant army, believe me,

"Yours very truly,

"D. HAIG, F.M."

"Paris, July 5, 1918.

"General Pershing,
  "Commander-in-Chief of the
    "American Forces in France.

"The American troops who took part in the Fourth of July ceremony on the Avenue President Wilson made a deep impression upon
all Paris. On this holiday so wholeheartedly celebrated by all our Allies, the splendid appearance of your soldiers aroused not only our enthusiasm but our unbounded confidence as well. I beg that you
transmit to your troops, with my compliments, the expression of my
sincere admiration.

"CLEMENCEAU."

"July 3, 1918.

"General Pershing,
  "Commander-in-Chief of the
    "American Forces in France.

"It is for independence that we all are fighting. With all our hearts
we celebrate with you the anniversary of Independence Day.

"GENERAL FOCH."

"Trianon, Versailles, July 4, 1918.

"General Pershing, HAEF.

"On this day of national festivity for the United States tnat all
Allied nations are solemnizing will you kindly accept the wishes
which I send you in my name and in the name of all Italian soldiers
present in France actually fighting or working for the great common
cause for the triumph of civilization and of right.

"GENERAL ROBILANT."

"Belgian Army, July 4, 1918.

"General Pershing,
  "Commander-in-Chief, American Expeditionary Forces.

"On this memorable day, July 4, 1918, when the Army of the United
States is celebrating Independence Day on the battlefield, I address
to you the cordial greetings and the respectful sympathy of the Belgian
Army which celebrates with you your national anniversary with the
spirit and the fervor of troops who have been fighting almost four years
without rest for the independence of their country. On this occasion
detachments from every arm will march beneath the folds of the
American Flag raised on the plain of Flanders. All our hearts are
united in one prayer for the success of the Allied armies and in the
expectation of that glorious day when your troops shall march in

their turn beneath the folds of our own Tricolor raised in our reconquered cities.

"DE CEUNINCK,
"Belgian Minister of War."

"Camp d'Auvours, July 4, 1918.

"Commander-in-Chief of the
"American Troops, H.A.E.F.

"At the moment when the Belgian troops at Camp d'Auvours, Sarthe, have just filed before the United States flag giving honor to it with all habitual ceremonies, I have the honor in the name of the officers and troops under my orders to transmit the expression of my respect and admiration for the great and chivalrous America.

"Major General Commanding,
"VERBIST."

"July 4, 1918.

"American Expeditionary Forces,
"HAEF.

"First Army send hearty greetings to their comrades of the American Army. We are all one in sentiment and determination to-day.

"GENERAL HORNE, B.E.F."

Regardless of the distinct understanding that our troops behind the British front were there for training and were not to be used except in an emergency, the British made constant efforts to get them into their lines. They had planned an attack by the Australians on the Fourth of July and requested Major General Read, Commander of the II Corps, to permit some of the troops of the 33d Division (Bell), which was then still in training, to take part. As the use of Americans at this time was directly contrary to the arrangement, naturally it did not meet with my approval, and on my visit to the II Corps on July 2d I advised Read that our troops should not participate. I also spoke to Marshal Haig about it when I saw him in Paris on the 3d, and he entirely agreed with my point of view. In telephone conversation with Read, further and positive instructions were given that our troops should be withdrawn. It was, therefore, somewhat of a surprise to learn on the following day that four companies of the 33d Division had taken part in the attack.

It seems that General Read, in accordance with my instructions, told General Rawlinson, Commander of the British Fourth Army, under whom the 33d was in training, that I did not want partially trained troops to participate. However, our units had become fully committed to the operation, and Rawlinson could make no change without instructions from his Commander-in-Chief. The Chief of Staff at British G.H.Q. then consented to leave our troops out, but when he learned from Rawlinson that it would compel the British to defer the operation he informed Read that no change could be made without orders from Marshal Haig, who, he said, could not be reached.

The incident, though relatively unimportant in itself, showed clearly the disposition of the British to assume control of our units, the very thing which I had made such strong efforts and had imposed so many conditions to prevent. Its immediate effect was to cause me to make the instructions so positive that nothing of the kind could occur again. It seems needless to add that the behavior of our troops in this operation was splendid. This division afterwards displayed the same eagerness to get at the enemy in several hard-fought engagements during the trying days of the Meuse-Argonne offensive.

(Diary) Chaumont, Tuesday, July 9, 1918. Have spent last few days on reorganization of Services of Supply, consulting with Generals Atterbury, McAndrew, and Hagood, and Colonel Eltinge.

Yesterday saw General Meriwether Walker, head of Motor Transport, and Colonel A. D. Andrews, Deputy Chief of Utilities. Melville E. Stone took luncheon with us yesterday and told me that the Associated Press, of which he is the head, was for America first, and if we needed its services to call upon him. Brigadier General Perelli arrived as Chief of Italian Mission. Had calls by Frederick Palmer and Casper Whitney.

To-day discussed corps and army organization and sector occupation with McAndrew, Fox Conner, and Fiske. Have recommended shipment of 120,000 tons of steel, besides copper, iron, lead, and lumber promised the British. Inefficient loading of transports and arrival of troops without equipment causing some confusion. Bulgarians reported tired of war. Allied Commander on Balkan Front telegraphs request for American troops. Received letter from General Bliss [1] concerning admiration of French for our troops.

In the month of June the amount of cargo discharged daily at all ports had increased to an average of 20,000 tons, including coal and oil, but due to continued shortage of rail facilities the corresponding transfers to depots and to the front were still falling short. This was a condition that we had been doing everything possible to overcome, but, having sown the wind, we were now about to harvest the whirlwind.

In order to meet what was considered by the Allies an extreme emergency, we had already devoted such a tremendous effort to the shipment of infantry and machine gun units, to the exclusion of the necessary personnel to keep the supply services abreast of requirements, that we were again facing a serious situation. Not only was personnel lacking, but there was need of material for completion of construction at ports, and for warehouses and railway improvement. Cargo ships were not being provided to increase supplies to a reasonable level. The shipment of locomotives, cars, and rails was behind and the railroads were not able to meet our demands. Instead of making the supreme effort during the preceding six or eight months in compliance with insistent and repeated cable demands for all these things, the War Department had been content to stand on an entirely inadequate program and had failed to live up to that.

As to the increase in the number of cargo vessels and shipments, it was feared by the War Department General Staff that the home ports, which were already congested, would not be able to handle the increased activity that would result. Concerning the situation at French ports, Washington again had expressed

[1] "From the time when your men began to do such fine work in the vicinity of Château-Thierry, I heard in all quarters the most enthusiastic expressions of admiration for them, accompanied in many cases by statements that the speaker believed that they had saved Paris. * * * It occurred to me that it would be a good thing to quietly put on record such statements, * * * so that when the history of the war comes to be written up these things will not be forgotten. There may be a tendency a year or so from now to minimize the credit which at the moment they gave to our troops. * * * "

doubt as to whether we should be able to handle a greater amount of cargo. The whole scheme of the War Department had been upset by the military crisis long since predicted. Yet the new demands of the situation required that an even higher rate of shipments should be carried out for several months to come.

Realizing that any expression of doubt on our part about handling cargo would probably cause a slowing down at home, from which it might be impossible later to recover, and which would cause far more embarrassment to us than any delay that might exist in the dispatch of freight, I continued to urge the War Department to send over cargo as rapidly as possible, giving no hint or statement which might be used later as a reason for not sending along everything they could.

It was a condition of affairs not entirely pleasing, but on the other hand not so gloomy as it appeared. It was merely a question of courage, persistence, and coöperation. Although difficult, it did not seem at all insuperable at the time.

It became necessary to examine the conditions in our Services of Supply very carefully in an effort to correct any defects in that organization which might be slowing us up. It appeared that the Transportation Department especially needed greater freedom of action. It was bound up with several other departments grouped under the Service of Utilities, which had been interposed in the organization in the belief that it would relieve the Commanding General of the S.O.S. of some of the details of administration. Unfortunately the scheme had not worked out that way. It would not be fair to say that there was any lack of inclination on the part of the personnel, which was straining every nerve to accomplish its task, but some unnecessary interference and faulty coöperation existed here and there for which it was difficult to fix the responsibility.

It was my idea to give the separate services as much independence of action as possible and yet have them linked up under the direction of the General Staff of the Commanding General, S.O.S., in such a way as to bring the activities into full coördination. After further consideration, it was decided to abolish the Service of Utilities, leaving the Transportation Department practically an independent agency. As such it was charged, as we have seen, with the operation and maintenance of railways and canals, of inland water transport and sea connection with England and other European countries, and of terminals, including unloading of ships. Its other obligations were the procurement of railway supplies, control of telegraph and telephone lines used by railways, and maintenance of all rolling stock. Construction was left with the Department of Construction and Forestry, while exclusive charge of motor vehicles with our forces was given to the Motor Transport Corps. All these services, including the Transportation Department, were to be directly under the Commanding General, Services of Supply, for proper coördination.

About this time the Allied Commander-in-Chief of the forces on the Bulgarian front sent a request through General Bartlett, our representative there, for American troops, as indicated by the following cablegram:

"July 8, 1918.

"Commander-in-Chief Allied forces on Balkan Front desires I report that Bulgarians are tired of war. Austria-Hungary is in unstable condition and her troops on this front are not the best. Line of least resistance to decisive victory is now through Balkan ways. With additional help of one American division without artillery Bulgaria can be defeated and Germany attacked through Austria-Hungary where Jugo-Slavs would aid Allies. American division should arrive with as little delay as possible for action before snow fall. All Greeks, Serbians and Slavs in the American Army should come to Balkan Front to encourage Greeks and Serbians and to discourage Bulgaria. Declaration of war by the United States against Bulgaria would greatly increase discouragement in latter country which now considers United States her friend on final peace congress. All British troops are now leaving Struma Section having been replaced by three Greek divisions. One of every four British infantry battalions are now leaving Balkans for another front."

Of course it was out of the question to send one of our divisions to the Balkan front, and the request was not seriously considered. It is quoted only to show how widely our troops would have been dispersed if we had not taken the firm stand that the Western Front was the place for our effort.

CHAPTER XXXVI

Conference with General Foch—Propose American Sector at Château-Thierry—Foch Declares for an American Army—Possible Operations Discussed—Kerensky and Intervention in Russia—French Independence Day—Postal Service—German Attack in Marne Salient Expected—Began on Fifteenth and Was Stopped—Our 3d and 42d Divisions Do Well—Situation Favorable for Allies

(Diary) Paris, Wednesday, July 10, 1918. Have issued orders commending the 1st and 2d Divisions. Went to Bombon to-day, taking Conner, Mott, and Boyd, for conference with Foch. Afterward went to 2d Division, northeast of La Ferté-sous-Jouarre, to bestow decorations. One of the men to receive the Distinguished Service Cross swam the river to be present.[1]

M Y visits to General Foch were usually by appointment. I went this time to discuss the assembly and the employment of our troops as an army. The first question considered was the withdrawal of those that were with the British. I said that it had been my intention from the beginning to have them transferred to the American sector as soon as it could be decided just where that would be. It was important that they should be taken before they became engaged in operations on the British front because it would be difficult to get them after that without causing some inconvenience to the British. I asked General Foch to take up the question with Sir Douglas Haig, but he said he would prefer that I should handle it.

Confronting the Château-Thierry salient we had the 3d (Dickman) and the 26th (Edwards) Divisions in line, the latter being a part of our I Corps, and there seemed to be an opportunity of adding other divisions then in the vicinity and forming our army

---

[1] Marine Gunner (later Lieutenant) Henry L. Hulbert, 5th Regiment, U. S. Marines, afterward killed in action while his division was aiding the French in the Champagne, Oct. 4, 1918. This gallant soldier had also received the Croix de Guerre with Palm, and the Navy Cross; and in 1899, in Samoa, received the Medal of Honor.

there. This was suggested for consideration only as a temporary arrangement, and I stated to General Foch that, "We should look beyond and decide upon a permanent front without delay." His attention was called to my tentative agreement with Pétain that the American sector should include the St. Mihiel salient, and to the fact that we had done a great amount of work in that region, such as the construction of railway sidings, yards, depots, air-dromes, and a regulating station which was nearing completion.

I went on to say that with American units scattered all along the Western Front, assigned to no particular zone for future operations, we were postponing the day when the American Army would be able to render its greatest help to the Allied cause. I stressed the point that we were thus dissipating our re-sources for lack of a plan and were not in position to utilize the full capacity of our facilities. Instead of thinking of the future, even the immediate future, we were merely temporizing. In short, if we were to do our part to the best advantage we should at once have a definite place on the front which could be served by our own lines of communication.

I again pointed out that the British were compelled to remain in the north and that the French were covering Paris and the area west of Verdun and that it seemed logical that we should hold to our original idea as to the location of an American sector. Also, that from a strategical point of view the new line resulting from the reduction of the St. Mihiel salient would afford a most favorable base for a later offensive toward the vital part of Germany which, if successful, would deprive her of a considerable part of her resources in iron and coal. I, therefore, strongly recommended to Foch that he approve the plan that Pétain and I had agreed upon for the reduction of the St. Mihiel salient as the first operation to be undertaken by the American Army.

In reply, he said that he was glad that our views on the situation were so nearly alike. He then said: "To-day, when there are a million Americans in France, I am going to be still more American than any of you. America must have her place in the war. America has the right to have her army organized as such. The American army must become an accomplished fact. Moreover, the cause of the Allies will be better served by an American army under its own chief than if its units are dispersed. Therefore, it is necessary at the earliest possible date to constitute an American army side by side with the French and British armies, and it should be as large as possible."

At one point in the conversation he dropped the remark that it might be possible by the end of July to constitute an American army with at least thirteen divisions. When asked about the artillery for some of our units whose artillery had not arrived, he said that Pétain would arrange that. He talked a great deal that day and went on to say that in order to bring victory to the Allies it would be necessary for them to have an incontestable numerical superiority. He laid particular stress on the view that the strength of the British and French divisions should be maintained and the number of American divisions increased as rapidly as possible. Temporarily, he said, as long as the present battle lasted he was going to ask the American Army to help the French Army by the loan of the divisions that had not yet received their artillery. He wanted them to be placed in quiet sectors or else be sent to complete their training in areas behind the lines where they would be available if necessary to assist the French troops in front of them. I agreed with the idea of putting newly arrived divisions in the inactive portions of the line and we left the details of assignment to be discussed by Weygand and Conner.[1]

With my objective always in mind, I again made the suggestion that the assembly of an American army as a temporary measure might take place in the vicinity of Château-Thierry, to which he promptly replied that this accorded with his plans. He then referred to a proposed attack that might occur between July 20th and 31st, and indicated that he expected the 1st and 2d Divisions

[1] According to the understanding, five of our new divisions were to go to the Vosges to relieve for active employment in case of necessity five which were there, provided certain artillery could be furnished them by the French. This involved sending the 29th (Morton) and 37th (Farnsworth) to relieve the 32d (Haan) and 77th (Duncan), and later the 90th (Allen), 89th (Winn), and 92d (Ballou) to relieve the 5th (McMahon), 82d (Burnham), and 35th (McClure), respectively.

to take part. He also said that an offensive would probably be made by the Allies in September to reduce the Marne salient, if it had not been reduced by that time. He mentioned the possibility of an operation in the region of Amiens for the purpose of freeing the railroads through that place. The impression this conference left on my mind was that although he had spoken of an early date General Foch did not think the formation of an American army possible before September or October.

In their mental processes Foch and Weygand were somewhat alike.[1] It had been frequently noticed that when Weygand expressed himself on any question under discussion, Foch was quite certain to be of the same opinion. During the conference and afterwards they laid stress on the view, which we all held, that every effort should be made to win the war in 1919. Foch said that the French and British armies and peoples were tired of the war and the minimum result required of the campaign of 1919 would be to free northern France and at least a part of Belgium. This would demand that the three Allies should utilize all available divisions in continuous attack.

The thought was expressed, especially by Weygand, that a certain spirit of emulation among the Allied armies would be necessary to coördination and that the attacks should be launched in the same general region, with interdependent objectives, a conception which would accord with the principle of concentration of effort. They pointed out that with the British lines extending to the vicinity of Amiens, the French would probably cover the front from there to about Reims, while the Americans, on account of the ports and railroads serving them, would be to the east. Their opinion, however, at that time was that the proper coördination of Allied attacks would forbid our going farther east than the sector Reims—Argonne. This distribution, they both thought, would correspond to the forces that would be available in 1919 and also to the peculiar necessities that governed the location of troops of the various nations.

The objective, it was stated, other than the enemy forces would

[1] See Footnote page 323, Volume I.

naturally be the railroad net to include the lateral railway from
Mézières via Cambrai toward Valenciennes and the north. If
this line were cut, it would throw the bulk of the enemy's traffic
on those lines through Liège and would force a considerable
portion of the army back against the rocky and heavily wooded
Ardennes. This would cause him much embarrassment and compel him to relinquish the territory in northern France and at least
a part of Belgium. Both Foch and Weygand viewed the terrain
of the Arras-Argonne Front as lending itself to offensive movements, whereas the railroad systems and fortresses of Metz and
Saarburg would give a certain advantage to the German defense
of Lorraine; also that an attack in the region of Nancy would
be more in the nature of a diversion. I took the view that operations on different portions of the Western Front if coördinated
as to time would be more confusing to the enemy than if the
armies were fighting side by side. Moreover, an offensive to
the northeast in Lorraine would directly threaten a region that
was vital to Germany. The strongest reason advanced at the
time in support of their general conception of an Allied offensive
was that the spirit of rivalry would be aroused among the armies
operating in one great zone. It was argued that this feature would
be missed if the Americans should attack in Lorraine while the
British and French attacked in the north.

As to the immediate future, it was evident that some further
action on the part of the enemy in the Marne salient might be
expected before very long. His position there was not comfortable
and, furthermore, a drive from there seemed to offer him the
best chance of success under the circumstances. But the Allies
were watching for indications of his intentions in order to strike
a counterblow. It was certain that our troops would be called
upon to participate in any Allied activity in that vicinity.

While nothing definite was then decided, the exchange of
views, although rather general in character, covering the probable operations to be undertaken during the fall and in the following year, did furnish several factors to be considered in the
study regarding the employment of the American Army. Gen-

eral Foch asked me to come and let him know if at any time I had any suggestions to make and added that he expected very soon to call the Commanders-in-Chief together for a conference.

(Diary) Paris, Friday, July 12, 1918. Visited Liggett's headquarters (I Corps) at La Ferté-sous-Jouarre yesterday. Called on 4th Division (Cameron) at Lizy-sur-Ourcq. Inspected positions of its 7th Brigade, Brigadier General B. A. Poore, commanding. Returned to Liggett's for the night.

Saw the 28th (Muir) at La Houssière to-day and went to front in sector of Brigadier General Wm. Weigel's brigade. Took lunch with Harbord at Nanteuil-sur-Marne, where his brigade of the 2d Division is resting. He told of a marine who had captured seventy-five German prisoners single-handed, at which I remarked that if he told such stories as that it was little wonder that he was popular with the Marines.[1] Visited 26th Division (Edwards) at Genevrois Farm to bestow decorations. At Paris Miss Anne Morgan and Mrs. Dyke came to talk of the important work they are doing in the devastated regions. Building program for Medical Department falling behind. Number of alien laborers increasing. Serious situation as to motor transport cabled to Washington. An intelligence agent obtained Kerensky's views on Russian situation.

As we have seen, Russia had come to be regarded as a possible recruiting ground for the German armies and various suggestions of ways and means to counteract German influence had been made. Apropos of the apprehensions of the Allies, it was not without interest to get the views of Kerensky, who, in command of the Russian armies, had at one time met with considerable temporary success in attempting to stem the tide of revolution.

One of our intelligence officers who had known Kerensky met him in Paris and was told that Trotsky desired the intervention of American troops in Russia, to be landed in Vladivostok. He said that Trotsky was personally opposed to Allied intervention and that if the Japanese participated they would meet with opposition unless they should be preceded by American troops. If Americans were accompanied by British and French, he said, both Lenin and Trotsky would inform Russian peasants

---

[1] It appears that at 5:30 A.M. on June 26th, four German officers and seventy-eight men had surrendered to one of his men and were brought in as prisoners.

that Allied forces had landed to deprive them of their property and liberty. He characterized Lenin and Trotsky as being in the pay of the Germans and said the real governor of Russia was the German Ambassador. Kerensky advised propaganda in favor of American aid and said that all Cossacks and 100,000 Czecho-Slovaks would join them because the Russians believed in the disinterested motives of Americans in Europe. He suggested, however, that if we should intervene the entry should be by way of Archangel.

The question of sending troops there was also presented from another source. When our Ambassador to Russia, Mr. David R. Francis, was in Paris in June, 1918, he strongly advo-cated our intervention and thought 100,000 men would save the nation. He urged me to recommend it, but I was opposed in principle to any undertaking that would deplete our strength in France and thought that such a diversion would only lead to complications and would not affect the final result an iota. It was my belief that our task clearly lay on the Western Front and that we would have all we could do to beat the enemy there. But, as mentioned later, Allied forces were sent both to Arch-angel and Vladivostok.

The fact is that the tendency persisted on the part of the Allied Governments to send expeditions here and there in pursuit of political aims. They were prone to lose sight of the fundamental fact that the real objective was the German Army. Once that was beaten, the political and naval power of Germany would collapse.

(Diary) Chaumont, Sunday, July 14, 1918. Had interesting talk with Mr. John Bass in Paris yesterday on Italian situation. General Rogers reported many shortages in quartermaster supplies. Motored to Provins; had dinner with General Pétain, who expects German advance soon. Arrived at Chaumont late last night.

This morning presided at exercises of *lycée* and presented prizes. The children of the school gave me a beautiful volume, "Episodes from the History of France," for my son, which we shall long treasure. Held reception this afternoon for civil and military officials.

Our mail service improving under Davis. Have recently discussed possibilities of making purchases in Japan.

The celebration in Chaumont of the French national holiday and similar occasions in which French and Americans joined, served not only to relieve the strain of this period of the war but gave us a closer and clearer understanding of the French people and their hopes and fears. On this particular day their spirits were high. "Liberté, Fraternité, Egalité" are too often only empty words that fail to inspire, but when uttered by a people in the throes of war, with everything at stake, the cry carries a special appeal to patriotic instincts that only those who have witnessed its effect can fully realize. The genuine gratitude they felt toward us was manifest in a thousand ways and the fraternal spirit on both sides was dominant. I have often thought since that if nations could but be guided under all circumstances by the sincere and sympathetic sentiments that then so strongly united in common purpose those who fought side by side, how much it would mean to the people of the world.

The prompt dispatch and delivery of mail was difficult, yet its bearing on the morale of the army and the folks at home made it very important. As far back as June, 1917, the Postmaster General had offered to aid in establishing an organization to assist in handling the mail for our forces and had sent over a superintendent and several assistants. While our numbers were still limited, the mail service went reasonably well, but as they increased the problem became most difficult and a complete reorganization was necessary. Some of the things that caused confusion were that divisions were disrupted to provide the special troops needed in the great emergency and that other units had usually been reconstituted at the last moment before embarkation and records of assignments were not kept up to date. Moreover, the public did not understand the composition of units, and as a result letters were, in a vast number of cases, misdirected and often completely lost.

In May the Postal Service was placed under control of the Adjutant General, A.E.F., and reorganized under the direction of Brigadier General R. C. Davis, the Adjutant General. An officer of extended postal experience was sent to the States with a full understanding of conditions to arrange for giving publicity to instructions regarding the address of mail and to supervise shipment from points of embarkation. A military postal organization was established at each port of debarkation where it was expected to receive mail, and a railway mail service was organized along our lines of communication. A central post office in connection with the Central Records Office of the Adjutant General's Department, A.E.F., was established; corps and divisions were directed to organize postal departments; and it was arranged to forward mail to units at the front along with supplies from the regulating stations.

This is a matter that might have been simplified by previous joint consideration by the General Staff and the Post Office Department, with regulations laid down beforehand for the guidance of all concerned. As a result of our efforts, there was considerable improvement, but the mail service never became entirely satisfactory.

(Diary) Chaumont, Wednesday, July 17, 1918. Another German attack broke Monday. Our 42d, part of the 28th, and the 3d Divisions became engaged. The latter counterattacked and captured 600 prisoners. Advised Foch that the 32d and 29th Divisions are available at once. Five other divisions have been placed at his disposal. Situation yesterday more favorable for Allies. General Bullard assigned to III Corps and General Wright to V Corps.

The battle lines in the Marne salient, with some local exceptions, had stood without material change since early in June. It was evident, as stated in my cable to Washington, quoted in a previous chapter,[1] that the question of interior transportation and supply was troublesome and could not be regarded by the enemy as satisfactory. His effort of June 9th to improve his exposed position near Soissons and to make a further advance which would possibly open the route to the French capital had met with little success.

No further offensives of consequence against the British in Flanders having been immediately undertaken, interest was cen-

[1] Chapter XXXII.

tered on the Champagne front as the most probable place to expect the next blow. The American and French divisions that had been quietly concentrated in reserve west of the Marne salient for use with either the French or British, as circumstances might require, most of them carefully hidden in the forest of Villers-Cotterêts and vicinity, were now about to get into the picture.

The intelligence services of all the Allied armies had been exerting every endeavor to discover the enemy's plans, with the result that for some days it appeared almost certain that his next move would be directed toward the southeast, on the right and left of Reims. On the evening of the 14th, a French raiding party from General Gouraud's Fourth Army, then holding that part of the line east of Reims, luckily secured prisoners who confirmed this belief and who gave the exact hour fixed for the attack, which they said was to take place on the following morning.

Our 3d Division, still in line south of the Marne, faced the enemy between Jaulgonne and Château-Thierry, and the 26th held a sector between Torcy and Vaux. Infantry elements of the 28th Division were south of the Marne, serving with the two French divisions on either side of the 3d; several companies of the 42d were in the main line of resistance and the rest occupied a support position behind Gouraud's front; the 4th went into line the night of the 16th; the 1st Division was in reserve north of Meaux, and the 2d near Château-Thierry.

The German offensive was launched on the early morning of the 15th, as expected, but at the very beginning their formations were more or less broken up and their forces seriously weakened by heavy Allied counter-artillery fire. The enemy concentrated his artillery on the French first line, from which practically all troops had been withdrawn to the second and main defensive line. The first position was taken by the enemy without difficulty, but as the barrage lifted for the attack on the second line he was met again with violent artillery fire and with unexpected infantry resistance and suffered further serious losses. By evening, thanks to the strong and skillful defense by the French and our 42d Division, which became engaged and sustained relatively heavy losses, the situation on General Gouraud's army front in Champagne was very satisfactory. The conduct of the 42d on this and succeeding days brought high praise from the French Army Commander.

Farther west, the enemy succeeded in crossing the Marne, penetrating in one place as far as five miles. In a determined attempt to force a crossing near Mézy he struck our 3d Division, which was posted along the river, and the fighting became intense, some units of the 30th and 38th Infantry Regiments which were holding the front lines being attacked from both the front and flanks. The brilliant conduct of these units, however, threw the enemy's effort into confusion and by noon of the next day he had nothing to show in most of the 3d Division sector for his careful preparations, except tremendous losses. The attacks against the division had stopped by noon of July 16th.

The Germans made but slight gains to the east of Reims, while to the southwest they got across the Marne and made some progress toward Épernay. The failure of their attack in Champagne and the relatively slight gains to which they were held to the west of Reims on the first day materially heartened the Allies. Although there were some ten divisions of the enemy remaining south of the Marne, the evident conclusion, judging from the results of the following two days and the losses he had suffered, was that he would be unable to continue the offensive.

Our I Corps, on the front from Château-Thierry to Belleau Wood, was in position to be expanded and there was the possibility of adding still another corps to that front. The original plan, which contemplated the first employment of this corps in the St. Mihiel region, with headquarters at Toul, like so many plans, had been upset temporarily by the changing situation caused by the successive German victories.

The Château-Thierry region now seemed to be further indicated as the sphere of activity for Americans for the time being. With one corps already in that vicinity, the first step had been taken. In addition to the seven American divisions in line or near the salient, there were nineteen others in France, five in quiet sectors to the east, five behind the British lines, five in training areas, two in depots, and two just arrived. So that we then had in France at that moment the equivalent of fifty-two French or average British divisions. Omitting the five in training areas, the two in depots, and the two just arrived, there remained for service

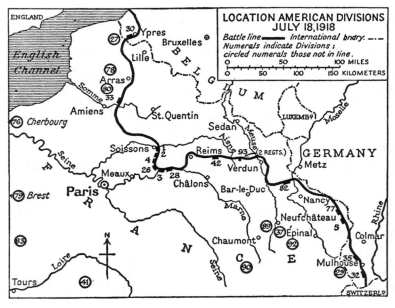

at the front a force of Americans equal in numbers to thirty-four Allied divisions.

Thus at this time the American combat reënforcements to the Allies more than offset the reënforcements which Germany had been able to bring from the Eastern to the Western Front after the collapse of Russia. Without the addition of the Americans the Allies would have been outnumbered by nearly 400,000 men.

Now that the Allied armies were no longer in jeopardy, it seemed opportune to push the formation of our own army near Château-Thierry for use against the Marne salient in the counteroffensive which I had frequently urged. The outlook for the Allies had changed materially since the crisis of early June. The enemy had been held in his most recent attacks and his losses were presumably heavy. He was losing the advantage of numbers and his superiority in every respect was passing.

CHAPTER XXXVII

American Forces Provide Superiority in Manpower—Counteroffensive Marne Salient—1st and 2d Divisions Arrowhead of Attack—Capture over 6,000 Prisoners—Germans Begin Retirement—Turning Point of War—Other American Divisions Take Part in Attack—Visit to Units Engaged—Confer with Pétain and Foch—American Sector Decided—Entertain Haig

(Diary) Provins, Saturday, July 20, 1918. The 1st and 2d Divisions, with Moroccan Division, pierced the Marne salient below Soissons on the 18th. The 4th and 26th Divisions also gained ground. Wrote M. Clemenceau protesting against French press publishing news of American activities.

Martin Egan back yesterday from visit to base ports impressed with improvement. Only 65 per cent of tonnage needed operating in our European service. Have requested 23,000 men qualified only for limited service to replace able men for combat.[1] Cabled War Department proposing four months' training program at home. Left for front after luncheon, accompanied by General Wright and Colonel Thomas H. Emerson. Spent the night at Montmirail.

To-day visited our troops in Marne sector.

WITH a preponderance of over 300,000 rifles, the Germans inflicted a crushing defeat on the British in March, followed by another in April, and in May achieved a striking victory against the French. Allied manpower rapidly dwindled to a dangerous degree and their morale almost reached the breaking point. In the supreme emergency, which, unfortunately, had not been wholly foreseen and only partially provided for, the necessity of greater effort by America had be-

[1] As showing the diversity of requirements, the following are some of the positions for which these men were needed: Forestry and general construction work, laborers, carpenters, chauffeurs, checkers for docks and depots, watchmen, kitchen helpers, cooks, mechanics, stenographers, storekeepers, telephone installers, telephone operators, typists, warehousemen, quartermaster clerks, engineer clerks, ambulance drivers, bakers, blacksmiths, canvas workers, cable splicers, draftsmen, electricians, finance men, harness workers, laundrymen, multiplex operators, photographers, punchers, sheetmetal workers, shoemakers, supervisors, tailors, toolmakers and wheelwrights.

come imperative. With the help of British shipping our troops, without which the Allied defeat would have been inevitable, had been pouring into France at a rate hitherto unbelievable.

Thanks to this unprecedented movement, Allied inferiority in March had been within three months transformed into Allied superiority of over 200,000 men. Biding their time, the Allies had waited until our arrivals should give them the preponderance.

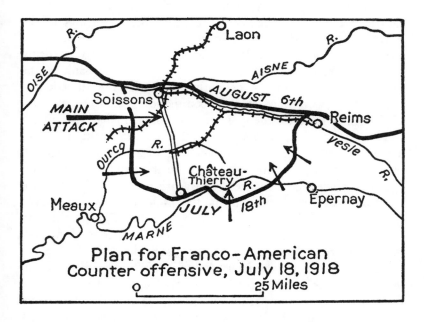

Plan for Franco-American
Counter offensive, July 18, 1918
0   25 Miles

When the Germans chose the front near Reims for their attack on July 15th, they played into the hands of the Allies. Plans already made provided for a counterattack against the base of the salient south of Soissons by the French Tenth Army, with our troops to pierce the line. Several French and American divisions had been held southwest of Soissons in readiness to participate. The youth and the enthusiasm of the vigorous young Americans, not yet war-weary, more than offset their lack of training and experience. With the German offensive suddenly frustrated, the moment had arrived for the counterblow that was destined to change the entire aspect of the war.

Our 1st (Summerall) and 2d (Harbord) Divisions were hastily assembled to form the American III Corps under General Bullard, but, as his corps staff had not yet been fully organized, these divisions became a part of the French XX Corps (Berdoulat). This corps, composed of these two divisions and the French 1st Moroccan Division, which had an excellent reputation, was assigned to the most important position on the left center of the French Tenth Army, commanded by General Mangin. The corps, which was four-fifths American, had the honor of being the spearhead of the thrust against this vulnerable flank of the salient, an honor which it gallantly sustained. The direction of the attack was eastward over the commanding plateau just south of Soissons and across the main road leading to Château-Thierry.

The 1st Division, recently relieved from the Cantigny sector and en route to a rest area, was north of Meaux when it received orders on the 13th to move by truck to the front. After a hurried departure, the advance troops early on the 16th reached the Forest of Retz[1] and during the night the division moved through the forest to its eastern edge. On the night of the 17th its columns marched forward over muddy and congested roads toward the front, where they arrived just in the nick of time.

The 2d Division was recuperating near Montreuil-aux-Lions when the order came on the 14th to move toward the lines south of Soissons. Starting by truck on the afternoon of the 16th, dawn on the 17th found the infantry and machine gun elements arriving at the Forest of Retz, the artillery and trains having gone before. That night the movement toward the front, through the dark forest, was made with extreme difficulty. The narrow roads had now become crowded, troops lost their direction and there was serious doubt whether they would be at their line of departure by the appointed hour of 4:35 A.M., on the 18th. With most commendable energy and initiative the officers led their commands

---

[1] This forest, which lay near the western face of the salient, was also known as the Forest of Villers-Cotterêts.

forward, winding in and out through the almost inextricable confusion of wheeled vehicles. One of the battalions assigned to lead in the attack, which had been on the march most of the night, was forced to move at a run for the last few hundred yards, reaching its place just as the barrage started.[1]

The 2d Division headquarters found itself on the 16th with no knowledge of the terrain and no detailed instructions for the attack. Going toward the front over the congested roads, Harbord and his Chief of Staff on the evening of the 16th found the headquarters of the French XX Corps at Retheuil, where they were given the directive for the attack, from which they issued the division orders for distribution the following day.

The country over which the XX Corps advanced consisted of a succession of wooded ravines that lay across the line of advance. Scarcely any roads led toward the front. The German main defenses along the ridges of the Soissons plateau were naturally strong. With the added obstacle of his entrenchments the enemy evidently felt himself reasonably secure. It was harvest time and the ripening grain that covered the rolling landscape gave excellent cover for the enemy's infantry and machine guns and also helped to hide our advance.

Without the usual preliminary artillery preparation, the assaulting battalions, accompanied by light tanks, plunged forward behind the barrage. The enemy was caught by surprise and the 1st and 2d Divisions, supported by the Moroccan Division in the center, quickly overran his forward positions and broke through the zone of his light artillery. Though constantly confronted by fresh enemy troops, this American-Moroccan corps took the lead and its progress was beyond expectations. By noon it had captured half of the great plateau on its front, with many prisoners, and later the forward elements reached the day's objective.

The 2d Division encountered and overcame strong opposition, especially at Vierzy. In a determined assault launched after 6 P.M., the town was captured and a line overlooking the valley of

[1] One unnecessary cause of delay reported was that the French officer in charge of the truck trains insisted upon counting the men carried and obtaining receipts for their transportation.

the Crise River was occupied. The 1st Division had also carried everything before it, capturing fortified farmhouses and other points where it met stiff resistance, finally taking Missy-aux-Bois and establishing its front line slightly beyond that town.

The attack of the corps was resumed on the morning of the 19th against the German lines which had been heavily reënforced with machine guns and artillery during the night. The 1st Division, leading the French division on its left, encountered fire from both the front and left flank. Tanks were sent to its as-

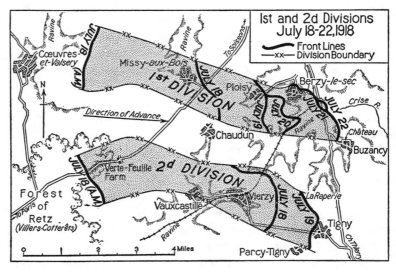

sistance and with close artillery support the division was enabled slowly to gain ground, but at considerable cost.

The 2d Division, with the reserves of the first day in the lead, forged ahead against stout opposition to the main Château-Thierry road, but was compelled to withdraw to the vicinity of La Raperie. After very severe fighting, it finally established a line just west of Tigny, with the road under the control of its guns. The division was relieved by a French division on the night of the 19th, having advanced 6½ miles, captured 3,000 prisoners and 75 guns, and sustained about 5,000 casualties.

On the 20th, the 1st Division doggedly continued its progress in spite of a determined stand by the Germans in front of Berzy-le-Sec, which the French attempted to take without success. In the afternoon Summerall directed that the town be taken by the 1st Division, but the effort failed. However, on the 21st, assisted by the skillful use of artillery and with consummate dash, in the face of intense artillery and machine gun fire, the town was captured by the 2d Brigade (Buck). Meanwhile, the right of the division and the French division which had relieved the Moroccans, had crossed the Soissons—Château-Thierry highway and reached the château of Buzancy. The line now ran parallel to the Crise, with Soissons commanded by our artillery.

The 1st Division, throughout four days of constant fighting, had advanced nearly 7 miles, taken 3,500 prisoners and 68 guns from seven different German divisions employed against it, and had suffered about 7,200 casualties.

The thrust of the XX Corps, in conjunction with the Franco-American attacks farther south, along the western face of the salient, was made with such dash and power that the enemy's position within the salient was rendered untenable. As a result he was forced into the decision of retiring from the salient, and the movement began on the 20th. We had snatched the initiative from the Germans almost in an instant. They made no more formidable attacks, but from that moment until the end of the war they were on the defensive. The magnificent conduct of our 1st and 2d Divisions and the Moroccan Division marked the turning of the tide. Pétain said it could not have been done without our divisions.

General Mangin, who commanded the French Tenth Army, said this about it in his general orders:

"Officers, noncommissioned officers and soldiers of the United States III Corps, shoulder to shoulder with your French comrades you were thrown into the counteroffensive battle which commenced on the 18th of July.

"You rushed into the fight as to a fête.

"Your magnificent courage completely routed a surprised enemy and your indomitable tenacity checked the counterattacks of his fresh divisions.

"You have shown yourselves worthy sons of your great country and you were admired by your brothers-in-arms.

"Ninety-one guns, 7,200 prisoners, immense booty, ten kilometers of country reconquered. This is your portion of the spoil of victory.

"Furthermore, you have really felt your superiority over the barbarous enemy of the whole human race against whom the children of Liberty are striving.

"To attack him is to vanquish him.

"American Comrades: I am grateful to you for the blood so generously spilled on the soil of my country.

"I am proud to have commanded you during such days and to have fought with you for the deliverance of the world.

"MANGIN."

The German Chancellor, Von Hertling, said later:

"We expected grave events in Paris for the end of July. That was on the 15th. On the 18th even the most optimistic among us understood that all was lost. The history of the world was played out in three days."

Field Marshal von Hindenburg, in "Out of My Life," says:

"From the purely military point of view it was of the greatest and most fateful importance that we had lost the initiative to the enemy and were at first not strong enough to recover it ourselves. We had been compelled to draw upon a large part of the reserves which we intended to use for the attack in Flanders. This meant the end of our hopes of dealing our long-planned decisive blow at the English army.

"In these circumstances the steady arrival of American reënforcements must be particularly valuable for the enemy. Even if these reënforcements were not yet quite up to the level of modern requirements in a purely military sense, mere numerical superiority had a far greater effect at this stage when our units had suffered so heavily.

"The effect of our failure on the country and our allies was even greater, judging by our first impressions. How many hopes, cherished during the last few months, had probably collapsed at one blow! How many calculations had been scattered to the winds!"

The following extracts from a special report by Colonel, later Brigadier General, Paul B. Malone, who commanded the 23d Infantry regiment of the 2d Division in this battle, give a vivid picture of the difficulties which the troops of the division encountered in reaching the line of deployment, and their progress thereafter:

"The road to the front was found completely blocked, the troops endeavoring to thread their way through and between vehicles of all kinds. It began raining early in the evening and the night became so dark that it was impossible to see at more than a pace distance. No opportunity of any kind could be given to the company or platoon commanders to reconnoiter the way to the front, through an intricate network of roads and trails in the forest. * * * Proceeding to the Post of Command of the French Regimental Commander I stationed noncommissioned officers to guide the troops as best they could in the proper direction. At 2:30 A.M. the Regimental Adjutant reported that all three battalions had secured ammunition and were moving along their proper routes to the front. The French troops at the front were sending in reports that the American troops to relieve them had not arrived, and throughout the night the most disquieting reports constantly arrived, indicating that our troops were lost in the woods.

"The attack was to start at 4:35 A.M. At about ten minutes to four the Sergeant Major of the First Battalion arrived at my P.C. [Post of Command] with the information that Companies 'A' and 'B' had lost their way and that he thought only a small portion of the First Battalion had reached position for the attack. A moment later I was advised that two battalions of the Marines were then passing the P.C. en route to the front, from which it was apparent that they could not possibly reach the jumping-off trenches in time. I immediately left the P.C. with my entire staff, the French regimental commander, all of his runners and all of mine. The French regimental commander turned over all of his runners to the Marines and Lieutenant Colonel Feland placed them with his troops to guide them as rapidly as possible to the front. I personally moved to the front with Companies 'A' and 'B,' picking up along the way some troops of the 9th Infantry and the 23d Infantry that had been lost in the darkness. It seemed futile to hope that any attack under such circumstances could be a success. Nevertheless, the troops were led as rapidly as possible along the road through the woods and at 4:35 A.M. our artillery barrage came down with a crash. A guide led me for a few minutes in the wrong direction but the proper direction was finally recovered and at 5:00 A.M. myself and this detachment, with my staff officers and runners, emerged from the eastern extremity of the Forêt de Retz at the proper point prescribed in the orders for the attack. The attack was already under way, the Second Battalion leading the attack had gone over the top at H hour (4:35 A.M.), but to reach its position it had been necessary to advance during the last ten minutes at a run, the men reaching the jumping-off trenches breathless and exhausted. * * *

"From the time the troops left the vicinity of Montreuil-aux-Lions (near Château-Thierry) they had received no food and practically no water; they had had no sleep and had fought continuously since the beginning of the operation. * * * No more difficult circumstances could have confronted a command than that which presented itself to this regiment on the night of July 17th-18th.

"Without reconnaissance of any kind it was compelled to move through an absolutely unknown terrain during a night which was intensely dark and rainy, to thread its way through a road blocked to a standstill with traffic of all kinds, find its jumping-off place of which nothing was previously known, form in three echelons for an attack, all three of which must move in harmony under an artillery barrage, the exact timing of which could not be secured because of the unknown incidents of the attack, and attack over a terrain which it had not previously seen, the attack changing in direction twice during its progress. The troops actually ran to their destination and met the enemy in an entrenched position with no other weapon than the rifle; yet they were completely and overwhelmingly successful."

While the 1st and 2d Divisions were waging a bitter contest for the possession of the crucial point near Soissons, our troops around the western rim of the salient also had been steadily driving ahead. The brigades of the 4th Division (Cameron) were at first assigned to French divisions. In the attack of July 18th, one brigade captured Noroy, and on the 19th advanced about two and one-half miles. The other brigade, in the attack of the 18th, assisted in the capture of Hautevesnes and Courchamps, took Chevillon and made further substantial gains. On the 19th and 20th, it made a gain of about two miles.

The I Corps (Liggett), serving with the French Sixth Army and composed of our 26th and the French 167th Divisions, took part in the movement. Attacking from the line near Belleau, the 26th Division (Edwards) captured the villages of Torcy and Belleau on July 18th and elements reached the base of the dominating Hill 193, which was in the sector of the French division. On the 19th and 20th the French failed to take Hill 193, which commanded the Allied lines, but on the 20th the 26th Division succeeded in taking Gonetrie Farm and secured a foothold on Hill 190. On the 21st, it was found that the Germans had withdrawn during the night and the division moved forward with little or no opposition until it reached the new German line near Épieds, east of the Soissons—Château-Thierry highway. On the 22d Trugny was taken and a foothold secured in Épieds, but a strong German counterattack forced a retirement to Breteuil Wood.

Although the success of the 1st and 2d Divisions near Soissons on the first two days of the attack had started the withdrawal of the German armies, they fought desperately from position to position and their retirement was skillfully conducted throughout in an effort to save men and matériel from capture. They were faced with the problem of saving what they could from the enormous quantities of supplies and equipment which had been brought into the salient. A subsequent statement of the Germans declared that their artillery column alone would occupy a road space of 375 miles. To obtain the necessary time for the removal of stores and matériel their retreat was conducted by stages, and the successive defense lines were prepared accordingly.

In the counteroffensive beginning July 18th, the French and American troops east of Château-Thierry did not advance immediately. On the 20th, however, patrols from the 3d Division (Dickman) discovered that the Germans had withdrawn and on the 21st the division crossed the Marne in pursuit, capturing Mont St. Père and driving machine guns out of Chartèves. Jaulgonne was taken on the 22d and gains made beyond the town, but the ground could not be held. On the 23d, the division wrested Mont l'Evèque Wood from the Germans, who that night retired to the line Vincelles-Coincy, leaving machine guns to delay our advance on Le Charmel.

On the 20th, I visited the commanders of our units engaged and found all roads west of the salient greatly congested. No one who has not been an eye-witness can visualize the confusion in traffic conditions that exists immediately behind the lines during the progress of a great modern battle. It is a most difficult problem to regulate circulation over the roads and keep them from becoming seriously blocked, especially at night, when vehicles must travel without lights and frequent halts are necessary due to accidents of various sorts.

On this trip, my first call was at the headquarters of the 3d Division, where General Dickman gave me details of the fighting on July 15th, when his troops showed such remarkable coolness and heroism in repulsing the Germans who assaulted and partially surrounded some units of his division.

Going from there to the 28th Division (Muir), farther to the east, I found that several companies of its 55th Brigade, through some misinterpretation of instructions, had been assigned to French battalions and were serving in the front lines at the time of the attack on the 15th. The French gave way before the German assault, but our companies, which had not been told that the French were retiring, gallantly held their positions and as a result found themselves surrounded and only fought their way to the rear under the greatest difficulties. This was another striking illustration of the danger of having our small units serve in Allied divisions.

At the headquarters of the I Corps, I reviewed Liggett's situation and found his divisions making satisfactory progress. We went forward to the 26th Division which, with the French division comprising this corps, was attacking the enemy, who was stubbornly fighting to cover his retirement.

While traveling northward through the Forest of Villers-Cotterêts it was almost impossible to make any headway, as the road was filled with columns moving in both directions over the badly cut-up road. In the middle of the forest, at the main cross-roads, I met General Mangin, the Army Commander, trudging along on foot, followed by his automobile, which was working its way through the jam of troops, trucks, artillery, wagons, and ambulances, including some with wounded. Although we talked but a moment, it was long enough for him to speak in high praise of the brilliant dash of the American divisions under his command. Moving on toward the front, we soon found ourselves at the command post of the 1st Division, sheltered in an underground quarry west of Cœuvres-et-Valsery. The Chief of Staff, Colonel Campbell King, gave me a full account of the fighting and explained the division's position. Leaving a message of congratulations for Summerall, who was still somewhere on the battlefield, we proceeded on our journey.

Arriving later at Taillefontaine, we located General Bullard, who, much to his regret and my own, had not been able to organize his III Corps Staff in time to take command of our 1st and 2d Divisions in this attack. However, he was just as elated over their work as if he had commanded them himself. En route from there to the 2d Division, which had just been withdrawn from the line, we passed a Scottish division going toward the front to relieve our 1st. At the headquarters of the 2d, I saw General Harbord, who always wore his tin hat, and his Chief of Staff, Colonel Preston Brown. They were both in fine spirits and could hardly find words to express their enthusiasm over the achievements of the division and I was happy to congratulate them on its splendid conduct. I recall saying to Harbord that even though the 1st and 2d Divisions should never fire another shot they had made themselves and their commanders immortal.

Having received a telephone request from General Pétain to meet him that evening for dinner and a conference, I went on to Provins. On account of being held back by traffic in reaching the 1st and 2d Divisions, darkness overtook us and we were also caught in a heavy rain storm. We were delayed further by crowded roads and by time lost examining sign-boards and maps, but about 1:30 in the morning we finally reached Provins, where I spent the night with our Chief of Mission, Major Paul H. Clark.

(Diary) Paris, Sunday, July 21, 1918. Saw Pétain this morning. He said that all French commanders were enthusiastic over American troops. Held conference with him about employment of other divisions and reached an agreement which we jointly presented to Foch this afternoon. This being Belgian national holiday, I telegraphed the greetings of the A.E.F. to His Majesty, the King, commanding the

Belgian Army. Chemical Warfare Service organization officially approved. War Department cables difficulties of diverting tonnage for shipment horses and suggests expedition of motor transport instead.

With every new demonstration of the efficiency of Americans in battle, the French became louder in their praise, and it looked as though they were ready to welcome the formation of an American army as soon as the various elements could be assembled. In talking it over with Pétain, I proposed anew that we should now take positive steps to plan for a sector for the American Army near Château-Thierry, or at some other active part of the front. I also suggested that we should have a quiet front of our own where we could send exhausted divisions from the battle line for rest and recuperation and where untrained divisions could go for preliminary line experience. Moreover, it was very important that an active sector be chosen at once in order to plan definitely the necessary installations. To all of this he agreed in principle.

I told him that I expected to take command of the American First Army when it was organized, and that, while retaining entire independence regarding plans and the conduct of operations, it seemed best in the beginning to place our army on the same footing as the French armies in order to secure their full coöperation. The practical effect of this would be that the French would handle many intricate questions concerning the civil population behind the lines and would feel under obligations to provide French artillery, aviation, truck transportation and tanks, much of which we still lacked and which could be supplied and managed efficiently only by the most intimate coördination between the French and ourselves.

In the first appearance of an American army beside the Allied armies, it was clearly my place to take personal command, which I was now in position to do, as our problems of supply were soon to be under efficient direction that would largely relieve me from the necessity of constant supervision. Furthermore, it accorded with my own desire from the purely military point of view.

Regarding the rest sector, Pétain and I agreed that it could be on the southern side of the St. Mihiel salient for the present, both of us having in mind our previous plan to make this the active American front later on. With the understanding that we should limit our conversation with General Foch and not go too much into details about the future, we went to see him at Bombon and laid the proposal before him. After some discussion and the approval of Pétain, he agreed to think the matter over and let me know.

(Diary) Paris, Tuesday, July 23, 1918. Saw Dawes yesterday about Spanish decree forbidding exportation of horses. McFadden working on problem. Mott brought letter from Foch approving Toul sector for Americans. Visited our wounded in Paris hospitals; impressed by their fine spirit. Mr. Nitti, Italian Prime Minister, requests more American troops for Italy. Our divisions progressing in Marne sector against strong enemy resistance.

Met Mr. Stettinius, Assistant Secretary of War, to-day and am certain he will be very valuable in handling munitions and financial questions.

Sir Douglas Haig, General Lawrence, Colonels Bacon and Boyd took dinner with me this evening.

The horse supply question now became more serious, due to a Spanish decree, which had been issued on July 22d, forbidding the exportation of horses. It looked as though this would prevent us from obtaining the 25,000 or 35,000 that we had hoped to get. It was said, and was doubtless true, that the embargo had been laid to force our War Trade Board to permit the shipment to Spain of cotton and other raw materials and manufactured articles required by her industries. After consultation with Dawes, the task of handling this matter was delegated to Mr. George Mc-Fadden, who had an intimate knowledge of the situation. I went over the question with him and concurred in his opinion that the War Trade Board should be urged to make some trade concessions to Spain. He cabled Washington, recommending that the State, Treasury, and War Departments should agree upon the policy to be followed, and also suggesting in some detail the method of procedure.

Spain was then in the throes of economic and commercial depression, with her cotton mills at Barcelona operating only three days per week and with three-fourths of her railway service discontinued for lack of equipment and fuel. It was believed that concessions on our part would influence Spanish public opinion in favor of the Allies and make it possible for us to obtain at least the 17,000 animals we had already contracted for. Eventually an export permit for upwards of 40,000 animals was granted, but only a few were received prior to the Armistice.

On the evening of the 23d, I had the pleasure of Marshal Haig's company at dinner. It was always interesting to talk with him and as we had not met for some time we discussed recent events, especially the success of the combined French and American counteroffensive. It was recalled that before the enemy's offensive of May 27th the French had thought that he intended to make a further effort against the British, and had declined to take the view that he was likely to attack on the Aisne. The French believed, Sir Douglas said, that the strength in reserves behind the armies of Prince Rupprecht, which confronted the British, led to that conclusion. On the other hand, they seemed to overlook their own front, which was very weak in reserves, a considerable number of which had been sent to aid the British. Sir Douglas referred to the fact that several British divisions sent to the French front for rest had been used against the German attack. He said that reports indicated that all of Prince Rupprecht's army was still in front of the British, with thirty to forty divisions in reserve.

Sir Douglas was as aggressive as ever and was then planning to start another offensive in about three weeks. Under the circumstances I was expecting a definite request for the use of the five American divisions remaining in the British area. I was prepared, however, to decline, well knowing that if they should become involved in this operation it would be impossible for me to obtain them in time to organize an American army as planned. Marshal Haig seemed somewhat apprehensive as to what might be proposed at the conference we were to have with the Allied Commander-in-Chief the next day. I outlined my project for uniting our divisions as an army but did not mention the probable early recall of our units from his front.

CHAPTER XXXVIII

Conference of Commanders-in-Chief—Initiative with the Allies—Plans Approved—Preliminary Operations—St. Mihiel American Task—First Army Organization Under Way—American Troops Ordered to Russia —President's Declaration of Aims and Purposes of the United States— Harbord to Command Services of Supply—Proposal that Washington Control Supply—Letters from and to Secretary of War

(Diary) Chaumont, Wednesday, July 24, 1918. To-day attended conference of Commanders-in-Chief at General Foch's headquarters to discuss plans for offensive operations. Present: Generals Foch, Pétain, Weygand and Buat; Field Marshal Haig and General Lawrence; and Colonel Conner, Chief of Operations, Boyd and Hughes with me. Told General Foch after the conference that Washington directed sending troops to Murmansk if he approved. He offered no objections. Pétain and I confirmed plan to group American divisions under the I Corps. Went to I Corps headquarters, located in tumbledown house at Buire; also went to 26th Division. Returned to Chaumont this evening. Orders for organization of First Army issued to-day, to take effect August 10th.

THERE was a pronounced air of good feeling and confidence as we assembled for this conference. General Foch began by reading from notes giving a résumé of the general situation as it existed at the moment, with which, of course, we were all familiar. He stated that he proposed no definite plan but submitted his remarks to us as the basis of discussion. The main point was that the fifth German offensive of the year had been checked and the Allied counteroffensive beginning July 18th had transformed it into defeat. It was the general opinion that every advantage should be taken of this fact and that the Allies should continue their attacks with as much vigor as possible. Foch stated with satisfaction that we had now reached an equality in the numbers of combatants and an actual superiority in reserves. As the enemy would soon be required to relieve a considerable number of tired divisions from the active front, the Allies would rapidly gain further superiority through the constantly increasing number of Americans. All information went to show that the enemy had two armies, so to speak, he continued, one an exhausted holding army and the other a shock army, already weakened, maneuvering behind this frail front. Unquestionably we had material advantage in aviation and tanks and, to a smaller degree, in artillery, although this would be augmented by the arrival of personnel and armament of American artillery.

As to the reserve strength behind the Allies, it would soon be powerful indeed if the rate of 250,000 per month at which the Americans were pouring in could be maintained. One could sense an approaching crisis, on the enemy's side, probably not so very remote, because of the difficulty which he was having in keeping up the effective strength of his units. Beyond these advantages of material force in our favor, there was also the moral ascendancy we had gained by our recent victories and his failures. Foch also felt, as we all did, that the Allies now held the initiative and that from this time on they should abandon the defensive attitude that had been so long imposed upon them and continue the offensive without cessation. He mentioned a series of operations on the different fronts which should aim at results of immediate importance to subsequent progress. These preliminary actions would be of limited extent and would be executed as rapidly as possible with the number of troops available. He then pointed out the following offensives which it was evident would be indispensable to later operations:

The release of the Paris-Avricourt railroad in the Marne region as the minimum result of present (Franco-American) operations;

The freeing of the Paris-Amiens railroad by a concerted action of the British and French;

The release of the Paris-Avricourt railroad in the region of Commercy by the reduction of the St. Mihiel salient by the American Army. By thus reducing the front, it would bring the Allies within reach of the Briey region and permit action on a larger scale between the Meuse and Moselle.

Further offensives were foreseen having in view the recapture of the mining section to the north by definitely driving the enemy from the region of Dunkirk and Calais.

With the armies working together, operations could be continued at such brief intervals as to prevent the enemy from using his reserves to advantage and without giving him time to build up depleted units. No one could tell then just how far these efforts might take us, but possibly they would, if successful, pave the way for something more important in the late summer or autumn, which in turn would still further increase our advantage. No one suggested that the plans of the moment or those to follow might be carried so far as to terminate the war in 1918. Concerning the part each should play, Foch then asked expressions of opinion of the respective Commanders-in-Chief as to how these or any other operations that we might propose should be conducted.

Marshal Haig gave his views and plans, which agreed with the general outline suggested, as did General Pétain, who wanted further to consider the possibilities. As far as these preliminary operations applied to the Americans, they were simply a restatement of the plans we had been leading up to ever since our entry into the war. I, therefore, advised him that details of organization and supply were receiving every consideration in preparation of the American Army to do its part.

In this connection, I brought up again the question of obtaining artillery, and the understanding that we should have the coöperation of the French in this respect was confirmed. The progress by the United States in the manufacture of guns was discussed and the hope was expressed that it might reach a point which would enable the French to turn their attention to making shells, and this brought out the critical situation regarding steel. I had been urging haste in our home production of artillery and remarked that we had all learned from experience that programs for manufacture of munitions had rarely been fully met.

The pressing need of cross-country transportation was then considered and it was agreed to urge upon our respective Governments the utmost celerity in this regard. General Foch suggested the importance of tanks, but we were without tanks and there was little prospect that the plan of joint production by the British and ourselves, previously undertaken, would provide them in any quantity for use in the immediate future. The proposal that we should develop our own tanks at home had come to naught. Marshal Haig reported that the British had three brigades with 700 or 800 tanks in all, but General Pétain said the French were short. Finally, however, the hope was held out by both of them that they would be able to let us have some tanks by the time we should need them.

While this conference was primarily held for the exchange of views, it decidedly confirmed the principle of coöperation and emphasized the wisdom of having a coördinating head for the Allied forces. The conclusions regarding operations, though more or less tentative, became the basis of action for the future. The general plans definitely contemplated that the American forces would constitute an independent army.

Frequent references have already been made to the difficulties and delays encountered in forming a distinctive American army, which I had contended was essential to Allied success. Not only was it demanded by the existing situation but by all the circumstances of our participation in the war. Not the least important consideration was that until such an army should be actually formed and successfully carry out an operation our position before our people at home would not be enviable.

Although General Pétain and I, in accordance with our first conversation, more than a year before, had definitely planned the transfer of the line north of Toul to American control, the demands for our divisions during April and May had been so great that this could not be done. Later, when it was agreed that the Americans should take over the sector as soon as four divisions could be united there, the German assault on the Chemin des Dames had disrupted the arrangement and our most effective divisions had to be sent to the Château-Thierry front. Thus each successive German offensive had brought a crisis followed by pressure for modifications of plans, and each had operated to delay the time when an American army could be assembled.

It was imperative that we should meet these conditons as they arose, although sending our regiments, brigades or divisions to aid the Allied armies caused a wide dispersion of our units that made it difficult to assemble them now that the time had come to take that step. The worst feature was that the special shipments of infantry and machine gunners made the organization of corps and armies impossible without obtaining from the French or British, at least temporarily, the units corresponding to those we had omitted.

The situation, however, demanded a very definite understanding. The Allies were resuming offensive operations, the enemy seemed to be entirely committed to the defensive and we now had more than 1,200,000 American soldiers on French soil. The important part our divisions had played gave me every reason to press my determination to have our own army. It was a matter of no special importance for the moment where our combat units should be assembled, whether near Château-Thierry or elsewhere, as any front other than that in the northeast would probably not be permanent.

While at General Foch's headquarters I arranged with General Pétain for the expansion of the I Corps, then operating in the Marne sector, by which four American divisions were to be placed in the line with two in reserve. It was tentatively understood between us that the III Corps should be placed beside the I Corps to form an army on that front. At that time it was also planned to form a second army in the St. Mihiel sector as soon as practicable. My formal order creating the First Army was issued on July 24th, to take effect on August 10th, with headquarters at La Ferté-sous-Jouarre.

The Supreme War Council was prone to listen to suggestions for the use of Allied troops at various places other than the Western Front. One of these, on which the British seemed to be especially insistent, was to send troops to help the so-called White Army in Russia in order to keep open the communications through Murmansk. I was opposed to the idea, as it would simply mean scattering our resources, all of which were needed to build up the A.E.F. But the President was prevailed upon to help and I was directed to send a regiment provided General Foch had no objections. As apparently he had already considered the question, he gave his approval. The 339th Infantry, Lieutenant Colonel George E. Stewart commanding, together with one battalion of engineers, one field hospital company and one ambulance company, were designated for this service.

Now that we were to assume the offensive and our divisions were likely to be sent into battle at once upon arrival, it was more important than ever that those yet to come should receive careful training prior to reaching France. A few days before I had again drawn attention to the defects we had found and emphasized as strongly as possible the urgency of greater supervision of training at home. As a guide, I sent to Washington an intensive four months' program based upon our experience and also recommended that officers of all grades be subjected to the most careful general staff inspections during their period of preparation.

A recent conference with Mr. Shearman and Colonel Bruce Palmer revealed facts of the utmost significance and I again urged an increase in shipping. For the time being, sufficient deadweight cargo tonnage had been placed in our service to give us, with a 60-day turn-around, a little more than 600,000 tons of freight per month, but this was not nearly enough to keep our supplies going. According to our information only one-quarter of the 126,000 tons so far built at home for the Shipping Board, not all suitable for transatlantic service, and less than half of the 500,000 tons of Dutch and 200,000 tons of Swedish and other shipping taken over, had been allotted to the Army. Restating it as my judgment that the successful outcome of the war was dependent upon the fulfillment of the 80-division program, which could not be transported and supplied with the tonnage allotted, I urged that no less than 500,000 tons then employed on commercial routes be withdrawn for use in supplying our forces.

Realizing that the hesitancy of the War Department to increase cargo tonnage was partly on account of the fear of swamping both their ports and our own, I again stated emphatically that the increased tonnage could and would be handled at our end of the line with reasonable rapidity. While conditions were improving at the ports, I had already planned certain changes, which will appear later.

(Diary) Chaumont, Sunday, July 28, 1918. Saw Foulois on Thursday about aviation for the First Army. Representative Isaac Siegel called to urge independent welfare organization for Jewish soldiers. Conferred with Mr. Stettinius on Friday. Tardieu wants priority on Liberty motors; Stettinius will handle. Cable received giving President's statement to Allies. Discussed First Army organization with Logan and Moseley. Need for trucks, motor cars, ambulances, motorcycles and horses urgently reiterated by cable. Harbord spent the night with us. Appointed him Chief of S.O.S., much to his regret. General Kernan designated from Washington as representative at conference with Germans at Berne on handling prisoners.

General Trenchard, British Air Chief, and Lord Weir, British Air Minister, came yesterday to consider aiding us in aviation.

M. Claveille and Atterbury came this morning to talk over railway matters; discharge of cargo and evacuation improving; French coöperating better. Congratulations received from the Secretary of War on work being done by our army; also from Chief of Staff, Japanese Army.[1] Germans continue giving way in Marne salient. Am leaving to-night on inspection trip S.O.S.

The statement of "Aims and Purposes of the United States" which the President handed the Ambassadors of Great Britain,

[1] "July 28, 1918. Accept our hearty and grateful congratulations on the brilliant work done by your Army. The whole country is thrilled with pride in our soldiers. We follow eagerly every move they make. Their courage and success make us all prouder than ever that we are Americans and are represented by such heroic soldiers. They are worthy of their country and the cause.
"BAKER."

"July 28, 1918. Please accept my sincere congratulations on the recent brilliant success won by your gallant army on the French battlefield. I am looking forward with absolute confidence to the continued favorable development of the situation, and I feel fortified in my conviction of the final triumph of our common cause.
"GENERAL BARON Y UYEHARA."

France and Italy at this time, and which was cabled to me, set forth at some length in diplomatic language the position of the United States in the war. It began by saying: "The whole heart of the people of the United States is in the winning of this war. The controlling purpose of the Government of the United States is to do anything that is necessary and effective to win it." The statement then said in substance that the war could be won only by common council and intimate concert of action. It further said that our Government had adopted a plan for fighting on the Western Front using all its resources; that it had put into the plan the entire energy of the Nation and that it was then considering the possibility of increasing its effort; but, that if the larger program were at all feasible, the industrial processes and the shipping facilities of the associated powers would be taxed to the utmost.

The reasons given for not diverting any part of the American military forces from the Western Front to other points or objectives were that the instrumentalities to handle our army in France had been created at great expense and they did not exist elsewhere. Moreover, while the army had been sent a great distance, it was much farther to any other field of action. The President said: "The United States Government therefore very respectfully requests its associates to accept its deliberate judgment that it should not dissipate its forces by attempting important operations elsewhere." In the statement the Italian front was considered a part of the line of the Western Front and sending troops there would be, of course, subject to the decision of the Supreme Command.

As to Russia, it was made clear that intervention was out of the question, as it would serve no useful purpose nor be of advantage in the prosecution of the war. Russia should not be used in an attempt to make an attack on Germany from the east. The only justifiable reason for entering Russia, the President said, would be to aid the Czecho-Slovakians to consolidate their forces and to steady any efforts at self-government or self-defense in which the Russians might accept assistance. It was set forth that the Government of the United States by restricting its own action did not wish to be understood as seeking, even by implication, to influence the action or define the policies of its associates.

The statement referred to the willingness of our Government to coöperate with the Allies and send a small force to Vladivostok, where the necessity seemed immediate, and with the approval of the Supreme Command to send another to Murmansk to guard stores and make it safe for Russian forces to come together in the north. It was also stated that solemn assurance by the governments united for action should be given the people of Russia that no interference with her political sovereignty or intervention in internal affairs or impairment of territorial integrity was intended.

The statement gave no promise that the 80-division project had been adopted; in fact, it implied some misgiving as to whether such an extensive plan could be carried out by our Government. It did, however, as a result of its frankness, no doubt put an end to the importunities of the Allies to send American troops here and there and confirmed the attitude that I had taken that the war must be won on the Western Front.

In view of the decision for the assembly of corps and divisions to form our army, it became urgent that the plans for its organization be hastened with all possible speed. The outlines had been determined and members of the First Army staff were at work on the details, yet several questions pertaining to final selection of troops and their assignments had to be decided and directions given to the staff.

In view of our increased program, consideration had to be given to improvement in the general supply system. Although the recent reorganization had helped, it had been my purpose for some time to make changes in personnel in the S.O.S., particularly in the position of commander, which demanded great administrative ability. After much thought, the choice fell on General Harbord. His knowledge of organization, his personality, his energy and his loyalty made him the outstanding selection.

Reluctance to lose his services in command of troops, where he had shown himself to be a brilliant leader, caused me to delay until his division could be relieved from the active front.

I had recently received a letter from the Secretary of War which confirmed reports reaching my headquarters from other sources, in which he stated that it had been proposed that General George W. Goethals be sent over to take charge of the Services of Supply. The idea was that he would have coördinate authority with me and be in control of supplies from the source at home, thence across the Atlantic and up to the Zone of the Armies, and be directly under orders from Washington. The theory was that this arrangement would enable me to devote my time exclusively to military operations. The Secretary wished to know what I thought of the suggestion.

I much appreciated the Secretary's desire to relieve me of every burden that might interfere with the direction of operations, but there appeared to be an exaggerated view concerning the personal attention required in handling the details of administration. As a principle of military organization, the suggestion did not meet with my approval. The command had been organized carefully with just this situation in view and the supply system was fulfilling its functions as an essential part of the organic military structure so far as the conditions of delayed material and of limited and inexperienced personnel would permit. I was in control through my General Staff, which in turn was handling directly a multitude of questions immediately vital to military success. The system, to be successful, could have no divided authority or responsibility.

The man who directed the armies was the one to control their supply through a military commander responsible to him alone. This military principle, under the peculiar circumstances, could not be violated without inviting failure. It was applied in the British armies and as far as possible in the French. In each of the Allied armies the general in charge of the Services of Supply and the Lines of Communication of their forces was subordinate to the Commander-in-Chief. In our case it only remained to invest the commanding general of the supply system with necessary authority to enable him to take the initiative under my general direction.

One example borrowed from my experience in October will illustrate the soundness of the principle. During the battle of the Meuse-Argonne our situation at the front was such that the S.O.S. had to be literally stripped of every available man and all means of transportation—animals, trucks, and railroad rolling stock—that could possibly be spared. Assistance was given cheerfully, but it was done in compliance with my orders. One can imagine the chances of failure if it had been necessary to request these things from an official responsible not to me but to the War Department at Washington. The officer or group of officers who proposed such a scheme to the Secretary could not have had the success of the High Command in France very deeply at heart or else they lacked understanding of the basic principles of organization.

A reply to the Secretary of War regarding his suggestion concerning Goethals was sent at once by cable, in which I urged him not to permit any violation of the foregoing principles, and asked him to await my letter, which he advised he would do. The real answer, however, was the assignment of Harbord to command the Services of Supply. No further action was taken with reference to the proposed assignment of Goethals. I should have been glad to have him under other conditions.

The following letter from the Secretary containing his reference to the command of the supply system is given in full, especially because of his discussion of other important matters under consideration at the time, and because it shows in detail the personal attention the Secretary himself gave to such questions:

"July 6, 1918.

"My Dear General Pershing:

"I have your letter of June 18,[1] which reached me promptly. I have been studying with more than ordinary care and interest the dispatches of the past week or two with reference to the enlargement of our

[1] Chapter XXXII.

military effort and program. When your cablegram suggesting a 60-division [1] program came I immediately set about the necessary inquiries to discover just how far it fell within the range of industrial possibility. When the 100-division program came it occurred to me that we ought to study the situation with the view of determining the maximum amount we can do. I have the feeling that this war has gone on long enough and if any exertion on our part or any sacrifice can speed its successful termination even by a single day, we should make it. We are therefore now having studies made to show the things necessary to be done for three possible programs, one involving 60, one 80, and the other 100 divisions by the first of July, 1919. As soon as these programs are worked out we will, in consultation with the War Industries Board, determine how far manufacturing facilities already in existence or possible to be created can supply the necessary material, and the assistance we shall have to have in the way of heavy artillery and transportation from the British and French. It will then be possible to take up with those Governments a frank exhibition of the possibilities and to arrange for concerted action among us which will lead to the increase in our effort which you and General Foch recommend. In the meantime, I have asked the British Government to continue the troop ships which they have had in our service during June through July and August, and have told them frankly that we are considering an enlargement of our program which may require for a time at least the uninterrupted service of all the ships which we have been using. If we are able in July and August to match the performance of June, it will mean another half-million men in France, as the June embarkation figures from this country show slightly more than 279,000 men. Our own ships carried during that month something more than 100,000, which is, of course, doing better than our part as we originally calculated it. I think it highly important that neither General Foch nor the British and French Governments should assume our ability to carry out an enlarged program until we ourselves have studied it. There is no disposition on the part of the United States to shrink from any sacrifice or any effort, and yet experience has taught us that great as our capacity is in industry it takes time to build new factories, get the necessary machine tools, and bring together the raw materials for any large increase in industrial output, and I am especially concerned that there should be no disappointment on the part of our Allies. I would very much rather they expect less and receive more, than to expect more and be disappointed in the result. One of the happy effects of the recent accelerated shipment

[1] Evidently this refers to the 66-division program.

of troops has been that we have out-stripped our promises and, if I judge correctly the effect of this in Europe, it has been most agreeable and heartening.

"The Operations Committee of the General Staff is pressing forward the necessary studies. They involve, of course, questions of clothing, small arms, ammunition, transportation, and training. On the latter subject I am beginning to be fairly free from doubts; the troops which we have recently sent you have admittedly been of an uneven quality, chiefly because we have made up deficiencies in divisions about to sail by taking men from other divisions, with consequent disorganization of those divisions from which men were repeatedly taken, and when we got to a place where we could no longer carry out this process, fairly raw men had to be used in order to keep divisions from sailing short. The plan inaugurated by General March of having replacement divisions in this country from which deficiencies could be supplied without robbing other divisions and disorganizing them, seems to me to solve the problem, and the divisions which come to you in August and September will, I am sure, show highly beneficial results from this policy. In the meantime, we have discovered two things about training in this country which apparently nobody knew or thought of before we went into the war; first, that while it may take nine months or a year to train raw recruits into soldiers in peace time, when there is no inspiration from an existing struggle, it takes no such length of time now when the great dramatic battles are being fought and men are eager to qualify themselves to participate in them. We are certainly able to get more training into a man now in three months than would be possible in nine months of peace-time training. And, second, we have learned that to keep men too long in training camps in this country makes them go stale and probably does as much harm by the spirit of impatience and restlessness aroused as it does good by the longer drilling. The men in our training camps are champing at the bit, and this applies not only to the officers, who naturally want their professional opportunity, but to the men as well. Indeed, one of the difficulties in America is to make people content with the lot which keeps them here for any length of time, so impatient are we all, military men and civilians alike, to get to France where the real work is being done. As a consequence of these discoveries, I feel that we will be perfectly safe if we have a million men in training in the United States at all times. That will enable us to feed them out to you at the rate of 250,000 a month and bring that number in by draft at the other end, which will always give us an adequate supply of men who have had as much training as they can profitably secure here in the

United States. The finishing touches in any event will have to be given in France, and I think you will find that men who have had four months' training here are pretty nearly ready for use in association with your veteran and experienced troops, and that no prolonged period of European training, for infantry at least, will be found necessary. This makes the problem very simple from the point of view of the draft and the training camps. A number of the camps originally established by us have now been developed for specialized technical uses, but we still have a large number, and I think an adequate number, of camps which can be enlarged without great expense, and there seems little likelihood of our being obliged to resort to the billeting system, although of course we should not hesitate to do it if the need arose.

"All accounts which we receive in this country of the conduct of our men are most stimulating and encouraging. Apparently the common opinion is that we have rendered valuable, if not indispensable, service already, in a purely military way, in the great battles. I saw a letter a day or two ago from Mr. Cravath to Mr. Leffingwell, in which he gave the opinion of British and French men of affairs on the subject of the American troops, and it was enthusiastic. I was a little afraid that too enthusiastic comment might create a feeling of resentment on the part of our allies. Their men, of course, have stood these attacks for a long time, and it would only be human if they resented the newcomers getting too much attention at the expense of organizations which are battle-scarred and have had their valor tested in great conflicts; and I have a little feared, too, that if our people here at home were fed too many stories of success they might get the notion that this great task is going to be easy for Americans and be ill-prepared for any reverse, no matter how slight, which might come. For that reason I have exercised a good deal of self-restraint in my own discussion with the newspapermen and in such public addresses as I have made, seeking always to couple up the British and the French with our American soldiers and to make the whole war a matter of common effort, rather than of our own national effort. This has been especially easy because the spirit of America is now very high. The country is thoroughly unified and is waiting only to be shown how it can make further effective sacrifices and efforts. It occurs to me in this connection that it might be wise for you in your communiqués, from time to time, to refer to slight repulses suffered by our men; but of course I do not want our men to be repulsed merely to balance the news.

"On the 1st of July I wrote the President that 1,019,000 men had embarked from the United States for France. There had been so much speculation about numbers that it seemed necessary to be frank and tell the facts. The American people are accustomed to demanding the facts and there was some impatience manifested with the Department for its continued policy of silence on this subject. I realized when I made the statement that in all likelihood I should have to discontinue further reference to numbers, at least further specific references. The Germans, French, and British of course make no such announcements, and our allies will not like to have us adopting a different course. There are doubtless good military reasons for not being very generous with information of this kind, which finds its way to the enemy and enables them to make more certain calculations. Still, if the rate of shipments which we have maintained for the last two or three months can be kept up for another six months, I am not very sure that exact news carried to Germany of the arrival of Americans in France might not be helpful to us, rather than harmful. The German Government cannot fail to be impressed by this steady stream of fresh soldiers to the Western front.

"The President and I have had several conferences about your situation in France, both of us desiring in every possible way to relieve you of unnecessary burdens, but of course to leave you with all the authority necessary to secure the best results from your forces and to supply all the support and assistance we possibly can. As the American troops in France become more and more numerous and the battle initiative on some parts of the front passes to you, the purely military part of your task will necessarily take more and more of your time, and both the President and I want to feel that the planning and executing of military undertakings has your personal consideration and that your mind is free for that as far as possible. The American people think of you as their 'fighting General,' and I want them to have that idea more and more brought home to them. For these reasons, it seems to me that if some plan could be devised by which you would be free from any necessity of giving attention to services of supply it would help, and one plan in that direction which suggested itself was to send General Goethals over to take charge of the services of supply, establishing a direct relationship between him and Washington and allowing you to rely upon him just as you would rely upon the supply departments of the War Department if your military operations were being conducted in America, instead of in France. Such a plan would place General Goethals rather in a coördinate than a subordinate relationship to you, but of course it would transfer all of the supply responsibilities from you to him and you could then forget about docks, railroads, storage houses, and all the other vast industrial undertakings to which up to now you have given a good deal of your time and, as you know, we all think with superb success. I would be very glad to know what you think about this suggestion. I realize that France is very far from the United States and that our reliance upon cables makes a very difficult means of communication, so that you may prefer to have the supply system as one of your responsibilities. I would be grateful if you would think the problem over and tell me quite frankly just what you think on the subject. The President and I will consider your reply together, and you may rely upon our being guided only by confidence in your judgment and the deep desire to aid you.

"One other aspect of your burdens the President feels can be somewhat lightened by a larger use of General Bliss as diplomatic intermediary. The President is adopting as a definite rule of action an insistence upon Inter-Allied military questions being referred to the Permanent Military Representatives. Our difficulty here has been that the British representative would present something for consideration without the knowledge of the French, or the French without the knowledge of the British, and when we took the matter up for decision we would sometimes find that the other nation felt aggrieved at not being consulted. As each of the Allied Nations is represented at Versailles, the President is now uniformly saying with regard to all Inter-Allied military questions, that their presentation to him should come through the Permanent Military Representatives who, in a way, are a kind of staff for General Foch and undoubtedly maintain such close relations with him as to make any proposition which they consider one upon which his views are ascertained.[1] As the President deals in matters of military diplomacy with General Bliss, it would seem that he could with propriety relieve you of some part of the conferences and consultations which in the early days you were obliged to have with the British War Office and the French War Office, thus simplifying the presentation of Inter-Allied questions to the President.

"Mr. Stettinius will leave very shortly for Europe; I enclose you copy of a letter which I have given him, outlining the inquiries which I desire to have him make. You will find him a very considerate man in the matter of demands upon your time, as he is accustomed to

[1] The Military Representatives were advisers to the Supreme War Council and their recommendations were presented to the Council in the form of joint (unanimous) notes which took effect only upon approval by the Council. In case the recommendation affected the American Government or Army, the approval of President Wilson was also required. General Bliss was the intermediary between the Council and the President. The Military Representatives had no relation to the Supreme Commander, Marshal Foch.

dealing with busy men and not prolonging conferences beyond their useful limit.

"It seems not unlikely at present that I shall myself come over to Europe in connection with our enlarged military program. If we find that our ability to do the thing depends upon French and British coöperation it will be a good deal simpler to put the whole question up to the British and French Cabinets and get definite agreements of coöperation and concerted action. Cablegrams are of course inconclusive and uncertain, and I constantly find that even letters fail to carry just the spirit in which they are dictated. When I write you, of course I know that our personal relations and knowledge of each other are too cordial and entire to allow any sort of misunderstanding, but I haven't the same acquaintance with the British and French Cabinet officers, and with them the presumptions do not obtain which are always implied in our correspondence. I confess I am somewhat moved to this idea of the necessity for my going by my desire to go; it is a tremendous inspiration to see our forces and to look at the work which you and they have done.

"Cordially yours,

"Newton D. Baker
"*Secretary of War.*"

In reply, the following letter was sent the Secretary by return messenger:

"July 28, 1918.

"My Dear Mr. Secretary:

"I have your letter of July 6th and have gone over it very carefully.

"I realize that a very large undertaking has been proposed in the 80 to 100 division program, and that to carry it out is going to require very great sacrifices on our part. But, as you say, the war has gone on long enough and should be brought to a close as early as it is possible for us to do it.

"The main reason for an extreme effort on our part next year is the stimulating effect that our immediate entry into the war in a large way will have upon our allies. If we should not demonstrate our wish thus to bring the war to a speedy end our allies might not hold on over another year, and we shall need every ounce of fight they have left in them to win, not that we have not the men and the resources at home, but that if left to carry on the war alone, even on French soil, we would soon come to the limit of our ability to bring them over and supply them.

"I realize that we shall be put to it to furnish all the equipment, the aviation, the artillery, the ammunition, the tanks, and especially the horses, but if we can win next year it will be worth the supreme effort necessary to provide all these things. I do not, of course, overlook the shipping, nor the very strenuous work necessary at this end to handle the immense quantity of freight that will be required. Our port facilities must be increased, our railroads must be improved, and we must have a large increase in cars and locomotives. These things must come along rapidly from now on. We are preparing estimates for what we shall need and will forward them by cable as soon as finished.

"Just now we are passing through a very critical time. When the shipment of infantry and machine guns was increased during May, June and July, of course we had to reduce, or rather postpone, the corresponding troops for our service of the rear, with the result that we now find ourselves shorthanded and unable to handle as quickly as we should like the increase of supplies incident to the great expansion of our combatant forces.

"To add to the difficulties there has been a shortage of replacements in men, as we have had to throw all available troops into the lines to stop the German advance. So that we have not even had any troops to spare for work to help out the rear, making it appear that we are unnecessarily falling behind in unloading ships. I have cabled a request for service of the rear troops to be sent at once and hope they will not be delayed. We have a lot to do to catch up and get our ports and lines of communication in shape to meet the heavy demands that are to be made upon them.

"On June 23d, when Mr. Clemenceau was at my headquarters for the conference, I had an opportunity to speak about the use of our troops. I told him that they were being wasted and that instead of the Allies being always on the defensive, an American Army should be formed at once to strike an offensive blow and turn the tide of the war.[1] He was very much impressed at such boldness, as he had heard only of our men going into French divisions as platoons or at most as regiments. Soon after that Pétain was called to Paris and I have heard was told my views. Anyway Pétain soon began to take another view. * * *

"Our troops have done well for new troops and the part they have taken has encouraged our allies, especially the French, to go in and help put over a counteroffensive. This offensive, between Soissons and

[1] In conversation with M. Clemenceau it was further suggested that we could put in at least six fresh divisions, and possibly eight, for a counteroffensive south of Soissons or Reims, and stress was laid on the fact that we were still on the defensive and that in my opinion opportunities were being lost by not using our troops for a counteroffensive, which I urged upon him as well as upon Foch and Pétain.

Château-Thierry, was planned some time ago, to be undertaken especially in the event of the Germans attempting to push their line south of the Marne; or to the east between the Marne and Reims. I had conferred with General Pétain and had arranged to put the 1st, 2d, and 26th Divisions in the attack north of the Marne, supported by the 4th, while the 3d and 28th were to be used south of the Marne. As it turned out, all these troops were engaged with results you already know. The participation by our troops made this offensive possible and in fact the brunt of it fell to them. Our divisions in this advance completely outstepped the French and had to slow down their speed occasionally for them to catch up.

"Two American corps are now organized and on the active front. These are to be organized into the Field Army which will take its place in line under my immediate command on August 10th. We shall occupy a sector north of the Marne and probably replace the 6th French Army. At the same time we shall take over a permanent sector north of Toul and Nancy, where I shall organize a second army at an early date. After that we shall soon have troops enough for a third army. So that before long I shall have to relinquish command of the Field Army and command the group.

"I have had to insist very strongly, in the face of determined opposition, to get our troops out of leading strings. You know the French and British have always advanced the idea that we should not form divisions until our men had three or four months with them. We have found, however, that only a short time was necessary to learn all they know, as it is confined to trench warfare almost entirely, and I have insisted on open warfare training. To get this training, it has been necessary to unite our men under our own commanders, which is now being done rapidly.

"The additional fact that training with these worn-out French and British troops, if continued, is detrimental, is another reason for haste in forming our own units and conducting our own training. The morale of the Allies is low and association with them has had a bad effect upon our men. To counteract the talk our men have heard, we have had to say to our troops, through their officers, that we had come over to brace up the Allies and help them win and that they must pay no attention to loose remarks along that line by their Allied comrades.

"The fact is that our officers and men are far and away superior to the tired Europeans. High officers of the Allies have often dropped derogatory remarks about our poorly trained staff and high commanders, which our men have stood as long as they can. Even Mr.

Tardieu said some of these things to me a few days ago. I replied, in rather forcible language, that we had now been patronized as long as we would stand for it, and I wished to hear no more of that sort of nonsense. Orders have now been given by the French that all of our troops in sectors with the French would be placed under our own officers and that American division commanders would be given command of their own sectors. This has come about since my insistence forced the French to agree to the formation of an American Field Army.

"At a conference called by General Foch last Wednesday, the 24th instant, plans for assuming the offensive this year were discussed, as well as tentative plans for 1919. This is the first time the American Army has been recognized as a participant, as such, alongside the Allies. I shall give you from time to time an outline of what our plans are, but hope you will soon be here so that I may discuss them with you.

"I entirely agree with what you say regarding General Bliss as a diplomatic intermediary. However, very little of my time has been taken up with that sort of thing, except as it concerned questions of troop shipments and their use with British and French. As you know, I have the highest regard for General Bliss and our relations have been the most pleasant. I think he is admirably fitted to represent the President in many of these perplexing diplomatic questions that come up. He has excellent judgment, and is very highly regarded by the Allied official world.

"Mr. Stettinius has arrived and we have had several conferences. I am very much delighted to have him here. His presence is going to relieve me entirely of all those difficult questions pertaining to the allocation of materials, and the determination of manufacturing programs and the like. His action will be able to prevent the continuous flow of cablegrams from the Allies to our War Department on all these subjects.

"On the subject of General Goethals, I have about covered it in my cablegram of to-day. I thank you very much for referring this matter to me. Mr. Secretary, our organization here is working well. It is founded upon sound principles. May I not emphasize again the principle of unity of command and responsibility. It has always been my understanding that you believed that full power should be given to the man on the spot and responsible for results. I would say this regardless of the person in command. Our organization here is so bound up with operations, and training, and supply, and transportation of troops, that it would be impossible to make it function if the control of our service of the rear were placed in Washington. Please let us not make the mistake of handicapping our army here by attempting to control these things from Washington, or by introducing any coördinate authority. All matters pertaining to these forces, after their arrival in France, should be under the General Staff here where they are being and can be handled satisfactorily.

"Mr. Secretary, I have been more or less puzzled about this question of sending over General Goethals. I thought he was in charge of transportation over there and that he was considered necessary in that position. So, it is difficult to see just why he should have been proposed for this place. I do not wish to appear unappreciative of any suggestion from you because I know that it is your desire to do the best possible to help, and have satisfied myself by a knowledge of this fact. I do think, however, that General Harbord can handle it as well as, or better than, any one I know; besides, I have every confidence in General Harbord and know that he is going to pull in the team. I should have put Harbord in some time ago but his division was in the line. Now it goes to a quiet sector and his services can be spared.

"May I say a word about our training. Our successes here should not be hastily accepted as the basis for conclusions on the possibilities of building up efficient units by intensive training for short periods. Four months should be the minimum for drafts that are to enter as replacements in among old soldiers in organized units. But, it requires a much longer time than that to build units from the ground up. Eight or nine months, or even a year, would be better, so that if we could get all of next year's army in the ranks by November we should be much better prepared in the Spring for the immense task we are preparing for.

"May I again express my warm appreciation of your confidence, and say also how gratifying it is to me to enjoy the personal relations that exist between us.

"Will you please convey to the President my best compliments and the Army's faith in his leadership.

"With very warm regards and sincere good wishes, I am
"Very faithfully,
"JOHN J. PERSHING."

CHAPTER XXXIX

Inspect Services of Supply with Harbord—At Headquarters, Tours—Confer with Supply Chiefs—Visit Wounded—Bordeaux Works Immense—La Rochelle—Nantes and St. Nazaire Activities—Brest Well Organized—Other Installations—S.O.S. Monument to American Initiative

(Diary) Paris, Monday, August 5, 1918. Returned yesterday from tour of principal installations and activities of Services of Supply with Harbord, McAndrew and other staff officers, including Colonels Wilgus, Andrews and Boyd, Major Bowditch, and Lieutenant Adamson. General Foch called informally after my return.

Held conference to-day on transfer of greater authority to Commanding General, S.O.S. Saw Felton, Atterbury, and Langfitt on needs of port improvements and rail transportation.

THIS trip of inspection was made to note the progress and acquaint myself, the Chief of Staff, and General Harbord, by actual observation, with conditions in the S.O.S., and also with a view to making such changes in personnel and such improvements in methods as would insure the complete fulfillment of the increased obligations imposed upon that service by the enlarged troop and supply program that had been undertaken. Our first stop was on the 29th, at Tours, which, being the location of the Headquarters of the S.O.S., with a large American military garrison of 2,400 officers and 4,360 men, had become a center of great activity. After the usual greetings from the préfect, the mayor and the local French commander, we went

Note: Total strength of the A.E.F. on July 31st, 54,224 officers, 1,114,838 enlisted men.

Divisional units arriving during July included elements of the following divisions: 36th Division (National Guard, Texas and Oklahoma), Maj. Gen. William R. Smith; 76th Division (National Army, New England and New York), Maj. Gen. Harry F. Hodges; 79th Division (National Army, northeastern Pennsylvania, Maryland and District of Columbia), Maj. Gen. Joseph E. Kuhn; 91st Division (National Army, Nebraska, Montana, Wyoming, Utah, Alaska, Washington, Oregon, California, and Idaho), Brig. Gen. Frederick S. Foltz.

directly to General Kernan's headquarters to meet and confer with the several chiefs of services.

Speaking for the Medical Department, Brigadier General Ireland said that although short of personnel his organization was working satisfactorily, and that he then had 59,000 beds in the various hospitals from seaports to battle front. For the present he felt prepared to meet any ordinary emergency, but as to the future, a greater number of buildings for hospitals would be required. Although we had considerable new construction under way at various points, I had already urged the French Minister of War to let us have more buildings.

Brigadier General Jadwin, the head of the Department of Construction and Forestry, gave an account of good progress, in spite of lack of building material before our own sawmills had reached capacity output. This department had charge of the building of docks, the erection of storehouses at ports and depots, and of general construction.

The Chief Quartermaster, Brigadier General Rogers, stated briefly that the quantities of food and clothing on hand were ample to meet the immediate requirements of the forces. His Department had accumulated at various storage plants and base ports 45,000,000 rations, or about 90,000 tons, equivalent to forty days for the command. There was a shortage of horses, forage and labor. The 80,000 horses promised by the French would be only about one-half the number required for the forces then in France, but a study was under way with a view to reducing the number of horses needed by using motor transportation instead. There were only about 32,000 non-American laborers of all nationalities available, including prisoners of war, and every effort was being made by the Labor Bureau to obtain more from France, Italy, and Spain. We also had about 50,000 American labor and forestry troops, including 3,000 combatant troops, on this work.

The Motor Transport Service, under Brigadier General Meriwether Walker, was increasing in efficiency, but there was difficulty in obtaining trained chauffeurs and mechanics. Only about half the number of automobiles and trucks actually needed in the S.O.S. at that time had reached France.

The Chief of Aviation, Major General Patrick, said that while our planes were arriving in increasing numbers, we were far behind expectations and still dependent upon the French. We had only one-third the number of squadrons in combat service that we expected. Our Liberty motors, in the opinion of the Air Service, had proved to be the last word, and it was thought then that there would be no further delay in supplying our own and Allied needs.

Brigadier General C. B. Wheeler, the Chief of Ordnance, who had succeeded Brigadier General Williams, said that the automatic supplies were coming regularly. Thus far no guns had been received from home and we should probably have to rely upon the Allies for the larger program. The indications were, however, that the French would be unable to produce enough for both their army and ours. The powder and explosive program was up to requirements, but on account of lack of steel the manufacture of ammunition for artillery, which had also been left to the French, was slowing down.

The task of the Services of Supply was very great and its successful accomplishment vital, yet, even from the beginning, the idea prevailed in the minds of its personnel, especially at the ports, that they were not exactly doing the work of soldiers, and hence, their efforts lacked enthusiasm. So, beginning with Tours, I took every opportunity during this trip to speak directly to groups of officers and men, giving them an account of the splendid conduct of our soldiers in battle and impressing upon them that forwarding supplies of food and ammunition to the front was quite as important as the actual fighting.

We visited every activity at Tours, beginning with the Central Records Office, established by Brigadier General Davis as a large branch of the Adjutant General's Office, where the personal record of every man in the A.E.F. was kept. At Camp de Grasse, near the city, we found the railway operators, numbering thousands, comfortably situated in portable barracks. Certain engineer troops were kept at Tours for railway work, ready to respond to calls from any direction. The well-managed camp of German prisoners contained several hundred men used as laborers.

A number of British women, known as the Women's Auxiliary Army Corps, were lent to us by their Government to assist in clerical work. The 250 women located at Tours occupied neat and comfortable temporary barracks and presented a very military appearance on parade. Some fifty of them were ill in quarters at the time and I gave instructions that they should be transferred to our hospital. This force with us eventually numbered about 5,000. Its members rendered valuable and efficient service with our forces, releasing an equal number of men for duty elsewhere.

The base hospital at Tours was filled with men wounded in the recent engagements. They were receiving the best of care under the efficient group of medical officers and nurses. In speaking to the men in our hospitals during this tour of inspection, I told them how much the country appreciated their services and assured them that no pains would be spared to hasten their recovery.

Passing through one of the wards of this hospital, I spoke to a fine-looking young soldier who was sitting up in bed and asked him where he was wounded, meaning to inquire as to the nature of his wound. In reply, he said: "Do you remember, Sir, just where the road skirts a small grove and turns to the left across a wheatfield, and then leads up over the brow of the hill? Well! right there, Sir." He was clearly describing the advance south of Soissons which pierced the Château-Thierry salient. Of course, I was not there at the time, but it touched me that he should feel that I must have been very close to him.

The Aviation Instruction Center for Observers gave us a favorable impression in every particular. While there I said a few words to the smart-looking company of mechanicians on the importance of their work.

At the end of our inspection, Boyd and I went for a walk and incidentally visited the fine old *pension* in which I had spent two happy months with my family back in 1908. The beautiful garden, the shade trees, the swing, the children's sand pile, all were the same, but the management had changed and I was a stranger.

On the way to our train, I went to the Y.M.C.A. hut and was greeted by the large crowd of men who had finished their day's work and had gathered there to enjoy the facilities for reading and recreation which our people at home, through the Y.M.C.A., so generously provided our troops abroad.

During the evening, Eltinge, the Deputy Chief of Staff, at Chaumont, reported by telephone to my train that the Supreme War Council had recommended that the United States establish a few training camps in Italy, with the idea that the presence of American soldiers would stimulate the morale of the Italians. I was as much opposed to any dispersion of our forces as ever and at once telegraphed General Foch to that effect. Although he was also against it, I feared he might be persuaded to recommend it, and that the War Department might fail to see that it was not the innocent proposition it appeared to be. My telegram seemed to settle the question, as nothing more was heard of it.

We left Tours that night and arrived the next morning at Bordeaux, where we were met by the base commander and General Hallouin, the French military commander. This base section covered fourteen French political departments, and all American establishments within this territory were under the commanding general of the section. Our main interests there centered around the docks at Bordeaux and Bassens. Other activities included the base depot at St. Sulpice, the large refrigeration plant, the engine terminal and other railroad facilities, the stevedore camp and the rest and embarkation camps at Grange Neuve and Génicart. There were smaller depots at Coutras and Sursol, with ammunition storage facilities at St. Loubès. Farther out were the extensive artillery training camps at Souge and Le Courneau, the remount stations and hospitals of various types located throughout the section, and numerous sawmills established by our Forestry Bureau in different forests.

The inspection began at the receiving camps for incoming troops, where everything was found in excellent condition. The next stop was at the main storage plant for the port, at St. Sulpice. Over half of the construction was then completed and everything appeared to be in fine shape.

Speaking to the colored stevedores for a few minutes I referred to my service with a colored regiment and how proud we were of its conduct in the Spanish-American War. Among other things, I told them that later they might be given the honor of serving as combat troops at the front. At the conclusion of the talk, Colonel Boyd asked one of the corporals if he understood what I had said, and inquired whether he would like to take part in the fighting. After some hesitation, the corporal replied, very seriously, that he understood, but said he hoped the Colonel would please tell the General that he was very well satisfied where he was.

On the opposite bank of the Gironde River and about six miles below Bordeaux lies Bassens, where the French had ten berths which they turned over to us. Near them we constructed an additional ten berths. My inspection showed that the unloading of ships was being carried on in a perfunctory sort of way, with apparently little realization of the necessity for haste. I minced no words in demanding a change to a more energetic attitude by all concerned.

We next visited the combined artillery and balloon training camp at Souge, several miles west of Bordeaux, where the artillery brigade of the 27th Division seemed to be making good progress under Brigadier General G. A. Wingate.

At the base hospital we found about 500 of our wounded, most of whom were soon to be sent home. No matter how severely wounded they were, I never heard a word of complaint from any of our men. There could not have been found in the hospitals of any army a more cheerful lot. Their fine courage was a lesson in fortitude; indeed, an inspiration. Some would never again see the light of day, others would never be able to walk again, but they all seemed proud of their sacrifice, which many of their countrymen are often prone to forget all too soon.

Considering the extreme importance to us of Bordeaux as one of our ports, the general conditions were not satisfactory. There was a lack of appreciation by the officials of the urgency of expediting the turn-around of vessels, and virile direction seemed to be wanting. In view of the necessity of promptly meeting our new obligations, several of the officers at base headquarters were replaced by others of greater activity.

The following day found us at La Rochelle, later the headquarters of Base Section No. 7, embracing the territorial department of Charente-Inférieure. A large part of our coal was received through the ports of this section, which included, among other activities, our main storage depot for oil and gasoline at La Pallice, and a cement plant at Mortagne.

Brigadier General Charles Gerhardt was in command of this section and at an early hour, under his guidance, we started on our inspection, visiting the docks, the well-kept camp and the car shops, where cars from home were being assembled by the 35th Engineers at the rate of sixty per day. This work was well systematized and the energy put into their task by the personnel was very gratifying.

We went by train to Nantes, where we were met by Colonel J. S. Sewell, commanding Base Section No. 1, Colonel E. T. Smith, commanding Nantes, and the préfect and other French officials. Nantes, some thirty miles up the Loire from St. Nazaire, was the second port in importance in this base section, but it was available only for vessels of light draft. The permanent warehouses assigned to us were rapidly being filled, making temporary structures necessary later on. The motor reception park was manned by a smart-looking lot of men doing their work well and promptly sending forward the limited amount of motor transport as it arrived. The two base hospitals there, both with many sick and wounded, presented every sign of good management.

The next day, August 1st, was spent at St. Nazaire, our principal port of entry, and the headquarters of the base section commander. Beginning the inspection at the remount station, we found it well regulated and sufficient in accommodations. The horses and mules recently arrived were in good condition, considering the sea voyage, and were receiving special attention by the veterinary hospital force. There was a camp for 2,400 stevedores, which was clean and neat, though somewhat cramped, and a casual camp with 16,000 men just in from the States.

At the Locomotive Repair and Erection Plant, the 19th Engineers, working at high pressure, were setting up American locomotives, then being received in parts. This labor was avoided when, upon our insistence, locomotives were shipped in vessels with holds large enough to take them without being dismantled. This method of transporting locomotives across the Atlantic had never before been undertaken, but loading was accomplished successfully at home, not without considerable difficulty, and eventually only complete engines were shipped. I spoke to the men of the 19th Regiment during the noon hour, and also to over 5,000 laborers and stevedores assembled in the broad square near the docks.

Montoir, the port depot of St. Nazaire, probably the largest of its kind ever planned or constructed, was the last word in efficient arrangement. It covered about 2,000 acres and, as planned, required over 200 miles of track, with over 4,000,000 square feet of storehouses and 10,000,000 square feet of open storage space. An engine pulling a flat car took us around the plant, and I used the rear end of the car as a speaking platform. At no place was there more enthusiasm for their work than that shown by the 2,000 railway troops at Montoir.

To supplement the port accommodations at St. Nazaire, the construction of a wharf with berths for eight vessels at once was begun on the Loire River at Montoir. Due to lack of material, it was not completed before the Armistice, but three berths were finished in January, 1919.

The base hospital at Savenay, near St. Nazaire, was the main point for the assembly of the sick and severely wounded being sent home. All patients there maintained the same cheerful attitude that was the surprise and admiration of those who so tenderly looked after their welfare.

The base section of St. Nazaire included five geographical departments and embraced several towns in which there were A.E.F. activities. Angers was one where we had a large training base for incoming engineer casuals, and where a base hospital and a replacement depot for railway troops were located. At Coëtquidan and Meucon there were artillery training camps and aerial observation schools. At Saumur was the large artillery school for officers.

Continuing our journey, we arrived at Brest, the headquarters of Base Section No. 5, on the morning of the 2d and found the Commanding General, G. H. Harries, and staff at the station to meet us. Brest was our leading port of debarkation. The section included four French territorial departments. Cherbourg was the other important landing port for troops in this base section. A large locomotive terminal and repair shop was located at Rennes and a coal port at Granville.

It was a reminder of frontier days to see Harries. After the campaign of 1890-1891 against the Sioux Indians, I was sent to Pine Ridge Agency, South Dakota, to command a company of Ogallala Sioux Scouts and Harries was there as a member of a commission sent to investigate the Indians' troubles and settle their differences with the Government. At Harries' headquarters at Brest we met Admiral Henry B. Wilson, who, under Admiral Sims, was commanding the Naval District. It was very gratifying to hear from both of these commanders how perfectly they were pulling together.

After an inspection of the storehouses and the new construction for additional storage on the piers, I asked for the chief stevedore, Major John O'Neil, who came up apparently quite embarrassed. To put him at ease, I took him by the arm and we walked together to where some lighters were being unloaded. As the port had made the record of handling 42,000 arriving troops and their baggage on May 24th, entirely with lighters, I asked him to tell me about it. By this time he had regained his composure, and pointing to two officers, each down in the bottom of a lighter directing the work, he said, "Sir, do you see those two captains down there in their shirt sleeves? Well, that's the secret. I say to them, 'Don't stand off somewhere and puff yourselves up in your uniforms, but take off your Sam Brownes and your coats and get down close to your men.' Of course, those captains have now become experts. I did the same thing when I started, but since they are trained I manage things generally and they carry out my orders. I can wear my uniform now that I have won the right to wear it." "Well," I said, "O'Neil, you're just the man that I have been looking for, and I am going to send you to every port we use to show them your secret."

We next went to the large French infantry barracks at Pont-anezen, which were utilized for incoming troops, a part of Major General W. R. Smith's 36th Division being there at the time. The new arrivals were impatient when they could not be promptly moved to the front, which was often the case, and these men were no exception. There was a German officers' prison camp at Fort Penfield, nearby, which we found in satisfactory condition. Incidentally, it was everywhere noticeable that whether in prison or at work the German soldier always retained his military bearing and his excellent discipline.

Of the three remaining base sections, none of which we visited at this time, the most important was that which embraced all the American agencies in the British Isles engaged in forwarding troops and supplies to France, with headquarters in London. Large numbers of air service personnel were trained in this section, and we had several base hospitals there. Rest camps for our troops were located along the route from Liverpool to Southampton.

There was another base section established on the French side of the Channel for receiving troops and supplies arriving from England. With headquarters at Le Havre, it embraced also the ports of Rouen, Boulogne, and Calais. The only other base section in operation at this time was on the Mediterranean, with headquarters at Marseille, which was used mainly for freight.

What was called the Intermediate Section covered all territory lying between Base Sections 1 and 2 and the French Zone of the Armies. It included the two great storage depots of Gièvres and Montierchaume, an ordnance depot and repair shops at Méhun-sur-Yèvre, a large replacement depot at St. Aignan, and the reclassification camp for officers at Blois. The main air service training center at Issoudun, a large air service production center and acceptance park at Romorantin, an aviation instruction center at Clermont-Ferrand, large hospital centers at Mars, Mesves-sur-Loire, and Allerey, and base hospitals at Châteauroux and Orléans were also in this section. The section headquarters was at Nevers, which was also the center for hospital trains and the location of a locomotive repair shop. The motor transport repair shops were at Verneuil and the Central Records Office of our forces was located at Bourges, after its removal from Tours.

The final link in the system of supply was the distribution to troops at the front, which was accomplished through the regulating stations in the Advance Section. We constructed two of these stations, one at Is-sur-Tille and another at Liffol-le-Grand, and used one at St. Dizier turned over to us by the French during the St. Mihiel operation. The details of distribution by the regulating stations have already been given in Chapter XI.

After leaving Brest, we arrived the next day, August 3d, at Blois, where Colonel H. R. Lee, commanding, met us at the station. At the reclassification camp for the A.E.F., officers found unfitted for a particular assignment were examined as to fitness for other duty and those recommended for discharge were assembled there until their cases could be disposed of.

From Blois we went to the replacement depot at St. Aignan, where part of the 41st Division was encamped. Our next stop was at Selles-sur-Cher, one of our many remount stations, commanded by Captain A. Devereux, of international polo fame. We then went to Gièvres, our greatest supply depot, which has been fully described in Chapter XXIII.

Near Gièvres was Romorantin, one of our large air service centers. We saw here several DeHaviland airplanes equipped with Liberty motors, and the well-kept camp sheltering about 1,000 railway troops. These men were all skilled workmen, but with most commendable spirit were doing any kind of work assigned to them.

The next stop was at Montierchaume, near Châteauroux, where another large depot was under construction. It was being built in anticipation of the enlarged program for the A.E.F. Our trip ended with a brief visit to Méhun, our mammoth ordnance station, with its large storehouses and shops designed to repair ordnance of all sorts, including the relining of worn-out artillery up to 155-millimeter guns.

The development that had taken place at the ports and along our lines of communication had surpassed our calculations, even though there had been a constant shortage of labor and material and a much larger flow of troops than had been anticipated. Although we had visited but a small proportion of the numerous activities, the system and local management, except in one or two instances, were encouraging. The principal criticism of S.O.S. administration up to that time was its lack of coördinating direction, initiative, and driving-force.

Our railway authorities had already caused the repair of 13,000 French freight cars and the number eventually reached over 57,000, besides a total of 1,900 damaged engines. They had risen to every emergency in a remarkable way, confronted as they had been during the preceding months by the unusual demands on rolling stock. In handling supplies for the front, the railroads had been so successful that even with our units widely scattered, supply trains had rarely failed to reach their destinations on time, and the number of our troops that went without food a single day through fault of the railway service was negligible.

Notwithstanding the difficulties encountered in perfecting the organization of the S.O.S. and the several changes that had been found necessary, the solutions of the problems generally were being worked out through the coöperation of able men in every line. With the recent adjustment of details, it was evident that the organization of this vast structure was now on a sound basis. With the expected improvement in methods and a more aggressive spirit in some quarters, there could be no question of the capability of the S.O.S. to fulfill the utmost requirements that might be imposed upon it provided the needs in personnel and material from home were reasonably met. My visit of inspection accompanied by the new commanding general of the S.O.S. had the effect of impressing the personnel with the vital significance of increased effort.

In order to relieve G.H.Q. of many details involved in handling questions of supply, which had been retained under its direct supervision during the formative period, it was decided to transfer to the S.O.S. the control of procurement, reception, maintenance, and distribution of supplies. Large questions of policy, the immediate direction of military transportation and supply in the Zone of the Armies, and the determination of quantities and the control of munitions remained under G.H.Q. The promise with which the new arrangement began almost immediately to operate afforded a definite indication of early and permanent improvement.

Some idea of the magnitude of this great supply organization of the A.E.F. may be obtained by giving the numbers of men employed in this problem of supply. On August 1st there were 1,169,062 officers and enlisted men in the A.E.F., of whom 275,-000 pertained to the S.O.S.; and even this was below requirements, as the proportion estimated for the work was somewhat less than one man in three. An adequate conception of the immense business organization behind the lines cannot be given by a mere recital of territory embraced or numbers of men employed. There was scarcely a town in France south of the latitude of Paris that had rail connections with our main railroad arteries to the front that did not boast some important American activity connected with the S.O.S.

Speaking of the situation in a cable to the Secretary of War, dated August 7th, I said, among other things:

"I have just returned from a thorough inspection of the Services of Supply, having spent a day at each of the western ports of France and visited all of the principal depots, remount stations and hospitals.* * * The results are especially gratifying in view of the handicap of the shortage of labor and material that has existed since April on account of tonnage being devoted to transportation of combatant troops to the exclusion of S.O.S. troops. I am satisfied now that we have builded properly and that there is no question whatever that the ports and our Services of Supply will be able to provide for the needs of our extended program.

" * * * Right now there is a capacity approximating 25,000 tons per day at all our ports including Marseille and this will continue to increase *pari passu* with our needs. Port efficiency will increase with experience and additional men and equipment.

" * * * With the increased personnel and material called for, the rail facilities will be adequate. There need be no worry as to our ability to handle supplies as fast as our expanding tonnage will require. Even with scant labor supply, we have repaired about 13,000 French cars and a proportionate number of engines.

" * * * Notwithstanding the scattered units of the command, supply trains have never failed to reach our troops, who have never been short of food for a day.[1] * * *

"The work of engineers in construction is now only a matter of men and material, both of which are in sight. * * * The great warehouses at Gièvres, Châteauroux, Méhun, and Is-sur-Tille are well advanced and will prove adequate for all requirements.

" * * * A change of the system to one of coördinate control is not indicated. Although there has been some lack of push in the S.O.S. yet I am as confident of the perfect working of the organization under the selected head, General Harbord, as I am of ultimate military victory. He has taken hold in splendid fashion. I shall transfer to him the entire subject of routine supply and related subjects, including transaction of cable business with the War Department on such subjects. There is no sort of doubt in my mind that the Services of Supply with him at its head, under direction of the General Staff, will continue to function satisfactorily regardless of the size of this command, leaving me free to devote my attention to the military problems.

" * * * There is no line of cleavage between the supply of troops and their tactical operations. All must be under one head to insure success. It is a sound military principle the wisdom of which the experience gained in all wars has clearly shown."

[1] This was true when the cable was sent, but during operations there were instances when it would not apply.

Regarding our rail situation in its relation to railway procurement at home, it was fortunate that Mr. Samuel M. Felton, who was in charge, should have been in France at this time. With the limited amount of sea transportation available, he had done everything possible to help equip and man our railways, but the immediate cry was still for more locomotives, more cars, and more port equipment. Despite the ever-increasing demands, we had received only about 7,600 cars, with about 21,000 on order that we had urgently asked for. Looking into the next year, to meet our program of 3,000,000 men, and allowing for all the cars that could be built or repaired in France or obtained elsewhere, we would need to receive from home over 60,000 more by the following July.

As to locomotives, it was the same story. We had obtained only 555 from the States and our actual needs by July, 1919, would be about 3,000 more, or 250 per month from then on.

Many other essential articles vitally needed to equip our docks for the prompt discharge of vessels had not yet arrived. Cablegrams that would fill volumes had been sent on all these matters, but there seems never to have been a clear conception at home of their relative importance. It is likely, however, that troop shipments during recent months had absorbed the attention of the home authorities to such an extent that many other important demands were postponed. Whatever may have been the reason for not meeting our requirements, the effect was to retard materially the necessary expansion of our supply system and thus to delay seriously the upbuilding in France of a well-balanced force. As indicated in my cable to the Secretary of War, it was simply a question of obtaining from home the necessary men, material and equipment.

CHAPTER XL

Reduction of Château-Thierry Salient Completed—President Poincaré's Visit to Chaumont—Mr. Hoover Discusses Allied Food Supply—I Take Command of First Army—33d Division Attacks with British—King George Visits 33d Division—Bestows Decorations—Withdraw Divisions from British—Vicissitudes of Forming Independent Army —Foch Suggests Control of Allied Supply Under One Head—War Department Appears Swamped

(Diary) La Ferté-sous-Jouarre, Saturday, August 10, 1918. The enemy has been pushed beyond the Vesle River.

M. Poincaré came to Chaumont Tuesday to present me with decoration of Grand Cross of the Legion of Honor. Mr. Hoover and M. Boret, French Minister of Agriculture, came for conference. Colonel the Marquis Saigo, Japanese Army, whom I knew in Manchuria, took dinner with us. In reply to inquiry from Washington, cabled that A.E.F. does not pay for trenches used or occupied.[1] Commanding General, French XXXVIII Corps, highly commends the 28th and 32d Divisions.[2]

Talked Wednesday with Mr. Shearman, of the Shipping Board, who is returning to Washington in the interest of our shipping. Also

[1] My cablegram, dated August 7th, was as follows: "Reference your cablegram 1766, the following statement of facts and explanation is made by Director of Renting, Requisition and Claims Service. 'Paragraph 1. The American E. F. have not paid rent for trenches occupied or used for offensive or defensive purposes, nor, so far as I know, has any request or suggestion that payment for such use been made. Paragraph 2. In divisional areas back of the line used for training purposes, the lands are leased. Where trenches are constructed on such land for training purposes the damages to the land caused by such construction are paid for under exactly the same principles as if such damage to land occurred in the United States.' "

[2] The following order was issued by General de Mondésir:

"The time having now come for him to hand over the command of the zone of battle to General Bullard, commanding the III Corps, A.E.F., General de Mondésir, commanding the French XXXVIII Corps, addresses all his thanks to the splendid troops of the 28th and 32d American Divisions, who have proved during the pursuit which is still being continued not only their courage but also their staying qualities.

"The casualties, the toils and hardships due to the difficulties of bringing up rations during the marching and fighting of this period were unable to break their high morale, their élan, and their war-like spirit.

"General de Mondésir is proud to have commanded them. He hopes that the day will come when he will have them next to him as comrades in our common fight."

saw Brigadier General W. D. Connor, leaving to command Bordeaux District. Sent Foch congratulations on his appointment as Marshal of France.

On Thursday considered First Army plans with Chief of Staff and Chief of Operations. Discussed tractor and railway artillery with Chief of Artillery. Martin Egan came for brief talk. Combined French and British attack begun between Montdidier and Albert going well. Left for Paris.

Called at Sarcus yesterday concerning transfer of First Army to St. Mihiel sector, receiving Foch's approval. Later, de Chambrun went with me to see Pétain, with whom an understanding was reached on details.

Advised Major General Degoutte, who came to call to-day, of agreement with Pétain to leave two divisions on Vesle front temporarily. Orders from Washington establish the Army of the United States, placing Regulars, National Guard and National Army on same footing. First American air squadron completely equipped by American production crossed the German lines on the 7th.

WE have seen how the powerful attack by our 1st and 2d Divisions south of Soissons beginning on July 18th seized the initiative from the enemy, hastened his withdrawal from the south bank of the Marne, and forced upon him the decision to retire from the salient. In the vigorous Franco-American offensive against the enemy, our attacks were directed northward through the center of his position, driving him back relentlessly from one position to another, and finally breaking through his determined stand on the Ourcq River and compelling his withdrawal beyond the Vesle.

It will be recalled that the 26th Division had crossed the Château-Thierry—Soissons road and was attacking Epieds on July 23d. That night, the division was reënforced by a brigade of the 28th Division, which on July 24th took up the pursuit of the enemy, who had withdrawn to La Croix Rouge Farm. Up to this time, the 26th Division had progressed nearly 11 miles, captured 250 prisoners, and suffered about 5,000 casualties. The division front was taken over on July 25th by the 42d Division, which later also replaced two adjoining French divisions and occupied the entire front of the I Corps, about two miles in extent.

The 3d Division, it will be remembered, was north of the Marne, engaged before Le Charmel, on July 23d. On the following day, the division advanced to a line just south of the town, which was captured on July 25th. Operations carried out the next day in coöperation with a French division and the 42d Division on its left were only partially successful. The 42d captured the strongly held La Croix Rouge Farm, but the French division could not advance. The leading battalions of the 3d

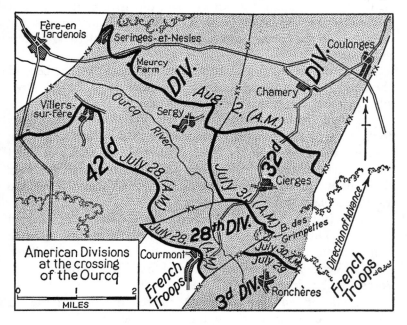

American Divisions at the crossing of the Ourcq

Division entered Le Charmel, but were withdrawn after dark. During the night, the hard-pressed Germans retired to the Ourcq River.

On July 27th, the 28th Division relieved a French division near Courmont, and the 3d Division occupied a line southeast of that town. During the morning of the 28th, the 3d Division captured Ronchères, and the 28th Division crossed the Ourcq, but was unable to hold its gains north of the river. Neither the 3d Division nor the 28th Division on its left was able to make progress against the Bois des Grimpettes on July 29th, but on the following day these woods were captured by the 28th Division in a hard-fought attack made jointly with the 32d Division, which had relieved the 3d Division that morning. That night the 28th Division also was relieved by the 32d.

The 3d Division had been in the line continuously for about two months and had taken part in three major operations. It had aided in stopping the last German offensive of the war and had advanced ten miles through difficult country stubbornly defended by the enemy. Its casualties were about 6,000 officers and men.

The 42d Division, on July 28th, had established its line beyond the Ourcq, and on the 29th, assisted by elements of the 4th Division, captured Sergy and Seringes-et-Nesles.

The enemy made an obstinate defense along the strong ridges to the north of the Ourcq River and some of the bitterest fighting of the war occurred on this line. However, his efforts to hold were of no avail against the gallant and persistent attacks of our divisions and on the night of August 1st he withdrew to the Vesle River, about ten miles farther back.[1]

On August 3d, the 42d Division in the I Corps was relieved by the 4th Division. The III Corps (Bullard) relieved the French corps on the right of our I Corps, so when the lines stabilized on the Vesle River we had for the first time two American corps side by side.

The 6th Brigade (3d Division) entered the line in the III Corps east of Fismes on August 6th, while the 28th Division relieved the 32d Division at Fismes on the 7th. The 77th Division took over the front of the 4th Division in the I Corps near

_____

[1] The American communiqué of August 3d read as follows: "The full fruits of victory in the counteroffensive begun so gloriously by Franco-American troops on July 18th were reaped to-day when the enemy, who met his second defeat on the Marne, was driven in confusion beyond the line of the Vesle.

"The enemy, in spite of suffering the severest losses, has proved incapable of stemming the onslaught of our troops fighting for liberty side by side with the French, British, and Italian veterans. In the course of the operations 8,400 prisoners and 133 guns have been captured by our men alone."

Bazoches on August 12th. Elements of all these units succeeded in crossing the Vesle River, encountering tenacious defense. The bridgeheads established at Fismette and in the vicinity of Château du Diable became localities of intense hand-to-hand fighting.

Thus the Second Battle of the Marne came to an end. Our strenuous efforts to place sufficient American troops in battle in time to deprive the enemy of victory in the summer of 1918 bore fruit in the Allied counteroffensive against the German salient about Château-Thierry. While our forces had played important rôles in halting earlier German offensives, there were available here for the first time sufficient American divisions to join with those of the Allies in striking a decisive blow. The power of American arms brought to bear in the Marne salient made it possible to crush the last enemy offensive and commit him entirely to the defensive. He suffered a costly and disastrous defeat by the determined attacks of our 1st, 2d, 3d, 4th, 26th, 28th, 32d, 42d, and 77th Divisions, which constituted a force equal to eighteen Allied divisions. To these should be added considerable numbers of American air units and corps artillery, medical and transportation troops. The preponderance of Americans at the critical periods of this offensive, coupled with their successes in the vital areas of the battle, brought about this victory. Nearly 300,000 American soldiers were engaged in these operations, sustaining more than 50,000 casualties.

While the battle was in progress, arrangements for the formation of the American First Army, to be composed of the I and III Corps comprising the American divisions then on the battlefield, had been completed, and transfer of command from the French to the Americans was planned for August 10th. However, the favorable turn of the situation, resulting in a slowing down of activity along the Vesle River by August 6th and the discontinuance for the time being of further extensive offensive operations in that direction, made it inexpedient for the First Army to assume command on that front.

The situation to the north also affected this decision. On August 8th, the French and British armies had combined, under

Marshal Haig, in a drive against the German lines between Montdidier and Albert. The attack came as a surprise to the Germans
and was the beginning of a splendid success. By the end of the
first day, an advance of more than six miles had been attained.
The time appeared propitious for activity farther east.

The First American Army had been recognized as an accomplished fact, with headquarters at La Ferté-sous-Jouarre. Now it
seemed advisable to begin preparations immediately to carry out
the plan of campaign adopted on July 24th, providing for a distinctly American operation against the St. Mihiel salient.

I motored to Sarcus on August 9th, and, after discussing with
Marshal Foch the changed conditions in the Marne sector and
the practical stabilization of the front on the Vesle, I suggested
shifting the First Army Headquarters to the St. Mihiel region,
where it could begin immediate preparations for the proposed
offensive. We roughly considered the outline of my plans and,
as expected, he at once acquiesced in the transfer. Returning to
Paris the same afternoon, I then went to Provins to talk the
matter over further with General Pétain. We took stock of
available units for the St. Mihiel operation and he said that
I could count on him definitely to do everything within his power
to furnish whatever we might require. Having thus reached a
general understanding regarding the preliminary details of the
move, and after spending the night at the quarters of Major Clark,
I drove the following morning to La Ferté-sous-Jouarre to take
formal command of the First Army and to give instructions to
my staff regarding the movement of headquarters to Neufchâteau.

The French Government had expressed a desire to bestow
their decorations on American officers and men and advised that
they wished to confer upon me the Grand Cross of the Legion
of Honor. As Congress had recently granted permission for
members of our forces to receive foreign decorations, the French
Government was informed accordingly, and it was for this purpose that M. Poincaré paid his first brief visit to Chaumont on
August 6th. I met him at the station with a military escort

General Ferdinand Foch, field commander of the French forces, confers with General Pershing in his quarterss at Val des Écoliers, Chaumont, France, on June 17, 1918. (National Archives photograph)

General Pershing and King George V of England review a contingent of U.S. Marines near Chaumont, France, in the fall of 1918. (National Archives photograph)

General Pershing and the King and Queen of Belgium enter the Hotel de Ville in Chaumont, France, to attend a reception on March 20, 1919. The mayor of Chaumont is on the left. (National Archives photograph)

General Pershing leads his staff down the Champs-Élysées in Paris during a victory parade on July 14, 1919. (National Archnives photograph)

Baseball star Babe Ruth enlists in the U.S. Army in 1924 and is welcomed on board by General Pershing. (The photograph is a reproduction from the collections of the Library of Congress.)

General Pershing places a wreath on the Tomb of the Unknown Soldier of World War I on Memorial Day, November 11, 1938. (National Archives photograph)

and conducted him to my headquarters, where the senior officers of the staff were presented. After that formality, we repaired to the small area of barracks, where the headquarters troop and band were drawn up in line for the ceremony.

Meanwhile, the entire headquarters personnel, consisting of several hundred men and women, had turned out to witness the proceedings. Both national airs were played and the troops were presented to the President, after which he addressed me briefly in perfect English and pinned on the decoration. He said:

"I am very glad to present to you to-day, before your gallant staff and your brave soldiers, the insignia of the high distinction bestowed upon you by the French Government.

"It is an especial pleasure to take this opportunity of congratulating you and your splendid army for the great successes already attained and for the precious services you render to right and freedom."

I replied thanking him for the honor and saying:

"I value this decoration as a mark of recognition by France of the services of the American Army and of friendship for the American people."

Then, according to the French custom, he kissed me on both cheeks, but not without some difficulty, as he was not so tall as I and it was necessary for him to rise on tiptoe and for me to lean somewhat forward.

I was not insensible to the high personal honor, but regarded it mainly as an appreciation on the part of the French Government of the assistance America had already given to the cause. Without implying the slightest criticism of the form of salutation used in the ceremony, I cannot refrain from confessing my embarrassment, especially as I could hear the restrained laughter of the irreverent Americans in the area who witnessed my situation, no doubt with sympathy. I thought that M. Poincaré himself was probably quite as much embarrassed as I was. Moreover, he must have heard the suppressed mirth as plainly as I did.

At this time there was some apprehension as to food supply for the civilian population of the Allies, especially for certain districts in France. Mr. Herbert Hoover, who came to Chaumont in company with the French Minister of Agriculture, was conversant with the food situation in general. He thought that England could be of immediate assistance, but I was not so hopeful, feeling that her stores must be low due to the employment of so much of her shipping to carry American troops, but I was willing to accept his views and assured him that in any event we would stand ready to assist.

My days, from the time of my arrival in France, had always been too short, but it now seemed that several days of arduous work had to be crowded into one. The sphere of our activities had become extended and many important matters required my personal attention, necessitating a great deal of travel. After the hurried trip to the Services of Supply, it was necessary to spend a day or so here or there—at Paris, Chaumont, on the Marne, or in the St. Mihiel region—holding frequent conferences with Foch, Pétain, Haig and others. I was much relieved to have the S.O.S. in good hands.

(Diary) Chaumont, Tuesday, August 13, 1918. Came through Paris Sunday and directed the Chief of Staff by telephone to announce to the press the formation of American First Army. Went to 33d Division, which was still engaged in British offensive.

King George visited the Division Headquarters Monday and decorated General Bliss, me, and several men of the 33d. Went to see Field Marshal Haig to arrange release of three of our divisions. Returned to Paris and saw Winston Churchill, Lord Weir, and Stettinius about artillery and aviation. British can provide us with additional artillery.

Told Clemenceau this morning of my talk with Sir Douglas and asked Mott to advise Marshal Foch. Have asked for Hugh S. Gibson, now in Paris, to supervise propaganda in enemy countries.[1] Returned to Chaumont in afternoon.

The 33d Division (Bell) was still in training when the combined attack of the British and French in the Montdidier-Albert

---

[1] This request was disapproved, as the Department did not think it wise that Mr. Gibson, who was in the Diplomatic Service, should be associated with that work, the responsibility for propaganda having been placed upon the Committee on Public Information.

sector began on August 8th. The division was attached to the British III Corps for the operation, the 131st Regiment of Infantry being assigned to the British 58th Division. This regiment joined in the attack on August 9th and captured in splendid fashion the Morlancourt—Chipilly ridge north of the Somme. During the next few days, it extended its gains and finally reached a line just west of Bray-sur-Somme. The other three regiments of the division were not engaged. The 131st Infantry was relieved on August 20th, having advanced over three miles and suffered heavy casualties.

I motored to the British front on Sunday to be present at 33d Division Headquarters, near Molliens-aux-Bois, on the occasion of the visit of His Majesty, King George, who was then spending some days with his armies. General Bliss had preceded me and we both spent the night there. That evening General Bell, in relating the details of the participation of his troops with the British, said that their services had been urgently requested and that they had acquitted themselves well.

The King and his suite arrived on the morning of the 12th, having come for the purpose of presenting decorations, especially to selected men of the 33d Division who had participated in the recent attacks of the British army. Soon after his arrival, the King invited General Bliss and me to his room, where he bestowed upon me the Grand Cross of the Order of the Bath, and upon General Bliss the order of St. Michael and St. George. The presentations were informal, as he simply handed the decorations to us in turn, at the same time expressing his appreciation of American assistance.

His Majesty, speaking of the employment of the American troops, said he was anxious to have as many as possible serve with the British Army, that their presence had an excellent effect in stimulating the morale of his men, and that although the British troops had never lost spirit they had been very sorely tried. He remarked that he was not a politician and did not see things from their point of view, but he thought it would be advantageous to have some Americans serving with his armies.

He suggested that our troops might be brought in through the port of Dunkirk, which could be placed at our disposal. He spoke of the friendly sentiments he held for America and of how much it would mean after the war to be able to say that the two English-speaking peoples had fought side by side in this great struggle.

I expressed entire agreement that friendly relations ought to be stronger after the war, but explained that we were now forming an army of our own and would require practically all our troops as soon as they could be brought together. He said he appreciated that fact but hoped that some divisions might continue with the British, but of course I could make no promises. At the conclusion of our brief conversation, we accompanied the King to the place where the men were assembled for the ceremony. He was gracious in his compliments as he pinned the decorations on our men, and needless to say the recipients were extremely proud of the honor conferred upon them.

As soon as the King departed, I left with Boyd for Sir Douglas Haig's advance headquarters to ask for the relief of some of the American divisions then with the British armies. When last at Marshal Foch's headquarters I had suggested that he should make the request of Marshal Haig for these divisions. But he had hesitated, for some reason, which I presumed to be either the coolness that was said to have arisen between him and Marshal Haig regarding the active use he had made of some British divisions sent to the French front near the Marne salient to recuperate, or his knowledge of how badly our troops were needed on the British front. In any event, he asked me to discuss the matter myself with Marshal Haig.

We found the Marshal on his train near Wiry-au-Mont and took luncheon with him and his staff, during which we chatted about everything except the object of my visit. Repairing to his office car after lunch, I brought up the subject and spoke to the Field Marshal of the letter he had written me a few days before saying that he would like to use some of our American divisions in an attack he was about to undertake. I referred to our plans then in progress to form an American army for the reduction of the St. Mihiel salient and said that I should be compelled to withdraw from his front at least three of the five American divisions still there in training. Referring to the conference with Marshal Foch in July, I pointed out that under the circumstances it would not be possible to leave our troops here and there among the Allies any longer, as their services would be required with our own armies.

In reply, he said that he had understood that the American divisions had been sent there to be trained and to serve on the British front and that now, just as they had become useful, it was proposed to take them away. He had hoped, he said, that these divisions would remain and was disappointed to have them removed. I reminded him of our agreement that these troops were at all times to be under my orders and that while they had been placed behind his armies for training they were to be used there in battle only to meet an emergency. I emphasized the fact that we were all fighting a common enemy and that in my opinion the best way to help toward victory was for the Americans to fight under their own flag and their own officers.

I could well understand the Field Marshal's feelings. His armies had suffered very heavy casualties, were worn with continuous fighting, and defeat had stared them in the face. Now that the tide had apparently turned and the offensive was to be resumed, it could not have been otherwise than disheartening to have our large divisions of vigorous, keen young Americans transferred to another field of action. I gave him my assurance that his desire was fully appreciated and that I regretted the necessity which impelled me to make this decision just at this moment, but in accordance with our agreement I must insist on having them. He acknowledged the understanding and said that although he needed our troops he realized my position and my reasons for their withdrawal. He then concluded, in his frank, straightforward way: "Pershing, of course you shall have them, there can never be any difference between us." On leaving British headquarters with the matter satisfactorily arranged, I felt that Marshal

Foch would be much relieved that his intervention would not be required.

On the following morning I called on M. Clemenceau and told him of my visit to British Army Headquarters and we spoke of the progress toward the formation of an American army. A record of what he said, as set down in my notes, is as follows:

> "M. Clemenceau told me that when I first began insisting on using American divisions in an American army under an American command, he frankly did not agree with me, but that he wished to say to me now that I was right and that every one who was against me on this proposition was wrong; that he fully agreed with me now and thought that the Americans should operate separately as an American army."

We then discussed a telegram he had received from Lloyd George endeavoring to arrange for a number of American divisions to be retained with the British. This message was handed to me by M. Clemenceau. In part Mr. Lloyd George said:

> "I did not ask for the transfer of American divisions to the British front. The brilliant part taken by them in the second great Marne victory has more than justified the use General Foch made of them. What I asked was that a few American divisions at most from among those recently arrived in France and which could not be put in the line without some training should be sent to complete their training behind British lines. My purpose was to form a reserve capable of being used in the critical situation of a break in our front by the enemy, permitting the holding with our local reserves until the arrival of divisions from the general reserve of the Allied Armies on the Western Front. I did not consider my demand excessive for it must not be forgotten that the greater part of the American troops were brought to France by British shipping and that because of the sacrifices made to furnish this shipping our people have the right to expect that more than five divisions of the twenty-eight now in France should be put in training behind our lines. We are informed that a serious attack on the British front is still probable now. I do not wish to hamper you now, but in the interest of that unity of command for which I made so great an effort, I urgently ask you to support the very modest request made by me from our Commander-in-Chief."

Not only were the British anxious to get our units, but the whole question of the employment of American troops continued to be considered among the Allies. One program which the British clung to contemplated the use of Dunkirk as the supply port for an American army which they hoped would be sent to their front for service under their control. M. Clemenceau told me that the Italian Ambassador and Mr. Lloyd George had been in conference in London regarding the disposition of our troops, the former urging that every influence be brought to bear upon Marshal Foch and myself to obtain divisions for Italy. This was not the first time that the British had shown an interest in having our units go to Italy, having previously suggested that they be grouped with the British forces there.

Another proposal which was again submitted to Marshal Foch about this time was that of placing American infantry and other services in the reduced divisions of all the principal Allies—British, French, and Italian—but the French had changed their attitude and were opposed to any of these schemes, none of which thereafter came up for formal consideration. I could not believe that Mr. Lloyd George was lending himself to any of these plans in view of his positive declaration at the Abbeville Conference in favor of the formation and use of an American army as such. The impression left on our minds was, first, that the British desired to discourage the concentration of our forces into one army, and, second, that perhaps there was a desire to check the growth of too friendly relations between Americans and French.

(Diary) Chaumont, Thursday, August 15, 1918. Senator J. Hamilton Lewis had luncheon with us yesterday. Several Congressmen and naval officers visited us to-day.[1] Foch suggests single control of supply systems, which I do not favor. Wrote Sir Douglas Haig approving request that 27th and 30th Divisions remain with British temporarily to function under our II Corps. Doctor Jacob Gould Schurman, of Cornell University, called.

Marshal Foch sent copy of proposed cable to President Wilson

[1] The party included: Representatives L. P. Padgett, J. J. Riordan, F. C. Hicks, S. E. Mudd, W. B. Oliver, W. J. Browning, and Paymaster J. S. Higgins, U. S. N., who took luncheon with us, the others being Representatives J. A. Peters, W. W. Venable, J. C. Wilson, J. R. Farr, J. R. Connelly, W. L. Hensley, T. S. Butler and T. D. Schall and Captain R. H. Jackson and Lieutenant M. H. Anderson of the Navy.

urging the 100-division plan. I sent back word to Foch that it would probably irritate the President and advised against sending it.

Our members of Congress from home were always welcome and particular care was taken to give them opportunity to become acquainted as far as practicable with our plans and the state of our preparations. The members of this group of Representatives were intensely interested, each one especially so in what the units from his own section of the country were doing. They were shown through our organization at General Headquarters and the projects we were about to undertake were explained to them. As representatives elected by the people, their personal and official interest in our effort and their expressed belief in our success were encouraging.

In its practical application through the Military Board of Allied Supply, our theory of pooling certain supplies was proving effective in solving a number of questions of greater or less importance. There was, however, a tendency to carry it beyond the limits under which it operated and the suggestion was presented that it be made general, with the entire control under one supreme head. In order to get my views, Marshal Foch sent one of his officers to discuss it with my staff, but I thought we had gone as far as it was safe to go in this direction. The matter of handling our supplies was bound up with our system of ports, depots, and means of transportation to such an extent that the control could not be delegated to any other authority.

While strategical use of the armies had been placed in the hands of the Allied Commander-in-Chief, the responsibility for their tactical direction necessarily remained in the hands of their respective commanders. If there had been a general mingling of units regardless of national integrity, then a general supply system applicable to the entire front under a single head might have been logical. But it was only by establishing the principle of unanimity that even the Inter-Allied Board was made acceptable, as no Commander-in-Chief would forego control of his supplies any more than he would yield the military command over his army. The system was already giving excellent service and in my opinion it was more satisfactory than any plan of arbitrary control could be. Among other things, such problems as procurement of labor, storage facilities, and forage supply were in process of solution. A reserve of light railway[1] material and of motor transport, though small, was being formed and systematic methods of handling traffic were being studied.

I took early occasion to explain my views to Marshal Foch and convinced him that the suggestion of a supreme head for supplies was not practicable, at the same time urging an extension of the scope of authority of the Inter-Allied Board as far as possible without interfering with the machinery of supply behind each army.

(Diary) Neufchâteau, Sunday, August 18, 1918. Saw press correspondents on Friday and gave confidential talk on plans. General Ireland came to report difficulties in obtaining buildings for hospitals, and although the French have been generous, I have asked M. Clemenceau for further concessions. Delay at Washington in answering cables indicates they must be swamped.

General George W. Read (II Corps) came for conference yesterday. Went to Neufchâteau to-day and worked with First Army staff. Tonnage falling off, many idle berths at ports. Cable reports that recommendations for promotion have finally been approved.

As it was the policy to let the press have just as much information as could safely be given out, the correspondents came in occasionally to receive news of our progress and plans. Although most of what was told them at these meetings was confidential, it gave them a background for intelligent action and their patriotic interest was sufficient safeguard that the information would not be divulged. It was understood that the publication of news

[1] The 60-centimeter railway, about 20 inches between rails, was used immediately behind the lines to transport ammunition and other supplies and was often used to carry troops and remove the wounded. The track came in sections and was easily and quickly laid, though oftentimes on soft ground a foundation of stone or the use of wooden ties was necessary. The engines and cars were relatively small, but the cars were supposed to carry about ten tons and often carried more than that. The operation of these lines was conducted by the engineers under the organization known as the Light Railway Department.

had to be limited and I think the members of the press fully appreciated the necessity of the restrictions imposed.

The decrease in the number of transport arrivals at this time caused some apprehension. The accumulation of the immense quantity of supplies needed could only be assured by a constant flow from home ports. Improvement in the rapidity of discharging cargo was almost instantaneous with the change made in the administrative personnel of the Services of Supply. This, combined with the fewer vessels arriving, had left many idle berths. A loss in tonnage deliveries could not readily be made up by sending very large groups of transports later on, as that would produce a certain amount of congestion and consequent delay of vessels. We were constantly increasing the capacity of our ports and were now able to discharge 25,000 tons a day, but only about 16,000 tons per day were arriving.

With the great number of our troops then in France and the continued arrival of others, there was danger of running still further behind in many things of which we were already short. Our imperative needs in motor transport, rolling stock for railways, and construction material were not being met, and yet they were indispensable. At that moment, when we were asking the French to lend us trucks, they made the same request of us. We actually needed 1,300 automobiles, thousands of trucks, and all other kinds of motor vehicles. The ambulance situation was critical, several sanitary units were completely immobile, and twenty base hospitals had arrived without equipment. The Ordnance Department was little better off, with shortages of machine guns, carts, and trench mortar ammunition. The Quartermaster Corps needed rolling kitchens, combat wagons, water carts, and many other things, without which troops were practically confined to training areas. The Signal Corps reported lack of many essentials of unit equipment for battle. It was not believed that the Secretary of War himself was being kept informed of these matters and often in reporting conditions it was requested that his especial attention be called to the cablegrams.

The following shows my thought at the time, as expressed to the Secretary of War:

"France, August 17, 1918.

"DEAR MR. SECRETARY:

"Inasmuch as you asked me to speak to you frankly I know you will permit me to refer to the subject of coöperation between here and the General Staff at Washington. I do so only to give you my point of view and possibly aid you in getting over some difficult places which I am sure you must encounter and which are beginning to affect us here. There is an impression here that our cablegrams are not being carefully studied and thoroughly coördinated. There seems to be energy enough behind things, but, perhaps, it is not as well directed by the Staff as it might be. It may possibly be due to faulty General Staff organization, which, as nearly as I can learn, has not yet reached that point of perfection which would enable all these matters to be handled systematically. In any event, there is not the satisfactory teamwork with us over here that should exist. It is not easy for me, at this distance, to understand all the reasons, but it may be due to a disinclination to accept our views.

"I fully realize that it may be difficult to get the perfection that you should have and that there may be some of the personnel that is not entirely satisfactory. In order to have full coöperation, there must, of course, be entire sympathy and unity of purpose. The system should be one thoroughly tested out, such as is in operation here, and upon which every successful army organization must depend. I have at times doubted whether you will get it going smoothly without taking some one who has actually gone through this organization here from beginning to end, as you know this is the only general staff organization that our army has ever had. All this comes to my mind following the idea of an occasional change, of which you spoke when here as being your intention.

*　　*　　*　　*　　*　　*　　*

"With very high personal and official regard, I am,
"Faithfully yours,
"JOHN J. PERSHING."

The tonnage allotted to our use was less in July than in June, notwithstanding our greater need. Consequently, it was again urged that more tonnage be pressed into service. Only a limited amount of the new tonnage from our own yards was then in military use and continuance of British assistance had become doubtful.

The following cable from Mr. Lloyd George to M. Clemenceau, handed to me by the latter some days before, showed some doubt about the continuance of aid, despite the confident assurances which Mr. Lloyd George and Lord Milner had given when the increased program was discussed:

"Recent dispatches from Washington give reason to believe that the United States Government has abandoned its program for putting 100 divisions on the Western front by July, 1919, and that the greatest possible number would only comprise 80 divisions.[1] We have also been advised that this program reduced can only be realized if Great Britain should continue to furnish its help for naval transportation. Because of the serious character of this information, I immediately made a preliminary study of the questions with Minister of Naval Transportation, Sir Joseph Maclay. I regret to declare that we shall not be able to continue our help as far as cargoes of merchandise are concerned and that we shall probably have to cut down tonnage assigned for troop transportation. In the last few months we have lost several troop transports of large tonnage. * * *

"In Lancashire 40,000 cotton workers, at least, are idle because of lack of raw material and to increase the cotton supply we have been forced to cut short our program for cereal supply. Another very serious difficulty results from the lack of coal by reason of our need of manpower to keep the armies going in the recent military crisis. The coal situation is giving me the greatest anxiety because the situation in France and Italy as well as our own munition production depend upon a suitable coal supply. By reason of the lack of coal a large number of ships have been subjected to delay in our ports and our whole program of naval transportation has been shaken up by this fact. This increases our difficulty to help the Americans in executing their program with regard to merchant shipping. While continuing to do our best for the Allies in the future as we have in the past, I think it best to let you know without delay what difficulties we may meet in attempting to realize the American program in its entirety."

[1] This would equal 160 French or British divisions, which was a larger force than the combined armies of the French and British then on the Western Front.

CHAPTER XLI

Preparations for St. Mihiel Offensive Begun—Composition of First Army
—Concentration Half Million Men—French Services Required—First
Army Staff Working Well—Colored Troops—Conferences with
Foch and Pétain—Two Divisions Left with British—Heavy Artillery
Delayed—St. Mihiel Postponed—Urge Maximum Effort at Home—
Recommend Withdrawal Allied Instructors in Training—Advance
Headquarters, Ligny-en-Barrois—Ruse Near Belfort Successful—
Cabled President Wilson Suggesting Possibility of Victory, 1918

(Diary) Chaumont, Thursday, August 22, 1918. Left Neufchâteau
Monday to inspect new divisions. Stopped to see General de Castelnau,
Commander of French Group of Armies, and express appreciation for
his coöperation. Spent the night at Belfort.

On Tuesday saw 29th Division (Morton) in line near there. Visited
Bandholtz's and M. A. Reckord's brigades in trenches.

Spent yesterday with 92d Division (Ballou). Colored officers deficient in training.

To-day at First Army Headquarters considered engineer, tank and
artillery questions with Brigadier Generals J. J. Morrow, Rockenbach,
and E. F. McGlachlin, respectively. Major Generals Dickman and
Cameron appointed corps commanders. Had letter from Tardieu on
control of commodity prices in our areas. Sent letter to Marshal Foch
requesting fifteen to seventeen observation squadrons and three night
bombardment groups for St. Mihiel attack.

THE final decision that the First Army would undertake
the reduction of the St. Mihiel salient as its first operation
was transmitted to army headquarters on August 10th,
and the army staff immediately began the development of plans
for the concentration of the troops necessary for its execution.

It was certain that the psychological effect on the enemy
of success in this first operation by the American Army, as
well as on the Allies, our own troops, and our people at home,
would be of signal importance. The attack must, therefore, not

only carry through, but a serious hostile reaction must be made impossible.

The headquarters of the First Army were transferred to Neufchâteau between August 11th and 16th. The special army troops assembled north of Château-Thierry were moved eastward during the same period. Neufchâteau was centrally located with reference to all parts of the front from St. Mihiel to the Swiss frontier, and as considerable American activity had been carried on there for many months, we thought that its selection would probably keep the enemy in ignorance as to the exact sector we were to occupy.

The corps and divisions placed at the disposal of the First Army for the St. Mihiel operation and their condition may be summarized as follows:

> The 1st and 2d Divisions were excellent as to training, equipment and morale. They had attacked July 18th in the Soissons drive.
>
> The 3d, 4th, 26th and 42d Divisions were of fine morale and considerable experience, as they had fought in the defense about Château-Thierry and in the advance toward the Vesle River.
>
> The 89th and 90th Divisions were going through their sector training on the front between Toul and the Moselle River, and the 5th and 35th Divisions were taking their sector training in the Vosges.
>
> The 33d, 78th, 80th and 82d Divisions had been training in rear of the British front, one brigade of the 33d having had front-line service with the British. The 91st Division had never been in the front line and had received less than four weeks' training in France.
>
> As to Corps Headquarters, the I Corps was well organized and had operated in the Aisne-Marne defensive and offensive. IV and V Corps Headquarters had taken no part in operations and had very few corps troops.
>
> Except for one brigade of corps artillery and three or four air service squadrons, all of the American corps and army troops to be employed were at this time in their preliminary training period in France.

The final instruction of the divisions for the coming operation was directed by the Training Section of General Headquarters. The equipment of these units, their supply, and the handling of replacements devolved upon the First Army, as did the reception, equipment and supply of thousands of corps and army troops arriving from the Services of Supply or directly from transports. Preparations were being hastened in the hope that the St. Mihiel attack might be made by the 7th of September. Our divisions were scattered and it seemed doubtful whether sufficient rail or truck transportation could be found to bring them in the area, together with the corps and army troops and auxiliaries, before the rainy season, which usually starts about the middle of September and which, it was said, might seriously hinder operations in that sector. It was necessary to assemble in all 550,000 troops for this operation, and this gigantic task, imposed mainly upon the First Army General Staff, which itself was yet in the formative state, might well have caused dismay, even under the most favorable circumstances.

The almost total inactivity on the St. Mihiel front since 1916 made many installations necessary in preparation for an operation of such magnitude. The telephone and telegraph lines, to insure effective communication throughout the area, needed many miles of wire. Artillery ammunition, calculated on the basis of at least five days of battle, was necessary in the amount of about 3,300,000 rounds. Engineering material for building roads across no-man's-land behind the advancing army ran into thousands of tons. Railway spurs, advance depots, and hospital accommodations for sick and wounded had to be provided and aviation fields prepared. Many other things were required, such as the construction of light railways for distribution beyond the railheads, personnel and equipment pertaining to searchlights, the development of water supply, installations for sound and flash ranging for artillery, arrangements for traffic control and the camouflage of positions, roads and material. Each item was the subject of consideration by qualified specialists and all had to be coördinated by the newly formed staff.

The actual movement for the concentration of the more than one-half million men, whether by rail, truck, or on foot, generally took place at night. The troops bivouacked during the day in forests or other sheltered places hidden from the observation of enemy airplanes, resuming the movement at nightfall.

The rail and most of the truck transport belonged to the French and was handled by them. Changes were constantly necessary in schedules on account of the nonarrival of trucks as planned, usually due to their being used elsewhere by the French.

All ranks of the staff and line were filled with enthusiasm at the prospect of the coming operation. Officers of the rapidly expanding First Army Staff worked with the greatest energy under their new responsibilities. The French officers assigned to my headquarters gave material assistance in expediting the arrival of French troops and in handling the civilian population within the Zone of the Armies. These officers were deeply interested and the spirit of coöperation between French and Americans in the untiring efforts given to preparation foretold the favorable outcome of our first offensive.

During my visit to the 92d Division (colored) it was learned that the situation as to training, especially of colored officers, was not entirely satisfactory. This National Army division had been in the service since October, 1917, and was composed of units from different parts of the United States. None of the junior officers had received more than superficial training and most of them were unaccustomed to the management of men. The general officers of the division, who had all served with colored regiments of the Regular Army, were not sanguine regarding the possibility of reaching a high standard of instruction among their troops.

It was well known that the time and attention that must be devoted to training colored troops in order to raise their level of efficiency to the average were considerably greater than for white regiments. More responsibility rested upon officers of colored regiments owing to the lower capacity and lack of education of the personnel. In the new army, with hastily trained colored officers relatively below white officers in general ability and in previous preparation, the problem of attaining battle efficiency for colored troops was vastly more difficult. It would have been much wiser to have followed the long experience of our Regular Army and provided these colored units with selected white officers.

On account of the rapidly increasing numbers of American troops in France, M. Tardieu, Commissioner General for Franco-American Affairs, writing on behalf of the Minister of Agriculture and Supplies, called attention to the necessity of controlling prices on sales of articles of food and drink. The French Government desired to prevent excessive charges, not only to benefit us, but to avoid the increased cost of living for the French people themselves. The efforts of the French Minister and M. Tardieu to regulate prices to our soldiers proved to be only partially successful, but the attempt was nevertheless much appreciated.

(Diary) Chaumont, Sunday, August 25, 1918. Harbord came up on Friday; reported increasing activity in S.O.S. Have cabled for 39,000 extra engineer and service troops for port expansion. Conferred with Colonel Andrews. Major Perkins, Red Cross, has requested service in the army.

Went yesterday for conference with Foch on operations. Franklin Roosevelt, Assistant Secretary of Navy, called. Had dinner with Pétain at Chantilly.

General Bliss came to-day to propose coöperation in urging the 100-division program. General Bridges, British Army, called to discuss machine gun organization, training, and repartition of lines. Told him that we were not in favor of training with the Allies. Lunched with Dawes; discussed Allied Board activities. Saw Foch at Bombon again to-day and reached Chaumont at 10:30 P.M.

My visit to Marshal Foch on the 24th was to discuss preparation for the coming operation in the St. Mihiel sector and especially to urge haste in the assignment of the required French auxiliary units. In our conversation, Marshal Foch referred to the letter he had written the previous day requesting that our 27th and 30th Divisions, which were still with the British, should remain there. He considered it important, he said, to have them ready to assist if necessary in the British operations then in progress. I replied that not only were these troops needed with our own army but they were eager to serve under their own flag. Moreover, it had been clearly understood that they should join the American Army when it was formed. I think Foch fully appreciated the situation and the sentiment involved, but he said the battle was going well on the British front from Arras to the Oise and he hoped that it would extend farther and produce still greater results. Therefore, he wanted to count on the assistance of our two divisions.

While he did not give any other reason, I thought it probable that he also wished thus to satisfy the demand of the British for their share of American troops. Moreover, it was certain that he would also ask for American divisions to aid the French and his action in this case would make the latter request appear more consistent. I felt that if our divisions should once become engaged in battle as part of another army it would be unlikely that they could be withdrawn, yet, under the circumstances, I accepted military emergency as the real reason for the request and assented, with the understanding that these divisions should not remain with the British indefinitely.

I was opposed to the suggestion made by Mr. Lloyd George in his telegram to M. Clemenceau that we should leave a few of our divisions behind the British lines, and felt that compliance with Foch's request for two divisions temporarily was as far as I could go. Our experience with the British had shown that, due to differences in national characteristics and military systems, the instruction and training of our troops by them retarded our progress.

As it was likely that further demands would be made on us, I told Foch that it should be definitely understood that we would thereafter instruct our troops according to our own methods and use them in our own army. He took the view that Mr. Lloyd George should not complain as to where our troops were used so long as they were winning victories, a view which, if given general application, might cause the continued dispersion of our units. I wished to be of assistance so far as consistent with the formation of an active, independent American army and when he asked that two other divisions be held for use wherever they might be needed I agreed only after much the same discussion as before and under the condition that such assignment, when it came, would be only temporary.

We then took up the question of tanks, to find, not at all to my surprise, that the British now said they could not spare any, although at the conference on July 24th it was understood that they would be able to furnish us some heavy tanks when we needed them. Foch said the French would let us have five battalions of light tanks, three with French personnel and two to be manned by Americans. I later sent my tank commander, Brigadier General Rockenbach, to confer with the British in an endeavor to obtain an equitable allotment of the heavy type, but without success.

The shortage in tanks made it necessary to plan for greater artillery or other preparation to overcome obstacles such as barbed wire entanglements and concrete machine gun shelters, or pill boxes, as they were called. Steps had already been taken to procure an extra supply of wire cutters, and the interest was such that various other means were improvised by engineers and by the troops themselves to enable them to cross the sea of entanglements on the St. Mihiel front.

I went from Bombon to Pétain's headquarters at Chantilly to talk over various details with him. We fixed the boundary between the American sector and that of the French Second Army, which was to attack on our left with six divisions. When we took up the questions of truck transport and additional artillery, he told me that he had issued orders directing all services to give us every assistance. He also said that all the aviation that we had asked for would be brought into the sector, and more besides. It could not yet be definitely determined how much artillery the French could furnish, as a considerable number of the necessary heavy guns were to come from Mangin's Tenth Army, which was then preparing for an operation. I was anxious to begin the attack by the 7th of September, if possible, or by the 10th at the latest, but it looked as though the delay in getting these guns would make it necessary to postpone the date until perhaps the 12th. General Pétain and I felt that it would be necessary to have this heavy artillery to insure our success. But there was danger of being held up by the mud in the plain of the Woëvre if the operation should be deferred too long. Moreover, it was desirable that the attack should be made before the season closed, as the Woëvre would be very difficult in the spring.

Returning to Bombon the following afternoon for further conference with Marshal Foch, I asked him particularly to expedite the arrival of the artillery, advising him that in order to save time the necessary reconnaissance had already been made and the positions for the guns chosen. I pointed out that we should hasten the St. Mihiel operation in order to have more time to prepare for subsequent offensives. We had to wait for the heavy artillery from Mangin's army, however, and were held up until the 12th and there was no way to avoid it.

Marshal Foch and I also spoke of the large program proposed for America in 1919. I mentioned the coming visit of the Secretary of War and suggested that we should get together upon his arrival and go thoroughly into all questions involved. In order that Foch might visualize our problem and be prepared to discuss it with the Secretary, I explained that our War Department feared we should not be able to provide supplies for the contemplated large increase in our forces, but that I thought there should be no hesitation, at least as to subsistence, as we were not making war in a barren country and there would be no danger of serious shortage of food.

Speaking of shipping, I said that we might obtain more for military purposes if only our Government could be induced to commandeer additional tonnage from commercial channels. As to the British, there seemed to be considerable doubt whether they would make much more of an effort, in view of the cable Mr. Lloyd George had sent M. Clemenceau and also of his statement that the amount of tonnage the United Kingdom might furnish could not be determined until after the American Government had declared how much it could provide.

The Marshal really needed no coaching, as he was thoroughly committed to the larger program. He said that in his opinion the Allies should make every effort to win the war in 1919, that the British were tired, that the French were worn out, and that we must hasten the arrival of American divisions. He said that he was doing and would continue to do all in his power to obtain the necessary sea transportation and that his requests had included the British, American and Italian shipping. I suggested that he should go into these details in his conversation with our Secretary of War.

Feeling that possibly Allied effort might be weakened by peace propaganda, then being circulated, I said positively, "We must not let the people listen to rumors that the Germans are ready to make peace; there should be no peace until Germany is completely crushed. We should emphasize this point. We have pacifists who are lukewarm * * * and too much inclined to accept any proposition to have the war stopped."

In support of the 100-division program, General Bliss came to see me and suggested closer coöperation between us in advocating its adoption. As no definite advice had been received from the War Department regarding the greater plans, I continued to urge that the 80-division program be completed by April, 1919, and the 100-division by July, basing my action in recommending the higher number mainly on the probability that the War Department would thus be spurred on to greater effort.

It was my thought also, and I so advised the War Department by cable on the 17th, that if we ourselves should decide to send over 100 divisions the Allies would be the more willing to concede additional tonnage and supplies. Moreover, it was certain that if our people at home could be brought to realize the possible eventual demands, they would be prepared for the necessary sacrifice the effort would entail and we should be all the more likely to attain at least the 80-division program. I conferred with Mr. Hoover on the question of food supply, with Mr. Stettinius on production of munitions, and with Marshal Foch on the military requirements, and all agreed that the maximum should be the goal. Hence, with the thought that insistence would at least insure the 80-division plan being carried out, it was again recommended that there be no hesitation or delay in entering upon the larger plan. I sent the following letter to the Secretary on the subject:

"France, August 17, 1918.

"DEAR MR. SECRETARY:

"I hope you will pardon me for referring so persistently to the large program for next year already recommended by Marshal Foch and myself, but I consider it such a vital matter and so important to our success within a reasonable time that I cannot refrain from again impressing it upon you, knowing that you will fully understand my motives.

"It seems to me that there has never been a full realization of our urgent requirements by those who control the Government's shipping, and this control, as understood over here, rests largely with Mr. Hurley's Board. But whoever may control, they must prepare to meet the program that the Government decides upon, regardless of temporary commercial or other sacrifices that it might entail upon our people. There will be little use for shipping, or little advantage in keeping up commerce if we lose this war. I firmly believe, Mr. Secretary, that if these interests could realize the vital need for more tonnage, they would stand ready to meet it as far as possible, even to the abandonment of certain fruit and other trade with South America.

"The food question, in general and in particular, must, of course, be given every consideration, but after all the fact remains that we are not making war in a country destitute of food supplies and that France has fairly good crops this year. French food supplies, with what England can furnish, would always tide us over any temporary emergency that might arise. Of course, I realize that all in all it is going to require considerable sacrifice to make the necessary saving in Allied food, but with 220,000,000 people in the Allied European countries the supply of 2,000,000 or 3,000,000 men, even though our contribution might be limited, is not likely so to deplete stocks as ever to bring us anywhere near the danger point of starvation. Therefore the question of food should not frighten us off.

"I sincerely hope that the President may decide on the 100-division program as a minimum and establish that as the aim toward which every energy shall be directed. Such a decision would stimulate our Allies to further effort, which, in itself, would be also of almost vital significance. Our own various supply departments and shipping interests, as well as those of our Allies, will then be brought to realize that much greater concessions will have to be made in order to carry out this high purpose of our Government. I am afraid that now they are inclined to hold back and discuss the matter and wonder whether it can be done or not. My strong opinion is that a leap must be made into this big program, and that those who fail to follow must take the consequences. Even though we may fall short, we shall have shown our full appreciation of its importance and our desire to carry it out.

"I am enclosing a copy of my cable of to-day on this subject.

"With expression of my high personal and official esteem, believe me, as always,

"Faithfully yours,

"JOHN J. PERSHING."

In a cablegram dated September 25th the War Department informed me that the 80-division program had been approved by the President and Secretary of War on July 26th. The message expressed the view that it would be impracticable to carry out any larger plan, citing the lack of camp space for having more than eighteen divisions in training at home at the same time. The cable made it clear that the War Department expected to have eighty divisions, or approximately 3,200,000 men, actually in France by July, 1919.

(Diary) Ligny-en-Barrois, Thursday, August 29, 1918. At G.H.Q. all day Monday. Conferred with Andrews, Moseley, Bethel and Eltinge. Saw Walter Damrosch, who has assisted in improving our bands.

Sent cable Tuesday supporting Liberty Loan.[1] Cabled objections

[1] "The men of the American Expeditionary Forces expect that the Fourth Liberty Loan will be subscribed.

"In the camps and villages of France we have been training and preparing these many months for the supreme test. In the ports and along the roads that reach from the sea to the battle front, we have been organizing, constructing, and achieving.

"We have toiled cheerfully against the day of battle, and the spirit that has urged us on through the discomfort and drudgery of the winter, in muddy field and sodden trench, in storm-swept port, in rain and sunshine, has been the determination to be worthy of those whom we left behind when we crossed the seas. By the side of the Allied veterans of the four years' conflict we have made a beginning as proof of what we hope to accomplish.

"The news of America awake, of the national spirit more strong, more unified, more determined day by day thrills us all. We have a thousand proofs that our people are behind us. The past successful loans, the fleets that are being launched, the voluntary to plan of starting school at home for higher commanders with French and British instructors. Issued General Order [1] commending I and III Corps.

Went to Neufchâteau Tuesday afternoon to confer with First Army Staff and returned yesterday. Sent de Marenches to French G.H.Q. to see about tanks, airplanes, and gas shells. Washington complains not receiving prompt report of casualties. Received Sir Connop Guthrie, British Shipping Board, and stressed Allied obligation to pool shipping. Saw Moseley regarding St. Dizier regulating station.

Arrived at Ligny-en-Barrois this morning. Visited headquarters I Corps (Liggett) and IV Corps (Dickman). Preparations for attack going well. Sent confidential message to the President.

I was very desirous of improving the music of the bands throughout the A.E.F., particularly on account of its beneficial effect upon the morale of the troops. For this purpose a number of musicians were selected from the various regimental bands and assembled in Chaumont for instruction. My idea also was to organize our bands so that it would be possible to separate each one into three parts when necessary to furnish music to the battalions, especially on the march. Out of the assembly of musicians grew the Headquarters Band. To Mr. Damrosch is largely due the credit for the development of this very remarkable organiza-

economies willingly undergone for the cause of world freedom, make us proud that we represent you.

"The American spirit of liberty and freedom urges us to continue until the end. It is the knowledge of that spirit which makes us certain that our people at home will stand behind us as they have from the beginning so that we may return soon to you, the victory won."

[1] France, August 28, 1918.

General Orders }
No. 143. }

It fills me with pride to record in General Orders a tribute to the service and achievements of the First and Third Corps, comprising the 1st, 2d, 3d, 4th, 26th, 28th, 32d and 42d Divisions of the American Expeditionary Forces.

You came to the battlefield at the crucial hour of the Allied cause. For almost four years the most formidable army the world had as yet seen had pressed its invasion of France, and stood threatening its capital. At no time had that army been more powerful or menacing than when, on July 15th, it struck again to destroy in one great battle the brave men opposed to it and to enforce its brutal will upon the world and civilization.

Three days later, in conjunction with our Allies, you counterattacked. The Allied Armies gained a brilliant victory that marks the turning point of the war. You did more than give our brave Allies the support to which as a nation our faith was pledged.

tion, in which many of the bandsmen from different units of the army had an opportunity to serve. Most of these men were returned to their own bands, thus exerting an excellent influence on the music of the A.E.F.

The question of training came up again, this time through the receipt of a cable saying that an advanced course of military instruction for higher commanders would be conducted at home by selected French and British officers. Our experience in France and our observation of the results of training at home under foreign officers did not point to the success of this higher course. As we had already abandoned the use of such instructors in the A.E.F., I cabled my objections to the plan, and suggested that competent American officers be employed. My cable stated that too much tutelage by Allied officers tended to rob our officers of a sense of responsibility and initiative. It was well known that many of these officers sent to the States were not professional soldiers, but were men whose knowledge was limited to personal experience in subordinate grades in trench warfare. Moreover, the French doctrine, as well as the British, was based upon the cautious advance of infantry with prescribed objectives, where obstacles had been destroyed and resistance largely broken by artillery. The French infantryman, as has been already stated, did not rely upon his rifle and made little use of its great power. The infantry of both the French and British were poor skirmishers as a result of extended service in the trenches. Our mission required an aggressive offensive based on self-reliant infantry.

The organization of our army was radically different from that of any of the Allied armies and we could not become imitators

You proved that our altruism, our pacific spirit, our sense of justice have not blunted our virility or our courage. You have shown that American initiative and energy are as fit for the test of war as for the pursuits of peace. You have justly won the unstinted praise of our Allies and the eternal gratitude of our countrymen.

We have paid for our success in the lives of many of our brave comrades. We shall cherish their memory always, and claim for our history and our literature their bravery, achievement and sacrifice.

This order will be read to all organizations at the first assembly formation after its receipt.

JOHN J. PERSHING,
General, Commander-in-Chief.

of methods which applied especially to armies in which initiative was more or less repressed by infinite attention to detail in directives prepared for their guidance. It was my belief, as cabled the War Department, that efficiency could be attained only by adherence to our own doctrines based upon thorough appreciation of the American temperament, qualifications and deficiencies. I recommended the withdrawal of all instruction in the United States from the hands of Allied instructors. This recommendation was promptly approved by the Chief of Staff, who entirely agreed with my views.

In preparation for the coming offensives, the Advance Headquarters of the First Army was moved from Neufchâteau on August 29th to Ligny-en-Barrois, a small town some twenty-five miles southwest of St. Mihiel. It was from Ligny that activities were directed during the St. Mihiel operation.

When we arrived, the French General who was being relieved and his Chief of Staff, all dressed up in their red trousers and blue coats, came formally to turn over the command. The Chief of Staff carried two large volumes, each consisting of about 150 pages, the first being the Offensive Plan and the second the Defensive Plan for the St. Mihiel salient. These they presented to me with considerable ceremony. My orders had been already prepared, the one for the attack comprising six pages and the one for the defense eight pages. This incident is cited merely to show the difference between planning for trench warfare, to which the French were inclined, and open warfare, which we expected to conduct.

At Ligny-en-Barrois we were in close touch with the front. The I Corps Headquarters was established at Saizerais, northeast of Toul, and the IV at Toul, as both corps were to be engaged on the south side of the salient. During my visit on the 29th, I went over their plans and examined the progress they were making in the assembly of troops. Each corps headquarters was charged with the location and general control of divisions and other elements arriving within the sector of the corps for assignment to its organization.

The I Corps staff had gained much experience in the Marne battle and although the staff of the IV Corps was without such experience both were well handled during the St. Mihiel battle and later.

The considerable circulation of troops in the St. Mihiel area naturally started our officers and men and the people talking about the possibility of an attack against the salient. It was feared that the enemy would hear rumors to this effect and conclude that the danger was immediate and either reënforce his position or withdraw to a line farther back. Up to this time our movements had not been definite enough to indicate the exact sector in which the attack was to be made. However, it was thought advisable to attract the enemy's attention elsewhere. Hoping that it would reach his ear, the news was quietly given out at headquarters that our first offensive might be in the direction of Mulhouse, in the Rhine valley beyond the Vosges Mountains, northeast of Belfort.[1]

It was also decided to make a diversion in that direction and as a preliminary step an officer was sent to lease necessary buildings in Belfort for the use of headquarters. At the same time, confidential instructions were given to Major General Bundy, commanding the VI Corps, to proceed to Belfort with a limited staff and prepare detailed plans for an offensive in the direction of Mulhouse and the heights to the southeast, with the object of eventually establishing our line along the Rhine. In the letter of instructions seven divisions were mentioned as having been designated for the attack and three officers from each of these units were detailed to report to General Bundy to assist in reconnaissance work. He was directed to expedite preparations and was informed that the movement would probably begin about September 8th, under my personal command.

The presence of a major general and an active staff in Belfort must have caused some apprehension among the Germans. In any event, two days later reports began to come in that a hospital

---

[1] To further this rumor, division radios were secretly directed to become active north of Lunéville.

and considerable numbers of the population were moving to the other side of the Rhine. Meanwhile, plans were being prepared in all seriousness, when one day Colonel A. L. Conger, who was in the secret and was acting as my representative, carelessly (?) left in his room at the hotel, as directed, a copy of instructions to the commander of the VI Corps, only to find upon his return that it had disappeared, no doubt at the hands of some spy. This apparently served to confirm the worst of German fears, for within a few days one of his reserve divisions was reported moving up to that front while another was sent to Mulhouse and two more to the Vosges farther north. The French staff gave valuable assistance by circulating false rumors about our plans. So the ruse apparently had been successful and the result quieted our anxiety over the situation for the time being.

The progress of the Allies since July 18th had been greater than expected and as a consequence the Allied program had been extended. At the same time, the weakness among Germany's allies was becoming more evident. With the prospect of three months of seasonable weather for active operations on a large scale, with every assurance of victory in our first independent offensive, and confidence in the plans in preparation for further offensives to follow, it seemed to me not unreasonable to hope for the successful conclusion of the war in 1918. In order that President Wilson might be apprised of my views, I sent word to him that there was such a possibility, and suggested that the utmost pressure, both diplomatic and commercial, be brought to bear upon neutrals as well as upon Germany's allies to the end that Germany might be forced to regard a continuance of the war as futile.

CHAPTER XLII

Thirty-second Division at Juvigny—St. Mihiel Transferred to American Command—Foch Makes Impossible Proposition—Would Break up American Army—Decline Approval—Conference with Pétain—Further Discussion with Foch—Agreement Reached—Americans Assigned to Meuse-Argonne Front—Lord Reading Advocates American Army near British—Diaz Requests Twenty-five American Divisions

(Diary) Paris, Monday, September 2, 1918. Our 32d Division has done splendid work in attack as part of French Tenth Army.

On Friday, the 30th, assumed command over definite American sector extending from Port-sur-Seille to Watronville. That same evening Marshal Foch called at Ligny-en-Barrois and proposed a new American front and the assignment of several divisions of the French armies, which I flatly disapproved.

On Saturday at Nettancourt saw Pétain, who disagrees with Foch's idea and favors an American sector from the Moselle to the Argonne. Had dinner with Pétain on his train. Generals McAndrew and Conner conferred with Weygand, Foch's Chief of Staff.

Visited the I and IV Corps Headquarters yesterday. Pétain and I met Marshal Foch this afternoon and after prolonged discussion reached an understanding with him regarding American operations.

THE attack of the French Tenth Army which began on the morning of August 29th was undertaken to force the retirement of the enemy from the Vesle and Aisne Rivers. On its relief from the Vesle on August 7th, the 32d Division (Haan) was assigned to the Tenth Army and entered the line

NOTE: Total strength of the A.E.F. on August 31st, 61,061 officers, 1,354,067 enlisted men.

Among divisional units arriving in August were elements of the following divisions: 7th Division (Regular Army), Brig. Gen. Charles H. Barth; 39th Division (National Guard, Arkansas, Mississippi and Louisiana), Maj. Gen. Henry C. Hodges, Jr.; 40th Division (National Guard, California, Colorado, Utah, Arizona and New Mexico), Maj. Gen. Frederick S. Strong; 81st Division (National Army, North Carolina, South Carolina, Florida, and Porto Rico), Maj. Gen. Charles J. Bailey; 85th Division (National Army, Michigan and Wisconsin), Maj. Gen. Chase W. Kennedy; 88th Division (National Army, North Dakota, Minnesota, Iowa and Illinois), Brig. Gen. William D. Beach.

on August 28th, immediately undertaking a series of local operations, in which gains were made in the face of very heavy fire. The ravines and the numerous caves in the region provided ideal cover for the defending troops. The general attack of the army on the following day met with but slight success, the enemy resisting desperately along his entire front, but on the 30th, by a flank attack from the south, the 32d Division captured Juvigny, pushing a small salient into the German lines. Hard fighting

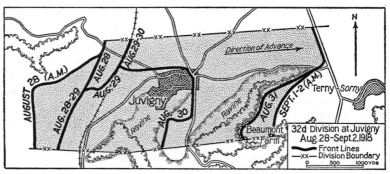

continued on the 31st, but by the end of the day the division had reached the important Soissons-St. Quentin road, where it was relieved on September 3d. The 32d Division had advanced nearly three miles and its success contributed greatly to the forced withdrawal of the German line to the Aisne River.

As pre-arranged between General Pétain and myself, the sector from Port-sur-Seille (east of the Moselle River) to Watronville (north of Les Eparges), forty-two miles in extent, then occupied by the entire French Eighth Army and a part of the French Second Army, was transferred to my command on August 30th. The front included the St. Mihiel salient, and embraced the permanent fortresses around Toul. We had three divisions in line on the southern face of the salient, but the mass of our battle troops were not to take over the trenches until the night before the attack.

As we have seen, there had been a great deal of discussion leading up to the agreement regarding the St. Mihiel offensive.

On August 16th, preliminary instructions had been issued by me and these had been supplemented from time to time by verbal directions, and now everything was moving smoothly toward readiness for the attack, with Marieulles—Mars-la-Tour—Etain as the objective. In my conversation with Foch as late as August 25th, he had even suggested the extension of our front on the west of the salient. Two French corps in the sector had been assigned to my command and arrangements for the transfer to the area of auxiliary troops and services had been agreed upon with no hint that he was not in full accord with our plans.

On August 30th, the day when I assumed command of the sector, Marshal Foch, accompanied by Weygand, his Chief of Staff, came to my residence at Ligny-en-Barrois and after the usual exchange of greetings he presented an entirely new plan for the employment of the American Army. He began by saying that the German armies were in more or less disorder from recent attacks by the Allies and that we must not allow them to reorganize, that the British would continue their attack in the direction of Cambrai and St. Quentin and the French toward Mesnil. Then, much to my surprise, he proposed that the objectives in the St. Mihiel operation should be restricted and the attack be made on the southern face only, and that upon its completion two other operations be undertaken by combined Americans and French, a number of our divisions going *under French command*. His plans, defining the operations after St. Mihiel, were as follows:

"(a) An attack between the Meuse and the Argonne executed by the French Second Army reënforced by a few American divisions (4 or 6), to be prepared at once and launched as soon as possible after that in Woëvre.

"(b) A French-American attack extending from the Argonne to the Souain road, to be prepared also without any delay so that it may be launched a few days after the preceding one. This attack will be executed by: On the right, an American army acting on each side of the Aisne—on the left the French Fourth Army extending its action to the Souain road."

He said, "I realize that I am presenting a number of new ideas and that you will probably need time to think them over, but I should like your first impressions," which I did not hesitate a moment to give.

I said, "Well, Marshal, this is a very sudden change. We are going forward as already recommended to you and approved by you, and I cannot understand why you want these changes. Moreover, I think that to make an attack in the salient with limited objectives would cost little less than to carry out the original idea, which would put us in much better position."

He then said, "That is true, but the fate of the 1918 campaign will be decided in the Aisne region and I wish to limit the Woëvre (St. Mihiel) attack so that the Americans can participate in the Meuse offensive, which will produce still greater results."

"But," I said, "Marshal Foch, here on the very day that you turn over a sector to the American Army, and almost on the eve of an offensive, you ask me to reduce the operation so that you can take away several of my divisions and assign some to the French Second Army [1] and use others to form an American army to operate on the Aisne in conjunction with the French Fourth Army, leaving me with little to do except hold what will become a quiet sector after the St. Mihiel offensive. This virtually destroys the American army that we have been trying so long to form."

He suggested that if I could give a satisfactory solution which would permit the execution of the operations in view he would be glad, but he did not think it possible. He said that he had studied the question carefully and had sincerely looked for some way to avoid dividing the American Army, but he did not believe it could be found.

I suggested that, "One way might be to withdraw the Americans from other sectors and put them in with their right on the Meuse and let them extend as far to the west as possible."

He then said, "That might be considered, although it would

[1] With the American First Army then in the St. Mihiel sector, the French Second Army was the next on our left and the French Fourth Army on the left of the Second.

be difficult to execute the St. Mihiel operation and have time to shift the command to another front for an operation there, but there would be no objection to relieving American divisions from the Woëvre (St. Mihiel) by tired French divisions later so that they could be sent to one or both of the proposed American groups."

He then requested me to send reserve divisions toward the Aisne while the St. Mihiel battle was going on and said that later, having made studies and general preparation for the attack, I could go and take command when the army was formed.

Referring again to the St. Mihiel operation, I argued that there would be less risk if we should attack on both sides of the salient. He seemed to think there was danger of our becoming too deeply involved in that sector, although in the conference in July he had stated that clearing the salient would bring us within reach of the Briey Basin and permit action on a larger scale between the Meuse and the Moselle.

However, he now clung to the idea that the objective should be the line Regniéville—Thiaucourt—Vigneulles and that the attack should be made only on the southern face. But I did not think it wise, at this eleventh hour, to make changes in our solution of the problem. I was willing to accept the limited objectives, but held out in favor of the secondary attack from the west.

Supporting his plans further, Marshal Foch suggested that for the operation in the Aisne he could put General Degoutte, who was thoroughly familiar with that region, and General Malcor, who was also acquainted with the country, having been Chief of Artillery of the Fourth Army, at my disposal to aid an American staff, while I was engaged in the Woëvre. This was only a roundabout way of attempting to assign General Degoutte to command our forces. Many officers who had served under him on the Vesle felt that because of his orders American troops had been unnecessarily sacrificed, so for both reasons I disapproved the suggestion. The Marshal then restated his proposal and added that if the two American contingents, one being the group assigned to the French Second Army and the other the proposed

American army on the opposite side of the Argonne, should eventually join hands, he could only see advantage in this.

The further we proceeded in the discussion the more apparent it became to me that the result of any of these proposals would be to prevent, or at least seriously delay, the formation of a distinct American army. In this event, it was certain that despite the contribution of our splendid units whatever success might be attained would be counted as the achievement of the French armies and our participation regarded entirely secondary.

I asked why these Americans which he proposed should go to the Aisne should not replace French divisions in the French Second Army, then between the Meuse River and the Argonne Forest. In other words, why should not the Americans take over the whole sector then occupied by the French Second Army west of the Meuse, thus making the French troops relieved available to reënforce the French Fourth Army. I repeated what I had often said that the American Government and people expected the army to act as a unit and not be dispersed in this way. I pointed out that each time we were about to complete the organization of our army some proposition like this was presented to prevent it.

Marshal Foch then said, "Do you wish to take part in the battle?" I replied, "Most assuredly, but as an American Army and in no other way." He argued that there would not be time, whereupon I said, "If you will assign me a sector I will take it at once." He asked, "Where would it be?" I replied, "Wherever you say." He then referred to our lack of artillery and other auxiliary troops. I reminded him that the French had insisted on our shipping to France only infantry and machine gun units and had said that they would supply us temporarily with auxiliary troops when needed. I pointed out that he himself had made repeated and urgent requests for such shipments and had promised that we should be furnished whatever units were necessary to complete our organization until our artillery and other troops should arrive. I then demanded that he fulfill these promises.

He said, "It is now August 30th, and the attack must begin on September 15th; it is a question of time," adding that he was quite ready to listen to any proposition, but we must start on the 15th. My reply was that I was willing to send divisions west of the Argonne Forest as part of an American army, but that I did not approve of putting any divisions in the French Second Army. He then asserted that this would not leave the Second Army enough troops with which to attack.

Among my other suggestions, one was that we should operate east of the Meuse River, and another that we should have two armies, one west and the other east of the Argonne Forest. Both proposals were rejected. When I offered definitely to extend the front of our army to include the sector between the Meuse and the Argonne, he said this had been his original idea.

However, he pleaded lack of time, and continued to reiterate his requests for the adoption of his plan until I was provoked to say: "Marshal Foch, you have no authority as Allied Commander-in-Chief to call upon me to yield up my command of the American Army and have it scattered among the Allied forces where it will not be an American army at all."

He was apparently surprised at my remark, and said, "I must insist upon the arrangement," to which I replied, as we both rose from the table where we sat, "Marshal Foch, you may insist all you please, but I decline absolutely to agree to your plan. While our army will fight wherever you may decide, it will not fight except as an independent American army." I then pointed out to him that I had depended upon him to assist in completing the organization of our army, and that we had all been criticized for parcelling out our troops here and there. I drew his attention to the message President Wilson had sent to the embassies in Washington stating that the American Army should fight as such on the Western Front.

He said he was disposed to do what he could toward forming an American army. He then picked up his maps and papers and left, very pale and apparently exhausted, saying at the door, as he handed me the memorandum of his proposal, that he thought that after careful study I would arrive at the same conclusion he had.

The impression this meeting left on my mind was that Marshal Foch was inclined to approve the formation of an American army, but had allowed himself to be persuaded that after the reduction of the St. Mihiel salient it should be split up as proposed. With the added support of American divisions, making the Second Army largely American, Foch's advisers no doubt thought that the French themselves would then be able to push forward and cut Germany's vital lines of communication.

I was ready to use our forces wherever it seemed best, but not under French commanders, except as a temporary measure. The plan suggested for the American participation in these operations, with a considerable number of our divisions under their command, was not in any sense acceptable to me. It was directly contrary to my belief that an American army under its own flag could best serve the Allied cause.

An enormous amount of preparation had been made in our area in the construction of roads, railroads, regulating stations, hospitals, and other installations looking to the use and supply of our armies on a particular front. Our divisions had already begun to move up to their battle positions. Moreover, the inherent disinclination of our troops to serve under Allied commanders had grown to open disapproval and if continued under the changes proposed would have been entirely destructive of American morale.

Because of its importance, the principal points of my formal reply to Foch of August 31st are given below:

"I have carefully examined your note of August 30th, in which you point out the fact that the successes already obtained are far beyond those foreseen by your decision of July 24th. I agree with you that it is now essential to exploit to the utmost the present situation.

"* * * I can no longer agree to any plan which involves a dispersion of our units. This is a matter whose importance is such as to demand very frank discussion. Briefly, American officers and soldiers alike are, after one experience, no longer willing to be incorporated in other armies, even though such incorporation be by larger units. The older American divisions have encountered so much difficulty in their service with the French and British that it is inadvisable to consider the return of such divisions to French or British control. The same is true of our corps staffs.

"It has been said that the American Army is a fiction and that it cannot now be actually formed because it lacks artillery and services. Unfortunately, this lack is evident. But our shortages in this respect are due to the fact that America brought over infantry and machine gunners to the virtual exclusion of the services and auxiliaries. Permit me also to recall that when this decision was made, there was coupled with it a promise that the Allies would undertake to provide the necessary services and auxiliaries, and that you yourself have repeatedly guaranteed the formation of a real American army. It seems to me that it is far more appropriate at the present moment for the Allies temporarily to furnish the American Army with the services and auxiliaries it needs than for the Allies to expect further delay in the formation of an American army. I am writing faithfully my own ideas, which are those not only of every American officer and soldier, but also of my Government.

"* * * Since our arrival in France our plans, not only with the consent but at the initiative of the French authorities, have been based on the organization of the American Army on the front St. Mihiel-Belfort. All our depots, hospitals, training areas and other installations are located with reference to this front, and a change of these plans cannot be easily made. For instance, the care of our wounded must be foreseen. We have already had very grave difficulty and no little dissatisfaction in those of our divisions serving under conditions which made us dependent on the French for the handling and care of our sick and wounded.

"With reference to the objective to be considered in the St. Mihiel operation, I agree, of course, with you that an advance to the line Thiaucourt-Vigneulles would accomplish the primary result sought by the operation. I think, however, that it is advisable, even in limiting the result sought, to make the attack north of Les Éparges, at least as a secondary operation. Unfortunately, both the French and the Americans have talked and it now seems certain that the enemy is aware of the approaching attack. Nevertheless, I believe that the attack should be made and that decision as to the extent to which any success should be exploited should be reserved. To do this it seems essential that I should hold available all the divisions I am now concentrating for the St. Mihiel operation.

"The number of American divisions which will be available immediately after the attack cannot, of course, be foretold with any certainty. However, it would appear entirely impracticable to carry out the St. Mihiel operation and to assemble the 12 to 16 American divisions for an attack in the direction of Mézières between the 15th and 20th of September. In fact, it would be necessary to begin at once the movements preliminary to the assembly of the 12 or 16 divisions contemplated by your note. It is improbable that any of the divisions actually engaged in the St. Mihiel operation could be withdrawn and placed in position for the Mézières operation by September 20th. Then, too, the second-line divisions which will not become involved even in the limited attack can hardly exceed six, and these could not be the most experienced divisions.

"Assuming, however, that six of the divisions from the St. Mihiel operation would be available, we should still have to find six to ten divisions in order to make up the 12 to 16 divisions which your note contemplates for employment in the Mézières operation, and we must seek these divisions elsewhere. * * *

"It seems apparent to me that it is impracticable to carry out even the limited St. Mihiel operation and yet assemble 12 to 16 American divisions, suitable for undertaking an offensive, by September 15th or 20th. It therefore follows that the St. Mihiel operation must be abandoned or that the Mézières operation must be postponed if 12 to 16 American divisions are to participate in the latter operation. Moreover, if the St. Mihiel operation is carried out, it is only after its completion that it would be practicable to fix a date upon which it would be possible to have available 12 to 16 American divisions fit for a powerful offensive.

" * * * In your capacity as Allied Commander-in-Chief, it is your province to decide as to the strategy of operations, and I abide by your decisions.

"Finally, however, there is one thing that must not be done and that is to disperse the American forces among the Allied armies; the danger of destroying by such dispersion the fine morale of the American soldier is too great, to say nothing of the results to be obtained by using the American Army as a whole. If you decide to utilize American forces in attacking in the direction of Mézières, I accept that decision, even though it complicates my supply system and the care of sick and wounded, but I do insist that the American Army must be employed as a whole, either east of the Argonne or west of the Argonne, and not four or five divisions here and six or seven there."

In my letter I also brought out the possibility that the American Army could carry out the St. Mihiel offensive and immediately thereafter attack in the vicinity of Belfort or Lunéville; the entire sector from St. Mihiel to the Swiss Border being eventually turned over to us. It was my plan that after the above operations we should advance either to the northeast or to the east.

On the afternoon of the 31st, General Pétain and I held a conference on his train at Nettancourt to consider the change in arrangements that would be required by the limited St. Mihiel operation. The point first to be decided was whether or not the attack planned against the western face of the salient should be abandoned. Originally three or four American divisions, with five or six French divisions on their left, were to make this assault, while the principal blow was being struck by a wholly American force against the southern face. The newly proposed operations would make unnecessary the participation of the six French divisions and at least two of the American divisions.

Being decidedly of the opinion that an attack on the western face would be necessary to give us the maximum benefit from the effort to be made north of Toul, I proposed that there should be at least one or preferably two divisions in the attack from the west, to support the seven divisions in the first line on the southern face. Opening a map on which he had sketched a project for this offensive, Pétain showed exactly the same dispositions and number of divisions which I had planned in an independent study. It was our opinion that once Marshal Foch had determined the strategical use of an army by prescribing the direction and extent of its employment, the details were solely the province of the Commander-in-Chief of the army concerned and that Foch had nothing further to do with it.

We then considered the question of putting the American Army astride the Aisne as proposed by the Marshal. A glance at the map showed the difficulty of working along the valley of the Aisne, as the heights of the left bank dominated those on the right, while deep ravines and projecting ridges offered serious obstacles. The main objection, however, was that, in addition to putting units under the French, our army would be separated into two parts, with a French army between them. Pétain was strongly of my opinion that this should not be done, but that the American Army in the Woëvre should continue to hold that sector and expand from there.

We agreed that, beginning with the Moselle, its then eastern flank, the American front could gradually be extended to the west as the forces increased. By retaining its position in the Woëvre, it would, in fact, be possible to widen its front in either or both directions. We concluded that eventually the American First Army might extend to Douaumont, the Second to the Suippe River and the Third to Reims, relieving the French Second Army and then the Fourth. Pétain thought the Americans would later deliver the final blow.

Referring to Metz, I expressed the view that it would have a tremendous moral and material effect on Germany if we should make an advance in that direction. Pétain considered that it could not well be undertaken until after the line had been straightened out along the Meuse. It was evident that the Marshal thought all could be settled on the left of that line. I referred to the dependence of Germany on the mines north of Metz and pointed out how jealously guarded that region was by the Germans. Eventually, Pétain thought, developments should lead to offensives in two directions, one toward Belgium and the other toward Metz, but he did not think the latter would be feasible until the Germans were back of the Ardennes. He was, however, anxious to see it carried out.

Marshal Foch did not favor an extended operation east of the Meuse on account of lack of communications, he said, although, as we have seen, he had previously suggested it. In my opinion, an advance in that direction would encounter less elaborate defenses than west of the Meuse and it was the shortest route to the German line of communications and supply.

After some further discussion, Pétain definitely proposed that he should transfer to the Americans the whole of the front from the Moselle River to the Argonne Forest, which was what I had suggested to Foch the day before, as he opposed an advance to the northeast. In the event that we should attack between the Meuse and the Argonne, Pétain thought all that could be done before winter would be to take Montfaucon, and that we could not contemplate this attack to the west of the Meuse until the St. Mihiel salient had been reduced.

My Chief of Staff, McAndrew, and Chief of Operations, Fox Conner, were sent to confer with Weygand on the 1st of September and returned to Ligny-en-Barrois with word that Marshal Foch desired to see General Pétain and me the following day. Motoring to Pétain's headquarters with Boyd and de Marenches, we found McAndrew and Conner had preceded us, and after lunch we went to Bombon. The others present at the conference were Marshal Foch and his immediate staff and General Pétain with his Chief of Staff, General Buat, and Colonels Dufieux and Payot.

As a result of the several conversations that had taken place since the 30th, it seemed probable that we would reach an understanding. When we met, there was little of the atmosphere of the meeting of August 30th. In opening the conference, Foch referred to the note he had handed me at that time and to my reply and asked for my observations. Stating my opinion that we should unite in carrying out vigorous offensives to the fullest possible extent, I explained that if it should be deemed necessary to abandon the St. Mihiel project in order to begin the larger offensive, which he had decided should be west of the Meuse, I would abide by his decision.

I would have regretted, however, to leave the salient unmolested. One reason was that it had been in possession of the Germans since September, 1914, and covered a very sensitive section behind the enemy's position on the Western Front, which included the Mézières—Sedan—Metz railway system and the Briey iron basin. Moreover, its reduction would relieve the threat against the French region opposite, including the railway from Paris to the east, and would afford the victors a new line of departure for further operations toward the northeast. If left undisturbed, it would render precarious the circulation in the rear of an army operating west of the Meuse or on the Nancy front. Finally, and this was a very important consideration, Pétain and I believed that its capture by the Americans would immensely stimulate Allied morale.

Taking up my reply, Marshal Foch said that, if he understood me correctly, I wished to postpone the St. Mihiel operation and concentrate entirely upon operations west of the Meuse. I explained that this was not exactly correct, but that to begin an operation west of the Meuse between the 15th and 20th of September, as he had suggested, would be impossible if we were to conduct the St. Mihiel offensive on the 10th, unless we could have plenty of transportation.

In the ensuing discussion, while there was considerable sparring, including a review of the number and state of preparation of our divisions and the length of front we should take over, it was agreed that the American Army should operate as a unit under its own commander on the Meuse-Argonne front. In my opinion, with which some of the French fully agreed, none of the Allied troops had the morale or the aggressive spirit to overcome the difficulties to be met in that sector.

Marshal Foch concluded that the date for the operation should be postponed so that we could first carry out the limited attack at St. Mihiel. We finally reached the definite understanding that after St. Mihiel our First Army should prepare to begin this second offensive not later than September 25th. The French Fourth Army was to advance at the same time west of the Argonne. The line from the Moselle to the Argonne, ninety miles long, was to be under my command and was to include certain French divisions to be left in the sector, the details of boundaries between the French and American sectors to be settled by General Pétain and myself.

Our commitments now represented a gigantic task, a task involving the execution of the major operation against the St. Mihiel salient and the transfer of certain troops employed in that battle, together with many others, to a new front, and the initiation of the second battle, all in the brief space of two weeks. Plans for this second concentration involved the movement of some

600,000 men and 2,700 guns, more than half of which would have to be transferred from the battlefield of St. Mihiel by only three roads, almost entirely during the hours of darkness. In other words, we had undertaken to launch with practically the same army, within the next twenty-four days, two great attacks on battlefields sixty miles apart.

Each of the Allied armies already occupied its own front, and the necessary installations, more complicated than the public utility services of a great city, were established. We were confronted with the problem of taking over an inactive portion of the line and had to put in many facilities required in an active sector. The time was very short. A million tons of supplies and munitions had to be transported to the Meuse-Argonne front before the day of the attack. As most of our truck transportation was involved at this time in connection with the St. Mihiel operation, only a limited amount was at once available for use in preparing for the second attack. When viewed as a whole, it is believed that history gives no parallel of such an undertaking with so large an army.

At that moment, it could not be said that my staff in the First Army was perfect, but it had done exceedingly well so far and was being rapidly whipped into shape under the able direction of Colonel H. A. Drum, the First Army Chief of Staff, and his principal assistants. The staffs of two of the four army corps had gained profitable experience, but the other two had just recently been organized. It was only my absolute faith in the energy and resourcefulness of our officers of both staff and line and the resolute and aggressive courage of our soldiers that permitted me to accept such a prodigious undertaking.

It was a relief to have a decision. While certain changes were necessary in plans under way, nevertheless the limits placed on the St. Mihiel operation made the preliminary work somewhat lighter. In spite of this fact, the additional burden on my First Army staff imposed by the second offensive was so great that I at once assigned several officers from G.H.Q. to assist. Immediate instructions were issued to carry out the amended program.

(Diary) Ligny-en-Barrois, Friday, September 6, 1918. On Tuesday Lord Reading called on me in Paris to discuss shipping. He also pointed out the advantages of having the American Army near the British. General Diaz came to request American divisions. Arrived at Ligny-en-Barrois 11 P.M.

Spent Wednesday at First Army Headquarters, reaching Chaumont for dinner. General Ireland reported 100,000 hospital beds available. Held conference yesterday on instruction of divisions. Returned to Ligny, stopping at aviation center, Colombey-les-Belles.

Harbord came up to-day, giving encouraging account of race between ports in handling cargo. Sent cable urging that army artillery, engineers, signal troops and field hospitals be hurried over. Reports indicate President urging economic and political pressure against Germany by Scandinavian countries.

In my discussion of shipping with Lord Reading, the increase of British tonnage for our use seemed to hinge on the allotment of a greater proportion of our troops for service with their armies. He advocated having the American Army near theirs, especially maintaining that our supply and equipment would really be facilitated, all of which was a repetition of arguments other British officials had advanced. But the question as to the employment of our troops was settled. Lord Reading's engaging personality made it interesting to talk with him, even though we were on different sides of the question, he as an advocate without particular conviction and I entrenched behind the sound principle involved.

Later in the day, General Diaz, the Italian Commander-in-Chief, with whom I was on very friendly terms, called to see me, and in the course of our conversation it developed that the real purpose of his visit was to ask that American troops be sent for service with the Italian armies. In framing his request, he at first mentioned twenty divisions, and as I showed no evidence of surprise, having become quite accustomed to that sort of thing, he possibly thought that was a favorable sign, so while the interpreter was translating what he had said he interrupted and raised the number to twenty-five divisions. With all the auxiliary services that would have been required to constitute an army of that many divisions, it would have reached the modest total of 1,000,000 men.

This request, coming from one in his position, was so astonishing that it was difficult to regard it seriously. In reply, it seemed unnecessary to go into details, so I merely let him know very politely that we were in need of troops ourselves and could not send any more to Italy. But taking up the question of operations, I suggested to General Diaz that it would be of immense help to the Allies if the Italian armies could assume the offensive also and take advantage of the situation in which the Germans found themselves with all their forces in France engaged on the defensive. He said his staff was studying the matter, but that if his troops should attack now he would have no reserves left for operations the following spring, a course of reasoning which was not easy to follow.

Other conferences filled a busy day, to which was added a motor trip to Ligny-en-Barrois, with a brief stop at Vitry-le-François for dinner. This journey took me through portions of the scene of the First Battle of the Marne, where the successive phases of the battle could be traced by the crosses over the graves of those who had fallen. Whenever I passed through this district I could not help thinking of the dreadful toll in human life that modern war demanded. As we were now about to enter into an active campaign, the thought came to me, perhaps as never before, that many an American boy would likewise be buried on the battlefield before the contest in which we were engaged should come to an end.

Since the war the remains of those of our men who were left in France have been gathered into a few cemeteries, where they lie in precise rows under the shadow of our own flag within the sacred limits of their small bit of America. Most of these spots mark the field of valor where they fell and each has become a shrine where devoted comrades and countrymen may come in remembrance of American youth who consecrated their lives to a sublime cause. It has been a great privilege for me to be at the head of the commission to erect suitable monuments in our cemeteries and on our battlefields, through which a grateful people may commemorate the heroism of their sons. But no matter what else we may do to beautify the hallowed ground where our dead lie buried, nothing can ever take the place of the white marble crosses and stars that mark their graves. These stand as memorials of sacrifice and as symbols of our faith in immortality.

CHAPTER XLIII

Preparations for St. Mihiel Completed—Description of Terrain—Plan of Battle—Order of Battle—Attack Begins—Objectives Taken First Day—Salient Wiped Out—Visit Town with Pétain—Our Victory Inspiring—Congratulatory Messages—Clemenceau on our Front—President and Madame Poincaré Visit Ruins of Home

(Diary) Ligny-en-Barrois, Tuesday, September 10, 1918. On Saturday visited 90th, 2d and 89th Divisions and found much enthusiasm regarding the coming offensive. Presented decorations to men of the 1st, 3d and 42d.

Chief of French Aviation, General Duval, came Sunday to place French air units under our control.

General Pétain called Monday and seemed surprised at completeness of our plans of attack.

Secretary Baker arrived at Brest on the 8th and came from Paris this morning. He at once visited various corps and division headquarters. Final conference was held this afternoon with corps commanders and their chiefs of staff. Germans seem to suspect an attack by Americans.[1] Mr. Baker speaks highly of officers and men of the *Mount Vernon*.[2]

[1] Extract from German paper, *Taeglische Rundschau*, of Sept. 1st: "General von Siebert foresees an early blow from American forces. Even though the German official communiqué says 'all is well and our front holds good,' and though French and British attacks have failed and their fronts have not been enlarged lately, there is another danger against which we must guard; a danger coming from the south, on the Aisne-Vesle. We must reckon with America's strength and numbers we have learned to know and understand. We shall see soon in what form they intend to participate. * * * As Americans pay strict attention to clock-like working of their machine, we must expect them to take their time while making minute studies and preparations for their attack."

[2] Mr. Baker sent the Secretary of the Navy on Sept. 8th, through our headquarters, the following message: "I have just visited and viewed the *Mount Vernon*. The high spirited morale of its men and the masterful seamanship of its Captain and officers makes such a stirring story of heroism that I wish all the nation might know the splendid way in which that huge transport met and foiled the attempt to destroy it at sea. The traditions of your service are enriched by the conduct in this emergency." It will be recalled that this vessel was torpedoed 250 miles out of Brest and though seriously damaged was successfully brought back into port.

THE actual concentration of troops and matériel to form our First Army was begun in the St. Mihiel region in early August.[1] The greater part of the American troops had previously been serving at other points along the Western Front. As railway and motor transport became available, units were brought from the British front, from the French armies about Château-Thierry, and from the Vosges. They were assembled in billeting areas some distance behind the battle lines, where they received necessary replacements and equipment and continued their training.

The transfer of certain auxiliary units and the French artillery could not be carried out until after September 2d, as much of the motor transportation which came from the French was in use farther west. On account of the scarcity of roads and the necessity for the crossing of columns, complete march tables had to be prepared by First Army Headquarters for this concentration, which was conducted with efficiency and celerity. The organization of the First Army was completed in the back areas. Beginning at the end of August, the battle concentration was started, when all combatant units were quietly moved to their battle positions.

The aviation force, consisting of nearly 1,400 planes, under Colonel Mitchell, was the strongest that had been assembled up to that time. It included the British Independent Bombing Squadrons, under General Trenchard, which Marshal Haig had

---

[1] We had 3,010 artillery guns of all calibers, none of which were of American manufacture. Of the total, 1,681 were manned by Americans and 1,329 by French. Before the attack, 40,000 tons of ammunition were placed in dumps. Signal communication consisted of telegraph and telephone lines, radio and pigeons. The central switchboard was at Ligny-en-Barrois with 38 circuits with separate nets for command, supply, artillery, air service and utilities. There were 19 railheads for daily supplies such as food, clothing and equipment. In addition to our own limited motor transportation, we borrowed from the French trucks capable of moving at one time 2,000 tons of material and 20,000 men. The Medical Department provided 15,000 beds for the southern and 5,900 for the western attack and 65 evacuation trains for patients. Engineers provided material, including rolling stock and shops, for the reconstruction and operation of over 45 miles of standard gauge and 250 miles of light railways. A bridge of 200 feet at Griscourt was built, and 15 miles of road reconstructed. Road rock used was over 100,000 tons. 120 water points were established, furnishing 1,200,000 gallons per day, replenished by night trips of railroad or truck water trains.

generously sent and which were particularly useful for attacking important rail centers in rear of the enemy's line. General Pétain placed at our disposal a French air division of 600 planes. Thus we started with a superiority over the enemy in the air which was maintained throughout the offensive.

Unfortunately, we could obtain no heavy tanks and only 267

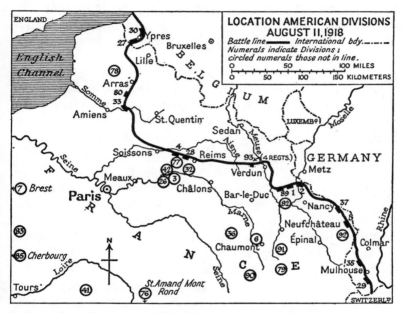

light tanks, which were all of French manufacture, and of these 154 were manned by American troops.

In addition to the American divisions, four French divisions, three of which were then serving under the French II Colonial Corps around the tip of the salient, were assigned to our army for the operation. The total strength of the First Army when ready for battle was about 550,000 American and 110,000 French troops.

The engineers were on hand with personnel and material to begin the reconstruction of roads and light railways. The signal troops were there to extend communications. Arrangements to give medical aid were ready, many installations having been taken over from the French, who assisted us materially in this work. The size and shape of the salient made it necessary to organize two systems of supply, one to serve troops operating against the southern face and the other those attacking from the west.

The preliminary arrangements were completed expeditiously and efficiently, and the First Army was now ready to undertake its first independent operation. Except for delay in the arrival of part of the French heavy artillery, the attack could have been made as early as the 10th.

The St. Mihiel salient lay between the Meuse and the Moselle Rivers and was roughly outlined by the triangle Pont-à-Mousson, St. Mihiel, Verdun. On the western side of this area the wooded heights of the Meuse extend along the east bank of the river. Beyond these heights lies the broad plain of the Woëvre with its large forest areas and numerous lakes and swamps. High wooded bluffs follow both banks of the Moselle, and the deep ravines and heavy forests on the western bank offer difficult terrain for offensive operations. Between the Moselle and Meuse Rivers, the only stream of any importance is the Rupt de Mad, which flows northeast through Thiaucourt and empties into the Moselle.

The principal forests in the plain of the Woëvre are the Bois le Prêtre, the Bois de Mort Mare and the Bois de Vigneulles. From the heights of Loupmont and Montsec, and from the steep eastern bluff of the heights of the Meuse, practically every portion of the plain can be seen.

Our possession of the eastern edge of the heights of the Meuse northwest of Les Éparges was a distinct advantage. But farther south the enemy held sections of these heights, which gave him important observation stations and enabled him to conceal masses of artillery that could fire either against our lines to the south on the plain of the Woëvre or to the west into the valley of the Meuse. It was, therefore, especially advisable, in order to prevent the concentration of his artillery fire in one direction, for us to attack the enemy from the west face of the salient in conjunction with our attack against the southern face.

The main rail lines and roads run along the river valleys, with subsidiaries passing through the heart of the salient and along the eastern slope of the heights of the Meuse.

The Woëvre is seriously affected by the wet season which begins about the middle of September. In dry weather, the water supply is difficult, while during the rainy period the country becomes flooded, making many of the roads impassable.

During the period of four years' occupation, the Germans had strengthened the natural defensive features by elaborate fortifications and by a dense network of barbed wire that covered the entire front. There were four or five defensive positions, the first of which included the outpost system, the fourth being the Hindenburg Line, back of which were a series of detached works, and in rear the permanent fortifications of Metz and Thionville. The strength of the defenses had been fully demonstrated earlier in the war when powerful efforts by the French against various points of the line had been defeated with heavy losses.

The salient was practically a great field fortress. It had, however, the characteristic weakness of all salients in that it could be attacked from both flanks in converging operations. Our heaviest blow was to be from the south where there were no great natural features to be overcome, while the secondary attack was to come from the west and join the main drive in the heart of the salient. The accompanying sketch illustrates the essentials of the First Army's plan for this offensive.

In our original plans it had been my purpose after crushing the salient to continue the offensive through the Hindenburg Line and as much farther as possible, depending upon the success attained and the opposition that developed.

As we have seen, however, the agreement reached in conference on September 2d limited the operations to the reduction of the salient itself. The basic features of the plan were not altered, but its objectives were defined and the number of troops to be employed was reduced.

A tactical surprise was essential to success, as the strength of the position would permit small forces of the enemy to inflict heavy losses on attacking troops. The sector had been quiet for some time and was usually occupied by seven enemy divisions in the front line, with two in reserve. It was estimated that the enemy could reënforce it by two divisions in two days, two more in three days, and as many divisions as were available in four days.

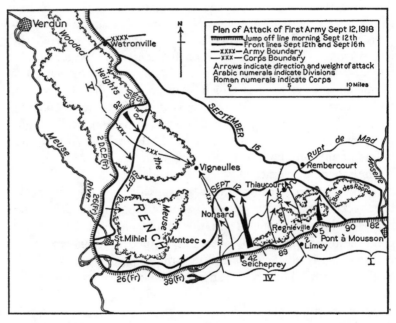

From captured documents and other sources of information, it seemed reasonable to conclude that the enemy had prepared a plan for withdrawal from the salient to the Hindenburg Line in case of heavy Allied pressure. There was no doubt he was aware that an American attack was impending. Therefore, it was possible that he might increase his strength on our front. In that case, our task would be more difficult and as anything short of complete success would undoubtedly be seized upon to our disadvantage by those of the Allies who opposed the policy of forming an American army, no chances of a repulse in our first battle could be taken. These considerations prompted the decision to use some of our most experienced divisions along with the others.

As the plans for the battle neared completion, the duration of the preliminary artillery bombardment came up for consideration as affecting the element of surprise. Practically all previous attacks by the Allies had been preceded by severe bombardments, in some instances lasting for days. In the event that we should pursue the same method the enemy would of course be fully warned of our intentions. I decided, therefore, that there should be only enough preliminary artillery fire to disconcert the enemy and still not leave him time to withdraw or bring up reserves in any number before we could strike. A reasonable amount of firing would give encouragement to our own troops and would be especially advantageous in case rain should make the ground difficult for the tanks. The length of time for the preliminary bombardment was therefore fixed at four hours, which proved to be wise.

In the order of battle for the main attack, the I Corps (Liggett) was on the right, with the 82d Division (Burnham) astride the Moselle, and the 90th (Allen), the 5th (McMahon), and the 2d (Lejeune) in order from east to west. Then came the IV Corps (Dickman) with the 89th Division (Wright), the 42d Division (Menoher), and the 1st Division (Summerall). The V Corps (Cameron), with the 26th Division (Edwards), and part of the 4th Division (Hines), assisted by the French 15th Colonial Division, was to conduct the secondary attack against the western face. In this corps the 26th Division alone was to make a deep advance, directed southeast toward Vigneulles.

At the point of the salient was the French II Colonial Corps composed of the French 39th and 26th Infantry Divisions and the 2d Dismounted Cavalry Division. This corps was to make a supporting advance on the left of the principal drive from the south, and also on the right of the western attack. Troops at the apex were to hold the enemy in their front.

Of the three American corps and nine divisions in the front

line, the IV and V Corps and the 5th, 82d, 89th and 90th Divisions had never before been engaged in offensive combat. Our divisions in reserve were, for the I corps, the 78th (McRae); for the IV Corps, the 3d (Buck); and for the V Corps, the 4th Division (Hines). The army reserve consisted of the 35th (Traub), 91st (Johnston), and 80th (Cronkhite) Divisions.

On the date of the attack the enemy had in the salient proper the equivalent of nine divisions in line, and one in reserve. These troops consisted of one division and two brigades of the Metz group, four divisions of the Bavarian I Corps, and three of the Combres group, V Corps, with one division in reserve. The sector was under the command of General von Fuchs.

The plan presented an especial difficulty in that the troops on the south were required to make a change in direction of sixty degrees during the advance. The long-range guns of Metz covered the Moselle valley as far as Pagny-sur-Moselle, and the enemy's positions on the heights to the east and west of the Moselle gave each other mutual support. These factors made it advisable not to attempt initially to carry the heights on the west bank of the river.

The infantry deployment along the line of departure was delayed generally until the night of September 11th-12th to avoid the possibility of the enemy gaining information of the additional strength on his front by the capture of prisoners. The artillery went into position from two to three nights before the attack.

(Diary) Ligny-en-Barrois, Friday, September 13, 1918. The First Army attacked yesterday and the reduction of St. Mihiel salient is complete. Our troops behaved splendidly. The Secretary of War visited two corps headquarters; returned to Ligny much delighted at our success.

Pétain and I went to the town of St. Mihiel to-day and were warmly greeted by the people. This is my birthday and a very happy one.

The attack on the southern face of the salient started at 5:00 o'clock on the morning of the 12th, and before that hour I went with several staff officers to old Fort Gironville, situated on a commanding height overlooking the battlefield from the south. The secondary attack on the west was launched at 8:00 A.M. as an element of surprise and in order to give more time for artillery preparation there.

A drizzling rain and mist prevented us from getting a clear view, but the progress of our troops could be followed by the barrage which preceded them. Notwithstanding a heavy rainfall on the night of the 11th-12th, the weather gave us an advantage, as the mist partially screened our movements from the enemy. There was a chill breeze blowing and its direction was such that no sound of firing could be heard from the artillery in our immediate front, although the more distant artillery bombardment on the western face was heard distinctly.

The sky over the battlefield, both before and after dawn, aflame with exploding shells, star signals, burning supply dumps and villages, presented a scene at once picturesque and terrible. The exultation in our minds that here, at last, after seventeen months of effort, an American army was fighting under its own flag was tempered by the realization of the sacrifice of life on both sides, and yet fate had willed it thus and we must carry through. Confidence in our troops dispelled every doubt of ultimate victory.

As we returned from Gironville, groups of prisoners were already being marched to stockades in the rear. About 9 o'clock reports began to come in to army headquarters at Ligny from all portions of the twenty-five mile front that everything was going well, with losses light.

Mr. Baker returned from his observation point near the battlefield much elated over the success of the troops. He had been a witness to the first effort of an American army and it was a proud day for him to feel that as Secretary of War his directing hand had led to such results. He took much pleasure in going about to all parts of the army, and scorned being treated as a guest.

Thanks to the thorough preparation beforehand, the wire entanglements were more easily overcome than we had expected.

Trained teams of pioneers and engineers, with bangalore torpedoes,[1] wire cutters and axes, assisted in opening gaps in the masses of barbed wire protecting the German positions. The leading troops themselves carried along rolls of chicken wire which was thrown across entanglements here and there, forming a kind of bridge for the infantry. In all their offensives the Allies had spent days in destroying these obstructions with artillery fire, or had used a large number of heavy tanks, but we had only a few light tanks, which were ineffective for such work. The fact that we had smothered the enemy artillery was an advantage, as it enabled the leading waves deliberately to do their work without serious loss.

The quick passage through these entanglements by our troops excited no little surprise among the French, who sent a large number of officers and noncommissioned officers to St. Mihiel several days later to see how it had been done.[2] One of these officers, after his reconnaissance, remarked in all seriousness that the Americans had the advantage over Frenchmen because of their long legs and large feet.

In making our dispositions for battle our older divisions, the 1st, 2d, and 42d, had been given positions on the southern face opposite the open spaces to enable them to flank the wooded areas quickly, thus aiding the advance of less experienced units assigned to these areas. The whole line, pivoting as planned on the 82d Division on the right, advanced resolutely to the attack. The entire operation was carried through with dash and precision.

---

[1] A bangalore torpedo is a long tin or sheet-iron tube containing T.N.T.

[2] The following extract is from General Pétain's order: "It is desirable for a certain number of French officers, noncommissioned officers and soldiers to visit the terrain so that they can fully understand the manner in which the American infantry has been able, during the last attacks carried out by the American First Army, to overcome the obstacles encountered during the advance and not destroyed by artillery or by tanks.

"The American units have cut themselves a passage with wire-cutters through the thick bands of wire or they have walked over these wire entanglements with much skill, rapidity and decision. It is interesting that our infantry soldiers should see for themselves the nature of the difficulties thus overcome and that they should persuade themselves that they also are capable of doing as much on occasion."

By afternoon the troops had pushed beyond their scheduled objectives and by evening had reached the second day's objective on most of the southern front. The divisions of the IV Corps and those on the left of the I Corps overwhelmed the hostile garrisons and quickly overran their positions, carrying the fighting into the open. The German resistance on this part of the front was disorganized by the rapidity of our advance and was soon overcome.

When the 1st Division, on the marching flank of the southern attack, had broken through the hostile forward positions, the squadron of cavalry attached to the IV Corps was passed through the breach. At 1:45 P.M. it pushed forward to reconnoiter the roads toward Vigneulles, but encountering machine guns in position, was forced to retire.

On the western face of the salient progress was not so satisfactory. The 26th Division, in its attempt to make a deep advance toward Vigneulles, met with considerable resistance and except for a battalion sent from the division reserve had not reached the day's objective.

The French at the tip of the salient had attempted to follow up the flanks of our successful penetrations, but made only small advances. Upon the request of General Blondlat, commanding the French II Colonial Corps, a regiment of the 80th Division, in reserve, was sent to his assistance.

On the afternoon of the 12th, learning that the roads leading out of the salient between the two attacks were filled with retreating enemy troops, with their trains and artillery, I gave orders to the commanders of the IV and V Corps to push forward without delay. Using the telephone myself, I directed the commander of the V Corps to send at least one regiment of the 26th Division toward Vigneulles with all possible speed. That evening, a strong force from the 51st Brigade pushed boldly forward and reached Vigneulles at 2:15 A.M. on the 13th. It immediately made dispositions that effectively closed the roads leading out of the salient west of that point. In the IV Corps the 2d Brigade of the 1st Division advanced in force about dawn of the 13th, its leading elements reaching Vigneulles by 6:00 A.M. The salient was closed and our troops were masters of the field.

The troops continued to advance on the 13th, when the line was established approximately along the final objectives set for this offensive. In view of the favorable situation that had been developed just west of the Moselle River by our successes farther to the left, a limited attack, in accordance with our previous plans, was made on that part of the front by elements of the 82d and 90th Divisions, with good results. During the night, our troops were engaged in organizing their new positions for defense, preparatory to the withdrawal of divisions and corps troops for participation in the Meuse-Argonne battle. On September 14th, 15th, and 16th, local operations continued, consisting of strong reconnaissances and the occupation of better ground for defensive purposes. Beginning on the 13th, several counterattacks were repulsed. The line as finally established was: Haudiomont—Fresnes-en-Woëvre—Doncourt—Jaulny—Vandières.

Reports received during the 13th and 14th indicated that the enemy was retreating in considerable disorder. Without doubt, an immediate continuation of the advance would have carried us well beyond the Hindenburg Line and possibly into Metz, and the temptation to press on was very great, but we would probably have become involved and delayed the greater Meuse-Argonne operation, to which we were wholly committed.

During the fighting from September 12th to 16th, the German 125th, 8th Landwehr, 88th and 28th Divisions reënforced the enemy's line and several other divisions arrived in reserve positions. On September 16th in front of the First Army there were ten German divisions and two brigades in line and seven divisions in reserve.

Nearly 16,000 prisoners were taken and some 450 enemy guns had fallen into our hands. Our casualties numbered about 7,000. As the enemy retreated he set fire to many large supply dumps and several villages. The few remaining French inhabitants who found themselves within our lines were overjoyed to be released from the domination of the enemy, but many were left destitute by the burning of their homes at the very moment of deliverance.

On the 13th, General Pétain came by my headquarters and we went together to St. Mihiel, where the people, including the children carrying French flags, gave us a welcome which may well be imagined when one realizes that they had been held as prisoners, entirely out of touch with their own countrymen, for four years, though always within sight of the French lines. They had heard only such vague reports of the war as their captors cared to furnish them, which were mainly accounts of German successes, and they were quite ignorant of the momentous events that had taken place during the previous two months.

The people were assembled at the Hôtel de Ville, where we talked with the assistant mayor. He told us that in their retreat the Germans had taken away all the Frenchmen between the ages of sixteen and forty-five years. Fortunately, the flight was so rapid that these prisoners were abandoned after a ten-mile march and returned to St. Mihiel the following day. The assistant mayor said the Germans had treated the inhabitants well.

General Pétain explained to the people that although the French troops had driven the enemy through St. Mihiel, they were serving as a part of the American Army and were able to reoccupy the town because the American attacks had crushed in the salient on the south and west. He arranged to reëstablish the city government and give aid to the people and we departed. Just as we were leaving the town we met Secretary Baker entering and I regretted that he could not have gone in with General Pétain and me.

On my visit to several corps and division headquarters the following day, I found all jubilant over the victory and overflowing with incidents of the fighting, reciting many feats of heroism among the troops. In one or two cases, the keen rivalry between adjoining divisions had resulted in friendly controversies between them as to which should have the credit for the capture of certain localities. Important villages along their boundaries were sometimes entered by elements of each without the knowledge of the other, and these instances formed the basis of claims for honors which were upheld with insistence by the units concerned. However, distinction in achievement among the attacking troops on the southern face could not be made with any assurance, as all had done more than was expected of them.

It is never difficult to discover the attitude of a commander, as it is almost certain to be reflected in his unit. If the commander lacks energy or is disloyal, his officers and men are likely to be affected accordingly. If he is aggressive and loyal, his command will show it. I recall one incident which illustrates the point. In the course of a conversation with one division commander he was asked the condition of his unit, to which he replied that the men were very tired. Whereupon, I remarked that there could be no reason for that, as they had been in the line only a short time, and I added with some emphasis that it was probably the division commander who was tired. Not long afterward his division lost its cohesion in battle and became much disorganized. He was relieved and another commander appointed, who was tireless and efficient, and under him the division served with exceptional distinction.

The reduction of the St. Mihiel salient completed the first task of the American Army. Its elimination freed the Paris—Nancy rail communications and the roads that paralleled the Meuse north from St. Mihiel. These at once became available for our use in the greater offensive to be undertaken immediately. We had restored to France 200 square miles of territory and had placed our army in a favorable situation for further operations. The new American position in the Woëvre, almost within reach of Metz, now stood as a threat against the great fortress on the Moselle that defended Germany on that part of the front. I was somewhat familiar with the strength of the fortifications, having visited Metz and the surrounding country, including the battlefields of 1870, some years before, little dreaming, however, that one day an American army would be so near and be so eager to measure swords with the defenders.

This striking victory completely demonstrated the wisdom of

building up a distinct American army. No form of propaganda could overcome the depressing effect on the enemy's morale of the fact that a new adversary had been able to put a formidable army in the field against him which, in its first offensive, could win such an important engagement. This result, after nearly a year and a half of working and waiting, must have tremendously heartened our people at home, as it gave them a tangible reason to believe that our contribution to the war would be the deciding factor. It inspired our troops with unlimited confidence which was to stand them in good stead against the weary days and nights of battle they were to experience later on. The St. Mihiel victory probably did more than any single operation of the war to encourage the tired Allies. After the years of doubt and despair, of suffering and loss, it brought them assurance of the final defeat of an enemy whose armies had seemed well-nigh invincible. The French people of all classes were loud in their praise of Americans.

Many were the messages of congratulation that poured into the First Army Headquarters from all sources, some of which are quoted, as follows:

"Pershing,
       "Amexforce, Paris.
    "Accept my warmest congratulations on the brilliant achievements of the Army under your command. The boys have done what we expected of them and done it in a way we most admire. We are deeply proud of them and of their Chief. Please convey to all concerned my grateful and affectionate thanks.
                                                "Woodrow Wilson."

"My dear General:
    "The American First Army, under your command, on this first day has won a magnificent victory by a maneuver as skillfully prepared as it was valiantly executed. I extend to you as well as to the officers and to the troops under your command my warmest congratulations.
                                                "Marshal Foch."

"General Pershing,
       "Headquarters,
          "American Expeditionary Forces.
    "All ranks of the British Armies in France welcome with unbounded admiration and pleasure the victory which has attended the initial

offensive of the great American Army under your personal command. I beg you to accept and to convey to all ranks my best congratulations and those of all ranks of the British under my command.

"HAIG."

(Diary) Ligny-en-Barrois, Sunday, September 15, 1918. Met M. Clemenceau at station and sent Colonel Quekemeyer and Captain de Marenches with him into recaptured territory. President and Madame Poincaré came to-day to Sampigny, their home town; took luncheon with them on his train. Sent Colonel Boyd with the President, who went to Thiaucourt. Troops made minor advances yesterday and to-day to straighten line and secure advantageous ground. Stettinius, in coöperation with Chief of Ordnance, directed by the Secretary to negotiate with Allies for ordnance material.

On Sunday, M. Clemenceau, who usually spent that day on some portion of the front, came to visit our army and was most enthusiastic in his congratulations. He wished to go over the field and particularly to visit Thiaucourt, but it seemed to me still too dangerous and I said, "Mr. President, we cannot take the chance of losing a Prime Minister." Moreover, the roads were filled with traffic moving in both directions, so, much to his disappointment, I gave instructions that he should not be allowed to go.

During luncheon with President and Madame Poincaré they expressed themselves as being much pleased at our success, especially so because Sampigny was no longer under the enemy's guns. After lunch we visited the site of their residence only to find that it had been completely demolished by German artillery. It had been a beautiful though modest house and its location especially well chosen to give one a fine view of the Meuse valley. It was a sad occasion for them as they looked over the ruins, but they accepted it in the usual courageous French way by saying simply, *"C'est la guerre,"* as did thousands of others in northern France, many of whose homes had been destroyed leaving scarcely a trace.

As we strolled about, two American artillerymen whose brigade happened to be billeted in the village came forward. When I told

them who the visitors were, they seemed to regard my remarks as an introduction. Both walked up and warmly shook
hands with the President and Madame Poincaré, and then
quietly went about with us. It was just another illustration of
our democracy and the President and his wife were very gracious,
though much amused by the cordial and rather unconventional
manner of their guests. I returned to army headquarters leaving
the President and Madame Poincaré to be escorted by Colonel
Boyd, who was compelled by the President's insistence to take
them to Thiaucourt. M. Clemenceau, who dined with me that
evening, was much annoyed when he learned about it, since I
had denied him the opportunity to go that far to the front.

CHAPTER XLIV

Red Cross Coöperation—Cable for Auxiliary Services—No Improvement in
Rifle Training in United States—Visit St. Mihiel with Marshal Foch—
We Turn to the Meuse-Argonne—Simultaneous Allied Attacks Planned
—Meuse-Argonne Vital Front—Description of Sector—German Defen-
sive Lines—Concentration Hurried—Complicated Movements—Use of
Partially Trained Divisions—Visit to Verdun

(Diary) Ligny-en-Barrois, Wednesday, September 18, 1918. Spent
Monday visiting front line divisions. Tuesday had discussion with
McAndrew on new offensive. Conferred with Personnel Section on
promotions. Martin Egan, also Mr. Julius Rosenwald, who has been
visiting the front, came to luncheon.

Mr. Davison, General Ireland, Colonel Wadhams, and Mr. Perkins
came to-day to discuss Red Cross matters. Called at headquarters
French corps and division commanders serving in the First Army. All
appear to be very efficient. Visited Hattonchâtel, from which German
lines can be plainly seen.

THE experience in the St. Mihiel battle brought out the
necessity of closer coöperation between the Red Cross and
the Medical Corps hospital services. Mr. Davison, the head
of the Red Cross, and General Ireland, Chief Surgeon, had
worked out a plan by which certain elements of the Red Cross
personnel would be taken into the Medical Corps. I think that
Mr. Davison had some doubt as to how the proposal would be
received, for, when I approved it without a moment's hesitation,
he seemed somewhat surprised. The American Red Cross represented in rather a personal way all those who had contributed
to its support, and I felt that it should be given a definite status
with respect to the care of our sick and wounded, although the
scheme was never entirely put into effect.

In recognition of the devoted service of the Red Cross, the
following order was published to the A.E.F. on October 3d:

"The American Red Cross is the recognized national organization for relief work with the Army and Navy in time of war. It is through this organization that the men and women of America contribute their funds and their labor for the relief and comfort of the men in service.

"To the millions of women whose hearts and hands are consecrated to the service, to the millions of men, rich and poor alike, throughout the country who have contributed and sacrificed, and even to the millions of children of our schools who are doing their part, it should be made clear that the relief and comfort contributed by them through the American Red Cross to the men in service is essential.

"The Commander-in-Chief desires to express for the entire American Expeditionary Forces the deep sense of appreciation of the services being rendered by the American Red Cross."

Having completed one major operation successfully and being now engaged in preparing for a second, our lack of personnel for certain services and our deficiencies in material became still more disturbing. In our cables to Washington every possible emphasis was laid on the urgency of supplying the items we needed most. In addition, our requirements for 1919 must be foreseen and provided for. In explaining the situation to the War Department, one of my cables stated that "as a consequence, before deciding upon any plan of operations, I must have assurance of not only sufficient fighting troops for the execution of the plan, but also sufficient labor and S.O.S. troops to permit of necessary construction that must be completed in advance." As to the training and shipment of later divisions, it was pointed out that they should be called into service in ample time to provide efficient units, it being important "that divisions should be organized far enough ahead so that the flow of fully trained divisions may keep every available troop transport busy from now on until the program is completed."

During the formative period most of our special services had only temporary personnel, that is, they were manned by officers and men from other branches. This was objectionable and was conducive neither to the esprit de corps nor the efficiency which permanent interest and status would inspire. In anticipation of another year of activity, cables had been sent the latter part of

May requesting authority to place the Chemical Warfare Service, Motor Transport Service, Transportation Corps, and Army Service Corps on a permanent footing. It was essential that their officers should be appointed with their proper grades, instead of being detailed temporarily and separated from their regular assignments. Although these services were established by War Department orders within a reasonable time, full details of organization had not yet been received, and we were forced to limp along with detailed personnel until the necessary action was taken.

Among our troops recently arrived there was a serious lack of training in the use of the rifle. It seemed inexcusable to send over men who were deficient in this very elementary step in preparation, even though there may not have been time to train them otherwise. The idea apparently prevailed at home that three months' instruction was sufficient, but it was never conceded by me that this was anything like adequate. Even though the shipment of troops was much more rapid than was ever expected, making it often necessary to send units whether their personnel was trained or untrained, some instruction in the use of the rifle should have been given. As already pointed out, this deficiency might have been avoided by beginning earlier in the spring to increase the monthly drafts. The following cable on this subject was sent on September 15th:

"Am mailing you report on serious lack of training in replacements recently arrived from Camp Lee, Virginia. These men have received little instruction gas defense, bayonet exercise and combat, interior guard, march discipline, school of soldier, care and use of rifle. Some had never handled a rifle. Nevertheless these men had been in service about two months. Essential replacements should receive instruction in fundamentals before departure United States provided flow of replacements not thereby impeded. Current shortage in replacements requires men to be sent to first line divisions within five or six days after arrival in France. Unfair individual and ruinous efficiency his organization send recruits into battle without adequate training. Thorough instruction in United States must be given in school of soldier, use individual field equipment, personal hygiene, first aid, military courtesy. Particularly important infantry be given rifle practice to include 600 yards in United States. Do not understand why this condition should prevail with anything like proper supervision over training in camps at home. Suggest fullest investigation of methods and policies as to instruction."

(Diary) Ligny-en-Barrois, Saturday, September 21, 1918. Visited St. Mihiel yesterday with Marshal Foch, drove to Hattonchâtel, overlooking St. Mihiel battlefield, thence back to Ligny for lunch. Am very busy these days in preparation for the coming offensive. The staff is carrying a tremendous burden efficiently.

To-day held conference with Pétain at Nettancourt; discussed co-operation with Fourth Army. Saw Hirschauer, who says the discipline and concealment of our infantry best he has ever seen, but road discipline not so good. Took luncheon with Liggett (I Corps) at Rarécourt; called on Cameron (V Corps) at Ville-sur-Cousances; then on Bullard (III Corps) at Rampont; found them all busy and everything moving up to schedule. Saw Claudel, French XVII Corps, and went over the situation on his front. He thinks the Germans do not anticipate our attack. Visited citadel at Verdun. First Army Headquarters moved to Souilly. Complete requirements for December cabled Washington.

Marshal Foch and I, accompanied by General Weygand and my aide, Colonel Boyd, went to St. Mihiel, where we found the people generally going about their business as though nothing had happened. The destruction of buildings was not so great as might have been expected and the work of reconstruction had already begun. Marshal Foch was very devout and wanted especially to visit the cathedral. When we entered, he reverently knelt, and following his example all of us did likewise, remaining some minutes at our devotions. Weygand told me that it was Foch's custom to visit church whenever he had an opportunity. We went from there to Hattonchâtel, where we had a fine view overlooking the St. Mihiel battlefield, and as we stood on this prominent point Foch spoke with enthusiasm regarding the battle. We returned to my quarters at Ligny-en-Barrois for luncheon, having spent a very interesting half-day.

In accordance with the understanding of September 2d, we were now moving rapidly toward our second great offensive. Questions concerning the concentration and supply of the elements of the First Army in the battle areas were being worked out by the staff of that army, which was given every possible assistance by the staff at G.H.Q. In my dual capacity as Commander-in-Chief and Commander of the First Army, I was able promptly to place every facility of the A.E.F. at the disposition of the First Army. With the Headquarters General Staff and the Services of Supply both in excellent working order, the business of the A.E.F., once general directions were given, was well conducted and I was free to devote my time to operations.

The general plan of action of the Allied armies, as agreed upon at the conference of Commanders-in-Chief on July 24th, was, to state it simply and briefly, that the offensive should continue, each army driving forward as rapidly as possible. The Allied and American operations during the summer had resulted in the reduction of the Château-Thierry, Amiens and St. Mihiel salients, and our greater offensive would soon combine with those of the Allies. Immediately west of the Meuse River the battle lines had remained practically unchanged since 1917. It was on this front that the American Army was to play its part. In accordance with Marshal Foch's idea, offensives were to be launched by the Allies as follows:

"(a) A British-French attack on the general line St. Quentin-Cambrai, advancing between the Oise and the Scarpe Rivers.

"(b) A French-American attack on the general line Reims-Verdun, advancing between the Suippe and the Meuse Rivers.

"(c) A combined Allied attack east of Ypres.

"(d) Between the attacks mentioned above, liaison was to be maintained by intervening armies."

The operations were to be as nearly simultaneous as possible all along the Western Front. If successful they would force the enemy either to disperse his reserves and weaken his defense generally, or else concentrate his reserve power at what appeared to be the vital points, to the jeopardy of the remainder of his line. The disposition of the Belgian, British, French, and American armies between the North Sea and Verdun was such that they would naturally converge as they advanced. So long as the enemy could hold his ground on the east of this battle line, frontal attacks farther west might drive him back on his successive positions, yet a decision would be long delayed.

His main line of communication and supply ran through Carignan, Sedan and Mézières. If that should be interrupted before he could withdraw his armies from France and Belgium, the communications in the narrow avenue between the Ardennes Forest and the Dutch frontier were so limited that he would be unable adequately to supply his forces or to evacuate them before his ruin would be accomplished. As our objective was the Sedan—Carignan railroad, it was evident that the sector assigned to the American Army was opposite the most sensitive part of the German front then being attacked.

The danger confronting the enemy made it imperative that he should hold on in front of the American Army to the limit of his resources. From his point of view this was the vital portion of his defensive line, because here it was closer to his main artery of supply (Carignan—Sedan—Mézières) than at any other point. He could afford to retire his armies gradually from all fronts west of the Meuse except ours, where he must hold until the last. The strategical value of success against this part of the enemy's line had been apparent from the beginning, and his preparations for its defense had been thoroughly carried out.

The operation against this important sector was to consist of an attack by the American First Army between the Meuse River and the Argonne Forest, supported by the French Fourth Army to the west of the Argonne. Our thrust east of the forest, by threatening the left flank of the enemy's position in front of the French Fourth Army, on the Aisne River, would force his withdrawal, and the combined or successive advances of both armies would throw him back on the line Stenay—Le Chesne—Attigny, and eventually on Mézières.

Once the Argonne should be captured, these two armies would continue their joint attacks in the general direction of Mézières and Sedan, with the object of severing the enemy's line of rail communications between Carignan and Sedan. The bulk of his armies farther west would be cut off as the Ardennes, a rugged, heavily wooded area, would limit them to the line of communication and supply through Liège.

At this moment, the American First Army, holding the sector from the Moselle River to Watronville, southeast of Verdun, and flushed with success, stood as a menace against the German lines that protected Metz and the Briey iron region. The second offensive about to take place required the extension of our lines to the north of Verdun, and from there to the western edge of the Argonne Forest, giving us a total front of ninety-four miles, or one-third of the total active portion of the lines from the North Sea to the Moselle.

The area between the Meuse River and the Argonne Forest was ideal for defensive fighting. On the east, the heights of the Meuse commanded that river valley and on the west the rugged, high hills of the Argonne Forest dominated the valley of the Aire River. In the center, the watershed between the Aire and the Meuse Rivers commanded both valleys, with the heights of Montfaucon, Cunel, Romagne and of the Bois de Barricourt standing out as natural strong points. From these heights, observation points completely covered the entire area in front of the German lines.

The terrain over which the attack was to be made formed a defile blocked by three successive barriers, the heights of Montfaucon, then those of Cunel and Romagne, and farther back the ridges of the Bois de Barricourt and of the Bois de Bourgogne. The Meuse River was unfordable and the Aire River fordable only in places. In addition to the heavy forest of the Argonne, there were numerous woods with heavy undergrowth which were serious obstacles.

These natural defenses were strengthened by every artificial means imaginable, such as fortified strongpoints, dugouts, successive lines of trenches, and an unlimited number of concrete machine gun emplacements. A dense network of wire entanglements covered every position. With the advantage of commanding ground, the enemy was peculiarly well located to pour oblique and flanking artillery fire on any assailant attempting to advance within range between the Meuse and the Argonne. It was small wonder that the enemy had rested for four years on this front without being seriously molested. He felt secure in the knowledge that even with few divisions to hold these defenses his east and west lines of rail communication in rear would be well protected against the probability of interference.

The system of defensive positions prepared by the Germans

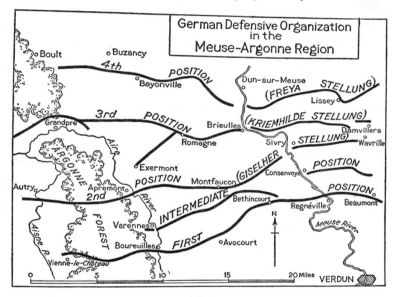

along the Western Front and farther back toward Germany consisted of four distinct lines extending from Metz to the northwest. These lines were widely separated near their greatest dip toward Paris, but converged as they approached that portion of the front protecting the communications which were the objective of the American Army. The location of these successive lines opposite the First Army is shown on the accompanying sketch.

Rapid concentration of the large force required for the battle was most urgent, and even before the beginning of the St. Mihiel offensive troops of some of the services were en route. At the end of the first day's fighting at St. Mihiel the success of the attack was assured, and, as prearranged, I immediately directed the transfer of certain combat troops from that battlefield to the Meuse-Argonne region. Army reserves, corps reserves and all spare artillery were moving by trucks and otherwise over circuitous routes to the new battle front, and other combat troops from the St. Mihiel area were now able to use the route near the tip of the former salient made available by our recent success.

In the area behind our Meuse-Argonne battle front, restricted as it was by the curve in the German line from Verdun to the south, there were but three standard gauge railroads available for the movement of troops and their supplies. One ran east and west between Ste. Menehould and Verdun, another north from Bar-le-Duc to Clermont-en-Argonne, and the third, northeast from Bar-le-Duc via Commercy and St. Mihiel to Souilly and Verdun.

There were only three roads leading into no-man's-land, one through Esnes, another through Avocourt and a third through Varennes; one for each corps. None of them, even though in good repair, was more than adequate for the normal supply of the attacking divisions dependent upon it. We realized that any excess of traffic would likely cause serious congestion, so that the greatest preparations were made to rebuild these roads by calling to that front all available engineer personnel and accumulating beforehand as much road material as possible.

On September 3d the French Second Army held the front from Watronville to the Argonne Forest with three army corps. In vacating the sector the French had to move two corps headquarters with corps troops, eleven divisions, and several army units, leaving the French XVII Corps behind to become a part of our army.

Our concentration required the entrance into the area of three corps headquarters with corps troops, fifteen divisions, and several thousand army troops. All movements were made under cover of darkness, by rail, autobus and marching. Approximately

220,000 men were moved out of the sector and 600,000 into it, making a grand total of 820,000 men handled.

As in the concentration prior to St. Mihiel, the route and length of each day's march for each unit had to be prescribed in order to prevent road congestion and insure the necessary daily delivery of supplies. It was a stupendous task and a delicate one to move such numbers of troops in addition to the large quantities of supplies, ammunition and hospital equipment required.[1] That it was carried out in the brief period available without arousing the suspicions of the enemy indicates the precision and smoothness with which it was calculated and accomplished. The battle at St. Mihiel followed the plan so closely, however, that it was possible to withdraw troops exactly as intended. It seldom happens in war that plans can be so precisely carried out as was possible in this instance. The details of the movements of troops connected with this concentration were worked out and their execution conducted under the able direction of Colonel George C. Marshall, Jr., of the Operations Section of the General Staff, First Army.

A well-known British war correspondent, an ex-officer of the British Army, in writing for the London *Post* said of this concentration:

"Few people in England know that this operation (the Argonne-Meuse Offensive), was preceded by one of the most interesting and difficult Staff operations of the war, namely, the transfer within four-

[1] Some idea can be formed of the amount of material involved by the following: Of artillery used in the Meuse-Argonne battle there were 3,980 guns of all calibers, most of which were in position for the opening of the battle; American gunners manned 2,516 and French 1,464. Artillery ammunition amounting to 40,000 tons was placed by September 25th, replenished by 12 to 14 trainloads, or 3,000 tons, daily; the amount fired by the divisional and corps artillery reached 350,000 rounds daily. There were 19 railheads for the automatic supply of the army. Depots established were: 12 for ordnance, 24 ammunition, 9 gas and oil, 9 quartermaster supplies, 12 engineer supplies, 8 engineer water supply, 6 chemical warfare, besides depots for medical, signal, motor, and tank supplies. There were 34 evacuation hospitals. The total number of animals was 93,032. Of motor transportation there were 3,500 truck tons capable of carrying 20,000 men in one load; 428,000 men were transported to the area by truck, average haul 48 miles. Light railway lines constructed and rebuilt 164 miles, and 215 miles were operated. As to standard gauge, we built 12 miles, Aubréville to Apremont, and reconstructed 65 miles.

teen days of the bulk of the 1st American Army from the Metz front to that of the Meuse-Argonne, and its replacement by the 2nd American Army. No less than 10 divisions began the Meuse-Argonne attack on September 26, * * * * while there stood in reserve, all eventually to be thrown into the fight, the 1st, 2nd, 3rd, 5th, 29th, 32nd, 82nd and 92nd Divisions. A comparison of these divisional units with those which fought at St. Mihiel shows that 10 divisions were withdrawn from the Metz front and aligned for the new operation. It was a fine piece of Staff work and no other Staff could have done it better."

On the new front, the army ammunition dumps were piling up and equipment for road building and for light railways was going forward. Hospital arrangements were being perfected, signal communications going in, remount stations constructed, battalion replacement camps located, and work had begun on a new railroad line from Aubréville to Varennes that had been projected to give us necessary additional rail transportation. Regulating stations, especially at St. Dizier, had to be greatly expanded and completely organized under American personnel in order to distribute efficiently the vastly multiplied volume of freight that must be provided before and during the battle. Aviation fields were being occupied by the constant arrival of the personnel and matériel of our squadrons. The services of water supply, camouflage and sound and flash ranging were being rapidly installed.

Specific instructions were sent to all troops calling attention to defects noticed during the St. Mihiel battle, such as ineffective liaison between units, passage through woods, regulation of barrages and the use of accompanying guns. The training staff was kept on the go to assist those divisions which would have no further opportunity to hold practice maneuvers with their artillery and the air service. Further instruction of the military police, who had lacked experience in the previous offensive, was carried out as far as possible, especially in the duty of controlling the immense amount of traffic even then crowding the area.

As we have seen, some of our most experienced divisions, the 1st, 2d, 26th and 42d, were used at St. Mihiel. This prevented their transfer to the Meuse-Argonne in time to open the fight, and compelled the employment of some divisions which had not entirely completed their period of training. Four of the nine divisions that were to lead the assault were without their own artillery and had brigades of that arm assigned to them with which they had never previously been in contact. It was realized that difficulties were likely to develop in handling these organizations in battle for the first time. Therefore instructions for the opening phases were made to cover as far as possible the details of maneuver ordinarily taught beforehand through combat exercises.

As Verdun was soon to become a part of my command, I went on the 21st to see the town and make a casual inspection of the citadel. The commanding officer showed me the various chambers, including those occupied by the local civil authorities during the period of the German drive to wrest the stronghold from the French, and finally we reached the Officers' Club. As we entered, my eye fell upon Pétain's famous declaration, *"On ne passe pas,"* in bold letters on the wall opposite me. It would be difficult to describe my feelings, and as I stopped in my tracks the party, realizing the reason, with one accord remained silent for some minutes.

Several years later, at the dedication of the Ossuary near Douaumont, it was my privilege to speak, and I addressed myself as follows to the distinguished commander who uttered the above inspiring phrase:

"The poignant horror of the tragedy enacted here has been brought home to me anew, and my triumphant sense of victory has been entirely overwhelmed by my sympathy for the men who fell, the victims of the sacrifice. Their patience and courage, their unalterable will to follow to the end the long and dolorous road of martyrdom which they were treading, have been celebrated in words more appropriate than any I could utter. But the grief of the man who commanded them has been too often forgotten by all who have commented on these battles. I have often felt, when you and I were together, that I could read your thoughts and follow your mind as it reviewed the days and weeks of your struggles on this soil, when your country's fate hung in the balance. Only those who know the kindness of your heart can appreciate the weight of sorrow which it carried. The fall of each one of your soldiers was a stab in the heart of his general, and the impassive expression under which you hide your feelings masked constant and unremitting grief.

"As an old friend and comrade in arms, I feel my thoughts dwelling on those who did not return, and like you, I think of them with infinite sympathy."

CHAPTER XLV

First Army Takes Command of Meuse-Argonne Sector—Order of Battle
—Plan of Battle—Battle Begins—Strong Defense Encountered—
Montfaucon Taken—Counterattacks—New Divisions Yield—Success
of First Four Days—Difficult Problems—Visit by M. Clemenceau—
27th and 30th Divisions Attack with British

(Diary) Souilly, Wednesday, September 25, 1918. Assumed command of Meuse-Argonne sector the 22d. General Gouraud, commanding the French Fourth Army, called to discuss joint operation.

General Deletoille, Director of the Zones des Étapes, reported on Monday and was given charge of relations with civil authorities in our area. Have spent the past three days working with staff on final details of preparation.

To-day visited headquarters of all front line divisions. Satisfied that they appreciate and understand their missions.

THE I, V, and III Corps Headquarters, located at Rarécourt, Ville-sur-Cousances and Rampont, respectively, worked in coöperation with the corresponding units of the French Second Army, which, under General Hirschauer's able and friendly direction, did everything possible to expedite preparations. He was of the greatest assistance in helping to place installations and in assigning units that were moved into the sector during the two weeks preceding the battle. The command passed to the First Army on September 22d and at that time, except for the XVII Corps, the last of the French troops and two Italian divisions serving with them were withdrawn, leaving a few detachments in the first line trenches which were maintained until the night of the 25th.

On the front of the American Army, the tactical missions varied for the different sectors. It was not intended to attempt a further advance on the Moselle-Watronville front, but to hold that portion of our line for the time being and utilize all available divisions for the extension of the front west of the Meuse. On that part of our line from Watronville northwest to the Meuse it was planned to keep the enemy busy by demonstrations while the attack between the Meuse and the Argonne was developing.

Of the eighteen enemy divisions on our front from the Moselle west, with twelve in reserve, five were in line between the Meuse and the Argonne. Judging from the number in the vicinity of Metz, it seemed probable that the German commander expected a renewal of the offensive in the St. Mihiel sector. It was estimated that the enemy could reënforce the front of attack between the Meuse and the Argonne with four divisions the first day, two the second, and nine the third day.

At the beginning of this battle most of the light and heavy guns, including corps and army artillery matériel and supply trains, as at St. Mihiel, were provided by the French, some by the British, and practically none from home. We had 189 light tanks, all of French manufacture, 25 per cent of which were handled by French personnel, but no heavy tanks could be obtained. In aviation, we had 821 airplanes, over 600 of which were flown by American aviators.

The order of battle of the First Army from the Moselle River to the Meuse River for September 25th, from east to west, was as follows: The IV Corps (Dickman) with the French 69th Division and our 90th (Allen), 78th (McRae), 89th (Wright) and 42d (Menoher) Divisions in line and the 5th (McMahon) in reserve; French II Colonial Corps with the French 39th and 2d Divisions and our 26th Division (Edwards) in line; French XVII Corps with the French 15th, 10th and 18th Divisions in line and the French 26th Division in reserve.

In the order of battle on the Meuse-Argonne front, from east to west, the III Corps (Bullard) was on the right, with the 33d Division (Bell) nearest the Meuse to cover the river and protect the flank of the army, the 80th Division (Cronkhite) in the center, and the 4th Division (Hines) on the left, with the 3d Division (Buck) in reserve. The V Corps (Cameron) consisted of the 79th Division (Kuhn) facing Montfaucon, the 37th (Farnsworth), and the 91st (Johnston), in that order, while the 32d Division (Haan) was in reserve. The I Corps (Liggett) was on the left of the army with the 35th Division (Traub) on its right, the 28th Division (Muir) next, west of the Aire River, and the 77th Division (Alexander) facing the Argonne, with the French 5th Cavalry Division and the American 92d Division (colored) (Ballou) in reserve, except one regiment which was attached to the French Fourth Army. The 1st Division (Summerall), the 29th (Morton), and the 82d (Burnham) formed the army reserve.

In accordance with the principal mission, which remained the

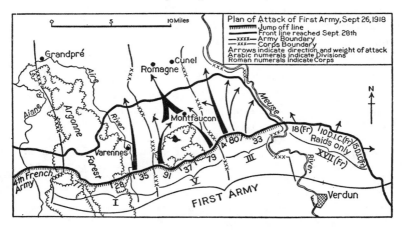

same throughout this offensive, the main attack by the First Army was to be launched west of the Meuse River, its right to be covered by the river and by the operations of the French XVII Corps on the east of the river, that corps being a part of our army. Our left was to be supported by a simultaneous advance by the French Fourth Army. Our attack, to include the Argonne Forest, was to be driven with all possible strength in the general direction of Mézières. The operations of the American First Army and the French Fourth Army were to be coördinated under agreement between General Pétain and myself.

The first operation of our army was to have for its objective the Hindenburg position on the front Brieulles-sur-Meuse—Romagne-sous-Montfaucon—Grandpré, with a following development in the direction of Buzancy—Mézières in order to force the enemy beyond the Meuse and outflank his positions on the Vouziers—Rethel line from the east.

In conjunction with our advance, which would outflank the enemy's position south of the Aisne, the French Fourth Army, by attacking successively the positions between the Aisne and the Suippe Rivers, would be able to occupy the line Vouziers—Rethel. After that it would operate in the directions of the plateau east of the Rethel—Signy-l'Abbaye road.

A liaison detachment under the French Fourth Army was designated to operate along the western edge of the Argonne Forest as a connecting link between the French and American armies.

In detail, it was actually planned by the First Army to make:

(a) An advance of ten miles to force the enemy to evacuate the Argonne Forest and insure our junction with the French Fourth Army at Grandpré.

(b) Then, a further advance of about ten miles to the line Stenay—Le Chesne to outflank the enemy's position along the Aisne River in front of the French Fourth Army and clear the way for our advance on Mézières or Sedan.

(c) An operation to clear the heights east of the Meuse River, either by an attack in an easterly direction or by an attack northwards along the east bank of the Meuse River between Beaumont and Sivry-sur-Meuse, to clear the crest south of Bois de la Grand Montagne, or by a combination of these two attacks.

The plan for the initial attack was based on penetrating the enemy's third position by capturing the commanding heights of Romagne.

The V Corps, after outflanking the Bois de Montfaucon and the Bois de Cheppy, and passing the hostile second position near Montfaucon, was to drive on, without waiting for adjacent corps, and penetrate the hostile third position about Romagne. The III Corps' main mission was to support the advance of the V Corps by turning Montfaucon from the east and protecting the right flank along the Meuse River. At the same time the I Corps, on the left, was to assist the advance by flanking the Argonne Forest from the east and protecting the left of the V Corps. The artillery of the two flank corps was specially charged with suppressing the enemy guns located on the dominating heights of the Meuse, to the east, and those in the Argonne Forest, to the west.

Thus, in the initial advance two salients were to be driven into the German defenses, one to the east and one to the west of Montfaucon. These two advances would carry the enemy's second position and outflank Montfaucon. The troops driving in the two salients just mentioned, having been joined by the troops attacking in the interval, would advance until the penetration of the third hostile position about Romagne and Cunel had been accomplished.

Our purpose was to effect a tactical surprise if possible and overcome the enemy's first and second positions in the area of Montfaucon and capture the commanding heights (Côte Dame Marie) of his third position before he could bring up strong reënforcements. This plan would require a rapid advance of ten miles through a densely fortified zone. From an estimate of the enemy's reserves and their location, it was realized that we must capture Montfaucon and seize Côte Dame Marie by the end of the second day.

It was thought reasonable to count on the vigor and the aggressive spirit of our troops to make up in a measure for their inexperience, but at the same time the fact was not overlooked that lack of technical skill might considerably reduce the chances of complete success against well organized resistance of experienced defenders. General Pétain had already given it as his opinion that we should not be able to get farther than Montfaucon before winter. Foreseeing clearly the difficulty under the existing conditions of reaching in one stride an objective ten miles away, alternative plans were made to continue with more deliberation but with every determination to win in the contest which, if not successful in the first rush, was certain to become extremely severe.

On the afternoon of the day before the attack I visited the headquarters of corps and divisions to give a word of encouragement here and there to the leaders upon whom our success on the following days would depend. They were all alert and confident and I returned feeling that all would go as planned.

(Diary) Souilly, Monday, September 30, 1918. Our attack started well Thursday morning and good advances were made along the whole front. Montfaucon was captured on Friday. The Secretary of War left for Paris. Assistant Secretary of War John D. Ryan took lunch with us.

Visited all American corps headquarters on Saturday. Approved Muir's request for temporary assignment of Brigadier General Nolan and Colonel Conger to 28th Division to replace inefficient officers. Gave orders yesterday for the relief from front line of 35th, 37th and 79th Divisions and their replacement by 1st, 32d and 3d Divisions.

German resistance stubborn. Yesterday counterattacks forced us to give ground in places. Our II Corps, with the British, attacked and broke through the Hindenburg Line. General Pétain called, much pleased at our progress. M. Clemenceau, who also came, very enthusiastic and started to Montfaucon, but road congestion prevented his reaching there. Some counterattacks to-day repulsed.

First Phase—Meuse-Argonne Operations

The Meuse-Argonne offensive opened on the morning of September 26th. To call it a battle may be a misnomer, yet it was a battle, the greatest, the most prolonged in American history. Through forty-seven days we were engaged in a persistent struggle with the enemy to smash through his defenses. The attack started on a front of twenty-four miles, which gradually extended until the enemy was being actively assailed from the Argonne Forest to the Moselle River, a distance of about ninety miles.

In all, more than 1,200,000 men were employed and the attack was driven thirty-two miles to the north and fourteen miles to the northeast before the Armistice terminated hostilities. The numbers engaged, the diverse character of the fighting and the terrain, the numerous crises, and the brilliant feats of individuals and units make a detailed description of the battle extremely complicated and necessarily confusing to the reader. The outstanding fact that I desire to emphasize is that once started the battle was maintained continuously, aggressively, and relentlessly to the end. All difficulties were overridden in one tremendous sustained effort to terminate the war then and there in a victorious manner.

After three hours' violent artillery preparation, the attack began at 5:30 A.M. At the same time, to divert the enemy's attention elsewhere, local raids and demonstrations were made on the Meuse-Moselle front. The French Fourth Army (Gouraud) to our left, on the west of the Argonne Forest, began its advance half an hour later. The battle opened favorably. Our attack at that particular place and at that time evidently came as a surprise to the enemy and our troops were enabled quickly to overrun his forward positions. The vast network of undestroyed barbed wire, the deep ravines, the dense woods, and the heavy fog made it difficult to coördinate the movements of the assaulting infantry, especially of some divisions in battle for the first time, yet the advance throughout was extremely vigorous.

The III Corps (Bullard), nearest the Meuse, carried the enemy's second position before dark. The 33d Division (Bell), wheeling to the right as it advanced, occupied the west bank of the Meuse to protect the flank of the army. The Bois de Forges, with its difficult terrain and strong machine gun defenses, was carried in splendid fashion.

The right of the 80th Division (Cronkhite) had by noon cleared the Bois Juré in the face of machine gun fire and established its line north of Dannevoux. On its left, after an all-day fight, the division forced its way through the strong positions on Hill 262 and reached the northern slopes of that hill.

The 4th Division (Hines), on the left of the 80th, took Septsarges and firmly established itself in the woods to the north. It was abreast of Nantillois and its left was more than a mile beyond Montfaucon, but through some misinterpretation of the orders by the III Corps the opportunity to capture Montfaucon that day was lost. Three counterattacks against the division during the afternoon were broken up.

In the center, the V Corps (Cameron), with the exception of the 91st Division (Johnston), on its left, fell short of its objectives. The 79th Division (Kuhn), on the right of the corps, took Malancourt but in the open ground beyond encountered considerable opposition and the advanced elements were not in position before Montfaucon until late afternoon. The attack of the division launched against this strongpoint early in the evening was met by the fire of artillery and machine guns from the southern slopes of the hill which held up further progress.

The 37th Division (Farnsworth), in the center of the V Corps, after overcoming strong machine gun fire, pushed through the Bois de Montfaucon, and its attacks in the afternoon carried the line up to west of Montfaucon. The left of its line, facing stiff opposition, cleaned up the woods in its front and established itself just south of Ivoiry.

The 91st Division (Johnston) overcame strong initial resistance and advanced rapidly to Épinonville, which it entered but did not hold. Crossing into the sector of the 35th Division during the day, it occupied Véry.

On the left of the Army, the I Corps (Liggett) made excellent progress. The 35th Division (Traub) cleverly captured the strong position of Vauquois and took Cheppy against stubborn opposition. Elements of the division reached the corps objective east of Charpentry but were withdrawn to a line west of Véry. On the left, the division captured that part of Varennes east of the Aire River, but was held up between Varennes and Cheppy. At this time, a fresh regiment took the lead, giving a new impetus to the attack, and pushed the line forward to the high ground south of Charpentry.

In the 28th Division (Muir) the right brigade captured the western half of Varennes and continued about a mile farther. The left brigade, facing the eastern spurs of the Argonne, which constituted the enemy's chief defense of that forest, was unable to overcome the intense machine gun fire from the vicinity of Champ Mahaut. The 77th Division (Alexander) in the difficult terrain of the Argonne made some progress.

The advance on the first day was generally rapid, as the forward elements of the German defensive zone were usually not strongly held and they had not yet been reënforced in any numbers. By the second day, however, his nearby reserves had arrived, and the enemy took full advantage of the stand at Montfaucon on the first day to strengthen his defenses.

The Germans made every use of the favorable terrain to oppose our advance by cross and enfilading artillery fire, especially from the bluffs on the eastern edge of the Argonne Forest and the heights east of the Meuse. His light guns and the extensive use of machine guns along his lines of defense, in the hands of well trained troops, were serious obstacles, and the advance after the second day was more difficult.

By the evening of the 27th, the V Corps was almost abreast of the I and III on its flanks. The 79th Division captured Montfaucon on the morning of the 27th, and on the 28th Nantillois and the Bois de Beuge were passed despite determined resistance. Twice on the 28th elements of the division penetrated the Bois des Ogons but could not hold on. Again on the 29th it attacked the wood, severe casualties once more compelling retirement to the ridge north of Nantillois. Other troops of the division advanced more than a mile beyond the Bois de Beuge but were forced to fall back.

I went to III Corps headquarters on the 28th to confer with Bullard, who spoke well of the divisions under his command. The 80th had taken the Bois de la Côte Lemont after hard fighting, but assault after assault made with dogged determination across the open space toward Brieulles-sur-Meuse was rolled back by the galling fire of the enemy from the town and its vicinity and by the artillery firing from the east of the Meuse.

The 33d Division maintained its position on the 27th and 28th and on the 29th relieved the 80th Division by extending its left along the northeastern edge of Bois de la Côte Lemont, where it occupied difficult ground under the dominating heights east of the Meuse.

The 4th Division captured Nantillois on the 27th but was forced by enemy counterattacks to retire. The town was retaken and held on the following day by troops of the 4th and 79th Divisions. After three days of almost continuous fighting, the 4th had taken the Bois de Brieulles and entered the Bois des Ogons, but could not hold the latter against counterattacks and the deadly machine gun and artillery fire of the enemy. The fortitude and courage of the 4th Division in these operations were inspiring.

The 37th Division on the 27th attempted to advance beyond the Ivoiry—Montfaucon road but each time it reached there was driven back by heavy shelling. On the 28th, however, it pushed forward to a position north of the Cierges—Nantillois road. Cierges was entered but not held. On the following day it again attacked Cierges but the advance was abruptly halted by concentrated artillery fire.

The 91st Division on the 27th encountered strong opposition at Épinonville, which was reached but could not be retained. Eclisfontaine was taken but was evacuated as an artillery barrage was to be laid on the road through the town during the night. Épinonville was finally captured on the 28th and the Bois de Cierges was occupied after hard fighting. Two attacks of the division from the Bois de Cierges on the 29th crumbled under fierce artillery and enfilading machine gun fire, but on the third attack, despite severe losses, Gesnes was taken. The full advantage of this important gain was lost, however, through the inability of the 37th Division to advance its left. This placed the right flank of the 91st in a dangerous position and it had to be withdrawn. During the afternoon the 35th Division was subjected to a heavy counterattack which also involved the left of the 91st, but made no progress against it.

Three new German divisions had appeared by September 30th on the front of the I Corps and the battle continued with increased intensity. The 35th Division was stopped by heavy fire soon after its attack opened on September 27th, but later in the day it captured Charpentry and advanced to the ridge northeast, though suffering severe casualties. When I called to see General Traub at his P.C. at Cheppy, on the 28th, his communications with his front had been seriously damaged and it was difficult to tell what was happening. The division, however, took Montrebeau Wood on that day. Early on the morning of the 29th a detachment reached Exermont valley, but being nearly surrounded withdrew to the starting-point. Encountering very heavy artillery fire and an advance of the German 52d and 5th Guard Divisions, the 35th withdrew from Montrebeau Wood, which it had taken the day before. The 35th suffered greater casualties than any other division during these four days of continuous fighting.

On my visit to the headquarters of the 28th Division, then at Varennes, General Muir complained of a lack of trained officers. Two general staff officers, General Nolan and Colonel Conger, were there at the time, and I assigned them both temporarily to the division. Though subjected to strong artillery and machine gun fire from the bluffs of the Argonne, the 28th Division captured Montblainville on September 27th. It could make only slight headway, however, against firm opposition from positions in the vicinity of Champ Mahaut, but carried them on the 28th and also captured Apremont. On the 29th, after repulsing a German counterattack, a slight advance was made against the defenses of Le Chêne Tondu.[1]

The 77th Division encountered stiff resistance in the Argonne on the 27th and was held to a small gain, but moved forward about a mile on the 28th. On the 29th its right was advanced with but little opposition.

During the first four days of fighting, the First Army, west of the Meuse, had made a maximum advance of about eight miles,

[1] Brig. Gen. Edward Sigerfoos, while en route to assume command of the 56th Brigade, 28th Division, was struck by shell fragments on Sept. 29th, near Apremont, and died of wounds on Oct. 7th.

reaching the line Bois de la Côte Lemont—Nantillois—Apremont. The enemy had been struck a blow so powerful that the extreme gravity of his situation in France was obvious to him. From the North Sea to the Meuse his tired divisions had been battered, and nowhere with more dogged resolution than in front of the American First Army, his most sensitive point. The initial moves of the German Government to stop the fighting occurred at this time and without doubt because of the results of these four days of battle.

The enemy must have realized that the complete loss of his positions on the west bank of the Meuse was only a question of a short time. Meanwhile, he had to hold his third line of defense on our front as long as possible to protect his vital artery of communications and the flank of his troops opposing the French Fourth Army. He was, therefore, compelled to weaken his power of resistance on other fronts to provide reënforcements for his struggle with our First Army. It should be recorded that in this dire extremity the Germans defended every foot of ground with desperate tenacity and with the rare skill of experienced soldiers.

The enemy quickly brought up reënforcements, one division arriving on the afternoon of the 26th. By the 30th he had added six fresh divisions to his lines with five more ready in close reserve. The 76th Reserve Division entered in the Argonne, the 5th Guard Division on the Aire, the 52d near Exermont, the 115th Division near Cierges, the 37th Division west of Nantillois, and the 5th Bavarian Division near Nantillois. Our initial gains had been made against eleven enemy divisions.

The difficulties encountered by our inexperienced divisions during this phase of the fighting were not easily overcome. Liaison between the various echelons was hard to maintain owing to the broken nature of the terrain and the numerous wooded areas. Supported in most instances by artillery units with which they had never before maneuvered, perfect teamwork between the artillery and the infantry was not at once attained. The tanks gave valuable assistance at the start, but they became especial targets for the enemy's artillery and their numbers were rapidly diminished.

The question of supply during the Meuse-Argonne operation, especially in the beginning, gave us much concern. The three roads crossing no-man's-land over which artillery and supply trains had to move were impassable in many places. After four years of neglect and frequent bombardment, scarcely more than traces were left. In addition to having been blown up in spots where repair was difficult, they were further damaged by the explosion of contact mines planted by the retreating enemy. The French earlier in the war had also blown enormous craters in these roads to hinder the German advance. Trucks and artillery were delayed and could often be gotten forward only by the troops hauling them by ropes. The whole terrain in front of the enemy's first line was one continuous area of deep shell holes. After the sunshine of the first day, the heavy rainfall on the second and third days added immeasurably to the task of road repair. Considerable portions of the roads over no-man's-land had to be entirely rebuilt.

Notwithstanding the limited time available and the scarcity of labor, the task of moving combat troops, supplies and ammunition under the circumstances was accomplished in a most commendable manner, due mainly to the energetic work of pioneer, road, railroad, and truck train troops. Most of the divisional artillery and a considerable portion of the corps artillery got forward on the first day, and all but a few batteries of heavy artillery on the second day.

During the first four days, especially, although we had a superiority in the number of guns, the enemy's artillery had the advantage of hidden flank positions on the heights of the Meuse and in the Argonne. It had almost full play on the more exposed elements of the advance, and its cross-fire caused us many casualties. The tremendous numbers of machine guns, located in inaccessible places, gave us much trouble.

The tenacity with which the eastern heights of the Argonne Forest were held by the Germans is indicated in the orders of their divisions and the corps holding the Argonne and Aire valley sectors. The corps advised the Argonne sector on September 26th to reënforce the eastern edge of the forest; on the 27th positive orders were issued that the troops in the Aire valley were to be supported with every piece of artillery in the Argonne. The artillery so concentrated along the edge of the forest poured its deadly flanking fire into the 28th, 35th and 91st Divisions, particularly the 35th. A German account written on the 28th gives the number of tanks shot to pieces in the vicinity of Chaudron Farm and Montblainville as thirty. By the morning of the 28th, according to German report, there were thirteen batteries enfilading the American attack from the eastern rim of the Argonne.

Telephone communications were difficult to maintain, mainly due to destruction wrought by the enemy's artillery, although somewhat due to the inexperience of our personnel. In the V Corps the signal battalion joined on the eve of battle and had to learn its duties under fire. Without some means of sending messages between the elements of a command, there can, of course, be no direction and no concerted action, and consequently little chance of success.

The severity of the fighting, the heavy casualties, and the intermingling of troops in some of our divisions were such that it seemed advisable to place in the line more experienced divisions which had now become available. It was also thought best to limit activities to local attacks for two or three days. The 32d (Haan) and the 3d (Buck) Divisions were brought in to relieve the 37th (Farnsworth) and 79th (Kuhn), and the 1st Division (Summerall) took the place of the 35th (Traub). The 91st (Johnston) was withdrawn to corps reserve and the 92d (Ballou) was placed at the disposal of the French XXXVIII Corps, which was on the left of the I Corps.

These changes, involving the movement of more than 125,000 men over the limited routes available, already severely taxed with the transportation of ammunition, food, and the evacuation of wounded, were successfully made and the army was ready for the renewal of its attacks.

It was a matter of keen regret that the veteran 2d Division was not on hand at this time, but at Marshal Foch's earnest request it had been sent to General Gouraud to assist the French Fourth Army, which was held up at Somme Py. At no time did I refuse to comply with Foch's requests to send divisions to the assistance of the Allies, no matter how inconvenient it may have been. I always insisted, however, that these divisions should operate as American units and should return to my command when they had accomplished their emergency mission.

It was one thing to fight a battle with well trained, well organized and experienced troops, but quite another matter to take relatively green troops and organize, train and fight them at the same time. Some of our divisions that lacked training could not have been considered available for this operation had it not been for our belief that the morale of the enemy in general was rather low and that this was the opportunity to throw our full strength into the battle with the intention of winning the war in 1918.

During this phase and throughout the battle, I frequently visited corps and divisions to give personal encouragement to commanders and staffs, to point out deficiencies, to adjust difficulties, to keep myself directly informed as to progress, and to indicate the most advantageous methods of handling the troops in these attacks. In order to keep in closer touch with the activities of our forces, my personal staff and other officers especially qualified for this duty were sent to the front to observe the progress of the different units.

On Sunday, the 29th, M. Clemenceau came to visit the First Army. He was pleased with our progress and was especially delighted at the capture of Montfaucon. He insisted on going there notwithstanding my warning that it was dangerous to do so and that the roads were filled with traffic. I felt real solicitude for his safety as Montfaucon was a prominent target for the enemy's artillery. The road he took was crowded with trucks that morning, due especially to the trains of the 1st Division, which was going to the front to relieve the 35th. He failed to reach Montfaucon and left rather disappointed, thinking, no doubt, that our transportation was hopelessly swamped, as we soon began to hear of criticisms to that effect not only by the French but even by some Americans.

The truth is that while the roads were at times congested in places, no such general condition existed. This is shown by the relief of three divisions by three others, making a large increase in the number of men handled over the roads at this time, in addition to the heavy regular traffic. Under the circumstances, the movement of the truck trains required for this purpose was especially well managed. The number of troops moved in this change was greater than the entire Northern Army in the battle of the Wilderness. There was no major offensive during the World War in which a certain amount of congestion on roads leading to the front did not occur until those across no-man's-land could be opened up and put in good shape. I have already referred to the confused conditions behind Mangin's army during his attack on the Château-Thierry salient in July, and this was another case in point.

Good reports came in regarding the operations on the 29th of our II Corps (Read), which was with General Rawlinson's British Fourth Army. With both the 30th (Lewis) and the 27th (O'Ryan) Divisions in line, this corps formed the main wedge in the attack against that portion of the German lines which included the Bellicourt tunnel of the Cambrai—St. Quentin Canal. This tunnel, which is about 6,500 yards in length, served as an excellent shelter for the protection of German troops in that sector.

The II Corps, attacking on September 29th against stiff resistance, gallantly captured the ridge of the tunnel, which was a part of the Hindenburg Line. The 30th Division did especially well. It broke through the Hindenburg Line on its entire front and took Bellicourt and part of Nauroy by noon of the 29th. The Australian 5th Division, coming up at this time, continued the attack with elements of the 30th Division and the line advanced a considerable distance.

The 27th Division, due to no fault of its own, had been unable to take full advantage of the accompanying barrage, which was laid down over 1,000 yards ahead of the line from which the troops started the attack. Despite the handicap, it took the

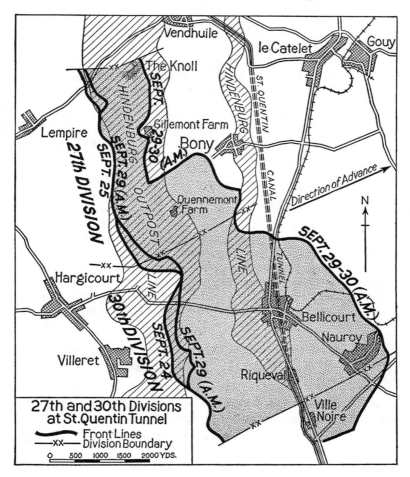

27th and 30th Divisions
at St. Quentin Tunnel
Front Lines
—xx— Division Boundary
0   500 1000 1500 2000 YDS.

enemy trenches of the Hindenburg Line south of Bony, captured The Knoll, and established its line south from that position to a point just west of Gillemont Farm.

CHAPTER XLVI

New Proposal by Foch—Would Divide First Army—Flatly Disapprove—
Motor Transport Woefully Short—Rail Transportation Inadequate—
Shipments Haphazard—Mr. Baker Obtains Additional Tonnage from
British—Personnel Falling Behind—Secretary's Departure—Letters
Exchanged

(Diary) Souilly, Thursday, October 3, 1918. Was surprised Tuesday by proposal of Marshal Foch, brought by General Weygand, to
interject the French Second Army between us and French Fourth
Army, which I disapproved.

Claudel [1] came yesterday to discuss an attack by his corps which
he had been directed to prepare. Sent letter to the Secretary of War.

Minor engagements have occurred since the 29th. Captured positions being consolidated.

This afternoon saw corps commanders about the attack to-morrow.
Roads rapidly improving and conditions better.

Serious situation as to motor transport again cabled to Washington.
Shortage in tonnage reducing supplies to danger point. The French
have agreed to import locomotives and turn over cars made for them
in the United States. Atterbury has cabled Felton complete rail requirements.

A S noted in the diary, the proposal from Marshal Foch,
brought by Weygand, contemplated placing the French
Second Army between the American First and the French
Fourth Armies. It was suggested by Weygand that the Second
Army should take over those divisions from the left of our First

[1] General Claudel commanded the French XVII Corps at Verdun, which formed a
part of the American First Army.

NOTE: Total strength of the A.E.F. on September 30th, 71,172 officers, 1,634,220 enlisted
men.

Divisional units arriving in September included elements of the following divisions:
34th Division (National Guard, Nebraska, Iowa, South Dakota, North Dakota and
Minnesota), Brig. Gen. John A. Johnston; 84th Division (National Army, Kentucky,
Indiana and southern Illinois), Maj. Gen. Harry C. Hale; 86th Division (National
Army, Wisconsin and Illinois), Maj. Gen. Charles H. Martin; 87th Division (National
Army, Arkansas, Louisiana, Mississippi and Alabama), Maj. Gen. Samuel D. Sturgis.

Army that were in and near the Argonne Forest, leaving the rest of the army under my command. The idea seemed to be that this would accelerate the advance. The plan was similar to the one of August 30th, which had been so firmly opposed that I thought the matter settled once for all.

Just what prompted the proposal was not clear. However, I suspected at the time that it was made in deference to some suggestion or direction from Clemenceau, who often jumped at conclusions. Although he might not have expert knowledge of military situations or of operations, this would not have deterred him from judging as though he were quite competent to do so.

As Chairman of the Supreme War Council, Clemenceau had been granted no authority to issue directions to the Allied Commander-in-Chief. But in his capacity as Prime Minister he had authority over Marshal Foch as an officer of the French Army. The Marshal fully realized this, and although he had been chosen by the Allied Governments and was responsible to them jointly, his tenure of office naturally depended upon their pleasure, and especially upon that of his own Prime Minister. This would readily account for any action he might take at the suggestion of the latter.

The proposition Weygand submitted was not sound because the different features of that front were interdependent and the advantages they afforded the enemy's defense could best be overcome by a strong attacking force under one control. Another objection was that there was only one road leading to the part of our front which was proposed for the French Second Army and its use by two different armies would have resulted in many complications. Moreover, the fact was again overlooked that our men seriously objected to service in the French Army. I pointed out these objections to Weygand and told him that the change, in my opinion, instead of increasing Allied progress would retard it. He left with the view that I was right, and my reply by letter disapproving the plan seemed to settle the matter. So we continued our attacks as planned.

We were woefully deficient in motor transportation now that we had undertaken large operations, although the shipment of motor vehicles had been repeatedly urged upon the War Department. Once more we were almost wholly dependent upon the French for land transport to move our troops and to handle about half of our ammunition supply. To carry on operations, we had to strip the S.O.S. of trucks, and this seriously interfered with work at the base ports, with construction projects at other points, and with supply of troops in general. The shortage of ambulances to move the sick and wounded was critical and we had been compelled to borrow fifteen American ambulance sections from Italy. But we had reached the point where we were no longer able to borrow. This condition was not easy to reconcile with the suggestion from Washington made a short time before that motor transportation be largely substituted for horses.

All these facts were pointed out plainly to the War Department, but we received little encouragement. According to the Department's detailed program of shipments, just received, the best we could expect in the near future was only about one-fifth of our requirements. After another urgent cable, we were promised 10,000 motor vehicles in October but the promise was only partially fulfilled. The question was to some extent dependent upon tonnage, although the shipping authorities continuously failed to take advantage of deck space available on most of our transports.

The following quotation from my cable to the Chief of Staff on the subject, sent September 13th, will indicate our situation:

"At the present time our ability to supply and maneuver our forces depends largely on motor transportation. The shortage in motor transportation is particularly embarrassing now due to shortage of horses for our horse-drawn transport. We are able to carry out present plans due to fact that we have been able to borrow temporarily large numbers of trucks and ambulances from French. We have also borrowed fifteen American ambulance sections from Italy. The shortage of ambulances to move our wounded is critical. * * * The most important plans and operations depend upon certainty that the home government will deliver at French ports material and equipment called for. It is urged that foregoing be given most serious consideration.

* * * The need of motor transportation is urgent. It is not understood why greater advantage has not been taken of deck space to ship motor trucks. Trucks do not overburden dock accommodations or require railroad transportation * * * . Can you not impress this upon shipping authorities?"

The absence of motor vehicles would not have been quite so serious if we had not been in such a crippled state as to horses. Due to lack of animals our divisional transport and artillery were rapidly becoming immobilized. We still hoped to obtain a number from the French, and from Spain and Portugal, but after cutting down the requirements as far as possible we needed 30,000 per month additional from home from October to June, 1919, even with our full quota of motor vehicles. It became evident in July that to meet our pressing needs the shipment of horses would have to be resumed and a request was cabled July 16th for 25,000 per month. It was not to be expected that shipments could begin at once, but it was disappointing that in the three months preceding our entry into battle we should receive less than 2,000 horses.

In the matter of locomotives and cars the situation continued much the same and came to such a pass that the French said they could do no more. They offered to import for us as many locomotives as could be produced in excess of our monthly program, the non-fulfillment of which had left us short, and to turn over sufficient cars manufactured on their orders to bring monthly shipments up to 7,500. As to rails, they suggested that if there was not enough steel for shell production and for rails we should abandon railroad repair and tear up existing track at home, as both they and the British had done. Marshal Foch urged increased rail facilities as necessary to win the war and himself submitted the above suggestions.

In considering questions of supply, we were always forced back to the subject of shipping. Our tonnage allotments were not keeping up to our increasing demands. In July, for instance, we were allotted 475,000 tons against my request for 750,000, and we received 438,000 tons. It was the same in August, when we were allotted 700,000 tons and received 511,000, and on the basis of receipts for the first two weeks of September it seemed probable we would run some 200,000 tons short in that month.[1] The situation was so grave that in my cable of October 3d setting forth the deficiencies I said, "Unless supplies are furnished when and as called for, our armies will cease to operate."

To aggravate matters, shipments seemed to be haphazard. For instance, there were sent in August 50,000 tons of quartermaster supplies of which we already had a surplus, and in that month the shipments showed a deficiency of 50,000 tons pertaining to the transportation department and motor transport. In cabling these facts to Washington, I stated, "You must prepare to ship supplies we request instead of shipping excess amounts of supplies of which we have a due proportion."

To get an idea of the situation, it may be noted that for June, July, and August, shipments of Ordnance material were 33 per cent short of estimated allotments, in Signal Corps material 52 per cent, in Chemical Warfare requirements 51 per cent, in Medical Corps supplies 23 per cent, in railway transportation, principally rolling stock, 20 per cent, while in motor transport we were desperate as the deficiency was 81 per cent.

It was next to impossible to consider with complacency a situation which left us not only short of supplies but almost without modern means to move our armies. When a nation is forced into war without preparation, neither men nor equipment are at once forthcoming and time is required to develop the flow of all that is needed, which is difficult because of the pressure for haste from all quarters. Yet after nearly eighteen months of war it would be reasonable to expect that the organization at home would have been more nearly able to provide adequate equipment and supplies, and to handle shipments more systematically. It was fortunate indeed that we were not operating alone, for, in that case, the failure to meet our demands would have caused us serious trouble, if not irreparable disaster.

[1] The difference in the amount of supplies asked for by the A.E.F. and the amount received in September was 330,000 tons and in October 398,000 tons.

There was hope, however, of some improvement in the tonnage situation. The Emergency Fleet Corporation of the Shipping Board at home, under the energetic and able direction of Mr. Charles M. Schwab, was turning out new ships at a greatly increased rate. Undoubtedly, had the war lasted a few months longer, our deficiency in this respect would have been entirely overcome.

As for the immediate future, when Mr. Baker came back from England to be with us at the beginning of the Meuse-Argonne battle, he brought the welcome news that he had succeeded in getting an allotment of 200,000 tons of shipping from the British, on the condition that we should help them out later in the shipment of cereals, if it should become necessary. He cabled the President asking approval of an agreement he wished to make with Lord Reading that there would be no diversion of tonnage from the amount needed for the maintenance of our forces in Europe if we would agree to coöperate with the Allies by using our tonnage for their supply programs as their needs should become paramount.

The arrivals of personnel were not keeping up with the 80-division program, even as construed in Washington. Our contention was that these eighty divisions should be combat troops, and that in addition we should have a corresponding number for the various units connected with the S.O.S., but Washington took another view. At any rate, for the forces then in France there was needed to balance the command, 129,000 army troops, 93,000 corps troops, 83,000 S.O.S. troops and 65,000 replacements. In order to make definite plans for the future, it was necessary for us to have the troops for the various purposes in due proportion. However, it was evident from the correspondence that in the opinion of the War Department 3,000,000 men would be the highest number that could be trained, transported, and supplied.

The Secretary was now about to leave for home and as it was not possible for me to see him again I wrote him touching on these and other matters that had been the subject of conversation:

"France, October 2, 1918.

"My dear Mr. Secretary:

"I very much regret that it will be impossible for me to meet you in Paris before you leave for the States. It seems that I have not had more than a glimpse of you, and our conversations have been so few and so short that I feel as though I had not brought out clearly many things of mutual interest and importance. Our whole problem here is of such magnitude that details sometimes are apt to get little attention, and yet only by carefully watching these details shall we be able to keep the machinery going. If one part of the mechanism gets weak, then, under great stress, the whole might fail. It all requires the most watchful care. There is no one quite so sensitive to this as the engineer who is getting the machinery into perfect working order, putting it under way, and trying to keep it moving until it has attained its full momentum, and then holding it there in a true course.

"The one general principle, which you so clearly understand, much to my gratification, and the enforcement of which will insure perfect coöperation, is that the General Staff and every supply department at Washington should strive to provide us promptly with the necessary personnel and material in the order called for, the whole scheme, of course, to be coördinated by your General Staff. As you know, our personnel and some kinds of material and supplies, including transportation, are in a very unbalanced condition. I hope that your own high position and your personal force will serve to regulate many of these matters with which no one but yourself over there can be familiar.

"In sending General McAndrew up to Paris to see you, I have asked him to take certain cables which illustrate our situation and show the insistence with which we have placed our needs before the Department, and the apparent routine attitude with which they are too often viewed at the other end. Of course, it may be difficult for them to see the problem as we see it, but that is all the more reason for their accepting our view instead of adhering to their own.

"The operations here have gone very well, but, due to the rains and the condition of the roads, have not gone forward as rapidly nor as far as I had hoped. But this terrain over which we now operate is the most difficult on the Western Front. Our losses so far have been moderate. I have taken out three of the newest divisions and replaced them by older ones. We shall be prepared to advance again in a day or two more.

"I did not mean to write at such length, but our success here depends so much upon the coöperative support that the General Staff and the supply departments, including shipping, at Washington give us that I have ventured again to appear garrulous. No doubt it will be much improved upon your return. If I have seemed too positive, it is because I am prompted by my wish and by your own strong desire to have things go as we have planned.

"May I ask you to convey to the President my most cordial greetings and very best wishes.

"Believe me, with warmest personal and official regard,

"Yours sincerely,   "JOHN J. PERSHING."

Written on the same date, his letter advised me of shipping and other matters of great interest:

"France, October 2, 1918.

"MY DEAR GENERAL PERSHING:

"I am returning to Paris to-day, having completed, so far as it can be done, the shipping matters in London. On Friday night I shall go to Brest and thence home. I am taking back to the United States with me, Mr. Ryan, General Hines, Mr. Hostetler, Mr. Day and Mr. Gifford, who came over with Mr. Stettinius. Before we leave, General Hines is going to see General McAndrew for a final talk about shipping matters. I think we will all go home to the United States with fresh enthusiasm for our end of the work and I hope you will soon feel in Europe the effect of our work in the States.

"The four main problems are, of course, the shipping of motor transport, animal transport, general supplies and of men. In addition to these I will assuredly be mindful of the discussion of the promotion question and the schools question.

"As you know, the British have already placed at our disposal for October sailings, substantially 200,000 tons cargo carrying capacity of ships. In London we found every disposition to assist us to the full extent of the needs of the eighty-division program, and after very careful studies of the question the whole matter was brought up at the Inter-Allied Maritime Council in session attended by Lord Reading and me. Apparently the only obstacle grew out of a fear on the part of the European Allies that the diversion of tonnage from their cereal import program at this time would leave them short of food later in the year. They were aware of the fact that our shipbuilding progress would, on present appearance, give us a surplus of ships beyond our Army needs beginning in March, 1919, but they wanted some sort of assurance that we would use this surplus to replenish their food stocks. As it is obvious that we cannot allow this period of the civil populations of the European Allies to be broken by insufficient food, I felt quite ready to give the necessary assurance and we have now this understanding embodied in the resolutions of the Inter-Allied Maritime Council, namely that the eighty-division American Military Program is approved and thought necessary. Shipping to effect it is to be placed at our disposal with the understanding that should a food, or other need of any of the European Allies become so pressing as to become critical, the United States will confer through the Inter-Allied Maritime Council with the representatives of other nations and participate with them in meeting the crisis out of any surplus shipping it may have or any such other way as the character of the crisis dictates. In effect this amounts to a present approval of our program with the reservation that in view of the constantly changing situation we are all free to meet any new crisis should it arise, by fresh consultations and determinations.

"Among the ships already diverted to our use are three horse-ships and I impressed upon the executives of the Maritime Council the importance of further diversion of ships of the same kind. One result of this arrangement will be that the Inter-Allied Maritime Council will be constantly studying America's need for shipping and this of course will mean principally the Army need. I stated to the Council quite frankly that America could never under any circumstances regard any other need as paramount to the necessary supplies of so much of our Army as is in Europe at any given time. This position was recognized as just and Messrs. Stevens and Rublee, who represent the United States on the Maritime Council, have assured me that they will keep themselves constantly advised as to the Army needs and represent them for us in the deliberations of the Maritime Council so that no diversion of shipping will be made by that body which will prejudice the necessary supplies of the Army.

"I hope to see General Harbord and to explain to him the importance of keeping Messrs. Stevens and Rublee fully acquainted with the Army needs from time to time and have arranged to have Mr. Morrow come to France and confer with General Harbord frequently so that he can be the means of inter-communication between our S.O.S. Headquarters and Mr. Stevens and Mr. Rublee. I am told that you have already met Mr. Morrow and I need not therefore enlarge upon his splendid abilities and fine spirit. It may be that he may ask to see you should any peculiarly difficult question arise and I am therefore explaining in detail the service which he has undertaken to perform and its importance in assuring the continuance of the necessary shipping for our use.

"I had rather expected that the Italian delegates to the Maritime Council might raise some question about American troops serving in Italy. They did not bring up the subject, nor was anything said at the meeting of the Council by the British on that subject, but an interesting incident took place about which I feel that you ought to have for your information a rather detailed account.

" * * * The conversation was very general until dinner time, but as soon as we had finished dinner, the Prime Minister brought up the shipping question. Sir Joseph Maclay, who was present, was called on to state the situation, which he did in a few words, and I made a brief comment which was accepted by everybody as showing that we were all in hearty accord and would be able to work out the problem. Then Mr. Lloyd George squared himself around and said that he had something which he felt it very important to say to me and to say with great frankness. We all kept quiet and he talked, I should say, for half an hour without interruption. I cannot of course reproduce verbally what he said, but in effect it was this:

"That the British had brought over from the United States an enormous number of troops in the firm expectation that they would be trained with the British and would assist the British in their Flanders fighting. That they had gone to great lengths to supply and equip our troops and finally had some ten divisions of them about ready to engage in conflict and included in Sir Douglas Haig's plans of attack, when suddenly the five best trained divisions were taken away just at the time when they would have been of most service with Sir Douglas Haig's troops. That later, of the five divisions then with the British, three were taken away and that he was informed that the other two came near being taken away so that the effect of the whole business was that for all their pains and sacrifices for training our troops there and equipping them they had gotten no good out of them whatever, and that the American troops had not been of any service to the British. That at one time when some American troops were about to go into action with the British, peremptory orders had been issued that they should not go into action as they were not adequately trained.

"From this he went on to say that he was earnestly desirous for opportunity of the American and British soldiers to fraternize. He felt that large issues to the future peace of the world depended upon the American and British peoples understanding one another and that much the best hope of such an understanding grew out of intermingling our soldiers so that they could learn to know one another, but that it seemed to him that there was some influence at work to monopolize American soldiers for the assistance of the French and to keep them from the association of the British.

"When he had about finished, I replied to him that I was profoundly surprised at the feeling he expressed, since Lord Reading and I had quite definitely understood in Washington, and our understanding had been set up in a memorandum of which copy had been sent him, that the American troops brought over by the British were expedited because of the lack of reserves by the British and French, which would be made up by August 1st. That I had stated to Lord Reading and put into the memorandum that these American troops assigned for training with the British were to be subject to your call at any time at your discretion and that their training and use was constantly to be such as you directed. I had, therefore, no thought that there could be any ground for misunderstanding your right to take the American troops at any time you wanted them. I pointed out to him that the President and I had repeatedly, both verbally and in writing, insisted that the American Army as such was the thing we were trying to create. That we had no intention of feeding our soldiers into the French or British Army and intended to have an American army in exactly the same sense that Great Britain had a British army and France a French army. That we all recognized the right of Marshal Foch to send divisions of Americans or French or British from one part of the line to another for particular operations or to create a composite reserve which would have troops of all three nations for use as reserves, but with that exception American troops in France were as completely under your control as British troops in France were under the control of Sir Douglas Haig. I then took up the question as to whether American troops had been of any service to the British and told him quite frankly that I did not see how it was possible to hold the view he had expressed for three reasons at least. First— the work of our troops at Château-Thierry and elsewhere had been so valuable a contribution to the whole cause, and I had been repeatedly told, in France by Frenchmen and in England by Englishmen, that they had saved the whole situation. Second—that our occupation of a substantial portion of the line in Lorraine and our operations there had undoubtedly both cost the enemy heavily and required the German high command to remove divisions from the British fronts, thus rendering Sir Douglas Haig's operations easier by diminishing the forces opposed to him; and third, I pointed out that our soldiers actually with the British at this time were bearing their full share of the heavy fighting and I said this must have been going on for some time, since I have visited several hospitals in England which are filled with wounded American soldiers, many of whom have been from three to five weeks in the hospitals recovering from wounds received by them in August, when according to the original understanding they would not have been with the British at all but would have been back with your Army.

"Long as this account of the conversation is, it is nevertheless but a summary of it. It left on my mind a very strong feeling that Lloyd George frankly wants Americans to remain with the British both as a stimulus and for the fraternization which he describes and that he is very suspicious that the French are desiring to monopolize the Americans and so come out of the war as our principal friends without there having been any real opportunity for coöperation and understanding between the British and Americans.

"I, of course, gave him no assurances whatever, and when he asked me what expectations I thought he ought to have about the use of American troops I replied shortly that I thought he ought to expect the American Army as such to exist in the same sense as the British Army and to be used there as a whole or by the detachment of divisions here and there wherever the largest good could be accomplished for the cause in the judgment of the Commander-in-Chief as he considered the problem from time to time.

"In the course of his statement that the American troops had been of no service to the British he pointed out that we had relieved the French of some forty or forty-five miles of front line and I remarked that when we took over forty miles of the entire front that was a help because it enabled the French and British to hold the remainder of the line more strongly with the same aggregate force. He then asked me whether I thought the French ought to take over some portion of the line held by the British in view of the fact that the Americans had relieved the French of so much of their portion of the line. I told him I knew nothing about the way that such matters were decided but that it would seem equable to have the relief afforded by the American assumption of a portion of the line insure to the benefit of both the French and the British in some such way.

"I am particular to describe this part of the conversation to you because I thought I could see an intention on his part to press Marshal Foch to take over for the French Army some part of the present British lines and he may quote me on the subject to the Marshal. I should be sorry to have the Marshal imagine that I undertook to express any opinion on such a subject beyond the mere generality that the American relief ought to be, as far as just and practicable, a benefit to both of our Allies in the line.

"The dinner party broke up pleasantly enough by our turning the conversation to other subjects. Later Lord Reading and Lord Milner communicated to me privately to the effect that they were very glad that the Prime Minister had brought up the subject and that we had discussed it so frankly. They were both perfectly proper in their attitude but as far as they could, gave me to understand that they were glad he had it off his chest and were equally glad that I had stood my ground and argued it out. So far as I can learn neither Lord Reading nor Lord Milner has had any special sympathy with the Prime Minister's view in this matter, although, of course, he is the head of the Government and they are loyal to his expressed views.

"I spoke with General Read, whose corps is participating very heavily in the present fighting, and I venture to suggest that it be not withdrawn from the British section for the immediate present. It will doubtless need to be rested up after this fighting is over and I would imagine it might be given its rest with the British so as to prolong its stay in their area and not immediately raise the question again, but I make this suggestion entirely subject to your own determinations which were originally made final and from which I have allowed nothing to be subtracted.

"I delivered your message of invitation to Lord Milner and he seemed heartily pleased at your having thought to convey a special invitation to visit your front through me. Last night, just before I left London, Lord Milner took me aside and said as a parting word, about this: 'I want to say to you, Mr. Secretary, that all my relations with your officers and your Army have been and are most cordial and sympathetic. I have had no disagreements or misunderstandings with them. From General Pershing down, I regard them highly and there is not likely to be any misunderstanding between us.' He told me that he had planned to visit you, but found out that the battle was on and knew that a visit would be more acceptable a little later so doubtless he will go over to see you pretty soon.

"I ought not to add a word to this long letter, but cannot leave France without thanking you heartily for all these fresh kindnesses you have shown me on this visit. Colonel Collins has been so graciously helpful and is personally so charming a companion that every minute of my stay here has been made delightful, and, of course, the opportunity to see your great Army in action was the crowning event of a very interesting visit which I hope sincerely will prove useful to you in your work.

"With cordial regards, believe me

"Sincerely yours,

"NEWTON D. BAKER."

The Secretary's letter impressed me, as did almost every communication received from him, with his earnest purpose to do everything possible for our success. His desire to aid in the solution of the multitude of problems which confronted me, his clear comprehension of their magnitude, his sympathy, his infinite tact and understanding, were qualities that served to lighten my burden and inspire loyalty to his direction of America's military effort. No American general in the field ever received the perfect support accorded me by Mr. Baker. His attitude throughout the war, in so far as it concerned me personally and the Army in France, is a model for the guidance of future secretaries in such an emergency.

CHAPTER XLVII

Vigorous Attacks Continued—Terrific Hand-to-Hand Fighting—I Corps Makes Important Gains—1st Division, I Corps, Drives Through—Other Corps Advance—French Fourth Army Stopped—Helped by Brilliant Work of 2d Division—Heavy Casualties, Much Sickness—Relief of "Lost Battalion"—Attack Extended East of the Meuse—Second Corps Does Well with British

(Diary) Souilly, Sunday, October 6, 1918. General attack in the Meuse-Argonne resumed the 4th, meeting stubborn resistance. Communications improving.

General Pétain took lunch with us yesterday; fully appreciates difficulty of our task. Summerall's 1st and Hines' 4th Divisions did well yesterday. Everything quiet on Dickman's IV Corps front in St. Mihiel sector. Conferred with Provost Marshal General Bandholtz; road circulation going better.

Our advance continued to-day. Mr. Baker cabled Washington directing appointment of general officers recommended by me.

Second Phase—Meuse-Argonne Operations

THE period of the battle from October 1st to the 11th involved the heaviest strain on the army and on me. There was little time to make readjustments among the troops heavily engaged, without giving the enemy a respite in which to strengthen his defenses and bring up reserves. The battle could not be delayed while roads were being built or repaired and supplies brought up. The weather was cold and rainy and not the kind to inspire energetic action on the part of troops unaccustomed to the damp, raw climate. A few commanders lacking in those stern qualities essential to battle leadership or in physical stamina so necessary under these conditions were inclined to pessimism or inertia. An exhibition of either of these tendencies was quickly reflected in the troops. The real leaders, those indomitable characters whose spirits rose to master every difficulty, stood forth, a tower of strength to me during this period of the fighting. For the thing to do was to drive forward with all possible force.

Our army in the Meuse-Argonne was confronted by the enemy strongly fortified on his main position of defense—the Hinden-

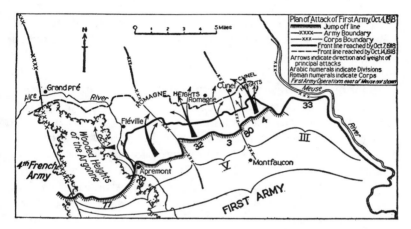

burg Line.[1] Romagne heights was a part of this defensive area and its dominating feature was Côte Dame Marie, which lay west of the town of Romagne and southeast of Landres-et-St. Georges. The approaches to the area could be plainly seen from the enemy's observation points and were covered thoroughly by his flanking artillery. The Cunel heights were flanked by fire

[1] The German estimate of the importance of holding this front is shown by the following order to his army issued by General von der Marwitz:

"October 1, 1918.

"According to information in our hands, the enemy intends to attack the 5th Army east of the Meuse in order to reach Longuyon. The objective of this attack is the cutting of the railroad line Longuyon-Sedan, which is the main line of communication (Lebensader) of the Western Army. Furthermore, the enemy hopes to compel us to discontinue the exploitation of the iron mines of Briey, the possession of which is a great factor in our steel production. The 5th Army once again may have to bear the brunt of the fighting of the coming weeks on which the security of the Fatherland may depend. The fate of a large portion of the Western Front, perhaps of our nation, depends on the firm holding of the Verdun front. The Fatherland believes that every commander and every soldier realizes the greatness of his task, and that every one will fulfill his duties to the utmost. If this is done, the enemy's attack will be shattered."

on the east from the heights of the Meuse and on the west from the heights of Romagne. The latter positions were supported by fire from Cunel heights and the heights of the Argonne Forest about Châtel-Chéhéry and Cornay. In other words the German positions then occupied in that sector afforded each other mutual support.

In the entire area on our front, as well as on the dominating heights mentioned, the large groups of woods were staggered in such a way that local flanking maneuvers caused excessive losses. Concealed in each group of woods were machine guns without number, covering the flanks and front of adjacent woods, and the timber lessened the effectiveness of our artillery fire. These machine gun positions were usually carried by direct infantry assault, with accompanying artillery. Such operations had to be carefully planned and executed to insure success.

The purpose of our attack on October 4th was to carry the above important positions or make gains that would lead to their capture. I visited our three corps headquarters on the day preceding this attack to discuss the plans with corps commanders. They all realized that we had hard fighting ahead of us, but they were acting with great vigor and determination and were confident of the outcome. The III Corps (Bullard) and the V (Cameron), acting in concert, were to take the heights of Cunel and Romagne. Their main effort was to be made against the western flank of Cunel heights, to avoid the enemy's fire from east of the Meuse. They were also to move against the eastern flank of Romagne heights. Heavy counterbattery fire with high explosives and gas was to be maintained and the observation stations beyond the Meuse were to be blinded by similar fire and smoke screens. The I Corps (Liggett) was to neutralize the flanking fire from the Argonne and was also to assist the V Corps by capturing the western portion of Romagne heights. Its plans involved a drive against the enemy east of Fléville to gain space for an attack northwest through Cornay and Châtel-Chéhéry, which would outflank the Argonne Forest.

To correct certain defects disclosed by our initial advance, special instructions were sent out regarding flanking maneuvers, mixing of units, and close coöperation between commanders.

Our order of battle to the west of the Meuse from right to left was as follows: III Corps (Bullard), with the 33d Division (Bell), the 4th (Hines), and the 80th (Cronkhite) in the front line; the V Corps (Cameron), with the 3d Division (Buck) and the 32d (Haan), both fresh, in line, with the 42d (Menoher) and the 91st (Johnston) in reserve; the I Corps (Liggett), with the 1st Division (Summerall), the 28th (Muir), and the 77th (Alexander) in line, and the 82d (Duncan) and the French 5th Cavalry Division in reserve. The army reserves were the 29th Division (Morton), the 35th (Traub), and the 92d (Ballou).

Between the Meuse and the Moselle the order of battle remained unchanged except that the 42d Division had been transferred to the reserve of the V Corps.

The general attack was resumed at 5:00 A.M. on October 4th, meeting desperate resistance by the enemy. In this attack, the 4th Division of the III Corps, in three days' bitter fighting, captured and held the Bois de Fays, making a gain of over a mile. Advances into the Bois de Peut de Faux were forced back by vicious counterattacks. In similar hard fighting, the 80th Division gained a foothold in the Bois des Ogons against very heavy machine gun fire.

In the attack of the V Corps, the 3d Division pushed forward in the face of strong resistance. During the next two days this division extended its gains, but could make no headway against the Bois de Cunel. The 32d Division, which had taken Cierges on October 1st, advanced to just south of Gesnes on the 4th, despite very severe hostile fire, and on the next day captured that town.

On the left of the army, the I Corps was very successful. The 1st Division, in a fine display of power on October 4th, drove a deep wedge into the enemy's line which was of great value in affording space for the attack toward the Argonne which was to be launched later. The fighting here was characterized by the stubborn nature of the German resistance and the offensive spirit of the division. In spite of heavy casualties, its determination was in no way weakened and by the evening of the 5th it had taken Arietal Farm and with great courage captured Hill 240. Its gains at this time totalled three miles.

The right of the 28th Division fought its way down the Aire River in liaison with the 1st and captured Chéhéry. The left of the division encountered much opposition and made but slight gain notwithstanding its repeated attacks. The division was now facing west for nearly three miles along the Aire River. The 77th Division between September 29th and October 4th continued its attacks in the Argonne, advancing about a mile over difficult terrain. In the assault of October 2d, a mixed battalion of the division moved forward more rapidly than the troops on its right and left and was completely surrounded by the enemy. It became popularly known as the "Lost Battalion." For several days every effort by the 77th Division to relieve this beleaguered force was unsuccessful and attempts by the Germans to compel its surrender were without avail.

Throughout this period the fighting was severe, with innumerable hand-to-hand combats between the opposing infantry. On the whole our new divisions were showing greater technical skill and their interior communications were much improved. By October 6th the attack had reached the general line: Bois de la Côte Lemont—Fléville—Le Chêne Tondu.

The enemy's lines were being reënforced by his best divisions, the total number then confronting the First Army having been increased to twenty-seven in line and seventeen in reserve. The Germans supported the defense by the use of innumerable machine guns and intense artillery fire from dominating crests and forests. That the danger which they foresaw from our violent attacks caused them grave apprehension was shown by their continued withdrawal of troops from other parts of the front for use against us. Although we were attacking, our estimate was that the enemy losses at least equalled our own.

In the meantime the French Fourth Army, on our left, had been held up at Blanc Mont. As a consequence, Marshal Foch

appealed to me for assistance. Although I was loath to spare
any troops from our front, so serious was our own replacement
situation, I sent, in accordance with my promise, the 2d Division
(Lejeune), which was followed later by the 36th (W. R. Smith).
On October 3d, the 2d Division, accompanied by French tanks, in

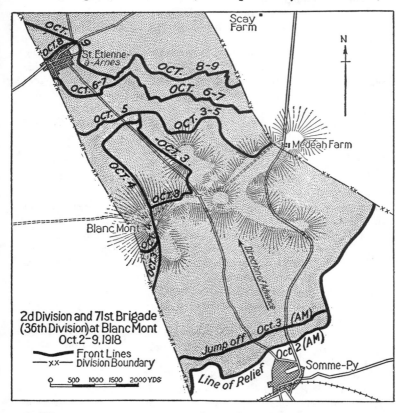

a brilliant maneuver against heavy machine gun resistance,
stormed and captured the dominating German positions on the
Médéah Farm—Blanc Mont Ridge, and continued on toward
St. Étienne, which was taken on October 8th with the assistance
of a brigade of the 36th Division. This success carried forward
the French divisions on its right and left, and, as reported by

General Gouraud, enabled the whole Fourth Army to advance.

The importance of this aid to the French Fourth Army is indicated by the following extracts from the French résumé of operations:

"The two brigades were side by side, the 4th Brigade of Marines on the left, and the 3d Brigade of Infantry on the right. Each of these two brigades had at its disposition a battalion of light tanks. * * *

"After a short but extremely violent artillery preparation the attack started at 5:50 A.M. on the 3d of October. Despite a considerable number of machine guns and heavy artillery fire, the two brigades with admirable dash attained the assigned objective, Blanc Mont—Médéah. In the course of its advance, the 5th Regiment of Marines sent a detachment to the XI Corps to help it clean out the German trenches. During this time, the division was subjected to violent artillery fire, as well as machine gun fire upon its left flank.

"At 4:00 P.M. the attack started anew. In the woods, filled with machine guns, the advance continued, and at 6:30 P.M., the forward movements of the American 2d Division reached the line marked by the Scay Farm and the crossroads at a point one kilometer south of St. Etienne-à-Arnes.

"The advance realized by the American 2d Division during the course of the day was remarkable, and reached a depth of about six kilometers. Numerous prisoners, cannon, machine guns, and material of all kinds, fell into its hands.

"The rapid advance of the XXI Corps, and, in particular that of the American 2d Division, on October 3d, brought about the most favorable results.

"The enemy, placed by this rapid advance of the center of the Fourth Army in a very difficult position upon the Monts, as well as in the valley of the Suippe, decided to evacuate the Monts and to retreat upon the Arnes and the Suippe. * * *

"On the 8th of October, a new attack took place on the whole Army front; the XXI Corps, strengthened by tanks, was directed to advance in the direction of Machault. The attack started at 5:15 A.M. The American 2d Division occupied St. Etienne-à-Arnes."

The 2d Division was relieved by the 36th on the night of October 9th-10th. During the night of the 10th the enemy withdrew, and the 36th went forward in pursuit, reaching the Aisne River on the 13th and establishing its line on the south bank.

The division maintained its position there until the night of the 28th-29th, when it was relieved by the French.

Although all classes of transportation were badly needed, it was imperative at this time to increase the rail facilities in the zone of our army. Truck trains were now being handled regularly and efficiently, yet the enormous supply of artillery ammunition that had to be brought up was beginning to bear heavily on them. The French were demanding the return of their trucks for use behind their own lines farther to the west, where transportation was also being overtaxed.

Our supply system was on a well regulated basis under the able coördination of Brigadier General Moseley and his assistants at G.H.Q., although we sorely felt the deficiencies in motor vehicles. These operations were hard on horse flesh, but our losses were being partially replaced from the limited numbers in the French armies, mainly through Marshal Foch's direct orders, and some were obtained from the British. Colonel John L. DeWitt, as the coördinator of supplies for the First Army, displayed rare ability in meeting the tremendous demands and overcoming the difficulties of transportation.

Influenza in the Army had assumed very serious proportions, over 16,000 cases additional having been reported during the week ending October 5th. Large numbers of cases were brought in by our troop ships. The total number of cases of influenza treated in hospitals was nearly 70,000, of whom many developed a grave form of pneumonia. The death rate from influenza rose to 32 per cent of cases for the A.E.F. and was as high as 80 per cent in some groups.

Although short of equipment and personnel, especially nurses,[1] the medical units of the First Army gave splendid service, regardless of the arduous character of their duties. In many instances they were under constant exposure on or near the battlefields for long periods. Their supply truck trains and ambulance trains went back and forth at all times, and were often hit by artillery

---

[1] In a cable dated October 3d it was requested that 1,500 nurses be sent to France at the earliest practicable date.

fire or shot up from airplanes. Evacuation hospitals were frequently bombed, and several nurses were wounded. Altogether, the Medical Department deserves the greatest praise for its services in this operation.

It was recognized that our divisions were required on other parts of the front to sustain and encourage the Allies and often to aid at points where the other armies were unable to advance without our help. At the same time, the absence with the French and British of four divisions, among which were some of our best, made it necessary to keep units in line on our front without the normal withdrawal for rest and refitting. Five of our divisions were kept in line on the active front for an average of twenty-four days of continuous service.

Once our army was committed to continuous attacks, the replacement of men became a problem of vital importance. The losses were mounting daily and the number of effectives was decreasing at a rapid rate. Casualties since September 26th had grown to nearly 75,000, and our need for replacements had increased to 80,000. It was necessary at this stage to reduce the size of our infantry companies from 250 to 175 men, and to keep up their strength even to this reduced figure some of our combat divisions had to be broken up and the men used as replacements. The offensive had to be continued without cessation, regardless of the expedients required to fill the depletion in our ranks.

On October 3d the following cable was sent supporting previous cables on the same subject:

"Over 50,000 of the replacements requested for the months of July, August, and September have not arrived. Due to extreme seriousness of the replacement situation it is necessary to utilize the personnel of the 84th and 86th Divisions for replacement purposes. Combat divisions are short over 80,000 men. Vitally important that all replacements due, including 55,000 requested for October, be sent early in October. If necessary, some divisions in the United States should be stripped of trained men and such men shipped as replacements at once."

(Diary) Souilly, Saturday, October 12, 1918. Series of attacks on different portions of front began the 7th, Germans fighting desperately to hold us. Confidential reports from the Inspector General (Brewster) and his assistants indicate improved conditions. Dawes reports petty criticisms in Paris of our supply management.

Visited French XVII Corps (Claudel) Monday to give final directions concerning attack next day.

Lewis' 30th Division, with the British, attacked on the 8th.

Colonel Logan, Tardieu and Ganne came Wednesday to discuss horse and forage questions.

Orders for organization of Second Army issued Thursday. Liggett will command First and Bullard the Second.

Discussed operations with Chief of Staff and Chief of Operations yesterday. Attack progressing well.

Liggett dined with us to-day on my train. Saw a number of officers, including Harbord, Patrick, Dickman and Hines, discussing with each some detail of his task. Important gains made during last few days.

The operations carried out between October 7th and 11th consisted of four specific attacks, as follows:

(1) October 7th. The I Corps, employing the 82d Division between the 1st and 28th Divisions, attacked the eastern edge of the Argonne Forest.

(2) October 8th. The French XVII Corps, reënforced by the American 33d and 29th Divisions, attacked east of the Meuse on the front Beaumont—Brabant-sur-Meuse, with the object of seizing the heights there.

(3) October 9th. The V Corps, reënforced by including within its front the 1st Division, to which was attached a brigade from the 91st Division, attacked the heights of the Bois de Romagne.

(4) October 10th-11th. A general attack on the 20-mile front from Beaumont west to the Aire River.

The French Fourth Army had not been able to keep abreast of the American First Army and it was evident that clearing the Argonne Forest would materially aid its advance. The opportunity presented itself just at this time. Although on October 6th the enemy continued to hold the heights of Cunel and Romagne, nevertheless sufficient space had been secured along the Aire River to warrant an attack to the west with the object of striking the rear of the enemy's positions in the Argonne Forest. There was another important factor that entered into the decision to force the withdrawal of the enemy from the Argonne at this time. This was the predicament of the "Lost Battalion," already mentioned, which, under Major C. W. Whittlesey, had been holding out near Binarville since October 2d. As efforts to relieve it had so far failed, the men had consumed their rations and expended most of their ammunition. Our aviators had attempted to drop small amounts of food to them, but, as learned later, they had not been successful. The battalion was resisting heroically against great odds.

Pursuant to the plan, an attack was made by the 28th and 82d Divisions against the left and rear of the enemy's positions in the region of Châtel-Chéhéry and Cornay. After a night march of eight miles, the 82d Division (Duncan) entered the line between the 28th (Muir) and the 1st (Summerall). In a series of daring movements to the west by the 28th and 82d Divisions, Châtel-Chéhéry and the dominating hills northwest of Apremont were captured.

The 82d Division captured Hill 180 with dash on the 7th, but the attack against Cornay was broken up by heavy fire. After occupying the hill north of Châtel-Chéhéry, which had been taken over from the 28th Division, the 82d suffered severe casualties in repulsing an enemy counterattack. On the 8th, while executing a change of direction from west to north, elements of the division entered Cornay, but heavy shelling, claimed to be from our own artillery, forced their retirement. The town was again occupied on the following day, but was recaptured by a counterattack of the fresh German 41st Division. On this same day the 82d Division took over the front of the 28th and made a substantial advance.

The 28th Division on October 7th captured Châtel-Chéhéry in splendid fashion. Troops of the division crossed into the sector of the 82d Division and occupied a portion of the hill north of the town which had menaced its flank. The 28th advanced again on the 8th against heavy machine gun fire and on the following day was relieved by the 82d Division. For twelve days it had faced the almost impregnable defenses of the Aire with fine courage and endurance and had well earned a rest.

Although the continued operation of these two divisions was attended by severe fighting, the results were immediate. The enemy was forced to withdraw from that region, the Argonne Forest was cleared, and the 77th Division was enabled to advance to the relief of its "Lost Battalion." It then pushed on to the north in pursuit of the retreating enemy.

On my visit to the French XVII Corps, east of the Meuse, I reviewed with General Claudel the plans for his attack the fol-

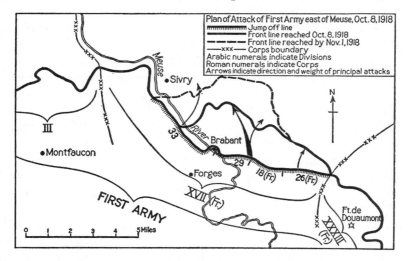

lowing day, October 8th. The object of the operation was to seize the heights northwest of Beaumont. At that time, the corps consisted of two French divisions and the two American divisions, 33d and 29th, making it two-thirds American in numerical strength. Though opposed by strong German resistance, the assault was successfully conducted and our lines were further advanced during the next few days to the commanding ground between Beaumont and Richêne Hill.

In a well directed operation, the 33d Division (Bell) crossed the Meuse early on the morning of the 8th by means of bridges constructed during the night, captured Consenvoye and progressed up the neighboring slopes. On the following day a further advance was made, but heavy fire from the Borne de Cornouiller and the failure of the troops on the right to keep up forced a retirement to the morning line. This ground was re-taken despite strong resistance and by the night of the 10th the division had established itself on the west slopes of Richêne Hill.

The 58th Brigade of the 29th Division (Morton), under com-mand of the French 18th Division, against considerable opposi-tion pushed forward into the woods south of Richêne Hill on the 8th and during the next two days completed the capture of those woods. Its 57th Brigade, also under the French 18th Division, on the 12th made important gains in the Bois d'Ormont.

This advance of the French XVII Corps deprived the enemy of many important observation points and battery positions. The main purpose of the attack, however, was to increase the fighting front of the army and thus engage and consume the maximum number of German divisions. In this latter respect, the attack was particularly successful, aimed as it was directly at the pivot of the German line on the Western Front. From this time on until the Armistice, the threat in this region forced the enemy to maintain east of the Meuse at least two additional divisions.

The narrowness of the ridge east of and parallel to the Meuse River and the difficulty of the terrain limited the number of troops that could be employed there. This restriction, coupled with the heavy hostile artillery fire directed from the vicinity of Romagne-sous-les-Côtes and from north of Damvillers, prevented a deeper advance or the clearing of the heights of the Meuse until we were able to attack from south of Dun-sur-Meuse, as originally planned.

In conjunction with the operations by the French XVII Corps, the V Corps (Cameron) attacked in force on October 9th and continued its efforts during the next two days. The 3d Division (Buck) progressed on the 9th and after fierce fighting seized Madeleine Farm, which had previously proved a stumbling-block, and partially cleared the Bois de Cunel. On the following day it completed the possession of that wood and on the 11th ex-tended its gains to the northwest.

The 32d Division (Haan) reached Romagne on October 9th, and penetrated the enemy trenches on Côte Dame Marie on the 10th, but was driven from the latter and established its lines on the southern slopes of the hill.

The 91st Division (Johnston), on the left of the 32d Division, fought all day on the 9th for possession of Hill 255, suffering heavy casualties, and on the following day occupied the position. The advance then continued until stopped at Hill 288 and the Côte Dame Marie. The division was relieved on the night of October 11th.

The 1st Division (Summerall) in a resolute attack captured the difficult enemy positions on and near Hill 272 on October 9th and established its line on the north slope of the Côte de Maldah on the 10th. It also was relieved on the 11th. During the operations of the 9th and 10th, the 181st Brigade (John B. McDonald) of the 91st Division was attached to the 1st Division, and was transferred to the 32d Division on the night of the 10th.

The advance of the III Corps (Bullard) was bitterly contested by the enemy, but on October 10th the 4th Division (Hines) fought its way forward beyond the Cunel—Brieulles road. Two determined assaults against the Bois de Peut de Faux were broken up, but on the third attempt the northern edge of that wood was attained. The division gained the far side of the Bois de Forêt on the 11th against severe opposition.

The 80th Division (Cronkhite) on the 9th pushed forward in the face of very heavy fire to a short distance north of the Bois des Ogons. The division's attacks continued and when relieved two days later it had reached a line slightly south and east of Cunel.

On the front of the I Corps (Liggett) the opposition encountered on the 10th was less determined and the 82d Division (Duncan) by midnight had established its line beyond Marcq; while the line of the 77th Division (Alexander) ran westward from there. On the 11th, however, the fighting was severe, yet the 82d, regardless of heavy casualties, advanced to a position north of Sommerance. This town, though in the sector of the 1st Division, was occupied by the 82d to protect its own flank.

On the night of October 11th our line ran from east to west roughly as follows: Molleville Farm—Bois de la Côte Lemont— part of Bois de Forêt—South of Côte Dame Marie—Sommerance —Grandpré.

While these operations on our First Army front were in progress, the 30th Division (Lewis) of the II Corps (Read) attacked on October 8th as a part of the British Fourth Army, aiding materially in the general advance of that army. The attack, although meeting considerable opposition, was successful and the progress continued for three days. When relieved on the night of the 11th, the 30th Division had driven the enemy back seven miles and had reached the Selle River.

CHAPTER XLVIII

Second Army Organized—Liggett takes First, Bullard Second—General Attack Resumed—Côte Dame Marie Captured—Hindenburg Line Broken—Germans Treating for Peace—Diplomatic Correspondence—Foch Fears President Wilson may Commit Allies too Deeply—British Views on Armistice

(Diary) Souilly, Wednesday, October 16, 1918. On Sunday, visited Pétain at Provins to discuss organization of group of armies. Called on Marshal Foch at Bombon and pointed out strength of Germans on our front. Told him of organization of group of armies. Spent the night in Paris and returned here Monday. Visited several corps and divisions yesterday.

Remained to-day at Souilly. Saw Chief of Staff regarding promotions. Brigadier General Wm. Chamberlaine came to confer on use of naval railroad artillery. Received cable from Griscom giving British views of armistice. Marshal Foch requests two divisions be sent to Belgian front to reënforce French Sixth Army near Ypres, which is making slow progress. Have selected 37th and 91st. Colonel Walter D. McCaw appointed Chief Surgeon, A.E.F., and Brigadier General John H. Rice, Chief Ordnance Officer.[1] Discussed with Mitchell better employment of aviation. War Department expects increase of shipping and promises motor transport, railway material and horses for November.

THE broadening of the front of attack to the east of the Meuse, and the probability that we should soon become engaged along our whole line made it advisable to establish another army. Accordingly the Second Army was formed of troops then on the front extending from the Moselle to Fresnes-en-Woëvre and placed under the command of Major General Bullard on the 12th. The remainder of our front, from

[1] The appointment of Col. McCaw followed the relief of Maj. Gen. Ireland, who was returned to Washington to become Surgeon General of the Army; and that of Brig. Gen. Rice to relieve Brig. Gen. Charles B. Wheeler in order that he might be available for service on the Inter-Allied Board of Ordnance.

Fresnes-en-Woëvre to the Argonne Forest, inclusive, remained under the First Army, to which Major General Liggett was assigned. Both commanders were recommended by me for promotion to the grade of lieutenant general.

My status now became that of Commander of a Group of Armies. Major General Summerall was placed in command of the V Corps to relieve Major General Cameron, who was given command of the 4th Division. Major General Hines was promoted to the command of the III Corps in place of General Bullard. Major General Dickman, commanding the IV Corps, was given the I Corps, and Major General Muir the IV. These changes generally took effect on the 12th, but I retained the immediate command of the First Army until the 16th.

The higher commanders and their staffs of the First Army, as well as the troops of all arms, were gaining in efficiency with every day of actual experience in battle. Nevertheless, I insisted that commanders should make closer examinations of the details of plans and give greater personal attention to their execution. Against the strong and thoroughly organized defense of the enemy, only the most determined and well directed efforts could insure success. Granting that the local plans were sound and arrangements perfected for support by the artillery, aviation, machine guns, and tanks, if any, it was the skill of the officers and men of the smaller units in the front lines that determined the final result of the battle.

On the particular visit to corps and divisions made on the 15th, I saw Generals Summerall and Hines, commanding the V and III Corps, respectively, and went to the command posts of the 5th, 3d, 89th, 32d and 42d Divisions, or saw their commanders. They were all very aggressive, but some of our troops had been forced out of captured positions by enemy counterattacks. It was, therefore, impressed upon every one that ground once taken should be quickly organized for defense and then held at all hazards.

In the series of attacks which began on the 7th and continued up to the 12th, the enemy contested every inch of ground and the severe fighting that occurred before positions could be captured was scarcely realized outside of our own army. Our troops were engaged in some of the most bitter fighting of the war, forcing their way through dense woods, over hills and across deep ravines, against German defense conducted with a skill only equalled by that of the French in front of Verdun in 1916. Yet all our corps advanced their lines, the V capturing elements of the Hindenburg Line, which our troops were now facing.

Early in the Meuse-Argonne offensive, most of the French air division was withdrawn from the First Army front. This considerably reduced our strength in aviation, and the German fliers began to do more serious damage to our troops. Therefore, it was necessary to concentrate our attention on the enemy's aviation and to make every effort to obtain superiority over it. The tendency of our air force at first was to attach too much significance to flights beyond the enemy's lines in an endeavor to interrupt his communications. However, this was of secondary importance during the battle, as aviators were then expected to protect and assist our ground troops. In other words, they were to drive off hostile airplanes and procure for the infantry and artillery information concerning the enemy's movements.

The best results were not obtained until we sent additional aviators to serve awhile with the infantry and study the problem from its point of view. Selected infantry and artillery officers were also sent to fly with air pilots. Once in command of the air, the enemy's artillery and ground troops became the object of their attacks. Individually, our aviators were unsurpassed in boldness, in fortitude, and in skill. These daring fliers who fought their opponents in the air vied with their fearless comrades of the infantry who grappled with the enemy on foot. Men of both arms left a record of heroic deeds that will remain a brilliant page in the annals of warfare.

Third Phase—Meuse-Argonne Operations

The increasing intensity of the resistance in our front indicated the enemy's fear of losing his hold on this vital sector before he could retire his armies facing the Allies farther to the west. His retirement in front of the Allies was being accelerated by our persistent gains in the east. He was clearly trying to save himself from complete disaster, which it was urgent that we should strive all the more vigorously to hasten.

The attacks during the preceding phase, although reaching the Hindenburg Line and even capturing portions of that position near Romagne and Cunel, left in the enemy's hands the strong defenses in the Bois de Romagne and the Bois de Bantheville,

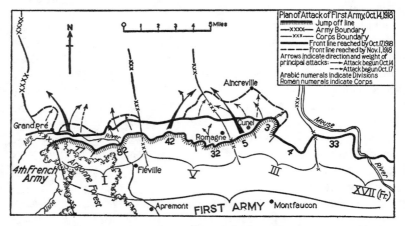

both of which had to be reduced before further considerable progress could be made. To the west of Romagne heights, we faced the strongly fortified position which included Côte de Châtillon, Landres-et-St. Georges, St. Juvin, Bois des Loges, and Grandpré.

Plans for a general attack were prepared, based on the following:

(a) The French XVII Corps, under our army, was to continue its offensive east of the Meuse River.

(b) The III and V Corps, with fresh divisions (the 5th and 42d), were to drive salients through the hostile positions on both flanks of the Bois de Romagne and of the Bois de Bantheville.

(c) The I Corps was to hold the enemy on its left flank while advancing its right in conjunction with the left of the V Corps.

(d) The French Fourth Army, which had now come up on our left and held the south bank of the Aire and the west bank of the Aisne as far as Vouziers, was ordered by General Pétain to attack on the same day, so as to outflank the enemy opposing our left.

We had set October 15th as the date for this offensive, but upon the request of the French Fourth Army, which intended to attack on the 14th, our arrangements were hastily changed to conform with theirs.

The order of battle in the Meuse-Argonne was now, from right to left: the French XVII Corps east of the Meuse, with the French 10th Colonial, 26th, and 18th Divisions and the American 29th (Morton) and 33d (Bell) Divisions; west of the Meuse the III Corps (Hines), with the 4th Division (Cameron), 3d (Buck), and 5th (McMahon); then the V Corps (Summerall), with the 32d Division (Haan) and 42d (Menoher); and on the left the I Corps (Dickman), with the 82d Division (Duncan) and the 77th (Alexander). On the front of our offensive the enemy had the equivalent of twenty-four divisions actually in the front line.

Our attacks on the 14th, 15th and 16th in conjunction with Gouraud's French Fourth Army met violent opposition, especially at the beginning, and although ground was often taken and retaken several times, our lines were steadily pushed forward.

On the east of the Meuse, in the French XVII Corps, the 33d Division had made some progress, and the 29th Division, despite the difficult terrain and severe casualties, had entered the woods north of Molleville Farm.

The III Corps was held up by very heavy machine gun and artillery fire from the Bois de Bantheville and the Bois des Rappes, in spite of precautions to neutralize these localities. The 4th Division remained inactive during this period. The 3d Division made a small gain west of the Bois de Forêt and cleaned up the eastern edge of the wood north of Cunel in conjunction with the 5th Division, but could make little headway northward. The 5th Division, in the face of intense fire on its front and flanks, on the 14th reached the top of the slopes northeast of Romagne and cleared the wood north of Cunel. Elements of the division pushed through to the northern edge of the Bois des Rappes, but were withdrawn.

By dint of the superior determination of our troops, the enemy's lines were broken at a vital point by the V Corps. Unstinted praise must be given the 32d Division. Notwithstanding heavy losses, its 64th Brigade (Edwin B. Winans) on October 14th brilliantly captured Côte Dame Marie, perhaps the most important strong point of the Hindenburg Line on the Western Front. The town of Romagne and the eastern half of Bois de Romagne were also taken by this division on that day; while on the following day its line was advanced about a mile to the southern edge of the Bois de Bantheville.

The 42d Division fought aggressively against the most obstinate defense, forcing its way through the western half of Bois de Romagne, its 84th Brigade (Douglas MacArthur) scaling the precipitous heights of the Côte de Châtillon and carrying its line on beyond that position. The desperate resistance on the left of the division, south of St. Georges and Landres-et-St. Georges, however, could not be overcome.

The advance of the I Corps was to a large extent dependent upon that of the V Corps, the left of which had been held up. The 82d Division, on the right of the I Corps, attacked October 14th and pushed forward to north of the St. Juvin—St. Georges road, but during the next two days had only slight success. The 77th Division forced a crossing of the Aire River on the 14th and took St. Juvin. On the following day it moved against Grandpré and after an all-day attempt occupied the island south of the town. On the 16th, the southern part of Grandpré was reached, but all attempts to take the northern part of the town were repulsed. The division was then relieved by the 78th Division.

The importance of these operations can hardly be overestimated. The capture of the Romagne heights, especially their dominating feature, Côte Dame Marie, was a decisive blow. We now occupied the enemy's strongest fortified position on that front and flanked his line on the Aisne and on the Heights of the Meuse. Unless he could recapture the positions we held, our successes would compel him to retire from his lines to the north, as we were within heavy artillery range of his railroad communications.

The main objective of our initial attack of September 26th had now been reached. Failing to capture it in our first attempt, the army had deliberately, systematically, and doggedly stuck to the task in the face of many difficulties and discouragements. The persistent and vigorous effort with which divisions forced their way forward to the goal is the outstanding glory of our service in France.

Our ranks had become further depleted by this severe fighting and we now had to use as replacements the personnel of two more recently arrived divisions, although even these were not enough. In all, we skeletonized four combat divisions and three depot divisions to obtain men for units at the front. Much greater numbers of replacements would have been available if they had been sent in groups as such. It was a source of much regret to me that these organized units should have to be stripped of men, but there was no alternative.

We were also in need of balloons and their personnel, none having arrived from home since July. Although fifty-two companies had been requested for August and September, there seemed to be no hope of receiving them within a reasonable time. A shortage in balloons always existed in our forces and as usual we sponged on the French. But at this time they did not have much more than half the numbers they needed themselves and our demands were creating a serious situation in their army. The loss of observation balloons was very heavy during the continuous fighting of this great battle. Balloons were especially good targets for airplanes. Many of our aviators became expert at destroying those of the enemy. They would wait until about dusk, then, approaching from a great height, swoop down and often surprise several in one flight.

The pressure of the American Army in this great offensive profoundly impressed the enemy. On October 3d Marshal von Hindenburg sent the following letter to the German Chancellor:

"The High Command insists on its demand of Sunday, September 29th, for the immediate forwarding of an offer of peace to our enemies. * * * There is now no longer any possible hope of forcing peace on the enemy. * * * The situation grows more desperate every day and may force the High Command to grave decisions. * * *"

The Chancellor yielded to this pressure and on October 6th telegraphed, through the Swiss Government, to President Wilson:

"The German Government requests the President of the United States to take in hand the restoration of peace, acquaint all belligerent states with this request, and invite them to send plenipotentiaries for the purpose of opening negotiations. It accepts the program set forth by the President of the United States in his message to Congress on January 8 and in his later addresses, especially the speech of September 27, as a basis for peace negotiations. With a view to avoiding further bloodshed, the German Government requests the immediate conclusion of an armistice on land and water and in the air.

"MAX, PRINCE VON BADEN,
"Imperial Chancellor."

Although we knew through our Intelligence Section that the enemy had sued for an armistice, we had no first-hand knowledge of the negotiations that followed. The development of the situation was so interesting and was so skillfully handled by President Wilson that the various notes that passed between the two Governments are given, some in condensed form.

On October 8th, in reply to the Chancellor's note, the following statement of the President's views was communicated to the German Government by Secretary of State Lansing:

"Before making reply to the request of the Imperial German Government, and in order that that reply shall be as candid and as straightforward as the momentous interests involved require, the President of the United States deems it necessary to assure himself of the exact meaning of the note of the Imperial Chancellor. Does the Imperial Chancellor mean that the Imperial German Government accepts the terms laid down by the President in his address to the Congress of the United States on January 8 last and in subsequent addresses, and that its object in entering into discussions would be only to agree upon the practical details of their application?

"The President feels bound to say with regard to the suggestion of an armistice that he would not feel at liberty to propose a cessation of arms to the Governments with which the Government of the United States is associated against the Central Powers so long as the Armies of those powers are upon their soil. The good faith of any discussion would manifestly depend upon the consent of the Central Powers immediately to withdraw their forces everywhere from the invaded territory.

"The President also feels that he is justified in asking whether the Imperial Chancellor is speaking merely for the constituted authorities of the empire who have so far conducted the war. He deems the answer to these questions vital from every point of view."

The German reply to this message, sent on October 12th, was as follows:

"In reply to the questions of the President of the United States of America the German Government hereby declares:

"The German Government has accepted the terms laid down by President Wilson in his address of January 8 and in his subsequent addresses on the foundation of a permanent peace of justice. Consequently its object in entering into discussions would be only to agree upon practical details of the application of these terms.

"The German Government assumes that the Governments of the powers associated with the Government of the United States also take the position taken by President Wilson in his address.

"The German Government in accordance with the Austro-Hungarian Government, for the purpose of bringing about an armistice, declares itself ready to comply with the propositions of the President in regard to evacuation.

"The German Government suggests that the President may occasion the meeting of a mixed commission for making the necessary arrangements concerning the evacuation. The present German Government, which has undertaken the responsibility for this step toward peace, has been formed by conferences and in agreement with the great majority of the Reichstag. The Chancellor, supported in all his actions by the will of this majority, speaks in the name of the German Government and of the German People."

The next note was from our Government:

"Washington, October 14, 1918.

"The unqualified acceptance by the present German Government and by a large majority of the German Reichstag of the terms laid down by the President of the United States of America in his address to the Congress of the United States on the 8th of January, 1918, and in his subsequent addresses, justifies the President in making a frank and direct statement of his decision with regard to the communications of the German Government of the eighth and twelfth of October, 1918.

"It must be clearly understood that the process of evacuation and the conditions of an armistice are matters which must be left to the judgment and advice of the military advisers of the Government of the United States and the Allied Governments, and the President feels it his duty to say that no arrangement can be accepted by the Government of the United States which does not provide absolutely satisfactory safeguards and guarantees of the maintenance of the present military supremacy of the armies of the United States and of the Allies in the field. He feels confident that he can safely assume that this will also be the judgment and decision of the Allied Governments."

The message went on to say that the President felt it his duty to add that an armistice could not be granted so long as the armed forces of Germany continued illegal and inhuman practices. The persistence by Germany of the sinking of passenger ships and small boats was cited, and reference was made to the destruction of villages as the armies retired. Continuing, it read in part:

"It is necessary also, in order that there may be no possibility of misunderstanding, that the President should very solemnly call the attention of the Government of Germany to the language and plain intent of one of the terms of peace which the German Government has now accepted. It is contained in the address of the President, delivered at Mount Vernon, on the Fourth of July last. It is as follows:

" 'The destruction of every arbitrary power anywhere that can separately, secretly, and of its single choice disturb the peace of the world; or, if it cannot be presently destroyed, at least its reduction to virtual impotency.'

*   *   *   *   *   *   *

"It is indispensable that the Governments associated against Germany should know beyond peradventure with whom they are dealing. The President will make a separate reply to the Royal and Imperial Government of Austria-Hungary."

In reply, the German Government sent the following:

"Berlin, October 20, 1918.

"In accepting the proposal for an evacuation of the occupied territories, the German Government has started from the assumption that the procedure of this evacuation and of the conditions of an armistice should be left to the judgment of the military advisers, and that the actual standard of power on both sides in the field has to form the basis for arrangements safeguarding and guaranteeing this standard. The German Government suggests to the President that an opportunity should be brought about for fixing the details. It trusts that the President of the United States will approve of no demand which would be irreconcilable with the honor of the German people and with opening a way to a peace of justice."

The German Government protested against the reproach of illegal actions by its land and sea forces and disclaimed any purpose to do such things. It then claimed that a new government had been formed, guaranteed by constitutional safeguards, with which the President could deal.

The State Department then sent the following:

"October 23, 1918.

"Having received the solemn and explicit assurance of the German Government that it unreservedly accepts the terms of peace laid down in his address to the Congress of the United States on the eighth of January, 1918, and the principles of settlement enunciated in his subsequent addresses, particularly the address of the twenty-seventh of September, and that it desires to discuss the details of their application, and that this wish and purpose emanate, not from those who have hitherto dictated German policy and conducted the present war on Germany's behalf, but from Ministers who speak for the majority of the Reichstag and for an overwhelming majority of the German people, and having received also the explicit promise of the present German Government that the humane rules of civilized warfare will be observed both on land and sea by the German armed forces, the President of the United States feels that he cannot decline to take up with the Governments with which the Government of the United States is associated the question of an armistice.

"He deems it his duty to say again, however, that the only armistice he would feel justified in submitting for consideration would be one which should leave the United States and the powers associated with her in a position to enforce any arrangements that may be entered into and to make a renewal of hostilities on the part of Germany impossible.

"The President has, therefore, transmitted his correspondence with the present German authorities to the Governments with which the Government of the United States is associated as a belligerent. * * * Should such terms of armistice be suggested, their acceptance by Germany will afford the best concrete evidence of her unequivocal acceptance of the terms and principles of peace from which the whole action proceeds. * * *

"Feeling that the whole peace of the world depends now on plain speaking and straightforward action, the President deems it his duty to say, without any attempt to soften what may seem harsh words, that the nations of the world do not and cannot trust the word of those who have hitherto been the masters of German policy, and to point out once more that in concluding peace and attempting to undo the infinite injuries and injustices of this war the Government of the United States cannot deal with any but veritable representatives of the German people, who have been assured of a genuine constitutional standing as the real rulers of Germany.

"If it must deal with the military masters and the monarchial autocrats of Germany now, or if it is likely to have to deal with them later in regard to the international obligations of the German Empire, it must demand, not peace negotiations, but surrender. Nothing can be gained by leaving this essential thing unsaid."

To this, Germany replied:

"Berlin, October 27, 1918.

"The German Government has taken cognizance of the answer of the President of the United States. The President is aware of the far-reaching changes which have been carried out and are being carried out in the German constitutional structure, and that peace negotiations are being conducted by a people's Government in whose hands rests, both actually and constitutionally, the power to make the deciding conclusions. The military powers are also subject to it. The German Government now awaits proposals for an armistice, which shall be the first step toward a just peace as the President has described it in his proclamation."

The President's messages were transmitted to the Allied Governments and upon receipt of their replies, the following note was sent:

"November 5, 1918.

"In my note of October 23, 1918, I advised you that the President had transmitted his correspondence with the German authorities to the Governments with which the Government of the United States is associated as a belligerent. * * * The President is now in receipt of a memorandum of observations by the Allied Governments on this correspondence, which is as follows:

"The Allied Governments have given careful consideration to the correspondence which has passed between the President of the United States and the German Government. Subject to the qualifications which follow, they declare their willingness to make peace with the Government of Germany on the terms of peace laid down in the President's address to Congress of January, 1918, and the principles of settlement enunciated in his subsequent addresses. They must point out, however, that Clause 2, relating to what is usually described as the freedom of the seas is open to various interpretations, some of which they could not accept. They must, therefore, reserve to themselves complete freedom on this subject when they enter the peace conference. Further, in the conditions of peace laid down in his address to Congress of January 8, 1918, the President declared that invaded territories must be restored as well as evacuated and freed. The Allied Governments feel that no doubt ought to be allowed to exist as to what this provision implies. By it they understand that compensation will be made by Germany for all damage done to the civilian population of the Allies and their property by the aggression of Germany by land, by sea and from the air.

"I am instructed by the President to say that he is in agreement with the interpretation set forth in the last paragraph of the memorandum above quoted. I am further instructed by the President to request you to notify the German Government that Marshal Foch has been authorized by the Government of the United States and the Allied Governments to receive properly accredited representatives of the German Government and to communicate to them terms of an armistice."

While these diplomatic negotiations were in progress, our own and Allied offensives continued to produce favorable results, and it became more and more evident that the time must soon come when we should have to consider terms and conditions under which hostilities might cease. The discussion of armistice terms in a general way by the Allies had in fact begun. In my conversation with Marshal Foch on the 13th he spoke of the notes that had been exchanged between the Germans and President Wilson and expressed some apprehension about how far the President might commit the Allies. He said he hoped the President would not become involved in a long correspondence and allow himself to be duped by the Germans, and added that so far Mr. Wilson had not consulted the Allies. I replied that he need not have any fear on that score, as of course Mr. Wilson would not act alone. In this discussion I gained the impression that Foch favored demanding the surrender of the German armies.

At my request, Lieutenant Colonel Griscom ascertained and cabled me the views of Lord Milner and General Sir Henry Wilson. Briefly, Lord Milner said that he occupied a middle position between those demanding unconditional surrender and those who wanted peace immediately on the best terms possible. He thought an armistice should be granted only on condition that Germany lay down her heavy guns and give some naval guarantee such as the possession of Heligoland.

General Wilson was in doubt whether it would be possible to inflict a crushing victory before winter, as the British Army was very tired and the French more so, and the Americans not yet prepared to use their great force, but he thought that armistice conditions should make it impossible for Germany to resume operations. He regretted President Wilson's suggestion of German evacuation of Allied territory because he would prefer to fight the Germans where they were than on their own frontiers with a much shortened line. He said the Germans should be required to abandon their heavy guns and retire to the east bank of the Rhine, and in addition to the surrender of Heligoland should also give up some warships and submarines.

General Wilson voiced the extreme British army viewpoint, but the more conservative element in government circles advised against pushing Germany too far for fear of having no government there strong enough to make peace. They feared that wide-spread revolutions in Germany might unsettle Allied countries and imperil constitutional monarchies. These hints gave the general attitude of the British as it was expressed later on when the time came to dictate the terms.

CHAPTER XLIX

Situation of First Army in Mid-October—Operations Preliminary to Resumption of General Offensive—II Corps with British—General Attack Set for October 28th—Senlis Conference at which Commanders-in-Chief Discuss Armistice Terms—My Views Cabled Washington—President's Comments—My Recommendation for Demanding Unconditional Surrender

(Diary) Souilly, Sunday, October 20, 1918. Admiral Plunkett came Thursday to discuss use of Navy 14-inch railway guns. Spent Friday and Saturday at Chaumont. Sir Arthur Paget came to visit our front; lunched with us on Friday. Representatives Glass, Whaley and Byrnes had dinner with us at Chaumont on Saturday. Brought Fox Conner to Souilly; discussed offensive operations with Liggett Sunday. Some straggling reported; directed energetic measures against it. Received reports of interesting gossip floating around Paris. French desire American director of railways; I have recommended Daniel Willard, of the Baltimore and Ohio.

Fourth Phase—Meuse-Argonne Operations

THE First Army was a tried and seasoned force equal to the best on the Western Front at the time I placed it under the immediate command of Major General Liggett. In order that the Army might understand the value of its recent achievements and realize the urgency of continued vigorous effort, I sent the following message to the new First Army Commander on October 17th:

"Please have the following transmitted as a telegram to Corps and Division Commanders:

"Now that Germany and the Central Powers are losing, they are begging for an armistice. Their request is an acknowledgment of weakness and clearly means that the Allies are winning the war. That is the best of reasons for our pushing the war more vigorously at this moment. Germany's desire is only to gain time to restore order among her forces, but she must be given no opportunity to recuperate and we

350

must strike harder than ever. Our strong blows are telling, and continuous pressure by us has compelled the enemy to meet us, enabling our Allies to gain on other parts of the line. There can be no conclusion to this war until Germany is brought to her knees.

"Pershing."

The enemy's most important defensive position[1] on the Romagne heights was in our firm possession, and his final defeat was merely a question of time. He had fought desperately to hold his ground, but had been compelled to give way steadily before our effective blows. We could have gone forward without special preparation and succeeded, within a reasonable time, in driving the enemy from the field, but the situation led to the conclusion that his complete defeat could best be accomplished in one powerful stroke by a well organized offensive.

The difficult and continuous attacks since September 26th had been very trying on our troops and had resulted in a certain loss of cohesion. It was, therefore, deemed advisable to take a few days for the replacement of tired units, the renewal of supplies, and the improvement of communications.

The 28th of October was tentatively designated as the date for the beginning of the next general advance, but the French Fourth Army, which was to support our attack on the left, notified us as late as the 27th that it could not get ready in time, so the attack of both armies was fixed for November 1st.

In accordance with instructions issued by me on the 16th, two important preliminary operations were carried out during this period: (1) operations against the Bois des Loges and Bois de Bourgogne to clear the woods east of the Aisne and north of the Aire and thus flank that part of the hostile line on the Aisne, and (2) local operations to secure a suitable line of departure for the general attack.

The I Corps (Dickman), in conjunction with the French Fourth Army, was directed to clear the Bois des Loges and the southern part of the Bois de Bourgogne. An advance in this

---

[1] "The pressure which the fresh American masses were putting upon our most sensitive point in the region of the Meuse was too strong." Marshal von Hindenburg in "Out of my Life."

vicinity would flank the enemy on the Aisne in front of the French and also turn his defenses east of the Bois des Loges which were holding up the I Corps. A study of the characteristics of the terrain will show the difficulties of the task. The enemy, realizing the importance of this position, employed his best troops to defend it.

The fighting on the 78th Division (McRae) front, for a period of ten days, was very severe, especially near the Bois des Loges and Grandpré. Frequent counterattacks, coupled with flanking machine gun and artillery fire, forced our troops back in several instances. However, on October 25th, the I Corps succeeded in gaining a footing on the high ground west of Grandpré and, by October 27th, had driven the enemy from that town. The Bois des Loges remained in the enemy's hands. The above maneuver carried the right of the French Fourth Army forward and a line was thus secured on the left of our Army especially advantageous for the general attack. These engagements had a material effect on the final phase, as they drew some of the enemy's strength to the I Corps front and away from the center, where our main drive was to be made.

Farther to the right, where we had pierced the Hindenburg Line on the Cunel and Romagne heights, it was desirable to force the enemy from the Bois des Rappes, Bois Clairs Chênes and the high ground to the east, and to secure the northern edge of the Bois de Bantheville. These preliminary operations were successfully carried out by the III and V Corps. Some very intense local battles took place during this period.

The 3d Division (Brown)[1] of the III Corps captured Bois Clairs Chênes early on October 20th, then lost the wood in a counterattack, and later in the day recaptured it. On the 22d, the division cleared the Bois de Forêt. The 5th Division (Ely) was unsuccessful in its attacks of October 18th, 19th and 20th against the Bois des Rappes, but on October 21st took the wood, and held it against counterattacks.

[1] On October 18th, Brig. Gen. Preston Brown and Maj. Gen. Hanson E. Ely took command of the 3d and 5th Divisions, respectively.

Although the terrain was difficult and the resistance most determined, the 32d Division (Haan) of the V Corps by night of October 18th had reached the middle of the Bois de Bantheville. Here it was relieved by the 89th Division (Wright), which, on October 20th and 21st, cleared the remainder of the wood.

By the 23d of October, the line of the III and V Corps ran north of Bois Clairs Chênes, Bois des Rappes, and along the northern and western flanks of the Bois de Bantheville and Côte de Chatillon, and then south of Landres-et-St. Georges. This gave us an excellent position in the center and on the right from which to start the next general attack.

To the east of the Meuse, the French XVII Corps, reënforced by the 29th Division (Morton) and the 26th Division (Edwards), continued to progress locally, forcing the enemy to employ fresh troops on that front. The 29th Division captured the ridge north of Molleville Farm on October 23d; while the 26th Division made some gains, and on October 27th, under Brigadier General Frank E. Bamford,[1] penetrated the wood east of the farm.

In the remaining days of this phase local successes continued, especially in the III Corps, Aincreville being captured by the 5th Division on October 30th.

During the Meuse-Argonne battle my personal quarters were on my train, which lay partially hidden in the woods on a spur near Souilly. While there I spent a portion of each day at official headquarters giving directions regarding operations and deciding other important questions. I usually occupied the rest of the day at the front in close touch with corps and divisions. Although I had now relinquished the immediate command of the First Army, its activities and those of the Second Army, carried out under my direction, required close supervision.

Farther west, our II Corps (Read), with the British Fourth Army, was engaged on October 17th south of Le Cateau in the Battle of the Selle. This Corps, with the 30th (Lewis) and 27th (O'Ryan) Divisions in line from right to left, crossed the Selle

[1] Brig. Gen. Bamford took command of the 26th Division on Oct. 25th.

River and advanced four miles in the face of strong resistance, capturing 1,600 prisoners and 12 guns.

The 30th Division captured Molain and St.-Martin-Rivière on the 17th, but heavy fire from Ribeauville prevented further advance until late the following day, when the operations of the British on the right forced the enemy to evacuate the town. Continuing on October 19th, the division captured Mazinghien and was then relieved.

The 27th Division had several hard fights along the railroad southeast of St. Souplet, at Bandival Farm and at the hamlet of Arbre Guernon, all of which were taken on October 17th. By October 19th, the division occupied a position east of the Mazinghien—Basuel road, where it was relieved on October 21st.

Marshal Haig sent the following message to General Read regarding the operations of the II Corps:

> "I wish to express to you personally and to all the officers and men serving under you my warm appreciation of the very valuable and gallant services rendered by you throughout the recent operations with the Fourth British Army. Called upon to attack positions of great strength, held by a determined enemy, all ranks of the 27th and 30th American Divisions under your command displayed an energy, courage and determination in attack which proved irresistible. It does not need me to tell you that in the heavy fighting of the past three weeks you have earned the lasting esteem and admiration of your British Comrades-in-Arms, whose success you so nobly shared."

During the previous weeks of furious fighting against obstinate resistance, the First Army had captured the strongest defenses on the Western Front, and was now engaged in local operations which were preparatory to effective delivery of the final blow. In the face of these splendid achievements, rumors reached me that the French Prime Minister, claiming we were not making satisfactory headway, was contemplating another move to interfere with our control of our own troops and force their distribution more generally among the Allied armies. Certainly, M. Clemenceau was aware of our steady progress and of the fact that we had attained a dominating position. The end was clearly approaching. It was obvious, therefore, that any attempt on his part to discredit our accomplishments would be purely a political gesture designed to minimize America's prestige at the peace conference.

(Diary) Souilly, Thursday, October 24, 1918. Admiral Mayo and party came to visit the army on Monday and had luncheon on my train.

Had conference with M. Clemenceau in Paris on Tuesday and found him in excellent spirits. Talked with Ambassador Sharp and General Bliss about possibility of armistice.

Visited Marshal Foch at Senlis on Wednesday and lunched with Marshal Haig at Bertincourt. Latter takes milder view as to armistice terms than Foch. Captain de Marenches takes up with French the question of civilian services in rear of our armies, which they now want us to handle.

Returned to Souilly this morning. Liggett and Drum came for final consultation on our next operation. Influenza increasing.

In the original plans for the Meuse-Argonne offensive, it was my purpose, after the capture of the Hindenburg Line, to drive through the center of the enemy's position, seize the Bois de Barricourt ridge, and immediately thereafter, by an advance westward to Boult-aux-Bois, outflank the Bois de Bourgogne and the enemy's forces facing the French Fourth Army on the Aisne. The First Army had already issued detailed battle plans for such an attack, to start October 28th, when General Maistre,[1] the representative of Marshal Foch, who had recently been sent to coordinate the activities of the French Fourth Army and our First Army, presented the Marshal's views (set forth in a letter dated October 21st) to the effect that our main blow should be directed along the eastern flank of the Bois de Bourgogne. But, in my opinion, with which General Liggett agreed, the execution of the original plan would be productive of greater results. This plan had been adopted prior to the Meuse-Argonne attack after full discussion with the Chief of Staff, First Army, Gen-

[1] General Maistre commanded a Group of Armies which included the French Fourth Army.

eral Drum, and mainly at his suggestion. Of course, it was quite beyond the Marshal's province to give instructions regarding the tactical conduct of operations. I therefore disregarded his directions and issued the following formal instructions to the Commanding General, First Army:

"October 21, 1918.

*　　*　　*　　*　　*　　*　　*

"2. The First Army will prepare to launch a general attack on October 28th with the object of securing control of Buzancy and the heights immediately to the east of that place. The minimum objective to be reached the first day is marked by the general line: heights south of Aincreville—Bois de Barricourt—hills north of Sivry-les-Buzancy—Bois des Loges. Immediately after reaching the general line above indicated you will proceed to free the Bois de Bourgogne from the enemy and to gain possession of the heights surrounding Briquenay. The operations of your left flank will be conducted in closest liaison with the right of the French Fourth Army. All plans will be made for following up any opportunities to gain possession of the high ground north and northeast of Buzancy.

"3. While preparing for the general attack as above ordered, you will constantly bear in mind that the present situation demands that there be no relaxation in the pressure now exerted on the enemy. You will therefore so time the local operations which are necessary preliminaries to the general attack as to continue the present pressure and will take immediate advantage of any favorable opportunity to advance your lines.

"4. East of the Meuse you will for the present confine your offensive operations to the local attacks necessary to improve your present position."

The changes of divisions and other adjustments necessary in preparation for this attack were being rapidly carried out. Except for those units in the Argonne, which utilized German dugouts, all of our troops had been without shelter of any sort, as none existed north of the Clermont—Verdun road, so that relief for rest and recuperation during this period entailed movements of considerable distance.

The demands of incessant battle had compelled our divisions to fight to the limit of their capacity. Troops were held in line and pushed to the attack until deemed incapable of further effort because of casualties or exhaustion; artillery once engaged was seldom withdrawn. Our men as a whole showed unrivaled fortitude in this continuous fighting during inclement weather and under the many disadvantages of position. Through such experience, the Army had developed into a powerful machine, and, with the short respite for readjustment, we had supreme confidence in its ability to carry on successfully.[1]

While the high pressure of our dogged attacks was severe on our troops, it was calamitous to the enemy. He had been so hard pressed that once a division was engaged in the fight it became practically impossible to effect its relief. The enemy was forced to meet recurring crises by breaking up tactical organizations and hurriedly sending detachments to different portions of the line.

Every member of the American Expeditionary Forces, from the front line to the base ports, was straining every nerve. Extraordinary efforts were exerted by the entire Services of Supply to meet the enormous demands made upon it. Obstacles which seemed insurmountable were overcome daily in hastening the movements of replacements, ammunition, and supplies to the front, and of sick and wounded to the rear. It was this spirit of determination animating every member of the A.E.F. that made it impossible for the enemy to maintain the struggle until 1919.

On October 26th, Marshal Foch published certain suggestions concerning tactical operations which were most pleasing to me, as they embodied those principles of open warfare for which I had been contending ever since our arrival in France. The following extract will illustrate his ideas at this time:

"Troops thrown into the attack have only to know the direction of attack. In this direction they go as far as they can without any thought of alignment, attacking and maneuvering the enemy who resists, the most advanced units working to help those who are momentarily stopped. In this manner they operate, not toward lines indicated ahead of time according to the terrain, but against the enemy, with whom they never lose contact once they have gained it."

[1] On October 23d, the combat strength of the A.E.F. was 1,256,478, of which 592,300 were in the First Army. The First Army also included approximately 100,000 French combat troops.

No doubt these excellent suggestions were intended for the French armies, as Marshal Foch surely was acquainted with our instructions issued October 25th, directing independent action by army corps in pursuing the enemy to the line of the Meuse River south of Sedan, and also the following instructions which I had issued to the whole American Army on September 5, 1918:

"Combat Instructions (extract)

"From a tactical point of view, the method of combat in trench warfare presents a marked contrast to that employed in open warfare, and the attempt by assaulting infantry to use trench warfare methods in an open warfare combat will be successful only at great cost. Trench warfare is marked by uniform formations, the regulation of space and time by higher commands down to the smallest details * * * fixed distances and intervals between units and individuals * * * little initiative * * *. Open warfare is marked by * * * irregularity of formations, comparatively little regulation of space and time by higher commanders, the greatest possible use of the infantry's own fire power to enable it to get forward, variable distances and intervals between units and individuals * * * brief orders and the greatest possible use of individual initiative by all troops engaged in the action. * * * The infantry commander must oppose machine guns by fire from his rifles, his automatics and his rifle grenades and must close with their crews under cover of this fire and of ground beyond their flanks. * * * The success of every unit from the platoon to the division must be exploited to the fullest extent. Where strong resistance is encountered, reënforcements must not be thrown in to make a frontal attack at this point, but must be pushed through gaps created by successful units, to attack these strong points in the flank or rear."

Now that the end was in prospect, everybody was in much better mood. M. Clemenceau was in fine humor when I saw him at his office on the 22d, and was profuse in his compliments on the success of our army. The object of my visit was to urge his assistance in obtaining more horses for our artillery, which was almost immobile. The French had furnished us 130,000 horses, but they were of inferior quality and were rapidly used up. He hesitated, however, to make a further requisition now that we appeared to be nearing the end of the war.

(Diary) Paris, Monday, October 28, 1918. Met Marshal Foch and Allied Commanders at Senlis Friday to consider terms of armistice. Pétain's views were stiffer than Marshal Haig's and mine more stringent than either. Yesterday sent Mr. House copy of cable reporting conference. Have been laid up with grippe since Saturday.

Although Marshal Foch had told me some days before that if his opinion should be asked regarding the terms of an armistice he expected to call the Commanders-in-Chief together and get their views, I had not made a detailed study of the terms that should be imposed, especially as I had expected some word from Washington on the subject. Having discussed the question in a general way with the Chief of Staff, McAndrew, the Chief of Operations, Fox Conner, and the Judge Advocate, Bethel, they were directed to meet me at Senlis, and we went over the details briefly before the conference.

This meeting of the Commanders-in-Chief was quite in contrast to the one held in July to consider joint action by the armies on the Western Front. What momentous events had taken place in three months! During that short period the Germans had lost the initiative and had been driven steadily backward from their extreme southern and western positions until now they faced certain defeat.

At the opening of the conference, Marshal Foch said in substance: "You are doubtless aware that the Germans are negotiating for an armistice through the intermediary of the American Government, and declare themselves ready to accept the Fourteen Points of President Wilson as a basis." He went on to say that he had called us together to obtain our views and that he thought "the terms should be such as to render Germany powerless to recommence operations in case hostilities are resumed." One of his officers then read aloud from a newspaper the Fourteen Points.

I expressed the opinion that commanders-in-chief should act only on the authority of their respective Governments, and inquired whether the Governments had referred this question to us with directions to draw up the conditions to be imposed in case they should deem it possible to grant an armistice. Marshal Foch replied that the French Government, with the approval of the Allied and Associated Powers, had directed him to take up the question with the Commanders-in-Chief, and he considered that we were justified in drafting the conditions of an eventual armistice. Although I was in favor of demanding the surrender of the German armies, I accepted this as a conference to decide upon the terms in case an armistice should be granted.

Foch then asked my opinion as to conditions that should be imposed. I replied that as it was a matter of greater concern to both Great Britain and France than to the United States and as their armies had been engaged longer and had suffered more than ours, I thought it appropriate for Sir Douglas Haig and General Pétain to express their views first.

Marshal Haig, being called on, said in substance that the German Army was far from being disintegrated and was still capable of withdrawing to a shorter front and making a stand against equal or greater forces. On the other hand, the Allies were pretty well exhausted. The total shortage of men for the British and French armies, he said, was about 250,000 each, with none available to fill the gaps. As to the American Army, he said something of its lack of training and experience, but later modified his statement, saying in effect that our army was not yet complete and that some time must elapse before it would be large enough to relieve the diminishing Allied armies. He thought the terms should be such that the Germans would not hesitate to accept them. He then proposed the following:

1st. Immediate and complete evacuation of invaded Belgian and French territory.

2d. Occupation by the Allies of Alsace, Lorraine, and the fortresses of Metz and Strasbourg.

3d. Restitution of all rolling stock seized by the Germans in France and Belgium, or its equivalent.

4th. Repatriation of inhabitants of invaded territory.

These conditions, Sir Douglas pointed out, would place us on the German frontier in case of a renewal of hostilities, and we could carry on the war in German territory. The armistice would give the Americans time to build up their army. He continued, "If hostilities should be resumed, I would prefer to find the Germans entrenched behind their old frontier of 1870 than to find them on the right bank of the Rhine."

Marshal Foch then remarked:

"It cannot be said that the German Army is not defeated. Although we are not able to tell its exact condition, still we are dealing with an army that has been pounded every day for three months, an army that is now losing on a front of 400 kilometers, that, since July 15th, has lost more than 250,000 prisoners and 4,000 guns; an army that is, physically and morally, thoroughly beaten. Certainly, the Allied armies are not new, but victorious armies are never fresh. In this matter the question is relative; the German armies are far more exhausted than ours. Certainly the British and French armies are tired; certainly the American Army is a young army, but it is full of idealism and strength and ardor. It has already won victories and is now on the eve of another victory; and nothing gives wings to an army like victory. When one hunts a wild beast and finally comes upon him at bay, one then faces greater danger, but it is not the time to stop, it is time to redouble one's blows without paying any attention to those he, himself, receives."

General Pétain spoke next and spread out a map of the Western Front showing territory between the existing positions and the Rhine, with lines drawn in red indicating proposed stages of retirement of the German armies. He said that in his opinion the best way to render them incapable of further fighting was to deprive them of their matériel, and he recommended that they be required to withdraw promptly according to the schedule he had prepared. If this movement should begin at once, he thought it would be impossible for the Germans to remove their matériel, especially the heavy guns and ammunition. He also suggested that they be required to return to the Allies 5,000 locomotives and 100,000 freight cars. His opinion was that the German armies should retire to the east of the Rhine and that the Allies should establish bridgeheads at Mayence, Coblenz and Cologne.

Marshal Foch then asked my views, which were stated in substance, and the exact terms submitted later in detail:

"The general view that an armistice should provide guarantees against a resumption of hostilities, give the Allies a decided advantage, and be unfavorable to Germany in case hostilities should be resumed, meets with my approval. I think that the damage done by the war to the interests of the powers with which the United States is associated against Germany has been so great that there should be no tendency toward leniency.

"The present military situation is very favorable to the Allies. The German forces since the beginning of the counteroffensive on July 18th have been constantly in retreat and have not been able to recover since that time. The condition of the French and British armies can best be judged by the fact that they have been continuously on the offensive since then and that they are now attacking with as much vigor as ever. As to the American Army, the part it has taken in the operations since July 18th has not been inconsiderable. It is constantly increasing in strength and training; its staffs, its services and its higher commanders have improved by experience, so there is every reason to suppose that the American Army will be able to take the part expected of it in the event of resumption of hostilities.

"I therefore propose:

"1st. The evacuation of France and Belgium within thirty days and of all other foreign territory occupied by Germany without delay.

"2d. The withdrawal of the German armies from Alsace-Lorraine and occupation of those territories by the Allied armies.

"3d. Withdrawal of German armies to the east of the Rhine and the possession of such bridgeheads on the eastern side of the Rhine by the Allies as may be necessary to insure their control of that river.

"4th. The unrestricted transportation of the American Army and its material across the seas.

"5th. The immediate repatriation of all nationals of foreign territory now or heretofore occupied during the war by Germany.

"6th. Surrender of all U-boats and U-boat bases to the control of a neutral power until their disposition is otherwise determined.

"7th. Return to France and Belgium of all railroad rolling stock that has been seized by Germany from those countries."

When I mentioned the surrender of submarines, Marshal Haig interrupted, saying:

"That is none of our affair. It is a matter for the Admiralty to decide."

I replied inviting attention to the fact that the American Army was operating 3,000 miles from home, that the German submarines constituted a formidable menace to our sea communications and that their surrender was a matter of vital importance to us. I said that while the number to be delivered could be decided by the naval authorities, this condition should be exacted so that if hostilities were resumed we should have our communications free from danger.

Marshal Foch said:

"The suggestion of General Pershing regarding submarines seems to me a reasonable one and his demand well founded."

The Marshal expressed his thanks for what I had said and repeated that while it was true the American Army was still young, its spirit was splendid and it was tremendously increasing every day in efficiency and in numbers. He then asked Marshal Haig whether, in view of what General Pétain and I had said, he cared to modify his views on the terms of an armistice, to which Haig replied in the negative. The conference ended here with Marshal Foch's request that each of us submit in writing what we had proposed.

Upon my return to Paris, I cabled a report of the proceedings of the conference to Washington, including my proposals. It may be noted that the views of Marshal Haig were included generally in paragraphs number one, two, five and seven of my proposal, and those of General Pétain were covered practically by paragraphs one, two, three and seven.

Marshal Foch did not definitely express his views at the conference, but on the following day submitted his report to M. Clemenceau. His recommendations embraced the main points proposed by the Commanders-in-Chief and were accepted by the Supreme War Council with practically no change.

(Diary) Paris, Wednesday, October 30, 1918. Cable giving the President's views received yesterday, to which I replied favoring demand for unconditional surrender.

The doctor let me out this morning. Went to Foreign Office, where Bliss and I met Generals Sir Henry Wilson, Sackville-West (British), Di Robilant (Italian), and Belin (French), to consider terms of armistice to be granted Austria, which, as submitted to the Supreme

War Council, included general evacuation of foreign territory and demobilization of armies. Left at 11 P.M. by train for Souilly.

On Sunday Lieutenant Colonel Griscom called to get my views on the terms of the armistice for Mr. House, who did not come himself, fearing that he might catch the grippe. I sent him a copy of my cable of the 25th and also offered to go to see him, but he preferred to wait until Tuesday morning before the meeting of the Supreme War Council. The meeting was later postponed until Wednesday afternoon. Meanwhile, Mr. House sent Frazier with a message to the effect that the military considerations of an armistice had not yet been discussed and that he wanted me to get in touch with Marshals Foch and Haig to see if their views could be reconciled. Although Foch had not expressed his views at the conference, it was evident that, if he favored an armistice, his terms would be greatly at variance with those proposed by Haig. Consequently, it did not seem advisable for me to follow the suggestion.

Inasmuch as no intimation had been sent to me regarding the President's attitude toward granting an armistice to the German armies, and feeling that I could not sit by without expressing my opinion, I prepared a letter to send to the Supreme War Council, giving my views for consideration in case a decision had not been finally reached. In my estimation, the German armies were so badly beaten that they would have no other recourse than to surrender if called upon to do so.

The President's comments on my cable of the 25th were received on the 29th:

"Replying to your cablegram from London,[1] October 26th, the President directs me to say that he is relying upon your counsel and advice in this matter, and in making the following comments he will be glad to have you feel entirely free to bring to his attention any consideration he may have overlooked which in your judgment ought to be weighed before settling finally. * * *

"In general, the President approves of your first, in subparagraph,

[1] My cable was not sent from London, but it frequently happened that the place of origin was not included in cables forwarded through London to Washington.

but suggests wisdom of retention of at least part of German heavy guns, in pledge, and specific enumeration of territory to be evacuated other than France and Belgium. This has to do especially with territory to the East and Southeast, but should not Luxembourg be also included?

"With regard to your second, in subparagraph, the President raises the question as to whether it is necessary for Allied or American (forces) actually to occupy Alsace and Lorraine when evacuated under armistice.

"With regard to your third, in subparagraph, the President doubts advisability of requiring Allied or American occupation on eastern side of the Rhine, as that is practically an invasion of German soil under armistice.

"The President concurs in your fourth, in subparagraph, to the extent of continuing transportation for supplies of troops then in France but would not insist on right to increase American forces during armistice.

"With regard to your fifth, in subparagraph, if this means repatriation of troops now in German Army which have been recruited from non-German soil occupied by Germans, or repatriation of civil population deported from occupied territory, the President approves.

"With regard to your sixth, the President believes it would be enough to require internment of U-boats in neutral waters, as a further pledge and also to further unrestricted transportation of American material referred to in your fourth, but does not think terms of armistice should suggest ultimate disposition of such U-boats, nor that U-boat bases should be occupied under armistice, as that would mean Allied or American occupation of German soil not now in their possession.

"Your seventh, in subparagraph, the President approves.

"In general, the President feels the terms of the armistice should be rigid enough to secure us against renewal of hostilities by Germany but not humiliating beyond that necessity, as such terms would throw the advantage to the military party in Germany.

"The President would be glad to have you confer with Colonel House, who is now in France, showing him copies of your dispatch and this answer, and generally discuss with him all phases of this subject."

Upon receipt of this cable I handed to Mr. House on the 30th, for presentation to the Supreme War Council, the letter I had prepared, and in view of the first paragraph of the message I also cabled the substance of the letter to Washington:

"Paris, October 30, 1918.

"To the Allied Supreme War Council,
   "Paris.

"Gentlemen:

"In considering the question of whether or not Germany's request for an armistice should be granted, the following expresses my opinion from the military point of view:

"1. Judging by their excellent conduct during the past three months, the British, French, Belgian and American Armies appear capable of continuing the offensive indefinitely. Their morale is high and the prospects of certain victory should keep it so.

"2. The American Army is constantly increasing in strength and experience, and should be able to take an increasingly important part in the Allied offensive. Its growth both in personnel and matériel, with such reserves as the Allies may furnish, not counting the Italian Army, should be more than equal to the combined losses of the Allied armies.

"3. German manpower is constantly diminishing and her armies have lost over 300,000 prisoners and over one-third of their artillery during the past three months in their effort to extricate themselves from a difficult situation and avoid disaster.

"4. The estimated strength of the Allies on the Western Front, not counting Italy, and of Germany, in rifles is:

Allies 1,563,000
Germany 1,134,000
An advantage in favor of the Allies
of 37 per cent.

"In guns:

Allies 22,413
Germany 16,495
An advantage of 35 per cent in favor
of the Allies.

"If Italy's forces should be added to the Western Front we should have a still greater advantage.

"5. Germany's morale is undoubtedly low, her Allies have deserted her one by one and she can no longer hope to win. Therefore we should take full advantage of the situation and continue the offensive until we compel her unconditional surrender.

"6. An armistice would revivify the low spirits of the German Army and enable it to reorganize and resist later on, and would deprive the Allies of the full measure of victory by failing to press their present advantage to its complete military end.

"7. As the apparent humility of German leaders in talking of peace may be feigned, the Allies should distrust their sincerity and their motives. The appeal for an armistice is undoubtedly to enable the withdrawal from a critical situation to one more advantageous.

"8. On the other hand, the internal political conditions of Germany, if correctly reported, are such that she is practically forced to ask for an armistice to save the overthrow of her present Government, a consummation which should be sought by the Allies as precedent to permanent peace.

"9. A cessation of hostilities short of capitulation postpones, if it does not render impossible, the imposition of satisfactory peace terms, because it would allow Germany to withdraw her army with its present strength, ready to resume hostilities if terms were not satisfactory to her.

"10. An armistice would lead the Allied armies to believe this the end of fighting and it would be difficult, if not impossible, to resume hostilities with our present advantage in morale in the event of failure to secure at a peace conference what we have fought for.

"11. By agreeing to an armistice under the present favorable military situation of the Allies and accepting the principle of a negotiated peace rather than a dictated peace the Allies would jeopardize the moral position they now hold and possibly lose the chance actually to secure world peace on terms that would insure its permanence.

"12. It is the experience of history that victorious armies are prone to overestimate the enemy's strength and too eagerly seek an opportunity for peace. This mistake is likely to be made now on account of the reputation Germany has gained through her victories of the last four years.

"13. Finally, I believe the complete victory can only be obtained by continuing the war until we force unconditional surrender from Germany, but if the Allied Governments decide to grant an armistice, the terms should be so rigid that under no circumstances could Germany again take up arms.

"Respectfully submitted:

"JOHN J. PERSHING,
"Commander-in-Chief, A.E.F."

That evening I received a note from Mr. House asking me about the views of the other Commanders-in-Chief. In conversation with my aide, Colonel Boyd, Mr. House said that the question as to whether an armistice should be granted was purely political and that all the Prime Ministers were in favor of it. He had shown my letter, he said, to Clemenceau and to Lloyd George. I then wrote him a note to the effect that my opinion was based upon military considerations. I also advised Marshal Foch, through Colonel Mott, that I thought we should demand unconditional surrender. The following day a message came to me at Souilly from Colonel Mott saying that the Marshal was much pleased, as he held similar views.

The correspondence which led up to the Armistice began, as we have seen, as far back as October 6th, by the application of the German Government to President Wilson for an armistice on the basis of the Fourteen Points set forth in his speech to Congress on January 8, 1918. The exchange of notes continued during the month, until finally the Germans accepted the very frank statement by the President, conveyed in the State Department message of October 23d, that "the nations of the world do not and cannot trust the word of those who have hitherto been the masters of German policy," and that "the Government of the United States cannot deal with any but veritable representatives of the German people, who have been assured of a genuine constitutional standing as the real rulers of Germany. If it must deal with the military masters and the monarchial autocrats of Germany now, or if it is likely to have to deal with them later in regard to the international obligations of the German Empire, it must demand, not peace negotiations, but surrender." German compliance with the President's demands was expressed in a note of October 27th, and on November 5th the Germans were advised to apply to Marshal Foch for terms of an armistice.

In the light of later events, we know Germany was more nearly beaten than the Allied leaders realized at that time and was, in fact, in no position to resume the fighting even though her Government had remained intact. Her last division was in line, her supply system was demoralized, and the congestion behind her lines made it practically impossible for her to move her armies in the face of the aggressive Allies. Instead of requiring the German forces to retire at once, leaving material, arms and equipment behind, the Armistice terms permitted them to march back to their homeland with colors flying and bands playing, posing as the victims of political conditions.

If unconditional surrender had been demanded,[1] the Germans would, without doubt, have been compelled to yield, and their troops would have returned to Germany without arms, virtually as paroled prisoners of war. The surrender of the German armies would have been an advantage to the Allies in the enforcement of peace terms and would have been a greater deterrent against possible future German aggression.

---

[1] In conversation with M. Poincaré some time after the war, he told me that, as President of the Republic, he was in favor of demanding the surrender of the German armies, but that M. Clemenceau, his Prime Minister, insisted upon granting them an armistice.

CHAPTER L

Preparations for General Attack—Plan of Maneuver—Attack Begins November 1st—Enemy Overwhelmed—First Army Forces Crossings of Meuse—Drive Relentless—We Reach Sedan on the 7th—German Delegates meet Foch to Discuss Terms of Armistice—Advance Continues in Meuse-Argonne—Second Army Assumes Offensive—37th and 91st Divisions in Flanders—Foch Appeals to Commanders-in-Chief for Decisive Results

(Diary) Souilly, Sunday, November 3, 1918. Returned here Thursday morning. Visited all corps commanders in afternoon.

General attack resumed Friday morning and our troops everywhere successful.

Arrived in Paris yesterday at Mr. House's request to attend meeting of Supreme War Council, Commanding Generals, and Chiefs of Staff, at Ministry of War, to consider Austrian situation. Austrians given until midnight November 3d-4th to accept terms of Armistice. Met with military men in afternoon to determine procedure in case of refusal of terms. Afterward attended meeting of Supreme War Council at Versailles, where general situation was discussed. Drove back with Mr. House; had satisfactory talk. Awarded first Distinguished Service Medal by the President; cabled appreciation.

Returned to Souilly this morning. The rapid progress of First Army continues. Discussed with General Maistre our proposed advance on Sedan.

Last Phase—Meuse-Argonne Operations

THE American Army had been able for the first time in the war to prepare for an offensive with some deliberation, under reasonably normal conditions, and more nearly on an equal footing with the other armies. It was already on the front of attack, the weather had taken a favorable turn,

NOTE: Strength of the A.E.F. on October 31st, 76,800 officers, 1,790,823 enlisted men. Divisional units arriving in October included elements of the following divisions: 8th Division (Regular Army), Maj. Gen. Eli A. Helmick; 31st Division (National Guard, Georgia, Alabama and Florida), Brig. Gen. Walter A. Harris; 38th Division (National Guard, Indiana, Kentucky and West Virginia), Maj. Gen. Robert L. Howze.

and the morale of the troops was lifted even higher than before. Our staffs and troops had become veterans. French special units of artillery, pioneers, engineers, rail and service troops had been largely replaced by Americans. The army was operating in a sector which had been under its control for a month and more. Hitherto, as on September 12th and 26th, we had held the front but a brief period instead of being several months on the ground as was usually the case with the Allies.

Preparatory to this general attack, the front line had been reorganized, inefficient commanders had been replaced by active, energetic men, and large quantities of ammunition, supplies and equipment had been brought up. Our line occupied favorable positions from which to start this offensive. From east of Landres-et-St. Georges to the Meuse we were beyond the Hindenburg Line defenses and at the Côte de Châtillon we flanked the enemy's positions in and near Landres-et-St. Georges. Having gained the northern edge of the Bois de Bantheville, we were within striking distance of the heights of Barricourt.

The terrain presented a configuration somewhat similar to that encountered in our initial attack. On the east, overlooking the Meuse River at Dun-sur-Meuse, is a main ridge (called Barricourt ridge), which runs northwest via Buzancy to Stonne. On the west is the high wooded country of Bois de Loges and Bois de Bourgogne. Between these two commanding areas of high ground is lower, rolling country.

We had learned from reports and from photographs taken by our aviators that the enemy had greatly strengthened the most prominent points back of his lines, while captured documents indicated his intention of organizing a position along the west slopes of the Barricourt ridge. The eastern spurs of this ridge commanded all the crossings of the Meuse and formed a connecting link with the high ground east of the river about Côte Saint-Germain.

Our plans, as already indicated, contemplated first a deep penetration in the center of the front west of the Meuse with the object of capturing Barricourt ridge, and, next, a drive to the left to effect a junction with the French Fourth Army near Boult-aux-Bois. The capture of the ridge would give us a flank position which would compel the enemy to withdraw to the east of the river. As previously stated, the operation was to be carried

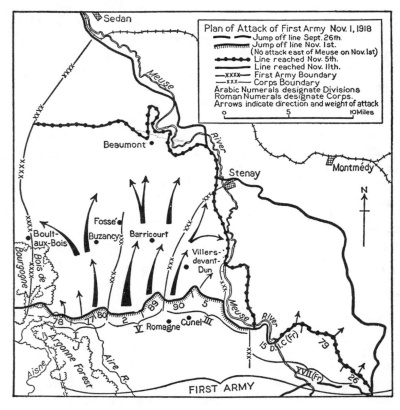

out in coöperation with the French Fourth Army and both armies were in readiness on November 1st.

The order of battle and general plan of the First Army are well illustrated by the accompanying sketch. On the right, the III Corps (Hines), composed, from right to left, of the 5th Division (Ely) and 90th (Allen), was to support the right of the V Corps, turning the east flank of the Bois de Barricourt and carrying the

Barricourt ridge at Villers-devant-Dun. The V. Corps (Summerall), in the center, with the 89th Division (Wright) and 2d (Lejeune), as the wedge, was to drive to the north, carrying the ridge west of Barricourt and Fossé. The I Corps (Dickman), on the left, consisting of the 80th Division (Cronkhite), 77th (Alexander) and 78th (McRae), was to protect the left of the V. Corps and later to strike toward Boult-aux-Bois. The 1st Division (Parker) and the 42d (Menoher) were placed in close reserve in rear of the V Corps to be passed through the 2d and 80th Divisions when needed to add impetus to the attack.

The personnel of our artillery had quickly absorbed the traditions and the efficiency of this branch of the Regular Army. The value of close coöperation with the infantry was soon recognized, especially where these units of the division were trained together. The advance shipments of infantry and machine gun units prevented combined practice in many divisions, which had to enter the lines supported by strange artillery. A shortage had often compelled us to keep some artillery units in the line to support successive divisions. Notwithstanding such handicaps, the battle efficiency developed in our artillery was unsurpassed in any army. This was shown especially by the striking success in this offensive of the well-planned system of artillery fire which materially aided the infantry's initial penetration of the enemy's lines.

Special arrangements were made for the artillery to employ persistent (mustard) gas against the eastern edge of the Bois de Bourgogne and other selected points. The strongest enemy positions were to be engaged from the front by specified units while all others were to push forward rapidly between these points. In the two-hour violent artillery preparation which preceded the commencement of the attack, all sensitive places such as known batteries, ammunition dumps, strongholds and crossroads were systematically and effectively bombarded.

Three batteries of naval 14-inch guns on railway mounts and manned by naval personnel had been brought into the battle on

October 23d. These guns, with their long range, were used to good advantage against the enemy's main lines of railway communication.

As an aid to our infantry, machine guns were of great value. Capable of direct and overhead fire, and readily concealed in flank positions, the machine gun, alone or in mass, was the primary weapon of the defense. On the offensive our machine guns, often carried long distances, were kept well forward, and played an important rôle in our attacks. In the same way, despite the difficulties, single light artillery guns were advanced with the troops for use against enemy machine gun nests.

The effectiveness of the machine gun was well demonstrated by the exploit of one of our men near Cunel.[1] Repairing and mounting in an abandoned tank a captured machine gun, and holding his position under a hostile barrage and against direct artillery fire, he broke up two counterattacks against our lines.

One serious deficiency, which imposed a harder task on our splendid infantrymen and subjected them to the certainty of additional losses, but which, however, could not be remedied, was the lack of tanks, only eighteen being available instead of several hundred which were sorely needed. It seems strange that, with American genius for manufacturing from iron and steel, we should find ourselves after a year and a half of war almost completely without those mechanical contrivances which had exercised such a great influence on the Western Front in reducing infantry losses. As usual, the American soldier discounted the odds placed against him and carried the day by his dash and courage.

The infantry advanced to the assault at 5:30 on the morning of the 1st, following an accurate barrage of artillery and machine gun fire, which beat down German resistance over a zone 1,200 yards in depth. Squadrons of swift-flying combat planes drove the enemy planes from the air and fired on the hostile infantry, while the bombing squadrons harassed important

---

[1] Private John L. Barkley, Co. K, 4th Infantry, 3d Division. For this feat Private Barkley was awarded the Medal of Honor.

points behind the enemy's lines. The attack went forward with precision, gaining momentum with every mile. For the first time, the enemy's lines were completely broken through. Although he had been badly beaten on all parts of the front, he had hitherto been able to avoid this disaster. By the magnificent dash of our First Army, however, the enemy now found himself in the same situation that had confronted the Allies earlier in the war.

The V Corps, in the center, drove a wedge into the German defenses, swept through the zone of their artillery, and by night had reached the heights of Barricourt, five miles from the front of departure. The enemy's lines here had been decisively crushed, thanks to the splendid performances of the 89th and 2d Divisions.

The III Corps had strongly supported the V Corps, the 90th Division carrying all its objectives without a reverse and the 5th Division, on its right, reaching the Meuse, north of Brieulles, and capturing Cléry-le-Grand.

On the left of the Army, in the I Corps, the 80th Division cooperated with the 2d Division in the capture of Imécourt and reached the corps objective north of Sivry. The remainder of the corps was unable, in spite of great efforts, to make much headway against the strong defense of the Bois des Loges, although the 78th Division did gain a foothold in that wood.

In the meantime, the French Fourth Army, after having been driven back from the Grandpré—Olizy road, was unable to advance beyond the line of the Aisne River, and did not penetrate the Bois de Bourgogne until the American First Army relieved the pressure on its front by capturing Briquenay on November 2d.

By the evening of November 1st, the situation of the enemy was so serious that he had either to deliver a strong counterattack or to withdraw from all territory south of the line, Buzancy—Boult-aux-Bois. The blow struck by the First Army had, however, given him such a shock that he was unable to take strong offensive action, although he still offered serious resistance.

The attack continued with vigor on November 2d and 3d, the III Corps hurling the enemy beyond the Meuse near Dun-sur-Meuse and Stenay. The 5th Division on the 2d captured Doulcon and the 90th took Villers-devant-Dun. On the following day, the 90th pushed through the woods on its front and established its line along the heights overlooking the river in the neighborhood of Villefranche.

In the V Corps, the 89th Division on the 2d captured Tailly in the face of heavy machine gun fire, and on the following day seized Barricourt and drove the enemy backward to Beauclair. The 3d Brigade (Colonel James C. Rhea) of the 2d Division daringly marched through the Bois de la Folie during the night of November 2d, and captured the high ground east and north of Fossé early in the morning of the 3d. That night, this brigade, by another perilous march through the extensive Forêt de Dieulet, passed completely beyond the enemy's lines and captured German troops in their billets. By midnight the head of the column was in firm possession of La Tuilerie Farm, just south of Beaumont. This exploit reversed a scene of the Franco-Prussian War where a French division was surprised in its bivouac around Beaumont, in the opening phase of the Battle of Sedan, by a German night advance through the same forest.

The success of the attack in the center on November 1st compelled the retirement of the enemy on November 2d along the entire front of the I Corps and in front of the right of the French Fourth Army. The 80th Division on the 2d reached the new German defensive position, broke through it, and took Buzancy. On the following day, against heavy fire, the 80th established its line along the road running southeast from St. Pierremont.

The 77th Division now succeeded in passing Champigneulles and by the night of the 2d had reached Harricourt. On the following morning, it drove the enemy to the hill north of St. Pierremont, where it was held up by heavy machine gun fire.

The 78th Division captured the Bois des Loges on the 2d and established its line along the eastern edge of the Bois de

Bourgogne north to Briquenay, and continuing on the 3d captured Germont and Verrières.

(Diary) Souilly, Thursday, November 7, 1918. Had long talk with Stettinius about ordnance on Monday. Visited Second Army Headquarters and found indications of withdrawal on that front. Issued orders the 5th for operations by First and Second Armies in the direction of Briey-Longwy. Spent the day at front. Went through Grandpré, overtaking Dickman's I Corps Headquarters at Harricourt; he was pushing troops toward Sedan. Returned through St. Juvin and found traffic in difficulties, many trucks having run off the road in the darkness. Gave directions to use lights on all motor transport.

Received letter from Marshal Foch to-day asking for six American divisions for new offensive south of Metz. Our advance has been continuous. Troops reached the heights of Sedan last night. German delegates are meeting Foch to consider terms of armistice. Recommended Harbord and McAndrew for promotion to grade of Lieutenant General.[1]

By November 4th, the enemy, greatly disorganized, was retiring before the vigorous pursuit of our troops on the entire front of the First Army. His withdrawal was strongly protected by cleverly placed machine guns and well organized delaying operations.

The following telegram came to me on the afternoon of the 5th:

"The operations begun on November 1st by the First American Army, due to the valor of the command, (and) to the energy and bravery of the troops, have already assured results of great importance. I am happy to send you my congratulations. * * *

"Foch."

Our success had been so striking since the beginning of the November 1st attack that I felt full advantage should be taken of the possibility of destroying the armies on our front and seizing the region upon which Germany largely depended for her supply

[1] This recommendation met with Secretary Baker's favor, but unfortunately the Tables of Organization made no provision for appointments to that grade except in the line of the army.

of iron and coal. In accordance with these views, the following order was issued on November 5th to the First and Second Armies:

"1. The energetic action of the 1st Army should completely expel the enemy from the region between the MEUSE and the BAR within the next few days. The results obtained by this Army have been felt on the entire front from the MOSELLE to HOLLAND. * * *

"It is desired that, in carrying out the directions that are outlined herein, Corps and Division Commanders push troops forward wherever resistance is broken, without regard for fixed objectives and without fear for their flanks. Special attention will be given to impress upon all officers and soldiers that energy, boldness and open warfare methods are demanded by the present situation.

"2. The 1st and 2nd Armies will at once prepare to undertake operations with the ultimate purpose of destroying the enemy's organization and driving him beyond the existing frontier in the region of BRIEY and LONGWY.

"3. As preliminaries of this offensive, the 1st Army will:

"(a) Complete the occupation of the region between the MEUSE and the BAR.

"(b) Complete the present operation of driving the enemy from the heights of the MEUSE north of VERDUN and south of the FORÊT DE WOËVRE.

"(c) Conduct an offensive with the object of driving the enemy beyond the THINTE and the CHIERS. * * *

"4. The 2nd Army will:

"(a) Conduct raids and local operations in accordance with verbal instructions already given.

"(b) Advance its line between the MOSELLE and the ETANG LACHAUSSÉE toward GORZE and CHAMBLEY.

"(c) Prepare plans for an attack in the direction of BRIEY along the axis FRESNES—CONFLANS—BRIEY. * * * "

Between the Meuse and Chiers Rivers, north and northeast of Stenay, there was a very strong position which commanded the crossings in that vicinity. I believed that if we should cross the river south of Stenay and move in the direction of Montmédy we could turn this position and would have an excellent opportunity to capture large numbers of German troops driven back on the line Sedan—Montmédy. By this maneuver we would also be in an advantageous position to advance on the important supply areas of Longwy and Briey.

In the First Army, an attack by the III Corps to the east across the Meuse, south of Dun-sur-Meuse, in conjunction with the northward movement by the French XVII Corps, was prepared as a preliminary to a new line of advance to the east.

On November 3d, 4th and 5th, the 5th Division of the III Corps, in a brilliant maneuver on a wide front, effected crossings of the Meuse and established bridgeheads south of Dun-sur-Meuse. The heights of the Meuse were gradually cleared by the III Corps and the French II Colonial Corps, which had relieved the French XVII Corps. Now, for the first time since 1914, the French positions around Verdun were completely free from the menace of these heights.

In these operations, the 5th Division, assisted by a regiment of the 32d, on November 5th had captured Milly and established its line from there south to the Bois de Châtillon. By night of the 9th, it had advanced to Remoiville and north of Mouzay.

Our front of attack was also extended to the south and by November 10th an excellent line of departure was secured for an offensive in the direction of Montmédy. The 79th Division (Kuhn), in the French II Colonial Corps, met decided opposition in its attacks of the 4th, 5th, and 6th against the Borne de Cornouiller and this strong point was finally taken on the 7th. On the following day the 79th, with units of the 26th Division (Bamford) attached, advanced on its entire front, and on the 9th took Wavrille.

Between November 3d and 7th the 26th Division, on the right of the 79th, made no attack. On the 8th it took up the pursuit of the retiring enemy and by night of the 9th occupied a line which included Ville-devant-Chaumont.

The 81st Division (Bailey) entered the line as the right division of the French II Colonial Corps on November 7th, relieving the

35th Division (Traub). Attacking on the 9th against stiff defense, it captured Manheulles and Moranville.

In these last days of the fighting some of our troops, including the 81st, operated with a serious shortage of animals, which made it impossible to employ all their artillery in close support of the infantry, and often required the men to drag their guns by hand. The 6th Division (Gordon), which unfortunately did not get into battle, pulled a large part of its transportation many miles by hand in attempting to reach the rapidly moving battle front south of Sedan, where it was planned to use this division in case of necessity.

Taking up again the account of our great drive northward, the 89th Division, V Corps, overcoming stubborn opposition, captured Beaufort on the 4th and reached the Meuse. The Forêt de Jaulnay was cleaned up on the following day and Cesse was occupied. The 2d Division in its attack of the 4th suffered heavy losses and made slight headway, but during the next two days it continued rapidly and by night of the 6th reached the Meuse south of Villemontry.

In the I Corps, the 80th Division on the 4th, in spite of the enemy's stand, captured Vaux-en-Dieulet and Sommauthe. The enemy retired during the night and the division took up the pursuit, overcoming vigorous rearguard resistance until reaching a line north and west of Beaumont. During the night of the 5th, its progress continued, the division being relieved the next morning.

The 77th Division was effectively opposed on the 4th north and east of Oches, but on the 5th its line was pushed forward to the north of Stonne and La Besace. By night of the 6th, the 77th had reached the Meuse; Remilly and Villers being entered by its patrols.

The 78th Division on the 4th captured Les Petites Armoises, and on the following morning advanced more than a mile to the north. The 42d Division relieved the 78th on this line, and by the 6th established itself north of Bulson.

On the morning of November 6th, the 1st Division, V Corps,

took over the front of the 80th Division, I Corps, and at once made a rapid advance to Yoncq, reaching the general line of the Meuse in the vicinity of Villemontry.

It was the ambition of the First Army and mine that our troops should capture Sedan, which the French had lost in a decisive battle in 1870. I suggested to General Maistre that the prescribed boundary line between our First and the French Fourth Army might be ignored in case we should outrun the French, to which he offered no objection, but on the contrary warmly approved.

To reach the objective the left boundary of the First Army would have to be disregarded, as Sedan lay to the northwest beyond that limit. On the afternoon of November 5th, the I Corps was directed to bend its energies to capture Sedan *"assisted on its right by the V Corps."* A misconception in the V Corps of the exact intent of the orders resulted in the 1st Division erroneously going beyond the left boundary of the V Corps and marching directly across the sector of the I Corps during the late afternoon of the 6th and throughout the night. The troops of the 1st Division carried out this unnecessary forced march in fine spirit despite their tired condition.

Considerable confusion resulted in the 42d and 77th Divisions, and their advance was delayed, as roads became blocked by the columns of the 1st Division. The 42d and the 1st then began a race for the honor of capturing Sedan. Part of these divisions had entered the zone of the French Fourth Army and were waging a fight with the enemy for the possession of the heights south and west of Sedan. The morning of the 7th found men of the 42d and the 1st Divisions on the heights overlooking the city.

Under normal conditions the action of the officer or officers responsible for this movement of the 1st Division directly across the zones of action of two other divisions could not have been overlooked, but the splendid record of that unit and the approach of the end of hostilities suggested leniency.

The enemy's main line of communications was now within range of the machine guns of the First Army, which had driven him twenty-four miles since the 1st of November. His position on the Western Front was no longer tenable and he urged immediate consideration of an armistice.

Between November 1st and 7th the western boundary of the First Army was changed several times by Marshal Foch, and the notification in more than one instance reached Army Headquarters too late to be transmitted to the troops in time to become effective. On the 7th of November the left of our army was limited by Mouzon, the original boundary not having been definitely fixed as far north as Sedan. However, this change was not effected until after the Armistice, as the French Fourth Army was not prepared before that time to take over that sector.

> (Diary) Paris, Saturday, November 9, 1918. Had telephone message from Foch yesterday that when hostilities cease troops should hold their lines.
>
> Arrived here to-day by motor to discuss with Foch further operations but found him absent. Word received from Mr. House that the Italians want three or four American regiments sent to Austria with their troops. Went to Neuilly hospital to see our patients. Had talk with Bishop Brent. Japanese Prince Torihito, representing the Emperor, presented me with the highest grade of Order of the Rising Sun.

Late on November 9th Marshal Foch, then in conference with German representatives regarding the terms of the Armistice, sent telegraphic instructions to all Commanders-in-Chief from which it might be inferred that he was uncertain regarding the outcome of negotiations and wished to let the enemy know that there could be no further delay. The following was the message received:

> "The enemy, disorganized by our repeated attack, retreats along the entire front.
>
> "It is important to coördinate and expedite our movements.
>
> "I appeal to the energy and the initiative of the Commanders-in-Chief and of their armies to make decisive the results obtained."

Orders in response to this appeal were immediately issued and their execution by the First Army was under way on November

10th and 11th. Yet here again no sort of urging was necessary. Our troops were determined not to give the enemy any respite. Already the crossing of the Meuse had been planned for the whole army and the V Corps got over during the night of the 10th-11th. Part of the 89th Division crossed on rafts just west of Pouilly, and others in the rear of the 90th Division.

The 2d Division was unable to force a crossing at Mouzon, as planned, but about a mile south of Villemontry the engineers of the division, with exceptional rapidity and skill, threw two bridges across, over which one regiment passed. The 77th Division, now on the left of the V Corps, sent over patrols only on the 10th and 11th, the low ground north of the river opposite its front being flooded due to heavy rains and to damming operations by the Germans.

The I Corps from November 6th to 10th was withdrawing its divisions to points on the Meuse between Dun-sur-Meuse and Verdun, preparatory to a general attack which would have as its object the turning of the enemy's strong position in front of the V Corps.

East of the Meuse, the First Army advanced in conjunction with the Second Army, which had been earnestly preparing for this moment ever since its organization. The Second Army, from left to right, was composed of the French XVII Corps, with the 33d Division (Bell) in line, and the 35th (Traub) in reserve; the IV Corps (Muir), with the 28th Division (Hay) and the 7th (Wittenmyer) in line, and the 4th (Hersey) in reserve; and the VI Corps (Menoher), with the 92d (colored) Division (Ballou) in line; and the 88th Division (Weigel) in the Army reserve. This order of battle is shown on the accompanying sketch.

Under the instructions issued by me on November 5th for the advance of the First and Second Armies, which received approval of Marshal Foch in a personal note of November 8th, the Second Army made progress along its entire front in the direction of the Briey iron basin during the last three days of hostilities. In view of the stubborn resistance encountered, and the extended

fronts held by its divisions, the gains realized reflected credit on
that command.

Attacking on the 10th, the 33d Division reached the Bois
d'Harville and captured Marchéville, but was forced to retire.
The 28th Division occupied a part of the Bois des Haudronvilles
Bas, as well as Marimbois Farm. The 7th Division took and held
against counterattack Hill 323. The 92d Division captured the
Bois Fréhaut.

On the front of the First Army, the 90th Division (Allen), on

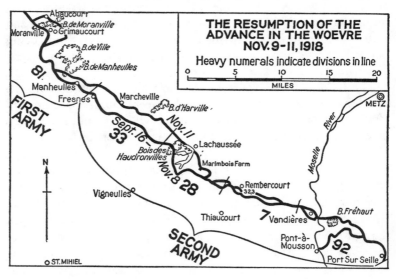

THE RESUMPTION OF THE
ADVANCE IN THE WOEVRE
NOV. 9-11, 1918

Heavy numerals indicate divisions in line

the left of the III Corps (Hines), had crossed the Meuse on the
9th and attacked on the 10th, meeting decided opposition
throughout the day. Elements of the division entered Stenay
but were unable to clean up the town; while others, after hard
fighting in the nearby wood, reached but could not take Baâlon.
The 5th Division (Ely) captured Jametz and cleared the Forêt
de Woëvre. The 32d Division (Haan) reëntered the line on the
9th as the right division of the III Corps and made substantial
progress. On the 10th the division moved forward until stopped
by heavy fire from east of the Thinte River.

In the French II Colonial Corps, the 79th Division (Kuhn) engaged the enemy on the 10th and captured Chaumont-devant-Damvillers, while the 26th Division (Bamford) took Ville-devant-Chaumont. The 81st Division (Bailey) continued its attack on the 9th, cleaning up the remainder of the Bois de Moranville and taking Abaucourt. After hard fighting, Grimaucourt was captured, but was later evacuated, the line being established west of the town.

Meanwhile other of our divisions were engaged on distant fronts. In Flanders, our 37th and 91st Divisions, which had been sent to the French Sixth Army at Marshal Foch's request, entered the battle on October 31st. The Cruyshautem ridge was taken by the 37th Division (Farnsworth) on the first day, while the 91st (Johnston), advancing against intense fire, seized the strongly defended wooded area in its front. Both divisions moved forward rapidly to the Escaut River on the following day in pursuit of the enemy. Despite resistance, crossings of the river were effected by the 37th on November 2d and 3d, the division being relieved on the following day. Audenarde was occupied by the 91st Division on the 2d, and the division was relieved on the 3d by the French.

Both divisions reëntered the line for the general attack of the French Sixth Army on November 10th. The 37th Division was directed to relieve two French divisions east of the Escaut on the morning of the 10th, but these divisions had been unable to cross and were relieved on the west bank. In spite of severe losses, the 37th succeeded in again crossing the river and moved forward on the following day, advancing two and a half miles eastward. The 91st Division met slight opposition on the 10th and none on the morning of the 11th, reaching a line east of Boucle-Saint-Blaise.

In the First Army, the V Corps advanced rapidly the morning of the 11th. Elements of the 89th Division occupied Stenay and established a line on the hill to the north. Pouilly-sur-Meuse was mopped up early in the morning and Autreville was occupied. The 2d Division advanced to the ridge west of Moulins; while the 77th Division held its line of the 10th.

In the III Corps, on the morning of the 11th, the 90th Division entered Baâlon, and the 5th and 32d Divisions were preparing to attack. The 79th Division of the French II Colonial Corps attacked against the Côte de Romagne and advanced a short distance; the 26th Division made slight gains; and the 81st Division again took Grimaucourt.

On the front of the Second Army, the attack of the 33d Division on the 11th was held up. The 28th Division carried its line

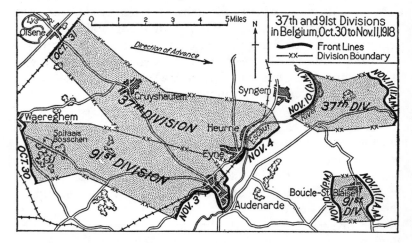

forward north of Marimbois Farm; the 7th Division made no attack; and the 92d Division attacked but did not hold all its gains.

The line of the First Army on November 11th extended from Fresnes-en-Woëvre to Pont-Maugis. The Second Army line ran from Port-sur-Seille to Fresnes-en-Woëvre. Thus both American armies were now in position to carry out the offensive as directed by my orders of November 5th, which was what I had planned and advocated when Marshal Foch insisted that there should be a converging movement of all the armies west of the Meuse, with Mézières—Sedan as the objective of the American First Army.

As noted in the diary of November 7th, Marshal Foch had requested that six American divisions be held in readiness to join in a Franco-American offensive in the direction of Château-Salins, to start from the sector east of the Moselle River. The plan was agreed to, but with the understanding that our troops should be employed as a group under our own command. This combined attack was to begin on November 14th, with twenty French divisions under General Mangin, and a force of six American divisions under General Bullard. It was my intention to have this force known thereafter as the Second Army. I then expected to give General Dickman the command of the old Second Army, which would become the Third, to hold the St. Mihiel front. Of the divisions designated for the operation toward Château-Salins, the 3d, 4th, 29th, and 36th, then in reserve, were scheduled to move eastward on November 11th, while the 28th and 35th were being withdrawn from line on the Second Army front.

CHAPTER LI

Armistice—Résumé—Decoration Foch, Joffre, Pétain and Haig—Call on Clemenceau

(Diary) Chaumont, Monday, November 11, 1918. Arrived here yesterday morning from Paris. Miss Margaret Wilson dined with us last night.

This morning at 6 o'clock message came from Marshal Foch, through Colonel Mott, that hostilities would cease at 11 A.M. Had information on tentative plans for following up Germans. Sent congratulations to the King of Belgium by Comte d'Oultremont on glorious outcome of the war. Assistant Secretary of War F. P. Keppel came to dine. Left on my train for Paris at 11 P.M., taking General McAndrew, Colonels Boyd and Quekemeyer, Lieutenant Colonel Griscom, and Captain Hughes.

A S the conference between Marshal Foch and the German delegates proceeded, and in anticipation of advices regarding the Armistice, telephone lines were kept constantly open between my headquarters and those of the First and Second Armies. When word came to me at 6 A.M. that hostilities would cease at 11:00 A.M., directions to that effect were immediately sent to our armies. Our troops had been advancing rapidly during the preceding two days and although every effort was made to reach them promptly a few could not be overtaken before the prescribed hour.

Between September 26th and November 11th, twenty-two American and six French divisions, with an approximate fighting strength of 500,000 men, on a front extending from southeast of Verdun to the Argonne Forest, had engaged and decisively beaten forty-three different German divisions, with an estimated fighting strength of 470,000. Of the twenty-two American divisions, four had at different times during this period been in action on fronts other than our own.

The enemy suffered an estimated loss of over 100,000 casualties in this battle and the First Army about 117,000. The total strength of the First Army, including 135,000 French troops, reached 1,031,000 men. It captured 26,000 prisoners, 874 cannon, 3,000 machine guns and large quantities of material.

The transportation and supply of divisions to and from our front during this battle was a gigantic task. There were twenty-six American and seven French divisions, besides hundreds of thousands of corps and army troops, moved in and out of the American zone. A total of 173,000 men were evacuated to the rear and more than 100,000 replacements were received.

It need hardly be restated that our entry into the war gave the Allies the preponderance of force vitally necessary to outweigh the tremendous increase in the strength of the Germans on the Western Front, due to the collapse of Russia and the consequent release of German divisions employed against her. From the military point of view, we began to aid the Allies early in 1918, when our divisions with insufficient training to take an active part in battle were sent to the inactive front to relieve French divisions, in order that they might be used where needed in the fighting line.

The assistance we gave the Allies in combat began in May with the successful attack of one of our divisions at Cantigny. This was followed early in June by the entrance into battle of the two divisions that stopped the German advance on Paris near Château-Thierry, and by three others that were put in the defensive line. In July two American divisions, with one Moroccan division, formed the spearhead of the counterattack against the Château-Thierry salient, in which nine of our divisions participated. There was a total of approximately 300,000 American troops engaged in this Second Battle of the Marne, which involved very severe fighting, and was not completed until the Germans were driven beyond the Vesle in August. In the middle of September an army of 550,000 Americans reduced the St. Mihiel salient. The latter part of September our great battle of the Meuse-Argonne was begun, lasting through forty-seven days of intense fighting and ending brilliantly for our First and Second Armies on November 11th, after more than 1,200,000 American soldiers had participated.

It was a time to forget the hardships and the difficulties, except to record them with the glorious history of our achievements. In praise and thanks for the decisive victories of our armies and in guidance for the future, the following order was issued:

"G. H. Q.

"American Expeditionary Forces.

"General Orders⎱
  "No. 203. ⎰   "France, Nov. 12, 1918.

"The enemy has capitulated. It is fitting that I address myself in thanks directly to the officers and soldiers of the American Expeditionary Forces who by their heroic efforts have made possible this glorious result. Our armies, hurriedly raised and hastily trained, met a veteran enemy, and by courage, discipline and skill always defeated him. Without complaint you have endured incessant toil, privation and danger. You have seen many of your comrades make the supreme sacrifice that freedom may live. I thank you for the patience and courage with which you have endured. I congratulate you upon the splendid fruits of victory which your heroism and the blood of our gallant dead are now presenting to our nation. Your deeds will live forever on the most glorious pages of America's history.

"These things you have done. There remains now a harder task which will test your soldierly qualities to the utmost. Succeed in this and little note will be taken and few praises will be sung; fail, and the light of your glorious achievements of the past will sadly be dimmed. But you will not fail. Every natural tendency may urge towards relaxation in discipline, in conduct, in appearance, in everything that marks the soldier. Yet you will remember that each officer and each soldier is the representative in Europe of his people and that his brilliant deeds of yesterday permit no action of to-day to pass unnoticed by friend or by foe. You will meet this test as gallantly as you have met the tests of the battlefield. Sustained by your high ideals and inspired by the heroic part you have played, you will carry back to our people the proud consciousness of a new Americanism born of sacrifice. Whether you stand on hostile territory or on the friendly soil of France, you will so bear yourself in discipline, appearance and respect for all civil rights that you will confirm for all time the pride and love which every American feels for your uniform and for you.

"JOHN J. PERSHING,
"General, Commander-in-Chief.

"Official:
  "ROBERT C. DAVIS,
    "Adjutant General."

The experience of the World War only confirmed the lessons of the past. The divisions with little training, while aggressive and courageous, were lacking in the ready skill of habit. They were capable of powerful blows, but their blows were apt to be awkward—teamwork was often not well understood. Flexible and resourceful divisions cannot be created by a few maneuvers or by a few months' association of their elements. On the other hand, without the keen intelligence, the endurance, the willingness, and the enthusiasm displayed in the training areas and on the battlefields, the decisive results obtained would have been impossible.

The Meuse-Argonne battle presented numerous difficulties, seemingly insurmountable. The success stands out as one of the great achievements in the history of American arms. Suddenly conceived and hurried in plan and preparation; complicated by close association with a preceding major operation; directed against stubborn defense of the vital point of the Western Front; attended by cold and inclement weather; and fought largely by partially trained troops; this battle was prosecuted with an unselfish and heroic spirit of courage and fortitude which demanded eventual victory. Physically strong, virile, and aggressive, the morale of the American soldier during this most trying period was superb.

Upon the young commanders of platoons, companies, and battalions fell the heaviest burden. They not only suffered all the dangers and rigors of battle but carried the responsibility of caring for and directing their men, often newly arrived and with but little training. Where these leaders lacked practical knowledge of tactics, they supplied the deficiency by fearless onslaughts against the enemy's line. Yet, quick to learn, they soon developed on the field into skilled leaders who inspired their men with increasing confidence.

To the higher commanders and their staffs great credit is due for the successful performance of an exceptionally complicated and arduous task. The problems born of inexperience multiply with each increase of strength, and the division, corps, and particularly the army headquarters were confronted by questions of superlative difficulty. The importance of their work is rarely realized or appreciated. The army staff at one time was involved in serving a front of ninety-four miles and a force of approximately one million men. With typical American directness of action and intensity of purpose, each member carried out his duties despite all obstacles.

Deeds of daring were legion. It is not intended to discriminate in favor of those whose heroic services have been recognized. There were thousands of others who bore themselves with equal gallantry but whose deeds are known only by the victorious results they helped to achieve. However, as typifying the spirit of the rank and file of our great army, I would mention Lieutenant Samuel Woodfill, 5th Division, who attacked single-handed a series of German machine gun nests near Cunel and dispatched the crews of each in turn until reduced to the necessity of assaulting the last detachment with a pick; Sergeant Alvin C. York, of the 82d Division, who stood off and captured 132 Germans after his patrol was literally surrounded and outnumbered ten to one; and Major Charles W. Whittlesey and his men of the 77th Division, who, when their battalion was cut off in the Argonne, refused to surrender and held out until finally relieved.

There is little to add in praise of the spirit of determination that stimulated each individual soldier to overcome the hardships and difficulties that fell to his lot. With fortitude and perseverance he gave his every energy to the accomplishment of his task, whether it required him to charge the enemy's guns or play the less conspicuous rôle of forwarding supplies. In their devotion, their valor, and in the loyal fulfillment of their obligations, the officers and men of the American Expeditionary Forces have left a heritage of which those who follow may ever be proud.

While we extol the virtues of the men who had the privilege of serving America in the ranks of her armies, it must be remembered that they received their inspiration of loyalty and of devotion to the country's cause from those at home. They were but the chosen representatives of the American people, whose resolute spirit they transformed into victory on the field of honor.

We who were in France were conscious always of the indefatigable efforts made to supply us with the men and materials necessary for our success. Individual officers and men, no matter what their position or their duty, were inspired by patriotic determination to respond to the fullest extent possible to our calls. We became, in fact, a nation in arms, a nation imbued with and expressing the will to victory.

(Diary) Paris, Tuesday, November 12, 1918. Arrived in Paris this morning. Colonel Mott was here with instructions from Marshal Foch about following up the Germans. Held brief conference on subject with McAndrew and Harbord, and left immediately with Boyd and Quekemeyer for Marshal Foch's headquarters at Senlis. Met Marshal Foch for the first time since victory and the meeting was one to be remembered. By direction of the President, bestowed on him the Distinguished Service Medal. We returned to Paris in the afternoon to find pandemonium.

When I saw Marshal Foch he was in high spirits and said a great many complimentary things about the splendid work of the American Army, my cordial coöperation, and how he appreciated my straightforward methods. He said that he had always known my attitude on every question, because I stated it frankly and clearly and then lived up to it. I was equally enthusiastic in praise of his leadership. What was said and the realization that the victory was won and the war actually over affected us both deeply and for some moments we were speechless. Both of us were rather overcome by emotion as we embraced and each gave the other the time-honored French "accolade."

We pulled ourselves together shortly, as one of the objects of my visit was to decorate him with the Distinguished Service Medal, this being the first to be presented to any officer other than an American. He had directed a small guard of some fifteen or twenty territorial orderlies, under the command of a sergeant, to be formed in the yard in rear of his quarters, with two trumpeters to furnish the music. Standing in front of this command and facing him, I made a short speech in French and pinned on his blouse the token of our country's esteem and appreciation of his distinguished services. My aide handed one of his aides a signed copy of what I said. The Marshal spoke somewhat at length on how he valued the honor and how brilliantly the Americans had fought beside the Allies and was so moved that he could hardly finish what he had to say. He shook hands with me very cordially and stood holding my hand with both of his as he ordered the flourish of trumpets to close the ceremony.

I had luncheon with him, during which Weygand gave a brief account of the conference with the German delegates regarding the terms of the Armistice. He said that the Germans came across the line by automobile on the afternoon of November 7th and boarded a special railway coach sent by the French to meet them. During the night this car and the Marshal's were placed side by side in the forest between Compiègne and Soissons. The emissaries were ushered into the Marshal's presence and after producing their credentials were asked the object of their visit. They replied that they had come to discuss the terms of an armistice. The Marshal then made it clear that he, himself, was not requesting an armistice and *did not care to have one*. When asked if they wished an armistice, they replied that they did. The Marshal said if that was the case, here were the terms, a copy of which he handed them. The severity of the demands seemed to surprise them and they appeared very much depressed. They had no power to sign an armistice, they said, without the consent of the Chancellor, and after some little discussion they started an officer to the German capital with the terms.

They did not seem to object to turning over 5,000 cannon, but deplored the condition which required them to surrender 30,000 machine guns. They finally succeeded in getting this reduced to 25,000 machine guns on the ground that they might have some left for riot duty. In speaking of the danger of riots, the delegates were asked why they did not send some of their reserve divisions to maintain order in the interior. Their reply was that they had no divisions in reserve, as *every division that they had was actually in line.* Then they complained about the short time allowed for evacuation, stating that the German Army was in no condition to move, either forward or backward.

During the 9th and 10th, while waiting for instructions from their Government, the delegates talked very freely with Weygand about conditions in Germany and spoke particularly of the lack of food and the fear that there would be famine in places because of the bad transportation service.

A wireless message from the German Government authorizing the delegates to sign the Armistice was received about 11:00 P.M. on the 10th. It took until 5:00 A.M. the 11th to decode the message, complete the discussion and draw up the terms in the rough. In order to stop bloodshed, the last page of the conditions was written first, and this was signed a few minutes after 5:00 A.M. on the 11th. At that hour word was sent out to the armies that fighting would cease at 11:00 A.M.

After luncheon we drove back to Paris and everybody was still celebrating. It looked as though the whole population had gone entirely out of their minds. The city was turned into pandemonium. The streets and boulevards were packed with people singing and dancing and wearing all sorts of odd costumes. The crowds were doing the most clownish things. One could hardly hear his own voice, it was such a bedlam.

It was next to impossible for our automobile to make any headway through the mass of humanity. We were two hours in crossing the Place de la Concorde, the crowd was so dense and so riotous. It happened that I was recognized before we had gone very far and French men and women boarded the car, climbed on top of it and got inside, and no amount of persuasion would prevail upon them to let us pass. Finally a group of American soldiers, who were enjoying the hilarity, came along and seeing our helpless condition took charge and succeeded in making an opening sufficiently large to permit the car to be moved a yard or so at a time until we got free.   If all the ridiculous things done during those two or three days by dignified American and French men and women were recorded the reader would scarcely believe the story.   But this was Paris and the war was over.

(Diary) Paris, Thursday, November 14, 1918.   Yesterday conferred the Distinguished Service Medal on Marshal Joffre and on General Pétain.   Saw Mr. House, Stettinius, Atterbury and several others on variety of subjects.

To-day at Cambrai I decorated Marshal Haig.   Saw Lord Derby, who always speaks warmly of the relations between our two Governments.   Called on M. Clemenceau.

I went to the Ecole de Guerre, where Marshal Joffre had his quarters, and in a very simple ceremony that took place in his office I pinned our Distinguished Service Medal on his breast. Only a few staff officers were present, among them the Marshal's faithful Chief of Staff, Colonel Fabre, while the officers who accompanied me were Harbord, Boyd, and Quekemeyer.   This grand old French Commander-in-Chief was very proud of this recognition by our Government, but expressed himself in few words.   It gave me the greatest pleasure to make this presentation.

We next motored to Provins to confer the same decoration on General Pétain.   After luncheon, together with several of his generals and staff officers, we repaired to the front court, where a guard of about twenty soldiers was already formed.   Facing General Pétain, who stood in front of the command, I spoke a few words regarding his exceptional service to his country and thanked him for his uniform consideration and great assistance to our armies, and pinned on the medal.   It was especially gratifying to me to decorate Pétain, as my relations with him were always closer than with any of the other Allied officers and we had become fast friends.   He made some complimentary remarks about our Army and seemed much pleased and deeply appreciative of the recognition shown by our Government of his great abilities.

At Cambrai, where I went to decorate Field Marshal Sir Douglas Haig, a brigade of Highlanders, which included some of the most distinguished units of the British Army, was assembled for the occasion. The ceremony was very impressive. Marshal Haig stood opposite the center of the line, the very picture of the ideal soldier that he was. The band of bagpipes swung down the line playing a medley of Scottish airs in thrilling fashion. As the command stood at "Present Arms," I approached the Field Marshal and after a few words pinned our decoration on him. The march-past of the troops completed a memorable event.

Upon my arrival in Paris that afternoon, I hastened over to call on M. Clemenceau. To my mind, he was the greatest of French civil officials. Though some seventy-six years of age, he had the vigor, the fire, and the determination of a man of fifty. He will live long in history. I had not seen him since the cessation of hostilities and when we met he was much affected, and indeed demonstrative. We fell into each other's arms, choked up and had to wipe our eyes. We had no differences to discuss that day.

APPENDIX

GENERAL ORGANIZATION OF THE AMERICAN
EXPEDITIONARY FORCES NOVEMBER 1, 1918

APPENDIX

GENERAL ORGANIZATION OF THE AMERICAN EXPEDITIONARY FORCES NOVEMBER 1, 1918

GENERAL HEADQUARTERS

Commander-in-Chief:
GEN. JOHN J. PERSHING
Chief of Staff:
MAJ. GEN. JAMES W. MCANDREW
Deputy Chief of Staff:
BRIG. GEN. LEROY ELTINGE
Asst. Chief of Staff, G-1 (Administrative):
BRIG. GEN. AVERY D. ANDREWS
Asst. Chief of Staff, G-2 (Intelligence):
BRIG. GEN. DENNIS E. NOLAN
Asst. Chief of Staff, G-4 (Coördination):
BRIG. GEN. GEORGE V. H. MOSELEY
Secretary, General Staff:
LT. COL. ALBERT S. KUEGLE
Judge Advocate General:
BRIG. GEN. WALTER A. BETHEL
Chief of Artillery:
MAJ. GEN. ERNEST HINDS

Aides-de-Camp:
COL. CARL BOYD
COL. JOHN G. QUEKEMEYER
COL. EDWARD BOWDITCH, JR.
CAPT. JOHN C. HUGHES
COL. ADELBERT DE CHAMBRUN (French)
CAPT. CHARLES DE MARENCHES (French)
Asst. Chief of Staff, G-3 (Operations):
BRIG. GEN. FOX CONNER
Asst. Chief of Staff, G-5 (Training):
BRIG. GEN. HAROLD B. FISKE
Adjutant General:
BRIG. GEN. ROBERT C. DAVIS
Inspector General:
MAJ. GEN. ANDRÉ W. BREWSTER
Chief of Tank Corps:
BRIG. GEN. SAMUEL D. ROCKENBACH

SERVICES OF SUPPLY

Commander:
MAJ. GEN. JAMES G. HARBORD
Deputy Chief of Staff:
COL. JOHN P. MCADAMS
Asst. Chief of Staff, G-2:
LT. COL. CABOT WARD
Adjutant General:
COL. LOUIS H. BASH
Inspector General:
BRIG. GEN. THOMAS Q. DONALDSON
Chief Surgeon:
COL. WALTER D. MCCAW
Chief Engineer Officer:
MAJ. GEN. WILLIAM C. LANGFITT
Chief of Air Service:
MAJ. GEN. MASON M. PATRICK
Provost Marshal General:
BRIG. GEN. HARRY H. BANDHOLTZ
Director General of Transportation:
BRIG. GEN. WILLIAM W. ATTERBURY
Director Construction and Forestry:
BRIG. GEN. EDGAR JADWIN
Director Military Engineering and Engineer Supplies:
BRIG. GEN. JAMES F. MCINDOE

Chief of Staff:
BRIG. GEN. JOHSON HAGOOD
Asst. Chief of Staff, G-1:
COL. JAMES B. CAVANAUGH
Asst. Chief of Staff, G-4:
COL. HENRY C. SMITHER
Judge Advocate General:
COL. JOHN A. HULL
Chief Quartermaster:
MAJ. GEN. HARRY L. ROGERS
Chief Ordnance Officer:
BRIG. GEN. JOHN H. RICE
Chief Signal Officer:
BRIG. GEN. EDGAR RUSSEL
Chief of Chemical Warfare Service:
BRIG. GEN. AMOS A. FRIES
General Purchasing Agent:
BRIG. GEN. CHARLES G. DAWES
Director Motor Transport Corps:
BRIG. GEN. MERIWETHER L. WALKER
Director Light Railways:
BRIG. GEN. CHARLES H. MCKINSTRY
Director Renting, Requisition and Claims Service:
COL. JOHN A. HULL

SERVICES OF SUPPLY (*Continued*)

Director Army Service Corps:
COL. DOUGLAS SETTLE
Base Section No. 1:
COL. JOHN S. SEWELL
Base Section No. 3:
MAJ. GEN. JOHN BIDDLE
Base Section No. 5:
BRIG. GEN. GEORGE H. HARRIES
Base Section No. 7:
COL. WILLIAM KELLY
Intermediate Section:
BRIG. GEN. ARTHUR JOHNSON

Chief War Risk Insurance Section:
COL. HENRY D. LINDSLEY
Base Section No. 2:
BRIG. GEN. WILLIAM D. CONNOR
Base Section No. 4:
BRIG. GEN. RICHARD COULTER, JR.
Base Section No. 6:
COL. MELVIN W. ROWELL
Base Section No. 8:
BRIG. GEN. CHARLES G. TREAT
Advance Section:
BRIG. GEN. WILLIAM R. SAMPLE

District of Paris: BRIG. GEN. WILLIAM W. HARTS

FIRST ARMY

Commander:
LT. GEN. HUNTER LIGGETT
Deputy Chief of Staff:
COL. WALTER S. GRANT
Asst. Chief of Staff, G-2:
COL. WILLEY HOWELL
Asst. Chief of Staff, G-4:
COL. JOHN L. DEWITT
LT. COL. EDWARD G. MCCLEAVE
(Acting)
Chief of Air Service:
COL. THOMAS DEW. MILLING
Chief Signal Officer:
COL. PARKER HITT
Chief of Chemical Warfare Service:
COL. JOHN W. N. SCHULZ

Chief of Staff:
BRIG. GEN. HUGH A. DRUM
Asst. Chief of Staff, G-1:
COL. LEON B. KROMER
Asst. Chief of Staff, G-3:
COL. GEORGE C. MARSHALL, JR.
Asst. Chief of Staff, G-5:
COL. LEWIS H. WATKINS
Chief of Artillery:
MAJ. GEN. EDWARD F. MCGLACHLIN, JR.
Chief Engineer Officer:
COL. GEORGE R. SPALDING
Chief Surgeon:
COL. ALEXANDER N. STARK

SECOND ARMY

Commander:
LT. GEN. ROBERT L. BULLARD
Deputy Chief of Staff:
COL. DAVID L. STONE
Asst. Chief of Staff, G-2:
LT. COL. CHARLES F. THOMPSON
Asst. Chief of Staff, G-4:
COL. GEORGE P. TYNER
Chief of Artillery:
MAJ. GEN. WILLIAM LASSITER
Chief of Air Service:
COL. FRANK P. LAHM
Chief Surgeon:
COL. CHARLES R. REYNOLDS

Chief of Staff:
BRIG. GEN. STUART HEINTZELMAN
Asst. Chief of Staff, G-1:
COL. GEORGE K. WILSON
Asst. Chief of Staff, G-3:
COL. WILLIAM N. HASKELL
Asst. Chief of Staff, G-5:
COL. JAMES E. BELL
Chief Engineer Officer:
BRIG. GEN. HERBERT DEAKYNE
Chief Signal Officer:
COL. HANSON B. BLACK
Chief of Chemical Warfare Service:
LT. COL. BYRON C. GOSS

THIRD ARMY

(Organized after the Armistice; Commander, Maj. Gen. Joseph T. Dickman.)

I CORPS

Commander:
MAJ. GEN. JOSEPH T. DICKMAN
Asst. Chief of Staff, G-1:
LT. COL. GEORGE GRUNERT
Asst. Chief of Staff, G-3:
COL. JOHN C. MONTGOMERY

Chief of Staff:
BRIG. GEN. MALIN CRAIG
Asst. Chief of Staff, G-2:
COL. RICHARD H. WILLIAMS
Chief of Artillery:
MAJ. GEN. WILLIAM S. McNAIR (From Nov. 7)

II CORPS

Commander:
MAJ. GEN. GEORGE W. READ
Asst. Chief of Staff, G-1:
LT. COL. RICHARD K. HALE
Asst. Chief of Staff, G-3:
COL. FRED E. BUCHAN
LT. COL. LAWRENCE E. HOHL (Acting)

Chief of Staff:
BRIG. GEN. GEORGE S. SIMONDS
Asst. Chief of Staff, G-2:
LT. COL. KERR T. RIGGS
Asst. Chief of Staff, G-4:
LT. COL. JOHN P. TERRELL

III CORPS

Commander:
MAJ. GEN. JOHN L. HINES
Asst. Chief of Staff, G-1:
LT. COL. MARTIN C. SHALLENBERGER
Asst. Chief of Staff, G-3:
COL. ADNA R. CHAFFEE

Chief of Staff:
BRIG. GEN. CAMPBELL KING
Asst. Chief of Staff, G-2:
LT. COL. HORACE C. STEBBINS
Chief of Artillery:
MAJ. GEN. CLEMENT A. F. FLAGLER

IV CORPS

Commander:
MAJ. GEN. CHARLES H. MUIR
Asst. Chief of Staff, G-1:
LT. COL. JAMES A. ULIO
Asst. Chief of Staff, G-3:
COL. BERKELEY ENOCHS

Chief of Staff:
BRIG. GEN. BRIANT H. WELLS
Asst. Chief of Staff, G-2:
LT. COL. JOSEPH W. STILWELL
Chief of Artillery:
BRIG. GEN. WILLIAM M. CRUIKSHANK

V CORPS

Commander:
MAJ. GEN. CHARLES P. SUMMERALL
Asst. Chief of Staff, G-1:
COL. ALBERT W. FOREMAN
Asst. Chief of Staff, G-3:
COL. THOMAS H. EMERSON

Chief of Staff:
BRIG. GEN. WILSON B. BURTT
Asst. Chief of Staff, G-2:
LT. COL. GEORGE M. RUSSELL
Chief of Artillery:
BRIG. GEN. DWIGHT E. AULTMAN

VI CORPS

Commander:
MAJ. GEN. CHARLES C. BALLOU
Asst. Chief of Staff, G-1:
COL. CHARLES H. BRIDGES
Asst. Chief of Staff, G-3:
COL. GEORGE F. BALTZELL

Chief of Staff:
COL. EDGAR T. COLLINS
Asst. Chief of Staff, G-2:
LT. COL. SAMUEL T. MACKALL
Chief of Artillery:
BRIG. GEN. ALBERT J. BOWLEY (From Nov. 7)

VII CORPS

Commander:
(Chief of Staff, Acting)
Asst. Chief of Staff, G-1:
COL. CLYFFARD GAME

Chief of Staff:
COL. HERBERT J. BREES
Asst. Chief of Staff, G-2:
COL. GEORGE A. HERBST

Asst. Chief of Staff, G-3: MAJ. DAVID E. CAIN (Acting)

1ST DIVISION

Commander:
BRIG. GEN. FRANK PARKER

1st Infantry Brigade:
COL. HJALMER ERICKSON (*Ad interim*)

Chief of Staff:
COL. JOHN N. GREELY

2d Infantry Brigade:
BRIG. GEN. FRANCIS C. MARSHALL

1st Field Artillery Brigade: BRIG. GEN. HENRY W. BUTNER

2D DIVISION

Commander:
MAJ. GEN. JOHN A. LEJEUNE, U.S.M.C.

3d Infantry Brigade:
COL. ROBERT O. VAN HORN

Chief of Staff:
COL. JAMES C. RHEA

4th Infantry Brigade:
BRIG. GEN. WENDELL C. NEVILLE, U.S.M.C.

2d Field Artillery Brigade: BRIG. GEN. ALBERT J. BOWLEY

3D DIVISION

Commander:
BRIG. GEN. PRESTON BROWN

5th Infantry Brigade:
BRIG. GEN. FRED W. SLADEN

Chief of Staff:
COL. ROBERT McCLEAVE

6th Infantry Brigade:
BRIG. GEN. ORA E. HUNT

3d Field Artillery Brigade: BRIG. GEN. HARRY G. BISHOP

4TH DIVISION

Commander:
MAJ. GEN. MARK L. HERSEY

7th Infantry Brigade:
BRIG. GEN. BENJAMIN A. POORE

Chief of Staff:
COL. CHRISTIAN A. BACH

8th Infantry Brigade:
BRIG. GEN. EWING E. BOOTH

4th Field Artillery Brigade: BRIG. GEN. EDWIN B. BABBITT

5TH DIVISION

Commander:
MAJOR GEN HANSON E. ELY

9th Infantry Brigade:
BRIG. JOSEPH C. CASTNER

Chief of Staff:
COL. CLEMENT A. TROTT

10th Infantry Brigade:
BRIG. GEN. PAUL B. MALONE

5th Field Artillery Brigade: BRIG. GEN. WILLIAM C. RIVERS

6TH DIVISION

Commander:
MAJ. GEN. WALTER H. GORDON

11th Infantry Brigade:
BRIG. GEN. WILLIAM R. DASHIELL

Chief of Staff:
COL. JOSEPH W. BEACHAM, JR.

12th Infantry Brigade:
BRIG. GEN. JAMES B. ERWIN

6th Field Artillery Brigade: BRIG. GEN. EDWARD A. MILLAR
LT. COL. BALLARD LYERLY (*Ad interim*)

7TH DIVISION

Commander:
MAJ. GEN. EDMUND WITTENMYER

13th Infantry Brigade:
BRIG. GEN. ALFRED W. BJORNSTAD

Chief of Staff:
LT. COL. WILLIAM W. TAYLOR, JR.

14th Infantry Brigade:
BRIG. GEN. LUTZ WAHL

7th Field Artillery Brigade: BRIG. GEN. TIEMANN N. HORN

26TH DIVISION

Commander:
BRIG. GEN. FRANK E. BAMFORD

51st Infantry Brigade:
BRIG. GEN. GEORGE H. SHELTON

Chief of Staff:
COL. DUNCAN K. MAJOR, JR.

52d Infantry Brigade:
BRIG. GEN. CHARLES H. COLE

51st Field Artillery Brigade: COL. OTHO W. B. FARR

27TH DIVISION

Commander:
MAJ. GEN. JOHN F. O'RYAN
53d Infantry Brigade:
BRIG. GEN. CHARLES I. DeBEVOISE

Chief of Staff:
COL. STANLEY H. FORD
54th Infantry Brigade:
BRIG. GEN. PALMER E. PIERCE
COL. EDGAR S. JENNINGS (*Ad Interim*)

52d Field Artillery Brigade: BRIG. GEN. GEORGE A. WINGATE

28TH DIVISION

Commander:
MAJ. GEN. WILLIAM H. HAY
55th Infantry Brigade:
BRIG. GEN. FREDERICK D. EVANS

Chief of Staff:
COL. WALTER C. SWEENEY
56th Infantry Brigade:
BRIG. GEN. FRANK H. ALBRIGHT

53d Field Artillery Brigade: BRIG. GEN. WILLIAM G. PRICE, JR.

29TH DIVISION

Commander:
MAJ. GEN. CHARLES G. MORTON
57th Infantry Brigade:
BRIG. GEN. LaROY S. UPTON

Chief of Staff:
COL. SYDNEY A. CLOMAN
58th Infantry Brigade:
COL. JOHN McA. PALMER

54th Field Artillery Brigade: BRIG. GEN. LUCIUS R. HOLBROOK

30TH DIVISION

Commander:
MAJ. GEN. EDWARD M. LEWIS
59th Infantry Brigade:
BRIG. GEN. LAWRENCE D. TYSON

Chief of Staff:
COL. JOHN K. HERR
60th Infantry Brigade:
BRIG. GEN. SAMSON L. FAISON

55th Field Artillery Brigade: BRIG. GEN. JOHN W. KILBRETH, JR.

31ST DIVISION (Depot)

Commander:
BRIG. GEN. WALTER A. HARRIS
62d Infantry Brigade:
BRIG. GEN. ROBERT E. STEINER

61st Infantry Brigade:
DIVISION COMMANDER
56th Field Artillery Brigade:
BRIG. GEN. JOHN L. HAYDEN

32D DIVISION

Commander:
MAJ. GEN. WILLIAM G. HAAN
63d Infantry Brigade:
BRIG. GEN. FRANK R. McCOY

Chief of Staff:
COL. ROBERT McC. BECK, JR.
64th Infantry Brigade:
BRIG. GEN. EDWIN B. WINANS

57th Field Artillery Brigade: BRIG. GEN. GEORGE LeR. IRWIN

33D DIVISION

Commander:
MAJ. GEN. GEORGE BELL, JR.
65th Infantry Brigade:
BRIG. GEN. EDWARD L. KING

Chief of Staff:
BRIG. GEN. WILLIAM K. NAYLOR
66th Infantry Brigade:
BRIG. GEN. PAUL A. WOLF

58th Field Artillery Brigade: BRIG. GEN. HENRY D. TODD, JR.
BRIG. GEN. EDWARD A. MILLAR (*Ad interim*)

34TH DIVISION (Replacement)

Commander:
BRIG. GEN. JOHN A. JOHNSTON
67th Infantry Brigade:
BRIG. GEN. HUBERT A. ALLEN

Chief of Staff:
COL. WILLIAM H. RAYMOND
68th Infantry Brigade:
COL. WILLIAM T. MOLLISON

59th Field Artillery Brigade: COL. THOMAS W. HOLLYDAY

35TH DIVISION

Commander:
MAJ. GEN. PETER E. TRAUB
BRIG. GEN. THOMAS B. DUGAN (*Ad interim*)
69th Infantry Brigade:
BRIG. GEN. LOUIS M. NUTTMAN

Chief of Staff:
COL. HAMILTON S. HAWKINS
70th Infantry Brigade:
BRIG. GEN. THOMAS B. DUGAN
BRIG. GEN. CHARLES GERHARDT (*Ad interim*)

60th Field Artillery Brigade: BRIG. GEN. LUCIEN G. BERRY

36TH DIVISION

Commander:
MAJ. GEN. WILLIAM R. SMITH
71st Infantry Brigade:
BRIG. GEN. PEGRAM WHITWORTH

Chief of Staff:
COL. EZEKIAL J. WILLIAMS
72d Infantry Brigade:
BRIG. GEN. JOHN A. HULEN

61st Field Artillery Brigade: BRIG. GEN. JOHN E. STEPHENS

37TH DIVISION

Commander:
MAJ. GEN. CHARLES S. FARNSWORTH
73d Infantry Brigade:
BRIG. GEN. WILLIAM M. FASSETT

Chief of Staff:
COL. DANA T. MERRILL
74th Infantry Brigade:
BRIG. GEN. WILLIAM P. JACKSON

62d Field Artillery Brigade: BRIG. GEN. EDWIN BURR

38TH DIVISION (Replacement)

Commander:
MAJ. GEN. ROBERT L. HOWZE
75th Infantry Brigade:
BRIG. GEN. FRANK M. CALDWELL
COL. GEORGE T. SMITH (*Ad interim*)

Chief of Staff:
COL. JAMES B. GOWEN
76th Infantry Brigade:
COL. GEORGE H. HEALEY

63d Field Artillery Brigade: BRIG. GEN. AUGUSTINE McINTYRE

39TH DIVISION (Depot)

Commander:
MAJ. GEN. HENRY C. HODGES, JR.
77th Infantry Brigade:
BRIG. GEN. LUCIUS L. DURFEE

Chief of Staff:
COL. HENRY H. SHEEN (Acting)
78th Infantry Brigade:
BRIG. GEN. WILDS P. RICHARDSON
COL. GEORGE C. HOSKINS (*Ad interim*)

64th Field Artillery Brigade: BRIG. GEN. IRA A. HAYNES

40TH DIVISION (Depot)

Commander:
MAJ. GEN. FREDERICK S. STRONG
79th Infantry Brigade:
BRIG. GEN. ALEXANDER M. TUTHILL

Chief of Staff:
LT. COL. FRANCIS H. FARNUM (acting)
80th Infantry Brigade:
COL. CHARLES F. HUTCHINS (*Ad interim*)

65th Field Artillery Brigade: BRIG. GEN. RICHARD W. YOUNG

41ST DIVISION (Depot)

Commander:
BRIG. GEN. ELI K. COLE, U.S.M.C.
81st Infantry Brigade:
(Replacement)

Chief of Staff:
COL. OREN B. MEYER (Acting)
82d Infantry Brigade:
BRIG. GEN. EDWARD VOLLRATH

66th Field Artillery Brigade: COL. ERNEST D. SCOTT

42D DIVISION

Commander:
MAJ. GEN. CHARLES T. MENOHER
83d Infantry Brigade:
COL. HENRY J. REILLY

Chief of Staff:
COL. WILLIAM N. HUGHES, JR.
84th Infantry Brigade:
BRIG. GEN. DOUGLAS MacARTHUR

67th Field Artillery Brigade: BRIG. GEN. GEORGE G. GATLEY

76TH DIVISION (Depot)

Commander:
MAJ. GEN. HARRY F. HODGES
151st Infantry Brigade:
COL. PERCY W. ARNOLD

Chief of Staff:
LT. COL. GEORGE M. PEEK
152d Infantry Brigade:
COL. JOHN F. PRESTON

151st Field Artillery Brigade: BRIG. GEN. RICHMOND P. DAVIS

77TH DIVISION

Commander:
MAJ. GEN. ROBERT ALEXANDER
153d Infantry Brigade:
BRIG. GEN. WILLIAM R. SMEDBERG, JR.

Chief of Staff:
COL. CLARENCE O. SHERRILL
154th Infantry Brigade:
BRIG. GEN. HARRISON J. PRICE

152d Field Artillery Brigade: BRIG. GEN. MANUS McCLOSKEY

78TH DIVISION

Commander:
MAJ. GEN. JAMES H. McRAE
155th Infantry Brigade:
BRIG. GEN. SANFORD B. STANBERY

Chief of Staff:
COL. CHARLES D. HERRON
156th Infantry Brigade:
BRIG. GEN. JAMES T. DEAN

153d Field Artillery Brigade: BRIG. GEN. CLINT C. HEARN

79TH DIVISION

Commander:
MAJ. GEN. JOSEPH E. KUHN
157th Infantry Brigade:
BRIG. GEN. WILLIAM J. NICHOLSON

Chief of Staff:
COL. TENNEY ROSS
158th Infantry Brigade:
BRIG. GEN. EVAN M. JOHNSON

154th Field Artillery Brigade: BRIG. GEN. ANDREW HERO, JR.

80TH DIVISION

Commander:
MAJ. GEN. ADELBERT CRONKHITE
159th Infantry Brigade:
BRIG. GEN. GEORGE H. JAMERSON
MAJ. GEN. ADELBERT CRONKHITE (*Ad interim*)

Chief of Staff:
COL. WILLIAM H. WALDRON
160th Infantry Brigade:
BRIG. GEN. LLOYD M. BRETT

155th Field Artillery Brigade: COL. ROBERT S. WELSH

81ST DIVISION

Commander:
MAJ. GEN. CHARLES J. BAILEY
161st Infantry Brigade:
BRIG. GEN. GEORGE W. McIVER

Chief of Staff:
COL. CHARLES D. ROBERTS
162d Infantry Brigade:
BRIG. GEN. MUNROE McFARLAND

156th Field Artillery Brigade: BRIG. GEN. ANDREW MOSES

82D DIVISION

Commander:
MAJ. GEN. GEORGE B. DUNCAN
163d Infantry Brigade:
BRIG. GEN. MARCUS D. CRONIN

Chief of Staff:
COL. GORDON JOHNSTON
164th Infantry Brigade:
BRIG. GEN. JULIAN R. LINDSEY

157th Field Artillery Brigade: COL. EARLE D'A. PEARCE (*Ad interim*)

83D DIVISION (Depot)

Commander:
MAJ. GEN. EDWIN F. GLENN
165th Infantry Brigade:
BRIG. GEN. LOUIS C. COVELL

Chief of Staff:
COL. KENYON A. JOYCE
166th Infantry Brigade:
COL. WILLIAM H. ALLAIRE

158th Field Artillery Brigade: BRIG. GEN. ADRIAN S. FLEMING

84TH DIVISION (Replacement)

Commander:
MAJ. GEN. HARRY C. HALE
167th Infantry Brigade:
BRIG. GEN. DANIEL B. DEVORE

Chief of Staff:
COL. LAURENCE HALSTEAD
168th Infantry Brigade:
BRIG. GEN. WILBER E. WILDER

159th Field Artillery Brigade: COL. CHARLES M. BUNDEL

85TH DIVISION (Depot)

Commander:
MAJ. GEN. CHASE W. KENNEDY
169th Infantry Brigade:
COL. BENJAMIN W. ATKINSON *(Ad interim)*

Chief of Staff:
COL. JAMES M. KIMBROUGH, JR.
170th Infantry Brigade:
COL. GEORGE E. BALL *(Ad interim)*

160th Field Artillery Brigade: BRIG. GEN. GUY H. PRESTON

86TH DIVISION (Replacement)

Commander:
COL. GUY G. PALMER *(Ad interim)*
171st Infantry Brigade:
COL. GUY G. PALMER *(Ad interim)*

Chief of Staff:
LT. COL. CHARLES E. T. LULL (Acting)
172d Infantry Brigade:
COL. CHARLES R. HOWLAND *(Ad interim)*

161st Field Artillery Brigade: BRIG. GEN. OLIVER L. SPAULDING, JR.

87TH DIVISION

Commander:
MAJ. GEN. SAMUEL D. STURGIS
173d Infantry Brigade:
COL. JOHN O'SHEA *(Ad interim)*

Chief of Staff:
COL. HENRY R. RICHMOND
174th Infantry Brigade:
BRIG. GEN. WILLIAM F. MARTIN

162d Field Artillery Brigade: LT. COL. ROBERT R. LOVE *(Ad interim)*

88TH DIVISION

Commander:
MAJ. GEN. WILLIAM WEIGEL
175th Infantry Brigade:
BRIG. GEN. MERCH B. STEWART

Chief of Staff:
LT. COL. FAY W. BRABSON (Acting)
176th Infantry Brigade:
BRIG. GEN. WILLIAM D. BEACH

163d Field Artillery Brigade: BRIG. GEN. STEPHEN M. FOOTE

89TH DIVISION

Commander:
MAJ. GEN. WILLIAM M. WRIGHT
177th Infantry Brigade:
MAJ. GEN. FRANK L. WINN

Chief of Staff:
COL. JOHN C. H. LEE
178th Infantry Brigade:
BRIG. GEN. THOMAS G. HANSON

164th Field Artillery Brigade: BRIG. GEN. EDWARD T. DONNELLY

90TH DIVISION

Commander:
MAJ. GEN. HENRY T. ALLEN
179th Infantry Brigade:
BRIG. GEN. JOSEPH P. O'NEIL

Chief of Staff:
COL. JOHN J. KINGMAN
180th Infantry Brigade:
BRIG. GEN. ULYSSES G. McALEXANDER

165th Field Artillery Brigade: MAJ. RALPH B. FAIRCHILD *(Ad interim)*

91ST DIVISION

Commander:
MAJ. GEN. WILLIAM H. JOHNSTON
181st Infantry Brigade:
BRIG. GEN. JOHN B. McDONALD

Chief of Staff:
COL. HENRY C. JEWETT
182d Infantry Brigade:
BRIG. GEN. VERNON A. CALDWELL

166th Field Artillery Brigade: BRIG. GEN. BEVERLY F. BROWN
COL. LOUIS E. BENNETT *(Ad interim)*

92D DIVISION

Commander:
MAJ. GEN. CHARLES C. BALLOU
183d Infantry Brigade:
BRIG. GEN. MALVERN-HILL BARNUM

Chief of Staff:
COL. ALLEN J. GREER
184th Infantry Brigade:
COL. FRED R. BROWN *(Ad interim)*

167th Field Artillery Brigade: BRIG. GEN. JOHN H. SHERBURNE

INDEX

INDEX

411

412 INDEX

414 INDEX

416 INDEX

420 INDEX

Germany, military strength of, in 1914,
i. 4-6; violated Belgian neutrality, i. 6;
disregards pledge against use of poisonous gases, i. 165; dominates all Central
Powers, i. 173; estimated military
strength in spring, 1918, i. 233; Cle-
menceau's views on future of, ii. 119;
cables peace overtures to President Wil-
son, ii. 342; correspondence on armistice
proposals, ii. 343-348.
Germont, capture of, ii. 377.
Gesnes, capture of, ii. 298, 323.
Giardino, Gen., i. 357, 358.
Gibson, Hugh S., ii. 214.
Gièvres, i. 109, 182, 207, 211, 212, 345, ii.
108, 202.
Gifford, Mr., ii. 313.
Gillain, Gen., ii. 125.
Gillemont Farm, ii. 305.
Gironde River, i. 209.
Gironville, ii. 267.
Gisors, ii. 17.
Glass, Congressman, ii. 350.
Gleaves, Adm. Albert, i. 87.
Glenn, Gen. Edwin F., ii. 118, 129.
Globe, The, London, i. 379.
Goethals, Gen. George W., ii. 180, 181,
190, 191.
Gondrecourt, i. 88, 136, 163, 254.
Gonetrie Farm, capture of, ii. 165.
Goodwin, Congressman W. S., i. 208.
Gordon, Gen. Walter H., ii. 58, 380.
Gorrell, Lieut. E. S., i. 159.
Gorze, ii. 378.
Gough, Gen., i. 3, 115, 353, 355.
Gouraud, Gen., ii. 152, 153, 289, 295, 303,
326, 399.
Gourko, Gen., of Russian Army, i. 260.
Gouzeaucourt, i. 252.
Grand Cross of the Legion of Honor, be-
stowed on General Pershing, ii. 213.
Grand Cross of the Order of the Bath
presented to General Pershing, ii. 215.
Grande Couronne de Nancy, i. 202.
Grandpré, ii. 292, 338, 340, 377; capture
of, ii. 352.
Grange Neuve, ii. 196.
Granville, ii. 200.
Grasty, Charles H., i. 42, 201.
Graves, Prof. Henry, i. 105, 123.
Graves, Col. W. S., i. 100.
Great Britain, draft system adopted, i. 13.
Greble, Gen. E. St. J., i. 193, 211.
Grémévillers, ii. 55.
Gresham, Corp'l James B., i. 217.
Grimaucourt, capture of, ii. 386.
Griscom, Col. Lloyd C., i. 24, ii. 58, 134,
335, 348, 364, 388.
Groome, Col. John C., i. 133, ii. 88.

Guillaumat, Gen., i. 138, 140, ii. 29.
Guthrie, Sir Connop, ii. 236.
Gwynne, Bishop L. H., i. 283.

Haan, Gen. William G., i. 338, ii. 17,
113, 145, 291, 323, 339, 353, 369, 384.
Hagood, Gen. Johnson, i. 337, ii. 55, 133,
138.
Haig, Field Marshal Sir Douglas, i. 151,
310, 313, 352, ii. 1, 2, 3, 45, 129, 134,
143, 169, 170, 214, 216, 219, 260, 315;
coördination with French Army, i. 68;
entertains General Pershing, i. 112-115;
does not favor Supreme War Council,
i. 151; discussion on shipment by, and
training of American troops with, British, i. 264-269; suggests Southampton
for port of debarkation, i. 287-304; the
Haig-Pétain agreement, i. 353; asks for
engineers and artillerymen, i. 358; at the
battle on Amiens front, i. 362; at meeting Supreme War Council, Beauvais, i.
373-377; "Backs to the Wall" order to
British Army, i. 396; at Abbeville meeting of Supreme War Council, ii. 20-34;
requests artillerymen, ii. 41; criticizes
French tactics on the Chemin des
Dames, ii. 61; Independence Day greetings, ii. 135; discussion of plans for offensive operations, ii. 171-176; congratulations on St. Mihiel victory, ii.
273; appreciation for American assistance at battle of the Selle, ii. 354;
views on armistice proposals, ii. 360-
363; receives Distinguished Service
Medal, ii. 396.
Hale, Gen. Harry C., ii. 306.
Hall, Adm. W. R., i. 52.
Hamilton, Sir Ian, i. 139.
Hankey, Col. Sir Maurice, i. 373.
Harbord, Gen. James G., i. 19, 20, 43, 50,
62, 111, 126, 193, 200, 207, 248, 326,
337, 381, 386, ii. 5, 38, 48, 52, 84, 90,
148, 158, 159, 167, 177, 179, 191, 192,
229, 256, 314, 329, 377, 393, 396.
Hardinge, Lord, i. 54.
Harjes, Maj. Herman H., i. 74, 290.
Harricourt, ii. 376.
Harries, Gen. George H., ii. 200.
Harris, Gen. Walter A., ii. 370.
Hattonchâtel, ii. 279.
Haudiomont, ii. 270.
Hautevesnes, capture of, ii. 164.
Hay, Gen. William H., ii. 383.
Hay, Pvt. Merle D., i. 217.
Hayes, Ralph, i. 342.
Hayward, Col. William, ii. 97.
Hazebrouck, i. 397, ii. 26.
Headlam, Gen., i. 280.

430   INDEX

THE END